THE OFFICIAL
MANCHESTER UNITED

ILLUSTRATED ENCYCLOPEDIA

The Official
Manchester
United
Illustrated Encyclopedia

Editors Jillian Somerscales, Deborah Murrell, Louise Pritchard and Margaret Hynes
Designer Dominic Zwemmer

Editorial assistant Jane Bawden
Design assistant Anthony Cutting

Editorial Direction Christiane Gunzi
Art Direction Chez Picthall

Consultants and Contributors
Cliff Butler, Adam Bostock, Andy Mitten, Sam Pilger, Tom Tyrrell, Justyn Barnes, Sir Bobby Charlton, Frank Taylor OBE, David Meek, Tony Brown and Jim Ferguson

First published in Great Britain in 1998

Third edition published in 2001 by
Manchester United Books
an imprint of Carlton Books Ltd.
20 Mortimer Street, London W1T 3JW
in association with
Manchester United Football Club plc
Old Trafford, Manchester M16 0RA

Produced for Carlton Books Ltd by
Picthall & Gunzi Ltd

Reproduction by Colourscan, Singapore
Printed and bound in Italy

CIP data for this title is available from the British Library

ISBN 0-233-99964-7

Contents

Foreword by Sir Bobby Charlton

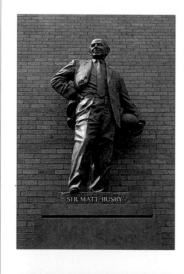

Foreword

by Sir Bobby Charlton

Manchester United is probably the most famous of all the English Association clubs worldwide, with supporters in almost every corner of this Earth. English football, indeed, is the most watched on TV globally, and United the most popular team. What has made this club the envy of the footballing world?

My own career has spanned a long period with this unique club, and I think the answer lies in the way our teams have approached the game. We have always felt that Manchester United meant excitement and adventure, which is what our fans have always expected. Indeed, the 1998/99 season, with the fantastic Treble win, was probably the most exciting time ever in the club's history, both for the fans and the team.

The great Sir Matt Busby set the pattern by playing exciting young footballers, and he allowed them the freedom to explore themselves. He played youngsters in their teens, and people thought he was foolhardy, but he had faith in their ability and it worked. The "Busby Babes", as they were called, had domestic success and Sir Matt pioneered them into Europe against the wishes of the authorities, which brought them international recognition too. While trying to win the European Cup, they were making friends everywhere, but what happened on 6th February, 1958 had a dramatic effect on both United's and England's future. On the way home from Belgrade, after qualifying for the semi-final, the plane crashed in Munich while taking off, and many of those great young players were killed. Sir Matt was severely injured, and the country was shocked that such a tragic end should come to talented youngsters of whom the greatest promise was predicted.

Jimmy Murphy took over the reins, and without Edwards, Taylor, Pegg, Jones, Whelan, Bent, Colman, and captain Byrne, he had to guide the club through a very traumatic period. Players were brought in to help during this emergency in the short term, aided by the survivors such as Gregg and Foulkes. A place in the Cup Final was attained and somehow United survived. As predicted by Sir Matt on his return, it took five years to get a team good enough again to go for honours – in 1963 they won the FA Cup, beating Leicester 3-1.

Soon Matt Busby physically had to hand over the control of the team to someone else, and a number of managers, such as McGuinness, O'Farrell, Sexton, Docherty, and Atkinson had spells in charge. But it was the Scot, Alex Ferguson, who gave the club the success that it had yearned for for so long when he arrived in the late '80s. He brought a swashbuckling style to the Premier League, and with the blooding of younger players such as Giggs, Beckham, Scholes, Butt and the Neville brothers, things were as the fans would wish it to be once more. There was great success in the '90s, and the United legend continued during Eric Cantona's time there, and into the new millennium.

The following pages will give a real thrill to all those who are interested in this great institution, and, for me, the pictures and stories will relive a great time at Old Trafford. Enjoy reading the encyclopedia, as I will.

Part One

The
HISTORY

The Early Years

Newton Heath LYR
The founder members of Newton Heath LYR. The LYR stood for Lancashire and Yorkshire Railway, distinguishing them from their rivals from the Motive Power Division of the company who were called Newton Heath Loco (motive).

The staff of Manchester's Piccadilly Station can reflect with satisfaction that Manchester United has an historically intimate relationship with the railway. The first-ever Manchester United footballers, though they played under a different name, were the men of the Carriage and Wagon department of the Lancashire and Yorkshire Railway at Newton Heath. They started the team of Newton Heath LYR in 1878. The railway workers were tough, diligent men who formed a powerful side. The team established itself at a ground in North Road, near the railway yard. At first they played against other departments of the LYR or against men from other railway companies. When the Football League formed in 1888, Newton Heath did not consider themselves to be good enough to compete with the likes of Preston North End and Blackburn Rovers, but their reputation grew and it was only four years before they joined the elite. The club had many ups and downs in its Newton Heath era, and there were times when it nearly went out of existence. But it survived, and was reborn in 1902 as Manchester United Football Club.

The Heathens
Taken in 1892, this is the earliest known photograph of the Newton Heath team. Sitting third from the left in the front row is Robert Donaldson. A former Blackburn Rovers player, Donaldson was the first Heathen to score a League goal – in their first League match against Blackburn Rovers. He was also the first to score a hat-trick a month later in a 10–1 victory over Wolves.

Newton Heath LYR

Soon after Newton Heath were formed, they began to dominate the local competitions. In 1888, they did not lose a home game until October, when they were beaten by a touring Canadian side. They started to look beyond Manchester for a game equal to their talents. In 1890, Newton Heath applied to join the Football League. The application was not a success. They received only one vote. So, together with other clubs not in the League, they formed an organization known as the Football Alliance. From there, Newton Heath campaigned vigorously to impress the authorities of the League. Eventually, after three further applications, they were accepted as members in the summer of 1892, as part of a League reshuffle. A second division was created and the First Division expanded. Newton Heath was elected to the First Division. Local rivals Ardwick, later to become Manchester City, joined the Second Division.

The Football League

Newton Heath's League career was neither distinguished nor particularly exciting. After being defeated by Blackburn in their first match, they went a further six games without a win, claiming only one point, in a 1–1 draw against Burnley. The Heathens, as they became known, finished their first season in the League at the bottom of the division, having conceded 85 goals and gained only 18 points. They only retained their place in the First Division by winning a play-off against Small Heath (later to become Birmingham City) from the Second Division.

Bank Street

As football entered the year 1893, it was time for Newton Heath to move home. The directors moved the club across the city to a ground at Bank Street in the Clayton district. There were hopes that a fresh pitch would be the arena for a new era of expansion but unfortunately Bank Street had problems. The surface was a strange mush of sand, mud and grass. A neighbouring factory belched out toxic fumes that blew over the stands if the wind was in the wrong direction. The novelty of Bank Street failed to give the team the necessary fillip. Newton Heath's second season ended even less successfully than their first. In 30 games, they won only six times and finished, once again, peering up the division from the bottom. This time they lost a play-off match against Liverpool and were relegated to the Second Division.

The Manchester Cup

Football teams in the Manchester area competed annually for the Manchester Cup. Newton Heath entered the competition for the first time in 1885, losing in the Final. They won the Cup the next year, and reached the Final again in 1887. As football became more popular, Newton Heath's success in this and other local competitions brought prestige to the Railway Company, and the men were allowed time off to train.

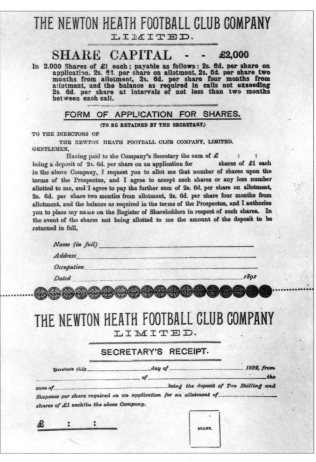

THE NEWTON HEATH FOOTBALL CLUB COMPANY
LIMITED.
SHARE CAPITAL - - £2,000

In 2,000 Shares of £1 each; payable as follows: 2s. 6d. per share on application; 2s. 6d. per share on allotment, 2s. 6d. per share two months from allotment, and the balance as required in calls not exceeding 2s. 6d. per share at intervals of not less than two months between each call.

FORM OF APPLICATION FOR SHARES.
(TO BE RETAINED BY THE SECRETARY.)

TO THE DIRECTORS OF
    THE NEWTON HEATH FOOTBALL CLUB COMPANY, LIMITED.
GENTLEMEN,
    Having paid to the Company's Secretary the sum of £   :   : being a deposit of 2s. 6d. per share on an application for   shares of £1 each in the above Company, I request you to allot me that number of shares upon the terms of the Prospectus, and I agree to accept such shares or any less number allotted to me, and I agree to pay the further sum of 2s. 6d. per share on allotment, 2s. 6d. per share two months from allotment, 2s. 6d. per share four months from allotment, and the balance as required in the terms of the Prospectus, and I authorise you to place my name on the Register of Shareholders in respect of such shares. In the event of the shares not being allotted to me the amount of the deposit to be returned in full.

Name (in full) _____
Address _____
Occupation _____
Dated _____1892

THE NEWTON HEATH FOOTBALL CLUB COMPANY
LIMITED.
SECRETARY'S RECEIPT.

Received this _____ day of _____ 1892, from _____
sum of _____ being the deposit of Two Shilling and Sixpence per share required on an application for an allotment of _____ shares of £1 eachin the above Company.

£   :   :

STAMP.

Record win

The Bank Street ground gave the Heathens one notable victory. On 9th March, 1895 Walsall Town Swifts were the visitors. The Swifts manager took one look at the pitch and registered an official complaint. How could his team be expected to play across the drab expanses of wet sand, tufted sparsely with failing grass? As a gesture of goodwill, the hosts tipped more sand over the pitch but the complaint was not withdrawn. The game went ahead and Newton Heath beat Walsall Town 14–0. Sadly, the result is known only in legend not in any official statistics because, in view of Walsall's prior complaint, the match was declared null and void.

Down and almost out

Newton Heath battled on in the Second Division. In 1897, they made the play-offs but failed to make it back into the First Division. In 1898, Manchester City leapfrogged over them into the First Division. In 1899, forward Henry Boyd was put on the transfer list following a string of disciplinary offences. Another forward, John Cunningham, was similarly ejected, and a third forward, Matthew Gillespie, was suspended for a time. This purging of its forward line made no change to the depressing rut into which Newton Heath had fallen. Morale fell, performances worsened and attendances dropped. The club's financial future looked more and more precarious.

Raising funds

On the right is an application form for £1 shares in Newton Heath Football Club, from 1892. The application form had to be returned to the secretary, A.H. Albut. He was the club's first full-time official, appointed in 1890, and he was working from a small terraced cottage at 33 Oldham Road, near the North Road ground.

The formation of Manchester United

On 9th January, 1902 William Healey, President of Newton Heath and one of its chief creditors, took the club to court to apply for its compulsory winding-up. He was owed £242 17s. 10d. – a lot of money in those days. The club, £2,600 in the red, was declared bankrupt. The *Manchester Evening News* reported that there was "no question of extinction. It is certain that when the immediate stress of financial resources has been removed, a big effort will be made to put the club on a much sounder basis than it has been for the past two years." But when the official receiver intervened before the next fixture and cancelled it, locking the gates at Bank Street, a "sound basis" seemed very far away.

Harry Stafford, the Heathens' full-back and captain, now became the club's most vigorous fund-raiser. A former boiler-maker, Stafford was a striking figure, almost dandyish in his white hat and garish waistcoat. He pulled together enough money to cover travel expenses to the next game – away to Bristol – and found an interim ground for the club at Harpurhey.

Funds are found

Stafford's fund-raising campaign was a success. He was able to enlist the help of the managing director of Manchester Breweries, John Henry Davies, and three other Manchester businessmen. They each invested £500 in return for a

direct interest in the running of the club. By mid-1902, Davies was installed as president of a newly upholstered Newton Heath. He was later to pay £60,000 to build a new stadium – Old Trafford.

A new name

Newton Heath was saved but it was decided that, in a spirit of renewal, the club should change its name. The team now had few ties with its origins, geographical or otherwise. The players were no longer railwaymen and the ground was no longer at Newton Heath. The names "Manchester Central" and "Manchester Celtic" were mooted but were dismissed for being too industrial or too Scottish. It was Louis Rocca, later to play a crucial role as Matt Busby's first super-scout, who suggested the new name. Newton Heath became Manchester United.

Men of influence

John Davies poses with his team and the English Cup in 1909. Sitting on his right is Charlie Roberts, who played for Manchester United from season 1903/04 until the First World War broke out in 1914.

The Grand Bazaar

The fund-raising bazaar of 1901 took place in St. James's Hall, Manchester. It did not raise a huge amount of cash but nonetheless contributed to the rescue of Newton Heath.

NEWTON HEATH FOOTBALL CLUB.

GRAND · BAZAAR,
REPRESENTING
"SUNNY LANDS,"

St. James's Hall,
Manchester,

Good to begin well, better to end well.

WEDNESDAY, FEBRUARY 27TH.
THURSDAY, FEBRUARY 28TH.
FRIDAY, MARCH 1ST.
SATURDAY, MARCH 2ND.

PRICES OF ADMISSION
FIRST DAY, 2s. 6d., after 6 p.m. 1s.
SECOND DAY, 1s. all day.
THIRD DAY, 1s., after 6 p.m. 6d.
FOURTH DAY, 6d. all day.

Season Tickets, 3s. 6d.
CHILDREN. HALF-PRICE.

Saved by a dog

In 1901, a fund-raising bazaar was organized. According to legend, it was indirectly one of the most important events in the history of Manchester United. It is said that Stafford had a St. Bernard dog, which was on show at the bazaar. One night it escaped. John Davies saw it and liked it. He asked Stafford if he could have it and Stafford asked him for a contribution to the funds in exchange. This chance meeting led to the saving of Newton Heath and the formation of Manchester United.

The Ernest Mangnall Era

Ernest Mangnall
Ernest Mangnall had been secretary at Burnley before joining United as manager.

If being rechristened "Manchester United" was one of the most significant events in the club's history, then another must have been the arrival of Ernest Mangnall in 1903. An old-fashioned passion for cycling (he once rode all the way from Land's End to John O'Groats) did not prevent Mangnall from being a modern manager. In an article for the *Manchester Evening News*, he wrote: "A great, intricate, almost delicate and, to the vast majority of the public, an incomprehensible piece of machinery is the modern, up-to-date, football club. It is a creation peculiarly by itself. There is nothing like it."

Mangnall was United's first real manager and he stayed at the club until 1912. As a team builder, he looked for a blending of young and old. In his first season, he picked 28 players for the first team as he searched for the right combination. He adhered to the dictum: "A ball should be used one day a week." The idea was that by Saturday, the players would be longing for the ball and would play madly for it. Mangnall took the club into the First Division, won two League championships, the FA Cup, Charity Shield (twice) and the Manchester Cup, and saw them move to the now famous ground of Old Trafford.

1903–1905

When Mangnall joined United, the club's finances were secure enough for him to venture on to the transfer market. By 1904, stalwarts such as keeper Harry Moger, forwards Charlie Sagar and John Picken, and half-backs Duckworth, Bell and Roberts had all arrived. They formed the beginnings of a team, which finished third in the Second Division at the end of the 1903/04 season. The next season, United had a run of 18 games without defeat, 16 of them wins. They finally finished third again in the division.

1905/06

This proved to be a magnificent season for United. In the first and second rounds of the FA Cup they had resounding wins; 7–1 over Staple Hill and 3–0 over Norwich City. Their third-round match was at home to Aston Villa on 20th February, 1906. A crowd of 40,000 made the trip to Clayton to watch the game and were rewarded with what the *Athletic News* called "a crop of extraordinary happenings". Aston Villa were five-time Cup winners and current holders, and four-time League champions. United won 5–1. The result was a huge overturning of expectations, and contained for Mangnall's United the seeds of future greatness. They would not always be identified with the marshy surface of their pitch at Clayton. For the first time since 1897, United were in the quarter-finals of the FA Cup, but here the run ended. They were beaten by Woolwich Arsenal 3–2. Mangnall's men, though doubtless disappointed, had other matters to attend to.

Leading the way
A committed activist in the early days of the Players' Union, Charlie Roberts was a natural captain whose quick thinking was matched only by his tremendous pace. He was a leader of fashion, wearing thigh-revealing shorts at a time when most players were keeping their knees covered.

The First Division

United's 12-year imprisonment in the Second Division was about to end. They finished the 1905/06 season in second place, four points behind Bristol City but nine points ahead of third place Chelsea, and were promoted. The *Manchester Evening News* commented: "Having obtained his ambition in reaching the Premier Division, Mr Davies (Club President) is determined to get together an XI that will be able to do honour to the city, and negotiations are already in progress with a view to strengthening the team." Negotiations were indeed in progress, but not quite in the way the public imagined. Ernest Mangnall was about to cause a sensation by signing four rather special players.

Manchester City in trouble

To understand the fuss, one has to go back two years, to Manchester City's FA Cup triumph of 1904. City were the pride of Manchester, but their victory served only to focus the hostile attention of the FA, which suspected the club of dealing in illegal wages and bonuses. An investigation followed which, while it uncovered no evidence of the suspected illegal practices, nonetheless turned up enough dirt to have the club fined £250 and the ground closed for a month. A few months later, an inquiry into the club, called the Clegg Inquiry, delivered findings that implicated Billy Meredith, City's right-winger, in attempted bribery. Meredith was suspended and in the investigations that followed almost the whole of Manchester City FC was taken apart. Five directors were dismissed and 17 players were banned from ever appearing for the club again. A date was set for their auction. Watching with interest was Ernest Mangnall. United, he knew, could not afford auction prices, so he made his move early. On 15th May, 1906, Manchester United announced the signing of Billy Meredith, and Mangnall

Billy Meredith
"The Welsh Wizard" in action for Manchester United against Queen's Park Rangers in the first-ever Charity Shield match, played at Stamford Bridge on 27th April, 1908. Only 6,000 people turned up for the match, which finished 1–1. Billy Meredith scored United's goal. It was a different story, though, in the replay at the same ground on 29th August, 1908. A crowd of 60,000 people witnessed a match that United dominated, winning 4–0.

Champions

The team and officials that put the name of Manchester United on the League championship trophy for the first time at the end of the 1907/08 season. The season included a run of 10 straight wins.

spent the close season secretly negotiating the transfers of Sandy Turnbull, Jimmy Bannister and Herbert Burgess. None of them could set foot on a pitch, since they were all suspended, but Ernest Mangnall could wait.

The ascendancy begins

Manchester United's new era began on New Year's Day, 1907. At home against Aston Villa, Mangnall unveiled his new team. On the right wing Billy Meredith was his usual self, setting up Sandy Turnbull for the game's only goal. Ex-blacksmith Herbert Burgess slotted in at full-back, and Jimmy Bannister looked comfortable in the forward line. In midfield were George Wall, Alex Bell, Dick Duckworth and Charlie Roberts, who was perhaps Mangnall's most inspired signing, from Grimsby. The new United won the championship in 1908.

The Outcasts

The start of the 1909/10 season was threatened by a players' strike. The Players' Union had been trying to affiliate to the Federation of Trade Unions, but the football authorities were worried that the players might get involved in other unions' strikes. The League decided that they would suspend any member of the Union, stop his wages and ban him from playing. Led by Meredith, most of the Manchester United players refused to leave the Union and were suspended. They started training independently as "The Outcasts". On 31st August, the authorities gave in. The Union was recognized, suspensions were lifted and back pay was allowed.

Their first Final

Manchester United's first FA Cup Final was against Bristol City. The match took place at London's Crystal Palace on 2nd April, 1909. It was a typical Final, with both teams paralysed by the occasion. The only goal was scored by Sandy Turnbull to give United the Cup.

Going for the Cup

United's 1909 Cup run began against Brighton, whom they beat 1-0. Another 1-0 win over Everton took them on to meet Blackburn Rovers. Forty thousand people came to watch the tie with great interest. United were a young team gathering momentum; Blackburn Rovers were a well established side with a solid defence. In the end it was a rout, with United winning 6-1. They bounced into the quarter-finals to meet Burnley from the Second Division. The referee was Herbert Bamlett who, 18 years later, would become United's manager. The match was stopped by blizzard conditions and replayed at Burnley four days later. The final score was 3-2 to United. In the semi-finals they faced the formidable Newcastle, who were chasing the Double that season. They beat them 1-0 and the Cup Final beckoned. United won the Final against Bristol City 1-0.

Leaving for City

In the middle of the 1909/10 season the club moved to Old Trafford. They ended their first season there in fifth place. They were League champions again in 1910/11, but fell to 13th place in 1911/12. Before the start of the 1912/13 season, Ernest Mangnall resigned. He left to join United's arch rivals, Manchester City.

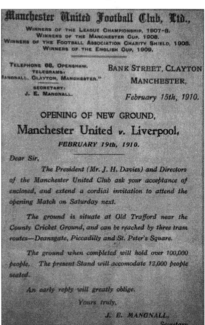

Old Trafford

Invitations were issued to VIPs to attend United's first match at Old Trafford - against Liverpool - on 19th February, 1910. The new ground was able to hold 100,000 fans. Two days before the match, the old wooden stand at the Bank Street ground collapsed, blown down by strong gales.

1912–1952

In the years between Mangnall's departure and the First World War, many of the big names at United reached the end of their playing careers, and as they left the game, so did the crowds. This had a bad effect on United's finances, which were dented further by the war when there was no football and therefore no money coming in, yet the club had to continue to pay for the running of Old Trafford. In 1921, United fans were dismayed to see their hero Billy Meredith rejoin his old club, Manchester City. At the end of that season United were relegated, having won only eight games. They had to wait until 1925 to return to the First Division. In December 1931, the club almost went bankrupt but was saved by a Manchester businessman, James Gibson. It was Gibson who was responsible for bringing the legendary Matt Busby to the club almost 14 years later. Between the wars, United's fortunes went up and down like a yo-yo. Attendances rose and fell and managers came and went. The team was relegated and promoted five times before the 1937/38 season and the start of 36 years in the top flight. In 1945, Busby took over as manager. The period when he was in charge - 25 years - was the most successful in United's history.

Team talk
Players and manager Scott Duncan discuss tactics during a training session at Old Trafford in October 1935. United won the Second Division title that season and were promoted, but they came straight back down again after winning only 10 games the following season.

Up and down

One of the worst cycles in the history of the club started on 8th October, 1926. The FA issued a statement to the press: "For improper conduct in his position as secretary/manager of the Manchester United football club, the Football Association have suspended Mr J.A. Chapman from taking part in football or football management during the present season." No reason was ever publicly given for the suspension. Half-back Clarence Hilditch became player-manager. He kept the team in the First Division but, without the time to enforce his own ideas, he unwittingly ushered in an era of managerial torpor and lack of initiative that almost destroyed United. Herbert Bamlett took over in 1927 and guided the club into a steady decline. In October 1927 club president J.H. Davies died, robbing Old Trafford of its principal benefactor. The situation became desperate.

Supporters' revolt

The Manchester United Supporters' Club proposed a five-point plan to the board. The supporters wanted: 1, a new manager; 2, an overhaul of the scouting system; 3, the signing of some quality players; 4, the election of five shareholders to the board; 5, the raising of capital through a new issue of shares. The board ignored them. The supporters issued a warning. If their demands were not taken seriously they would instigate a boycott of the game against Arsenal on 18th October. There was no reply. On the eve of the Arsenal match the Supporters' Club met and voted for a boycott but, despite this, 23,000 people turned up for Arsenal's visit. However, United played so badly that from then on only the most fanatical turned up to watch them. The stadium was almost empty for the final match of the season, against Middlesbrough.

Struggling on

Herbert Bamlett was sacked on 31st April, 1931. Walter Crickmer took over and, with the help of Louis Rocca, sometime scout and all-round fixer for the club, managed to keep United afloat. The brewery company that held the mortgage on Old Trafford agreed to allow it to lapse. Stretford Urban District Council, to whom United owed road charges, accepted an instalment plan, and the Inland Revenue relented on its immediate demands. Then, in December 1931, Crickmer was turned away from the bank. United's credit was exhausted and the end of the club seemed to be inevitable. It was then that someone approached James Gibson. Gibson was not a lover of football, but he loved Manchester and hated to see one of its institutions perish. He put £2,000 at the club's disposal and had control of the club within a week. According to Mr Greenhough of the Supporters' Club: "Mr Gibson would be looking for the sort of manager to whom he would give full control and allow to reorganize the club." These words would in due course be answered by a man who was at that moment toiling in the lower echelons at Manchester City - Matt Busby.

Saved

On the outbreak of war in 1939, football was effectively frozen. United were by then a viable First Division side, having finished the 1938/39 season in 14th place. More importantly, Gibson had established the Manchester United Junior Athletic Club, a hotbed of young talent that would sustain the club for years to come. In ensuring the future of United, Gibson had been aided by the administrative excellence of Walter Crickmer, the flair of Louis Rocca, and the unfailing support of the people of Manchester. He continued as chairman until June 1950, living to see the grand rewards of his initial commitment.

Pre-Busby bosses

Manchester United had six different managers between the eras of Ernest Mangnall, who left in 1912, and Matt Busby, who joined in 1945.

John Robson
1914–1921

John Chapman
1921–1926

Clarence Hilditch
1926–1927

Herbert Bamlett
1927–1931

Walter Crickmer
1931–1932, 1937–1945

Scott Duncan
1932–1937

War damage
The stadium at Old Trafford was a bombed-out hulk when Matt Busby arrived at Manchester United. At that time the team *played at Maine Road, paying £5,000 a year in rent to Manchester City. The club was practically bankrupt and many of its players were still in the armed forces.*

Busby arrives

On 15th February, 1945, Matt Busby travelled to Manchester to meet James Gibson. Busby was initially offered a three-year contract but, at his insistence, this was lengthened to five years. He knew that the work he had to do would take time and patience. He demanded the authority to appoint his own staff and act on his own judgement in all matters that pertained to the playing of the game. He asked for equal measures of power and responsibility, on a scale that had not previously been imagined.

The start of an era

Busby assumed managerial command of Manchester United mid-season, in October 1945. His first act was to call in Jimmy Murphy, whom he put in charge of the Reserve team. Murphy would also

be heavily involved with the junior players. Their partnership was to last for nearly 30 years.

The United players returned one by one from wartime service, not having seen much more than a season of first-team action. They were experienced professionals who were nonetheless fresh as novices and ready to learn from Busby. Busby prepared for the 1946/47 season by transfer-listing seven players, then beginning a series of positional changes. Johnny Carey finally found his home at full-back; John Aston discovered his as a defender; Henry Cockburn was turned from a forward into a wing-half. Jimmy Delaney was bought from Celtic to join Pearson, Rowley, Mitten and Morris and complete the "famous five" forwards. These key changes had immediate results. Manchester United ended the 1946/47 season as runners-up in the League. Then in 1948 they won the Cup, beating Blackpool 4–2 in a hard-fought Final. Gibson, who had been too ill to attend any of his team's Cup performances, welcomed the conquering heroes home with the words: "You have fulfilled my greatest ambition."

Busby's first great team
The United team of 1946/47, a mixture of Matt Busby's new signings and players who were already at the club when he arrived. They won the FA Cup in 1948, and became the first of Busby's three great teams.

New style of manager
Busby was a physical presence, magnetic and imposing. He astonished people by appearing at training sessions in his *tracksuit and training alongside his first team. He instilled in the players a desire to perform for him, to do their very best.*

Young for old

At the start of the 1948/49 season, unhappy mutterings began in the dressing room. The players wanted more money. Other clubs paid their players illegal bonuses, but Busby refused. The 1948 team had peaked and Busby's first stars were pushing 30. They wanted to cash in while they were still in the game.

The first player to go was Johnny Morris, sold to Derby in 1949 after a series of training-ground set-tos with Busby. Then, in the summer of 1950,

Charlie Mitten was lured to Colombia. Busby was not worried. He knew that there were some promising developments in the Youth and Reserve teams. Roger Byrne, Jeff Whitefoot, Jackie Blanchflower and Mark Jones were names that were beginning to be mentioned among the supporters. Roger Byrne was the first to make his debut, late in November 1951. He scored seven goals in the last six League games, making a vital contribution to the effort that secured United the 1951/52 League championship.

The Busby Babes

The "Busby Babes" were so named for their youth (most of them made their first-team debut for United as teenagers), and of course for their manager, Matt Busby. The name was coined after a game in November 1951 when Busby gave 18-year-old Jackie Blanchflower and 21-year-old Roger Byrne their debuts against Liverpool at Anfield. Both players had come up through the Youth and Reserve teams and Tom Jackson of the *Manchester Evening News* described them in his match report as "United's Babes". The name stuck and was soon joined to the name of the manager. The Busby Babes were born.

The main players in the Babes, other than Blanchflower and Byrne, were Bobby Charlton, Johnny Berry, Wilf McGuinness, Duncan Edwards, Tommy Taylor, Eddie Colman, Albert Scanlon, Ray Wood, Dennis Viollet, David Pegg, Mark Jones and Liam Whelan. Not all of them were "Babes" by the strictest definition. Not all of them came up through United's youth programme, and some were older than others, but all of them were part of a phenomenon that lit up English and European football in the '50s. The Busby Babes flourished between 1953 and 1958. Their reign ended with the Munich air disaster.

MUJAC

In 1938, the Manchester United Junior Athletic Club was formed. Its aim was to seek out talented young players and give them the chance to develop their abilities by working with professional coaches and trainers. Scouts went all over the nation to watch local and schoolboy football matches in an attempt both to give the best a chance and, of course, to bring them to United before other teams showed an interest.

The dream team

When Matt Busby arrived at Old Trafford in October 1945, he brought with him a vision. He foresaw a time when Manchester United, by combining diligent, attentive management with a vigorous youth development programme, could produce its own players and its own style. He wanted to build a system that would produce four or five teams, each one like a rung on a ladder, the top rung being the first team. The framework of this system was already in place. It had been there since 1938, when secretary Walter Crickmer and chairman James Gibson set up the Manchester United Junior Athletic Club.

The Manchester United Junior Athletic Club, or MUJAC, was responsible for the development of post-war heroes such as Johnny Morris and John Aston (Snr.), and he provided a model for the youth programme's future success.

In 1950, Joe Armstrong replaced Louis Rocca as United's chief scout. Like his predecessor, Armstrong kept his ear to the ground. He reassured anxious parents of young prospects, trading on the (by now) winning brand name of Manchester United, to acquire the talent that the club needed. It was Joe Armstrong who first spotted the enormous potential in schoolboys Bobby Charlton and Duncan Edwards.

Blackpool v United
Mark Jones and Bill Foulkes in action during the 0-0 draw against Blackpool in 1956. With two games left of the League season, the Babes were confirmed champions after the corresponding fixture at Old Trafford, when United beat their nearest rivals 2-1. The two goals were scored by Johnny Berry and Tommy Taylor.

The Babes are introduced

As the team that won the FA Cup in 1948 began to age and tire, the presence of boys from the Youth team began to be felt on the fringes of the first XI. The 1948 team made a last stand with its conquest of the League in 1952. From then on more and more new young talent was introduced into the first team.

While Busby had been assembling his first great team and guiding them towards the FA Cup triumph in 1948, coach Jimmy Murphy had been working in the lower echelons of the club. With Bert Whalley joining the coaching staff in 1947, the structure was complete. Along with trainers Bill Inglis and Tom Curry, Whalley and Murphy took the raw material of teenagers and shaped it with wisdom, preparing the boys for a life of football. Supplied with schoolboys of the calibre of Duncan Edwards and Bobby Charlton, Murphy worked tirelessly, training with his young charges sometimes into the twilight hours to sharpen up their game. The Youth team won the FA Youth Cup five times in a row from its introduction in 1952/53.

Duncan Edwards' debut

In April 1953, 16-year-old Duncan Edwards arrived at Old Trafford for his usual tour of duty with the ground staff,

Youth team triumph in Zurich

Having won the first FA Youth Cup in 1953, Manchester United's Youth team of 1953/54 were invited to enter the 1953/54 Blue Stars International Youth Tournament in Zurich.

only to be told by Matt Busby to get his boots on. He phoned his parents, then rushed back to his lodgings to tell his landlady the news. Other graduates from Mrs Watson's boarding house at 5 Birch Avenue included Mark Jones, David Pegg and Jackie Blanchflower, all of whom had already tasted first-team action.

Carey retires

A month later, on 23rd May, 1953, United's captain Johnny Carey announced his retirement as a player, aged 34. Pearson and Chilton both had brief captaincies, but in 1955 another full-back, Roger Byrne took over, to lead the Babes until his death at Munich.

As word spread of the extraordinary young talent being developed at Manchester United, attendances for the club's Youth games swelled dramatically. After his Youth team had beaten Wolves in the FA Youth Cup in May 1953, Busby took the players to Zurich, Switzerland, to compete in the International Youth Cup. There, Bobby Charlton and his teenage colleagues were exposed for the first time to the flair and pace of continental-style football, a style with which they would become closely identified when, three years later, Manchester United's European adventure began in earnest.

The Babes' boss was said to dislike their name, unhappy with its infantile connotations. Despite their years, Busby's players were fiercely mature. He preferred the swashbuckling name "Red Devils", which seemed a more accurate description. This new generation was bolder and brighter than anything football had seen before. They were both devils and babes. Their "demonic" power was offset by a pure enjoyment of the game, an innocent pleasure in the simple exercise of their skills. These were virtues that Busby had instilled in his team since his first day as manager.

was in Europe that the true legend of the Babes was forged. The grander scale of continental football - the arenas, the national fervour - seemed to suit the Babes, as did the exhilarating speed of the teams they faced. The first English team into Europe, their first tilt at the Cup took them to the semi-finals, where they were beaten by Real Madrid, but where they nonetheless thrilled a huge international audience.

The Babes won the English League again in 1957. They were undoubtedly the best team in the country and, because they were so young, everyone knew they had still not reached their full potential. In fact, they were within one match of winning the League and

On tour
After the championship-winning season of 1956/57, the victorious young team went on a victory parade around the streets of Manchester in an open-topped bus, watched by hordes of jubilant fans.

FA Cup Double in 1956/57. They faced Aston Villa in the FA Cup Final and were full of confidence until Ray Wood was injured by Peter McParland's charge at the United goal. No substitutes were allowed in those days and United lost the match 1–2.

Champions

The take-over of the first team by the Babes was gradual and carefully handled. By the mid-1950s, all the elements were in place and the young team began its ascent. Keen-eyed observers discerned the markings of greatness as early as November 1955, when United beat the League champions, Chelsea. Eddie Colman made his debut that day, combining with Edwards in defence to help United to a 3–0 victory. At the end of the season, Roger Byrne hoisted the League trophy aloft at Old Trafford. United were 11 points clear of their nearest challengers, Blackpool. Their championship run included 20 goals from Dennis Viollet.

The championship qualified United for the 1956/57 European Cup and a chance to test themselves against the greatest. It

Shattered
Only six minutes into the 1957 FA Cup Final, Aston Villa's Peter McParland headed the ball into Ray Wood's arms and kept running, crashing into the United keeper. Wood fractured his cheekbone and was carried from the field. United's hopes of the Double were lost.

Champions 1956/57
The stars of the 1956/57 season line up with their two trophies: the championship trophy (left) and the Charity Shield (right).

Last match
The Busby Babes lined up together for the last time on 5th February, 1958 in Belgrade. Left to right: Edwards, Colman, Jones, Morgans, Charlton, Viollet, Taylor, Foulkes, Gregg, Scanlon, Byrne.

End of an era

United headed once again for Europe the following season, hoping this time to win the trophy as part of a treble. They comfortably dispatched Shamrock Rovers and Dukla Prague in the first two rounds and were drawn against Red Star Belgrade in the quarter-finals. Many of the Babes did not want to go to Yugoslavia for the match, worried about going behind the Iron Curtain. Their worries turned out to be well-founded, but for a different reason. After a hard-fought 3–3 tie, the Babes emerged 5–4 winners on aggregate, but their progress towards the Cup was interrupted by an event that was to cast a shadow over all football. The tragedy of the Munich air disaster brought the era of the Busby Babes to a sudden end. The fellowship of youth, promise and achievement that the Babes had brought to United was all but destroyed, and the club entered a period of sombre renewal.

The Munich Air Disaster

On 6th February, 1958 a plane crash at Munich airport killed 21 people, including seven Manchester United players. The players were on their way home from a European Cup quarter-final against Red Star Belgrade. The plane had stopped at Munich for a routine refuelling. Back in Manchester the newspapers were first with the news. The headline "UNITED CUP XI: 28 DIE" was an exaggeration but it made little difference to the impact of the tragedy. The novelist H.E. Bates described his reaction to hearing about the tragedy on television's six o'clock news. "The screen seemed to go black. The normally urbane

voice of the announcer seemed to turn into a sledgehammer. My eyes went deathly cold and I sat listening with a frozen brain to that shocking list of casualties." As well as the players, United lost coach Bert Whalley, trainer Tom Curry and club secretary Walter Crickmer. Eight journalists also died. Left fighting for their lives in hospital were Matt Busby, Duncan Edwards, Johnny Berry and one of the pilots of the plane, Captain Ken Rayment. Rayment died soon after. Edwards was hurt so badly that he should have died immediately but he hung on for 15 days. He finally died of kidney failure on 21st February.

The crash

After a night of mild celebration in Belgrade, the Busby Babes boarded Flight 609 for Manchester, mid-morning. They were due to arrive home at 6:00 p.m. The chartered plane was an Elizabethan class G-ALZN A5 57, the *Lord Burghley*, piloted by Captain James Thain and his co-pilot and friend Captain Kenneth Rayment. Although Thain was in command, it had been agreed that Captain Rayment would fly the plane home. The atmosphere on board was subdued but content. There were two card tables across which the players could face each other. Their games petered out shortly before the plane began its descent to Munich airport for refuelling. Only when they had almost reached ground level did the passengers notice that it was snowing.

Aborted take-offs

The refuelling was scheduled to take no more than 20 minutes so the passengers remained on board. At 2:31 p.m., its tanks full, Flight 609 readied itself on the runway and received clearance to take off. As the plane picked up speed, the pilots heard an odd note from the engines and after 40 seconds they aborted the take-off. The sound they had heard suggested a phenomenon called "boost surging" – the result of rich fuel causing the engines to over-accelerate. The problem was not uncommon in Elizabethans and the pilots saw no reason for alarm. Deciding to compensate for the problem by letting the throttle out more slowly, they again

Flight 609
Passengers on the ill-fated Flight 609 board the plane. As well as Manchester United players and staff, the passengers included

attempted to take off at 2:34 p.m. Again the engines soared, and this time Thain and Rayment decided to taxi back to the terminal to discuss what to do.

Last moments

Informed of a "technical fault", the passengers disembarked. It was a curious moment of hiatus. They knocked about in the cafeteria, discussed going home via the Hook of Holland, and groaned at

journalists, a few supporters and associates. One Yugoslav writer Miro Radojic missed the plane at Belgrade after going home to get his passport which he had forgotten.

the prospect of overland travel. There was chat and nervous humour. Duncan Edwards must have thought that there would not be another attempt to take off that day. While the passengers were waiting in the airport cafeteria he took the opportunity to send a telegram to his landlady in Manchester, Mrs Dorman. It read: "ALL FLIGHTS CANCELLED FLYING TOMORROW = DUNCAN." The telegram was delivered at about 5:00 p.m. – after

The wreckage
The plane collided with a house, tearing off a wing and part of the tail. The cockpit hit a tree and the body hit a hut full of tyres and fuel, where it exploded into flames.

the crash. Edwards had been mistaken, because it wasn't long before the passengers were recalled to the plane. Having consulted the ground staff at Munich, Captains Thain and Rayment decided against an overnight stay at the airport for retuning of the engine. The boost surging seemed to be confined to the port engine and, since Elizabethans had the power to take off on a single engine, the pilots were satisfied that they could make it off the ground.

Third time – disaster

As the plane rushed into its third attempt to leave Munich, the passengers were frightened. The design of the plane meant that they could see each other's faces. Roger Byrne's shaky expression transmitted fear to his team mates. Johnny Berry voiced his belief that they were all about to be killed. Liam Whelan, a devout Catholic, answered that he was ready to die. Harry Gregg saw "snow coming off the

The Dead

The Munich air disaster closed the chapter on a team that was, despite its many triumphs, still not fully formed. For many, the tragedy felt like a physical blow. United, the standard-bearers of English football, lost eight players and three other members of staff. Forty years on, people still dream of what could have been.

Geoff Bent
Full-back
Aged 25

Roger Byrne
Full-back
Aged 28

Eddie Colman
Half-back
Aged 21

Duncan Edwards
Half-back
Aged 22

Mark Jones
Half-back
Aged 24

The aftermath

News of the crash moved quickly to Manchester. Mark Jones' wife, June, heard it in a supermarket. United players learned of the tragedy from ground staff. Jimmy Murphy, who had missed the trip due to commitments with the Welsh international side, heard it from Matt Busby's secretary, Alma George. Matt's son Sandy read it on placards. Murphy

Missing players
The programme for the Sheffield Wednesday match brought home the scale of United's loss. No-one knew in advance who would play and the team list was left empty.

flew out to Munich the next day. He walked around the wards to show the wounded that life would go on. Duncan Edwards asked Murphy what time kick-off was. Busby asked Murphy to take care of things for him.

The game goes on

Swallowing his grief, Jimmy Murphy got to work. Jack Crompton, once goalkeeper for the Cup-winning side of

1948, came back from his coaching job at Luton to help out, bringing new training routines and a freshness of spirit that was gladly felt by the players. Ernie Taylor was signed from Blackpool. On the day of their first match after the crash, only hours before the game, Murphy persuaded Stan Crowther to transfer from Aston Villa. United had been allowed to postpone the match – a fifth-round FA Cup tie against Sheffield Wednesday – until 19th February. Apart from the two new players, Murphy fielded a scratch team against Wednesday. The side was full of Reserve and Youth team players. They were led out on the pitch at Old Trafford by captain Bill Foulkes and, close behind him, Harry Gregg. Both Munich survivors, their entrance drew a roar from the crowd. Not surprisingly, Sheffield Wednesday were swamped by the occasion and United won 3-0.

After the game, Jimmy Murphy took his team to Blackpool, where they spent most of the rest of the season. FA Cup replays and the backlog of fixtures piled up by the crash gave them little time to think. They poured their energy into the Cup run, a crusade that kept the heart of the club beating. They reached the Final for a match against Bolton Wanderers. It was an amazing achievement in the circumstances but, in spite of the huge support of neutrals around the country, when Bolton's Nat Lofthouse scored the first goal United seemed to fall apart, finally exhausted. They lost 2-0.

Final injustice
Nat Lofthouse's second goal against United in the 1958 Cup Final is disputed to this day. As United's keeper Harry Gregg jumped to catch a cross, Nat Lofthouse charged in and pushed Gregg and the ball over the line. Gregg was knocked unconscious in the collision, and even Lofthouse was amazed that the goal was allowed to stand.

wheels like a speedboat". The plane rushed on, further than it had been before, but just as the pilot tried to take off, the *Lord Burghley* burst off the runway at high speed, skidded through a fence and across a road.

Gregg the hero

When the plane eventually came to a stop, there were no cries from inside, but gradually there was movement. Harry Gregg kicked his way out of the wreckage past the corpse of Bert Whalley. He was met by Captain Thain, uselessly holding a little fire-extinguisher and shouting at him to run because further explosions were imminent. Instead, Gregg plunged back into the plane to rescue a crying baby and her mother, who had fractured her skull and both legs. He dragged Dennis Viollet and Bobby Charlton clear of the wreckage by their waistbands. Busby was on the ground, complaining of pains in his chest and legs. Jackie Blanchflower was lying badly injured, with Roger Byrne dead across him. A stewardess stood nearby, paralysed with shock. At last cars and trucks arrived at the crash scene. Bodies were loaded into vehicles and rushed to Munich's Rechts der Isar hospital.

Fight for life
After the air crash Matt Busby was in a critical condition. His chest was shattered and his lungs punctured. Busby twice received the last rites, but he finally pulled through. He stayed in the Rechts der Isar hospital in Munich for 71 days before he was allowed to return home to Manchester.

David Pegg
Forward
Aged 22

Tommy Taylor
Forward
Aged 26

Liam Whelan
Forward
Aged 22

Walter Crickmer
Club secretary
Age unknown

Tom Curry
Trainer
Aged 64

Bert Whalley
Coach
Aged 45

The 1960s and 1970s

After the Munich disaster, Matt Busby said that it would take him five years to build a new team. The fans were behind him and United continued to be the best-supported club in the country, but they had to wait until 1963 for another trophy – the FA Cup. Then, from 1964 to 1968, United were League champions twice and finished second twice and fourth once. Their greatest achievement, however, came in 1968, when Manchester United became the first English club to win the European Cup. When Busby resigned as team manager in 1969 it was the end of an era. Busby had been in charge for 23 years and he was a hard act to follow. The 1970s were difficult years for the club, with the players having to adapt to four different managers in 10 years. After being relegated in 1974, United came up again immediately as Second Division champions, but they did not win the League again for almost 30 years.

The 1963 FA Cup Final
The end of Denis Law's first season at United saw him gain an FA Cup winners' medal. Law, who tormented Leicester City for much of the game, scored the first goal in United's 3-1 victory.

1959/1960
Dennis Viollet scores 32 League goals in the 1959/60 season, beating the record of 30 set by Jack Rowley in 1951/52. In 10 seasons, Viollet scored 159 goals in his 259 League appearances.

November 1960
Left-back Noel Cantwell signs for United. He plays an important part in Matt Busby's plans for rebuilding the team, and is to become club captain.

March 1962
United reach the semi-finals of the FA Cup, but lose 3–1 to Tottenham Hotspur at Hillsborough.

6th February, 1963
Pat Crerand joins United.

July 1962
Busby signs Denis Law for a record fee of £115,000. Law scores on his debut, earning the nickname "The King".

May 1963
United win the FA Cup, beating Leicester 3–1 in the Final. It is the side's first big success since the Munich disaster.

1963/64
Denis Law is voted European Footballer of the Year, having scored 46 goals in League and Cup games.

September 1963
George Best makes his debut, playing against West Bromwich Albion.

1964
The Youth team win the Youth Cup for the first time in seven years. In the team are promising youngsters such as Jimmy Rimmer, David Sadler, Bobby Noble, George Best, Willie Anderson and John Aston Jnr.

1960	1961	1962	1963	1964	1965

January 1962
Dennis Viollet leaves United to join Stoke in the Second Division.

1962/63
United finish 19th in the League out of 22, their lowest position with Matt Busby as manager.

1963/64
United finish second to Liverpool in the League, four points behind, qualifying them for the Fairs (now UEFA) Cup.

March 1964
United reach the semi-final of the FA Cup but lose to West Ham 1–3.

April 1964
John Connelly signs for Manchester United, completing Busby's third great team.

The 1970 FA Cup semi-final
George Best shoots towards the Leeds goal in the FA Cup semi-final in 1970. The match ended 0-0 and it took two replays before Leeds eventually beat United 1-0.

January 1971
George Best is suspended for six weeks after failing to turn up for training and for a disciplinary hearing at the FA.

December 1972
George Best and the management team are sacked. Tommy Docherty takes over as manager. Docherty signs George Graham, the first of nine Scotsmen.

January 1973
Sammy McIlroy is seriously injured in a car accident, but he recovers to come on as a substitute against Arsenal in the first game of the 1973/74 season.

May 1973
Charlton retires, having made a club record of 604 League appearances.

April 1974
Denis Law scores for Manchester City, confirming United's relegation to Division Two.

February 1972
Martin Buchan joins United.

1970	1971	1972	1973	1974	1975

March 1970
Leeds win the FA Cup semi-final against United in the 2nd replay.

May 1971
Nobby Stiles is transferred to Middlesbrough.

November 1971
Sammy McIlroy makes his debut against Manchester City, aged 17.

September 1972
United play Glasgow Celtic in Bobby Charlton's testimonial, watched by 60,358 people.

July 1973
Denis Law joins Manchester City on a free transfer.

September 1973
George Best returns.

May 1974
Stuart Pearson is signed from Hull City.

June 1970
Bill Foulkes retires from playing and becomes a coach.

December 1970
Third Division Aston Villa knock United out of the League Cup in the semi-finals, hastening McGuinness' removal as team manager after Christmas. He returns to training the Reserves and Busby temporarily takes over again.

1971
Frank O'Farrell is appointed manager in time for the new season. Matt Busby gives up his paid job and joins the board as a director.

Summer 1970
Ten players are put on the transfer list, including Denis Law.

Pitch invasion
When Denis Law sent United into the Second Division with his goal in 1974, the United fans invaded the pitch in an attempt to have the game abandoned. The game was stopped, but the result stood.

Best player
George Best came to prominence during the '60s, and became an icon for a generation.

Victory in Europe
Shay Brennan and Bobby Charlton parade the European Cup on a triumphant lap of honour after beating Benfica 4–1 in the Final at Wembley in 1968.

June 1966
Bobby Charlton, Nobby Stiles and John Connelly play for England in the country's World Cup triumph. Old Trafford is one of the venues.

1966/67
League champions again. United are unbeaten at home for the whole season and have the biggest away win – 6–1 against West Ham. During the season more than 1,000,000 people, the highest number since the war, watch the home games.

1964/65
United are League Champions again, for the first time since the Munich air disaster.

March 1966
George Best injures his knee in an FA Cup match. United cannot survive without him and lose the FA Cup semi-final to Everton and the European Cup semi-final to FK Partizan Belgrade.

September 1966
Alex Stepney joins United from Chelsea. Matt Busby later says that Stepney was one of the main reasons that they won the championship that season.

1967/68
A record average of more than 57,500 people attend League matches. United finish second in the League to rivals Manchester City. George Best is voted Footballer of the Year, having played 41 League games and scored his highest total of 28 goals.

September/October 1968
United play Estudiantes, the South American champions from Brazil, in the World Club championship. Over two bad-tempered legs, Estudiantes win 2–1 on aggregate.

August 1967
Brian Kidd makes his League debut, aged 18.

July 1968
Matt Busby is knighted for services to football.

April 1969
Wilf McGuinness is appointed team coach.

May 1969
Defence of the European Cup ends with a defeat by AC Milan in the semi-finals.

1965   **1966**   **1967**   **1968**   **1969**   **1970**

March 1965
Leeds beat United 1–0 in the FA Cup semi-final.

March 1967
David Herd breaks his leg scoring against Leicester City, marking the end of his United career.

May 1968
United are the first English club to win the European Cup.

January 1969
Busby announces that he will resign as team manager at the end of the season to become general manager.

December 1969
United lose to Manchester City in the semi-finals of the League Cup.

1965/66
Bobby Charlton is English and European Footballer of the Year.

Top of the League
Bill Foulkes raises the League trophy after United win the 1966/67 championship with a home draw against Stoke City.

May 1979
United and Arsenal play for the FA Cup in the "five-minute Final". Losing 2–0 with four minutes to go, United score twice, only for Arsenal to triumph with a 90th-minute winner.

1975/76
United finish third in the League, qualifying for the UEFA Cup.

January 1975
United lose 1–3 on aggregate to Norwich City in the League Cup semi-final.

1976/77
United go back into Europe after seven years out. Juventus knock them out in the second round.

May 1977
United win the FA Cup Final. Tommy Docherty's affair with Mary Brown becomes public; he is sacked, and Dave Sexton is appointed manager.

January 1978
Sexton's first major buy is Joe Jordan.

February 1978
Gordon McQueen signs for United.

November 1978
Gary Bailey makes his debut in goal.

1975   **1976**   **1977**   **1978**   **1979**   **1980**

February 1975
Steve Coppell arrives from Tranmere Rovers, coming on as a substitute against Cardiff City.

November 1975
Gordon Hill is bought from Millwall.

December 1976
Jimmy Greenhoff joins his brother Brian at United.

April 1978
Tommy Docherty, now manager of Derby, buys Gordon Hill from United.

August 1978
United win 4–0 at home in their centenary game against Real Madrid.

August 1979
Ray Wilkins signs for United. Stuart Pearson joins West Ham, having announced before the Cup Final in May that he would never play for United again.

April 1975
United are Second Division champions, and are promoted to the First Division again.

May 1976
Second Division side Southampton beat United 1–0 in the FA Cup Final.

Deflected glory
Lou Macari and Jimmy Greenhoff celebrate the winning goal in the 1977 FA Cup Final. The ball went into the net after Macari's shot was deflected off Greenhoff.

The 1980s and 1990s

During the 1980s and 1990s, football followers were to see the creation of another great team at Manchester United. Stars such as Mark Hughes, Bryan Robson, Eric Cantona and David Beckham all had their part to play. When Dave Sexton lost his job as manager in 1981, Ron Atkinson led the club for a relatively settled period of five-and-a-half years. United finished out of the top four in the League only once during his reign, won the FA Cup twice, and reached the Final of the League Cup once. It wasn't a bad record, but Atkinson never really won the hearts of the supporters. Alex Ferguson took his place and, with his new methods, gained the admiration of the fans as well as the respect of the players. His building up of the youth system at the club, and introduction of young players into the senior team, brought back memories of a previous young, talented Manchester United team. Fergie's Fledglings were born.

World class
After winning the FA Cup in 1983, the team posed as usual with the Cup. Unusually, the Cup then toured the city of Manchester without most of the players, who had to join their countries' international squads for the home International championship.

January 1980
Two Middlesbrough fans are killed at Ayrsome Park when a wall collapses as the fans leave the ground. United fans are accused of causing the tragedy.

February 1980
Louis Edwards dies of a heart attack and is succeeded as chairman by his son, Martin.

1980/81
Injuries cost United dearly as they win only three times in the first 12 League games and are knocked out of the League Cup by Coventry City.

April 1981
Manager Dave Sexton is sacked, although the team win seven games in a row at the end of the season – the best run since Busby was manager.

1981
United agree a sponsorship deal with Sharp.

1981/82
United finish third in the League, qualifying for the UEFA Cup.

February 1982
Sammy McIlroy leaves for Stoke City.

September 1982
Garry Birtles is sold back to Nottingham Forest for less than half what he cost.

March 1983
United lose the League (Milk) Cup Final 1–2 against Liverpool.

May 1983
United win the FA Cup against Brighton in a replay, destroying the Second Division club 4-0.

January 1984
Robert Maxwell tries, but fails, to take over United.

June 1984
Ray Wilkins is transferred to AC Milan.

1980 | **1981** | **1982** | **1983** | **1984** | **1985**

March 1980
Ipswich Town beat United 6–0 in the League in spite of the fact that Gary Bailey saves two penalties.

October 1980
Garry Birtles costs United £1,250,000 – a club record at the time.

June 1981
Ron Atkinson arrives at Old Trafford as manager.

October 1981
Bryan Robson signs for a record £1.5 million.

October 1982
Ray Wilkins fractures his cheekbone and loses the captaincy of both club and country to Bryan Robson.

October 1983
Mark Hughes comes on as substitute in a Milk Cup tie against Port Vale, his first game in the senior team.

Summer 1984
Atkinson signs Gordon Strachan from Aberdeen, Jesper Olsen from Dutch club Ajax, and Alan Brazil from Spurs.

May 1990
Liverpool win the championship, with United way behind in 13th place. Ferguson unwillingly drops Leighton for the FA Cup Final replay against Crystal Palace, hastening the end of his career. United win 1–0 and Bryan Robson becomes the first captain to win the FA Cup three times.

August 1981
Frank Stapleton signs for United for a fee of £900,000, set by a League tribunal.

Summer 1982
Atkinson signs Arnold Muhren.

1982
The Youth team reach the Final of the FA Youth Cup for the first time since 1964.

Summer 1991
United is floated on the Stock Exchange. First Division clubs resign from the Football League. Ferguson signs Peter Schmeichel and Paul Parker.

April 1992
United win the League (Rumbelows) Cup, beating Nottingham Forest 1–0 in the Final. Leeds win the championship, beating United by four points.

April 1993
The start of a run of seven wins in the last seven games of the season, to make United champions again after 26 years and winners of the first Premier Division championship.

January 1994
Sir Matt Busby dies, aged 84.

March 1994
Aston Villa beat United 3–1 in the League (Coca Cola) Cup Final.

1990 | **1991** | **1992** | **1993** | **1994** | **1995**

June 1990
Ferguson buys Denis Irwin from Oldham.

May 1991
English clubs are allowed back in Europe and United win the European Cup Winners' Cup. Andrei Kanchelskis arrives at Old Trafford.

Summer 1992
The Premier League is launched. Dion Dublin joins United and Mark Robins is sold to Norwich City.

July 1993
Roy Keane is signed for a British record transfer fee of £3.75 million.

October 1993
United lose in the European Cup to Turkish side Galatasaray.

May 1994
United beat Chelsea in the FA Cup Final, to complete the club's first-ever Double.

November 1992
Eric Cantona joins United.

Europe 1991
Mark Hughes scored both United's goals in the 1991 European Cup Winners' Cup Final. United won the Final against Barcelona 2-1.

Two years running
Steve Bruce and Bryan Robson with the Premiership trophy at the end of the 1992/93 season. United successfully defended the championship, winning again in 1993/94.

The 1985 FA Cup Final

Late in the second half, with the score at 0–0, Everton's Peter Reid came running through on goal. In an attempt to clear the ball, Kevin Moran mistimed his tackle, fouled Reid and became the first player ever to be sent off in an FA Cup Final. Down to 10 men, United mustered everything they had and, in extra time, Norman Whiteside scored the only goal of the match. United had won the Cup again.

April 1988
Alex Ferguson and Liverpool manager Kenny Dalglish clash after their teams draw 3–3 in a tense end-of-season match. Brian McClair scores his 20th League goal of the season in the 3–0 home win against Luton Town – the first player to do so since George Best, 20 years earlier.

September 1989
Paul Ince and Danny Wallace join United. The Knighton deal is announced as "off" because his backers are pulling out. Knighton tells the press that the deal is "on".

December 1987
Steve Bruce joins United from Norwich after two weeks of negotiations.

1988/89
"Fergie's Fledglings" begin to emerge.

September 1988
Lee Sharpe makes his debut for United. Ferguson had signed him secretly from Torquay at the end of the previous season.

Summer 1985
Due to the Heysel stadium tragedy, English clubs are banned from European competitions. Mark Hughes is voted Young Footballer of the Year.

1987/88
United finish second in the League to Liverpool, giving supporters cause to be optimistic for the next season.

January 1985
Bryan Robson dislocates his shoulder. The injury is to affect both his career and England's World Cup chances in '86.

November 1986
Ron Atkinson is sacked, together with assistant manager, Mick Brown. Alex Ferguson accepts the job the same day.

March 1987
Gary Bailey is forced to retire with a knee injury.

July 1987
Ferguson's first signings are Viv Anderson and Brian McClair.

May 1988
Goalkeeper Jim Leighton joins United from Aberdeen.

March 1989
Gordon Strachan is transferred to Leeds.

1985   **1986**   **1987**   **1988**   **1989**   **1990**

May 1985
Kevin Moran is the first player ever to be sent off in an FA Cup Final, for tripping Everton's Peter Reid. United win the match 1–0.

May 1986
Mark Hughes plays his last match for United before moving to Barcelona for £1.8 million.

June 1988
Mark Hughes re-signs for United.

August 1989
Martin Edwards announces that businessman Michael Knighton is to buy his majority share in the club. Ferguson buys Gary Pallister.

October 1989
Knighton withdraws his bid to buy Edwards' shares in exchange for a seat on the board.

1985/86
The team set a club record at the start of the season, winning the first 10 games.

First watch
Alex Ferguson watches his team during his first season in charge, learning about existing players at United.

Summer 1989
Norman Whiteside and Paul McGrath are sold to Everton and Aston Villa respectively.

June 1999
Alex Ferguson is knighted in the Queen's Birthday Honours list. Aston Villa's Mark Bosnich replaces Peter Schmeichel.

January 1995
Ferguson signs Andrew Cole. Eric Cantona attacks a Crystal Palace fan and is charged by the police with common assault. Cantona is banned for the rest of the season and the club fine him two weeks' wages.

May 1997
United become Premier champions for the fourth time in five seasons. Eric Cantona retires from football.

August 1998
Jaap Stam and Jesper Blomqvist join United just before Dwight Yorke, signed for a club record fee of £12.6m. United's total summer spending is £27.7m.

November 1998
Peter Schmeichel announces he will retire from English football at the end of the season.

April 1999
The BSkyB deal is rejected by the Office of Fair Trading.

1995   **1996**   **1997**   **1998**   **1999**   **2000**

March 1995
Cantona is sentenced to two weeks' imprisonment. The sentence is later changed to 120 hours of community service.

May 1995
United lose the championship to Blackburn by one point and lose the FA Cup to Everton by 1–0.

May 1996
United win the Double for the second time in three years. They beat Liverpool in the Cup Final and finish 4 points clear of Newcastle in the League.

June 1997
Teddy Sheringham signs for United.

May 1998
United are pipped at the post for the championship by Arsenal, who also win the Double.

September 1998
Satellite broadcasting company BSkyB launches a £623m bid to take control of United.

February 1999
Steve McClaren is appointed as the new full-time assistant manager. United win 8-1 at Nottingham Forest, setting a new record for an away team victory in the Premier League.

May 1999
United complete a 33-match unbeaten run by winning the Premiership title, the FA Cup, and the European Cup. It is the first-ever Treble of its kind by an English team, and only the third in European history.

December 1998
Brian Kidd stuns United when he leaves to become manager of Blackburn Rovers. Reserve coach Jim Ryan steps up to assist Alex Ferguson.

Summer 1995
Three of United's stars are sold – Hughes, Ince and Kanchelskis.

1999 European Cup
A glorious season reached a dramatic climax when Ole Gunnar Solskjaer scored the winning goal against Bayern Munich to clinch the European Cup and the Treble.

Summer 1999
United courted controversy when they announced, with the FA's support, their intent to withdraw from the FA Cup to ease fixture congestion and concentrate on the inaugural FIFA World Team Championship in Brazil, in January 2000.

Into the 21st Century

Manchester United may have failed to repeat their 1999 Champions League success in Europe in the first two seasons of the 21st century, but back on the home front they tightened their vice-like grip on the Premiership.

Claiming their sixth League title in the 1999/2000 season by a record 18 points, United did not ease off the pressure in the following season. On New Year's Day, 2001, they pulled away from the League's main contenders by increasing their eight-point margin by a further three points, with a win over West Ham.

Over the two seasons, United won 52 matches, drew 15, and lost only nine. In the process, they scored 176 goals while conceding only 76. Such solid performances led Sir Alex Ferguson to declare that this Manchester United team is the greatest in the club's history, better than the Busby Babes, the 1968 European Cup winners, and any of his earlier teams.

Giggs delivers again
Ryan Giggs celebrates his crucial goal against Coventry at Old Trafford in April 2001. This match proved to be United's last game before they became Champions, since their only challengers for the title, Arsenal, were decisively defeated later that day.

July 2000
Fresh from triumphing with France at Euro 2000, Fabien Barthez (below) signs for United from Monaco for £7.8 million.

Overwhelming support
During the 2000/01 season, more than 1.8 million fans filed through the Old Trafford turnstiles, to make Manchester United the best supported club in Britain.

January 2000
United compete in the inaugural FIFA Club World Championship in Brazil, but fail to make it past the group stage after drawing with Nexaca, losing to Vasca da Gama and beating South Melbourne.

June 2001
Steve McClaren leaves Manchester United after two and a half successful years as Sir Alex Ferguson's assistant, to become manager of Middlesbrough.

| 2000 | 2001 | 2002 | 2003 | 2004 | 2005 |

April 2000
United win their sixth Premiership title in eight years with a 3-1 victory over Southampton at The Dell.

April 2001
United's third consecutive Premiership title is handed to them when Arsenal lose 3-0 to Middlesbrough at Highbury. Ruud van Nistelrooy breaks the British transfer record when he signs for United from PSV Eindhoven for £19 million.

Spring 2001
For the the second consecutive season, Manchester United were knocked out of the European Cup at the quarter-final stage, by the eventual winners. In 2000, they lost to Real Madrid; in 2001 they were beaten over two legs by Bayern Munich.

The Trophies

European Champion Clubs' Cup winners
1968, 1999

European Cup Winners' Cup winners
1991

UEFA Super Cup winners
1991

Inter-Continental Cup
1999

First Division champions
1908, 1911, 1952, 1956, 1957, 1965, 1967

FA Cup winners
1909, 1948, 1963, 1977, 1983, 1985, 1990, 1994, 1996, 1999

Charity Shield winners
1908, 1911, 1952, 1956, 1957, 1983, 1993, 1994, 1996, 1997
Joint winner: 1965, 1967, 1977, 1990

Premier League champions
1993, 1994, 1996, 1997, 1999, 2000, 2001

League Cup winners
1992

Part Two

THE
GAMES:
HIGHLIGHTS

The League

In 1892, when Manchester United were still called Newton Heath, they were elected to the Football League. They did not compete as Manchester United until 1902, when they changed their name. They finished top in the First Division seven times and won the Second Division twice. Their record as champions is complemented by 10 seasons as runners-up, firmly establishing them among the elite of the English game. Although the club is famed the world over for its achievements, it has also had its low times. On 5th April, 1934, Manchester United met Millwall in a Second Division match at Old Trafford. United had to beat Millwall to avoid dropping into the Third Division North. United rose to the occasion winning 2-0. It was a vital result and two seasons later they were promoted to the First Division. In 1938, United were again promoted to the First Division, as runners-up, just before the League programme was abandoned because of the war. Their triumph ensured Matt Busby a First Division platform after the war to launch United into a glorious era. After Busby retired, United had to wait until the '90s and the start of the FA Premier League for another era of League success.

1907/08: 25th April, 1908
Manchester United 2
Preston North End 1
Manchester United finished the season with this victory over Preston North End as Ernest Mangnall led United to their first championship. They won the title by nine points and set a record of 52 points for the championship. Despite missing several regulars, including Sandy Turnbull, the result was never in doubt. Star man on the day was Billy Meredith.

1910/11: 29th April, 1911
Manchester United 5
Sunderland 1
A crowd of only 10,000 watched this match as United beat third-placed Sunderland to win the League for the second time. Terrible weather conditions and the fact that Aston Villa seemed certain to take the title at Liverpool combined to reduce interest in the fixture. When Sunderland were reduced to 10 men through injury, United scored with ease. Harold Halse

League debut of a legend
Duncan Edwards' League debut was in April 1953, when he played for the first team against Cardiff City. United lost 1-4.

claimed two, Sandy Turnbull and Enoch West scored one each, and the fifth was an own goal. Meanwhile, Liverpool beat Aston Villa 3-1 to give United the championship.

1935/36: 2nd May, 1936
(Second Division)
Hull City 1
Manchester United 1
United were already assured of promotion when they travelled to Hull for the last game of the season, but a draw would secure the Second Division title. Before 10 minutes were up, Tommy Bamford put United in the lead when he latched on to a long ball, beat the Hull defence and lobbed the ball over the goalkeeper and into the net. Just before half time, Hull equalized with a goal from Acquroff. The goal led to a tense second half but United held on to claim the title.

1946/47: 26th May, 1947
Manchester United 6
Sheffield United 2
This was Matt Busby's first full season in charge of Manchester United. In this last match, the team provided the fans with a glimpse of what was to come as they annihilated Sheffield United. Stan Pearson and Jack Rowley formed a striking partnership that was to serve United well over the next six years. Pearson opened the scoring when he shot home Rowley's cross, then Rowley knocked in the second after eight minutes and another after 14 minutes. Sheffield pulled two back by half time. In the second half, Johnny Morris made it 4-2, Rowley completed his hat-trick and Morris wrapped up the scoring. It was a splendid team effort but not enough to win the title. United finished runners-up behind Arsenal.

1951/52: 26th April, 1952
Manchester United 6
Arsenal 1
After five seasons of almost making it to the top of the Football League, Matt Busby won his first championship with a flourish. In the last match of the season, Arsenal, in second place, had a

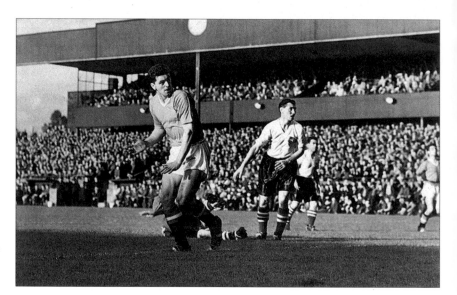

Top scorer Taylor
Tommy Taylor was one of the club's most lethal finishers, scoring 112 times in 163 League appearances. In this match against Preston North End in August '57, Taylor scored twice in United's 3-1 victory. Sadly, he played only four full seasons before his death at Munich.

faint mathematical chance of taking the title, but United had no intention of finishing second for a fourth time. Arsenal were already a weakened side and suffered a further blow when centre-half Shaw broke his wrist. After that, 10-man Arsenal were never in it. The match was a personal triumph for Jack Rowley, who scored three and laid on two. Rowley opened the scoring with a shot, then Pearson made it two when his effort was deflected. Rowley created the opening for Byrne to score the third. The fourth came from a carefully crafted lob after Rowley had outrun the Arsenal defence. Rowley then completed his hat-trick from the penalty spot and finally laid on the pass for Pearson to make it 6-1 and bring the title to Old Trafford for the first time in 41 years.

1952/53: 7th March, 1953
Manchester United 5
Preston North End 2
The man who provided most of the goals for the Busby Babes was Tommy Taylor. He averaged two goals every three matches for United. Taylor showed his potential immediately in his debut against Preston North End. He opened the scoring with a powerful header, outjumping the Preston defence to meet Rowley's cross. United added to their lead with two goals from Pegg and a blistering shot from Rowley that gave the goalkeeper no chance. As the game entered the closing stages, United put Preston under increasing pressure. Then Taylor caught a pass on his chest, wheeled and shot in one move to complete Manchester United's tally for the match in style.

1955/56: 27th August, 1955
Manchester United 3
West Bromwich Albion 1
Matt Busby knew that the team that won the title in 1952 was too old to sustain long-term success, so he fixed his sights on creating a young team that would last. In the third game of the 1955/56 season, against West Bromwich Albion, he fielded the youngest-ever side to play for Manchester United. The average age was only 22½. Busby's confidence in the youngsters was rewarded when they gave him a victory with goals from Lewis, Viollet and Scanlon.

End of an era

Dennis Viollet and Tommy Taylor attack the Arsenal goal at Highbury in February 1958. The game turned out to be a fitting goodbye to England from the Busby Babes.

1955/56: 21st April, 1956
Manchester United 1
Portsmouth 0

This victory over Portsmouth earned United two points and gave them the League title for the fourth time in their history. They finished 11 points clear of the runners-up Blackpool, a record that still stands. The match itself was not as important to United fans as the imminent presentation of the trophy, but the goal that gave them victory was worth watching. Portsmouth survived for a period in which United created four clear-cut chances but then their luck ran out. Edwards and Colman combined to provide Viollet with another chance, which this time he seized ruthlessly.

1956/57: 6th October, 1956
Manchester United 4
Charlton Athletic 2

Several of United's regulars were on international duty when this match was played, forcing Matt Busby to draft in some of his reserves for the game. Bobby Charlton was picked to make his debut for the first team and he responded in magnificent fashion, scoring two goals in the first half and narrowly missing out on a hat-trick. Further goals from Billy Whelan and Johnny Berry put the game beyond doubt, although the second half was not as convincing as the first.

1957/58: 1st February, 1958
Arsenal 4
Manchester United 5

More than 60,000 fans crammed into Highbury to see United on their first visit to London that season. They saw one of the finest games of attacking football. Nobody imagined that it was to be the last match on British soil for most of the Busby Babes. Duncan Edwards opened the scoring with a powerful drive. Bobby Charlton made it two, then Tommy Taylor scored the third. After the break, Arsenal began to press forward and were soon rewarded with a goal. David Herd, then playing for Arsenal, pulled one back and Nutt soon provided a cross for Bloomfield to make it 2-3. Within a minute Herd was on target again with a header and the scores were level. This time it was United who responded. Viollet gave United back the lead from a header and Taylor made it 5-3 from the tightest of angles. Arsenal were still not finished. Herd provided an opening for Tapscott who made the final score 4-5.

1962/63: 18th August, 1962
Manchester United 2
West Bromwich Albion 2

Denis Law found the net in his debut for United on the opening day of the season. David Herd, recently signed from Arsenal, scored first within two minutes of kick-off. Five minutes later Law sent the crowd into raptures. Giles sent in a chip and Law rose, hung in the air and flicked a header past Millington. The rest of the match did not live up to the glorious beginning. West Brom hit back with two goals in the last 15 minutes.

1963/64: 28th December, 1963
Manchester United 5
Burnley 1

Manchester United, seeking revenge for a 6-1 defeat by Burnley on Boxing Day, brought two teenagers into the team in a bid to even the score - Best and Anderson. Best duly scored his first goal for the club. David Herd opened the scoring after 11 minutes, Graham Moore made it 2-0 and Best made it 3-0 by half time. Midway through the second half, Moore grabbed his second and Herd rounded off the rout 20 minutes from time. Burnley's consolation came from Lochhead with two minutes to go.

1964/65: 26th April, 1965
Manchester United 3
Arsenal 1

United knew that if they won this fixture they would win the League championship with a game in hand, and would be the first squad to achieve Division One success since the Busby Babes in 1957/58. The match brought their North London rivals, Arsenal, to Old Trafford, where they succumbed to a near-constant wave of United's attacking play. As Denis Law grabbed two goals and George Best the other, United secured the championship. George Eastham scored Arsenal's consolation goal.

Laying down the Law

Law watches with baited breath as his team lays seige to the Arsenal goal at Old Trafford in April 1965. Law scored two of the three goals, and United won the championship for the first time since the Busby Babes.

Crowd pullers

Denis Law scores from the penalty spot at West Ham in May 1967. United fans had travelled south in their thousands to watch the match, swelling the crowd to 38,000 – the biggest at Upton Park since the war.

1966/67: 6th May, 1967
West Ham 1
Manchester United 6

Unbeaten in the League since Boxing Day, United came to London determined to put on a show worthy of soon-to-be champions. West Ham still boasted the World Cup-winning trio of Moore, Hurst and Peters but that didn't seem to impress United. Bobby Charlton, Pat Crerand and Bill Foulkes all scored within the first 10 minutes. George Best then made it 4-0 after an amazing individual run on 25 minutes. Charles had some consolation with a goal just after the interval, but he then had the frustration of conceding a penalty, which Law converted. Law also added the sixth and final goal of the match. The result ensured that United would be the League champions and would have another crack at the European Cup – which they went on to win at Wembley 12 months later.

1972/73: 20th January, 1973
Manchester United 2
West Ham 2

Tommy Docherty gave up the job as Scotland boss to manage United, and the Old Trafford board must have wondered if they'd hired the Scotland team too. For this match United fielded eight players who were either full Scotland internationals or went on to represent Scotland. In spite of this they were at the bottom of the First Division when West Ham came to Old Trafford. Pop Robson gave West Ham the lead with a header after 15 minutes. Best scored next with a well-judged lob – unfortunately not George, but Clyde Best, for West Ham. Lou Macari, playing in his debut, and Willie Morgan on the wing inspired a United revival. Bobby Charlton pulled one back from the penalty spot before Morgan laid on a goal for Macari 10 minutes from time.

1973/74: 27th April, 1974
Manchester United 0
Manchester City 1

One of the most well-known moments in the history of Manchester United took place in the afternoon of 27th April, 1974. Manchester United were facing relegation to the Second Division when they met their great rivals Manchester City, including former United hero Denis Law. Francis Lee broke forward for City and reached the 18-yard box. He pushed the ball forwards to Law, who flicked it with his heel into the goal. United's fate was sealed. Law had left Old Trafford less than 12 months earlier. He did not celebrate his goal but walked to the half-way line unmoved by his team mates' congratulations. The goal triggered a pitch invasion by United fans and the game was halted. A few minutes after the restart, the match was abandoned. The results of other matches played the same day meant that United were relegated to Division Two anyway, so this result was allowed to stand.

1974/75: 19th April, 1975
(Second Division)
Notts County 2
Manchester United 2

Manchester United's stay in the Second Division was brief. They lost only seven League matches and bounced straight back up to Division One. This draw against Notts County only served to confirm their return to the top flight as Second Division champions. The two goals came from Stewart Houston and Brian Greenhoff.

1979/80: 3rd May, 1980
Leeds United 2
Manchester United 0

Manchester United needed to win at Elland Road to keep their chances of the championship alive. United had shadowed Liverpool all season but five consecutive wins suggested that they might pull off a win. Unfortunately John Lukic gave a brilliant display in the Leeds goal. First he stopped Mickey Thomas, then he saved at point-blank range from Jimmy Greenhoff. He was beaten once, by Joe Jordan, but Jordan headed the ball over the bar. An injury to Martin Buchan forced Dave Sexton to reshuffle his side. He pulled Coppell back into defence but Leeds struck through Derek Parlane and Kevin Hird from the penalty spot. The title went to Anfield for the fourth time in five seasons. Runners-up spot was United's best performance in the League since 1968, but storm clouds were gathering for Sexton.

1980/81: 25th April, 1981
Manchester United 1
Norwich City 0

As in previous seasons, Dave Sexton's side finished their League programme with a run of victories. Their win over Norwich at Old Trafford was their sixth. Joe Jordan, top scorer with 15 goals that season, scored the goal. The win hoisted United up to eighth place, but it wasn't enough to save Sexton's job. Five days later he was sacked.

1981/82: 7th November, 1981
Sunderland 1
Manchester United 5

Steve Coppell set a club record when he lined up for Manchester United against Sunderland in November 1981. It was his 206th consecutive League appearance in a run that stretched back to January 1977.

Under Ron Atkinson, United had enjoyed a 12-match unbeaten run and this win made the total 13. Stapleton scored twice, Moran and Birtles each scored once, and the five-goal tally was completed by Robson.

For the record

England international Steve Coppell played almost 400 times for United. Between January 1977 and November 1981 he played 206 consecutive League games.

5th April, 1975 – Southampton v United

Lou Macari scores at the Dell in United's 1-0 victory over Southampton. Macari was one of the first Scottish internationals that Tommy Docherty brought to the club.

1984/85: 8th September, 1984
Manchester United 5
Newcastle United 0

Manchester United were unbeaten in their first four matches of the season but were still looking for their first win. Manager Ron Atkinson was convinced that some team was going to be on the receiving end of a landslide and Newcastle were the unlucky victims. The visitors held United at bay until the last minute of the first half. Then Jesper Olsen robbed John Ryan and slotted home the opening goal. After the break, Gordon Strachan scored from the spot, Mark Hughes got the third and Remi Moses illustrated United's control perfectly, scoring the fourth after a brilliant piece of team work and one-touch passing. The final goal was the result of a dazzling individual run by Gordon Strachan.

1985/86: 21st September, 1985
West Bromwich Albion 1
Manchester United 5

United made a storming start to the 1985/86 season with 10 wins in 10 matches. The ninth consecutive victory, against West Bromwich Albion, was the pick of the lot, and with only two months gone in the League campaign, put United nine points clear of Liverpool. There was a cost: Gordon Strachan dislocated his shoulder while scoring, but Alan Brazil took up the challenge, scoring twice. The other goals came from Frank Stapleton and Clayton Blackmore, with West Brom's reply coming from Crooks.

1986/87: 26th December, 1986
Liverpool 0
Manchester United 1

The Boxing Day result at Anfield made little impact on Manchester United's mid-table position, but it gave them their only away win of the season. Liverpool seemed invincible at the time so victory for United at Anfield in front of 40,000 people was sweet indeed. It took just one goal from Norman Whiteside to peg Liverpool back to fourth place in the First Division and give Alex Ferguson a welcome Christmas present.

1987/88: 4th April, 1988
Liverpool 3
Manchester United 3

Manchester United lay second in the table but were 11 points behind Liverpool when they arrived at Anfield. With only five matches left, United knew they had to take full points to stay in the championship race. After two minutes they were a goal up through Bryan Robson. Perhaps if United had been more adventurous they might have won, but they fell back to defend the lead and found themselves 3-1 down. Liverpool equalized through Peter Beardsley in the 38th minute, then two minutes later Beardsley crossed and Gary Gillespie headed home. Just after the interval, Steve McMahon made it three with a shot from 20 yards. United had no option but to attack again and Olsen and Whiteside came on as substitutes. A lucky break put United back in contention when a shot from Robson was deflected past Liverpool keeper Grobbelaar. When Colin Gibson was sent off for a second booking Liverpool moved in for the kill, but United had the final word. Gordon Strachan scored with 12 minutes to go, stretching his club's unbeaten run at Anfield to nine years. Liverpool eventually took the title and United finished runners-up.

Spectacular start
Neil Webb challenges for the ball against Arsenal in the opening League match of the 1989/90 season at Old Trafford. United won the game 4-1.

Brightwell celebrates for City
Brightwell scores for Manchester City in their 5-1 victory over United in September 1989. City have twice scored five against United since the war.

On a roll
Alan Brazil scores against West Bromwich Albion at the Hawthorns in September 1985. It was United's ninth straight win of 10. They went on to beat Southampton but drew their 11th game against Luton. A victory would have equalled Tottenham Hotspur's record of 11 consecutive wins at the start of a season.

1989/90: 19th August, 1989
Manchester United 4
Arsenal 1

Even the sight of Michael Knighton, who hoped to be chairman soon, juggling before the match did not eclipse United's rollicking start to the season. They beat the reigning champions decisively. Steve Bruce headed home a corner to give United the lead with just two minutes gone, and for the next 15 minutes Arsenal hardly had a look in. Although the visitors equalized through David Rocastle before half time, United were in no mood to be charitable. Hughes scored United's second 15 minutes after the break with a stunning angled drive. Ten minutes from the end, new signing Neil Webb lobbed John Lukic to make it three, and two minutes later Brian McClair completed Arsenal's misery with a fine left-foot shot. By the end of the season, the extravagances of this day were forgotten. United finished 13th in the table and Michael Knighton had to settle for joining the board at Carlisle.

1991/92: 26th April, 1992
Liverpool 2
Manchester United 0

Once again, Manchester United needed to win a difficult match at the end of the season to remain in contention for the League championship. Yet, three weeks before the match, United had been 8-1 on to win the League and most punters struggled to find anyone to bet against them. Maybe the pressure was too much for them but they then won only one in five matches leading up to the contest against Liverpool and they looked a less sure bet. United nerves were evident in the opening stages and it took Liverpool just 12 minutes to score when Rush beat Schmeichel after taking a fine pass from Barnes. To United's credit, they responded with everything they had. Ince, Bruce and Kanchelskis all hit the woodwork and Hughes sent the ball over the bar twice. Liverpool proved the deadlier of the two sides when it came to finishing and Walters ended United's hopes with a second goal. Leeds won the championship and this was made even more painful for United because they lost the title at Anfield.

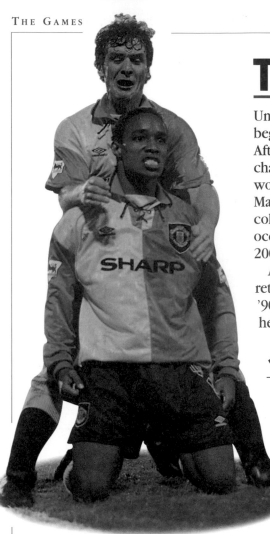

The Premier League

United have dominated English football since the beginning of the FA Premier League in 1992. After failing to win the old First Division championship for a quarter of a century, United won the revamped league at the first attempt in May 1993. Since then United have gone on to collect the Premiership title on six more occasions: in 1994, 1996, 1997, 1999, 2000 and 2001. They were runners-up in 1995 and 1998.

Alex Ferguson was hired in November 1986 to return United to greatness but it took until the '90s for his masterplan to reach fruition. By then he had assembled a team capable of becoming champions: the world's best goalkeeper, Peter Schmeichel, the defensive partnership of Pallister and Bruce, a midfield of pace and power in Giggs, Kanchelskis, Ince and Keane and the genius of Eric Cantona and Mark Hughes up front. The introduction of Beckham, Butt, Scholes and the Neville brothers during this period ensured further championships, while the addition of Cole, Solskjaer, Stam, Yorke and Barthez has seen Manchester United continue to dominate English football into the new millennium.

These are some of the most important and memorable games of the first nine seasons.

1992/93

Champions elect
Paul Ince celebrates with Mark Hughes after scoring the second goal in United's win over Crystal Palace in 1993. It was their last goal before being declared champions.

10th April, 1993
Manchester United 2
Sheffield Wednesday 1
In one of the most dramatic games Old Trafford has ever witnessed, Steve Bruce kept United on course for their first championship since 1967 when he turned defeat into victory with two late goals. At Easter the previous season the title had slipped away from United. A year on and they were in danger of letting it slip again when they went a goal down against Sheffield Wednesday. Bruce equalized with only four minutes of normal time remaining and then, seven minutes into injury time, he popped up in the penalty box again to head the winner beyond the Wednesday keeper Chris Woods. Alex Ferguson ran on to the pitch to celebrate while his assistant Brian Kidd knelt and thanked the heavens. It proved to be the turning point in the title race, helping United go to the top of the table, a position they were not to relinquish for two seasons.

21st April, 1993
Crystal Palace 0
Manchester United 2
United put the title within reach when they won this tense game. At half time it was goal-less, but United learned that their nearest rivals Aston Villa were losing 3–0 at Blackburn. If United won their match, they would almost certainly be champions. After 64 minutes, Cantona swung over a cross for Mark Hughes, who scored with a powerful volley. It was Hughes' 100th League goal for United and he called it "the most significant goal I have ever scored". Cantona was again the provider for United's second goal when he played the ball into Paul Ince's path. Ince surged into the penalty area and scored with a low shot.

3rd May, 1993
Manchester United 3
Blackburn Rovers 1
The result of this match was immaterial because United had been handed the championship 24 hours earlier when Oldham Athletic defeated Aston Villa. The evening was like a party. Thousands of people gathered at Old Trafford to celebrate Manchester United becoming champions for the first time in 26 years. The relief was palpable as fans enjoyed the end of their long wait. With the pressure of the title race gone, United could now enjoy their football.

Blackburn took the lead but United pulled level courtesy of a stunning Ryan Giggs 30-yard free kick. In the second half, Paul Ince gave United the lead, then Gary Pallister scored his first goal of the season in the last minute. After the game, Steve Bruce and Bryan Robson lifted the Premiership trophy, and the team did a slow lap of honour to complete a memorable night.

> ❝ *I have never experienced an atmosphere like tonight. You strive all your life for a feeling like this.* ❞
> **Alex Ferguson**

Aerial combat
United's Lee Sharpe and Nicky Marker of Blackburn challenge for the ball in May 1993. Sharpe scored only once that season but made 27 League appearances, playing his part in the Premiership campaign.

Equal forces
Paul Ince tackles his future team mate Steve McManaman as Manchester United and Liverpool fight out their thrilling draw of January 1994. United took a three-goal lead in the first half but Liverpool stormed back in the second half to level the game 3-3. It was the first time that a team managed by Alex Ferguson had surrendered a three-goal lead.

1993/94

23rd August, 1993
Aston Villa 1
Manchester United 2
This thrilling battle was a warning to the Premier clubs that United intended to retain their title. The game was played at great pace with both sides interested only in attack. United soaked up Villa's pressure, then hit them on the break, Sharpe giving United the lead. Atkinson then equalized just before half time. United claimed all three points when Sharpe scored again after running clear of the Villa defence and beating Spinks.

4th January, 1994
Liverpool 3
Manchester United 3
Two traditional football powers combined to produce this exciting game. United had a three-goal lead within 24 minutes. Steve Bruce opened the scoring with a header, Ryan Giggs beat Bruce

Grobbelaar with a chip and Denis Irwin scored from a 25-yard free kick. Liverpool refused to be humbled and Nigel Clough pulled two goals back before half time. In the second half United searched for another goal, but Ruddock equalized for Liverpool with 11 minutes to go. It was a classic match.

16th March, 1994
Manchester United 5
Sheffield Wednesday 0
Eric Cantona scored two and set up two goals in this victory, as United produced what the *Daily Mail* called "sublime football artistry". Ryan Giggs, Mark Hughes and Paul Ince all scored before the Frenchman registered his own two goals. In a campaign of brilliant displays that won United the championship for the second season in a row, Alex Ferguson called this one "the best performance of the season".

Power and pace
Andrei Kanchelskis attacks the Sheffield Wednesday defence during Manchester United's stunning 5-0 win over the Yorkshire side in March 1994. The Ukrainian's forays down the right wing were a major factor in United retaining the championship.

1994/95

10th November, 1994
Manchester United 5
Manchester City 0
This victory was a wonderful form of revenge for City's 5-1 triumph five years earlier, on what Alex Ferguson had called "one of the worst days of my career". The game was a show-case for Andrei Kanchelskis. City could not deal with the Ukrainian winger's pace and power, which brought him the first Manchester derby hat-trick since 1970. Eric Cantona, who assisted in all of Kanchelskis' goals, scored the opener while Mark Hughes added the other.

25th January, 1995
Crystal Palace 1
Manchester United 1
"On Sunday Eric took us to heaven with that wonderful goal to beat Blackburn. Three days later we have been taken to hell." So wrote Alex Ferguson in his diary after the events at Selhurst Park. Cantona was sent off for kicking Crystal Palace's Richard Shaw. As he made his way to the tunnel a Palace fan, Matthew Simmons, shouted abuse at him. Cantona jumped into the stands to kick and punch him. The match ended in a 1-1 draw but will always be remembered for Cantona's behaviour. His suspension until the end of the season effectively ended United's hope of a third consecutive title.

4th March, 1995
Manchester United 9
Ipswich Town 0
United produced what Ferguson called a "once in a lifetime" performance to

Record scorer
Andrew Cole scores against Ipswich in March 1995. His five goals in the game set a new Premiership record for United players.

rout Ipswich in their biggest League win for 103 years. Andrew Cole set a Premiership record with five goals in the game, Hughes scored twice and Ince and Keane both scored once.

14th May, 1995
West Ham 1
Manchester United 1
In order to snatch the title on the last day of the season, United had to beat West Ham and needed Blackburn Rovers to lose at Liverpool. At half time Blackburn were leading and United were a goal down. Early in the second half, United and Liverpool drew level when McClair scored. United laid siege to West Ham's goal but Miklosko saved headers from Lee Sharpe and Mark Hughes and denied Andrew Cole in the dying minutes. Blackburn lost 2-1 to Liverpool, but won their first title in 81 years.

Pipped at the post
Mark Hughes and Brian McClair trudge off the pitch at Upton Park after drawing 1-1 with West Ham on the last day of the 1994/95 season. United had not scored the goal that they needed to win the championship. Blackburn won the title by a single point.

King Eric
Eric Cantona threatens the Newcastle goal in March 1996. "Billed as the game of the season, it certainly lived up to it," observed the Daily Express. *"This was heart-stopping football on a stage fit for kings. The one who wore the crown last night was Eric Cantona."*

1995/96

16th September, 1995
Manchester United 3
Bolton Wanderers 0
United's youngsters (nine of the team's 14 players and substitutes were 21 or under) proved their potential right from the start. In their 3–0 win over Bolton, Paul Scholes scored twice but it was Giggs' goal that will be remembered – for its speed and precision. Intricate work between Scholes and Beckham set Cooke free on the right. He crossed the ball for Giggs to finish at the far post.

1st October, 1995
Manchester United 2
Liverpool 2
Old Trafford welcomed Eric Cantona back after his eight-month suspension with an almost religious fervour. Supporters had anticipated Liverpool's visit and Cantona's return like no game before. It took Cantona only 67 seconds to announce his return when he crossed the ball for Nicky Butt to score. Liverpool went ahead through two fine Robbie Fowler goals but, with 20 minutes to go, conceded a penalty. As if scripted, Cantona despatched the penalty to rescue the game for United.

4th March, 1996
Newcastle United 0
Manchester United 1
United were the first team in the 1995/96 season to defeat Newcastle at St. James's Park. Two months before, Newcastle had been 12 points clear but this win put United within one point. United withstood a relentless onslaught from Newcastle in the first half, and one of Peter Schmeichel's finest displays kept them in the game. United came forward in the second half. After six minutes Andrew Cole fed Phil Neville, who crossed, and Eric Cantona scored with a volley. United went on to win the title by four points from Newcastle.

1996/97

19th February, 1997
Arsenal 1
Manchester United 2
Manchester United's assured victory at Highbury gave fans a glimpse of what life might be like after Cantona, who was missing through injury. Andrew Cole and Ole Gunnar Solskjaer, paired for the first time, were exceptional. After 18 minutes, Cole ran on to a long Gary Neville pass, nipped in behind Tony Adams, then slipped past Lukic to score from a tight angle. Cole then laid on a goal for his partner after a stunning end-to-end move. Roy Keane cleared from an Arsenal corner and Giggs intercepted the ball before laying it off to Poborsky, who slipped it into Cole's path. Cole drove through the middle of the field and crossed the ball to Solskjaer. The Norwegian drilled a shot across Lukic into the far corner of the goal. Dennis Bergkamp gave Arsenal hope with a goal after 70 minutes, but United held out.

19th April, 1997
Liverpool 1
Manchester United 3
United's 3–1 win showed why they had established themselves as England's finest team in the '90s. Liverpool goalkeeper David James' generous role in the victory might have obscured United's sheer brilliance on the day. Intent on winning the game, United flooded the midfield and penetrated the Liverpool defence with ease. The first half was a tale of two heads. After 13 minutes Gary Pallister rose above the static Liverpool defence to plant David Beckham's cross in the top corner. Soon afterwards, United were caught unprepared as Liverpool took a quick corner, and an unmarked John Barnes headed down past Peter Schmeichel. As half time approached, Gary Pallister put United back in front with another firm header from a Beckham cross. The result was confirmed midway through the second half when David James flapped at a high Gary Neville cross and allowed Andrew Cole to bundle the ball into an empty net. United supporters then unfurled a banner that said, "M.U.F.C.: We won the League on Merseyside." In 1992, United's search for the title had failed at a jubilant and gloating Anfield. This victory avenged that defeat and took United to the brink of their fourth Premier League title in five years.

Cole's best
Andrew Cole eludes John Lukic before scoring United's first goal in their crucial win at Highbury in February 1997. Cole considers this goal one of his best for United.

1997/98

25th October, 1997
Manchester United 7
Barnsley 0
The morning newspapers on 25th October predicted Andrew Cole's imminent departure from Old Trafford but by the end of the day he had scored a hat-trick, which overwhelmed Barnsley and began his own renaissance. Cole delivered a masterclass in clinical finishing. For his first he latched on to a poor back-pass and fired past Watson. Sixty seconds later he scored with a low, first-time shot from the edge of the area and then, just before half time, he ran on to a through-ball from Giggs and placed the ball past the unfortunate Watson. It's rare that anyone upstages a hat-trick scorer, but Ryan Giggs nearly managed it. He complemented his running with the finishing that is too rarely seen from him in recent years, scoring two exquisite goals. United's sixth goal was awarded October's goal of the month. Incisive passing from Cole, Solskjaer and Giggs teed up Scholes, who chipped the ball over Watson. Poborsky back-heeled the seventh. United's performance left Barnsley's chairman John Dennis to predict that United would dominate English football for the decade.

14th March, 1998
Manchester United 0
Arsenal 1
Arsenal began to wrestle the title from Manchester United with this powerful performance that really proved their championship-winning credentials. The victory gave the London side a mathematical advantage that they would not surrender.
Arsenal's central midfield partnership of Petit and Vieira was superb, outmuscling United and forcing Alex Ferguson to concede, "we did not have the strength to beat Arsenal." Rarely has a side of Alex Ferguson's been so humbled.
Overmars was the main beneficiary of Arsenal's midfield dominance and it was he who scored Arsenal's winner in the 79th minute when he ran on to a nod down from Anelka and calmly placed the ball through Schmeichel's legs.

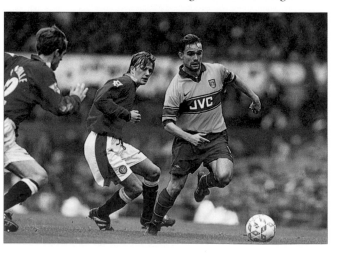

Left behind
Marc Overmars leaves Phil Neville and David Beckham in his wake during Arsenal's 1–0 win at Old Trafford. United had tried to sign the Dutchman themselves during the summer of 1995, but the deal fell apart as Overmars became injured.

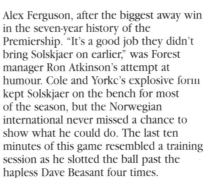

United celebrate winning the Premiership trophy in 1999 on the final day of the season. It was the first time they had won the title at home since 1967.

1998/99

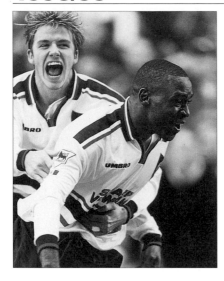

Forest flounder
Beckham and Andrew Cole celebrate one of Cole's two goals in the 8-1 record away win at Nottingham Forest. Forest manager Ron Atkinson conceded that, "United murdered us, they were quality all over the field."

17th October, 1998
Manchester United 5 Wimbledon 1
Wimbledon were the first team to suffer at the hands of the fledgling partnership of Andrew Cole and Dwight Yorke. During the next seven months they went on to score 53 goals between them

to become Europe's most prolific strikeforce. "The movement and sharpness of Cole and Yorke was fantastic," said a shocked Wimbledon keeper Neil Sullivan, "I couldn't believe this was only one of their first games together."

The pair clicked immediately. Cole at last seemed to have found the perfect partner. Yorke played behind the front line and fed Cole the balls he liked. Cole scored twice and Yorke once, with Beckham and Giggs getting the others. The game also marked the home debut of Wes Brown, who nearly got in on the act with two efforts of his own. A goal would have crowned one of the most exciting debuts Old Trafford has witnessed in a long while.

6th February, 1999
Nottingham Forest 1
Manchester United 8
Winning 4-1 deep into the second half United were coasting to victory with two goals each from Cole and Yorke. The game's main remaining interest was which one of them would get the hat-trick. Then on came Solskjaer and trumped them both by scoring four goals in the last ten minutes, the first time a substitute has ever scored so many.

"It's the best display of finishing in my time at United and, in terms of goal potential, we've never been stronger," said

Trafford triumph

Alex Ferguson, after the biggest away win in the seven-year history of the Premiership. "It's a good job they didn't bring Solskjaer on earlier," was Forest manager Ron Atkinson's attempt at humour. Cole and Yorke's explosive form kept Solskjaer on the bench for most of the season, but the Norwegian international never missed a chance to show what he could do. The last ten minutes of this game resembled a training session as he slotted the ball past the hapless Dave Beasant four times.

16th May, 1999
Manchester United 2
Tottenham Hotspur 1
Alex Ferguson finally realized his dream of seeing Manchester United win the championship at Old Trafford when they defeated Tottenham Hotspur 2-1 on the final day of the season.

With Arsenal only a point behind United at the start of play, only a win

would guarantee United their fifth title in seven years. The game didn't go according to plan as Tottenham took the lead after 25 minutes.

An injury caused uncertainty that Roy Keane would feature in this game but he played a true captain's role to inspire his team. "Keane was 150% fit because he wanted to be. That's the difference between him and others," observed his manager. United eventually equalized on the stroke of half time with a superb Beckham goal, curled into the top corner from a tight angle. Cole replaced Sheringham for the second half and with his first touch produced the goal that clinched the title. Collecting a long ball from Gary Neville, Cole brought it under control and lifted it over Ian Walker. Midway through the second half, news came that Arsenal had taken the lead at Highbury, but United continued to protect their lead and claimed the title by a point.

1999/2000

22nd August, 1999
Arsenal 1 Manchester United 2
After the unprecedented success of the previous Treble-winning season, there was a sense of how could United follow that? This exciting comeback win over Arsenal at Highbury certainly helped to re-energise both United players and fans at the start of the new season. United went behind to a goal from Freddie Ljungberg in the first half, but Roy Keane secured a dramatic win for United with two goals in the second half. Keane equalised for United when Andrew Cole

slipped the ball through to him and he then poked it past the Arsenal keeper, Manninger. Keane grabbed the winner in the final minute when he chested down a blocked shot from Ryan Giggs and nudged the ball past Manninger again.

22nd April, 2000
Southampton 1
Manchester United 3
Manchester United's large lead in the Premiership since Christmas made the eventual clinching of their sixth title in eight years slightly anti-climatic, but this

was still a memorable day in the south coast sunshine. The game, and the title race, was effectively over after only 15 minutes, after a trademark free-kick from David Beckham and an own goal from Francis Benali. Ole Gunnar Solskjaer sealed the game with a clinical strike in the 29th minute. United coasted through the second half and, at the final whistle, celebrated their title win at the Dell.

Beckham clinches it
Beckham curls in United's opening goal from a free kick in their 3-1 win at the Dell.

2000/2001

1st January, 2001
Manchester United 3
West Ham United 1
Manchester United have extensively won many of their games during the Ferguson era, but this one stands out for the way United utterly dominated their opponents, almost to the point of humiliation. West Ham were completely outplayed by United, who simply sprayed the ball around the pitch and left the Londoners chasing shadows. United made a Premiership side brimming with recognised names and international players look like a bunch of hapless amateurs. A typical Ole Gunnar Solskjaer finish and an own goal from Stuart Pearce in the first half was added to by a

diving header from Dwight Yorke in the second half, to secure a 3-1 win on a night when the scoreline didn't really reflect United's awesome dominance.

New Year's Day massacre
Norwegian striker Ole Gunnar Solskjaer challenges West Ham's Rigobert Song for the ball during United's New Year's Day victory over the Londoners at Old Trafford.

25th February, 2001
Manchester United 6 Arsenal 1
This game serves as the perfect example of the enormous gap between United and their nearest rivals, Arsenal, in the 2000/2001 season. On an unseasonably sunny day at Old Trafford, United tore the Londoners apart and punished them with some expert finishing. Arsenal manager, Arsene Wenger, could do nothing but concede the title to United

after the game. United took the lead through Dwight Yorke after only three minutes, but Thierry Henry restored parity for Arsenal soon afterwards. However, from here on United asserted their authority and knocked in five more goals, four of them before half time. Dwight Yorke scored twice more to complete his hat-trick, with Ole Gunnar Solskjaer, Teddy Sheringham and Roy Keane adding the other goals.

"It was one of our best performances of the season, we were so lethal up front whenever we got a chance we put it away," said Dutch defender Jaap Stam. "Funnily enough, I wouldn't say it was by far our most outstanding display of the season. We can play even better."

The FA Cup

In the global game of football, the FA Cup is recognized as one of the most romantic competitions in the world, with a history stretching back to 1871. Manchester United have been competing for the Cup for more than 100 years. In their first-ever season, as Newton Heath, they were beaten 6-1 in the first round by the holders Preston North End, and the club never progressed beyond the third round until they changed their name to Manchester United in 1902. Since then they have appeared in the Final on 15 occasions and have won the competition a record 10 times. But it's not just at Wembley that

Manchester United have contributed to the excitement of the FA Cup. Over the years, United teams have brought glamour and spectacle, drama and despair to millions of supporters worldwide. United fans have known the highs, such as three successive Finals between 1994 and 1996, and the lows, such as when they were knocked out of the Cup by Third Division Bristol Rovers in 1956. One thing is constant: regardless of the club's League status, the name of Manchester United provokes a universal murmur of anticipation every time it comes out in the FA Cup draw.

1889/90: Round 1: 18th Jan, 1890
Preston North End 6
Newton Heath 1

This was Newton Heath's first venture into what was the biggest competition in the country. Preston North End were the Cup holders and had completed the Double the previous season without losing a game. Newton Heath's one goal against the team nicknamed "The Invincibles" was considered a moral victory for the Alliance League club.

1902/03: Round 5: 7th Feb, 1903
Manchester United 2
Liverpool 1

Despite having the advantage of playing on home ground, Manchester United were not expected to progress much further than this fifth-round match. They were a struggling Second Division outfit while Liverpool were among the front runners in the First Division and favourites for the Cup. The United players, however, were not overawed by their illustrious visitors and scored despite battling against a strong wind. As the match progressed, the tension increased and Liverpool eventually had a man sent off, effectively ending their chances of a comeback.

1908/09: Final: 24th Apr, 1909
Manchester United 1
Bristol City 0

This was a Cup Final debut for both clubs and a crowd of more than 70,000 came to watch. The FA insisted on both sides wearing different colours from their traditional red and white, and United opted for a white strip trimmed with red. Having knocked out champions Newcastle in the semi-finals, United began the match as favourites. The star of the match was Billy Meredith, who gave City an object lesson in ball control, accurate passing and shooting, but Charlie Roberts, Dick Duckworth and Alex Bell all played their part in helping their side control the match from the start. Bristol City's top player, England international Billy Wedlock, failed to make an impact and when City did get possession, they proved too lightweight and short of pace to pose any real threat. With the wind in their

Spot the ball
Desperate defending cannot prevent the ball (just visible behind the post) from crossing the Bristol City goal line. Sandy Turnbull's effort brought about the only goal of the 1909 Final and gave United the FA Cup for the first time. The shirt that Turnbull wore during this match can be seen on permanent display in the Manchester United museum at Old Trafford.

favour, Manchester United took the lead midway through the first half when Harold Halse hit the crossbar and Sandy Turnbull followed up to power the ball home. The only real moment of concern came when United lost the services of full-back Vince Hayes, who went off injured. The reshuffled side managed to hold out and Hayes returned to finish the match in the forward line. Skipper Charlie Roberts had the honour of being the first Manchester United captain to step up and collect the famous trophy – proudly sporting the red rose of Lancashire on his shirt.

1925/26: Semi-final: 27th Mar, 1926
Manchester United 0
Manchester City 3

Although Manchester United's name first went into the hat for the FA Cup in 1902, it was almost 26 years before they were drawn to play local rivals Manchester City. At the time of this match, City were bottom of the First Division while United were several places above them. City surprised everyone, playing much better than was expected of a team of their lowly League status, and finished the first half 1-0 up. Manchester City goalkeeper Goodchild

made good saves from McPherson and Smith before Hicks, City's star forward, sent in a corner that was headed home by Browell after 15 minutes. United were by no means overwhelmed and City had Goodchild to thank on several more occasions. Then, 12 minutes from the end, the combination of Hicks and Browell proved deadly once more. A centre found Browell unmarked and he easily beat the United keeper Stewart to make it 2-0. Three minutes later, Hicks created yet another opening and although Stewart got a hand to Roberts' shot, he couldn't stop the ball going in off the post. It was the last victory City had that season. They lost the Final 1-0 to Bolton Wanderers and were relegated to the Second Division in the League, while United finished ninth.

1947/48: Final: 24th Apr, 1948
Manchester United 4
Blackpool 2

Matt Busby was hungry for success in Manchester United's first Final for nearly 40 years. Blackpool took the lead after 15 minutes with a penalty from Shimwell. After 30 minutes Jack Rowley side-footed home an equalizer. Blackpool re-took the lead 10 minutes before half time through Mortensen. They held on until the 70th minute when Rowley equalized again, with a header. Minutes later, Mortensen ran through only to be denied a goal by Crompton. That seemed to inspire United and Pearson soon put them ahead. Three minutes later, John Anderson wrapped up the game. His shot from 30 yards was deflected into the net, ending Blackpool's challenge.

United's top marksman
Jack Rowley outjumps Haywood of Blackpool during the 1948 FA Cup Final.

1956/57: Final: 4th May, 1957
Manchester United 1
Aston Villa 2

United entered this match hoping to complete the League and Cup double but after six minutes their goalkeeper Ray Wood was carried off on a stretcher. A blatant charge by Villa's Peter McParland had left him with concussion and a fractured cheekbone. There were no substitutes allowed, so Matt Busby reshuffled his team, putting Jackie Blanchflower in goal and Duncan Edwards at centre-half. Villa did not capitalize until the 68th minute. Then McParland scored twice in five minutes. By this time, Wood was playing out on the right wing, but he was still concussed and could make no effective contribution. With eight minutes left, Tommy Taylor scored for United. Wembley erupted and United believed they might force a replay. Busby sent Wood back into goal, but Villa held on.

1962/63: Final: 25th May, 1963
Manchester United 3
Leicester City 1

United were the outsiders for this game, having finished 19th in the League, while Leicester City had finished fourth. Straight from the whistle, they reversed the odds. Within 30 minutes United took the lead when Denis Law cracked an unstoppable shot past Gordon Banks. Minutes later he almost made it two from an individual run that left three Leicester defenders trailing. He beat Banks only to see his shot cleared off the line. Fifteen minutes after the break, United extended their lead. Banks could only parry a shot from Bobby Charlton, and David Herd pounced on the loose ball to score. With 10 minutes left, Keyworth scored for Leicester with a diving header. That seemed only to sharpen United's appetite. A header from Law rebounded off the post to a startled Banks. Then Banks fumbled a shot by Quixall and Herd was there once again to complete the scoring.

United v Liverpool – the 1977 FA Cup Final
Stuart Pearson holds off Liverpool's Tommy Smith, watched by Jimmy Greenhoff. Pearson and Greenhoff both scored in the 2-1 win over the League and European Cup champions.

Six of the Best
George Best scores one of his six goals in the 8-2 win over Northampton in the fifth round of the Cup in 1970. Harold Halse is the only other United player to have scored a double hat-trick, against Swindon in 1911.

1976/77: Final: 21st May, 1977
Manchester United 2
Liverpool 1

With the superb marshalling of captain Martin Buchan in the centre of United's defence, and with a bit of luck when Liverpool's Ray Kennedy hit the post, the first half was goal-less. The Final was decided in a few crazy minutes after half time, when Stuart Pearson scored with a low shot. Three minutes later Jimmy Case equalized for Liverpool, only for United to regain the lead two minutes after that with a freak deflection off Jimmy Greenhoff from a wayward Lou Macari shot.

1978/79: Final: 12th May, 1979
Manchester United 2
Arsenal 3

This match will be remembered for the most dramatic Cup Final climax in living memory. After 12 minutes, Arsenal's Liam Brady left Lou Macari trailing and created a chance from which Brian Talbot scored. Two minutes before half time, Brady again created a chance, this time for Stapleton to head past Gary Bailey. The score remained 2-0 until, with less than five minutes to go, the dramatic finale began with a goal for United, from Gordon McQueen. Before Arsenal could get back in their stride, Sammy McIlroy levelled the scores and extra time seemed inevitable. Then, as United were playing out the final seconds, Brady collected the ball in midfield and passed to Rix. Bailey missed the cross and Alan Sunderland beat Albiston to the ball to score the winner for Arsenal on 90 minutes.

1982/83: Semi-final: 16th Apr, 1983
Manchester United 2
Arsenal 1

Manchester United booked their second trip of the season to Wembley by coming back from a goal down at Villa Park to defeat Arsenal in the FA Cup semi-final. Tony Woodcock gave the Gunners the lead in the first half. Bryan Robson equalized for United in the second half before Norman Whiteside clinched victory with a wonderful long-range volley.

1982/83: Final: 21st May, 1983
Manchester United 2
Brighton 2

Manchester United were expected to make light work of relegated Brighton, but were ultimately fortunate to survive for a replay. Gordon Smith headed Brighton into a shock lead, which they held until half time. Ten minutes into the second half, United drew level when Frank Stapleton forced home Mike Duxbury's cross at the far post. When Ray Wilkins scored a stunning goal after 74 minutes, it looked as if United had won the Cup. Then, with three minutes remaining, Gary Stevens equalized for Brighton.

More drama was to follow in the last minute of extra time. Michael Robinson played in Gordon Smith with only the goalkeeper to beat. United fans held their breath as Smith took aim, but Bailey rushed out and blocked his shot, keeping Manchester United in the tie.

1982/83: Final replay:
26th May, 1983
Manchester United 4
Brighton 0

The Final was replayed four days later. Manchester United gave Brighton no second chances and crushed them 4–0. It was the highest score in an FA Cup Final for 80 years. Bryan Robson opened the scoring by driving in a low shot past Brighton's goalkeeper, Manchester-born Graham Moseley, and four minutes later Norman Whiteside glanced in a cross. Just before the interval, Robson made it three by tapping in a Frank Stapleton header on the line.

United strolled through the second half. They added one more goal when Arnold Muhren converted from the penalty spot. It was Ron Atkinson's first trophy and the ideal way for Sir Matt Busby, who was watching the match from the royal box, to celebrate his 74th birthday.

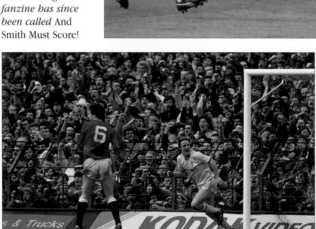

Vital save
Gary Bailey saves from Brighton's Gordon Smith in the 1983 FA Cup Final. A Brighton fanzine has since been called And Smith Must Score!

Onside
Despite being flagged offside by a linesman, Paul Walsh scores a last-minute equalizer for Liverpool at the end of extra time, taking the 1985 FA Cup semi-final to a replay.

Wright choice
There had been doubts that Wright would play in the 1990 Final, having broken his leg twice that season. Brought on as a substitute, he scored twice for Crystal Palace.

1989/90: Final: 12th May, 1990
Manchester United 3
Crystal Palace 3

In a poor season, Alex Ferguson's job was saved by United's run to the FA Cup Final. The prospect of their first trophy for five years placated Old Trafford's directors. After 120 minutes and six goals in the first game, United and Steve Coppell's Crystal Palace could not be separated. Palace went ahead through a Gary O'Reilly header but United drew level before half time, courtesy of a deflected Bryan Robson header. Mark Hughes' powerful volley gave United a 2–1 lead early in the second half and they looked to be coasting to victory until Crystal Palace introduced Ian Wright as a substitute. Wright's impact was immediate. On his first run at goal he skipped past Pallister before slotting the ball past Leighton. In extra time Palace went 3–2 up when Wright volleyed in a cross at the far post. Palace were just seven minutes from their first ever major trophy when Hughes scored his second to take the Final to a replay.

1984/85: Semi-final: 13th Apr, 1985
Manchester United 2
Liverpool 2

Manchester United overcame Liverpool to reach their ninth post-war Final, but only after two titanic games. In the first game United twice had the lead only for Liverpool to come back. After 69 minutes, Mark Hughes forced the ball into the net after Robson's shot had been blocked. United were four minutes from Wembley when Ronnie Whelan equalized for Liverpool. United regained the lead in extra time through Stapleton, only for Paul Walsh to equalize in the 120th minute. A linesman flagged Walsh offside but the referee ignored him.

1984/85: Semi-final replay:
17th Apr, 1985
Manchester United 2
Liverpool 1

In the replay, Paul McGrath gifted Liverpool the lead by heading into his own net in the first half. United stormed back with two sumptuous strikes in the second half. After swapping passes with Stapleton, Robson ran from the half-way line pursued by a group of Liverpool defenders. Just when it looked as if he would be caught, he unleashed a shot that flew into the top corner of the net. Twelve minutes later Strachan sent Hughes through and the Welshman drilled in United's winner.

1984/85: Final: 18th May, 1985
Manchester United 1
Everton 0

The game was uneventful until the 78th minute when Everton's Peter Reid seized upon a bad pass from Paul McGrath. Everton looked certain to test Gary Bailey in goal, but Reid was sent flying by Kevin Moran. The foul was more clumsy than intentional, but the referee pointed to the dressing room. Moran became the first person to be sent off in an FA Cup Final. Being down to 10 men steadied United into action. In extra time Hughes passed to Whiteside who ran into the area, steadied himself and curled a wonderful shot past Neville Southall.

A despairing dive
Everton's Neville Southall dives in a vain attempt to stop Norman Whiteside's curling shot. The goal won the 1985 FA Cup for United and ended Everton's Double hopes.

1989/90: Final replay:
17th May, 1990
Manchester United 1
Crystal Palace 0

Bryan Robson became the first man to lift the FA Cup three times at Wembley when Manchester United finally overcame Crystal Palace. Alex Ferguson called it "the greatest day of my life". The replay was a dull affair, largely due to Palace's spoiling tactics and over-physical approach. United's winning goal came after an hour. Neil Webb spotted Lee Martin's run and found him with a sweeping pass on the edge of the area. Martin chested down the ball and struck it past Nigel Martyn into the top corner of the net - only his second-ever goal.

1993/94: Semi-final: 10th Apr, 1994
Manchester United 1
Oldham Athletic 1

Mark Hughes rescued Manchester United's bid for the Double with one of the most important goals in the club's history. United's hope of winning an unprecedented domestic Treble had vanished after their defeat in the League Cup Final two weeks earlier. If they lost in the FA Cup semi-final at Wembley, United were in danger of finishing with nothing. Neil Pointon had given Oldham the lead in the second half of extra time to put the small Lancashire side on the brink of their first ever FA Cup Final. With only 46 seconds remaining, Brian McClair lobbed a hopeful ball into the area. Hughes fought his way past Fleming and struck a powerful volley beyond a helpless Hallworth into the top corner. It was a goal that showed Hughes at his most heroic and powerful best. Oldham's manager Joe Royle called it "a stroke of genius", while Alex Ferguson welcomed it as a "miracle".

Last goal
Bryan Robson scores in the Cup semi-final replay against Oldham. This was Robson's last goal for United and it made him, at 37, the oldest player ever to score for them.

1993/94: Semi-final replay: 13th Apr, 1994
Manchester United 4
Oldham Athletic 1

After being given such a scare in the first game at Wembley, United were a different team in the replay at Maine Road three days later. They dismissed Oldham 4–1 with goals from Irwin, Kanchelskis, Robson and Giggs.

Penalty for the Cup
Eric Cantona is mobbed by Roy Keane, Andrei Kanchelskis, Paul Ince and Ryan Giggs after scoring the first penalty against Chelsea in the 1994 FA Cup Final.

1993/94: Final: 14th May, 1994
Manchester United 4
Chelsea 0

Manchester United brushed aside Chelsea 4–0 to become only the fourth team this century to win the English League and FA Cup Double. Victory in the FA Cup Final completed a season in which United had produced arguably their finest-ever football. "Winning the double was a fitting tribute to Sir Matt," said Alex Ferguson. "The team performed in a way he would have appreciated". The final scoreline may have been comprehensive but United's first-half performance was not, and they were lucky that the scores were level at half time.

In the previous eight months Chelsea had twice beaten United 1–0 in the League with goals from Gavin Peacock, and Peacock nearly gave the Londoners the lead in this match. In the first half, his 20-yard shot hit the underside of the crossbar and bounced out. United reproduced their championship-winning form in the second half and won the game in the space of eight minutes. Eddie Newton brought Irwin down in the penalty area and the referee awarded a penalty to United on the hour. Eric Cantona took it and coolly sent Kharine diving in the wrong direction. Six minutes later referee David Ellery controversially awarded United another penalty, when Frank Sinclair pushed Andrei Kanchelskis in the area. Cantona again took the penalty, producing almost a carbon copy of the earlier shot and again sending Kharine the wrong way. Two minutes later Sinclair slipped in possession of the ball to let in Mark Hughes, who scored the third goal. United coasted through the rest of the match. Cantona missed an opportunity to score the first Cup Final hat-trick for 41 years, before United finally added a fourth goal in the last minute. Ince was set free of the Chelsea defence by a Mark Hughes pass. He rounded Kharine and squared it to Brian McClair to tap the ball into an empty net.

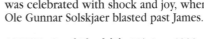

Winning goal
Paul Rideout heads Everton's winner in the 1995 FA Cup Final after Graeme Stuart's shot had cannoned off the underside of the bar. A pulled hamstring prevented Steve Bruce from clearing the ball before it crossed the line.

1994/95: Final: 20th May, 1995
Manchester United 0
Everton 1

A week after losing the League title, United failed to pick themselves up for the FA Cup Final and went down to a 1-0 defeat to Everton. "This is a game we would have won if we'd won the League," reflected Alex Ferguson. "It's five years since we've won nothing. Sometimes our players forget what defeat is like. They know now." Drained of confidence and deprived of Cantona, Cole, Giggs and Kanchelskis, United could not match Everton's hunger. Paul Rideout scored Everton's winner after half an hour and although United fought back in the second half they couldn't find a way past Neville Southall.

1995/96: Semi-final: 31st Mar, 1996
Manchester United 2
Chelsea 1

United secured their place in a record 14th FA Cup Final with a win over Chelsea that Alex Ferguson called, "the best semi-final in my time here."

Ruud Gullit put Chelsea 1-0 up 10 minutes before half time with a close-range header. United began to assert themselves in the second half and made it 1-1 after 55 minutes, when Phil Neville delivered a high cross from the by-line, which Cantona headed across for Cole to stab the ball over the line. Four minutes later, Beckham won the game by racing on

to a misplaced Craig Burley backpass and placing the ball past Hitchcock.

1995/96: Final: 11th May, 1996
Manchester United 1
Liverpool 0

Cantona completed his comeback by scoring the winning goal in the FA Cup Final with only four minutes remaining, to make United the first English club to ever win the Double twice. "It doesn't get much better than this," said Alex Ferguson, "Beating Liverpool, our great rivals, with four minutes to go was marvellous." Despite the thrilling finish, it was a disappointing Final. United reined in their attacking instincts to try to negate Liverpool's own attacking flair. The game looked destined to go into extra time until the 86th minute, when Beckham swung over a high cross which James could only punch straight to Cantona, who swivelled his body and hit a shot past four helpless defenders.

1998/99: Round 4: 24th Jan, 1999
Manchester United 2
Liverpool 1

Manchester United staged a dramatic comeback against their oldest rivals to keep them on course for the Treble. If this competition was United's third priority, no one had told the players. Despite trailing to a Michael Owen goal for most of the game, they never gave up. Even so, United were on the brink of going out of the Cup when Yorke finally claimed an equalizer after 88 minutes. If the equalizer was greeted

with relief, the winner a minute later was celebrated with shock and joy, when Ole Gunnar Solskjaer blasted past James.

1998/99: Semi Final (R): 14th Apr, 1999
Arsenal 1
Manchester United 2

In a game acclaimed as one of the greatest ever, United finally overcame Arsenal to make it to the FA Cup Final. Beckham gave United the lead in the first half, but Bergkamp's equalizer and Keane's dismissal returned the initiative to Arsenal. It looked as if it was over for United when Arsenal were awarded a last-minute penalty, but Schmeichel pushed away Bergkamp's effort to send the game into extra time. United were holding out for penalties until Giggs scored a goal labelled "the greatest ever scored." Picking the ball up in his own half he passed four Arsenal players before blasting the ball over David Seaman to spark off a joyous pitch invasion at Villa Park.

1998/99: Final: 22nd May, 1999
Manchester United 2
Newcastle United 0

For so long United's forgotten man, Teddy Sheringham came off the bench to win the FA Cup and complete United's

Semi-final stunner
Beckham wheels away after giving United the lead in the FA Cup semi-final replay against Arsenal. A stunning goal, it was to be overshadowed by Giggs' later effort!

third Double in six seasons with a Man of the Match performance. Sheringham replaced the injured Keane after only 8 minutes. Two minutes later he swapped passes with Scholes and fired United into the lead. Newcastle caused United few problems. David May said "I couldn't believe how easy that was." United won in the second half when Sheringham laid the ball back to Scholes, who drilled a low shot beyond Steve Harper.

A proud moment
Eric Cantona lifts the FA Cup in 1996 as United win the double Double. "I am a very proud man," said the Frenchman, "To score the last goal was something special."

The final frontier
Dwight Yorke takes the ball past Newcastle United's Dabizas and Charvet in the 1999 FA Cup Final. The Trinidad and Tobagan international started the game on the bench, but he replaced Andy Cole in the second half to claim his first-ever FA Cup Winners' medal.

The League Cup

For English League clubs the Football League Cup has neither the tradition of the FA Cup nor the glamour of the European competitions. Despite major sponsorship deals and name changes, it has always come third, as far as domestic trophies are concerned, behind the League championship and the FA Cup. Now that the winner qualifies for the UEFA Cup, the top sides may take it more seriously. The trophy has come to Old Trafford only once, in 1992, and the competition has otherwise been a catalogue of disappointments for United, punctuated by disasters and dreams of what might have been. For United fans the most disappointing defeat was in 1994. That season, United won the Charity Shield against Arsenal, beat Chelsea in the Final of the FA Cup and swept aside Blackburn Rovers and Newcastle United to take the Premiership. Victory over Aston Villa in the final of the League Cup would have meant they won every domestic trophy available to them, something no English club has ever achieved.

1960/61: Round 2: 2nd Nov, 1960
Bradford City 2
Manchester United 1

In the first year of the competition, Manchester United went to Third Division Bradford City in the second round. Not even a goal by the top marksman Dennis Viollet could inspire United and they lost to the club two divisions below them.

1966/67: Round 2: 14th Sep, 1966
Blackpool 5
Manchester United 1

United had a bye to the second round but got no further after this crushing defeat by Blackpool. A hat-trick by Ray Charnely and goals from Les Lea and Bobby Waddell earned Blackpool the victory. David Herd scored the only goal for United.

1982/83: Final: 26th Mar, 1983
Manchester United 1
Liverpool 2

Norman Whiteside gave Manchester United a dream start when he side-footed the opening goal home after 12 minutes.

First defeat
Mark Lawrenson gets in a tackle on Gordon McQueen during the 1983 Final. Injuries to McQueen and Kevin Moran forced United to reshuffle their team, a move that helped Liverpool get back into the game and win the Milk Cup in extra time.

Then, 30 minutes into the second half, Gordon McQueen was through on goal when Bruce Grobbelaar obstructed him 10 yards outside the box. Under new rules Grobbelaar should have been sent off but the referee awarded only a foul. United held on until the last 10 minutes when Alan Kennedy put the match into extra time. With 100 minutes played, Ronnie Whelan curled a shot around the Manchester United defence to score the winning goal.

1990/91: Round 4: 28th Nov, 1990
Arsenal 2
Manchester United 6

Arsenal were looking for a record unbeaten run with this match but United ran riot. Clayton Blackmore scored within 60 seconds, then Mark Hughes and Lee Sharpe both scored just before half time. After the break, Alan Smith revived Arsenal's hopes with goals on 48 and 68 minutes but Sharpe scored with a header after 75 minutes and completed his hat-trick five minutes later. Danny Wallace secured United's highest away win in the competition with a goal eight minutes from time.

1990/91: Final: 21st Apr, 1991
Manchester United 0
Sheffield Wednesday 1

Robbed of the trophy with United in 1983, Ron Atkinson won it with Wednesday in 1991. Wednesday had one shot on target, which was the only goal. After 38 minutes, Pallister attempted to clear a free kick from Worthington but headed to John Sheridan who scored.

1991/92: Final: 12th Apr, 1992
Manchester United 1
Nottingham Forest 0

Brian McClair's 23rd goal of the season won the League Cup for United for the first time. There were other chances for Ince and Bruce, and McClair saw a shot cleared off the line, but there were no more goals. Forest, who had won the trophy twice in the previous three years, had their one real chance saved when Schmeichel dived at the feet of Clough.

1993/94: Final: 27th Mar, 1994
Manchester United 1
Aston Villa 3

United dominated the opening period but, after 26 minutes, Villa broke quickly and Dalian Atkinson had the ball in the net before United could regroup. With 76 minutes gone, Dean Saunders scored when he tapped home a free kick by Kevin Richardson. Mark Hughes knocked in United's consolation goal eight minutes from time then, in the last minute, a Villa shot hit the post, Andrei Kanchelskis handled the ball and Saunders scored from the penalty.

Villa's Cup
Dalian Atkinson side-foots home Villa's first goal of the 1994 Final to put them on the way to winning the Coca Cola Cup.

1995/96: Round 2 (first leg): 20th Sep, 1995
Manchester United 0
York City 3

United went a goal down to York City when a shot from Paul Barnes was deflected into the net. Six minutes later, United's McGibbon was sent off for pulling down Barnes in the penalty area and Tony Barras scored from the spot. It was all over seven minutes into the second half when Barnes scored again. It was the first time that United had lost at Old Trafford for nine months.

League Cup winners
Ryan Giggs, aged only 18, enjoys the taste of success with Steve Bruce and Lee Sharpe, after winning the League (Rumbelows) Cup in 1992. Giggs was voted Young Player of the Year at the end of the season.

The Doubles and the Treble

Manchester United dominated English football in the 1990s. Their trophy haul from the decade included five titles, four FA Cups, two European trophies and the League Cup. The Double- and Treble-winning seasons of 1994, 1996 and 1999 were the most spectacular achievements.

A year after winning their first League championship for a generation, United went one better by becoming only the fourth team this century to win the League championship and FA Cup Double. Alex Ferguson then guided United to the Double again two years later. "It was so stunning as to be almost unbelievable," said the then England manager Terry Venables.

Alex Ferguson trumped even that in 1999, when he lead his team to the Treble of the League championship, FA Cup and European Cup. United were acclaimed as the greatest English club side of all time, while Ferguson was knighted for his services to football.

The Busby Babes and the 1968 European Cup-winning side will always be revered, but they never ruled English football as Alex Ferguson's team did in the 1990s.

United captains old and new
Steve Bruce, the current captain, and Bryan Robson, the former captain, hold the Premiership trophy aloft for the second successive season at Old Trafford, after the final game of the 1993-94 campaign against Coventry City. This was Bryan Robson's final appearance for United.

1993/94

No longer burdened by the long wait for the title, Manchester United captured the Double by playing some thrilling football. "With 26 years of frustration over we could approach our task with a clear mind," said Alex Ferguson, "we were much more relaxed and began to play with real authority."

This team was arguably United's finest ever. During the season, they won 41 of their 62 games, losing only 6 and scoring an incredible 125 goals. They were only a game away from winning an unprecedented domestic Treble. "We will never know what the side that perished at Munich could have achieved," said United's chairman Martin Edwards, "but this side is one of the greatest the club has ever had."

United patented a wonderful brand of fast, flowing, attacking football. With Giggs, Sharpe and Kanchelskis dashing down the wings and Hughes and Cantona leading the forward line, United were irresistible. Throughout the whole team each player was arguably the Premiership's best in their position. It is an eleven that supporters could instantly reel off: Schmeichel, Parker, Irwin, Bruce, Pallister, Kanchelskis, Keane, Ince, Giggs, Hughes and Cantona.

From Wembley to Wembley

United started the season where they would end it, at Wembley. They won the Charity Shield after a penalty shoot-out against Arsenal, then began their League campaign by winning five of their first six games. Their first loss was at the beginning of September at Chelsea, but United then went unbeaten for 34 matches, the longest run in their history. There seemed to be an invincibility about the team.

United were defeated in the League Cup Final against Aston Villa in March, but came back to retain the League before completing the Double with victory over Chelsea in the FA Cup Final. It was a fitting end to a season that saw the death of United's greatest manager, Sir Matt Busby, at the age of 84. "He would have been proud of the way we played," reflected Alex Ferguson.

United v Chelsea
Mark Hughes takes on Chelsea's Erland Johnsen. In United's 12th FA Cup Final, in 1994, they faced a Chelsea side that had already beaten them twice during the season. Here, the Welshman scored United's third goal to confirm United's first Double win.

1995/96

The title is won
Eric Cantona, David Beckham and Roy Keane congratulate Ryan Giggs after he scored United's third goal against Middlesbrough at the Riverside Stadium.

In the summer of 1995 Ferguson sold three heroes of the first Double: Hughes, Ince and Kanchelskis, and chose not to replace them by entering into the transfer market. Instead, he had faith in his young players: Beckham, Butt, Scholes, and the Nevilles. "I have always considered that the player you produce is better than the one you buy."

The season started badly for United when they went down 3-1 to Aston Villa on the opening day. It prompted the former Liverpool captain, Alan Hansen, to comment famously on *Match of the Day*: "You don't win anything with kids."

Eric Cantona returned from his eight-month ban at the beginning of October and galvanized the youngsters around him into action, but by Christmas Newcastle United had opened up a seemingly unassailable 12-point lead at the top of the table. Kevin Keegan's team were even being referred to as "Champions elect."

United rose to the challenge and from the end of January 1996, Cantona produced an inspired personal run of form by scoring the winner in a succession of 1-0 wins, against Newcastle in March's title decider, Coventry, Tottenham and Arsenal. United won all but two of their last 22 League and Cup games.

The FA Cup Final against Liverpool proved to be an uninspiring game, but it was immortalized by Cantona's winner four minutes from time. "It was a quite magnificent goal," said Alex Ferguson, "Eric Cantona makes the difference."

Alex Ferguson's faith in his youngsters had been vindicated: "I always knew our youngsters would deliver. To win the double Double was the culmination of the youth policy I began when I first arrived."

King Eric
Eric Cantona in typically regal pose is shadowed by Liverpool's John Barnes during the 1996 FA Cup Final. "He has behaved himself this season and has performed wonderfully well," said Sir Bobby Charlton. "A lot of people have had to eat humble pie over Eric Cantona."

1998/99

Manchester United's aim to topple Arsenal, the previous season's Double winners, didn't get off to a good start. United were humiliated 3-0 by Arsenal at the Charity Shield in August. At the end of September, in the Premiership, they went down to them by the same score.

United's triumvirate of new signings, Stam, Yorke and Blomqvist, soon found their form, however, and the team began to enjoy a golden autumn. They went through their six Champions League "Group of Death" games against Brondby, Bayern Munich and Barcelona unbeaten, scoring a record 20 goals to qualify for the quarter-finals. At home, Cole and Yorke struck up a prolific partnership to keep United challenging for the Premiership behind Aston Villa. United recorded convincing wins over Liverpool, Southampton, Wimbledon, Everton, Blackburn and Leeds, but then began to wobble around Christmas with a spell of just one win in nine games, including a Worthington Cup exit at the hands of Tottenham. United were so poor in the 3-2 home defeat to Middlesbrough, the game triggered an investigation at Old Trafford. It must have worked, as United were not to lose another game all season.

United went top of the Premiership for the first time in January, with a narrow 1-0 win at Charlton. They were less goal-shy on their trips to Leicester and Nottingham, where they ran up 6-2 and 8-1 wins respectively. Springtime saw United do battle in the knockout stages of the Champions League. They defeated Inter Milan 2-0 at Old Trafford and two weeks later gained a 1-1 draw in the San Siro to usher them through to the semi-finals. They returned to Italy to face Juventus. The Old Lady of Turin gave them a torrid time in the first leg but United secured a 1-1 draw. In the return leg at the Stadio Delle Alpi, United conceded two early goals but fought back to record their first win on Italian soil and book a place in the Barcelona Final.

Cole clinches championship
Andy Cole watches the ball beat Tottenham's Ian Walker to deliver Manchester United their fifth Premiership title in seven years, on the final day of the 1998/99 season.

Shooting stars
Manchester United's goalscorers Teddy Sheringham and Paul Scholes display the FA Cup to the fans, after defeating Newcastle 2-0 in the 1999 Cup Final at Wembley.

Race to the Finish

Arsenal pushed United all the way in the Premiership. At the start of the season's last week they were level on points and goal difference. Arsenal's defeat at Leeds handed United the advantage and on the final day United beat Tottenham to finish a point above Arsenal and secure their fifth title in seven years.

United added the FA Cup to the title, but almost went out to Liverpool in the fourth round, when two late goals saw them through. Two Yorke goals knocked Chelsea out after a replay before Giggs settled an FA Cup semi-final replay against Arsenal with an incredible goal. In a dull Final, Newcastle were beaten 2-0.

The Treble was completed on a balmy night in Barcelona when United scored twice in extra time to defeat Bayern Munich in the European Cup Final and so finish the greatest season in their 121-year history.

> *The most important factor was the spirit of the team. They just don't give in, they don't know how to.*
> **Alex Ferguson**

European euphoria
United's jubilant squad gather on the victory podium to lift the European Cup in the Nou Camp stadium in Barcelona, after their dramatic and late win over Bayern Munich. Alex Ferguson broke with tradition to lift it with match captain Peter Schmeichel.

Europe

Manchester United's reputation as European pioneers did not start with their 1957 campaign in Anderlecht, but in 1908, when Ernest Mangnall's championship-winning side toured in Austria and Hungary. The tour made headlines, not only for United's two recorded victories, 6-2 and 7-0 in Budapest, but also because a near-riot by Hungarian fans forced Mangnall to declare that he would never bring a side there again.

The European Cup was the first official inter-club contest, and Sir Matt Busby was eager to enter, although the Football League feared that European commitments might affect the quality of domestic competitions. Busby defied his critics and lead United to European Cup victory in 1968.

After a lull in the '70s and '80s, Sir Alex Ferguson re-established Manchester United as a European force during the '90s. United won the European Cup Winners' Cup in 1991 with victory over Barcelona in Rotterdam. They have been a constant presence in the Champions League in recent times, reaching the knock-out stages in five consecutive seasons between 1997 and 2001, and winning the trophy for the first time in 31 years with that dramatic victory over Bayern Munich in Barcelona in 1999.

European Cup 1956/57: Round 1 (2nd leg): 26th Sep, 1956
Manchester United 10
Anderlecht 0

The first night Manchester played host to European Cup football, more than 43,000 spectators were rewarded with one of the finest displays of football the competition has seen. It took eight minutes for United to extend their 2-0 lead from the first leg, when David Pegg wriggled past two defenders and his cross was met by Tommy Taylor, who headed in the first goal.

Anderlecht managed to stem the goal deluge for the next 20 minutes but United were not to be denied. Taylor was on target again from a short corner, then Dennis Viollet made it 3-0. Viollet added number four from an interception, then shot home from the edge of the penalty box for a hat-trick.

After the break United continued the rout. Tommy Taylor got his hat-trick, Billy Whelan made it 7-0, Dennis Viollet then added his own fourth goal, and Johnny Berry made it nine before Whelan scored goal number 10.

A Real test
Ray Wood saves from Real Madrid's di Stefano in the semi-final 1st leg of the European Cup at the Bernabeu Stadium, Madrid. United were competing with the very best in Europe at this critical stage in the competition. At that time, Real Madrid were the kings of Europe, having won the European Cup the previous season, in 1955/56. Tommy Taylor scored for United during the game in Spain, but they lost 1-3. In the semi-final 2nd leg at Old Trafford they drew 2-2.

The last goal
Bobby Charlton scores United's third goal against Red Star Belgrade, in the Busby Babes' last game before the Munich disaster.

United's stupendous victory could hardly be said to have been over an inferior side. Anderlecht were champions of Belgium for the third consecutive season, at a time when Belgian football was held in high regard.

European Cup 1957/58: Quarter-final (2nd leg): 5th Feb, 1958
Red Star Belgrade 3
Manchester United 3

It was the last time the Busby Babes took the field together, but they left their imprint on football history with a performance that fully justified a place in the semi-finals of the European Cup. United were 2-1 ahead from the first leg, and within two minutes they had extended their lead, from a shot by Dennis Viollet. It was a shock for Red Star Belgrade and evoked a bad tempered response. On the half hour Bobby Charlton piled on the pressure with the

kind of goal that was to become his trademark over the next 15 years. He dispossessed Kostic, accelerated over 10 yards and rifled in a shot from 30 yards. Two minutes later Red Star conceded another free kick and Charlton stepped in to make it 3-0. With the score now 5-1 on aggregate the tie should have been over, but Red Star got a break two

minutes after the interval, when Kostic fired home from all of 30 yards. Eight minutes later Foulkes lost his footing and appeared to pull down Tasic, who promptly converted the penalty awarded to put an entirely different complexion on the game. The United forwards had shone in the first half; now it was the turn of the defence, rallied by Foulkes and inspired by Gregg. They held Red Star at Bay until two minutes from the end, when Kostic equalized from a free kick, but it was too late to deny United their glory. However, within 48 hours the result was to become a mere footnote to more dramatic and tragic events.

European Cup 1965/66: Quarter-final (2nd leg): 9th Mar, 1966
Benfica 1
Manchester United 5

During this match, in the long wake of the Munich tragedy, United re-emerged as serious contenders for Europe's top prize. Benfica, twice winners of the European Cup and finalists four times in the previous five years, could justifiably have been considered favourites but, after a narrow 3-2 victory in the first leg, United had come to Europe's cathedral of football excellence, on the attack.

George Best called into question the pre-match presentation to Eusebio of the European Player of the Year award. After six minutes he jumped free to head home, and six minutes later he weaved past three defenders and silenced the

Portuguese crowd. Connelly scored a third goal from close range. Benfica got back into the match after the break - but only with an own goal by Shay Brennan. In the final 15 minutes Law laid on a goal for Crerand, then Charlton beat three men and fired home the fifth.

European Cup 1967/68: Final: 29th May, 1968
Manchester United 4
Benfica 1

The prize many believed the Babes had been robbed of in 1958 finally came home to United 10 years later. Both teams were tense, and the first half was punctuated by fouls and stoppages. The goals began with a header from Bobby Charlton in the second half, but David Sadler passed up a golden opportunity, and with 10 minutes to go the game was looking very tame. Then Jaime Graca got Benfica back into the game when he collected a knock down from Torres and

The best
The biggest club prize of all must surely be this stunning trophy - the European Cup that United won in 1968.

A Kidd's delight
In extra time at Wembley during the 1968 European Cup Final, Brian Kidd is in seventh heaven as he celebrates his 19th birthday, having just headed United's third goal.

equalized. Stepney then saved a blistering shot from Eusebio and kept United in the match at 1-1 after 90 minutes. Seven minutes into extra time Best scored. Next, Brian Kidd headed in a goal to celebrate his 19th birthday and Charlton headed another. Suddenly the game was over and the Cup was won.

European Cup Winners' Cup 1983/84: Quarter-final (2nd leg): 21st Mar, 1984
Manchester United 3
Barcelona 0

The crowd of 58,000 packed into Old Trafford in March 1984 were unaware that they were about to witness a great European performance from the Manchester United side. Trailing 2-0 from

the first leg in the Nou Camp Stadium, and with the world superstar Diego Maradona in the Barcelona side, there was probably little optimism from United's supporters. But right from the kick-off, United made their intentions clear, with Bryan Robson their driving force as captain. In the 25th minute, a Ray Wilkins corner was helped on by Graeme Hogg to Robson, who scored with a diving header. Robson then added a second goal, thumping the ball home after the keeper failed to hold a Wilkins drive. Then, after being set up by Norman Whiteside, Frank Stapleton sent Old Trafford into raptures with a third goal. Despite a few scary moments in the home penalty area, particularly when Barcelona had a penalty claim turned

down towards the end of the match, United had achieved a memorable result, and had successfully shackled the menace of Barcelona's captain, Maradona. At the end of United's superb 3-0 victory, Robson was mobbed and carried off by jubilant fans.

UEFA Cup 1984/85: Quarter-finals (2nd leg): 20th Mar, 1985
Videoton 1
Manchester United 0

Manchester United had dominated the first leg against Videoton, winning 1-0, and Wittman's shot after 19 minutes, which levelled the aggregate score, was one of the few opportunities Videoton took to explore the goal area over the two legs. Even going a goal behind on the night did not seem likely to prevent United from reaching the semi-final. But try as they might a combination of good goalkeeping by Diszil and squandered chances by Frank Stapleton, Norman Whiteside and Mark Hughes allowed Videoton to hold out through extra time. In the end it was missed penalties by Stapleton and Hughes that cost United a place in the semi-finals. Videoton won the shoot-out 5-4.

Captain Marvel
With a diving header, Robson (above) plants United's first goal against Barcelona. Blaming himself for missing chances in the first leg, he made amends in the second leg, and scored twice.

Video nasty
Atkinson (right) rallies players before the penalty shoot-out in Hungary against Videoton. Stapleton and Hughes missed, and United were out.

Doubly pleased
In 1991 Alex Ferguson became the first manager to win the European Cup Winners' Cup with both an English and Scottish side.

European Cup Winners' Cup 1990/91: Final: 15th May, 1991
Manchester United 2
Barcelona 1

On an unforgettable night in Rotterdam, Manchester United became the first English club to win a European trophy since the Heysel ban was lifted.

Two goals from Mark Hughes saw United victorious against his old club Barcelona. Sixty-nine minutes into the game, Steve Bruce headed a Bryan Robson free-kick towards the goal for Hughes to provide the finishing touch on the line. Five minutes later, Hughes latched on to a through ball from Robson, rounded the goalkeeper and fired in from an almost impossible angle.

Barcelona pulled a goal back through Koeman, but it wasn't enough to deny Manchester United their first European success since 1968.

Champions League 1997/98: 1st Oct, 1997
Manchester United 3
Juventus 2

Manchester United laid to rest the myth of Juventus' invincibility with a stirring win at Old Trafford.

The game started badly after 21 seconds, when Alessandro del Piero gave the Italians the lead. This was when United showed they had learned from their previous seasons in Europe. They played with all the signs of greatness.

Left foot forward
Beckham leaves del Piero in his wake during the Champions League clash against Juventus at Old Trafford in October 1997.

Eight minutes before half time Teddy Sheringham headed in United's equalizer. Juve's Deschamps was sent off in the second half, and four minutes later Scholes danced through the Juventus defence to put United 2-1 in front. Giggs confirmed the result with a thumping shot, later acclaimed as United's goal of the season, before Zidane scored a last minute consolation goal. This goal was irrelevant. United now knew they could compete with the best in Europe.

Champions League 1998/99: Quarter-final (1st leg): 3rd Mar, 1999
Manchester United 2
Inter Milan 0

In the build up to this clash all the talk had been about whether the great Ronaldo would play. In its aftermath, the Brazilian had been forgotten, replaced with talk about the stunning performances of Yorke and Beckham.

Manchester United triumphed over Inter Milan's collection of superstars with two almost identical goals in the first half. Twice Beckham swung in perfect crosses for Yorke to head past the Inter Milan goalkeeper Pagliuca. However, only some heroic defending from Henning Berg protected United's lead in the second half. Late on it looked certain that Francesco Colonnese would score after he had sidestepped Schmeichel, but Berg cleared the ball off the line to ensure that Inter Milan left with nothing. Two weeks later, United made it through to the semi-finals with a hard fought 1-1 draw in the hostile San Siro.

Champions League 1998/99: Semi-final (2nd leg): 21st Apr, 1999
Juventus 2
Manchester United 3

Manchester United overcame the mighty Juventus in the Stadio Delle Alpi to book a place in the Champions League Final for the first time since 1968.

In the first leg at Old Trafford Juventus

gave United a footballing masterclass but thanks to a late Ryan Giggs goal, his team escaped with a draw. In Turin, despite going two goals down, it was United who performed with the greater skill and passion. Alex Ferguson was moved to call it, "the best Manchester United have played in my time at the club."

Early on it looked as if United would again miss out on the Final, after Filippo Inzaghi scored twice to give Juventus a commanding 3-1 lead on aggregate. Driven on by Roy Keane, United levelled the game before half time, with goals from Keane himself and Dwight Yorke. A 2-2 draw would have been enough, but Andrew Cole scored a late goal that saw United through as winners.

Champions League 1998/99: Final: 26th May, 1999
Manchester United 2
Bayern Munich 1

Amid unprecedented scenes in the Nou Camp stadium, Manchester United scored twice in injury time to win the Champions League. "That was supernatural," said Gary Neville. "It certainly wasn't skill and ability that won us the game. It was something else, and I can't understand what it was."

Mario Basler gave Bayern Munich the lead after only six minutes and for the rest of the match Manchester United toiled away without reward. It looked as if Bayern Munich had triumphed when the assistant referee held up the board to indicate that there were just three more minutes left.

Keane as ever
Keane kick-starts United's comeback against Juventus by heading past Peruzzi. Keane's performance is regarded as his finest ever for the club as he managed to drag United back from the brink of defeat to usher them into the 1999 European Cup Final, despite picking up a yellow card which he knew would rule him out of the Barcelona game.

Manchester United then won a corner, Beckham swung it in, the ball made its way back out to Giggs whose shot was going wide until Sheringham steered it in to equalize. A minute later United again had a corner, which Sheringham glanced on to Solskjaer who poked it in to spark off bedlam amongst the 55,000 United fans packed in behind the goal.

Mauled in Munich
Dutch defender Jaap Stam deals with his disappointment at being knocked out of the Champions League by Bayern Munich.

Champions League 2000/01: Quarter-final: 3rd, 18th April, 2001
Bayern Munich (1) 2
Manchester United (0) 1

Manchester United's failure to build on their 1999 Champions League triumph was ruthlessly exposed over two legs by the eventual winners Bayern Munich, who won 3-1 on aggregate. After a similar defeat at the same stage to Real Madrid in the previous year, this was a particularly painful experience. In the first leg at Old Trafford, United lacked penetration, and allowed the Germans to soak up the pressure and score on the counter-attack through Paulo Sergio in the dying minutes of the game. In the second leg in Munich two weeks later, United's challenge was derailed in the first half by goals from Elber and Mehmet Scholl. A Ryan Giggs goal in the second half gave United hope, but they failed to score again and were knocked out of the competition.

Ole's moment
Ole Gunnar Solskjaer is mobbed by delirious team mates after scoring the goal that won the Champions League for Manchester United. "I woke up on the morning of the game and had a funny feeling it was going to be my night. I rang my mate in Norway and said, 'You'd better watch it,' said Solskjaer. "It was unbelievable. This is why I want to stay at United."

Part Three

OLD TRAFFORD

The Stadium

Old Trafford is the largest, most impressive club stadium in English football. The status of the ground is fitting, both of the fine team that plays there and of the huge worldwide support that United enjoys. Accommodating sell-out crowds of 55,000 during the Treble-winning season, the stadium's capacity has since been increased to 67,700. An extra tier was added to the East Stand and opened to spectators in January 2000, while an extra tier was also added to the West Stand soon afterwards. These developments, like the new North Stand in 1995/96, are based around a long-term strategy that can be traced back to the

first sketches. The official opening of the stadium was on 19th February, 1910 when a crowd of 50,000 people saw Liverpool win 4–3. Even then, Manchester United was called "Moneybags United" and was stigmatized for the lavish way in which it was run. One writer described Old Trafford as a "wonder to behold", and with a billiard room, massage room, gymnasium, and plunge bath under the country's only covered stand, he certainly had a point. Add to that a capacity of 80,000 and it is easy to understand why other teams and their supporters were so envious of Manchester United's ground.

The way it was
Even in this photograph, taken in about 1926, you can see the beginnings of today's Old Trafford. Since the early '20s the club's financial situation had been improving and attendances were rising. United's directors decided to buy the freehold from Manchester Breweries, and the deal was completed on 25th March, 1927.

Second largest stadium
The largest English stadium after Wembley, Old Trafford has grown so much over the years that newcomers to the ground need a map to find their way around!

Moving home

United's first home, while they were still Newton Heath, was at North Road, just northeast of the city centre. In 1893, the Heathens moved to Bank Street in Clayton. In 1902, poor crowds forced Newton Heath to go into liquidation. The club was rescued by J. H. Davies, who turned Newton Heath into Manchester United. Davies was an ambitious man and, despite the capacity of 50,000 at Bank Street, the ground was too hemmed in by factories to satisfy his vision for the future. After United won their first FA Cup, in 1909, he paid £60,000 to purchase a site five miles away, near Old Trafford cricket ground. The new ground was built by Messrs Brameld and Smith of Manchester under the supervision of Scottish architect Archibald Leitch, who designed many famous stands, including those at Ibrox and White Hart Lane.

Old Trafford was soon recognized as a quality venue, and staged its first FA Cup semi-finals within weeks of opening. In 1915 it was the venue for the FA Cup Final between Sheffield United and Chelsea. Shortly after the First World

War, two attendance records were set at Old Trafford. The first was in 1920 when 70,504 people paid to watch United play Aston Villa, a record that still stands as United's largest-ever League attendance. One year later just 13 people paid to see a Second Division fixture between Stockport County and Leicester City. Stockport's ground had been closed and, with relegation looming, their fans had decided to boycott the match. However, the record is slightly misleading as there were about 20,000 people still inside the ground who had paid to see United play Derby County earlier that day.

Between the wars

Old Trafford changed little between the two wars. In 1934 a cover was erected over the United Road terrace opposite the main stand, but with the club struggling and unemployment in the country rising, there was little cash for further developments. On 25th March, 1939, 79,962 people crammed into Old Trafford to watch an FA Cup semi-final between Wolves and Grimsby, the biggest crowd ever to pack the stadium.

The Second World War was to bring more problems to Old Trafford. The ground was close to the Trafford Park Industrial Estate, which was a prime target for German bombers, and on the night of 11th March, 1941, the stadium suffered direct hits from two German bombs. One nearly demolished the Main Stand and another hit the United Road terrace and scorched the pitch.

In August 1945, the War Damage Commission granted the club £4,800 to clear the debris and a further £17,474

to rebuild the stands. While Old Trafford was rebuilt, United played "home" games at Manchester City's Maine Road ground in Moss Side. City received £5,000 for every game that United played, plus a share of the gate receipts. United were attracting huge attendances,

so City reaped the rewards, but in November 1948 City gave United notice to quit, and on Wednesday 24th August, 1949, United ran out at Old Trafford once again to face Bolton Wanderers for their first League fixture at the ground since 1939.

Players' changing rooms
Situated beneath the Stretford End family stand, the spacious new changing rooms were first opened in 1993 to replace the old ones, which were under the Main Stand.

By 1954, the ground was back to full use and on 23rd March, 1957 Old Trafford's floodlights were turned on for the first time, when Bolton Wanderers were once again the visitors for another milestone in the stadium's history.

The Stretford End was covered in 1959, and 1,500 seats were added to the rear of this stand in 1962. In 1965 a cantilever stand was designed by Manchester architects Atherden Fuller, a company which remains involved with the redevelopment of Old Trafford. Built as Old Trafford prepared to stage games for the 1966 World Cup Finals, this stand along the United Road side of the ground reflected the fact that some spectators wanted to stand and others preferred to sit. Private boxes were also built at the rear of the stand.

Britain's biggest club stadium

With the addition of an extra tier on both the East and West stands in 2000, Old Trafford outgrew Celtic's Celtic Park and became the biggest club stadium in Britain.

When completed, the United Road Stand seated 10,000 people and had a covered standing paddock in front. It was the beginning of the stadium that we know today, and housed the United side that won the European Cup in 1968. In 1973, the cantilever was extended behind the Scoreboard End to add an additional 5,500 seats to what became known as "K" Stand.

The first fence

At the end of the 1973/74 season, Old Trafford had the unfortunate distinction of being the first stadium in the country to erect fences to prevent fans invading the pitch. In the last home game of the season, Denis Law, by then a Manchester City player, scored a goal that seemed to send United down to the Second Division and supporters caused havoc on the pitch. The club installed fences in time for the 1974/75 season.

The next part of the ground to be developed, between 1978 and 1984, was the Main Stand, which was given a new

The Munich Clock

The "Munich Clock" is a poignant memorial to all those who lost their lives in the 1958 air disaster. The club also has a stone tablet, listing all the players and club staff who died. This is now on display on the outside of the East Stand at Old Trafford.

Sir Matt Busby statue

The bronze life-size statue of Sir Matt Busby was erected following the great man's death in 1994. It now stands at the front of the East Stand overlooking the forecourt.

The new museum

The new "North Stand" was completed in 1996 and includes a spectacular new club museum, which opened in 1998.

cantilever roof in three sections. New club offices were added behind this stand. When the corner between the Main Stand and the Scoreboard End was developed into a family stand in 1985, it meant that the cantilever roof swept around 75 per cent of Old Trafford. The plan that chairman Louis Edwards and manager Sir Matt Busby had envisaged in the early '60s was to have been completed with a new Stretford End stand, including both a standing paddock and seating. As a result of the disaster at Hillsborough on 15th April, 1989, the plans had to be changed.

In 1992, the Stretford End and adjacent Stretford Paddock were used for the very last time in Norman Whiteside's testimonial. The following year a 10,164 all-seater stand costing £10 million took its place to make Old Trafford the most complete stadium in the country.

Concerns that the 44,800 all-seated capacity would be too small for a club of United's stature were soon confirmed. Despite a lack of atmosphere since the loss of the terraces, demand for tickets vastly exceeded the supply. In 1995 the club announced plans for a giant new stand on the United Road side of the ground. Seating 25,300 people, the stand would have the biggest cantilever roof in the world. This new "North Stand" was completed in 1996, but even then, United's first-team home games continued to sell out. It soon became clear that further expansion would be needed so, in May 1999, the club embarked on a three-year programme to redevelop the East and West stands. Within seven months, both of the stands had been extended, allowing an additional 12,000 fans to enjoy the Manchester United spectacle.

It's no wonder that Sir Bobby Charlton referred to Old Trafford as "a theatre of dreams." No surprise either that UEFA has given it their prestigious seal of approval, declaring it to be of grade "A" status. Anyone privileged enough to visit will soon tell you – the place United call "home" is a truly magnificent stadium.

Match Day

When Manchester United play at Old Trafford, the 90 minutes of football that the 67,700 football fans have paid to see represents just the tip of the iceberg in terms of all the organization that has gone into staging the event. Without the hundreds of individuals who put the show on the road, from ball-boys to broadcasters, a Manchester United home game wouldn't be the impressive spectacle that it is.

For a Premier League home game kicking off at 3:00 p.m., the main preparation will begin six weeks before the game, when the ticket office starts selling the 18,700 match tickets not allocated to United's 46,000 plus season ticket holders. As the demand for match tickets usually far exceeds the supply, tickets are offered to club members, and a lottery is held to determine the successful applicants. If the game is to be televised, the television company's outside broadcast unit starts setting up and laying cables a couple of days before the game. The first overseas United fans, including some from Scandinavia, usually arrive in the city about 24 hours before the game. They are followed by groups of Irish fans, many of whom spend the weekend in Manchester and take in the stadium tour.

The Stretford End
United supporters await the emergence of the teams. Since the building of the new players' changing rooms in 1993, players come on to the pitch from the corner on the right-hand side, beneath the Stretford End.

7:00 a.m. Pitch preparation

Work starts early on a match day. Depending upon the time of year, the pitch is rolled at about 7:00 a.m., and markings are painted on soon afterwards. Groundsman Keith Kent and his team of ground staff work throughout the year to keep the pitch in the best possible condition, but in the days leading up to a game they make sure that it gets plenty of water. Wet grass makes the pitch slicker and faster, which suits United's style of play. If rain is forecast, as it often is in Manchester, Keith will water the pitch more sparingly.

During the early morning, food and programmes are delivered, and all around the country, coaches depart for Old Trafford. From north, south, east and west, thousands of supporters set off, timing their arrival at Old Trafford for about 1:00 p.m.

Signing autographs
Autograph hunters besiege players old and new before the game at Old Trafford. Right, former player Norman Whiteside signs an autograph book on his way into the ground.

10:00 a.m. Police briefing

At about 10:00 a.m., the police gather at their headquarters on Talbot Road, just a short walk from the ground, for their pre-match briefing. The number of police on duty depends on the category of the game; the higher the likelihood of trouble, the more officers are on duty.

By mid-morning, the crowds start to gather on Sir Matt Busby Way, the stadium's main thoroughfare. Soon, the whole road resembles a bazaar in Istanbul, resounding with cries selling burgers, newspapers, T-shirts, fanzines and even match tickets. Queues form outside the huge megastore behind the Stretford End as supporters stock up on United souvenirs, and the pubs around the ground gradually fill up with United fans, friends old and new who follow the same pre-match ritual week after week, and year after year.

12:00 p.m. United players arrive

The players arrive individually by car at about midday. Until a couple of years ago players parked in the number one car park, opposite the Sir Matt Busby statue, and walked across the forecourt and through the tunnel to the players' entrance. Some players were taking so long to walk the 100 metres, because of autograph hunters, that they now park their cars behind the Stretford End, close to the new changing rooms. From there they are escorted to the players' entrance. At least there's no chance of their missing the kick-off. Once the players have gathered they eat a meal, usually pasta-based, for energy during the match. Then they go to the changing rooms, where they change out of the suits and ties that Alex Ferguson insists on, and into training gear for a warm-up on the pitch at around 2:15 p.m.

1:30 p.m. Away side arrives

At around 1:30 p.m. the first of the 3,000 away supporters arrive at the stadium in coaches, escorted by motorcycle police. The coaches are parked by Salford Quays and the supporters are escorted to the away section, between the East and South Stands. The away team's coach arrives at about the same time, and is escorted to the new changing rooms. Turnstiles around the stadium open and the first trickle of supporters enters the ground. Since Old Trafford has become an all-seater, fans enter the stadium much later because they don't have to find a vantage point on a terrace.

Old Trafford has approximately 5,000 executive seats including 180 executive boxes and many of the spectators using these facilities like to enjoy a meal or a drink before a game, keeping the catering staff in the various suites on three sides of the ground busy.

With 67,700 people descending upon one area in a short period of time, it's up to the police to make sure that everyone gets into the stadium without difficulty. Queues may build up outside turnstiles and the police, usually those on horseback, do their best to keep the queues flowing steadily and safely. Other police officers keep a watch on fans they know to be troublemakers and make sure that there is no conflict between rival supporters. If the police do have to arrest somebody, they can either take them away to nearby Stretford Police Station in one of the waiting police vans, or hold them in one of several cells inside the ground.

3:00 p.m. Kick-off

Once the game gets underway, the police and United's security officials monitor the crowd from the stadium control room, located behind the away

Keith Kent
United's groundsman, Keith Kent and his team have a full-time job keeping the pitch up to the boss's high standards.

The story goes that when Keith Kent first arrived at Old Trafford, one of his requests was for loads of earthworms to help aerate the pitch!

home. Up in the press box the print journalists busily prepare their copy for a deadline that could be as soon as 15 minutes after the final whistle. The radio journalists, including those from United's own radio station, which broadcasts on match days, summarize the game before heading into the Main Stand to view the after-match press conference. About 20 minutes after the final whistle both team managers, usually accompanied by one selected player, will speak to the gathered journalists about the game that has just been played. Many tabloid journalists choose to lead their match reports with post-match quotes given by the manager or player before writing about the game itself.

5:00 p.m. Litter collection

As the supporters file back out of Old Trafford towards waiting cars, trains, coaches and buses, the ground staff again replace any divots, and the manager speaks to his players about the game that they have just played, discussing good points, bad points and areas in which the team could improve. Then the players have a bath; the United changing room has a large plunge bath as well as individual baths and showers. After getting changed into their suits again, they either go straight home or go to the players' lounge, a small bar area nearby, where they can mingle with invited friends and family.

With the supporters and the police long gone and the players gradually drifting home, a large team of litter collectors descends upon Old Trafford and the surrounding streets to pick up the litter inevitably left by such a large crowd of people. By the time they have finished, the streets are looking tidy once again, and Old Trafford is ready and waiting ... to stage another game.

supporters and the Main Stand. Here, officials are surrounded by an enormous bank of monitors feeding pictures from the closed-circuit television cameras located both inside and outside the stadium. The officials look out for trouble and can zoom in on any offenders or areas of potential conflict. The cameras used at Old Trafford are so powerful that they can pick out the detail on a badge on a fan's shirt anywhere in the ground.

3:45 p.m. Half time

Half time is the busiest 15 minutes of the game for the various catering outlets around the ground selling pies, burgers and drinks. The ground staff are also busy, replacing any divots cut up during the first half.

During the second half of the game, the area outside the ground becomes almost as busy as the inside. Buses, taxis and private cars begin to congregate near Old Trafford, waiting to transport the thousands of supporters back into the city centre and beyond, once the game has finished.

4:45 p.m. The final whistle

As the referee blows the final whistle, the majority of supporters immediately start to leave the ground and head for

After the match
Sir Alex Ferguson and Peter Schmeichel being interviewed by members of the press after a game.

The control room
Closed-circuit TV monitors (left), showing images from all over the stadium, enable officials to keep a close eye on the behaviour of the supporters.

After the match
Alex Ferguson and Peter Schmeichel are interviewed by members of the press after a game.

The Strip

When Newton Heath first took to the field at their North Road ground in 1892, the players wore red-and-white quartered jerseys and blue shorts – a strange combination, even in those early days, but stranger kits were to come. From 1894 to 1896, the team wore distinctive green and gold jerseys with laced collars. In 1896, the green and gold jerseys were replaced by a kit that featured a white shirt with blue shorts but this new strip brought no better fortunes to the club, who struggled in the recently formed Second Division of the Football League. It wasn't until Newton Heath became Manchester United in 1902 that they started to wear the famous red shirts with white shorts.

During the 20th century, the football strip evolved from an unconventional jersey to a fashion accessory worn by millions of fans. Rival sports manufacturers now bid for the rights to mass-produce kits in a multi-million pound worldwide industry. Sporting a replica of the kit worn by your heroes is a trend that really took off in the 1970s and 1980s, and became hugely popular in the 1990s. At this time many clubs, including Manchester United, began to change their strips more and more frequently.

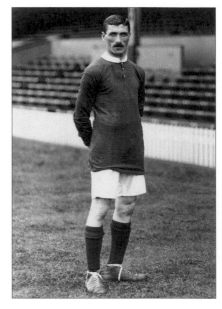

Early days
The simple red and white strip brought in by Davies remained pretty much the same for years, as this photograph of Billy Meredith in 1905/06 illustrates.

Red and white

When John Davies, a wealthy local brewer, took over as chairman of the club in 1902, the name Newton Heath disappeared for ever in favour of Manchester United. Davies was the man eventually responsible for United's move to Old Trafford, but one of his first moves was to change the colours of the first team strip to the famous red and white that we know and love today.

Initially football jerseys were made of wool, but wet weather, not uncommon in Manchester, would weigh the players down and it wasn't long before wool

The Heathens
This photograph shows the Heathens in 1892, in the early green and gold strip, which was to be revived a century later.

was superseded by the lighter cotton, flannel or cotton twill. Over the next few decades there were few changes to the United shirt, although from 1922 to 1927 players wore a white shirt bearing a deep red "V" around the neck. The red and white colour combination has remained the most popular. In 1934 United wore maroon shirts with white hoops, and they finished 20th in Division

Two, the club's lowest ever League position. The red shirt was duly recalled.

Although United have been known as the "Red Devils" for many decades, the red shirt has been notable by its absence for some of the club's greatest achievements. In 1948, when United beat Blackpool 4–2 to win their first FA Cup since 1909, a deep blue shirt was worn to prevent a colour clash with the

Revivalism
A green and gold strip, based on the Heathens' strip, was released in 1992/93 as a third kit, worn here by Steve Bruce.

Blackpool shirts. In United's finest hour, the European Cup win over Benfica at Wembley in 1968, the team wore royal blue shirts, produced especially for the game. In 1991, when United beat Barcelona in Rotterdam to lift the European Cup Winners' Cup, they played in special white shirts.

Styles changed very little after World War Two. The '50s again saw a plunging "V" neckline. Home shirts were red with a white "V", and away shirts were white with a red "V". In the '60s this "V" was

Twenties colours
For most of the '20s, the players wore white shirts with a deep red "V" neck, a shape that was to become popular again in the '50s.

1909
Sandy Turnbull wore this shirt in the 1909 FA Cup Final. He scored the only goal in United's 1-0 win over Bristol City.

1948
This was Charlie Mitten's shirt in the 1948 FA Cup Final against Blackpool. United won the match 4-2.

The Manchester badge
Liam Whelan and Duncan Edwards pose in shirts with badges, worn for the 1957 FA Cup Final at Wembley, against Aston Villa.

ditched in favour of a round collar, with the red and white trim still being reversed for home and away games.

The United strip didn't have a badge on the chest until the early 1970s, unless the team were playing in a Cup Final. Then, in the 1957 and 1963 FA Cup Finals for example, the badge of the Manchester County Football Association, featuring the Manchester coat of arms, was sewn on to the chest. The only exception to this tradition was in the 1958 FA Cup Final, just three months after the tragedy at Munich. For this poignant game, a symbolic badge was produced that featured a phoenix rising from the ashes. Sadly, if unsurprisingly, United lost, and it was to be 10 years before the club rose to greatness again.

In the main, football shirts stayed plain, functional and cotton until the late '70s, when synthetic materials became available, but football shorts had been getting shorter since the '60s, and long, baggy shorts were seen as a relic of days gone by. By the mid '80s shorts were so short that some players looked as though they were in severe discomfort. Italian clubs reintroduced longer shorts and English clubs soon did likewise, wearing the looser, more casual shorts that are still popular today. The multi-coloured goalkeeper's jerseys are designed to dazzle opposing strikers, and have become more garish over the years.

The United badge was added to shirts in 1973, and the whole kit underwent a major change in 1983, when the club signed its first shirt sponsorship with Sharp Electronics. Sharp, a Japanese company, have their UK base in Newton Heath, and United's association with Sharp was to continue for many years.

'60s style
Right, George Best wears a typical '60s round-necked shirt.

European Cup winners
This royal blue shirt was worn by George Best in the 1968 European Cup Final against Benfica, which United won 4–1.

Initially, however, television companies refused to cover matches played in sponsored shirts and for a time United wore the Sharp logo only for matches that would not be televised.

German sportswear giants Adidas produced United kits for over 10 years, right through the '80s to the early '90s. During this time, United had a red home

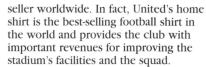

Replica strip
The first replica strip that supporters could buy was the Admiral strip, worn here by Stuart Pearson in the 1977 Cup Final.

shirt, a white away shirt and an all-blue third strip worn for away games at Southampton, Sunderland and Arsenal, whose home strips clashed with United's first two strips.

Manchester United changed their kit manufacturers from Adidas to Umbro in 1992. Umbro had strong links with Manchester; the company was formed in nearby Wilmslow in 1924. The Manchester United shirt is their biggest

Short and Sharp
Bryan Robson is seen here wearing the short shorts and the Sharp shirt of 1985/86.

seller worldwide. In fact, United's home shirt is the best-selling football shirt in the world and provides the club with important revenues for improving the stadium's facilities and the squad.

Today's shirts are worn as fashion items by fans keen to show their allegiance to Manchester United. The home and away kits are updated in two-year cycles, although there have been special kits for Europe, and kits such as the grey away kit in 1995/96, which lasted just nine months. First worn

1994
Steve Bruce's shirt, worn in the 1994 FA Cup Final, echoes the lace-up collars of earlier times.

competitively in a 3–1 defeat to Aston Villa, United didn't record a single victory in the kit. The final straw came at Southampton in early 1996. After going three goals behind to a team fighting relegation, United players complained that they couldn't see each other and changed strips at half time. They could not pull back the deficit, losing 3–1, and the dreaded grey kit was never worn again.

The red United home shirt is probably the most recognizable football shirt in the world. The full strip, with white shorts and black socks, is highly distinctive, and is a part of the tradition that has made Manchester United the worldwide institution that it is today.

1992
Steve Bruce wore this blue shirt in the 1992 League (Rumbelows) Cup Final. United beat Nottingham Forest 1–0.

1996
Eric Cantona scored the only goal in the 1996 FA Cup Final wearing this shirt. United beat Liverpool and became the first-ever double Double winners.

2001/2002
The 2001/2002 reversible away strip is gold on one side and white on the other. These colours were chosen to mark the 100th anniversary of Manchester United's change of name from Newton Heath in 1902.

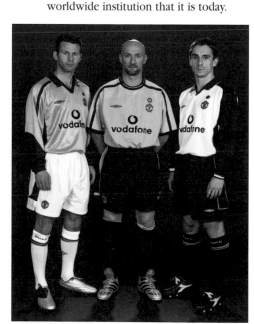

Memorabilia

Visit the new Manchester United museum and you'll get some idea of just how much football-related memorabilia there is. From old programmes to players' jerseys, football cigarette cards to cup winners' medals, there are all sorts of items that have played their part, however small, in the proud history of United. The museum, the first of its kind in England, was opened in 1986. In its first year, 25,000 people passed through its doors. In 1997, 192,000 people from all over the world visited the museum. It had become so successful that it had outgrown its original site so it was relocated to

three floors in Old Trafford's huge North Stand. The new museum opened in spring 1998. It is the definitive history of Manchester United, and has some unique memorabilia on display.

When people think of football memorabilia they usually picture a box of old programmes gathering dust and, for most supporters, programmes are the most accessible items of memorabilia. Collecting programmes has become so popular that some people make a living out of their hobby. It might be worth wiping the dust off any old programmes you own; you could have a rare example worth thousands of pounds.

Cigarette cards
Years ago, many people collected and swapped cigarette cards of their favourite players and teams. Today, they can be a valuable reminder of the great players.

Programmes

In 1997, a programme from Manchester United's postponed game against Wolverhampton Wanderers at Old Trafford in February 1958 was sold for £1,925. That price surpassed the £1,887 paid for a programme from United's 1958 game against Red Star Belgrade. The reason that these programmes fetched such high prices was because of their relevance to the Munich air disaster. United's game in Belgrade was the last time that the Busby Babes played together on a football field, and with so few United fans making the journey, practically no programmes came back to England. It's that scarcity that makes the price so high.

The United Review

The image of a United player shaking hands with a supporter, a design that has remained almost unchanged for years, gives the *United Review* one of the most distinctive mastheads of any British programme. It even has a collectors' club, with 250 members. Perhaps the most famous *United Review* is the one from the first post-Munich match, an FA Cup tie against Sheffield Wednesday. Under the heading "United Will Go On", the *Review* outlines what happened at Munich. The United team line-up was left blank because it wasn't known who would play until the last minute. Copies are only worth about £30 because 60,000 were printed, so there are plenty to satisfy the demand. In terms of sentiment, though, they're priceless.

Charlie Roberts' FA trial cap

Two of Roberts' medals, for representing the Football League against the Scottish League, in 1907 and 1911

Billy Porter's Manchester Cup winners' medal

Mark Jones' 1956 League championship winners' medal

Bobby Charlton's European Cup and World Cup winners' medals

While collecting programmes is the most popular method of accumulating football memorabilia, there has been a surge of interest in other items in the 1990s, influenced partly by the American obsession with sports memorabilia.

Medals

Medals always create a lot of interest, especially when they happen to be a European Cup winners' medal and a World Cup winners' medal, the two most prestigious medals that a player can win. In England, only Bobby Charlton and Nobby Stiles share the distinction of owning both medals.

Tickets

Up until the early 1990s it was possible to gain admittance to Old Trafford by paying cash at the turnstiles. A huge increase in the demand for tickets, at both home and away games, coupled with shrinking ground capacities, meant that supporters needed to buy a ticket in

advance for practically every single Manchester United game. Tickets for Cup Finals and big European games are always scarce and change hands for vastly inflated fees on the black market. Old and rare tickets, like programmes, are highly prized, especially if they also have sentimental value. These days, to avoid counterfeiting, tickets have holograms and watermarks.

Above, a ticket for the European Cup 2nd leg against Red Star Belgrade, 5th February, 1958.

Right, a ticket for the FA Cup Final that made United the double Double winners in 1996.

Originals and one-offs

The kit that a certain player wore in an important match or a League championship medal can be worth tens of thousands of pounds. A shirt worn by Eric Cantona in his last game for United was sold for £2,000 and the boots that Bryan Robson wore in his final game for

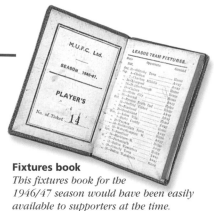

Fixtures book

This fixtures book for the 1946/47 season would have been easily available to supporters at the time.

Scarves

Scarves really took off in the 1960s and 1970s, when supporters used to tie them to their wrists. While scarves are still popular today, for many supporters the sight of a packed Stretford End, complete with a mass of swirling red and white scarves, is just a happy memory of the days before all-seater stadiums.

Rosettes

For important events, such as Cup Finals and championship victories, various kinds of rosettes are often produced.

Middlesbrough were auctioned for charity and raised £1,500.

The most intriguing pieces are usually one-offs, such as the telegram Duncan Edwards sent to his landlady telling her he would be home late from Munich.

Flags

Flags have been popular at United games for years, especially on a European away trip. Arguably the finest display of United flags was seen at Rotterdam for the 1991

The last telegram

Duncan Edwards telegrammed his landlady on the day of the Munich crash, telling her that engine problems meant he would be flying back the following day. Tragically, he never went home alive.

Cup Winners' Cup Final when 25,000 United supporters went to Holland to watch United beat Barcelona 2–1.

Look to the future

Some items are unlikely to find favour in the future. A 1970s United supporter's white butcher's coat covered in United badges will probably not accrue value with time, and the wooden rattle is unlikely to make a comeback.

The 1990s has seen the large clubs, including United, greatly expand their merchandise departments, and today you can buy practically anything with the United badge on, from duvets to desk lamps. Your green and gold third kit from 1993 might be lucky to see the light of day today but it's worth keeping hold of, since it might come back into fashion as "retro wear" one day.

Stylo boots

Football players frequently endorse products, such as football boots and sportswear. These side-lacing "Stylo" boots endorsed by George Best in the early 1970s may have raised a few eyebrows but they certainly didn't catch on.

Pennants

Before a big game, to commemorate the occasion, the opposing team captains often swap pennants.

Benfica pennant from the 1968 European Cup Final

Badges

Enamel pin badges became popular in the 1980s. There are a large number of collectors, and up to 75 badges dedicated to Manchester United.

Souvenir pennant produced for the 1991 European Cup Winners' Cup Final

Red Star Belgrade pennant from the 1958 European Cup

The ball with which George Best scored six goals in United's 8–2 win over Northampton Town on 7th February, 1970, signed by the team

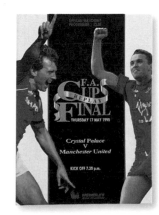

The Supporters

Sea of scarves
Even while United were in Division Two, their supporters were enthusiastic and loyal. Here, fans display a sea of scarves at Fulham on 5th October, 1974. It may have helped; United won the match 2–1.

Wherever you go in the world, from Beswick to Bangkok, Urmston to Uruguay, you'll never be far away from somebody with an allegiance to Manchester United. Although United have always been a big club in British football, it was the Munich air crash in 1958 that gave United the worldwide profile it has today. Under Sir Matt Busby, United's phoenix-like rise from the ashes to triumph in the European Cup a decade later won the club fans the world over. It is still the best supported club in English football, attracting the highest home crowds in the League for 31 out of the past 36 years.

A large percentage of the support comes from the local area, contradicting the '90s myth that no United fans come from Manchester. United's away following is one of the loudest in the country, and tickets at away grounds consistently sell out. The 1999 European Cup victory over Bayern Munich in Barcelona was witnessed by over 30,000 United supporters, and some estimates put the figure nearer 60,000. That is a level of support seldom seen on the Continent. Trips to Wembley for Cup Finals in the '90s became so frequent one writer claimed the stadium should be renamed "Old Trafford South".

United we stand

The majority of United's vocal support traditionally came from the Stretford End, a large bank of covered terracing with seats at the rear, behind the West End goal. Before 1992, when the Stretford End was demolished to make way for a new all-seater stand, it was not uncommon to see long queues snaking their way behind the stand as much as three or four hours before kick-off.

As kick-off approached, the noise level inside the ground would increase with the volume of people and at one time in the mid '70s, the noise from the Stretford End was so loud that it was likened to a jumbo jet at take-off point. It must have been quite intimidating to members of the visiting team.

Few deny that the Old Trafford atmosphere suffered when the Stretford End was demolished to make the stadium an all-seater. Despite that, for a big European match or a championship celebration day, there is no better place to be than Old Trafford when the whole ground seems to be singing and urging the team towards victory.

Crowd trouble

During the early '70s, United supporters, especially those who called themselves "Doc's Red Army", earned themselves a reputation for being unruly hooligans, causing trouble wherever they travelled. Old Trafford was the first English ground to install fences to keep supporters off the pitch, but later, in the wake of the Hillsborough disaster in 1989, these fences were taken down as safety inside stadiums became of paramount importance and hooliganism, fortunately, seemed to be on the decline.

Supporters' clubs

Despite the fact that the current ground capacity of Old Trafford is limited to 67,700 people, over 140,000 United fans are paid-up members of the club. Affiliated to the membership scheme are over 200 branches of the Manchester United Supporters' Club. The majority of these branches are based in the UK, and arrange travel for members to and from United games. United's support in Ireland is legendary and there are many branches, even in the smallest Irish towns, arranging regular travel to games in England. Amazingly enough, the largest supporters' club is one of the overseas branches, the Scandinavian Branch, which by 1998 had 28,000 paid-up members. From the USA to Mauritius, South Africa to Iceland, United's supporters have branches around the world, staffed with people keeping their loyal and enthusiastic members up to date with events at Old Trafford.

Manchester United's support can perhaps best be summed up by one of the most popular terrace anthems, which goes: "If the Reds should play, in

Home and away
Supporters from all over the world watch United's last League match of the championship winning 1993/94 season, at home against Coventry. The result was a 0–0 draw.

Rome or Mandalay, we'll be there." Judging by the reception that the players receive wherever they travel, this claim would be difficult to dispute.

United in respect
Following the death of Sir Matt Busby in January 1994, United supporters on their way into the ground showed their respect by hanging their club scarves over the street sign of the road named after him.

Doc's Red Army

The self-styled "Doc's Red Army", complete with white butchers' coats decorated with United badges, terrorized the opposition's supporters both home and away, and embarrassed Tommy Docherty by their behaviour. Following a pitch invasion in 1974, the club was forced to take action to curb the problem. Old Trafford installed fences to keep fans off the pitch, although later they were taken down in the interests of safety.

Hilditch: Clarence 1926–1927

United's first player-manager, Clarence Hilditch stepped into the breach after the controversial departure of John Chapman. His time as manager was brief, and he remained in the job only until the appointment of Herbert Bamlett. He then returned to the playing ranks until 1932, when he joined the coaching staff.

Mangnall: Ernest 1903–1912

It was the influence of Ernest Mangnall that led to the building of Manchester United's new stadium at Old Trafford in 1910. Appointed secretary at Burnley in March 1900, Mangnall moved to Manchester United in September 1903. He took charge as secretary with the side in the Second Division and after finishing third for two seasons, United won promotion in 1905/06. Mangnall's team, skippered by Charlie Roberts and including the legendary Billy Meredith, won the League championship and the FA Cup for the first time, and were the first winners of the FA Charity Shield at the beginning of the 1908/09 season. Mangnall resigned from United in 1912, moving across town to join Manchester City, where he was responsible for the building of the stadium at Maine Road. Ernest Mangnall retired from football in 1924 to become a part-time sports correspondent with a Sunday newspaper.

McGuinness: Wilf 1969–1970

A Busby Babe, Wilf McGuinness' playing career was cut short when he broke his leg badly in a Reserve match against Stoke in 1960. He retired at the age of 22. McGuinness was given the job of Youth team manager in 1961 and in June 1969 he became senior coach when Sir Matt Busby announced his retirement. He was appointed manager a year later, but held the post for just six months and returned to coaching the Reserves. McGuinness left the club in February 1971 and spent four years in Greek football as coach of Aris Salonika, then Panachaiki Patras. He returned to England to manage York City. A qualified physiotherapist, he had spells as manager with Hull City and Bury before retiring from football in 1992.

Murphy: Jimmy 1958

Although he was never officially appointed manager, the part Jimmy Murphy played in the rebuilding after Munich is enough to earn him his place alongside others who were. Murphy spurned many offers of managerial posts at other clubs to continue his work at Old Trafford. He joined Busby's coaching staff after the Second World War, and at the time of the air disaster was also manager of Wales. Sir Matt's right-hand man, he held the post of assistant manager at Manchester United until his retirement in 1971.

Training under Busby
Wilf McGuinness, in his playing days at United under Matt Busby in the mid-1950s, leapfrogs over Liam Whelan during a team training session.

O'Farrell: Frank 1971–1972

Despite United's strong links with Ireland, Frank O'Farrell is, to date, the only Irishman to manage the club. He was appointed in June 1971, leaving Leicester City weeks after they came top of the Second Division. The son of an engine driver from Cork, O'Farrell had a long playing career with West Ham before being appointed player-coach at Weymouth. He took them to the fourth round of the FA Cup in 1962, then became manager of Torquay in 1965, winning promotion from Division Four. Two years later he replaced Matt Gillies at Leicester. In the first part of the 1971/72 season, his United side won all but two of 20 League games, but from 1st January had just five more victories. O'Farrell brought Martin Buchan to the club but United's performance early in the 1972/73 season was pretty disastrous, and the final straw was a 5-0 defeat at the hands of Crystal Palace on 16th December. Frank O'Farrell was dismissed just three days later, on 19th December, 1972.

Robson: John 1914–1921

Two years after Ernest Mangnall resigned, John Robson was appointed as Manchester United's first official manager, responsible for team affairs. Mangnall's secretarial role was filled first by T.J. Wallworth, then by J.J. Bentley, who remained in the post following Robson's arrival from Brighton on 28th December, 1914. Robson worked under Bentley, with responsibility for the playing arrangements. With the First World War badly disrupting football, Robson's United remained a First Division club, but they were relegated in 1922, seven months after Robson resigned on health grounds. He remained at the club, however, as assistant to John Chapman.

Sexton: Dave 1977–1981

Having already replaced Tommy Docherty at Chelsea and Queen's Park Rangers, Dave Sexton replaced him again at United in 1977. The son of a professional boxer, Sexton was an expert coach. His side reached the FA Cup Final in 1979, but lost 2-3 against Arsenal, and were runners-up in the League to Liverpool in 1980. Under Sexton, Gary Bailey emerged from the ranks and Ray Wilkins arrived from Chelsea. However, in 1980, injuries to the team began to cause poor results. Sexton became the first United manager to spend £1 million on a player, buying Garry Birtles from Nottingham Forest, but his own days were numbered. United dispensed with his services on 30th April, 1981, and he went on to manage Coventry City before joining the England coaching staff.

Dedication
Jimmy Murphy was thoroughly dedicated to the game of football, to Matt Busby and to Manchester United. He was manager of Wales at the time of the Munich disaster, and in Cardiff for a national game when United were playing Red Star Belgrade in Yugoslavia. Murphy admits that his mind was more on the United game than on the game he was watching.

Training

Knowing the ropes
Wilf McGuinness describes training under Matt Busby: "On Tuesdays, we'd have a practice match … The other mornings, you'd run the track, a few laps to loosen up, then 10 sides of the pitch, a few sprints, a bit of gym work – or straight round the back for the game. We used to play on the car park, which was half cinders, half tar …"

In January 2000, after almost half a century at the Cliff, Manchester United moved into a new training ground on the southern outskirts of Manchester: the Trafford Training Centre (commonly known as Carrington).

For the previous fifty years, the Cliff training ground in Salford was an integral part of United. Opening in the early 1950s, it is where the great managers delivered their team talks and devised their tactics, and where many of United's finest players honed their skills and received treatment for any injuries. If Old Trafford is where the show is put on, the Cliff, and another training ground at Littleton Road, were where rehearsals took place.

The Cliff was full of character and memories, but the move had to be made for United to keep pace with the rest of Europe. Costing £14.3 million, Carrington extends over a 100-acre site and boasts nine outdoor pitches, an indoor swimming pool and state-of-the-art facilities for all the club's staff.

"The timing was appropriate as we move into a new era of club facilities," said Sir Alex Ferguson. "My staff toured Europe and beyond looking for the best. We believe we brought everything together in a way that made us the envy of the footballing world."

The training regime at United

When you watch Manchester United's elite squad in training, their level of commitment and concentration is striking. Alex Ferguson and his coaches understand that skill and fitness go hand in hand. The United coaching team's philosophy is simple: the harder a player works, the more chance he has of realizing his potential.

Pre-season training

United players start their pre-season training in early July. They train twice a day, five or six days a week. The morning session is from 10:30 a.m. until 12:30 p.m. This is followed by lunch at Carrington's canteen. After lunch, they regroup at 2:00 p.m. for another hour-long session, which may include some weight training and sprints. The first week of United's pre-season training is devoted to cardiovascular and aerobic work, which involves plenty of running and ballwork exercises to build up the players' stamina and break down any body fat that they may have gained during their summer holidays. In the second week of training, match situation games (with two teams of eleven players) are introduced, and more work is devoted to the tactical side of the game. As the football season approaches, a series of five or six pre-season friendly matches are played to translate all the players' hard groundwork at Carrington into match sharpness.

Season training

On a non-match day during the football season, there is one training session per day from 10:30 p.m. until 12:30 p.m. Players do not need to train in the afternoons because their basic level of fitness is now up to scratch through playing two or three games per week. The first 30 minutes of each morning session are spent warming up, stretching and jogging. During the winter, warming up is extremely important as it is easy to strain a muscle. The ballwork exercises are varied so that training sessions are never exactly the same.

For example, there may be five-a-side games, a "box", or "possession" (where two teams play on a small pitch without goals and try to keep hold of the ball).

Match tactics

On the days approaching a match, Alex Ferguson and his coaching staff assess the opposition, and during pre-match training they will work on specific tactics for the match. The day before a match, the manager's likely team selection might play a short practice game against eleven other squad members who are instructed to play like the opposition. If United have had a bad run of results, any problems identified on the video tape will be ironed out at Carrington. Players often choose to stay on for extra training if they feel that their game is below par. Eric Cantona was one player who believed in staying behind, and he would sometimes ask his team mates to help him practise his shooting. On free afternoons, players are instructed to rest and relax, and are rarely allowed on the golf course!

One-on-one
In one-on-one exercises, an attacking player has to try to dribble the ball past a defender, who tries to stop the attacker getting through.

Voices of experience
Jim Ryan and Mike Phelan issue instructions to a gathering of United players. The pair have both managed United's Reserve team and were promoted to work alongside Sir Alex Ferguson in the summer of 2001.

| 100 m | 75 m | 50 m | 25 m | 0 m |

Shuttle runs
For shuttle runs, a 100-metre track is marked out with cones at 25-metre intervals. The players set out from the ends of the track at regular intervals. As each individual player reaches a cone, he must change pace from a jog, to a run, to sprinting. These running exercises are repeated as many times as the coach specifies.

Free kicks
United's free kick takers, such as Beckham and Giggs, aim to whip the ball over the wall with swerve and power to beat the keeper. For practice, Beckham hangs a tyre from the crossbar, and tries to kick the ball through it from 25 yards.

Taking charge
Jim Ryan takes a moment to explain some tactics to his Manchester United charges during a training session at Carrington. He always makes his intentions very clear to the players.

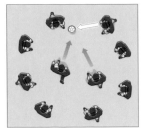

Keepy-uppy in pairs
This exercise promotes good touch and ball control. Two players, each with their own ball, aim to keep it in the air for as long as possible, using their heads, feet, knees and chest, occasionally passing to one another without letting either ball hit the ground.

Box
Eight players spread out within a marked area approximately 10 metres square. There are two tacklers in the middle, who have to try to intercept the ball, while the players on the perimeter aim to keep the ball moving quickly within the box.

Catching practice
This is a test of reflexes, agility and handling, as high and low balls are thrown to the left and right of the keeper. The coach and goalkeeper stand 10 metres apart. The goalkeeper must catch the ball, throw it back to the coach, recover, then dive for the next one.

In the gym

Training in Carrington's high-tech gym is a vital part of each player's schedule, and helps to build stamina and strength. Players recovering from injury also use the equipment to rebuild their weakened muscles. Below is the sort of gym circuit that might be given to an injury-free player at a good level of fitness:

Carrington's gym
Manchester United's gym at their Carrington training complex houses state-of-the-art equipment. Players, from apprentices to the first team, are permitted to use the gym's facilities to improve their strength, stamina and general fitness.

- *Exercise bike - cycling 1 mile*
- *Techno gym rowing - 500 metres*
- *Lateral pull downs - 50 reps (40 kg)*
- *Press-ups - 50 reps*
- *Step-ups - 100 reps (10 kg in each hand)*
- *Abdominal crunches - 60 reps*
- *Treadmill - 800 metres, 6% incline*
- *Bench press - 40 reps (40 kg)*
- *Boxercise - 1 minute uppercuts, 1 minute books*

Nutrition

The traditional footballer's steak and chips meal has been replaced in recent years with a low-fat, high-carbohydrate diet that includes plenty of fresh fruit and vegetables. United's resident dietitian is Trevor Lea, who designs the day-to-day menu at Carrington's canteen. On an average day, a typical menu might include roast chicken or lamb, pasta, or even curry and rice. Among the players' favourite desserts are apple crumble, syrup sponge, rice pudding and lemon meringue pie. Trevor Lea is not too concerned about calorie-counting, but he offers sound advice to individual players on their diet, and always makes sure that they keep up their fluid intake

during arduous training sessions. Measuring body fat is a way of ensuring that a player is eating the correct amount of food for the training he is doing. Winger Ryan Giggs has a low body fat ratio of around 8%, but a higher body fat ratio of 10-15% is acceptable for robust central defenders, such as Jaap Stam. Players' body fat is monitored throughout the season. In July, when players start pre-season training, they are checked to see how their body fat compares to their pre-summer level.

Trevor also advises injured players on their diet. For example, if a player has a bone injury, Trevor will make sure that he is getting enough calcium in his diet to aid recovery.

> *I just design a plan of eating which will give the player an acceptable level of body fat for their position, and most importantly, a level at which the individual player feels comfortable when they are playing.*
> **Trevor Lea**

Physiotherapy

The British game is fast, fierce and dangerous. Every professional player expects to be seriously injured at least once, and many will tell you that more often than not they carry a niggling injury as they play. Most injuries are caused by collisions between players, but improved flexibility can reduce the risk of injury, which is why players warm up, warm down and stretch carefully. For obvious reasons, footballers are most prone to lower-body injuries. Knees, ankles, calves, the groin area and hamstrings are all particularly vulnerable.

In the course of a match, it's the physiotherapist's job to attend to the injuries on the pitch. At times, the physiotherapist saves lives; in separate incidents in the 1980s, both Bryan Robson and Kevin Moran swallowed their tongue following head collisions, and it was their physiotherapist, Jim McGregor, who treated them.

Physiotherapists like McGregor and his successors David Fevre and Rob Swire,

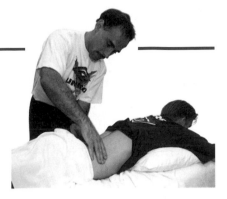

> *I'm always amazed at the players' powers of endurance. They've got a gritty determination to play through the pain barrier.*
> **David Fevre, United physio 1994-1999**

play an important role at a football club. On a match day their work can start as early as five hours before kick-off. They prepare the players for the rigours ahead with massage and manipulation, and strap up any limbs needing support. The senior physiotherapist, now Rob Swire, also has to assess the players he has treated during the week, and determine whether they are fit to play.

First team coaches

Sir Alex Ferguson's coaches have played a major role in the success he has enjoyed in his 15 years at Manchester United.

Archie Knox, who had come with Ferguson from Aberdeen, was at Ferguson's side during the difficult times of the late '80s. Just before United's fortunes began to change, Knox left for Glasgow Rangers in the summer of 1991, to become Walter Smith's assistant.

In the '90s, the period in which United won four Premiership titles and two FA Cups, Brian Kidd (below) was Ferguson's right-hand man. Kidd developed a reputation as an internationally respected coach and also helped bring through United's famous crop of youngsters including Giggs, Beckham, and scholes, before he was poached to become manager of Blackburn Rovers in December 1998.

The Derby County coach, Steve McClaren (above right), was drafted in to replace Kidd

in February 1999, and within a matter of months he had helped United to win the Treble.

Two Premiership titles in his first two full seasons as United coach always made it likely that, as with Brian Kidd before him, McClaren would be snapped up by a fellow Premiership side that was looking for a new manager.

Nearing the end of the 2000/2001 season, West Ham United, Southampton and Middlesbrough all invited McClaren to take up their vacant manager's positions. McClaren opted to succeed former United legend Bryan Robson as manager of Middlesbrough after the United board had made it clear to him that he would not be chosen to replace Sir Alex Ferguson in the summer of 2002.

In July 2001, Manchester United confirmed that former players, Jim Ryan and Mike Phelan, would become Assistant Manager and First Team Coach respectively.

Reserve and Youth Teams

Gigg Lane
United Reserves play their home matches during the winter months at Bury FC's Gigg Lane ground. This helps to preserve the playing surface at Old Trafford. Pontin's League rules allow this temporary migration because they stipulate that only half of a club's Reserve home fixtures must be played at their recognized stadium.

Manchester United's tradition for turning teenage prodigies into accomplished first-team stars dates back to Sir Matt Busby's pioneering work in the 1950s. Busby signed a host of promising schoolboy players, many of them from the Manchester area. Together, these "Busby Babes" won the FA Youth Cup in five successive years, from 1953 to 1957, and many of them went on to play for the first team. The average age of United's 1956 championship-winning side was just 22. The Babes were all set to dominate English and European competitions for many years when, in February 1958, the Munich air disaster so tragically intervened.

Inspired by Matt Busby, Alex Ferguson overhauled the ineffective youth system that he inherited in 1986. Within six years, his newly improved scouting and coaching network had an FA Youth Cup triumph. This victorious Youth team of 1992 emulated the Babes when several of its players were promoted to the first team and became household names. In 1996, Manchester United's League and FA Cup Double-winning side included six players aged 22 or under.

Reserves

A professional football club isn't about just one side competing for honours in the public eye. Behind the first team, there are several other sides. They are there to prepare players, both young and experienced, for the demands of senior football. For the developing youngster, the Reserve team is the penultimate rung on a ladder, bridging the gap between youth and senior levels. For older players, it can provide invaluable match practice as they recuperate from injury.

In daily training sessions, Reserve team coach Mike Phelan can have as many as 20 players to organize. Most of them are aged between 18 and 20 and are in either their first or second year as professional players. The main aim in training is to build on their two-year youth apprenticeships. While employing his own coaching methods, Mike encourages the Reserves to play in the same way as the first team. This familiarity with style and tactics makes the Reserve player's transition to senior level all the more comfortable. Links with foreign football clubs provides valuable experience overseas for some players, such as Danny Higginbotham, who played for Royal Antwerp in Belgium in 1998/99.

Competitions

Manchester United Reserves play in the new FA Premier Reserve League, competing with other professional Northern and Midland clubs, and the Manchester Senior Cup, against other local rivals. Youth competitions for Premiership clubs were restructured in 1998. United had previously entered "A" and "B" teams into Divisions One and Two respectively of the Lancashire League. In 1998/99 they entered the Northern division of the FA's Academy League for the first time. There are two age groups: Under 17s and Under 19s. These replaced the old "A" and "B" format. Manchester Youth also play in two knockout competitions, both for players aged 18 or under, the Lancashire FA Youth Cup, and the FA Youth Cup. The latter is a highly prestigious national competition.

> *What you're looking for is a ladder from the age of 16, when the kids first start in the "B" team. It's a ladder which raises their level and hopefully gets them playing the kind of quality football the first team play. That avenue for getting first-team players is just as valid as buying them.*
> **Jim Ryan, former coach**

The 1992 FA Youth Cup-winning team
Standing (left–right): John O'Kane, Nicky Butt, Simon Davies, Kevin Pilkington, Chris Casper, Gary Neville.
Seated (left–right): Ben Thornley, George Switzer, David Beckham, Rob Savage, Colin McKee. This team defeated Tottenham Hotspur in the semi-final and Crystal Palace 6–3 on aggregate in the two-legged Final. All bar Savage and Switzer have since played in United's first team.

Fledglings

Each season Alex Ferguson advances at least one new player to the first team:

- 1986/87: Gary Walsh, Tony Gill
- 1987/88: Deiniol Graham, Lee Martin
- 1988/89: Russell Beardsmore, Mark Robins, David Wilson
- 1989/90: Mark Bosnich
- 1990/91: Darren Ferguson, Ryan Giggs, Paul Wratten
- 1991/92: Ian Wilkinson
- 1992/93: Keith Gillespie, David Beckham, Nicky Butt, Gary Neville
- 1993/94: Colin McKee, Ben Thornley
- 1994/95: Chris Casper, Simon Davies, Phil Neville, John O'Kane, Kevin Pilkington, Graeme Tomlinson, Paul Scholes
- 1995/96: Terry Cooke, Pat McGibbon
- 1996/97: Michael Clegg, Michael Appleton
- 1997/98: Phil Mulryne, John Curtis, Michael Twiss, Ronnie Wallwork, Wes Brown, Danny Higginbotham
- 1998/99: Jonathan Greening, Alex Notman, Mark Wilson
- 1999/2000: Luke Chadwick, Paul Rachubka, John O'Shea, David Healy, Nick Culkin, Richard Wellens
- 2000/01: Bojan Djordjic, Michael Stewart, Danny Webber

Brian McClair

Three years after he finished his illustrious playing career at Manchester United, Brian McClair returned to the club as the Reserve team manager.

McClair had clocked up an impressive 470 games and 127 goals for United before, in June 1998, he left Old Trafford to join Motherwell. After six months there, he moved to Blackburn Rovers to become Brian Kidd's assistant manager. However, the duo departed Ewood Park in May 1999 following Blackburn's relegation.

It was at this point that McClair decided to take his coaching badges and, to this end, he became a regular visitor to United's training ground.

In the summer of 2001, Sir Alex Ferguson appointed McClair as the Reserve team manager to succeed Mike Phelan, who had been promoted to the first team coach position.

"Hopefully my experience (as a player) will show the boys what to do on the training pitch and challenge them," McClair has said. "They have to go out there and find their feet."

Youth coaches

Eric Harrison (right) became United's youth coach in 1981 and remained in this job until 1997. Since then, he has worked as a coaching advisor to United's Youth academy. Between 1981 and 1997 he guided the Youth team to numerous trophies, including two FA Youth Cups, and coached current footballing stars like David Beckham and Ryan Giggs.

The second year trainees (Under 19s) are now looked after by Dave Williams, while the first years (Under 17s) are coached by Neil Bailey.

Dave, a former Norwich City and Wales player and Reserve team coach at Leeds, was appointed in September 1997. Neil Bailey first began coaching at Stockport County and joined United from Blackpool in July 1995.

“ Even if they don't make it here, the players know they'll be able to make a living somewhere in the League. ”
Neil Bailey

Youth

Each summer, Manchester United sign a number of 16-year-old boys who have impressed the coaching staff through several years of playing and training with the club's School of Excellence. In accordance with new FA guidelines, this school was renamed in the summer of 1998 as the Manchester United Academy. Former chief scout Les Kershaw was appointed director of the Academy. The size of the apprenticeship intake can vary, depending on the quality of boys available. In July 1996, the club signed only six new trainees. In July 1997, they signed 18. The boys earn approximately £40 per week during their two-year apprenticeship. Local boys live at home; those from further afield live nearby in lodgings arranged by the club. Youth development officer David Bushell has overall responsibility for the young players' needs. It's his job to help the boys settle into their new routine and environment. On most days, the apprentices train with coaches Dave Williams and Neil Bailey in the morning and afternoon. One day a week, usually Thursday, is reserved for academic training at a local college. United are firm believers in providing the boys with the education they will need if they don't succeed in football.

The working week isn't solely devoted to football. The apprentices all have menial chores to complete, which could be anything from sweeping the floors at the training ground to cleaning the professional players' boots. This system helps to instil discipline in the young apprentices. At the end of their apprenticeships, the players are all assessed by the coaching staff. Ultimately it is Alex Ferguson who decides whether or not a player should be signed on a professional basis at the club. Some young players are released, but, wherever possible, Manchester United's staff help to find them new clubs.

Legendary Youth XI

A team made up of some of the great players who have graduated to Manchester United's first team from its Youth Team might look like this:

1: Goalkeeper
M. Bosnich 1989-91, 1999-2001 : Debut aged 18

2: Right-back
G. Neville 1992-
Debut aged 18

5: Centre-back
E. Colman 1955-58
Debut aged 21

6: Centre-back
B. Foulkes 1952-70
Debut aged 20

3: Left-back
P. Neville 1995-
Debut aged 18

7: Right-midfield
G. Best 1963-74
Debut aged 17

4: Central midfield
S. McIlroy 1971-82
Debut aged 17

8: Central midfield
D. Edwards 1953-58
Debut aged 16

11: Left-midfield
R. Giggs 1991-
Debut aged 17

10: Centre-forward
M. Hughes 1983-86, 1988-95: Debut aged 20

9: Centre-forward
B. Charlton 1956-1973: Debut aged 18

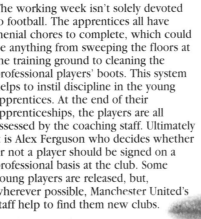

Luke Chadwick
Cambridge-born Luke Chadwick looks destined to enjoy a fine career at Manchester United. The young winger made his debut against Aston Villa in the Worthington Cup in October 1999, but his real breakthrough came in the 2000/01 season, when he made 23 appearances and scored two goals.

“ I can see a little of myself in him in the way that he loves taking people on. He has so much raw talent, and the rest, the crossing and finishing, will come with age and experience. ”
Ryan Giggs on Luke Chadwick

Michael Stewart
Michael Stewart signed for Manchester United in 1996 when he was sixteen. Just over three years later, United fans got their first glimpse of Stewart in the third round of the 2000/01 Worthington Cup against Watford. Later in the same season he was called up by Scotland to play for their Under-21 team, before making his League debut at the Riverside Stadium against Middlesbrough.

Reserve & Youth trophies won

- *Pontin's League (Reserves): champions 1994, 1996, 1997; runners-up 1998*
- *Lancashire League Division One ("A" team): champions 1987, 1988, 1990, 1991, 1993, 1995, 1996, 1997, 1998; runners-up 1989, 1992*
- *Lancashire League Division Two ("B" team): champions 1989, 1997; runners-up 1988, 1992, 1994, 1996*
- *FA Youth Cup (Youth team): winners 1992, 1995; runners-up 1993*
- *Lancashire FA Youth Cup (Youth Team): winners 1991, 1993, 1994, 1996, 1997*
- *Manchester Senior Cup (Reserves): 1999, 2000*

Players A–Z

This section includes all the players who have ever appeared in a competitive game for United (and Newton Heath), from 1886–2000/01, and is arranged alphabetically. The players' dates are from the season of their first to the season of their last first-team game, and their debut is their first-ever competitive first-team appearance, excluding the Charity Shield. International statistics are for a player's entire career, and heights, weights and fees are approximate. At the bottom of each page is a key to the terms used.

Ainsworth: Alf **F** 1934–1935

b. 31.7.1913, Manchester, England **d.** 25.4.1975 • *5ft 6in • 10st 6lb* • **Clubs** Ashton Utd; UTD; New Brighton Sep 1935 (WW2: Accrington Stanley, Bury, Rochdale, Southport, Oldham Athletic), re-registered New Brighton 10.8.1946, Congleton Town Dec 1947 **SU** 1933 (am.), 13.2.1934 (pro.) **UD** v Bury (h) 3.3.34 **FL** 2/gls 0 **T** 2/gls 0

Aitken: John **F** 1895–1896

b. dnk, Scotland **d.** nk • **Clubs** 5th King's Rifle Volunteers (Dumfries); NH; **SU** Jul 1895 **UD** v Crewe Alexandra (h) 7.9.1895, scored 1 **FL** 2/gls 1 **T** 2/gls 1

Albinson: George **HB** 1920–1921

b. 14.2.1897, Prestwich, Manchester, England **d.** 1975 • *5ft 9in • 10st 7lb* • **Clubs** UTD; Manchester City May 1921–May 1922, Crewe Alexandra Aug 1923–cs. 1925, Witton Albion, Daily Herald (Manchester) am. Feb 1935 **SU** May 1919 (pro.) **UD** v Liverpool (h) FAC 1 replay, 12.1.21 **FAC** 1/gls 0 **T** 1/gls 0

Albiston: Arthur **FB** 1974–1988

b. 14.7.1957, Edinburgh, Scotland • *5ft 7in • 11st 5lb* • **Clubs** UTD; West Bromwich Albion Aug 1988, Dundee Aug 1989 (on loan to Chesterfield Nov 1990), Chester City Aug 1991–cs. 1993 (on loan to Molde FC, Norway Aug 1992) **SU** Jul 1972 (appr.), Jul 1974 (pro.) **UD** v Manchester City (h) FLC 3, 9.10.74 **FL** 364(15)/gls 6 **FAC** 36/gls 0 **FLC** 38(2)/gls 1 **EUR** 26(1)/gls 0 **T** 464(18)/gls 7 **INT** (Scotland) 14/gls 0

It's a testament to the unswerving loyalty that Arthur Albiston gave to Manchester United that only five players have made more appearances in a United shirt than the Scottish full-back. It was during a Manchester Derby, in front of a 55,000-strong crowd, that Arthur Albiston made his senior debut. Even more dramatic was his FA Cup debut, which was in the 1977 final against Liverpool, in place of an injured Stewart Houston. Albiston played an integral part in United's success during the match, but felt he hadn't deserved his winners' medal, and offered it to Houston, in a touching gesture that was politely declined. Albiston's performance against Liverpool established him as a first-team regular, and he remained a consistent and dependable first-team member for the next 10 years. An almost unsung hero, Albiston's speed, quality distribution and ball control were a vital component in United's achievements. He appeared in four FA Cup finals, collecting three winners' medals, and also represented Scotland on 14 occasions.

Allan: Jack **F** 1904–1906

b. 1883, South Shields, England **d.** nk • *5ft 9in • 11st* • **Clubs** Bishop Auckland; UTD; Bishop Auckland cs. 1906 **SU** 1904 (pro.) **UD** v Burslem Port Vale (a) 3.9.1904, scored 2 **FL** 35/gls 21 **FAC** 1/gls 1 **T** 36/gls 22

Allen: Reg **GK** 1950–1953

b. 3.5.1919, Marylebone, London, England • *6ft • 12st 12lb* • **Clubs** Corona FC, Bromley 1937, Queen's Park Rangers May 1938; UTD; Altrincham **SU** Jun 1950 **UD** v Fulham (h) 19.8.50 **FL** 75/gls 0 **FAC** 5/gls 0 **T** 80/gls 0

Allman: Arthur **FB** 1914–1915

b. 24.12.1890, Milton, Stoke-on-Trent, England **d.** 22.12.1956 • *5ft 9in • 11st 2lb* • **Clubs** Smallthorne, Shrewsbury Town, Wolverhampton Wanderers cs. 1912, Swansea Town 1913; UTD (WW1: Stoke); Millwall Athletic Dec 1919, Aberaman 1921–22, Crewe Alexandra Aug 1922, Aberaman Jun 1924 **SU** May 1914 **TF** £150 **UD** v Sunderland (a) 6.2.1915 **FL** 12/gls 0 **T** 12/gls 0

Ambler: Alfred **HB** 1899–1900

b. dnk, Manchester, England **d.** nk • *5ft 7in • 11st 7lb* • **Clubs** Hyde Utd; NH; Colne FC, Stockport County May 1906, Exeter City cs. 1908, Colne FC cs. 1910 **SU** Aug 1899 **UD** v Gainsborough Trinity (h) 2.9.1899 **FL** 10/gls 1 **T** 10/gls 1

Anderson: George **F** 1911–1915

b. 1893, Cheetham, Manchester, England **d.** nk • *5ft 8in • 10st 10lb* • **Clubs** Broughton St. James', Broughton Wellington, Salford Utd, Bury Mar 1910; UTD **SU** Sep 1911 **TF** £50 **UD** v Everton (h) 9.9.1911 **FL** 80/gls 37 **FAC** 6/gls 2 **T** 86/gls 39

Anderson: John **HB** 1947–1949

b. 11.10.1921, Salford, Manchester, England • *5ft 6.5in • 11st* • **Clubs** UTD (WW2: Plymouth Argyle); Nottingham Forest Oct 1949, Peterborough Utd Aug 1952 (trainer-coach 1954) **SU** Mar 1938 (am.), Dec 1938 (pro.) **UD** v Middlesbrough (h) 20.12.47 **FL** 33/gls 1 **FAC** 6/gls 1 **T** 39/gls 2

Anderson: Trevor **F** 1973–1974

b. 3.3.1951, Belfast, N. Ireland • *5ft 9in • 9st 11lb* • **Clubs** Portadown; UTD; Swindon Town Nov 1974, Peterborough Utd Dec 1977, Linfield Jul 1979 (subsequently manager) **SU** Oct 1972 (pro.) **TF** £20,000 **UD** v Stoke City (a) 14.4.1973 **FL** 13(6)/gls 2 **T** 13(6)/gls 2 **INT** (N. Ireland) 22/gls 4

Anderson: Viv **FB** 1987–1991

b. 29.8.1956, Nottingham, England • *6ft .5in • 12st 4lb* • **Clubs** Nottingham Forest appr. Nov 1972, pro. Aug 1974, Arsenal Jul 1984; UTD; Sheffield Wednesday Jan 1991, Barnsley (player-manager) Jun 1993; Middlesbrough (asst. manager) May 1994–June 2001 **SU** Jul 1987 (pro.) **UD** v Southampton (a) 15.8.1987 **FL** 50(4)/gls 2 **FAC** 7/gls 1 **FLC** 6(1)/gls 1 **EUR** 1/gls 0 **T** 64(5)/gls 4 **INT** (England) 30/gls 2

Anderson: Willie **F** 1963–1967

b. 24.1.1947, Liverpool, England • *5ft 9in • 11st* • **Clubs** UTD; Aston Villa Jan 1967, Cardiff City Feb 1973 (on loan to Portland Timbers May–Aug 1975), Portland Timbers Apr 1977–Aug 1982 **SU** May 1962 (appr.), Feb 1964 (pro.) **UD** v Burnley (h) 28.12.1963 **FL** 7(2)/gls 0 **FAC** 2/gls 0 **EUR** 1/gls 0 **T** 10(2)/gls 0

Appleton: Michael **M** 1996–1997

b. 4.12.1975, Salford, Manchester, England • *5ft 9in • 12st 4lb* • **Clubs** UTD (on loan to Wimbledon Jun 1995, Lincoln City 1995–1996, and to Grimsby Town 1996–1997); Preston North End Aug 1997, West Bromwich Albion Jan 2001 **SU** 13.7.1992 (appr.), 1.7.1994 (pro.) **UD** v Swindon Town (h) FLC 3, 23.10.96 **FLC** 1(1)/gls 0 **T** 1(1)/gls 0

Arkesden: Tommy **F** 1902–1906

b. 1878, Warwick, England **d.** 25.6.1921 • *5ft 11in • 11st 4lb* • **Clubs** Burton Wanderers Jan 1896, Derby County Jan 1898, Burton Utd Jul 1901; UTD; Gainsborough Trinity Jul 1907–cs. 1908 **SU** Feb 1903 **UD** v Blackpool (a) 14.2.1903 **FL** 70/gls 28 **FAC** 9/gls 5 **T** 79/gls 33

Asquith: Beau **F** 1939–1940

b. 16.9.1910, Painthorpe, England **d.** 12.4.1977 • *5ft 10in • 11st 5lb* • **Clubs** Painthorpe Albion, Barnsley Jul 1933; UTD (WW2: Blackburn Rovers, Huddersfield Town, Chesterfield, Doncaster Rovers, Barnsley, Leeds Utd, Bradford, Rotherham Utd); Barnsley 1945–46 season, Bradford City Sep 1948, Scarborough–cs. 1950 **SU** May 1939 **UD** v Charlton Athletic (a) 2.9.1939 **FL** 1/gls 0 **T** 1/gls 0

Astley: Joe **FB** 1925–1927

b. 1899, Dudley, Birmingham, England **d.** 1967 • *5ft 9in • 11st 4lb* • **Clubs** Cradley Heath; UTD; Notts County Jun 1928, Northwich Victoria Aug 1929, Hyde Utd May 1930 **SU** Aug 1924 **UD** v Bolton Wanderers (a) 17.3.1926 **FL** 2/gls 0 **T** 2/gls 0

Aston (Snr.): John **FB** 1946–1954

b. 3.9.1921, Prestwich, Manchester, England • *5ft 11in • 12st 7lb* • **Clubs** Mujacs FC; UTD (WW2: Hyde Utd, Plymouth Argyle, Portsmouth, Hamilton Academical) 1954 (junior coach) Aug 1970–Dec 1972 (chief scout) **SU** Jan 1938 (am.), Dec 1939 (pro.) **UD** v Chelsea (h) 18.9.1946 **FL** 253/gls 29 **FAC** 29/gls 1 **T** 282/gls 30 **INT** (England) 17/gls 0

When Matt Busby switched John Aston from inside-forward to full-back, he did more than change the number on Aston's shirt. With his usual combination of insight and intuition, Busby brought out the best in his player. A graduate of the Manchester United Junior Athletic Club, Aston made his League debut against Chelsea in September 1946 as inside-forward, but as full-back he blossomed, bringing a forward's pace and accuracy to a defensive position. In the 1948 FA Cup Final, he had to contain the awesome Stanley Matthews. In a tight corner, as in the difficult 1950/51 season, John Aston could be moved up front, which accounts for the 15 goals he scored during that season. Before injury cut short his playing career, John Aston also won 17 England caps. After the Munich disaster he returned to Old Trafford as a Youth team coach. In 1970 Aston became chief scout for Manchester United, and remained closely associated with the team in which his son, John Aston Jnr., was now making his name.

Aston (Jnr.): John **F** 1964–1972

b. 28.6.1947, Manchester, England • *5ft 9.5in • 10st 12lb* • **Clubs** UTD (ground staff) Jul 1962; Luton Town Jul 1972, Mansfield Town Sep 1977, Blackburn Rovers Jul 1978–1980 **SU** Jun 1963 (appr.), Jul 1964 (pro.) **UD** v Leicester City (h) 12.4.1965 **FL** 139(16)/gls 25 **FAC** 5(2)/gls 1 **FLC** 12(3)/gls 0 **EUR** 8/gls 1 **T** 164(21)/gls 27

In the European Cup Final of 1968, John Aston truly rose to the occasion. Out on the left wing he routed Benfica's Adolfo, passing him repeatedly to shoot. It was Aston, too, who flew into defence to dispossess Eusebio. The match was the summit of his career. John Aston's father (John Aston Snr.) had given him a reputation to live up to. Aston Jnr. overcame this and settled in well at Old Trafford. However, as a less glamorous player than United's other forwards, he was often barracked by the home crowd for lack of imagination. Aston was nippy and direct, but the playful runs of Best and Law were making headlines.

Aston's commitment never wavered, and his pace never flagged. Matt Busby recognized his contribution to the side. Aston earned a League championship medal in 1967 and a European Cup winners' medal the following year. After breaking his leg he lost his first-team place and, in 1972, transferred to Luton Town for £30,000.

Bailey: Gary **GK** 1978–1986

b. 9.8.1958, Ipswich, England • *6ft 2in • 13st 12lb* • **Clubs** UTD; Kaiser Chiefs (South Africa) 1988–1990 **SU** Jan 1978 (pro.) **UD** v Ipswich Town (h) 18.11.78 **FL** 294/gls 0 **FAC** 31/gls 0 **FLC** 28/gls 0 **EUR** 20/gls 0 **T** 373/gls 0 **INT** (England) 2/gls 0

A supreme shot-stopper, Gary Bailey credited his success in the FA Cup Finals of 1983 and 1985 to a good-luck charm used by witch doctors. In his goal net he kept a padlock wrapped in red and white ribbons, to "lock out" the opposition. When a knee injury ended his football career in 1987, Gary Bailey found work as a sports presenter on South African TV.

Bain: David **F** 1922–1924

b. 5.8.1900, Rutherglen, Glasgow, Scotland **d.** nk • *5ft 10in • 11st 10lb* • **Clubs** Rutherglen Glencairn; UTD; Everton Jul 1924, Bristol City Nov 1928, Halifax Town Aug 1930, Rochdale Sep 1932–May 1934 **SU** May 1922 **UD** v Port Vale (a) 14.10.1922 **FL** 22/gls 9 **FAC** 1/gls 0 **T** 23/gls 9

Bain: James **F** 1899–1900

b. nk **d.** nk • **Clubs** Dundee Mar 1899; NH **SU** Sep 1899 **UD** v Loughborough Town (h) 16.9.1899, scored 1 **FL** 2/gls 1 **T** 2/gls 1

Bain: Jimmy **HB** 1924–1928

b. 6.2.1902, Rutherglen, Glasgow, Scotland **d.** 22.12.1969 • *5ft 9in • 11st 7lb* • **Clubs** Rutherglen Glencairn, Glasgow Strathclyde; UTD; Manchester Central Jul 1928, Brentford Nov 1928 (asst. manager) May 1934 (manager) Aug 1952–Jan 1953 **SU** Oct 1922 **UD** v Clapton Orient (h) 7.2.1925 **FL** 4/gls 0 **T** 4/gls 0

Bainbridge: Bill **F** 1945–1946

b. 9.3.1922, Gateshead, England • *5ft 10in • 11st 9lb* • **Clubs** Ashington (WW2: Hartlepools Utd); UTD; Bury May 1946, Tranmere Rovers Nov 1948–1953 **SU** Dec 1944 (pro.) **UD** v Accrington Stanley (h) FAC 3, 2nd leg, 9.1.1946, scored 1 **FAC** 1/gls 1 **T** 1/gls 1

Baird: Harry **F** 1936–1938

b. 17.8.1913, Belfast, N. Ireland **d.** 22.5.1973 • *5ft 9in • 11st 4lb* • **Clubs** Bangor FC (Ireland), Dunmurry FC, Linfield; UTD; Huddersfield Town Sep 1938, Ipswich Town Jun 1946 ("A" team coach Jun 1951–Jun 1953) **SU** Jan 1937 **TF** £3,500 **UD** v Sheffield Wednesday (a) 23.1.1937 **FL** 49/gls 15 **FAC** 4/gls 3 **T** 53/gls 18 **INT** (Ireland) 1/gls 0

Baldwin: Tommy **F** 1974–1975

b. 10.6.1945, Gateshead, England • *5ft 10in • 11st 6lb* • **Clubs** Arsenal am. Sep 1962, pro. Dec 1962, Chelsea Sep 1966, Millwall Nov 1974 (on loan to UTD Jan–Feb 1975); Seattle Sounders Apr–Aug 1975, Gravesend and Northfleet Aug 1976, Brentford (player-coach) Oct 1977–Mar 1980 **SU** Jan 1975 **UD** v Sunderland (a) 18.1.1975 **FL** 2/gls 0 **T** 2/gls 0

Ball: Billy **HB** 1902–1903

b. 1876, West Derby, Liverpool, England **d.** nk • **Clubs** Liverpool South End, Rock Ferry FC, Blackburn Rovers May 1897, Everton May 1898, Notts County May 1899, Blackburn Rovers May 1901; UTD **SU** Oct 1902 **UD** v Lincoln City (a) 8.11.1902 **FL** 4/gls 0 **T** 4/gls 0

Ball: Jack **F** 1929–1930; 1933–1934

b. 13.9.1907, Banks, Southport, England **d.** 6.2.1976 • *5ft 10in • 11st 8lb* • **Clubs** Croston FC, Southport am. Dec 1924, pro. Aug 1925, Darwen Sep 1927, Chorley Jan 1928; UTD; Sheffield Wednesday Jul 1930; UTD; Huddersfield Town Sep 1934, Luton Town Oct 1934, Excelsior Roubaix (France, player-coach) May 1936, Luton Town Jul 1936, Vauxhall Motors

KEY: **a**=away **am.**=amateur **appr.**=apprentice **b.**=born **c.**=circa **cs.**=close season **CWC**=Club World Cup **D**=Defender **d.**=died **dnk**=date not known **EUR**=European competitions **F**=Forward **FAC**=FA Cup **FB**=Full-back (defender) **FL**=Football League **FLC**=Football League Cup **GK**=Goalkeeper **gls**=goals **h**=home **HB**=Half-back (midfield) **INT**=International matches **M**=Midfield **NH**=Newton Heath **Newton Heath LYR**=Newton Heath Lancashire & Yorkshire Railway **nk**=not known **pro.**=professional **Q**=qualifying round **SU**=signed for United **sub**=substitute; substitute apps are in brackets after appearances **T**=total **TF**=transfer fee **TM**=Test match **U**=Utility **UD**=United debut **UTD**=Manchester United **v**=versus

(player-coach) cs. 1937, St. Albans City, Biggleswade c. 1940 **SU** 8.5.1929 **UD** v Leicester City (h) 11.9.1929, scored 1 **FL** 47/gls 17 **FAC** 3/gls 1 **FLC** 3/gls 1 **T** 53/gls 19

Ball: John FB 1947–1949

b. 15.3.1925, Ince, Wigan, England • *5ft 10in* • *10st 9lb* • **Clubs** Wigan Athletic (WW2: Gravesend); UTD; Bolton Wanderers Sep 1950 until his retirement in 1958, Wigan Athletic (manager) 1960–1963 **SU** Feb 1948 **UD** v Everton (a) 10.4.1948 **FL** 22/gls 0 **FAC** 1/gls 0 **T** 23/gls 0

Bamford: Tommy F 1934–1938

b. 2.9.1905, Port Talbot, Wales **d.** 12.12.1967 • *5ft 9in* • *11st 9lb* • **Clubs** Cardiff Docks XI, Cardiff Wednesday, Bridgend Town, Wrexham Apr 1929; UTD; Swansea Town Jun 1938 until his retirement in 1945/1946 **SU** Oct 1934 **UD** v Newcastle Utd (a) 20.10.1934, scored 1 **FL** 98/gls 53 **FAC** 11/gls 4 **T** 109/gls 57 **INT** (Wales) 5/gls 1

Thomas Bamford had an impeccable scoring record at Wrexham, netting a club record 174 League goals in 204 appearances. His tally of 44 in one season, 1933/34, is also a Wrexham record. Hampered by injuries, Bamford scored less prolifically for Manchester United but still managed 14 goals in 23 games to help them win the Division Two title in 1937/38.

Banks: Jack HB 1901–1903

b. 1871, West Bromwich, Birmingham, England **d.** 1947 • *5ft 9in* • *11st 5lb* • **Clubs** Oldbury Town, West Bromwich Albion Dec 1893; NH; Plymouth Argyle May 1903, Leyton cs. 1906, Exeter City (player-coach) Dec 1907 (trainer) cs. 1910, Barrow (trainer) cs. 1912 **SU** Aug 1901 **UD** v Gainsborough Trinity (h) 7.9.1901 **FL** 40/gls 0 **FAC** 4/gls 1 **T** 44/gls 1

Bannister: Jimmy F 1906–1910

b. 20.9.1880, Leyland, England **d.** nk • *5ft 7in* • *10st 7lb* • **Clubs** Leyland Temperance, Leyland FC, Chorley, Manchester City Sep 1902; UTD; Preston North End Oct 1909–cs 1912, Burslem Port Vale, Heywood FC Oct 1912 **SU** Dec 1906 **UD** v Aston Villa (h) 1.1.1907 **FL** 57/gls 7 **FAC** 4/gls 1 **T** 61/gls 8

Barber: Jack F 1922–1924

b. 8.1.1901, Salford, Manchester, England **d.** 30.3.1961 • *5ft 9in* • *11st 7lb* • **Clubs** Clayton FC; UTD; Southport May 1924, Halifax Town Aug 1926, Rochdale Jul 1927, Stockport County Aug 1931, Stockport County Oct 1932, Bacup Borough 1933 (secretary) 1938 **SU** May 1922 **UD** v Hull City (h) 6.1.1923 **FL** 3/gls 1 **FAC** 1/gls 1 **T** 4/gls 2

Barlow: Cyril FB 1919–1922

b. 22.1.1889, Newton Heath, Manchester, England **d.** nk • *5ft 8in* • *11st 8lb* • **Clubs** Northern Nomads; UTD; New Cross FC Oct 1922 **SU** Jul 1914 (am.), Dec 1919 (pro.) **UD** v Sunderland (h) 14.2.1920 **FL** 29/gls 0 **FAC** 1/gls 0 **T** 30/gls 0

Barnes: Peter F 1985–1987

b. 10.6.1957, Manchester, England • *5ft 10in* • *11st* • **Clubs** Manchester City pro. Jul 1974, West Bromwich Albion Jul 1979, Leeds Utd Aug 1981 (on loan to Real Betis, Spain, Aug 1982, to Melbourne JUST, Australia, Apr 1984, and to UTD May 1984), Coventry City Oct 1984; UTD; Manchester City Jan 1987 (on loan to Bolton Wanderers Oct 1987 and to Port Vale Dec 1987), Hull City Mar 1988, Drogheda Utd (Rep. of Ireland) 1988, Sporting Farense (Portugal) Aug–Sep 1988, Bolton Wanderers Nov 1988, Sunderland Feb 1989, Tampa Bay Rowdies (USA) Apr–Aug 1990, Northwich Victoria Aug–Oct 1990, Wrexham 1991, Radcliffe Borough 1991, Mossley cs. 1991–Oct 1991, Cliftonville Nov 1992 **SU** July 1985 (pro.) **TF** £50,000 **UD** v Nottingham Forest (a) 31.8.1985, scored 1 **FL** 19(1)/gls 2 **FLC** 5/gls 2 **T** 24(1)/gls 4 **INT** (England) 22/gls 4

Barrett: Frank GK 1896–1900

b. 2.8.1872, Dundee, Scotland **d.** 1907 • **Clubs** Dundee Harp, Dundee 1893; NH; New Brighton Tower May 1900, Arbroath Aug 1901, Manchester City Sep 1901, Dundee Nov 1902, Aberdeen 1903–1905 **SU** Sep 1896 (pro.) **UD** v Newcastle Utd (h) 26.9.1896 **FL** 118/gls 0 **TM** 4/gls 0 **FAC** 14/gls 0 **T** 136/gls 0

Capped by Scotland against Ireland and Wales, Frank Barrett kept a clean sheet on his Newton Heath debut in a 4-0 win over Newcastle United. In 1896/97, his safe ball-handling helped the club to reach the promotion play-offs in which they lost to Sunderland. When Frank died at the age of 35, Manchester United donated the generous sum of £14 (worth about £680 today) to his widow.

Barson: Frank HB 1922–1928

b. 10.4.1891, Grimethorpe, Sheffield, England **d.** 13.9.1968 • *6ft* • *12st 10lb* • **Clubs** Albion FC (Sheffield), Cammell Laird FC (Sheffield), Barnsley Aug 1911, Aston Villa Oct 1919; UTD; Watford May 1928, Hartlepools Utd (player-coach) May 1929, Wigan Borough am. Oct 1929, pro. Jul 1930, Rhyl Athletic (player-manager) Jun 1931, Stourbridge (manager) Jul 1935, Aston Villa (youth coach) Jul 1935 (senior coach/head trainer) Oct 1935, Swansea Town (trainer) Jul 1947–Feb 1954, Lye Town (trainer) Jul 1954 until his retirement in 1956 **SU** Aug 1922 **UD** v Wolverhampton Wanderers (a) 9.9.1922 **FL** 140/gls 4 **FAC** 12/gls 0 **T** 152/gls 4 **INT** (England) 1/gls 0

Barthez: Fabien GK 2000–

b. 28.6.1971, Lavelanet, France • *5ft 11in* • *12st 8lb* • **SU** 31.5.2000 (pro.) **TF** £7.8 million **UD** v Newcastle United (h) 20.8.2000 **FL** 30/gls 0 **EUR** 12/gls 0 **FAC** 1/gls 0 **T** 43 **INT** (France) 42/gls0

Fabien Barthez, the World Cup- and Euro 2000-winning French goalkeeper, arrived at United in the summer of 2000 from Monaco in a £7.8 million deal. He immediately began proving his reputation as the world's best goalkeeper, and after only one season, he was well on the way to attaining legendary status at Old Trafford. Agile, quick and a wonderful distributor of the ball, Barthez looks set to enjoy a successful career at Manchester United.

Beadsworth: Arthur F 1902–1903

b. 1876, Leicester, England **d.** 1917 • **Clubs** Hinckley Town, Leicester Fosse May 1900, Preston North End May 1902; UTD; Swindon Town cs. 1903, New Brompton cs. 1905, Burton Utd Aug 1906–1907 **SU** Oct 1902 **UD** v Woolwich Arsenal (a) 25.10.1902, scored 1 **FL** 9/gls 1 **FAC** 3/gls 1 **T** 12/gls 2

Beale: Robert GK 1912–1915

b. 8.1.1884, Maidstone, Kent, England **d.** 5.10.1950 • *5ft 11in* • *11st 6lb* • **Clubs** Maidstone Utd, Brighton & Hove Albion May 1905, Norwich City May 1908; UTD (guest at Arsenal season 1915–16); Gillingham July 1919; UTD again during season 1920–1921 (occasional Reserve team game) until his retirement cs. 1921 **SU** May 1912 **UD** v Woolwich Arsenal (a) 2.9.1912 **FL** 105/gls 0 **FAC** 7/gls 0 **T** 112/gls 0

Beardsley: Peter F 1982–1983

b. 18.1.1961, Longbenton, Newcastle upon Tyne, England • *5ft 8in* • *11st 7lb* • **Clubs** Carlisle Utd Aug 1979, Vancouver Whitecaps (Canada) May 1981; UTD; Vancouver Whitecaps (Canada) May 1983, Newcastle Utd Sep 1983, Liverpool Jul 1987, Everton Aug 1991, Newcastle Utd Jun 1993, Bolton Wanderers 1997 (on loan to Manchester City Feb 1998 and to Fulham Mar 1998), Fulham Nov 1998, Hartlepool Dec 1998, Doncaster Rovers Oct 1999–Nov 1999, Bolton (coach) Jun 2000 **SU** Sep 1982 (pro.) **TF** £250,000 **UD** v AFC Bournemouth (h) FLC 2, 1st leg, 6.10.82 **FLC** 1/gls 0 **T** 1/gls 0 **INT** (England) 59/gls 9

Ranked below Stapleton, Hughes and Whiteside in the United strikers' pecking order, Peter Beardsley was released after just one appearance. He later made a mockery of that decision by joining Liverpool for £1.9 million and winning two League championships. A quick-thinking passer and a neat dribbler, Peter was the perfect strike partner for Gary Lineker with England, and Andrew Cole at Newcastle.

Beardsmore: Russell M 1988–1991

b. 28.9.1968, Wigan, England • *5ft 8in* • *9st 7lb* • **Clubs** UTD (on loan to Blackburn

continued on p. 66

Beckham: David M 1992–

b. 2.5.1975, Leytonstone, London, England • *6ft* • *11st 2lb* • **Clubs** UTD **SU** 8.7.1991 (appr.), 23.1.1993 (pro.) **UD** v Brighton and Hove Albion (sub) (a) FLC 2, 2nd leg, 23.9.1992 **FL** 187(19)/gls 45 **FAC** 18(2)/gls 5 **FLC** 5(2)/gls 0 **EUR** 56(7)/gls 7 **CWC** 1 **T** 267(30)/gls 57 **INT** (England) 42/gls 4

A Manchester United fan since childhood, David Beckham has lived out his dreams at Old Trafford where he is already recognised as one of the club's greatest ever players. He is also one of the world's leading players of his generation. At the beginning of the 1995/96 season, with the departures of Ince and Kanchelskis, Beckham was given his chance in midfield. He played 32 times and scored eight goals, including the FA Cup semi-final winner against Chelsea. Criticized by commentator Alan Hansen on the first day of the season as being too young, Beckham and his colleagues had each picked up a championship medal and an FA Cup winners' medal by the end of the season. The following season, in the dying minutes of United's opening fixture against Wimbledon, Beckham had possession of the ball on the half-way line, looked up, saw the gap and scored a goal from 57 yards. It was a moment of inspiration. That goal started the David Beckham phenomenon. He was seen as the fresh new face of English football. In just one season Beckham made an effortless transition from promising youngster to England's main creative force. The autumn of 1996 saw him score a breathtaking string of goals from outside the area. Beckham had presence in midfield and the ability to hit long passes, and Glenn Hoddle must have seen something of himself in the young player. In September 1996 in Moldova, Hoddle gave Beckham his international debut, and he became the only ever-present player in England's World Cup qualifiers. A momentous season ended with Beckham collecting his second championship medal and being voted the PFA's Young Player of the Year.

In 1997/98 Beckham's relationship with the Spice Girls' Victoria Adams brought added pressure off the field, but he continued to impress on it. He was United's top scorer from midfield with 11 goals, and the team's leading provider of goals, with 22 assists.

Beckham will not look back fondly on the '98 World Cup in France. Hoddle questioned his focus and left him out of England's opening game against Tunisia. In the second game, against Romania, he replaced Ince, who was injured, and scored his first international goal with a free kick against Columbia. But Beckham's tournament ended in shame when he was sent off in the second-round match against Argentina for a retaliatory kick at an opponent. England eventually lost the tie on penalties, but many believed that it was Beckham's sending-off that cost England the game.

Opposition fans consequently barracked Beckham during 1998/99 but their jeers were often drowned by United supporters' cheers. Beckham rewarded the faithful with some brilliant performances, creating plenty of goals for the Cole-Yorke partnership. He notably set up both of Yorke's headers in the Champions League quarter-final against Inter Milan, and it was from his corner kicks that United scored twice in injury time of the Final, eventually winning the competition. All this, and he became a father too, when Victoria Adams gave birth to their son Brooklyn, on 4th March, 1999. David and Victoria were married in Ireland on 4th July, 1999.

Beckham's growing stature on the football field was rewarded when he finished as runner-up to the Brazilian, Rivaldo, in both the European Footballer of the Year and the FIFA World Player of the Year polls in 1999. Despite relentless media interest in the Beckhams as a celebrity couple, David's football has never wavered. In the autumn of 2000, his solid performances were rewarded when the caretaker England manager, Peter Taylor, made him captain. This appointment was endorsed by Sven Goran Eriksson when he became manager. Beckham responded with the best form of his international career, scoring three goals in four games for England in early 2001.

A great future
Beckham is likely to be at the forefront of English football well into this century. He influences games with his vision and passes.

Fact file

- **Youth medals**
  Beckham won an FA Youth Cup winners' medal in 1992.
- **Long-distance goal**
  The famous 57-yard goal against Wimbledon in August 1996 is the furthest successful strike at goal since the Premiership was founded in 1992.
- **Short-term loan**
  In March 1995, Beckham spent a month on loan at Third Division club Preston North End.
- **Kitted out**
  A true cockney Red, Beckham once turned up to a trial at Tottenham in a Manchester United kit.
- **Special feature**
  Beckham was the only player to feature in all of England's qualifiers for the 1998 World Cup finals in France.

"When you see a footballer of that standard in any company, he is something apart."
Tom Finney

Best: George F 1963–1974

b. 22.5.1946, Belfast, N. Ireland • 5ft 9in • 10st 3lb • Clubs UTD (ground staff) Aug 1961; Dunstable Town Jul 1974, Stockport County Nov 1975, Cork Celtic Jan 1976, Los Angeles Aztecs (USA) Apr–Aug 1976, Fulham Sep 1976, Los Angeles Aztecs (USA) May–Aug 1977 and Mar 1978, Fort Lauderdale Strikers (USA) Jun–Aug 1978 and Mar–Jul 1979, Hibernian Nov 1979, San Jose Earthquakes (USA) Apr–Aug 1980 and Mar–Aug 1981, AFC Bournemouth Mar 1983, Brisbane Lions (Australia) Jul 1983 SU 16.8.1961 (appr.), 22.5.1963 (pro.) UD v West Bromwich Albion (h) 14.9.1963 FL 361/gls 137 FAC 46/gls 21 FLC 25/gls 9 EUR 34/gls 11 T 466/gls 178 INT (N. Ireland) 37/gls 9

When he arrived in Manchester as a youngster, George Best hardly seemed a future star: "He looked more like a little jockey than a footballer. He was puny and he was petrified," said Mary Fullaway, his landlady. Even George himself seemed uncertain about his destiny. Only a couple of days after his arrival, he was so homesick that he took the ferry back to Northern Ireland, but his father sent him back.

Once settled, Best quickly revealed his ability, as Harry Gregg discovered: "One of the boys, the skinny one, brought the ball up to me and sent me diving the wrong way as he tapped it in at the other end. I thought any kid can get lucky once but he did it to me a second time. I had always prided myself that I could make forwards do what I wanted but this slip of a boy had just shaken his hips and had me diving at fresh air. I knew at that moment that Manchester United had a very rare talent on their hands."

Did you know?

- George Best's mother played hockey for Northern Ireland.
- In 1964 Best opened the first of his half a dozen clothes boutiques, in Sale, Cheshire. He has also owned a travel agency, a bar and two nightclubs.
- Best has been married twice and has a son, Calum Milan, by his first wife.
- In 1969, Best was given a miniature golden pair of the boots he endorsed, to mark record sales of 250,000 pairs.

The Belfast boy

It was not long before others noticed the young Irishman's potential, as he skipped through the "A" and "B" junior teams and helped win the FA Youth Cup in 1964. Early that season, after only a handful of Reserve games, he had made his League debut, aged 17. He did well enough but went back into the Reserves until 28th December, 1963, when he scored in a 5-1 win. This time he stayed in the team, beginning a career which saw him play 466 League, Cup and European games and score 178 goals. Best rarely missed a game, playing in 40, 41 or an ever-present 42 League matches in each of six consecutive seasons.

Best became a key figure not just for the goals, but for the way he made space for the other luminaries in the side, such as Bobby Charlton and Denis Law. He loved to take on opponents, and the fans loved to see him do it.

El Beatle

George Best was football's answer to the Beatles, with entertaining football and a rebel lifestyle to match the impact of the new music from Liverpool; indeed the Portuguese press admiringly christened him "El Beatle", after a European Cup match against Benfica in 1966.

The Reds had taken a narrow 3-2 lead in the first leg, and few thought it would be enough. Matt Busby's tactics were to play safe, especially in the opening stages, but after 20 minutes United had grabbed three goals, two of them from Best. His second was remarkable. Harry Gregg sent a goal kick down the middle for David Herd to head on. Best fastened on to the ball and weaved past three defenders to score a sensational goal. United won 5-1 and George Best came home a star. Busby said: "When we made our plans, George must have had cotton wool stuffed in his ears!"

United were now favourites to win the Cup, but they fell to Partizan Belgrade in the semi-finals. Best had played the first leg with a bad knee, and he missed the return to undergo a cartilage operation. The magic went out of the side. It

> " George Best, more than any one player brought the European Cup to Old Trafford. "
> **Harry Gregg**

showed how important Best had become. United won the championship in 1967, and in 1967/68, Best enjoyed his best-ever figures, scoring 28 League goals and inspiring the United side that became the first English club to win the European Cup. In the semi-final at home against Real Madrid, Best scored the first goal, then in the second leg scorched down the right wing to send the ball into the path of Bill Foulkes, out of his defensive position, who scored the goal that took United to the final.

A magnetic attraction

Best's balance and speed were entrancing to watch – the ball often appeared to be fastened to his boots. He also had sex appeal. Women flocked to see a player who became a cult figure as soccer interest accelerated through the '60s.

Aerobatics

Best beats Frank McClintock of Arsenal in an aerial duel in a League game at Old Trafford on 7th October, 1967. United won the match 1-0, with John Aston (Jnr.) getting the game's only goal. They went on to finish second in the League, three points behind local rivals Manchester City.

George Best: Career timeline

14th September, 1963
League debut v West Bromwich Albion

1961   1962   1963   1964

16th August, 1961
Signs as apprentice for United

22nd May, 1963
Signs professional forms

KEY: a=away am.=amateur appr.=apprentice b.=born c.=circa cs.=close season D=Defender d.=died dnk=date not known EUR=European competitions F=Forward FAC=FA Cup FB=Full-back (defender) FL=Football League FLC=Football League Cup GK=Goalkeeper gls=goals h=home HB=Half-back (midfield) INT=International matches M=Midfield NH=Newton Heath LYR=Newton Heath Lancashire & Yorkshire Railway nk=not known pro.=professional Q=qualifying round SU=signed for United sub=substitute; substitute apps are in brackets after appearances T=total TF=transfer fee TM=Test match U=Utility UD=United debut UTD=Manchester United v=versus

Player of the year

United fulfilled Matt Busby's European dream in a 4-1 win over Benfica, with Best scoring one of the goals. George Best was voted Player of the Year in both Northern Ireland and England, and later that season he became European Footballer of the Year. It was the pinnacle of his career. The only cloud was that he had been unable to make much difference on the international front. It wasn't a successful era for Northern Ireland, although Best will be remembered for taking England's World Cup defence apart in 1965, and for his display in a 1-0 win over Scotland in 1967. He entranced the crowd with dazzling skill on the ball, dropping his shoulder and surging past defenders.

Two seasons after the European triumph of 1968, United began to go downhill and Best was involved in a number of clashes with referees. Late nights and alcohol added to a downward spiral. Busby's retirement in 1969 was the beginning of the end. In 1969/70 Best was fined £100 and given a month's suspension for knocking the ball out of the referee's hands in a League Cup semi-final game against Manchester City. At the end of the season, playing for Northern Ireland, he was sent off for spitting and throwing mud at the referee.

Turbulent times

The United managers after Busby found George increasingly difficult to manage. In January 1972, during O'Farrell's first season, Best failed to turn up for training. He was dropped, fined two weeks' wages, given extra training and ordered to leave his luxury house and return to his digs.

> *George Best was the greatest player in the world.*
>
> **Pele**

Internationals

Best was capped for his country after just 21 first-team games for United. He went on to win 37 caps, but it was not a great time for Northern Ireland, and Best never played in a World Cup or European Championship. He produced some great individual displays, though, such as here against England.

Europe 1968

Best, wearing the number seven shirt, turns away in triumph after scoring United's all-important second goal, seven minutes into extra time of the European Cup Final. With the score level at 1-1 at the end of normal time, and with United tiring, Best finally lost his marker, took the ball around the goal keeper, and clipped it into an empty net.

At the end of the season he failed to report for Northern Ireland and, from Spain, announced his retirement. A few days later he apologized and said it had been a mistake. He was taken back because, despite his problems, he was still the club's top scorer, and he had missed only two games. O'Farrell also conceded that Best had always trained enthusiastically. His behaviour, however, didn't do much for team spirit. Willie Morgan once said: "George thought he was the James Bond of soccer. He had everything he wanted, money, girls and tremendous publicity. He lived from day to day and right up until the end he got away with it. When he missed training or ran away people made excuses for him. He didn't even have to bother to make them himself. He just didn't care."

In Best's last season Tommy Docherty sent him to live with Pat Crerand and his family in an effort to bring more order into his life. It didn't work, and Best played his final game for United on New Year's Day, 1974.

He has worked as a radio and television commentator and after-dinner speaker, also touring the country in a chat show act with Rodney Marsh.

George is still remembered fondly, and reports of his declining health in 2000 caused great public concern.

The downward slide

In 1968/69 Best's behaviour on and off the pitch was becoming more erratic, although he was still a nightmare for opposing defenders. Here, against Leicester City, Best scored once in a 3-2 victory at Old Trafford.

Fact file

- **International games**
Best won 37 caps for Northern Ireland in his career, but he never played in the finals of a major tournament.

- **Euro star**
Best won championship medals in 1965 and 1967 before winning the European Cup in 1968.

- **Youngest-ever**
In 1968, Best was made the youngest-ever European Footballer of the Year. He was
also named Player of the Year in both Northern Ireland and England.

- **High scorer**
In 1970, Best scored six goals in an 8-2 win against Northampton in the fifth round of the FA Cup. His best scoring season for United was 1967/68, when he scored 28 League goals.

- **All told**
In all competitions for United, Best made 466 appearances and scored 178 goals.

15th April, 1964
Debut for Northern Ireland v Wales

May 1967
Wins championship medal

May 1968
Top First Division scorer with 28 goals. Wins European Cup medal. Voted FWA Footballer of the Year

May 1969
Top United scorer with 19 goals

April 1970
Sent off playing for Northern Ireland v Scotland

May 1970
Top United scorer with 15 goals

May 1971
Top United scorer with 18 goals

August 1971
Sent off v Chelsea

May 1972
Fails to report for international duty with Northern Ireland and flees to Spain

June 1972
Returns to club after 17-day "retirement"

May 1973
Scores just four goals in 1972/73 season

1964	1965	1966	1967	1968	1969	1970	1971	1972	1973	1974	1975

30th April, 1964
Wins FA Youth Cup medal

May 1965
Wins championship medal

9th March, 1966
Named El Beatle after scoring twice v Benfica in 5-1 win

April 1968
Voted Northern Ireland Player of the Year

July 1968
Voted European Footballer of the Year

January 1970
Suspended for four weeks

January 1971
Suspended by United for two weeks. Also receives suspended six-week ban from FA and record £250 fine

January 1972
Fails to report for training, is fined and dropped from the team

May 1972
Top United scorer with 18 goals

Best played his last game for United on 1st January, 1974. Then he left, aged just 27, for a variety of clubs in England, Scotland and America where he commanded top money, though he never really recovered his earlier form.

Beardsmore: Russell **M** 1988–1991 *cont.*

Rovers Dec 1991); AFC Bournemouth Jun 1993 **SU** Jun 1985 (appr.), Oct 1986 (pro.) **UD** v West Ham (sub) (h) 24.09.1988 **FL** 30(26)/gls 4 **FAC** 4(4)/gls 0 **FLC** 3(1)/gls 0 **EUR** 1(2)/gls 0 **T** 38(33)/gls 4

Russell Beardsmore broke into the first team as a substitute in a 2–0 win over West Ham United on 24th September, 1988. The attacking midfielder then won the regional Barclays' Young Eagle of the Month award for January 1989 after starring in a 3–1 triumph over Liverpool. Lacking the physical strength to compete regularly at top level, he was released on a free transfer in 1993.

Beckett: R **GK** 1886–1887

b. nk **d.** nk • **Clubs** <u>Newton Heath LYR</u> **SU** Apr 1886 **UD** v Fleetwood Rangers (a) FAC 1, 30.10.1886 **FAC** 1/gls 0 **FLC** 1/gls 0 **T** 2/gls 0

Beckham: David **M** 1992–

See p.63.

Beddow: "Clem" (John) **F** 1904–1907

b. 1885, Burton-on-Trent, nr. Derby, England **d.** nk • *6ft 1in* • *13st* • **Clubs** Trent Rovers, Burton Utd Sep 1904; <u>UTD</u>; Burnley Jul 1907–cs. 1910 **SU** Feb 1905 **UD** v Barnsley (a) 25.2.1905 **FL** 33/gls 12 **FAC** 1/gls 3 **T** 34/gls 15

Behan: Billy **GK** 1933–1934

b. 3.8.1911, Dublin, Rep. of Ireland **d.** 1991 • **Clubs** Shelbourne; <u>UTD</u>; Shelbourne cs. 1934, Shamrock Rovers 1935, Drumcondra (manager) **SU** Sep 1933 **UD** v Bury (h) 3.3.1934 **FL** 1/gls 0 **T** 1/gls 0

Bell: Alex **HB** 1902–1913

b. 1882, Cape Town, South Africa **d.** 30.11.1934 • *5ft 10in* • *11st 10lb* • **Clubs** Ayr Spring Vale, Ayr Westerlea, Ayr Parkhouse; <u>UTD</u>; Blackburn Rovers Jul 1913–cs 1915, Clackmannan FC Sep 1921, Coventry City (trainer) Jul 1922, Manchester City (trainer) Jul 1925 until his death **SU** Jan 1903 (pro.) **TF** £700 **UD** v Glossop (a) 24.1.1903 **FL** 278/gls 10 **FAC** 28/gls 0 **T** 306/gls 10 **INT** (Scotland) 1/gls 0

In the successful period prior to the First World War, Alexander Bell was one of Manchester United's key players. Bell was born in South Africa, but his parents were Scottish, and he joined the club after being spotted in Scotland by ex-Newton Heath half-back Will Davidson. Arriving as a forward, Bell struggled to make an impact in that position, appearing only 11 times in his first two seasons. A switch to half-back, where the club was a little threadbare, reaped dividends and Bell became a regular in that position.

Although Bell may never have been a headline maker in his own right, his work behind the front line helped Manchester United to win two League championships and one FA Cup in the space of four seasons. In modern terms, Alex Bell was the complete midfielder, able to defend and attack to the same high standard. Occupying the left side of the half-back line, he was complemented to his right by attacking centre-half Charlie Roberts and right-half Dick Duckworth. Together the trio formed the basis of the side, collectively making more than 850 League and Cup appearances in United's colours. Roberts, who became a tobacconist after retirement, later named a brand of cigarette "Ducrobel" in their honour. A championship winner with United in 1908 and 1911, Alex Bell completed a hat-trick when he won the title in his first season with Blackburn Rovers, the club who signed him for £1,000 in July 1913.

Bennion: Ray **HB** 1921–1932

b. 1.9.1896, Summer Hill, Wrexham, Wales **d.** 12.3.1968 • *5ft 8in* • *11st 2lb* • **Clubs** Chrichton's Athletic (Saltney) 1919; <u>UTD</u>; Burnley Nov 1932 (coach cs. 1934, then trainer until his retirement in Feb 1964) **SU** Apr 1921 **UD** v Everton (a) 27.8.1921 **FL** 286/gls 2 **FAC** 15/gls 1 **T** 301/gls 3 **INT** (Wales) 10/gls 0

Welsh wing-half Ray Bennion had a miserable start to life at United, losing 5–0 to Everton on his debut and being relegated in his first season. His sterling support play helped the club to regain its top-flight status in 1925 and he played regularly until 1932, when he joined Burnley, the club he then coached for over 30 years.

Bent: Geoff **FB** 1954–1957

b. 27.9.1932, Salford, Manchester, England **d.** 6.2.1958 • *5ft 11in* • *11st 4lb* • **Clubs** <u>UTD</u> (trialist Aug 1948) until his death **SU** May 1949 (am.), Apr 1952 (pro.) **UD** v Burnley (a) 11.12.1954 **FL** 12/gls 0 **T** 12/gls 0

Geoffrey Bent was on the fringe of the Busby Babes. A good tackler and accurate passer, he was understudy to Roger Byrne, which gave him few chances to show his real worth. Bent only travelled to Munich because Byrne had an injury, but in the end Byrne was fit enough to play. Geoff Bent's trip to Munich had been unnecessary, and tragically, he died instantly when the United plane crashed in Munich.

Berg: Henning **D** 1997–2000

b. 1.9.1969, Eidsvell, Norway • *6ft* • *12st 4lb* • **Clubs** KFUM, Valerengen, SK Lillestrom Aug 92 (all Norwegian clubs), Blackburn Rovers Jan 1993–1997; <u>UTD</u>; Blackburn Rovers Dec 2000 **SU** 11.8.1997 (pro.) **TF** £5 million **UD** v Southampton (sub) (h) 13.8.1997 **FL** 33(10)/gls 1 **FAC** 7/gls 0 FLC 3/gls 0 **EUR** 8 (3)/gls 1 **T** 51(13)/gls 2 **INT** (Norway) 61/gls 6

Henning Berg will always be fondly remembered at Old Trafford for his two stunning goal-line clearances against Inter Milan in both legs of United's 1999 quarter-final, Champions League clash. Signed from Blackburn in 1997 for £5 million, a World record for a defender, Berg was a reliable player, but he never completely convinced Sir Alex Ferguson or the Old Trafford faithful. He rejoined Blackburn initially on loan, then permanently in December 2000.

Berry: Bill **F** 1906–1908

b. 1882, Sunderland, England **d.** nk • *5ft 7in* • *10st 12lb* • **Clubs** Oakhill, Sunderland Royal Rovers, Sunderland Sep 1902, Tottenham Hotspur cs. 1903; <u>UTD</u>; Stockport County Feb 1909–cs. 1910, Sunderland Royal Rovers **SU** Nov 1906 **UD** v Sheffield Wednesday (a) 17.11.1906 **FL** 13/gls 1 **FAC** 1/gls 0 **T** 14/gls 1

Berry: Johnny **F** 1951–1958

b. 1.6.1926, Aldershot, nr. Farnham England **d.** 1994 • *5ft 5in* • *10st* • **Clubs** Birmingham City am., pro. Sep 1944; <u>UTD</u> until his retirement in Feb 1958 **SU** Aug 1951 (pro.) **TF** £15,000 **UD** v Bolton Wanderers (a) 1.9.1951 **FL** 247/gls 37 **FAC** 15/gls 4 **EUR** 11/gls 3 **T** 273/gls 44 **INT** (England) 4/gls 0

In the United team of the '50s, John James Berry was unusual in having established a significant career outside Old Trafford. Berry was at Birmingham City when he caught Matt Busby's eye and Busby earmarked him as successor to Jimmy Delaney. United signed Berry in August 1951, and he arrived a fully developed player aged 25. All around Berry brilliant younger men were making their debuts, but he was never out of place, and his experience and maturity helped to balance the exuberance of the younger stars. Berry pursued the ball down his wing with a fire that much endeared him to the Old Trafford faithful. Once in possession, he would dispatch it at once to his waiting forwards. This was his role, to forge a path and supply the cross, and within its limits he excelled. Berry was also capable of a surprisingly hard shot. In United's 3–0 defeat of Atletico Bilbao in February 1957, he burrowed into the centre, picked up a short ball from Tommy Taylor and scored the final goal.

Berry's bravery and unselfishness earned him four full England caps and several "B" team appearances. With United he won three championship medals – in 1952, 1956 and 1957. He was showing no signs of flagging when his career was cut short by the Munich tragedy. Berry survived the crash, but severe injuries brought his playing days to an end.

Best: George **F** 1963–1974

See p.64.

Bielby: Paul **F** 1973–1974

b. 24.11.1956, Darlington, England • *5ft 9in* • *11st 4lb* • **Clubs** <u>UTD</u> (on loan to Hartlepool Utd Nov 1975); Hartlepool Utd Dec 1975, Huddersfield Town Aug 1978–Mar 1980 **SU** Jul 1972 (appr.), Nov 1973 (pro.) **UD** v Manchester City (a) 13.3.1974 **FL** 2(2)/gls 0 **T** 2(2)/gls 0

Birch: Brian **F** 1949–1952

b. 18.11.1931, Salford, Manchester, England • *5ft 6in* • *9st 7lb* • **Clubs** <u>UTD</u>; Wolverhampton Wanderers Mar 1952, Lincoln City Dec 1952, Boston Utd, Barrow Jun 1956, Exeter City Sep 1958, Oldham Athletic Jan 1960, Rochdale Mar 1961, Philippines coaching tour cs. 1962, Boston Utd Aug 1963, Mossley Sep 1963, coaching in Sydney (Australia) Feb 1964, Ellesmere Port until Jan 1967, Blackburn Rovers (junior coach) Nov 1967 **SU** May 1946 (am.), May 1948 (pro.) **UD** v West Bromwich Albion (h) 27.8.1949 **FL** 11/gls 4 **FAC** 4/gls 1 **T** 15/gls 5

Birchenough: Herbert **GK** 1902–1903

b. 1874, Crewe, England **d.** nk • **Clubs** Crewe Alexandra Sep 1892, Burslem Port Vale May 1898, Glossop Jan 1900; <u>UTD</u>; Crewe Alexandra May 1903 **SU** Oct 1902 **UD** v Woolwich Arsenal (a) 25.10.1902 **FL** 25/gls 0 **FAC** 5/gls 0 **T** 30/gls 0

Birkett: Cliff **F** 1950–1951

b. 17.9.1933, Haydock, nr. St. Helens, England • *5ft 8in* • *10st 6lb* • **Clubs** <u>UTD</u>; Southport Jun 1956, Compton's Recs cs. 1957, Wigan Rovers cs. 1959, Macclesfield Town Sep 1959 **SU** 1949 (am.), Oct 1950 (pro.) **UD** v Newcastle Utd (h) 2.12.1950 **FL** 9/gls 2 **FAC** 4/gls 0 **T** 13/gls 2

Birtles: Garry **F** 1980–1982

b. 27.7.1956, Nottingham, England • *5ft 11in* • *11st 8lb* • **Clubs** Long Eaton Rovers, Long Eaton Utd, Nottingham Forest Dec 1976; <u>UTD</u>; Nottingham Forest Sep 1982, Notts County Jun 1987, Grimsby Town Aug 1989–May 1992, Gresley Rovers (asst. manager) 1995–96, (manager) 1997–Feb 1999 **SU** Oct 1980 (pro.) **TF** £1.25 million **UD** v Stoke City (a) 22.10.1980 **FL** 57(1)/gls 11 **FAC** 4/gls 1 **FLC** 2/gls 0 **T** 63(1)/gls 12 **INT** (England) 3/gls 0

At Nottingham Forest Garry Birtles had been a prolific striker, winning two European Cups and one League Cup. Unfortunately, he never really settled away from his native Nottingham, failing to net a single League goal in his first season at Manchester United. He persevered for one more campaign before returning to Nottingham Forest, from where he moved to Notts County, then Grimsby, retiring in 1992.

Bissett: George **F** 1919–1921

b. 25.1.1897, Cowdenbeath, nr. Dunfermline, Scotland **d.** nk • *5ft 8in* • *11st* • **Clubs** Glencraig Thistle, Third Lanark 1914–1915, Army football; <u>UTD</u>; Wolverhampton Wanderers Nov 1921, Pontypridd Jan 1924, Southend Utd May 1924 until his retirement in Apr 1926 **SU** Nov 1919 **UD** v Burnley (h) 15.11.1919 **FL** 40/gls 10 **FAC** 2/gls 0 **T** 42/gls 10

Black: Dick **F** 1931–1934

b. dnk, Glasgow, Scotland **d.** nk • *5ft 7in* • *11st 6lb* • **Clubs** Greenock Morton; <u>UTD</u>; St. Mirren Nov 1934 **SU** 23.4.1932 **UD** v Bradford City (h) 23.4.1932 **FL** 8/gls 3 **T** 8/gls 3

Blackmore: Clayton **U** 1983–1994

b. 23.9.1964, Neath, nr. Swansea, Wales • *5ft 8in* • *11st 12lb* • **Clubs** <u>UTD</u>; Middlesbrough May 1994 (on loan to Bristol City Nov-Dec 1996), Barnsley Feb 1999, Notts County Jul 1999, Leigh RMI Aug 2000, Bangor City Nov 2000 **SU** June 1981 (appr.), Sep 1982 (pro.) **UD** v Nottingham Forest (a) 16.5.1984 **FL** 150(36)/gls 19 **FAC** 15(6)/gls 1 **FLC** 23(2)/gls 3 **EUR** 12/gls 2 **T** 200(44)/gls 25 **INT** (Wales) 39/gls 1

Before squad numbers were introduced in 1993/94, Clayton Blackmore wore every red shirt, from 2 to 14. Although he never really commanded one position, he did enjoy an extended run at left-back in 1990/91, when United won the Cup Winners' Cup. Nick-named "Sunbed", his accurate and powerful shooting made him a free-kick specialist.

Blackmore: Peter **F** 1899–1900

b. nk **d.** nk • **Clubs** <u>NH</u> **SU** Oct 1899 **UD** v New Brighton Tower (h) 21.10.1899 **FL** 1/gls 0 **FAC** 1/gls 0 **T** 2/gls 0

Blackstock: Tommy **FB** 1903–1907

b. 1882, Kirkaldy, Scotland **d.** 8.4.1907 • **Clubs** Dunniker Rangers, Blue Bell FC, Raith Athletic, Leith Athletic, Cowdenbeath; <u>UTD</u> until his death **SU** Jun 1903 **UD** v Woolwich Arsenal (a) 3.10.1903 **FL** 34/gls 0 **FAC** 4/gls 0 **T** 38/gls 0

Blanchflower: Jackie **HB** 1951–1958

b. 7.3.1933, Belfast, N. Ireland **d.** 2.9.1998 • *5ft 11in* • *11st 10lb* • **Clubs** Pitt Street Mission Belfast, Boyland FC; <u>UTD</u> **SU** May 1949 (am.), Mar 1950 (pro.) **UD** v Liverpool (a) 24.11.1951 **FL** 105/gls 26 **FAC** 6/gls 1 **EUR** 5/gls 0 **T** 116/gls 27 **INT** (N. Ireland) 12/gls 1

Brother of legendary Spurs captain Danny Blanchflower, John (Jackie) Blanchflower was an inside-right in United's forward line, scoring 13 goals in 1953/54. He later switched to centre half-back, and even played as emergency goal-keeper in the 1957 Cup Final defeat by Aston Villa. The injuries that Jackie Blanchflower sustained in the Munich air crash forced him to retire prematurely in 1958, aged just 24. He passed away in 1998 just two weeks after the Munich memorial match at Old Trafford.

Blew: Horace **FB** 1905–1906

b. 1878, Wrexham, Wales **d.** 1.2.1957 • *5ft 6in* • *10st* • **Clubs** Rhostyllen 1896–1897, Wrexham 1897–1911, Druids 1903, Bury Aug 1904; <u>UTD</u>; Manchester City Sep 1906, Brymbo 1910, Wrexham FC (on board) in 1920s **SU** Mar 1906 **UD** v Chelsea (h) 13.4.1906 **FL** 1/gls 0 **T** 1/gls 0

Blomqvist: Jesper **F** 1998–2001

b. 5.2.1974, Tavelsjo, Sweden • *5ft 9in* • *11st 3lb* • **Clubs** Tavelsjo IK, Umea, IFK Gothenburg (all Sweden) Aug 1994, AC Milan (Italy) 1996, Parma (Italy) 1997; <u>UTD</u> **SU** 21.7.1998 (pro.) **TF** £4.4 million **UD** v Charlton Athletic (h) 9.9.1998 **FL** 20(5)/gls 1 **FAC** 3(2)/gls 0 **FLC** 0(1)/gls 0 **EUR** 6(1)/gls 0 **T** 29(9)/gls 1 **INT** (Sweden) 29

Jesper Blomqvist has had a mixed time at Old Trafford. The Swedish winger was signed in the summer of 1998 from Italian side Parma, for £4.4 million, and during his first season he played an integral part in United's Treble success. This included a place in the final of the 1999 Champions League in Barcelona. The following two seasons were write-offs for Blomqvist, who spent both campaigns battling with injury.

Blott: Sam **F** 1909–1913

b. 1.1.1886, London, England **d.** 1969 • *5ft 9in* • *11st 7lb* • **Clubs** Southend Utd, Bradford cs. 1907, Southend Utd May 1908; <u>UTD</u>; Plymouth Argyle Jun 1913, Newport County Jun 1920–1921 **SU** May 1909 **UD** v Bradford City (h) 1.9.1909 **FL** 19/gls 2 **T** 19/gls 2

KEY: **a**=away **am.**=amateur **appr.**=apprentice **b.**=born **c.**=circa **cs.**=close season **CWC**=Club World Championship **D**=Defender **d.**=died **dnk**=date not known **EUR**=European competitions **F**=Forward **FAC**=FA Cup **FB**=Full-back (defender) **FL**=Football League **FLC**=Football League Cup **GK**=Goalkeeper **gls**=goals **h**=home **HB**=Half-back (midfield) **INT**=International matches **M**=Midfield <u>**NH**</u>=Newton Heath <u>**Newton Heath LYR**</u>=Newton Heath Lancashire & Yorkshire Railway **nk**=not known **pro.**=professional **Q**=qualifying round **SU**=signed for United **sub**=substitute; substitute apps are in brackets after appearances **T**=total **TF**=transfer fee **TM**=Test match **U**=Utility **UD**=United debut <u>**UTD**</u>=Manchester United **v**=versus

Bruce: Steve D 1987-1996

b. 31.12.1960, Corbridge, nr. Hexham, England • *6ft* • *13st* • **Clubs** Gillingham appr. Jul 1977, pro. Oct 1978, Norwich City Jul 1984; UTD; Birmingham City Jun 1996, Sheffield United (player-manager) Jul 1998, Huddersfield Town (manager) May 1999, Wigan Athletic (manager) Apr 2001, Crystal Palace (manager) May 2001 **SU** 17.12.1987 (pro.) **TF** £825,000 **UD** v Portsmouth (a) 19.12.1987 **FL** 312/gls 36 **FAC** 41/gls 3 **FLC** 31(2)/gls 6 **EUR** 23(1)/gls 6 **T** 407(3)/gls 51

As the 1993 title race reached its climax, Manchester United found themselves a goal down to Sheffield Wednesday with only four minutes remaining. At this point during the previous year United had faltered in the race, but Steve Bruce was not going to let it happen again. With two dramatic goals, the second deep into injury time, he single-handedly changed the destination of the championship. It is for great moments such as these that Bruce is so fondly remembered at Old Trafford.

Bruce was a product of the famous Wallsend Boys Club in the northeast, which also produced Alan Shearer and Peter Beardsley. Bruce had trials with several clubs, but the general verdict was that although he tried hard, he lacked genuine talent. Eventually, however, Bruce was signed by Gillingham. While there, he was voted the club's Player of the Year three times and capped by the England Youth team. Norwich City signed him for £135,000 in the summer of 1984, and Bruce helped in the club's rebirth, winning the League Cup in 1985 and the Second Division championship in 1986.

When Alex Ferguson arrived at Old Trafford in November 1986, one of United's problems was that too many of its central defenders were unreliable or injury-prone. Steve Bruce seemed to be the solution. "You'll love this boy," Norwich manager Ken Brown told Ferguson, "You will not find a more enthusiastic lad".

Bruce eventually joined United in December 1987, bringing with him not only enthusiasm, but also a determination that the team had previously lacked. After almost failing to make it as a professional, he wasn't going to give anything but his best.

His gritty style often overshadowed his playing ability; rather than clear the ball with an aimless header, Bruce would often take the ball down on his chest and play it on the ground. His seven-year partnership with Gary Pallister, whose pace and ball skills complemented Bruce's grit and organization, was integral to Manchester United's success.

For a period Bruce was the club's penalty taker, which helped increase his scoring rate; in eight-and-a-half seasons he scored 51 times. In 1990/91 he was United's joint top scorer in the League, with 13, and his overall total of 19 in that campaign is thought to be the biggest-ever total for a defender in a single season.

In 1992, Bruce took over from Bryan Robson as United captain. In Bruce's four years as captain he lifted three Premiership trophies, the FA Cup and the League Cup.

Last-gasp winner
Above, Bruce scores United's winning goal in injury time, in a League match against Sheffield Wednesday on 10th April, 1993. United won the match 2-1.

True grit
Bruce's mix of determination and leadership was an essential part of the most successful era in United's history. He led through example and had his team's absolute respect.

" It's quite remarkable that Bruce never won international honours. "
Terry Venables

In 1993 Steve Bruce led his team mates to collect the Premiership trophy. The next season he captained what was probably the finest-ever Manchester United side to the Double. In doing so, he became only the fourth footballer and the first Englishman in the 20th century to captain a side to the Double.

Although Bruce also captained an England "B" team, his failure to get a full cap was remarkable. After his eight years as England manager, Bobby Robson bumped into Bruce in Portugal and told him: "I made a mistake with you, son. I should have had you in my England team long before I finished". Bruce's mix of determination and leadership was an essential part of the most successful era in United's history. "When he passes on I want his body for medical research," joked Alex Ferguson, "he's unbelievable. It's hard to know what this man is made of".

In his final season, Bruce captained Manchester United to another Double, but he was left out of the season's final game and the Cup Final. However, his influence was felt beyond the football field, and he was a friend to United's young players. "He is the kind of person you strive to be," said Gary Neville, "everybody would go to him for advice". Not prepared to sit on the bench, Bruce was granted a free transfer and signed for First Division Birmingham City in June 1996. In the summer of 1998, Bruce took his first steps into management with Sheffield United. However, frustrated by the lack of funding for his squad, he resigned at the end of his first season. A new job in Yorkshire swiftly followed, at Huddersfield Town. However, Bruce remained there for only 16 months, leaving in October 2000 after a dismal run of six consecutive home game defeats.

In April 2001, Steve Bruce revived his managerial career by taking charge at Second Division Wigan Athletic for two months. Following his short spell there, he moved south to succeed caretaker manager Steve Kember at First Division Crystal Palace

Fact file

• **United's elite**
Bruce is one of only 27 players to have appeared in more than 300 League games for United.

• **Scoring record**
Steve Bruce scored 19 League and Cup goals in the 1990/91 season. This is said to be an all-time record for a defender.

• **Penalty score**
The highest number of penalties scored in a single season for United was 11, scored by Steve Bruce in 1990/91:

• **Games played**
When Bruce left Manchester United, he had played a total of 407 games for the club.

Steve Bruce: Career timeline

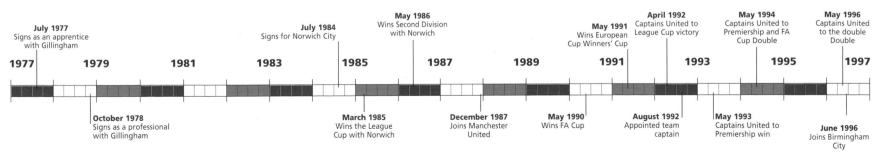

July 1977 — Signs as an apprentice with Gillingham
October 1978 — Signs as a professional with Gillingham
July 1984 — Signs for Norwich City
March 1985 — Wins the League Cup with Norwich
May 1986 — Wins Second Division with Norwich
December 1987 — Joins Manchester United
May 1990 — Wins FA Cup
May 1991 — Wins European Cup Winners' Cup
April 1992 — Captains United to League Cup victory
August 1992 — Appointed team captain
May 1993 — Captains United to Premiership win
May 1994 — Captains United to Premiership and FA Cup Double
May 1996 — Captains United to the double Double
June 1996 — Joins Birmingham City

1977 1979 1981 1983 1985 1987 1989 1991 1993 1995 1997

Bogan: Tommy **F** 1949–1951

b. 18.5.1920, Glasgow, Scotland **d.** 23.9.1993 • *5ft 9in* • *11st 2lb* • **Clubs** Strathclyde 1937, Blantyre Celtic 1939, Renfrew 1943, Hibernian Sep 1943, Glasgow Celtic Jan 1946, Preston North End Sep 1948; UTD; Aberdeen Mar 1951, Southampton Dec 1951, Blackburn Rovers Aug 1953, Macclesfield Town Jun 1954 **SU** Aug 1949 **UD** v Charlton Athletic (h) 8.10.1949 **FL** 29/gls 7 **FAC** 4/gls 0 **T** 33/gls 7

Bond: Ernie **F** 1951–1953

b. 4.5.1929, Preston, Lancashire, England • *5ft 6in* • *9st 11lb* • **Clubs** Preston North End am. Jun 1948, Leyland Motors; UTD; Carlisle Utd Sep 1952, Cowdenbeath Oct 1958 **SU** Dec 1950 **UD** v West Bromwich Albion (a) 18.8.1951 **FL** 20/gls 4 **FAC** 1/gls 0 **T** 21/gls 4

Bonthron: Bob **FB** 1903–1907

b. 1884, Dundee, Scotland **d.** nk • *5ft 10in* • *12st 4lb* • **Clubs** Raith Athletic, Raith Rovers cs. 1900, Dundee cs. 1902; UTD; Sunderland May 1907, Northampton Town cs. 1908, Birmingham Jul 1910, Leith Athletic Jul 1912 **SU** May 1903 **UD** v Bristol City (h) 5.9.1903 **FL** 119/gls 3 **FAC** 15/gls 0 **T** 134/gls 3

Booth: William **F** 1900–1901

b. dnk, Manchester, England **d.** nk • **Clubs** Edge Lane FC; NH **SU** Dec 1900 **UD** v Blackpool (h) 26.12.1900 **FL** 2/gls 0 **T** 2/gls 0

Bosnich: Mark **GK** 1989–1991, 1999–2001

b. 13.1.1972, Fairfield, Sydney, Australia • *6ft 2in* • *13st 7lb* • **Clubs** Croatia Sydney SFC (Aust.); UTD (non-contract) Jun 1989; Croatia Sydney SFC, Aston Villa Feb 1992; UTD Jul 1999; Chelsea Jan 2001 **UD** v Wimbledon (h) 30.4.1990 **FL** 3/gls 0 **T** 3/gls 0 **INT** (Australia) 14/gls 1

A former Manchester United apprentice, Mark Bosnich's great return to Old Trafford in the summer of 1999 ended in acrimony after only eighteen months. Re-signed from Aston Villa on a Bosman free transfer, the Australian goalkeeper was brought to United to succeed Peter Schmeichel. Despite some match-winning performances, most notably against Palmeiras in the Intercontinental Cup in November 1999, Sir Alex Ferguson soon seemed to regret his decision to bring Mark Bosnich back to the club. Ferguson even signed two more keepers, Massimo Taibi and Fabien Barthez, during Bosnich's brief stay, before he shipped him out to Chelsea on a free transfer in January 2001.

Boyd: Billy **F** 1934–1935

b. 27.11.1905, Cambuslang, Glasgow, Scotland **d.** 14.12.1967 • *5ft 7in* • *10st 12lb* • **Clubs** Regent Star Rutherglen, Larkhill Thistle, Clyde 1930, Sheffield Utd Dec 1933; UTD; Workington Sep 1935, Luton Town Dec 1935, Southampton Jul 1936, Weymouth Aug 1937 **SU** Feb 1935 **UD** v Swansea Town (a) 9.2.1935 **FL** 6/gls 4 **T** 6/gls 4 **INT** (Scotland) 2/gls 1

Boyd: Henry **F** 1896–1899

b. 1868, Pollockshaws, Glasgow, Scotland **d.** nk • *5ft 10in* • *11st 4lb* • **Clubs** Sunderland Albion, Burnley Aug 1892, West Bromwich Albion Oct 1892, Royal Arsenal May 1894; NH; Falkirk Aug 1899–1900 **SU** Jan 1897 **UD** v Loughborough Town (h) 6.2.1897, scored 1 **FL** 52/gls 32 **TM** 3/gls 2 **FAC** 7/gls 1 **T** 62/gls 35

Boyle: Tommy **F** 1928–1930

b. 1897, Sheffield, England **d.** nk • *5ft 9in* • *11st 7lb* • **Clubs** Bullcroft Colliery, Sheffield Utd Oct 1921; UTD; Macclesfield May 1930, Northampton Town (player-manager) Jul 1930, Scarborough (manager) May 1935 **SU** Mar 1929 **UD** v Derby County (a) 30.3.1929 **FL** 16/gls 6 **FAC** 1/gls 0 **T** 17/gls 6

Bradbury: Len **F** 1935–1937; 1938–1942

b. 1914, Northwich, England • *5ft 8in* • *11st 4lb* • **Clubs** Northwich Victoria am. 1934–1935; UTD; Northwich Victoria Jan 1937, Corinthians, Birmingham University, Moor Green FC, Corinthians, Manchester University; UTD **SU** May 1935 and Oct 1938 (am.) **UD** v Chelsea (a) 23.1.1939, scored 1 **FL** 2/gls 1 **T** 2/gls 1

Bradley: Warren **F** 1958–1962

b. 1914, Northwich, England • *5ft 8in* • *11st 4lb* 20.6.1933, Hyde, Manchester, England • *5ft 5in* • *10st 6lb* • **Clubs** Durham City, Bolton Wanderers am. Aug 1954, Bishop Auckland am. 1955; UTD; Bury Mar 1962, Northwich Victoria Jul 1963, Macclesfield Nov 1963, Bangor City cs. 1964, Macclesfield Apr 1966 **SU** Feb 1958 (am.), Nov 1958 (pro.) **UD** v Bolton Wanderers (a) 15.11.1958 **FL** 63/gls 20 **FAC** 3/gls 1 **T** 66/gls 21 **INT** (England) 3/gls 2

Bratt: Harold **HB** 1960–1961

b. 8.10.1939, Salford, Manchester, England • *5ft 10in* • *12st* • **Clubs** UTD; Doncaster Rovers May 1961–1963 **SU** 1956 1954 (am.), Nov 1957 (pro.) **UD** v Bradford City (a) FLC 2, 2.11.1960 **FLC** 1/gls 0 **T** 1/gls 0

Brazil: Alan **F** 1984–1986

b. 15.6.1959, Glasgow, Scotland • *5ft 11in* • *13st 1lb* • **Clubs** Ipswich Town appr. Aug 1975, pro. May 1977, Detroit Express (USA) May–Aug 1978, Tottenham Hotspur Mar 1983; UTD; Coventry City Jun 1986, Queen's Park Rangers Jun 1986–Jan 1987, Witham Town 1988, Chelmsford City 1988, FC Baden (Switzerland) 1988–1989, Chelmsford City 1989, Southend Manor 1989, Bury Town 1989–1990, Stambridge 1990, Chelmsford City 1991, Wivenhoe Town 1991 **SU** Jun 1984 (pro.) **TF** £625,000 **UD** v Watford (h) 25.8.1984 **FL** 18(13)/gls 8 **FAC** 0(1)/gls 0 **FLC** 4(3)/gls 3 **EUR** 2/gls 1 **T** 24(17)/gls 12 **INT** (Scotland) 13/gls 1

Brazil: Derek **D** 1988–1990

b. 14.12.1968, Dublin, Rep. of Ireland • *6ft* • *12st 1lb* • **Clubs** Manchester City, Tottenham Hotspur, Chelsea; UTD (on loan to Oldham Athletic Nov–Dec 1990, to Swansea City Sep 1991 and to Cardiff City 1992); Cardiff City Aug 1992–May 1996 **SU** Mar 1986 (pro.) **UD** v Everton (h) 10.5.1989 **FL** 0(2)/gls 0 **T** 0(2)/gls 0

Breedon: Jack **GK** 1935–1940

b. 29.12.1907, South Hiendley, Barnsley, Yorkshire, England • *5ft 10in* • *11st 3lb* • **Clubs** South Hiendley, Barnsley Sep 1928, Sheffield Wednesday Nov 1930; UTD (WW2: Bolton Wanderers, Manchester City); Burnley Oct 1945–cs. 1946, Halifax Town (manager) Aug 1945–Nov 1950, Bradford (manager) Jan–Oct 1955, Leeds Utd (scout) early 1960s **SU** Jul 1935 **UD** v Plymouth Argyle (a) 31.8.1935 **FL** 38/gls 0 **T** 38/gls 0

Breen: Tommy **GK** 1936–1939

b. 27.4.1917, Belfast, N. Ireland • *5ft 10in* • *11st 6lb* • **Clubs** Drogheda Utd, Belfast Celtic; UTD; Belfast Celtic 1939, Linfield, Shamrock Rovers, Newry Town, Glentoran **SU** Nov 1936 **UD** v Leeds Utd (a) 28.11.1936 **FL** 65/gls 0 **FAC** 6/gls 0 **T** 71/gls 0 **INT** (N. Ireland) 9/gls 0

Brennan: "Shay" (Seamus) **FB** 1957–1970

b. 6.5.1937, Manchester, England **d.** 9.6.2000 • *5ft 10in* • *10st 7lb* • **Clubs** UTD; Waterford (player-manager) Aug 1970 **SU** 22.4.1955 (pro.) **UD** v Sheffield Wednesday (h) FAC 5, 19.2.1958, scored 2 **FL** 291(1)/gls 3 **FAC** 36/gls 3 **FLC** 4/gls 0 **EUR** 24/gls 0 **T** 355(1)/gls 6 **INT** (Rep. of Ireland) 19/gls 0

Having played in United's FA Youth Cup-winning team in 1955, Seamus (Shay) Brennan was still waiting for a first-team try out at the time of the Munich disaster. A natural full-back, Brennan played outside-left in United's first match after the tragedy, a fifth-round FA Cup tie against Sheffield Wednesday, in replacement for David Pegg. Brennan scored twice, a rare triumph for a fledgling player.

As more senior players returned to action after the Munich disaster, Shay Brennan was selected less frequently, and he unfortunately missed the 1958 FA Cup Final. In 1959/60, however, he rejoined the first team as a mature right-back. He won League championship medals in 1965 and 1967, and played in the triumphant 1968 European Cup Final.

To supporters, Shay Brennan was a reassuring presence whose confident tackling and defensive work kept the midfield clear for action. Brennan's Irish parentage qualified him for a place in the Republic of Ireland team, and he earned 19 caps. Brennan left Manchester United to become player-manager at Waterford.

Brett: Frank **FB** 1921–1922

b. 10.3.1899, King's Norton, England **d.** 21.7.1988 • *5ft 11in* • *11st 7lb* • **Clubs** Redditch, Aston Villa am. Jul 1920; UTD; Aston Villa Aug 1922, Northampton Town May 1923, Brighton & Hove Albion May 1930, Tunbridge Wells Rangers Sep 1935, Hove FC am. Sep 1936 **SU** Feb 1921 **UD** v Everton (a) 27.8.1921 **FL** 10/gls 0 **T** 10/gls 0

Briggs: Ronnie **GK** 1960–1962

b. 29.3.1943, Belfast, N. Ireland • *6ft 2in* • *13st 3lb* • **Clubs** UTD; Swansea Town May 1964, Bristol Rovers Jun 1965–Jun 1968 **SU** 1958 (appr.), Mar 1960 (pro.) **UD** v Leicester City (a) 21.1.1961 **FL** 9/gls 0 **FAC** 2/gls 0 **T** 11/gls 0 **INT** (N. Ireland) 2/gls 0

Brooks: William **F** 1896–1897; 1898–1899

b. 1873, Stalybridge, Manchester, England **d.** nk • **Clubs** Stalybridge Rovers; NH; Stalybridge Rovers cs. 1897; NH; Stalybridge Rovers **SU** Feb 1896 and May 1898 **UD** v Loughborough Town (h) 22.10.1898, scored 2 **FL** 3/gls 3 **T** 3/gls 3

Broome: Albert **F** 1922–1923

b. 1900, Unsworth, nr. Bury, England • *5ft 10in* • *11st 1lb* • **Clubs** Northern Nomads, Oldham Athletic am. Oct 1921; UTD; Oldham Athletic Jul 1924; Welshpool FC Dec 1925, Stockport County Mar 1927, Mossley Aug 1928 **SU** Jan 1923 **UD** v Barnsley (a) 28.4.1923 **FL** 1/gls 0 **T** 1/gls 0

Broomfield: Herbert **GK** 1907–1908

b. 11.12.1878, Audlem, Nantwich, England **d.** nk • *6ft 1in* • *13st 10lb* • **Clubs** Northwich Wednesday, Northwich Victoria, Bolton Wanderers Dec 1902; UTD; Manchester City Jul 1908; UTD **SU** Apr 1907 (pro.), Oct 1910 (am.) **UD** v Woolwich Arsenal (a) 21.3.1908 **FL** 9/gls 0 **T** 9/gls 0

Brown: "Berry" (Robert) **GK** 1947–1948

b. 6.9.1927, West Hartlepool, England • *6ft 1in* • *11st 9lb* • **Clubs** UTD; Doncaster Rovers Jan 1949, Hartlepools Utd Aug 1951–Jun 1956 **SU** May 1946 (am.), Aug 1946 (pro.) **UD** v Sheffield Utd (a) 31.1.1948 **FL** 4/gls 0 **T** 4/gls 0

Brown: James **FB** 1892–1893

b. nk **d.** nk • **Clubs** NH; Dundee Aug 1893 **SU** Jun 1892 **UD** v Blackburn Rovers (a) 3.9.1892 **FL** 7/gls 0 **T** 7/gls 0

Brown: James **F** 1932–1934

b. 31.12.1908, Kilmarnock, Scotland • *6ft 1in* • *12st 8lb* • **Clubs** Plainfield FC, Bayonne Rovers (New Jersey, USA) 1927, Newark Skeeters (ASL) 1928–1929, New York Giants (ASL) 1930–1931, Brooklyn Wanderers (ASL) 1930–1931; UTD; Brentford May 1934, Tottenham Hotspur Sep 1936, Guildford City Jul 1937, Clydebank 1940, Greenwich High School (Connecticut, USA, coach) 1950–1951, Greenport Utd SC (USA, player-president) 1951–1952, Brunswick School (Greenwich, Connecticut, senior coach) 1953–1975, also Polish Falcons SC (USA, manager) 1957–1958 **SU** Sep 1932 **UD** v Grimsby Town (h) 17.9.1932, scored 1 **FL** 40/gls 17 **FAC** 1/gls 0 **T** 41/gls 17

Brown: James **HB** 1935–1939

b. 1907, Leith, Edinburgh, Scotland • *5ft 9in* • *11st 6lb* • **Clubs** East Fife season 1926–1927, Burnley May 1927; UTD; Bradford Feb 1939 until his retirement in WW2 **SU** Jun 1935 **TF** £1,000 **UD** v Plymouth Argyle (a) 31.8.1935 **FL** 102/gls 1 **FAC** 8/gls 0 **T** 110/gls 1

Brown: "Rimmer" (William) **F** 1896–1897

b. nk **d.** nk • *5ft 8in* • *10st 10lb* • **Clubs** Stalybridge Rovers, Chester; NH; Stockport County Dec 1896, Hurst Ramblers 1898–99 **SU** May 1896 **UD** v Gainsborough Trinity" (h) 1.9.1896 **FL** 7/gls 2 **T** 7/gls 2

Brown: Wesley **D** 1997–

b. 16.3.1979, Manchester, England • *6ft 1in* • *12st 2lb* • **Clubs** UTD **SU** 8.7.1996 (appr.), 4.11.1996 (pro.) **UD** v Leeds Utd (sub) (h) 4.5.1998 **FL** 37(7)/gls 0 **EUR** 12(3)/gls 0 **FAC** 3/gls 0 **FLC** 1(1)/gls 0 **T** 53(11)/gls 0 **INT** (England) 3/gls 0

A natural centre-back, Wesley Brown played at right-back during the autumn of 1998 while Gary Neville covered for the injured Ronny Johnsen. Strong, quick and composed on the ball, he was United's Young Player of the Year in the 1998/99 season. He made a senior England debut against Hungary on 28th April, 1999, and was a regular member of the Under-21s squad.

A knee injury sustained during training in August 1999 ruled Wesley out of play in the 1999/2000 season. He returned the following season and swiftly re-established his reputation as England's finest young defender. Sir Alex Ferguson hailed his recovery from injury as the best he had ever seen.

Bruce: Steve **D** 1987–1996

See p.67.

Bryant: Billy **F** 1934–1940

b. 26.11.1913, Shildon, nr. Bishop Auckland, England **d.** 1975 • *5ft 10in* • *11st 6lb* • **Clubs** Cockfield FC Aug 1931, Wolverhampton Wanderers Sep 1931, Wrexham Oct 1933; UTD (WW2: guest at Chester 1941–1942); Bradford City Nov 1945–1946, Altrincham, Stalybridge Celtic **SU** Oct 1934 **UD** v Blackpool (a) 31.11.34 **FL** 151/gls 44 **FAC** 9/gls 0 **T** 160/gls 44

Bryant: William **F** 1896–1899

b. 1874, Rotherham, England **d.** nk • *5ft 8in* • *11st 12lb* • **Clubs** Rotherham Town Aug 1894; NH; Blackburn Rovers Apr 1900–cs. 1902 **SU** Apr 1896 **UD** v Gainsborough Trinity (h) 1.9.1896 **FL** 109/gls 27 **TM** 4/gls 0 **FAC** 14/gls 6 **T** 127/gls 33

Buchan: George **F** 1973–1974

b. 2.5.1950, Aberdeen, Scotland • *5ft 7in* • *10st 11lb* • **Clubs** Aberdeen; UTD; Bury Aug 1974 (on loan to Motherwell Sep 1975–cs. 1976) **SU** May 1973 **UD** v West Ham Utd (sub) (h) 15.9.1973 **FL** (3)/gls 0 **FLC** (1)/gls 0 **T** (4)/gls 0

Buchan: Martin **D** 1971–1983

See p.69.

Buckle: Ted **F** 1946–1949

b. 28.10.1924, Southwark, London, England • *5ft 11in* • *11st* • **Clubs** Royal Navy football; UTD; Everton Nov 1949, Exeter City Jul 1955–Jun 1957, Prestatyn (player-manager) cs. 1957, Dolgellau (Welsh League) season 1961–1962 **SU** Oct 1945 (am.), Nov 1945 (pro.) **UD** v Charlton Athletic (h) 4.1.1947, scored 1 **FL** 20/gls 6 **FAC** 4/gls 1 **T** 24/gls 7

Buckley: Frank **HB** 1906–1907

b. 9.11.1882, Urmston, Manchester, England **d.** 22.12.1964 • *6ft* • *12st 9lb* • **Clubs** Aston Villa Apr 1903, Brighton & Hove Albion May 1905; UTD; Aston Villa May 1907, Manchester City Sep 1907, Birmingham Jul 1909, Derby County May 1911, Bradford City May 1914, Norwich City (manager) Mar 1919–1920, Blackpool (manager) Jun 1923, Wolverhampton Wanderers (secretary-manager May 1927, Notts County (manager) Mar 1944, Hull City (manager) May 1946, Leeds Utd (manager) May 1948, Walsall (manager) Apr 1953–Jun 1955 **SU** Jun 1906 **UD** v Derby County (h) 29.9.1906 **FL** 3/gls 0 **T** 3/gls 0

Bullock: Jimmy **F** 1930–1931

b. 25.3.1902, Gorton, Manchester, England **d.** 9.3.1977 • *5ft 9in* • *12st 1lb* • **Clubs** Gorton FC, Crewe Alexandra am. May 1921, Manchester City "A" team am. Mar 1922, Crewe Alexandra Feb 1924, Southampton Jul 1924, Chesterfield Jun 1929; UTD; Dundalk (Irish Free State League) Jun–Nov 1931, Llanelly Jul 1932, Hyde Utd Jun 1933 **SU** Sep 1930 **TF** £1,250 **UD** v Sheffield Wednesday (a) 20.9.1930 **FL** 10/gls 3 **T** 10/gls 3

Bunce: William **FB** 1902–1903

b. nk **d.** nk • **Clubs** Rochdale Athletic, Stockport County Dec 1900; UTD **SU** Jul 1902 **UD** v Chesterfield (h) 4.10.1902 **FL** 2/gls 0 **T** 2/gls 0

KEY: **a**=away **am.**=amateur **appr.**=apprentice **b.**=born **c.**=circa **cs.**=close season **CWC**=Club World Championship **D**=Defender **d.**=died **dnk**=date not known **EUR**=European competitions **F**=Forward **FAC**=FA Cup **FB**=Full-back (defender) **FL**=Football League **FLC**=Football League Cup **GK**=Goalkeeper **gls**=goals **h**=home **HB**=Half-back (midfield) **INT**=International matches **M**=Midfield **NH**=Newton Heath **Newton Heath LYR**=Newton Heath Lancashire & Yorkshire Railway **nk**=not known **pro.**=professional **Q**=qualifying round **SU**=signed for United **sub**=substitute; substitute apps are in brackets after appearances **T**=total **TF**=transfer fee **TM**=Test match **U**=Utility **UD**=United debut **UTD**=Manchester United **v**=versus

Buchan: Martin D 1971-1983

b. 6.3.1949, Aberdeen, Scotland • *5ft 10in* • *11st 7lb* • **Clubs** Banks o' Dee "A", Aberdeen 1965, pro. Aug 1966; UTD; Oldham Athletic Aug 1983-Oct 1984, Burnley (manager) Jun-Oct 1985 **SU** Mar 1972 (pro.) **TF** £125,000 **UD** v Tottenham Hotspur (a) 4.3.1972 **FL** 376/gls 4 **FAC** 39/gls 0 **FLC** 30/gls 0 **EUR** 10/gls 0 **T** 455/gls 4 **INT** (Scotland) 34/gls 0

Nobody can dispute the enormous contribution that Manchester United's long-serving defender, Martin Buchan, made to the club. Buchan had enjoyed a distinguished career at Aberdeen before he ventured south to Old Trafford. At 20, he was made club captain of the Dons, and a year later he skippered the team to a Scottish Cup victory. He was voted Scottish Player of the Year in 1971 and earned the first of his 34 Scotland caps in the same year. Towards the end of the 1971/72 season, Aberdeen decided to cash in on their young captain by selling him to a top English club. Plenty were interested, and it came as a surprise when Buchan chose United over the more successful Liverpool and Leeds clubs of that time. A class centre-back like Buchan was exactly what United needed, and he wasted no time in justifying the record £125,000 transfer fee that manager Frank O'Farrell paid.

United were in decline, with world-class players such as Charlton, Best and Law coming to the end of their careers playing alongside individuals who simply weren't of the same calibre. Six months after Buchan joined United, O'Farrell was sacked and Tommy Docherty brought in. United

continued to slide and were relegated in 1974, but with Buchan newly installed as captain, they bounced back at the first attempt by winning the Second Division championship in 1975.

After the adversity of his first two years at Old Trafford, the club's fortunes were improving and Buchan later described his years under Tommy Docherty as "the happiest days of my playing career".

United reached the FA Cup Final in 1976, but Southampton, surprisingly, won with a single goal. A year later United reached the final again, against Liverpool, and with Buchan

blotting out the threat of Kevin Keegan with a typically faultless performance, the Reds achieved a memorable 2-1 victory. Buchan also won the accolade of becoming the first post-war player to captain both a Scottish and English Cup-winning side. With Liverpool dominant in the League, Buchan's United honours were restricted to the Cups, and he picked up another FA Cup runners-up medal in the 1979 final defeat by Arsenal.

In the '80s, Buchan suffered badly from persistent injuries, and in August 1983 he bowed out of Old Trafford to spend a short spell playing at Oldham, and an even shorter one managing Burnley before leaving the game. Today, Buchan works for a sportswear company, promoting football boots.

Fact file

- **Bouncing back**
United were relegated to the Second Division in 1974, but with Buchan as their captain, they managed to win the Second Division championship in 1975 and regain their place in the First Division.

- **Award-winning**
First Division managers voted Buchan their Player of the Year in 1977.

- **Double honour**
Buchan became the first player since World War Two to captain both English and Scottish Cup-winning sides.

- **Scoring rate**
Buchan scored on just four occasions in his 455 United games - a goal every 111 games!

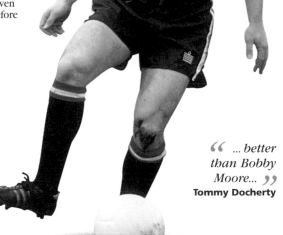

66 ...you didn't cross Martin Buchan, our captain. 99
Stewart Houston

66 ...better than Bobby Moore... 99
Tommy Docherty

Rock solid
United regained a place in the First Division in 1975 with spirit, passion and skill. Buchan's supreme confidence, discipline and leadership qualities made him the rock [at] the heart of United's defence.

Burgess: Herbert FB 1906-1910

b. 1883, Openshaw, Manchester, England **d.** 1954 • *5ft 5in* • *11st 2lb* • **Clubs** Gorton St. Francis' Openshaw Utd, Edge Lane FC, Moss Side FC, Glossop Apr 1900, Manchester City Jul 1903; UTD; (coach in Hungary, Spain, Italy, Austria, Denmark and Sweden), Ashton National FC Oct 1934 (trainer) **SU** Dec 1906 **UD** v Aston Villa (h) 1.1.1907 **FL** 49/gls 0 **FAC** 3/gls 0 **T** 52/gls 0

Burke: Ronnie F 1946-1949

b. 13.8.1921, Dormanstown, nr. Middlesbrough, England • *5ft 10in* • *12st 7lb* • **Clubs** St. Albans City, Luton Town am. Jun 1941 (WW2: Manchester City, Rotherham Utd, Liverpool); UTD; Huddersfield Town 1949, Rotherham Utd Mar 1953, Exeter City Jun 1955, Tunbridge Wells Rangers cs. 1957, Biggleswade Town 1959-1961 **SU** May 1946 (am.), Aug 1946 (pro.) **UD** v Sunderland (h) 26.10.1946 **FL** 28/gls 16 **FAC** 6/gls 6 **T** 34/gls 22

Ronnie Burke joined United after serving in the RAF during the war. Well-built and pacey, he constantly troubled defenders, as his 1946/47 record of nine goals in 13 games testifies. Unable to break the successful strike partnership of Rowley, Pearson and Morris, Burke was granted a transfer request in 1949. A good spell with Rotherham saw him notch up 54 goals in 73 games.

Burke: Tom HB 1886-1889

b. 1863, Wrexham, Wales **d.** 1914 • **Clubs** Wrexham Grosvenor, Wrexham February FC 1882, Wrexham Olympic 1884, Liverpool Cambrians; Newton Heath LYR; Wrexham Victoria 1890-1891 **SU** 1886 **UD** v Fleetwood Rangers (a) FAC 1, 30.10.1886 **FL** 1/gls 0 **FAC** 1/gls 0 **T** 2/gls 0 **INT** (Wales) 8/gls 1

Burns: Francis D 1967-1972

b. 17.10.1948, Glenboig, nr. Glasgow, Scotland • *5ft 9in* • *10st 10lb* • **Clubs** UTD; Southampton

Jun 1972, Preston North End Aug 1973, Shamrock Rovers 1981, Italia FC (Western Australia, manager) **SU** Jun 1964 (appr.), Oct 1965 (pro.) **UD** v West Ham Utd (a) 2.9.1967 **FL** 111(10)/gls 6 **FAC** 11(1)/gls 0 **FLC** 10(1)/gls 0 **EUR** 10(1)/gls 1 **T** 142(13)/gls 7 **INT** (Scotland) 1/gls 0

Former Scotland Schoolboys skipper Francis Burns was a competitive and cultured full-back who prided himself on his fitness. Playing 36 games in 1967/68, he was unlucky enough to be squeezed out of the European Cup-winning team by Shay Brennan. Burns' United career was curtailed by persistent cartilage problems, though he continued playing for other teams. Retiring from football in Ireland, he emigrated to Australia in 1987.

Butt: Nicky M 1992-

b. 21.1.1975, Manchester, England • *5ft 10in* • *11st 3lb* • **Clubs** UTD **SU** 8.7.1991 (appr.), 23.1.1993 (pro.) **UD** v Oldham Athletic (sub) (h) 21.11.1992 **FL** 164(42)/gls 19 **FAC** 18(2)/gls 1 **FLC** 5/gls 0 **EUR** 38(11)/gls 2 **T** 225(55)/gls 22 **INT** (England) 14/gls 0

When Alex Ferguson let Paul Ince depart for Italy in the summer of 1995, it was the biggest compliment he could pay to Nicky Butt. At the time Butt had only started 11 games, but Ferguson still believed he could anchor the United midfield, even at the young age of 20. Since then Butt has more than repaid his manager's faith in him, by being part of a United side that has won three Premiership titles, two FA Cups and a European Cup.

Nicky Butt was part of the great 1992 Youth team who were responsible for United's first FA Youth Cup win since 1964. Butt made his first-team debut in November 1992, significantly as a substitute for Paul Ince. He had to wait until the autumn of 1994

for another chance, but since then he has become a regular, and an integral part of United's success. While some of his more glamorous team mates might receive bigger headlines, Nicky Butt has few peers in the middle of the field where the ball needs to be won. Not many opponents get past him.

"He is without doubt one of the bravest players I have ever come across in all my time at Old Trafford," said his youth coach Eric Harrison, "he is the one you want by your side when the going gets tough". Nicky Butt continued in the vein of unsung hero in 1998/99, and only really attracted some attention in September, when he was sent off twice in the space of five days. He formed a new central midfield partnership with David Beckham for the Champions League Final, when Roy Keane and Paul Scholes were both suspended.

In recent seasons, the number of Butt's first-team appearances have been limited due to the successful central midfield partnership of Scholes and Keane, and for United's bigger games, Butt usually has to be satisfied with a place on the substitutes' bench. However, when he is called upon, he rarely lets United down, and during the 2000/01 season, he displayed a notable improvement in form.

Byrne: David F 1933-1934

b. 28.4.1905, Ringsend, Dublin, Rep. of Ireland • *5ft 7in* • *10st 9lb* • **Clubs** St. Brendan's (Dublin), Shamrock Rovers Aug 1926, Bradford City Nov 1927, Shelbourne cs. 1928, Shamrock Rovers 1929, Sheffield Utd Oct-Dec 1932, Shamrock Rovers; UTD; Coleraine Feb 1934, Larne Shamrock Rovers 1935, Hammond Lane FC 1936, Brideville FC 1937, Shelbourne 1938 **SU** May 1933 **UD** v Bury (a) 21.10.1933, scored 1 **FL** 4/gls 3 **T** 4/gls 3 **INT** (Rep. of Ireland) 3/gls 0

Byrne: Roger FB 1951-1958

See p.70.

Cairns: James FB 1894-1895

b. nk **d.** nk • **Clubs** Ardwick FC Mar 1892; NH **SU** Sep 1984 **UD** v Bury (a) 15.4.1895 **FL** 1/gls 0 **T** 1/gls 0

Cairns: James F 1898-1899

b. nk **d.** nk • **Clubs** Stevenston Thistle Jul 1895, Glossop North End, Lincoln City Sep 1897; NH; Berry's Association Nov 1898 **SU** Apr 1898 **UD** v Burslem Port Vale (h) 8.10.1898 **FL** 1/gls 0 **T** 1/gls 0

Campbell: William F 1893-1894

b. nk **d.** nk • **Clubs** Royal Arsenal, Preston North End Dec 1890, Middlesbrough cs. 1891, Darwen May 1892, Blackburn Rovers Aug 1893; NH; Notts County Mar 1894, Newark Oct 1894 **SU** Jan 1894 **UD** v Sheffield Utd (a) 25.11.1893 **FL** 5/gls 1 **T** 5/gls 1

Cantona: Eric F 1992-1997

See p.72.

Cantwell: Noel FB 1960-1967

b. 28.2.1932, Cork, Rep. of Ireland • *6ft* • *13st 3lb* • **Clubs** Western Rovers, Cork Athletic, West Ham Utd Sep 1952; UTD; Coventry City (manager) Oct 1967, Peterborough Utd (manager) Oct 1972-May 1977, New England Tea Men (NASL, coach) 1977-1978, Jacksonville Tea Men (NASL, coach) 1981-1982, Peterborough Utd (manager) Dec 1986 (general manager) 1988-Mar 1989 **SU** Nov 1960 (pro.) **TF** £29,500 **UD** v Cardiff City (a) 26.11.1960 **FL** 123/gls 6 **FAC** 14/gls 2 **EUR** 7/gls 0 **T** 144/gls 8 **INT** (Rep. of Ireland) 36/gls 14

In the wake of the Munich tragedy, Noel Cantwell was a cornerstone of Busby's rebuilding work. He became an inspirational leader in the United teams of the early 1960s and captained the side to victory in the 1963 FA Cup Final. As a player, Cantwell was both strong in the air

continued on p.78

Coppell: Steve **F** 1975–1983 *continued*

director), Feb 1997 (caretaker manager), May 1997 (manager), Manchester City (manager) Oct 1996–Nov 1996, Crystal Palace (manager) Feb 1997–Mar 1998, Jan 1999–Aug 2000, Brentford (manager) May 2001 **SU** Feb 1975 (pro.) **TF** £60,000 **UD** v Cardiff City (sub) (h) 1.3.1975 **FL** 320(2)/gls 54 **FAC** 36/gls 4 **FLC** 25/gls 9 **EUR** 11(1)/gls 3 **T** 392(3)/gls 70 **INT** (England) 42/gls 7

Despite playing professional football for only 10 years, Liverpool-born Steve Coppell made a big impact on the game for both club and country. For almost eight years Coppell was an automatic choice for Manchester United and England, until in 1983 injury robbed the game of the little winger's slick ball skills.

Following an impressive year with Third Division Tranmere Rovers, who he had joined while studying at Liverpool University, Coppell attracted the attentions of Manchester United manager Tommy Docherty. Coppell moved to Old Trafford in early 1975, and soon took over from Willie Morgan at right-wing.

Although Coppell's first full season at United ended in a disappointing 1-0 defeat by Second Division Southampton in the FA Cup Final, United were back at Wembley a year later. This time, in May 1977, United defeated Liverpool 2-1 and Coppell picked up the only Cup winners' medal of his career. He later earned two losers' medals, in the FA Cup in 1979 and the Milk (League) Cup in 1983.

During an England game against Hungary in 1981, Coppell seriously injured his knee in a tackle with Josef Roth. Despite three operations he never regained full fitness, and after struggling for 14 months he was forced to hang up his boots, aged just 28.

Coppell played 206 consecutive League games between 15th January, 1977 and 7th November, 1981, which is still a Manchester United record. The premature end to his career was a huge loss to United and England, who missed the winger's hard work, speed and ability with the ball. Coppell later went on to manage Crystal Palace.

Coupar: Jimmy **F** 1892–1893; 1901–1902

b. dnk, Dundee, Scotland **d.** nk • **Clubs** NH; St. Johnstone 1893–1894, Rotherham Town Oct 1894, Luton Town Jun 1897, Swindon Town 1898–1899, Linfield Aug 1899, Swindon Town 1899–1900; NH Sep 1901–cs. 1902 **SU** Jun 1892; Sep 1901 **UD** v Blackburn Rovers (a) 3.9.1892, scored 1 **FL** 32/gls 9 **TM** 2/gls 1 **T** 34/gls 10

Coyne: Peter **F** 1975–1976

b. 13.11.1958, Hartlepool, England • *5ft 9in* • *10st 7lb* • **Clubs** UTD; Ashton Utd Mar 1977, Crewe Alexandra Aug 1977, Hyde Utd cs. 1981, Swindon Town Aug 1984 (on loan to Aldershot Aug 1989), Colne Dynamos, Glossop, Radcliffe Borough **SU** Mar 1975 (appr.), Nov 1975 (pro.) **UD** v Leicester City (a) 24.4.1976, scored 1 **FL** 1(1)/gls 1 **T** 1(1)/gls 1

Craig: T. **F** 1889–1891

b. nk **d.** nk • **Clubs** Newton Heath LYR **SU** Dec 1889 **UD** v Preston North End (a) FAC 1, 18.1.1890, scored 1 **FAC** 2/gls 1 **T** 2/gls 1

Craven: Charlie **F** 1938–1939

b. 2.12.1909, Boston, England **d.** 30.3.1972 • *5ft 9in* • *10st 11lb* • **Clubs** Boston Trinity, Boston Town, Boston Utd, Grimsby Town May 1930; UTD; Tamworth Jun 1939 (WW2: Birmingham, Coventry City), Sutton Town cs. 1951 **SU** Jun 1938 **UD** v Middlesbrough (a) 27.8.1938 **FL** 11/gls 2 **T** 11/gls 2

Crerand: Pat **HB** 1962–1971

See left.

Crompton: Jack **GK** 1946–1956

b. 18.12.1921, Newton Heath, Manchester, England • *5ft 9in* • *11st 2lb* • **Clubs** Newton Heath Loco, Goslings FC, Oldham Athletic am. 1942–1943, Manchester City am. 1944; UTD (WW2: Stockport County); Luton Town (trainer) Oct 1956; UTD (trainer) Feb 1958; Luton Town (manager) summer 1962, Barrow (manager) 1971–1972, Bury (coach), Preston North End (asst. manager) May 1973; UTD (Reserve team trainer) 1974–1981 **SU** Jun 1944 (am.), Jan 1945 (pro.) **UD** v Grimsby Town (h) 31.8.1946 **FL** 191/gls 0 **FAC** 20/gls 0 **T** 211/gls 0

In the late '40s the solid figure of John (Jack) Crompton was a regular sight between the United goal posts. He came to United as an amateur from Oldham Athletic in 1944 and, although never a spectacular athlete, he was courageous and reliable. Matt Busby made him a staple of his post-war team. Crompton's most memorable flash of brilliance was in the 1948 Cup Final even though he had secretly had a back operation two days previously. Ten minutes from time, with the score at 2-2, he deflected a goal-bound header from Blackpool's Mortensen, and United went on to win with two more goals.

In 1950 Crompton lost his place to Reg Allen, bought from QPR. He regained it briefly in 1952/3 when Allen dropped out of the team, but by this time Old Trafford was buzzing with the advent of the Busby Babes, and Crompton's generation was gradually being replaced. Once Ray Wood staked his claim in goal, Jack Crompton's playing days were over. His one and only appearance of 1955/56, against Huddersfield Town on 22nd October, 1955, was his last for the club. He moved to a coaching post at Luton, but in the wake of the Munich air disaster he returned to Old Trafford as Jimmy Murphy's assistant and trainer to the decimated squad. Crompton was a tirelessly positive figure who did much to bolster the team, and he performed his duties with exemplary commitment until well after Busby's return. Crompton moved on to manage Barrow, and subsequently to assist Bobby Charlton at Preston North End, before reappearing at Old Trafford as Reserve team trainer, under Tommy Docherty.

Crooks: Garth **F** 1983–1984

b. 10.3.1958, Stoke-on-Trent, England • *5ft 8in* • *11st 2lb* • **Clubs** Stoke City Jul 1974 pro. Mar 1976, Tottenham Hotspur Jul 1980 (on loan to UTD), West Bromwich Albion Aug 1985, Charlton Athletic Mar 1987–Nov 1990 **SU** Nov 1983 **UD** v Watford (h) 19.11.1983 **FL** 6(1)/gls 2 **T** 6(1)/gls 2

Crowther: Stan **HB** 1957–1958

b. 3.9.1935, Bilston, Wolverhampton, England • *6ft 2in* • *13st 2lb* • **Clubs** West Bromwich Albion am., Bilston Town 1952, Aston Villa Aug 1955; UTD; Chelsea Dec 1958, Brighton & Hove Albion Mar 1961, Rugby Town Aug 1965, Hednesford Town cs. 1967 **SU** Feb 1958 **TF** £18,000 **UD** v Sheffield Wednesday (h) FAC 5, 19.2.1958 **FL** 13/gls 0 **FAC** 5/gls 0 **EUR** 2/gls 0 **T** 20/gls 0

Tough-tackling wing half-back Stanley Crowther spent only 10 months with United, as an emergency signing following the Munich air crash. Reluctantly leaving FA Cup holders Aston Villa, Crowther signed only one hour before his United debut in the club's emotional first game after the tragedy. An FA Cup runner-up in May, he was sold to Chelsea in December after losing his place to Wilf McGuinness.

Cruyff: Jordi **M** 1996–2000

b. 9.2.1974, Amsterdam, Holland • *6ft* • *11st* • **Clubs** Ajax (Holland, trainee), Barcelona (Spain); UTD (on loan to Celta Vigo); CD Alaves Jul 2000 **SU** 9.8.1996 (pro.) **TF** £1.5 million **UD** v Wimbledon (a) 17.8.1996 **FL** 15(19)/gls 8 **FAC** 0(1)/gls 0 **FLC** 5/gls 0 **EUR** 4(7)/gls 0 **CWC** 1(1)/gls 0 **T** 25(27)/gls 8 **INT** (Holland) 9/gls 1

Jordi Cruyff was at Old Trafford for the most successful era in Manchester United's history, but sadly for him, he played a very minor role in it all. In four seasons at United, Cruyff played in only 57 games, and was eligible for just one winners medal from the five trophies United won while he was there. The son of the Dutch legend, Johan Cruyff, Jordi enjoyed a good start to his United career after signing from Barcelona in the summer of 1996, but he soon found himself on the substitutes' bench and in the treatment room. At the end of the 1998/99 season he went out on loan to Spanish club Celta Vigo, before leaving United for another Spanish club, Alaves, in the summer of 2000. It was here that he began to revive his career, reaching the UEFA Cup final in May 2001.

Culkin: Nick **GK** 1999–

b. 6.7.1978, York, England • *6ft 3in* • *12st 13lb* • **Clubs** York City; UTD (on loan to Hull City for 4 league games 1999-2000 and to Bristol Rovers 2000-01) **SU** 1995 (appr.), 25.9.95 (pro.) **TF** £100,000 **UD** v Arsenal (a) 22.8.1999 **FL** (1)/gls 0 **T** (1)/gls 0

Cunningham: John **F** 1898–1899

b. dnk, Glasgow, Scotland **d.** nk • **Clubs** Benburb GC, Burnley Nov 1889, Glasgow Hibernian Dec 1889, Celtic 1890, Partick Thistle 1892, Heart of Midlothian Oct 1892, Rangers 1892, Glasgow Thistle Mar 1893, Preston North End Sep 1893, Sheffield Utd May 1897, Aston Villa Jun 1898; NH; Wigan County 1899, Barrow Aug 1901 **SU** Oct 1898 **UD** v Grimsby Town (h) 5.11.1898 **FL** 15/gls 2 **FAC** 2/gls 0 **T** 17/gls 2

Cunningham: Laurie **F** 1982–1983

b. 8.3.1956, London, England **d.** 15.8.1989 • *5ft 8in* • *11st* • **Clubs** Orient appr. Aug 1972, pro. Jul 1974, West Bromwich Albion Mar 1977, Real Madrid (Spain) Jul 1979; UTD (on loan) Mar–May 1983; Sporting Gijon (Spain) Aug 1983, Olympique Marseilles (France) Aug 1984 (on loan to Leicester City Oct 1985–May 1986), Rayo Vallecano (Spain) Aug 1986, RSC Charleroi (Belgium) Oct 1987, Wimbledon Feb 1988, Rayo Vellecano (Spain) Aug 1988 until his death **SU** Mar 1983 (pro.) **UD** v Norwich City (a) 30.4.1983 **FL** 3(2)/gls 1 **T** 3(2)/gls 1 **INT** (England) 6/gls 0

Laurence (Laurie) Cunningham was England's first black international footballer when he played for the Under-21 side in 1977. A European Cup runner-up with Real Madrid in 1981, he livened up United's attack in a two-month loan period, showing off his speed and close ball control. Laurie Cunningham died tragically in a car crash in Spain, a year after winning the FA Cup with Wimbledon.

Curry: Joe **HB** 1908–1911

b. 1887, Newcastle upon Tyne, England **d.** nk • *5ft 9in* • *11st 10lb* • **Clubs** Scotswood FC; UTD; Southampton Apr 1911–cs. 1912, West Stanley Jul 1913 **SU** Feb 1908 **UD** v Bradford City (h) 21.11.1908 **FL** 13/gls 0 **FAC** 1/gls 0 **T** 14/gls 0

Curtis: John **D** 1997–2000

b. 3.9.1978, Nuneaton, England • *5ft 10in* • *11st 7lb* • **Clubs** Utd (on loan to Barnsley), Blackburn Rovers Jun 2000 **SU** 10.7.95 (appr.), 23.9.95 (pro.) **UD** v Ipswich Town (a) FLC (3), 14.10.97 **FL** 4(9)/gls 0 **EUR** 0 **FAC** 0 **FLC** 5/gls 0 **T** 9(9)/gls 0

Dale: Billy **FB** 1928–1931

b. 17.2.1905, Manchester, England **d.** 1987 • *5ft 9.5in* • *10st 4lb* • **Clubs** Sandbach Ramblers; UTD; Manchester City Dec 1931, Ipswich Town May 1938, Norwich City Apr 1940 **SU** Apr 1925 (am.), May 1926 (pro.) **UD** v Leicester City (h) 25.8.1928 **FL** 64/gls 0 **FAC** 4/gls 0 **T** 68/gls 0

Dale: Herbert **F** 1890–1891

b. 1867, Stoke-on-Trent, England **d.** 1925 • **Clubs** Manchester FA; Newton Heath LYR **SU** 1887 **UD** v Bootle (a) FAC 2Q, 25.10.1890 **FL** 1/gls 0 **FAC** 1/gls 0 **T** 2/gls 0

Dale: Joe **F** 1947–1948

b. 3.7.1921, Northwich, England • **Clubs** Witton Albion; UTD; Port Vale Apr 1948, Witton Albion Oct 1948, Northwich Victoria (asst. manager) cs. 1959 **SU** Jun 1947 **UD** v Preston North End (a) 27.9.1947 **FL** 2/gls 0 **T** 2/gls 0

Dalton: Ted **FB** 1907–1908

b. nk **d.** nk • **Clubs** Pendlebury FC; UTD; Pendlebury FC Aug 1908, St. Helens Recs cs. 1909 **SU** Sep 1905 (am.), Jan 1906 (pro.) **UD** v Liverpool (a) 25.3.1908 **FL** 1/gls 0 **T** 1/gls 0

Daly: Gerry **M** 1973–1977

b. 30.4.1954, Cabra, Dublin, Rep. of Ireland • *5ft 9in* • *10st 1lb* • **Clubs** Bohemians; UTD; Derby County Mar 1977 (on loan to New England Tea Men May 1978 and May 1979), Coventry City Aug 1980 (on loan to Leicester City Jan 1983), Birmingham City Aug 1984, Shrewsbury Town Oct 1985, Stoke City Mar 1987, Doncaster Rovers Jul 1988, Telford Utd (player/asst. manager) Dec 1989 (manager) Jul 1990–1993 **SU** Apr 1973 (pro.) **TF** £20,000 **UD** v Arsenal (a) 25.8.1973 **FL** 107(4)/gls 23 **FAC** 9(1)/gls 5 **FLC** 17/gls 4 **EUR** 4/gls 0 **T** 137(5)/gls 32 **INT** (Rep. of Ireland) 48/gls 13

Gerard Daly's first season had an unhappy ending when United were relegated to Division Two. The energetic midfielder then aided the team's return to the top division and also their run to the 1976 FA Cup Final. Daly was a reliable penalty-taker for United with only one miss in 17, and a key player for Eire in an international career that spanned 14 years.

Davenport: Peter **F** 1985–1989

b. 24.3.1961, Birkenhead, England • *5ft 10in* • *11st 3lb* • **Clubs** Cammell Laird FC, Everton am., Nottingham Forest Jan 1982; UTD; Middlesbrough Nov 1988, Sunderland Jul 1990, Airdrieonians cs. 1993, St. Johnstone 1994, Stockport County 1995, Southport 1995 (asst. manager 1996), Macclesfield Town Jan 1997 (player-coach summer 1997, manager Jan–Dec 2000) **SU** Mar 1986 (pro.) **TF** £570,000 **UD** v Queen's Park Rangers (a) 15.3.1986 **FL** 72(19)/gls 22 **FAC** 2(2)/gls 0 **FLC** 8(2)/gls 4 **T** 82(23)/gls 26 **INT** (England) 1/gls 0

Released by Everton as an amateur, Peter Davenport scored prolifically enough for Nottingham Forest to earn an England cap against Eire in 1986. Despite finishing as Manchester United's top scorer with 14 in his first full season, 1986/87, Davenport moved on when Mark Hughes returned from Barcelona. An FA Cup runner-up with Sunderland in 1992, he scored his 100th English League goal in May 1998, for Macclesfield Town at Exeter City.

Davidson: Will **HB** 1893–1895

b. nk **d.** nk • **Clubs** Annbank; NH **SU** Jul 1893 **UD** v Burnley (h) 2.9.1893 **FL** 40/gls 2 **TM** 1/gls 0 **FAC** 3/gls 0 **T** 44/gls 2

Davies: Alan **F** 1981–1984

b. 5.12.1961, Manchester, England **d.** 4.2.1992 • *5ft 8in* • *11st 8lb* • **Clubs** UTD; Newcastle Utd Jul 1985 (on loan to Charlton Athletic Mar 1986 and to Carlisle Utd Nov 1986), Swansea City Aug 1987, Bradford City Jun 1989, Swansea City Aug 1990 until his death **SU** Jul 1978 (appr.), Dec 1978 (pro.) **UD** v Southampton (h) 1.5.1981 **FL** 6(1)/gls 0 **FAC** 2/gls 0 **EUR** 0(1)/gls 1 **T** 8(2)/gls 1 **INT** (Wales) 11/gls 0

Welsh international winger Alan Davies managed to win an FA Cup medal in 1983 and scored in the European Cup Winners' Cup semi-final against Juventus the following year. He was a fine dribbler but never a regular, even when Steve Coppell retired through injury. He was on Swansea's books when, tragically, he committed suicide in his car in 1992.

Davies: Joe **HB** 1886–1890

b. 1865, Cefn Mawr, nr. Wrexham, Wales **d.** 7.10.1943 • **Clubs** Druids; Newton Heath LYR; Wolverhampton Wanderers Aug 1890, Druids 1894–1895 **SU** 1886 **UD** v Fleetwood Rangers (a) FAC 1, 30.10.1886 **FAC** 2/gls 0 **T** 2/gls 0 **INT** (Wales) 7/gls 0

Davies: John **GK** 1892–1893

b. nk **d.** nk • **Clubs** NH **SU** Jul 1892 **UD** v Nottingham Forest (h) 14.1.1893 **FL** 7/gls 0 **TM** 2/gls 0 **FAC** 1/gls 0 **T** 10/gls 0

Davies: L. **F** 1886–1887

b. nk **d.** nk • **Clubs** Newton Heath LYR **SU** 1886 **UD** v Fleetwood Rangers (a) FAC 1, 30.10.1886 **FAC** 1/gls 0 **T** 1/gls 0

Davies: Ron **F** 1974–1975

b. 25.5.1942, Holywell, Wales • *6ft* • *11st 6lb* • **Clubs** Chester Jul 1959, Luton Town Oct 1962, Norwich City Sep 1963, Southampton Aug 1966, Portsmouth April 1973; UTD (on loan to Arcadia Shepherds, South Africa, Mar 1975, and to Millwall Nov 1975); Los Angeles Aztecs (USA) Apr 1976, Dorchester Town Sep 1976, Los Angeles Aztecs (USA) Apr 1977, Tulsa Roughnecks (USA) Jul 1978, Seattle Sounders (USA) Apr–Aug 1979, White Horse (Ampfield) 1982, Totton FC Apr 1982 **SU** Nov 1974 (pro.) **TF** £25,000 **UD** v Sunderland (sub) (h) 30.11.1974 **FL** 0(8)/gls 0 **FAC** 0(2)/gls 0 **T** 0(10)/gls 0 **INT** (Wales) 29/gls 8

Davies: Simon **M** 1994–1996

b. 23.4.1974, Middlewich, England • *6ft* • *11st 11lb* • **Clubs** UTD (on loan to Exeter City 1993 and to Huddersfield Town 1996), Luton Town Aug 1997, Macclesfield Town Dec 1998, Rochdale Aug 2000–Jun 2001 **SU** 9.7.1990 (appr.), 1.7.1992 (pro.) **UD** v Port Vale (a) FLC 2, 1st leg, 21.9.1994 **FL** 4(7)/gls **FLC** 4(2)/gls 0 **EUR** 2(1)/gls 1 **T** 10(10)/gls 1 **INT** (Wales) 1/gls 0

Davies: Wyn **F** 1972–1973

b. 20.3.1942, Caernarfon, Wales • *6ft 2in* • *12st 5lb* • **Clubs** Llanberis FC, Caernarfon Town 1959, Wrexham Apr 1960, Bolton Wanderers Mar 1962, Newcastle Utd Oct 1966, Manchester City Aug 1971; UTD; Blackpool Jun 1973 (on loan to Crystal Palace Aug 1973), Stockport County Aug 1975, Arcadia Shepherds (South Africa), Crewe Alexandra Aug 1976, Bangor City Aug 1978 **SU** Sep 1972 (pro.) **TF** £25,000 **UD** v Derby County (h) 23.9.1972, scored 1 **FL** 15(1)/gls 4 **FAC** 1/gls 0 **T** 16(1)/gls 4 **INT** (Wales) 34/gls 7

Dawson: Alex **F** 1957–1961

b. 21.2.1940, Aberdeen, Scotland • *5ft 10in* • *13st 6lb* • **Clubs** UTD; Preston North End Oct 1961, Bury Mar 1967, Brighton & Hove Albion Dec 1968 (on loan to Brentford Sep–Nov 1970), Corby Town Jul 1971–1973 **SU** Mar 1957 (pro.) **UD** v Burnley (h) 22.4.1957, scored 1 **FL** 80/gls 45 **FAC** 10/gls 8 **FLC** 3/gls 1 **T** 93/gls 54

Capped by England as a schoolboy, Alexander Dawson won two FA Youth Cups with Manchester United. At senior level, he was a fearsome forward who averaged more than one goal per two League matches. An FA Cup runner-up with United in 1958 and Preston in 1964, he scored a semi-final hat-trick against Fulham in 1958.

Dean: Harold **F** 1931–1932

b. dnk, Hulme, Manchester, England **d.** nk **Clubs** Old Trafford FC; UTD; Mossley Dec 1931 **SU** Sep 1931 (am.), **UD** v Chesterfield (h) 26.9.1931 **FL** 2/gls 0 **T** 2/gls 0

Delaney: Jimmy **F** 1946–1951

b. 3.9.1914, Cleland, nr. Motherwell, Scotland **d.** 26.9.1989 • *5ft 8.5in* • *12st* • **Clubs** Celtic Sep 1933; UTD; Aberdeen Nov 1950, Falkirk Dec 1951, Derry City Jan 1954, Cork Athletic (player-manager) 1955–1956, Elgin City 1956 until his retirement in Apr 1957 **SU** Feb 1946 (pro.) **TF** £4,000 **UD** v Grimsby Town (h) 31.8.1946 **FL** 164/gls 25 **FAC** 19/gls 3 **T** 183/gls 28 **INT** (Scotland) 13/gls 3

James Delaney was the first player that Matt Busby brought to United from another club. He had been playing for Celtic, with whom he had won two Scottish League championships and one Scottish Cup. Primarily a goal creator, the nippy winger's tendency to move inside with menace brought him a healthy number of goals of his own, including 79 goals in 178 matches for Celtic. Nicknamed "Brittle Bones" after a series of injuries in Scotland, Jimmy Delaney rarely missed a match with Manchester United. He helped Busby's first great side to win the FA Cup in 1948 and finish second in the League in 1947, 1948, 1949 and 1951.

Leaving the club at his own request midway through the 1950/51 season, Delaney rounded off his career in Ireland. In 1954, aged 40, he completed a unique hat-trick of English, Scottish and Irish Cup winners' medals when he won the FAI Cup with Derry City. Jimmy Delaney's international career with Scotland spanned 12 years, and included two appearances in wartime matches.

Dempsey: Mark **M** 1985–1986

b. 14.1.1964, Manchester, England • *5ft 8in* • *9st 12lb* • **Clubs** UTD (on loan to Swindon Town Jan–Feb 1985, and to Sheffield Utd Aug 1986); Sheffield Utd Sep 1986 (on loan to Chesterfield Sep 1988), Rotherham Utd Oct 1988, Macclesfield Town cs. 1991 **SU** May 1980 (appr.), Jan 1982 (pro.) **UD** v Ipswich Town (h) 7.12.1985 **FL** 1/gls 0 **EUR** 0(1)/gls 0 **T** 1(1)/gls 0

Denman: J. **FB** 1891–1892

b. nk **d.** nk • **Clubs** Newton Heath LYR **SU** Mar 1891 **UD** v Blackpool (h) FAC 4Q, 5.12.1891 **FAC** 1/gls 0 **T** 1/gls 0

Dennis: Billy **FB** 1923–1924

b. 21.9.1896, Mossley, nr. Oldham, England **d.** nk • *5ft 9in* • *12st* • **Clubs** Ashton PSA, Army football (WW1: Birkenhead Comets and Tranmere Rovers), Stalybridge Celtic 1918, Blackburn Rovers May 1919, Stalybridge Celtic Feb 1920; UTD; Chesterfield Feb 1924, Wigan Borough May 1928, Macclesfield May 1930, Hurst Jul 1931, Mossley (trainer) Oct 1934 **SU** May 1923 **UD** v Oldham Athletic (h) 13.10.1923 **FL** 3/gls 0 **T** 3/gls 0

Dewar: Neil **F** 1932–1933

b. 11.11.1908, Lochgilphead, Scotland • *5ft 11in* • *11st 10lb* • **Clubs** Lochgilphead Utd, Third Lanark Oct 1929; UTD; Sheffield Wednesday Dec 1933, Third Lanark Jul 1937 **SU** Feb 1933 **TF** £5,000 **UD** v Preston North End (a) 11.2.1933, scored 1 **FL** 36/gls 14 **T** 36/gls 14 **INT** (Scotland) 3/gls 4

Djordjic: Bojan **M** 1999–

b. 6.2.1982, Belgrade, Yugoslavia • *5ft 10in* • *11st* • **Clubs** Brommapojkarna IF; UTD **SU** 17.2.1999 (pro.) **UD** v Tottenham (a) 19.5.2001 **FL** 0(1)/gls 0 **T** 0(1)/gls 0

Doherty: John **F** 1952–1958

b. 12.3.1935, Manchester, England • *5ft 10in* • *11st 10lb* • **Clubs** UTD; Leicester City Oct 1957, Rugby Town (player-manager) Jul 1958, Altrincham Sep 1958, Hyde Utd (Reserve team trainer) June 1962, Burnley (chief scout) early 1980s **SU** May 1950 (am.), Mar 1952 (pro.) **UD** v Middlesbrough (h) 6.12.1952 **FL** 25/gls 7 **FAC** 1/gls 0 **T** 26/gls 7

John Doherty was a highly promising and intelligent young footballer when he joined United. Able to use both feet and boasting a powerful shot, Doherty scored four times in 16 games in the championship-winning season of 1955/56. Persistent knee problems stopped him fulfilling his potential with Manchester United or any subsequent team, and he retired from football prematurely at 23 years of age.

Donaghy: Bernard **F** 1905–1906

b. dnk, Londonderry, Ireland **d.** nk • *5ft 4in* • *10st 10lb* • **Clubs** Derry Celtic; UTD; Derry Celtic Aug 1906, Burnley Jul 1907–1908 **SU** Nov 1905 **UD** v Lincoln City (h) 4.11.1905 **FL** 3/gls 0 **T** 3/gls 0

Donaghy: Mal **D** 1988–1992

b. 13.9.1957, Belfast, N. Ireland • *5ft 11in* • *12st 6lb* • **Clubs** Post Office SC (Belfast), Cromac Albion, Larne Town 1978, Luton Town, Jun 1978; UTD (on loan to Luton Town Dec 1989–Jan 1990); Chelsea Aug 1992–May 1994 **SU** Oct 1988 (pro.) **TF** £650,000 **UD** v Everton (a) 30.10.1988 **FL** 76(13)/gls 0 **FAC** 10/gls 0 **FLC** 10(4)/gls 0 **EUR** 2(3)/gls 0 **T** 98(20)/gls 0 **INT** (N.Ireland) 89/gls 0

Former Gaelic footballer Mal Donaghy was a stalwart in Northern Ireland's defence during the 1980s, playing for them in the World Cups of 1982 and 1986. His fitness and consistency persuaded United to sign him at 31 as a central defensive partner for Steve Bruce, but he later switched to full-back. The signing of Paul Parker prompted his departure to Chelsea in 1992.

Donald: Ian **FB** 1972–1973

b. 28.11.1951, Aberdeen, Scotland • *5ft 10in* • *11st 6lb* • **Clubs** UTD; Partick Thistle Jan 1973, Arbroath 1973–1975, Aberdeen (director) 1980 (vice-chairman) 1986 (chairman) 1994 **SU** May 1968 (am.), Jul 1969 (pro.) **UD** v Portsmouth (h) FLC 3, 7.10.1970 **FL** 4/gls 0 **FLC** 2/gls 0 **T** 6/gls 0

Donaldson: Bob **F** 1892–1898

b. nk **d.** nk • *5ft 8in* • *12st 10lb* • **Clubs** Airdrieonians, Blackburn Rovers May 1891; NH; Luton Town Dec 1897, Glossop North End Aug 1898, Ashford 1899–1900 **SU** May 1892 (pro.) **UD** v Blackburn Rovers (a) 3.9.1892, scored 1 **FL** 131/gls 56 **TM** 8/gls 0 **FAC** 16/gls 10 **T** 155/gls 66

Robert Donaldson made history when he scored on his Newton Heath debut. It was the club's first-ever goal in the Football League, but the joy was short-lived because they lost the match at Blackburn 3–4 and eventually finished bottom of the table. A popular and powerful player, Bob Donaldson also scored Newton Heath's first League hat-trick.

Donnelly: (no initial known) **F** 1890–1891

b. nk **d.** nk • **Clubs** Newton Heath LYR **SU** 1890 **UD** v Bootle Reserves (a) FAC 2Q, 25.10.1890 **FAC** 1/gls 0 **T** 1/gls 0

Donnelly: Tony **FB** 1908–1913

b. 1886, Middleton, Manchester, England **d.** 1947 • *5ft 9.5in* • *11st 10lb* • **Clubs** Army football, Heywood Utd; UTD; Heywood Utd 1911–1912, Glentoran Jul 1913, Heywood Utd Oct 1913, Chester May 1914, Southampton Sep 1919, Middleton Borough Nov 1919 **SU** Jul 1908 **UD** v Sunderland (h) 15.3.1909 **FL** 34/gls 0 **FAC** 3/gls 0 **T** 37/gls 0

Dougan: Tommy **F** 1938–1939

b. dnk, Holytown, Motherwell, Scotland **d.** nk • *5ft 6.5in* • *9st 10lb* • **Clubs** Tunbridge Wells Rangers, Plymouth Argyle Dec 1936; UTD; Heart of Midlothian Sep 1940, Kilmarnock Feb 1946, Dunfermline Athletic Apr 1946 **SU** Mar 1939 **TF** £4,000 **UD** v Everton (h) 29.3.1939 **FL** 4/gls 0 **T** 4/gls 0

Doughty: Jack **F** 1886–1892

b. 1865, Bilston, England **d.** 1937 • **Clubs** Druids 1882; Newton Heath LYR **SU** 1886 (pro.) **UD** v Fleetwood Rangers (a) FAC 1, 30.10.1886, scored 2 **FAC** 3/gls 3 **T** 3/gls 3 **INT** (Wales) 8/gls 0

Doughty: Roger **HB** 1889–1892

b. 1868, Cannock Chase, Birmingham, England **d.** 19.12.1914 • **Clubs** Druids; Newton Heath LYR; Fairfield FC 1893, West Manchester 1894; NH 1896–1897 **SU** 1886 **UD** v Preston North End (a) FAC 1, 18.1.1890 **TM** 3/gls 0 **FAC** 5/gls 1 **T** 8/gls 1 **INT** (Wales) 2/gls 2

Douglas: William **GK** 1893–1896

b. dnk, Dundee, Scotland **d.** nk • **Clubs** Ardwick May 1890; NH; Derby County Feb 1896, Blackpool Jun 1896, Warmley FC 1898–1899, Dundee Aug 1899 **SU** Jan 1894 **UD** v Aston Villa (a) 3.2.1894 **FL** 55/gls 0 **TM** 1/gls 0 **FAC** 1/gls 0 **T** 57/gls 0

Dow: John **FB** 1893–1896

b. 1873, Dundee, Scotland **d.** nk **Clubs** Dundee FC; NH; Fairfield cs. 1897–Oct 1897, Glossop North End, Luton Town Sep 1898, Middlesbrough May 1900, West Ham Utd 1902–1903, Luton Town 1903–1905 **SU** Feb 1894 **UD** v Bolton Wanderers (h) 24.3.1894 **FL** 48/gls 6 **TM** 1/gls 0 **FAC** 1/gls 0 **T** 50/gls 6

Downie: Alex **HB** 1902–1910

b. 1876, Dunoon, Scotland **d.** 9.12.1953 • *5ft 9in* • *12st 4lb* • **Clubs** Glasgow Perthshire, Third Lanark Oct 1898, Bristol City season 1899–1900, Swindon Town Aug 1900; UTD; Oldham Athletic Oct 1909, Crewe Alexandra (player-coach) 1911–1912, Old Chorltonians (coach) **SU** Oct 1902 **UD** v Leicester Fosse (a) 22.11.1902, scored 1 **FL** 172/gls 12 **FAC** 19/gls 2 **T** 191/gls 14

Alexander Downie joined the club in its first season as Manchester United and he scored the only goal of his debut game. As part of an ever-changing half-back line he appeared in 22 League and Cup matches in 1902/03. It was only when the club signed Alex Bell and Charlie Roberts that the midfield positions really settled down. With them, Downie formed the first-choice trio in 1904/05 when United finished third in Division Two. His creative thinking and hard work helped them to clinch promotion the following season, when they finished second to his old club, Bristol City. Downie played the first half of the 1906/07 season in Division One but then lost his regular place to Dick Duckworth. An occasional deputy in the championship season of 1907/08, Downie missed out on the 1909 FA Cup triumph and was sold to Oldham Athletic later that year. He captained Oldham to promotion from Division Two in 1909/10.

Downie: John **F** 1948–1953

b. 19.7.1925, Lanark, Scotland • *5ft 9in* • *11st 10lb* • **Clubs** Lanark ATC, Bradford City am. Aug 1942, pro. Dec 1944; UTD; Luton Town Aug 1953, Hull City Jul 1954, King's Lynn Jul 1955, Mansfield Town Oct 1958, Darlington May 1959, Hyde Utd Jul 1960, Mossley cs. 1961, Stalybridge Celtic 1961–1962 **SU** Mar 1949 (pro.) **TF** £18,000 **UD** v Charlton Athletic (a) 5.3.1949, scored 1 **FL** 110/gls 35 **FAC** 5/gls 1 **T** 115/gls 36

John Downie became United's most expensive player when they signed him to replace Johnny Morris. Settling in well with two goals in his first two games, Downie justified the fee by helping the team to finish strongly as League runners-up. Three years later he contributed 11 goals to the team's cause as they won the 1951/52 League championship.

Draycott: Billy **HB** 1896–1899

b. 15.2.1869, Newhall, Derby, England **d.** nk • *5ft 7in* • *12st 3lb* • **Clubs** Stoke Sep 1889, Burton Wanderers Jun 1894; NH; Bedminster 1899, Bristol Rovers 1900, Wellingborough 1901, Luton Town 1902–1903 **SU** May 1896 **UD** v Gainsborough Trinity (h) 1.9.1896 **FL** 81/gls 6 **TM** 4/gls 0 **FAC** 10/gls 0 **T** 95/gls 6

Dublin: Dion **F** 1992–1994

b. 22.4.1969, Leicester, England • *6ft 2in* • *13st 7lb* • **Clubs** Oakham Utd, Norwich City Mar 1988, Cambridge Utd Aug 1988; UTD; Coventry City 1994, Aston Villa Nov 1998 **SU** 7.8.1992 (pro.) **TF** £1 million **UD** v Southampton (a) 24.8.1992, scored 1 **FL** 4(8)/gls 2 **FAC** 1(1)/gls 0 **FLC** 1(1)/gls 1 **EUR** 0(1)/gls 0 **T** 6(11)/gls 3 **INT** (England) 3/gls 0

Dion Dublin had mixed fortunes in his first month at Manchester United. Having scored in his debut game at Southampton, he broke his leg in his third game, against Crystal Palace. With Eric Cantona signing during his absence, Dion never regained a regular place in the team. He enjoyed more luck with Coventry City and then Aston Villa, who paid £5.75 million for his services in 1998.

Duckworth: Dick **HB** 1903–1914

b. dnk, Collyhurst, Manchester, England **d.** nk • *5ft 8in* • *11st 5lb* • **Clubs** Stretford FC, NH Athletic; UTD **SU** Oct 1903 (pro.) **UD** v Gainsborough Trinity (h) 19.12.1903, scored 1 **FL** 225/gls 11 **FAC** 26/gls 0 **T** 251/gls 11

Richard (Dick) Duckworth was a professional centre-forward on 7s. 6d. a week (today worth about £18) when he signed for United. Successfully switching to right half-back,

KEY: **a**=away **am.**=amateur **appr.**=apprentice **b.**=born **c.**=circa **cs.**=close season **CWC**=Club World Championship **D**=Defender **d.**=died **dnk**=date not known **EUR**=European competitions **F**=Forward **FAC**=FA Cup **FB**=Full-back (defender) **FL**=Football League **FLC**=Football League Cup **GK**=Goalkeeper **gls**=goals **h**=home **HB**=Half-back (midfield) **INT**=International matches **M**=Midfield **NH**=Newton Heath **Newton Heath LYR**=Newton Heath Lancashire & Yorkshire Railway **nk**=not known **pro.**=professional **Q**=qualifying round **SU**=signed for United **sub**=substitute; substitute apps are in brackets after appearances **T**=total **TF**=transfer fee **TM**=Test match **U**=Utility **UD**=United debut **UTD**=Manchester United **v**=versus

Duckworth joined Charlie Roberts and Alex Bell in a formidable midfield trio for United. After helping the club to win the League championship in 1908 and 1911 and the FA Cup in 1909, Duckworth retired in 1913.

Dunn: William **F** 1897–1898

b. dnk, Middlesbrough, England **d.** nk • **Clubs** South Bank; NH **SU** May 1897 **UD** v Lincoln City (h) 4.9.1897 **FL** 10/gls 0 **FAC** 2/gls 0 **T** 12/gls 0

Dunne: Pat **GK** 1964–1966

b. 9.2.1943, Dublin, Rep. of Ireland • *5ft 11in* • *12st 3lb* • **Clubs** Everton am. Jan 1959, pro. May 1960, Shamrock Rovers cs. 1962; UTD; Plymouth Argyle Feb 1967, Shamrock Rovers Nov 1970 **SU** May 1964 (pro.) **TF** £10,500 **UD** v Everton (a) 8.9.1964 **FL** 45/gls 0 **FAC** 7/gls 0 **FLC** 1/gls 0 **EUR** 13/gls 0 **T** 66/gls 0 **INT** (Rep. of Ireland) 5/gls 0

Dunne: Tony **D** 1960–1973

b. 24.7.1941, Dublin, Rep. of Ireland • *5ft 6.5in* • *10st 9lb* • **Clubs** Shelbourne; UTD; Bolton Wanderers Aug 1973, Detroit Express May–Jul 1979, Bolton Wanderers (coach) 1979–1981, Stenjker (Norway, coach) 1982–1983 **SU** Apr 1960 **TF** £5,000 **UD** v Burnley (a) 15.10.1960 **FL** 414/gls 2 **FAC** 54(1)/gls 0 **FLC** 21/gls 0 **EUR** 40/gls 0 **T** 529(1)/gls 2 **INT** (Rep. of Ireland) 33/gls 0

Patrick Anthony Dunne remains one of the best players ever to wear the number two or three shirt for Manchester United. Quick and brave when tackling, he used the ball simply and effectively whenever he was in possession, rarely giving it away.

Signed initially as cover for Noel Cantwell or Shay Brennan, Tony Dunne deputized for the latter in the 1963 FA Cup Final triumph. Over the next four seasons, he secured a regular place of his own, missing only six League games in all. During that time, United won two League championships in 1965 and 1967, and finished second in 1964. The pinnacle of Dunne's career was the 1968 European Cup run, when he played in every round and produced one of his greatest performances to help United win the Final. Capped as an amateur and a professional by his country, Dunne was voted Irish Footballer of the Year in 1969. Tony Dunne eventually clocked up more than 700 appearances in the game.

Duxbury: Mike **D** 1980–1990

b. 1.9.1959, Accrington, nr. Blackburn, England • *5ft 9in* • *11st 2lb* • **Clubs** UTD; Blackburn Rovers Aug 1990 (on loan to Bradford City Jan 1992), Bradford City Mar 1992, Hong Kong 1994–1996 **SU** Jul 1976 (appr.), Oct 1976 (pro.) **UD** v Birmingham (sub) (a) 23.8.1980 **FL** 274(25)/gls 6 **FAC** 20(5)/gls 1 **FLC** 32(2)/gls 0 **EUR** 17(1)/gls 0 **T** 343(33)/gls 7 **INT** (England) 10/gls 0

First appearing as a substitute in a 0–0 draw at Birmingham, versatile Michael Duxbury could play admirably in several different positions. In the FA Cup triumphs of 1983 and 1985 he peaked as an attacking full-back. Ending his career in Hong Kong with a friendly against England in 1996, he's since worked in Bolton as a P.E. teacher.

Dyer: Jimmy **F** 1905–1906

b. 24.8.1883, Blacker Hill, Barnsley, England **d.** nk • *5ft 10in* • *11st 7lb* • **Clubs** Wombwell FC, Barnsley Sep 1901, Doncaster Rovers 1903–1904, Ashton Town 1904–1905; UTD; West Ham Utd May 1908, Bradford Jul 1909–cs. 1910, Wombwell FC **SU** May 1905 **UD** v West Bromwich Albion (a) 14.10.1905 **FL** 1/gls 0 **T** 1/gls 0

Earp: John **F** 1886–1887

b. nk **d.** nk • **Clubs** Newton Heath LYR **SU** 1884 **UD** v Fleetwood Rangers (a) FAC 1, 30.10.1886 **FAC** 1/gls 0 **T** 1/gls 0

Edge: Alf **F** 1891–1892

b. 1865, Stoke-on-Trent, England **d.** 1941 • **Clubs** Goldenhill Wanderers, Stoke 1884; Newton Heath LYR; Notts Jardines cs. 1892, Stoke Oct 1892, Northwich Victoria Aug 1893, Ardwick Jan–May 1894 **SU** 1981 **UD** v Ardwick FAC 1Q, 3.10.1891 **FAC** 3/gls 3 **T** 3/gls 3

Edmonds: Hugh **GK** 1910–1912

b. 1884, Chryston, Scotland **d.** nk • *5ft 9.5in* • *12st* • **Clubs** Hamilton Academical, Belfast Distillery cs. 1907, Linfield, Bolton Wanderers Oct 1909; UTD; Glenavon (player-manager) cs. 1912, Belfast Distillery May 1913 **SU** Feb 1911 **UD** v Bristol City (h) 11.2.1911 **FL** 43/gls 0 **FAC** 7/gls 0 **T** 50/gls 0

Edwards: Duncan **HB** 1952–1958

See p.84.

Edwards: Paul **D** 1969–1972

b. 7.10.1947, Shaw, Oldham, England • *5ft 10in* • *10st 4lb* • **Clubs** UTD (on loan to Oldham Athletic Sep1972); Oldham Athletic Mar 1973 (on loan to Stockport County during Jan 1977), Stockport County Aug 1978–Jul 1980, Ashton Utd **SU** Dec 1963 (am.), Feb 1965 (pro.) **UD** v Everton (a) 19.8.1969 **FL** 52(2)/gls 0 **FAC** 10/gls 0 **FLC** 4/gls 1 **T** 66(2)/gls 1

Ellis: David **F** 1923–1924

b. 1900, Kirkaldy, Scotland **d.** nk • *5ft 8.5in* • *11st* • **Clubs** Glasgow Ashfield, Airdrieonians 1920, Maidstone Utd May 1922; UTD; St. Johnstone Sep 1924, Bradford City Aug 1926, Arthurlie FC 1928–1929 **SU** Jun 1923 **TF** £1,250 **UD** v Bristol City (a) 25.8.1923 **FL** 11/gls 0 **T** 11/gls 0

Erentz: Fred **FB** 1892–1902

b. 1870, Dundee, Scotland **d.** 6.4.1938 • *5ft 10.5in* • *12st 8lb* • **Clubs** NH **SU** Jun 1892 (pro.) **UD** v Blackburn Rovers (a) 3.9.1892 **FL** 280/gls 9 **TM** 7/gls 0 **FAC** 23/gls 0 **T** 310/gls 9

Fred C. Erentz was a key member of the Newton Heath side that entered the Football League for the first time in 1892. A consistent performer, his coolness under pressure made him the ideal penalty-taker. Despite a handsome financial offer to join his brother Harry at Tottenham, Fred played out his career at Manchester United, retiring through injury in 1902.

Erentz: Harry **FB** 1897–1898

b. 17.9.1874, Dundee, Scotland **d.** 19.7.1947 • *5ft 11in* • *12st 10lb* • **Clubs** Dundee Aug 1895, Oldham County Sep 1896; NH; Tottenham Hotspur May 1898, Swindon Town Dec 1904 until his retirement through injury, later trainer to the Corinthians **SU** May 1897 **UD** v Woolwich Arsenal (a) 8.1.1898 **FL** 6/gls 0 **FAC** 3/gls 0 **T** 9/gls 0

Evans: George **F** 1890–1891

b. nk **d.** nk • **Clubs** Newton Heath LYR **SU** 1890 **UD** v Higher Walton (h) FAC 1Q, 4.10.1890, scored 1 **FAC** 1/gls 1 **T** 1/gls 1

Evans: Sidney **F** 1923–1924

b. dnk, Darlaston, Walsall, England **d.** nk • *5ft 8in* • *11st 6lb* • **Clubs** Darlaston FC, Cardiff City Aug 1920; UTD; Pontypridd Aug 1925 **SU** May 1923 **TF** £ free **UD** v Crystal Palace (h) 12.4.1924 **FL** 6/gls 2 **T** 6/gls 2

Fall: Joe **GK** 1893–1894

b. 1872, Miles Platting, Manchester, England **d.** nk • *5ft 11in* • *12st 6lb* • **Clubs** Middlesbrough Ironopolis; NH; Small Heath May 1895, Altrincham 1896 **SU** Aug 1893 **UD** v Burnley (h) 2.9.1893 **FL** 23/gls 0 **TM** 1/gls 0 **FAC** 3/gls 0 **T** 27/gls 0

Farman: Alf **F** 1889–1895

b. 1869, Kings Norton, Birmingham, England **d.** nk • **Clubs** Birmingham Excelsior, Aston Villa, Bolton Wanderers Apr 1892; Newton Heath LYR **SU** 1889 (am.), Jun 1892 (pro.) **UD** v Blackburn Rovers (a) 3.9.1892 **FL** 51/gls 18 **TM** 3/gls 4 **FAC** 7/gls 6 **T** 61/gls 28

Alfred Farman's association with Newton Heath dates back to the club's amateur days in the Football Alliance, when he netted 25 goals in 60 games. He was equally prolific in the League, memorably scoring a match-winning hat-trick when the club staged its first-ever game at Bank Street, Clayton, on 2nd September, 1893 against Burnley.

Feehan: "Sonny" (John) **GK** 1949–1950

b. 17.9.1926, Dublin, Rep. of Ireland • *5ft 11in* • *12st 6lb* • **Clubs** Bohemians am. 1942, Waterford 1944; UTD; Northampton Town Aug 1950, Brentford Aug 1954–Jun 1959 **SU** Nov 1948 **UD** v Huddersfield Town (h) 5.11.1949 **FL** 12/gls 0 **FAC** 2/gls 0 **T** 14/gls 0

Felton: G. **HB** 1890–1891

b. nk **d.** nk • **Clubs** Newton Heath LYR **SU** Nov 1887 **UD** v Bootle Reserves (a) FAC Q2, 25.10.1890 **FAC** 1/gls 0 **T** 1/gls 0

Ferguson: Danny **F** 1927–1928

b. dnk, Flint, Wales • *5ft 8in* • *11st 2lb* • **Clubs** Rhyl Athletic; UTD; Reading May 1928, Accrington Stanley Jun 1929, Chester Mar 1932, Halifax Town Jul 1933, Stockport County Jul 1935, Macclesfield Jul 1936 **SU** Mar 1927 **UD** v Burnley (h) 7.4.1928 **FL** 4/gls 0 **T** 4/gls 0

Ferguson: Darren **M** 1990–1994

b. 9.2.1972, Glasgow, Scotland • *5ft 10in* • *10st 11lb* • **Clubs** UTD; Wolverhampton Wanderers Jan 1994, Sparta Rotterdam, Wrexham **SU** Jul 1988 (appr.), Jul 1990 (pro.) **UD** v Sheffield Utd (sub) (a) 26.2.1991 **FL** 20(7)/gls 0 **FLC** 2(1)/gls 0 **T** 22(8)/gls 0

Alex Ferguson's son Darren rose through the United ranks, eventually earning a place in his father's team in February 1991, when he came on as a substitute for Neil Webb at Sheffield United. During the early part of the 1992/93 championship season he proved to be skilled at passing the ball. Mainly a left-sided player, Darren's first-team opportunities were limited by Ryan Giggs and Lee Sharpe.

Ferguson: John **F** 1931–1932

b. 1904, Rowlands Gill, nr. Newcastle upon Tyne, England **d.** nk • *5ft 7in* • *11st* • **Clubs** Grimsby Town Oct 1926, Workington Aug 1927, Spen Black & White, Wolverhampton Wanderers Jan 1929, Watford Nov 1929, Burton Town Jul 1930; UTD; Derry City Dec 1931, Gateshead Utd Sep 1934 **SU** May 1931 **UD** v Bradford (a) 29.8.1931 **FL** 8/gls 1 **T** 8/gls 1

Ferrier: Ron **F** 1935–1938

b. 26.4.1914, Cleethorpes, England **d.** 11.10.1991 • *5ft 10.5in* • *11st 6lb* • **Clubs** Grimsby Wanderers, Grimsby Town May 1933; UTD; Oldham Athletic Mar 1938 (WW2: Reading, Grimsby Town, Southampton), Lincoln City Aug 1947, Grimsby Town (junior player-coach) Nov 1949, Lysaghts Sports Scunthorpe (player-coach) Jul 1950 **SU** May 1935 **UD** v Charlton Athletic (h) 4.9.1935 **FL** 18/gls 4 **FAC** 1/gls 0 **T** 19/gls 4

Fielding: Bill **GK** 1946–1947

b. 17.6.1915, Broadhurst, nr. Hyde, Manchester, England • *5ft 11in* • *11st 10lb* • **Clubs** Hurst, Cardiff City May 1936 (WW2: Stockport County, Bolton Wanderers), Bolton Wanderers Jun 1944; UTD **SU** nk **UD** v Nottingham Forest (h) FAC 4, 25.1.1947 **FL** 6/gls 0 **FAC** 1/gls 0 **T** 7/gls 0

Fisher: James **F** 1900–1902

b. dnk, Scotland **d.** nk • **Clubs** East Stirlingshire Jun 1895, St. Bernard FC Edinburgh May 1896, Aston Villa Jul 1897, Kings Park FC; NH **SU** Oct 1900 **UD** v Walsall (h) 20.10.1900 **FL** 42/gls 2 **FAC** 4/gls 1 **T** 46/gls 3

Fitchett: John **FB** 1902–1903; 1904–1905

b. 1874, Chorlton, England **d.** nk • *5ft 10in* • *11st 9lb* • **Clubs** Talbot FC, Bolton Wanderers May 1897, Southampton May 1902; UTD; Plymouth Argyle May 1903; UTD; Fulham May 1905, Sale Holmfield cs. 1906, Barrow Nov 1906, Exeter City Feb 1910 **SU** Mar 1903 and Jun 1904 **UD** v Leicester Fosse (h) 21.3.1903, scored 1 **FL** 16/gls 1 **FAC** 2/gls 0 **T** 18/gls 1

Fitton: Arthur **F** 1931–1932

b. 30.5.1902, Melton Mowbray, Leicester, England **d.** 1984 • *5ft 7in* • *11st* • **Clubs** Kinver FC, Cookley St. Peters, Kidderminster Harriers, West Bromwich Albion Oct 1922; UTD; Preston North End Dec 1932, Coventry May 1935, Kidderminster Harriers, West Bromwich Albion (asst. trainer) Oct 1948–Jul 1950 (senior trainer) Aug 1951–Jun 1956 **SU** Mar 1932 **UD** v Oldham Athletic (h) 26.3.1932, scored 1 **FL** 12/gls 2 **T** 12/gls 2

Fitzpatrick: John **D** 1964–1973

b. 18.8.1946, Aberdeen, Scotland • *5ft 6in* • *9st 12lb* • **Clubs** UTD (ground staff) Sep 1961 **SU** Jul 1962 (appr.), Sep 1963 (pro.) **UD** v Sunderland (a) 24.2.1965 **FL** 111(6)/gls 8 **FAC** 11/gls 1 **FLC** 12/gls 1 **EUR** 7/gls 0 **T** 141(6)/gls 10

An FA Youth Cup winner with United in 1964, John Fitzpatrick was United's first-ever League substitute when he replaced Denis Law at Tottenham on 16th October, 1965. A terrier-like full-back, John's aggressive style earned him an eight-week suspension in 1969. After missing virtually all of season 1971/72 through injury, his arthritic knee joints forced him to retire in 1973.

Fitzsimmons: David **HB** 1895–1896; 1899–1900

b. dnk, Annbank, Ayr, Scotland **d.** nk • **Clubs** Annbank FC; NH; Fairfield FC Aug 1896, Chorley 1897–1898, Wigan County Aug 1898; NH **SU** Jul 1895; Aug 1899 **UD** v Crewe Alexandra (h) 7.9.1895 **FL** 28/gls 0 **FAC** 3/gls 0 **T** 31/gls 0

Fitzsimmons: Tommy **F** 1892–1893

b. 21.10.1870, Annbank, Ayr, Scotland **d.** nk • **Clubs** Annbank FC; NH; Annbank FC 1894, St. Mirren Oct 1894, Annbank FC Nov 1894, Fairfield FC Sep 1895, Glossop North End Mar 1897, Fairfield FC cs. 1897, Oldham County Oct–Nov 1897, Chorley FC, Wigan County Aug 1898, Annbank FC Sep 1899 **SU** Nov 1892 **UD** v Aston Villa (h) 19.11.1892, scored 1 **FL** 27/gls 6 **TM** 2/gls 0 **FAC** 1/gls 0 **T** 30/gls 6

Fletcher: Peter **F** 1972–1973

b. 2.12.1953, Manchester, England • *6ft .5in* • *10st 13lb* • **Clubs** UTD; Hull City May 1973, Stockport County May 1976, Huddersfield Town Jul 1978–Jun 1982 **SU** Aug 1969 (appr.), Dec 1970 (pro.) **UD** v Derby County (a) 16.2.1974 **FL** 2(5)/gls 0 **T** 2(5)/gls 0

Foggon: Alan **F** 1976–1977

b. 23.2.1950, West Pelton, nr. Gateshead, England • *5ft 9in* • *11st* • **Clubs** Newcastle Utd appr. Aug 1965, pro. Nov 1967, Cardiff City Aug 1971, Middlesbrough Oct 1972, Rochester Lancers (NASL) Apr 1976, Hartford Bi-Centennials (NASL) Jun 1976; UTD; Sunderland Sep 1976, Southend Utd Jun 1977 (on loan to Hartlepool Utd Feb 1978), Consett Aug 1978, Whitley Bay **SU** Jul 1976 (pro.) **TF** £40,000 **UD** v Birmingham City (sub) (h) 21.8.1976 **FL** 0(3)/gls 0 **T** 0(3)/gls 0

Foley: G. **F** 1899–1900

b. nk **d.** nk • **Clubs** Ashford FC; NH **SU** Feb 1900 **UD** v Barnsley (h) 17.3.1900 **FL** 7/gls 1 **T** 7/gls 1

Ford: Joe **F** 1908–1910

b. 7.5.1886, Northwich, England **d.** nk • *5ft 9.5in* • *10st 6lb* • **Clubs** Witton Albion, Crewe Alexandra; UTD; Nottingham Forest Jun 1910, Goole Town cs. 1914 **SU** Oct 1907 **UD** v Aston Villa (h) 31.3.1909 **FL** 5/gls 0 **T** 5/gls 0

Forster: Tommy **HB** 1919–1922

b. 1894, Northwich, England **d.** nk • *5ft 6in* • *10st 7lb* • **Clubs** Northwich Victoria; UTD; Northwich Victoria cs. 1922 **SU** Jan 1916 **UD** v Burnley (a) 8.11.1919 **FL** 35/gls 0 **FAC** 1/gls 0 **T** 36/gls 0

Edwards: Duncan HB 1952–1958

b. 1.10.1936, Dudley, Birmingham, England **d.** 21.2.1958 • *5ft 11in* • *13st* • **Clubs** <u>UTD</u> until his death **SU** Jun 1952 (am.), 1.10.53 (pro.) **UD** v Cardiff City (h) 4.4.1953 **FL** 151/gls 20 **FAC** 12/gls 1 **EUR** 12/gls 0 **T** 175/gls 21 **INT** (England) 18/gls 5

It is generally agreed that the best United player of all time was Duncan Edwards. Matt Busby said of the 15-year-old giant that he looked and played like a man. In terms of achievement in football at a young age, he was the Ryan Giggs of his day.

At 16 years and 185 days old, Edwards became the youngest-ever player in the First Division. On making his England debut in the 7–2 win over Scotland in April 1955, aged 18 years and 183 days, he became the youngest England international this century. This record remained unbroken until Liverpool player Michael Owen's debut for England in February 1998.

Edwards went on to score five goals in the 18 games that he played for England, a healthy total for a left-half. The fact that he helped United to win the Youth Cup in the same month as he played his international debut underlines his "Manboy" nickname. Before his untimely death in the Munich tragedy, Edwards had already won three Youth Cups, two League titles and an FA Cup Finalists' medal.

Young colossus

Edwards' talent was first noticed when he was a star of Dudley Boys team. He went on to captain England Schoolboys, and several top clubs scrambled for his signature, but in June 1952 he joined United. Coach Jimmy Murphy did the groundwork in persuading Duncan's parents that he should come to Old Trafford, but Matt Busby clinched the move. Busby didn't have to sell United to Edwards. In his autobiography, Busby recalls, Duncan said: "I think Manchester United is the greatest team in the world. I'd give anything to play for you."

Within a year Edwards made his League debut, the youngest ever to play in the First Division. Frank Taylor, the only survivor among nine British journalists on the Munich plane, went to Edwards' first League game. United had a woeful 1–4 defeat at home to Cardiff that day, and Taylor reported that Edwards was heavily built and might have problems with his weight.

Power and skill

Despite his imposing appearance, Edwards was a gentle, unassuming man. He was well-liked by his team mates, who accepted that he was naturally capable of achieving more than them. The team would warm up by jogging along the sides of the pitch and walking across the ends. Most of them did four circuits, but Duncan Edwards did 10.

At left-back, Edwards usually wore the number six shirt, but he had the ability to play in virtually any position on the field. Wilf McGuinness credits Duncan Edwards' incredible versatility for most of his own early chances in the first team: "I never dreamt I could overtake him, but if Dennis Viollet (forward) or Roger Byrne (left-back) got injured, Duncan could be slotted in these positions and I would get a game. He could play as an attacker, creator or defender and be the best player on the pitch ... Once he was playing for the English League XI against the Scottish League. 2–0 down, Duncan was moved from wing-half to centre-forward. He scored a hat-trick to win the game."

Awesome and accurate
At first sight what set Duncan apart was his size, but he combined awesome power with a feathery touch. "He had legs like tree trunks, like Mark Hughes only bigger," remembers Wilf McGuinness, "but he wasn't all power. If the ball was hit like a bullet at him, he would let it hit his chest and kill it. He could dribble, give short one-twos and then unleash an accurate 50-yard pass."

Edwards v Charles

The only contemporary player who bore comparison with Edwards was Welsh star John Charles. But in a private conversation with Frank Taylor in 1957, Sir Matt Busby told Taylor why he rated Edwards the best player in the world: "He agreed that John Charles was a fantastic player: taller (6ft 2in against 5ft 11in), better in the air and perhaps better on the ball. But the difference was Duncan was always involved. Charles would drift out of games."

Sir Matt Busby's right-hand man Jimmy Murphy was perhaps Duncan's greatest admirer. Once in Murphy's other role as Welsh national team coach, he was delivering his team talk before a game against England. He spoke about each player in turn, highlighting their strengths and weaknesses. As he closed his tactical sermon, a Welsh player piped up: "You haven't mentioned Duncan

Edwards, boss." Murphy replied: "There's nothing to say that would help us."

Of the many talented Busby Babes, Edwards was the natural kingpin. Wilf McGuinness recalls one game that illustrates the point: "Pre-match, Jimmy Murphy was saying to the likes of David Pegg, Bobby Charlton and myself, 'I don't want you to have a Duncan Edwards complex and always pass to him. You're good enough players yourselves.' At half-time it was 0–0 and Jimmy changed his tune. He said, 'Right, this half, as soon as you get the ball, pass it to Duncan!'"

Tragedy

Of the eight Busby Babes killed in the Munich air crash, Edwards' innate strength and unconquerable spirit kept him alive for longest. For 15 days in the Rechts Der Isar hospital, he defied chronic kidney damage, broken ribs, a collapsed lung, a broken pelvis and a smashed right thigh, before his death at 2:16 a.m. on 21st February, 1958.

The greatest?

Sir Bobby Charlton describes Duncan Edwards as "The best player I've ever seen, the best footballer I've ever played with for United or England, the only player who ever made me feel inferior."

> *He is the greatest player of his age I have ever seen. Yet though he has soared up among the stars, his feet are still on the ground.*
> **Sir Matt Busby**

Making his fortune

Edwards supplemented his earnings by appearing in advertisements. When he died, he left approximately £9,000 in his will, a fortune for those days, and the equivalent in modern terms of about £117,630.

Fact file

• **League: youngest-ever**
On 4th April, 1953, Edwards became the youngest-ever footballer to play in the First Division when he made his debut for Manchester United v Cardiff City.

• **England: youngest-ever**
Duncan Edwards became England's youngest-ever debutant, playing against Scotland in April 1955, aged 18 years and 183 days. England won the game, 7–2.

• **Euro star**
Duncan Edwards was third in the European Footballer of the Year poll in 1957, behind Real Madrid's Alfredo di Stefano and fellow England player Billy Wright.

• **Captaining England**
Edwards captained England at both Schoolboy and Under-23 level.

• **Honours**
In his brief career at United, cut short by the Munich disaster, Duncan Edwards won six honours; three Youth Cups, two League titles and an FA Cup Finalists' medal.

KEY: a=away **am.**=amateur **appr.**=apprentice **b.**=born **c.**=circa **cs.**=close season **D**=Defender **d.**=died **dnk**=date not known **EUR**=European competitions **F**=Forward **FAC**=FA Cup **FB**=Full-back (defender) **FL**=Football League **FLC**=Football League Cup **GK**=Goalkeeper **gls**=goals **h**=home **HB**=Half-back (midfield) **INT**=International matches **M**=Midfield **NH**=Newton Heath <u>Newton Heath LYR</u>=Newton Heath Lancashire & Yorkshire Railway **nk**=not known **pro.**=professional **Q**=qualifying round **SU**=signed for United **sub**=substitute; substitute apps are in brackets after appearances **T**=total **TF**=transfer fee **TM**=Test match **U**=Utility **UD**=United debut <u>UTD</u>=Manchester United **v**=versus

This was extraordinary praise for someone who died years before average footballers reach their peak.

In 1957, United had reached the European Cup semi-final and were favourites to win it in 1958. If Edwards had come through Munich unscathed, United would almost certainly have won the European Cup before 1968.

At international level, Duncan was expected to take over the captaincy when Billy Wright retired. Edwards would have been 29 by the time of the 1966 World Cup, and some believe that it would have been him and not Bobby Moore who lifted the Jules Rimet trophy. Bobby Charlton certainly believed that Edwards would have held back Bobby Moore for some time, and Frank Taylor once said that if Duncan Edwards had lived, Bobby Moore would not even have won a cap, because there was no way Edwards would not have been chosen. As Bill Foulkes said: "Duncan had everything, he was powerful, technically as good as anyone, and he could read the game as if he'd been in the game for 30 years even when he was 17. He was a freak to be honest, mature beyond his years. He always behaved in the correct

> *Awesome is a word that is a bit over-used, but it was appropriate in Duncan's case. He had such presence, strength ... an aura.*
> **Sir Bobby Charlton**

way – everything he did was correct. He'd obviously been well-tutored when he was young. He was one of the boys, but he was also a gentleman, the model professional." Wilf McGuinness explains succinctly why Edwards was the greatest-ever United player: "Best, Law and Charlton were world class when they had the ball. Duncan was world class when United had the ball, and when the opposition had the ball he was our best defender. He was complete."

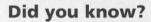

On English soil
Above, Edwards clears the ball from defence in his last game in England, against Arsenal at Highbury on 1st February, 1958. Edwards scored one goal in United's 5–4 win.

> *When I used to hear Muhammad Ali proclaim to the world that he was the greatest, I used to smile. You see, the greatest of them all was an English footballer named Duncan Edwards.*
> **Jimmy Murphy**

Did you know?

- *Edwards once got into trouble with the Manchester police ... for riding a bike with no lights. Matt Busby gave him a telling-off, too, for letting the side down.*
- *German fans gave Edwards the nickname "Boom Boom" after he scored a 25-yarder for England against West Germany in 1955. He struck the ball with such power that their goalkeeper finished in the back of the net with the ball.*
- *Edwards forced his way into the Dudley Boys team, average age 15, when he was just 11 years old.*
- *Edwards once scored six goals in one match, playing at centre-forward for England Under-23s.*

Gentle giant
In playing style, Edwards' nearest modern equivalent is Roy Keane, but Edwards was even bigger than Keane, and more placid.

In memoriam
This stained-glass window memorial to Duncan Edwards is one of two that can be seen at St. Francis' Church in Dudley, Worcestershire, where Edwards was born.

Duncan Edwards: Career timeline

1947
11-year-old Edwards plays for Dudley Boys (average age 15)

1st October, 1953
Signs pro. forms with United on his 17th birthday

February to April 1955
Plays centre-forward in place of injured Dennis Viollet

April 1957
United lose European Cup semi-final to Real Madrid, but win Division One championship

December 1957
Placed third in European Footballer of the Year poll

4th April, 1953
United debut v Cardiff City

April 1954
Wins Youth Cup again, scoring two goals

April 1956
United win Division One championship

1947	1948	1949	1950	1951	1952	1953	1954	1955	1956	1957	1958

June 1952
Joins United as an amateur

April 1953
Wins Youth Cup against Wolves

31st October, 1953
Henry Cockburn loses his first-team place to Edwards v Huddersfield Town

April 1955
Makes England debut. Wins third consecutive Youth Cup with United

26th September, 1956
Edwards' European Cup debut v Anderlecht. United win 10–0

5th February, 1958
Edwards' final game: 3–3 draw v Red Star Belgrade

6th February, 1958
Munich air crash

21st February, 1958
Edwards dies, aged 21 years, 143 days.

Foulkes: Bill **D** 1952–1970

b. 5.1.1932, St. Helens, England • *5ft 11in* • *11st 2lb* • **Clubs** UTD (youth coach) 1970; Chicago Sting (coach) 1975–1977, Tulsa Roughnecks (coach) 1978, Witney Town (manager) 1979–1980, San Jose Earthquakes (coach) 1980, Stenjker (Norway, manager), Lillestrom (Norway, manager), Viking Stavanger (Norway, manager), Mazda (Hiroshima, manager) Dec 1988–Jan 1992 **SU** Mar 1950 (am.), Aug 1951 (pro.) **UD** v Liverpool (a) 13.12.1952 **FL** 563(3)/gls 7 **FAC** 61/gls 0 **FLC** 3/gls 0 **EUR** 52/gls 2 **T** 679 (3)/gls 9 **INT** (England) 1/gls 0

Few players will ever have as long or eventful a Manchester United career as Bill Foulkes. For 18 seasons he was a permanent fixture and a rock at the heart of the United defence. Foulkes was 18 and playing for Whiston Boys Club when United scouts spotted him and invited him to Old Trafford for a trial. He made his first-team debut in December 1952, playing with an injured ankle, having falsely convinced Matt Busby of his fitness. The injury restricted Foulkes' appearances for the remainder of the season, but in the next season, he began to establish himself in the side.

In October 1954 Foulkes was picked for England. Surprisingly, even though he played First Division football for the next 16 years, and was capped twice at Under-23 level, this was his only full cap.

Foulkes was a regular member of the Busby Babes, and one of the few to survive the Munich air crash of 1958. Along with fellow

survivor Harry Gregg, he played against Sheffield Wednesday in the 5th round of the FA Cup only two weeks after the crash. Foulkes was made captain for the game, a post he retained for the rest of the season. For a while it looked as if United might lift some of the gloom with an FA Cup win, but they were defeated at Wembley by Bolton.

As Busby rebuilt his team, Foulkes continued to impress. Strong in the air, sure on the ground and never one to shirk a physical challenge, he had all the assets of a centre-half, and that was what he became. From that position, Foulkes gave United a stability that was essential to the rebuilding process.

Year in, year out, Foulkes was United's ever-dependable stopper. He was the most successful United player of his era, and was still a vital part of United's new and exciting side in 1965 and 1967, when he won two championship winners' medals.

In 1968, during United's European Cup quest, Foulkes scored the most sensational of his nine goals for the club. Having beaten Real Madrid 1–0 in the semi-final first leg at Old Trafford, United were trailing 3–1 at half time in the return game. Early in the second half Sadler scored to narrow the deficit, but United needed an equalizer to go through on aggregate. George Best tricked his way down the right wing. He squared the ball for Charlton, or perhaps Kidd to finish, but Foulkes had made his way forward. He side-footed the ball into the net to send United into the final. No one deserved the goal more. United went to the final to beat Benfica 4–1

in front of a 100,000-strong crowd. The final was the pinnacle of Foulkes' career, and it was an emotional evening for everyone, especially those who had survived Munich. United had rebuilt their shattered team and Foulkes had been a consistent contributor. The European Cup was the ultimate reward for his loyalty.

Did you know?

• Bill Foulkes' grandfather was captain of St. Helens Rugby League Club and also an international player. Bill's father played rugby for St. Helens and football for New Brighton.

• After United's European Cup success in 1968, Foulkes felt that he could achieve nothing greater, and wanted to retire. Only Busby finally persuaded him not to do so.

• Foulkes is the second oldest post-World War Two player to play for Manchester United. When he played at home to Southampton on 16th August, 1969 he was 37 years and 222 days old.

• After life at United, Foulkes coached in the United States, then managed in Norway, and in 1988, in Japan. He later became European scout for Japan's J-league.

• In 1992 Foulkes' medals and mementoes were sold at auction at Christie's in Glasgow. Twenty items realized almost £35,000.

Fact file

• **Serial player**
Foulkes' 61 FA Cup matches for United were all consecutive, played between January 1954 and January 1967.

• **Long term**
Over 18 seasons, Foulkes made 679 appearances for United, plus three as a substitute. Only Bobby Charlton has played for the club on more occasions.

• **European record**
Bill Foulkes made a record 52 European appearances for United.

• **One full cap**
Foulkes had only one full international cap, for England v N. Ireland in 1954.

• **Survivor**
Foulkes and Harry Gregg were the only two Munich survivors to play in Manchester United's next match, which was only two weeks after the air disaster in February, 1958.

1953/54 season
United goalkeeper, Ray Wood, and Bill Foulkes make a concerted effort to clear a corner kick from Tottenham Hotspur in a League game at White Hart Lane on 26th September, 1953. They drew 1–1.

Solid rock
Supporters said that Foulkes' body must have been quarried from rock. Here he is in action at Wembley in the 1963 FA Cup Final, where United defeated Leicester City 3–1.

Bill Foulkes: Career timeline

13th December, 1952
United League debut v Liverpool

April 1956
League champion with United

1958
Receives a second FA Cup losers' medal when Bolton Wanderers beat United 2–0 in the Final

May 1967
League champion with United

May 1968
European Cup winner with United

1950	1952	1954	1956	1958	1960	1962	1964	1966	1968	1970

1950
Arrives at United from Whiston Boys Club

October 1954
England debut v Northern Ireland

May 1957
League champion with United. Receives FA Cup losers' medal when Aston Villa beat United 2–1 in the Final

6th February, 1958
Escapes unhurt in the Munich disaster

19th February, 1958
Captains United in the side's first post-Munich fixture

May 1963
FA Cup winner with United

May 1965
League champion with United

When Foulkes finally retired from playing, in June 1970, he remained at United as a coach, before moving on to coach and manage football in other countries.

KEY: **a**=away **am.**=amateur **appr.**=apprentice **b.**=born **c.**=circa **cs.**=close season **D**=Defender **d.**=died **dnk**=date not known **EUR**=European competitions **F**=Forward **FAC**=FA Cup **FB**=Full-back (defender) **FL**=Football League **FLC**=Football League Cup **GK**=Goalkeeper **gls**=goals **h**=home **HB**=Half-back (midfield) **INT**=International matches **M**=Midfield **NH**=Newton Heath **Newton Heath LYR**=Newton Heath Lancashire & Yorkshire Railway **nk**=not known **pro.**=professional **Q**=Qualifying round **SU**=signed for United **sub**=substitute; substitute apps are in brackets after appearances **T**=total **TF**=transfer fee **TM**=Test match **U**=Utility **UD**=United debut **UTD**=Manchester United **v**=versus

Forsyth: Alex **FB** 1972-1978

b. 5.2.1952, Swinton, Lanarks, Scotland • *5ft 9in • 11st 11lb* • **Clubs** Arsenal ground staff 1967, Partick Thistle cs. 1968; UTD; Glasgow Rangers (on loan at beginning) Aug 1978–May 1979, Motherwell cs. 1982, Hamilton Academical cs. 1983 **SU** Dec 1972 (pro.) **TF** £100,000 **UD** v Arsenal (a) 6.1.1973 **FL** 99(2)/gls 4 **FAC** 10/gls 1 **FLC** 7/gls 0 **EUR** 0(1)/gls 0 **T** 116(3)/gls 5 **INT** (Scotland) 10/gls 0

Alexander "Bruce" Forsyth was signed by Tommy Docherty, the manager who had first capped him for Scotland. Although Forsyth established himself as a strong tackling full-back, he liked to test goalkeepers with his powerful shot. A Scottish League Cup winner with Partick Thistle in 1972 and a Second Division champion with United in 1975, Alex Forsyth lost his United place to the faster Jimmy Nicholl in 1977.

Fortune: Quinton **M** 1999-

b. 21.05.1977, Cape Town, South Africa • *5ft 11in • 11st 11lb* • **Clubs** Tottenham Hotspur, Atletico Madrid; UTD **SU** 2.8.1999 (pro.) **TF** £1.5 million **UD** v Newcastle United (sub) (h) 30.8.1999 **FL** 10(3)/gls 2 **FLC** 2/gls 0 **T** 13(7)/gls 2 **EUR** 1(4)/gls 0 **CWC** 1(1)/gls 2 **INT** (South Africa) 30/gls 1

Foulkes: Bill **D** 1952-1970

See left.

Fox: Position and dates not known

SU nk **UD** v Sheffield Wednesday FAC, 1914

Frame: Tommy **HB** 1932-1934

b. 5.9.1902, Burnbank, Scotland **d.** 17.1.1987 • *5ft 10in • 11st* • **Clubs** Burnbank Athletic, Cowdenbeath 1926; UTD; Southport Jun 1936, Rhyl Athletic Aug 1937, Bridgnorth Town 1938–1939 **SU** Sep 1932 **UD** v Preston North End (h) 1.10.1932 **FL** 51/gls 4 **FAC** 1/gls 0 **T** 52/gls 4

Gallimore: Stanley **F** 1930-1934

b. 14.4.1910, Bucklow Hill, Altrincham, England • *5ft 7.5in • 10st 8lb* • **Clubs** Witton Albion; UTD; Altrincham Jun 1934, Northwich Victoria cs. 1938 **SU** Sep 1929 (am.), Dec 1929 (pro.) **UD** v West Ham Utd (a) 11.10.1930 **FL** 72/gls 19 **FAC** 4/gls 1 **T** 76/gls 20

Stanley Gallimore was spotted as a teenage amateur player in the Cheshire league, and was still only 19 when he turned professional with United. Positioned at either inside-left or inside-right, he was more a supplier than a scorer of goals. He was troubled by knee injuries, and was released in 1932 but returned briefly in 1934 after a cartilage operation.

Gardner: Dick **F** 1935-1937

b. 1913, Birmingham, England • *5ft 9.5in • 11st 2lb* • **Clubs** Evesham Town, Birmingham am. Sep 1932, Notts County May 1933, Stourbridge 1935; UTD; Sheffield Utd May 1937–cs. 1938 **SU** May 1935 **UD** v Plymouth Argyle (h) 28.12.1935 **FL** 16/gls 1 **FAC** 2/gls 0 **T** 18/gls 1

Garton: Billy **D** 1984-1989

b. 15.3.1965, Salford, Manchester, England • *5ft 11in • 11st 11lb* • **Clubs** UTD (on loan to Birmingham City Mar–Apr 1986); Salford City (player-manager) Jun 1992, Witton Albion 1993–1994, Hyde Utd (manager) **SU** May 1981 (appr.), Mar 1983 (pro.) **UD** v Burnley (h) FLC 2, 1st leg, 26.9.1984 **FL** 39(2)/gls 0 **FAC** 3/gls 0 **FLC** 5(1)/gls 0 **EUR** (1)/gls 0 **T** 47(4)/gls 0

Garvey: James **GK** 1900-1901

b. 1878, Hulme, Manchester, England **d.** nk • *5ft 11in • 12st* • **Clubs** Wigan County; NH; Middleton FC, Stalybridge Rovers, Southport Central cs. 1902, Bradford City Feb–Nov 1905 **SU** May 1900 **UD** v Glossop (a) 1.9.1900 **FL** 6/gls 0 **T** 6/gls 0

Gaskell: David **GK** 1957-1967

b. 5.10.1940, Orrell, Wigan, England • *5ft 10in • 12st 9lb* • **Clubs** UTD (on loan to Wigan Athletic cs. 1968); Wrexham Jun 1969–Jun 1972, South African and Kuwaiti clubs (coach) **SU** Jul 1955 (am.), Oct 1957 (pro.) **UD** v Tottenham Hotspur (h) 30.11.1957 **FL** 96/gls 0 **FAC** 16/gls 0 **FLC** 1/gls 0 **EUR** 5/gls 0 **T** 118/gls 0

David Gaskell made a surprise debut aged 16 in the 1956 Charity Shield 1-0 win over Manchester City when he came on as a substitute for Ray Wood. He conceded four goals on his League debut, including a first-half hat-trick from Tottenham's Bobby Smith. Acrobatic and adventurous, Gaskell struggled to depose first-choice goalkeeper Harry Gregg, despite playing in the 1963 FA Cup Final victory.

Gaudie: Ralph **F** 1903-1904

b. 1876, Guisborough, Middlesbrough, England **d.** nk • **Clubs** South Bank, Sheffield Utd Nov 1897, Aston Villa Aug 1898, Woolwich Arsenal Oct 1899; UTD **SU** Aug 1903 **UD** v Bristol City (h) 5.9.1903 **FL** 7/gls 0 **FAC** 1/gls 0 **T** 8/gls 0

Gibson: Colin **D** 1985-1990

b. 6.6.1960, Bridport, England • *5ft 8in • 11st 1lb* • **Clubs** Portsmouth am., Aston Villa appr. Jul 1976, pro. Jul 1978; UTD (on loan to Port Vale Sep–Oct 1990); Leicester City Dec 1990, Blackpool Aug 1994, Walsall Sep 1994 **SU** Nov 1985 (pro.) **UD** v Watford (h) 30.11.1985 **FL** 74(5)/gls 9 **FAC** 8(1)/gls 0 **FLC** 7/gls 0 **T** 89(6)/gls 9

Gibson: Don **HB** 1950-1955

b. 12.5.1929, Manchester, England • *5ft 9.5in • 11st 4lb* • **Clubs** UTD; Sheffield Wednesday Jun 1955, Leyton Orient Jun 1960–Jun 1961, Buxton (player-manager) to Jan 1962 **SU** Nov 1946 (am.), Aug 1947 (pro.) **UD** v Bolton Wanderers (a) 26.3.1950 **FL** 108/gls 0 **FAC** 6/gls 0 **T** 114/gls 0

Gibson: Richard **F** 1921-1922

b. 1889, Holborn, London, England **d.** nk • *5ft 6in • 11st* • **Clubs** Sultan FC, Birmingham Sep 1911 (WW1: Leicester Fosse); UTD **SU** Jun 1921 **TF** £250 **UD** v Everton (a) 27.8.1921 **FL** 11/gls 0 **FAC** 1/gls 0 **T** 12/gls 0

Gibson: Terry **F** 1985-1987

b. 23.12.1962, Walthamstow, London, England • *5ft 4in • 10st 9lb* • **Clubs** Tottenham Hotspur appr. Apr 1979, pro. Jan 1980 (on loan to Gais, Sweden 1981), Coventry City Aug 1983; UTD; Wimbledon Aug 1987 (on loan to Swindon Town Mar 1992), Peterborough Utd (non-contract) Dec 1993, Barnet Feb 1994, Wycombe Wanderers **SU** nk **TF** £600,000 **UD** v Liverpool (a) 9.2.1986 **FL** 14(9)/gls 1 **FAC** 1(1)/gls 0 **FLC** 0(2)/gls 0 **T** 15(12)/gls 1

Gidman: John **FB** 1981-1986

b. 10.1.1954, Liverpool, England • *5ft 11in • 12st 6lb* • **Clubs** Liverpool appr. Jun 1969, Aston Villa appr. 1970, pro. Aug 1971, Everton Oct 1979; UTD; Manchester City Oct 1986, Stoke City Aug 1988, Darlington Feb–May 1989, King's Lynn (manager) July 1993 **SU** Aug 1981 (pro.) **TF** £450,000 (+ player exchange) **UD** v Coventry City (a) 29.8.81 **FL** 94(1)/gls 4 **FAC** 9/gls 0 **FLC** 5/gls 0 **EUR** 7(2)/gls 0 **T** 115(3)/gls 4 **INT** (England) 1/gls 0

John Gidman was Ron Atkinson's first signing for United, arriving from Everton in exchange for Mickey Thomas and £450,000. He was well-suited to United's attacking style, able to break quickly from defence to support the forwards. In 1985 he won the FA Cup with United, 11 years after his career nearly ended when a firework seriously injured his eye.

Giggs: Ryan **F** 1990-

See p.88.

Giles: Johnny **F** 1959-1963

b. 6.11.1940, Cabra, Dublin, Rep. of Ireland • *5ft 6in • 10st 13lb* • **Clubs** Home Farm; UTD; Leeds Utd Aug 1963, West Bromwich Albion (player-manager) Jun 1975, Shamrock Rovers (player-manager and executive director) Jul 1977, Philadelphia Fury (NASL) Jan 1978, Vancouver Whitecaps (Canada, coach) Nov 1980, West Bromwich Albion (manager) Feb 1984–Sep 1985 **SU** Jul 1956 (am.), Nov 1957 (pro.) **TF** £10 (signing-on fee) **UD** v Tottenham Hotspur (h) 12.9.1959 **FL** 99/gls 10 **FAC** 13/gls 2 **FLC** 2/gls 1 **T** 114/gls 13 **INT** (Rep. of Ireland) 59/gls 5

An FA Cup winner with United in 1963, Michael John Giles was blessed with great vision and good control in both feet. Giles requested and was granted a transfer to Leeds after being dropped by Matt Busby, and he received many medals in Yorkshire, including two League championships and two Fairs (UEFA) Cups. The former Republic of Ireland player and manager is now a respected football journalist.

Gill: Tony **D** 1986-1990

b. 6.3.1968, Bradford, England • *5ft 10in • 11st 4lb* • **Clubs** UTD until his retirement in Dec 1990 **SU** Jun 1984 (appr.), Mar 1986 (pro.) **UD** v Southampton (a) 3.1.1987 **FL** 5(5)/gls 1 **FAC** 2(2)/gls 1 **T** 7(7)/gls 2

Gillespie: Keith **F** 1992-1995

b. 18.2.1975, Larne, N. Ireland • *5ft 10in • 10st 11lb* • **Clubs** UTD (on loan for one month to Wigan Athletic Sep 1993), Newcastle Utd Jan 1995, Blackburn Rovers Dec 1998 **SU** Jul 1991 (appr.), Jan 1993 (pro.) **UD** v Bury (h) FAC 3, 5.1.93, scored 1 **FL** 3(6)/gls 1 **FAC** 1(1)/gls 1 **FLC** 3/gls 0 **T** 7(7)/gls 2 **INT** (N. Ireland) 26/gls 1

Keith Gillespie was a promising peer of Ryan Giggs in United's Youth team, with comparable pace and dribbling skills. But two years after his first-team debut, he left United as a £1 million component of the Andrew Cole transfer deal. A highly skilful forward, Keith realized his full potential with a first team place in Kevin Keegan's exciting Newcastle team. The Northern Ireland winger later became Brian Kidd's first signing at Blackburn Rovers for a fee of £2.3 million.

Gillespie: Matthew **F** 1896-1900

b. 24.12.1869, Strathclyde, Glasgow, Scotland **d.** nk • **Clubs** Strathclyde FC, Leith Athletic, Lincoln City Sep 1895; NH **SU** Nov 1896 (pro.) **UD** v Burton Wanderers (h) 24.10.1896 **FL** 74/gls 17 **TM** 4/gls 0 **FAC** 11/gls 4 **T** 89/gls 21

Matthew Gillespie scored a hat-trick on his debut for Newton Heath, in a friendly with local amateurs Fairfield. Unfortunately, it was not a sign of things to come, as shooting was not one of his strong points. Gillespie's strengths were his heading ability and an unselfish work rate which helped the club to the brink of promotion from League Division Two in 1896/97, his first season.

Gipps: Tommy **HB** 1912-1915

b. 1888, Walthamstow, England **d.** nk • *5ft 8in • 11st* • **Clubs** Walthamstow FC, Tottenham Hotspur pro. Oct 1907, Barrow cs. 1910; UTD **SU** May 1912 (pro.) **UD** v Chelsea (a) 25.12.1912 **FL** 23/gls 0 **T** 23/gls 0

Givens: Don **F** 1969-1970

b. 9.8.1949, Dublin, Rep. of Ireland • *5ft 11in • 11st 2lb* • **Clubs** Dublin Rangers; UTD; Luton Town Apr 1970, Queen's Park Rangers Jul 1972, Birmingham City Aug 1978 (on loan to AFC Bournemouth Mar 1980), Sheffield Utd Mar 1981, Xamax Neuchatel (Switzerland) Jun 1981–May 1987 **SU** Sep 1965 (appr.), Dec 1966 (pro.) **UD** v Everton (a) 19.8.1969 **FL** 4(4)/gls 1 **FLC** 1/gls 0 **T** 5(4)/gls 1 **INT** (Rep. of Ireland) 56/gls 19

Gladwin: George **HB** 1936-1939

b. 28.3.1907, Chesterfield, England • *5ft 7.5in • 12st* • **Clubs** Worksop Town, Doncaster Rovers Aug 1930; UTD (WW2: Wrexham, Doncaster Rovers, West Ham Utd) **SU** Feb 1937 **TF** £3,000 **UD** v Chelsea (a) 27.2.1937, scored 1 **FL** 27/gls 1 **FAC** 1/gls 0 **T** 28/gls 1

Godsmark: Gilbert **F** 1899-1900

b. 1877, Derby, England **d.** 1901 • **Clubs** Ashford FC; NH **SU** Jan 1900 **TF** £40 **UD** v Sheffield Wednesday (h) 3.2.1900 **FL** 9/gls 4 **T** 9/gls 4

Goldthorpe: Ernie **F** 1922-1925

b. 8.6.1898, Middleton, Leeds, England **d.** nk • *5ft 9in • 11st* • **Clubs** Tottenham Hotspur (and Army football) 1917–1919, Bradford City Jun 1919, Leeds Utd Jun 1920, Bradford City Mar 1922; UTD; Rotherham Utd Oct 1925 **SU** Nov 1922 **UD** v Fulham (h) 21.10.1922 **FL** 27/gls 15 **FAC** 3/gls 1 **T** 30/gls 16

Goodwin: Billy **F** 1920-1922

b. 1892, Staveley, nr. Chesterfield, England **d.** nk • *5ft 9in • 11st 7lb* • **Clubs** Old Staveley Primitives, Chesterfield FC, Blackburn Rovers Mar 1913, Exeter City May 1914; UTD; Southend Utd Aug 1922, Dartford Aug 1927 **SU** Jun 1920 (pro.) **TF** £640 **UD** v Bolton Wanderers (h) 28.8.1920 **FL** 7/gls 1 **T** 7/gls 1

Goodwin: Fred **HB** 1954-1960

b. 28.6.1933, Heywood, nr. Bury, England • *6ft 2in • 13st 2lb* • **Clubs** UTD; Leeds Utd Mar 1960, Scunthorpe Utd (player-manager) Dec 1964, New York Generals (USA, manager) Oct 1966, Brighton & Hove Albion (manager) Oct 1968, Birmingham City (manager) May 1970–Sep 1975, Minnesota Kicks (USA, manager) 1976 **SU** Oct 1953 (pro.) **UD** v Arsenal (h) 20.11.1954 **FL** 95/gls 7 **FAC** 8/gls 1 **EUR** 3/gls 0 **T** 106/gls 8

Fred Goodwin was one of Manchester United's best Reserve players, and was promoted to the first team following the Munich tragedy. An ever-present player in 1958/59, he used his physical stature and neat ball-passing to full effect as a half-back. After a broken leg ended his playing career at Leeds, Goodwin moved into management.

Goram: Andy **GK** 2001

b. 13.4.1964, Bury, England • *5ft 11in • 12st 13lb* • **Clubs** Oldham Athletic, Hibernian, Glasgow Rangers, Nottingham County, Sheffield United, Motherwell (on loan to UTD) **SU** on six-week loan **UD** v Coventry City (h) 14.4.2001 **FL** 2/gls 0 **T** 2 **INT** (Scotland) 43/gls 0

Gotheridge: J. **F** 1886-1887

b. nk **d.** nk • **Clubs** Newton Heath LYR; West Manchester FC **SU** Oct 1884 **UD** v Fleetwood Rangers (a) FAC 1, 30.10.1886 **FAC** 1/gls 0 **T** 1/gls 0

Gourlay: John **HB** 1898-1899

b. 1879, Scotland **d.** nk • **Clubs** Annbank Jan 1898; NH **SU** Feb 1899 **UD** v Loughborough Town (a) 18.2.1899 **FL** 1/gls 0 **T** 1/gls 0

Gouw, van der: Raimond **GK** 1996-

b. 24.3.1963, Oldenzaal, Holland • *6ft 2in • 13st 1lb* • **Clubs** Go Ahead Eagles 1985, Vitesse Arnhem 1988; UTD **SU** 1.7.1996 (pro.) **TF** £200,000 **UD** v Aston Villa (a) 21.9.1996 **CWC** 1/gls 0 **FL** 26(10)/gls 0 **EUR** 11/gls 0 **FAC** 1/gls 0 **FLC** 8/gls 0 **T** 47(10)/gls 0

Gowling: Alan **F** 1967-1972

b. 16.3.1949, Stockport, England • *6ft • 11st 10lb* • **Clubs** UTD; Huddersfield Town Jun 1972, Newcastle Utd Aug 1975, Bolton Wanderers Mar 1978, Preston North End Sep 1982–Jun 1983 **SU** Aug 1965 (am.), Aug 1967 (pro.) **UD** v Stoke City (a) 30.3.1968, scored 1 **FL** 64(7)/gls 18 **FAC** 6(2)/gls 2 **FLC** 7(1)/gls 1 **T** 77(10)/gls 21

Alan Gowling rose through United's ranks while studying for an economics degree. He scored on his first-team debut and later netted four against Southampton in 1971. Never a first-choice forward, he enjoyed his longest run in the side as a midfielder, in his final season, 1971/72. More recently, the former England Under-23 captain chaired the PFA and the Association of Former Manchester United Players.

Graham: Arthur **F** 1983-1985

b. 26.10.1952, Castlemilk, Glasgow, Scotland • *5ft 7.5in • 12st 5lb* • **Clubs** Cambuslang Rangers, Aberdeen 1969–1970, Leeds Utd Jul 1977; UTD; Bradford City Jun 1985, (junior coach) Feb 1987, (caretaker-manager) Jan–Feb 1989 **SU** Aug 1983 (pro.) **TF** £45,000 **UD** v Queen's Park Rangers (h) 27.8.1983 **FL** 33(4)/gls 5 **FAC** 1/gls 0 **FLC** 6/gls 1 **EUR** 6(1)/gls 1 **T** 46(5)/gls 7 **INT** (Scotland) 10/gls 2

Giggs: Ryan F 1990-

b. 29.11.1973, Cardiff, Wales • *5ft 11in* • *10st 7lb* • **Clubs** UTD **SU** 9.7.1990 (appr.), 29.11.1990 (pro.) **UD** v Everton (sub) (h) 2.3.1991 **FL** 291(30)/gls 64 **FAC** 36(3)/gls 7 **FLC** 17(4)/gls 6 **EUR** 51(3)/gls 13 **CWC** 2/gls 0 **T** 397(40)/gls 90 **INT** (Wales) 31/gls 7

The most naturally gifted player of his generation, Ryan Giggs was a footballing legend by the time he was 21. For flair and pure talent, Giggs is the obvious successor to George Best, and as legendary AC Milan coach Fabio Capello observed: "Like Best, there is a special fantasia about him".

Comparisons with George Best has often weighed heavily on other players, but Giggs seemed untouched by it, and has created his own considerable reputation. Alex Ferguson's decision to protect Giggs from the media has helped; in his first two seasons as a professional he did not give a single interview to the press. At the end of the 1990/91 season, aged 17, Giggs made his first-team debut as a substitute in a match against Everton. He was slight in build, but he could easily get past defenders with his pace.

When Lee Sharpe was injured, Giggs became a regular on the left-wing, as United went close to winning the 1992 League championship. At the end of his inaugural season Ryan Giggs was named as the PFA's Young Player of the Year.

Ryan Giggs' 17 goals and 14 assists from the left-wing position helped United to their first League championship and FA Cup Double in 1994. His goal against Queen's Park Rangers in February 1994 was sublime; he ran past four defenders and hit an unstoppable shot. "The boy's a genius," proclaimed the *Match of the Day* football commentator.

In the autumn of 1994, however, Giggs' form suffered. Most young players lose form after their initial burst on to the scene and not all respond well. Giggs responded by proving his greatness. From 1995/96 he developed into a more complete and mature player, opting to pass inside rather than fly down the wing at every opportunity, and working more as a team player. The goals returned too, with Giggs contributing 12 to the double Double-winning campaign.

In 1997, Ryan Giggs won his fourth championship medal, and finally dispelled doubts about his ability to perform on the highest stage of European football. He was United's inspiration in their 4-0 victory over Porto and he terrorized Juventus in October 1997, when United became the first English team to defeat the Italians for 18 years.

Giggs was a thorn in Juve's side again in 1998/99, scoring a last-minute goal against them in the Champions League semi-final at Old Trafford. He became a semi-final specialist, also producing one of the best goals of all time in the FA Cup semi-final replay at Villa Park. Running with the ball from inside his own half, Giggs dribbled around several defenders before shooting past England goalkeeper David Seaman to knock Arsenal out of the competition. Giggs went on to join Irwin, Keane and Schmeichel as one of only four players to win three League and FA Cup Doubles.

It is often forgotten that Ryan Giggs is a contemporary of Butt, Beckham, Scholes and the Nevilles. His extraordinary talent earned him an earlier call-up into the first team. As Tommy Docherty said: "He has achieved so much, but he is still years away from his prime, a frightening concept for defenders".

At the turn of the millennium Giggs freely confessed that he was in the finest form of his life, and his performances since then have not disproved this statement. In 2001, Giggs was among the final six players short-listed for both the Football Writers' Footballer of the Year and the PFA's Player of the Year awards.

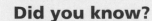

Did you know?

- Although Giggs is credited with scoring on his United debut, he is not sure that he even touched the ball.
- Giggs was the youngest footballer ever to publish an autobiography, in 1994.
- Giggs' father was Welsh international rugby player, Danny Wilson. Ryan captained England Schoolboys and first came to United as Ryan Wilson.
- The name Giggs is Ryan's mother's maiden name, which he adopted after his parents separated.
- One of Giggs' favourite snacks is mushy peas on toast.

" His talent is God-given. "
Brian Kidd

The usual flair
Giggs in full flight with the ball is a defender's nightmare. Here he holds off Liverpool's Jason McAteer and Michael Thomas at Old Trafford on 12th October, 1996. United won 1-0.

" *The way he moved, it was like a gazelle, lovely to watch.* "
Alex Ferguson

A unique blend
There is no finer sight than Giggs in full flow, with his unique blend of balance, pace and control. "A wee cocker spaniel chasing a piece of silver paper in the wind," is how Alex Ferguson has described him.

In the 1992/93 season, Giggs helped United to its first championship in 26 years. He produced flashes of genius, most notably at White Hart Lane when he glided through the Spurs defence to score, and then at a festive Old Trafford in the final home game against Blackburn, when he drove home a free kick from thirty yards.

The Welshman became one of the most marketed players in football's history. His image has appeared on everything imaginable; books, magazines, mugs and duvets. He has also been used to endorse an array of products from Citroën cars to Quorn!

Fact file

- **First-ever**
Ryan Giggs was the first-ever player to be voted PFA Young Player of the Year twice, in both 1992 and 1993.

- **Quickest goal**
Giggs scored Manchester United's quickest-ever goal, after just 15 seconds against Southampton in November 1995.

- **Youngest player**
Giggs is the youngest-ever player to earn a full international cap for Wales. He was just 17 years and 321 days old when he made his debut against Germany.

- **One of six**
Giggs is one of only four players ever to win three sets of English Double medals, in 1993/94, 1995/96 and 1998/99.

Ryan Giggs: Career timeline

9th July, 1990 United apprentice

May 1991 Full debut against Manchester City

April 1992 League Cup winner. Voted PFA Young Player of the Year

May 1992 Wins the FA Youth Cup

April 1993 Scores first goal for Wales against Belgium. Voted PFA Young Player of the Year for the second time

March 1997 Plays what he regards as his best-ever game to date in the 4-0 European Cup win against Porto

14th April, 1999 Scores the best goal of his career against Arsenal in the FA Cup semi-final replay

1997/98 Plagued by hamstring injury for much of the season

April 2000 Wins sixth Premiership title

August 2001 Old Trafford stages testimonial against Celtic, to celebrate Giggs' ten years at United

1988 1989 1990 1991 1992 1993 1994 1995 1996 1997 1998 1999 2000 2001 2002

February 1988 Signed associated schoolboy forms for United

29th November, 1990 Signs as a professional for United

2nd March, 1991 Debut as substitute against Everton

October 1991 Becomes the youngest-ever Welsh international at 17 years, 321 days

May 1993 Becomes FA Premiership champion with United

May 1994 Becomes FA Premiership champion and FA Cup winner – the Double

May 1996 Second FA Premiership and FA Cup wins – the double Double

May 1997 FA Premiership champion

9th December, 1998 Makes his 300th start for United's first team in a 1-1 draw with Bayern Munich

May 1999 Third FA Premiership and FA Cup Double wins, European Cup winner

April 2001 Wins seventh Premiership title and is nominated for the PFA Player of the Year award

KEY: **a**=away **am.**=amateur **appr.**=apprentice **b.**=born **c.**=circa **cs.**=close season **CWC**=Club World Championship **D**=Defender **d.**=died **dnk**=date not known **EUR**=European competitions **F**=Forward **FAC**=FA Cup **FB**=Full-back (defender) **FL**=Football League **FLC**=Football League Cup **GK**=Goalkeeper **gls**=goals **h**=home **HB**=Half-back (midfield) **INT**=International matches **M**=Midfield **NH**=Newton Heath **Newton Heath LYR**=Newton Heath Lancashire & Yorkshire Railway **nk**=not known **pro.**=professional **Q**=qualifying round **SU**=signed for United **sub**=substitute; substitute apps are in brackets after appearances **T**=total **TF**=transfer fee **TM**=Test match **U**=Utility **UD**=United debut **UTD**=Manchester United **v**=versus

Graham: Deiniol F 1987–1990

b. 4.10.1969, Cannock, nr. Stafford, England • *5ft 11in* • *10st 11lb* • **Clubs** UTD; Barnsley Aug 1991 (on loan to Preston North End Oct 1992 and to Carlisle Utd Nov 1993), Stockport County Jun 1994, Scunthorpe Utd 1995, Emley **SU** Jul 1986 (appr.), Oct 1987 (pro.) **UD** v Wimbledon (a) 21.11.1987 **FL** 1(1)/gls 0 **FAC** (1)/gls 1 **FLC** (1)/gls 0 **T** 1(3)/gls 1

Graham: George M 1972–1974

b. 30.11.1944, Bargeddie, Glasgow, Scotland • *5ft 11in* • *11st 10lb* • **Clubs** Aston Villa (ground staff) 1959, pro. Dec 1961, Chelsea Jun 1964, Arsenal Sep 1966; UTD; Portsmouth Nov 1974, Crystal Palace Nov 1976–1980 (on loan to California Surf Mar–Jul 1978), (youth coach) May 1980, Queen's Park Rangers (coach) 1981, Millwall (manager) Dec 1982, Arsenal (manager) May 1986, Leeds Utd (manager) Sep 1996, Tottenahm Hotspur (manager) 1998, sacked Mar 2001 **SU** Dec 1972 (pro.) **TF** £120,000 **UD** v Arsenal (a) 6.1.1973 **FL** 41(2)/gls 2 **FAC** 2/gls 0 **FLC** 1/gls 0 **T** 44(2)/gls 2 **INT** (Scotland) 12/gls 3

Latterly a highly successful manager, George Graham won the Double as a player with Arsenal in 1971. He was Tommy Docherty's first signing for United and was appointed captain when Bobby Charlton retired. Nicknamed "Stroller", he was a creative player who specialized in setting up his team mates. However, his laid-back approach annoyed some fans and he lost his place during the relegation season, 1973/74.

Graham: John F 1893–1894

b. nk **d.** nk • *5ft 11in* • *12st 4lb* • **Clubs** Blyth FC; NH **SU** Nov 1893 **UD** v Wolverhampton Wanderers (h) 11.11.1893 **FL** 4/gls 0 **T** 4/gls 0

Grassam: Billy F 1903–1904

b. 20.11.1878, Larbert, nr. Falkirk, Scotland **d.** nk • *5ft 9in* • *11st 6lb* • **Clubs** Redcliffe Thistle 1896, Glasgow Maryhill 1897, Burslem Port Vale Jul 1899, West Ham Utd cs. 1900, Celtic May 1903; UTD; Leyton FC cs. 1905, West Ham Utd Dec 1905, Brentford 1909 **SU** Sep 1903 **UD** v Woolwich Arsenal (a) 3.10.1903 **FL** 29/gls 13 **FAC** 8/gls 1 **T** 37/gls 14

Greaves: Ian FB 1954–1960

b. 26.5.1932, Shaw, Oldham, England • *6ft* • *12st 4lb* • **Clubs** Buxton Utd; UTD; Lincoln City Dec 1960, Oldham Athletic May 1961, Altrincham Jun 1963, Huddersfield Town (coach) Aug 1964 (manager) Jun 1968, Plymouth Argyle (coach) Jul 1974, Bolton Wanderers (asst. manager) Aug 1974 (manager) Oct 1974, Hereford Utd (asst. manager) Feb 1980, Oxford Utd (manager) Dec 1980, Wolverhampton Wanderers (manager) Feb–Sep 1983, Mansfield Town (manager) Jan 1983–Feb 1989, Bury (coach); UTD (scout); Emley (manager) 1991–1992, Manchester City (scout) **SU** May 1953 **UD** v Woverhampton Wanderers (a) 2.10.1954 **FL** 67/gls 0 **FAC** 6/gls 0 **EUR** 2/gls 0 **T** 75/gls 0

Green: Eddie F 1933–1934

b. dnk, Tewkesbury, England **d.** nk • *5ft 11in* • *12st 4lb* • **Clubs** Bournemouth & Boscombe Athletic am. Feb 1929, pro. Mar 1929, Derby County May 1931; UTD; Stockport County Jul 1934, Cheltenham Town Jun 1936 **SU** Jun 1933 (pro.) **UD** v Plymouth Argyle (a) 26.8.1933 **FL** 9/gls 4 **T** 9/gls 4

Greenhoff: Brian D 1973–1979

b. 28.4.1953, Barnsley, England • *5ft 9in* • *10st 11lb* • **Clubs** UTD; Leeds Utd Aug 1979 (on loan to Hong Kong), Rochdale Dec 1983–1984 **SU** Aug 1968 (appr.), Jun 1970 (pro.) **UD** v Ipswich Town (a) 8.9.1973 **FL** 218(3)/gls 13 **FAC** 24/gls 2 **FLC** 19/gls 2 **EUR** 6/gls 0 **T** 267(3)/gls 17 **INT** (England) 18/gls 0

Greenhoff established himself as a midfielder in the side that won the Second Division in 1974/75. He then switched to centre-half, playing alongside Buchan in the FA Cup Finals of 1976 and 1977 when the line-up also featured his brother Jimmy. Brian's hard work was rewarded with England caps at full, "B" and Under-23 levels.

Greenhoff: Jimmy F 1976–1981

b. 19.6.1946, Barnsley, England • *5ft 10in* • *11st 12lb* • **Clubs** Leeds Utd appr. Jun 1961, pro. Aug1963, Birmingham City Aug 1968, Stoke City Aug 1969; UTD; Crewe Alexandra Dec 1980, Toronto Blizzard (Canada, player-coach) Mar 1981, Port Vale Aug 1981, Rochdale (player-manager) Mar 1983–Mar 1984, Port Vale (coach) **SU** Nov 1976 (pro.) **TF** £120,000 **UD** v Leicester City (a) 20.11.1976 **FL** 94(3)/gls 26 **FAC** 18(1)/gls 9 **FLC** 4/gls 1 **EUR** 2/gls 0 **T** 118(4)/gls 36

James Greenhoff was the ideal player to boost United's flagging fortunes when he joined the club from Stoke City in November 1976 for a £120,000 fee. Tommy Docherty's once thrilling side had lost its characteristic spark and Jimmy Greenhoff was the inspiration needed when he teamed up with his younger brother, Brian, at Old Trafford. Greenhoff was 30 when he signed, but blessed with a fine first touch, impeccable ball control and a habit of scoring spectacular goals, he immediately struck up a formidable partnership with fellow striker Stuart Pearson.

Greenhoff's finest moment in a red shirt came during the 1977 FA Cup Final when he scored the winner – something of a fluke – against Liverpool. However, he was on the losing side in the 1979 FA Cup Final against Arsenal, and left the club in December 1980. After United, Greenhoff played for Crewe and Toronto Blizzard, and made the last of over 650 Football League appearances with Rochdale, on 3rd December, 1983.

Greening: Jonathan F 1998–

b. 2.1.1979, Scarborough, England • *6ft* • *11st 3lb* • **Clubs** York City Aug 1996; UTD **SU** 26.3.1998 (pro.) **UD** v Bury (h) 28.10.1998 **FL** 4(10)/gls 0 **FAC** (1)/gls 0 **FLC** 6/gls 0 **EUR** 2(1)/gls 0 **CWC** 1/gls 0 **T** 13(12)/gls 0

Greenwood: Wilson F 1900–1901

b. 1868, Padiham, Burnley, England **d.** 1943 • *5ft 6in* • *11st* • **Clubs** Blue Star Burnley, Brierfield, Accrington, Sheffield Utd Jan 1895, Rossendale FC cs. 1895, Rochdale Athletic 1896, Warmley Nov 1897, Grimsby Town May 1898; NH **SU** Oct 1900 **UD** v Walsall (h) 20.10.1900 **FL** 3/gls 0 **T** 3/gls 0

Gregg MBE: Harry GK 1957–1967

b. 25.10.1932, Magherafelt, nr. Londonderry, N. Ireland • *6ft* • *12st 8lb* • **Clubs** Linfield Rangers, Linfield Swifts, Coleraine, Doncaster Rovers Oct 1952; UTD; Stoke City Dec 1966, Shrewsbury Town (manager) cs. 1968, Swansea City (manager) Nov 1972, Crewe Alexandra (manager) 1975–1978, Kitan Sports Club (Kuwait, manager-coach); UTD (coaching staff) Nov 1978–Jun 1981; Swansea City (coach) 1982, Swindon Town (asst. manager) Jul 1984–Apr 1985, Carlisle Utd (manager) May 1986–1987 **SU** Dec 1957 (pro.) **TF** £23,000 **UD** v Leicester City (h) 21.12.1957 **FL** 210/gls 0 **FAC** 24/gls 0 **FLC** 2/gls 0 **EUR** 11/gls 0 **T** 247/gls 0 **INT** (N. Ireland) 25/gls 0

In December 1957, United were making their second great assault on the European Cup and Matt Busby needed a tough goalkeeper. Busby paid Doncaster Rovers £23,000 for Henry (Harry) Gregg, a record fee for a keeper. Gregg had an imposing physical presence, and was the natural master of his line. He also liked to venture off the line, assuming command of the whole area. He clashed boldly with opposing forwards and encouraged United's defence through example and encouragement. In the course of his career Harry Gregg gained 25 caps for his country.

Gregg had been with United for barely two months when the entire destiny of the club was recast at a stroke. He emerged almost unscathed from the air crash at Munich, but plunged back into the wreckage and rescued, among others, a mother and baby. Gregg and Bill Foulkes were the only Munich survivors fit enough to resume their duties immediately, and they led Jimmy Murphy's patched-up team into its first match. Throughout United's hectic, emotional 1958 FA Cup campaign, Gregg was a tower of strength. He deserved better than a runners-up medal, his only honour with the club.

Harry Gregg's later years at Old Trafford were overshadowed by injury. A damaged shoulder never fully righted itself, and the apparently indestructible keeper often played in considerable pain. Despite an operation in 1961/62 he was gradually forced out of the game. He left Manchester United for Stoke in 1966, to be replaced by David Gaskell.

Griffiths: Billy HB 1898–1905

b. dnk, Manchester, England **d.** nk • **Clubs** Berry's Association FC; NH; Atherton Church House cs. 1905 **SU** Feb 1899 **UD** v Woolwich Arsenal (h) 1.4.1899 **FL** 157/gls 27 **FAC** 18/gls 3 **T** 175/gls 30

William Griffiths worked in a shoe polish factory before he laced up his boots for Newton Heath. His best season was 1903/04, the club's second campaign as Manchester United. Scoring two on the opening day, he finished as joint top scorer with 11 goals in 30 games. Despite this, he lost his place in the team to Charlie Roberts in 1904/05.

Griffiths: Clive D 1973–1974

b. 22.1.1955, Pontypridd, Wales • *5ft 10in* • *11st 6lb* • **Clubs** UTD (on loan to Plymouth Argyle Jul–Nov 1974 and to Tranmere Rovers Oct 1975–Apr 1976); Chicago Sting (NASL) Apr 1976, Tulsa Roughnecks (NASL) Mar–Aug 1980 **SU** Jun 1970 (am.), Jan 1972 (pro.) **UD** v Burnley (a) 27.10.1973 **FL** 7/gls 0 **T** 7/gls 0

Griffiths: Jack FB 1933–1940

b. dnk, Fenton, Stoke-on-Trent, England • *5ft 11in* • *11st 8lb* • **Clubs** Shirebrook FC, Wolverhampton Wanderers May 1929, Bolton Wanderers Jun 1932; UTD (WW2: Notts County, Stoke City, West Bromwich Albion, Derby County, Port Vale); Hyde Utd (player-coach) May 1946 **SU** Mar 1934 **UD** v Fulham (h) 17.3.1934 **FL** 168/gls 1 **FAC** 8/gls 0 **T** 176/gls 1

After frustrating spells at both Wolverhampton and Bolton Wanderers, John (Jack) Griffiths' career blossomed at United. Replacing Jack Silcock in the United defence, Griffiths' explosive pace enabled him to match and outstrip many a forward. He missed only one game in the Division Two title-winning season of 1935/36, and scored his only goal on April Fool's Day 1936 in a 2–2 draw with Fulham.

Grimes: Ashley M/D 1977–1983

b. 2.8.1957, Dublin, Rep. of Ireland • *5ft 11in* • *10st 4lb* • **Clubs** Stella Maris; UTD (trialist Aug 1972); Bohemians; UTD; Coventry City Aug 1983, Luton Town Aug 1984, Osasuna (Spain) Aug 1990, Stoke City (coach and non-contract player) Jan 1992 **SU** Mar 1977 (pro.) **TF** £20,000 **UD** v Birmingham City (sub) (a) 20.8.1977 **FL** 62(28)/gls 10 **FAC** 5/gls 1 **FLC** 6/gls 0 **EUR** 4(2)/gls 0 **T** 77(30)/gls 11 **INT** (Rep. of Ireland) 18/gls 1

In 1972 Ashley Grimes had a trial with Manchester United, but he was turned away, and it wasn't until 1977 that Tommy Docherty finally signed him up. The energetic, left-sided player never really established himself as a first choice, and watched from the bench as United won the FA Cup in 1983. Grimes enjoyed more limelight at Luton Town, with whom he won the League Cup in 1988.

Grimshaw: Tony D 1975–1976

b. 8.12.1957, Manchester, England • *5ft 6.5in* • *10st* • **Clubs** UTD **SU** Apr 1974 (appr.), Dec 1974 (pro.) **UD** v Brentford (sub) (h) FLC 2, 10.9.1975 **FL** 0(1)/gls 0 **FLC** 0(1)/gls 0 **T** 0(2)/gls 0

Grimwood: John HB 1919–1927

b. 25.10.1898, Marsden, South Shields, England **d.** 26.12.1977 • *5ft 10in* • *11st 4lb* • **Clubs** Marsden Rescue FC, South Shields; UTD; Aldershot Town Jun 1927, Blackpool Sep 1927, Altrincham Sep 1928, Taylor Bros. Manchester am. Nov 1932 **SU** May 1919 **UD** v Manchester City (a) 11.10.1919 **FL** 196/gls 8 **FAC** 9/gls 0 **T** 205/gls 8

Grundy: John F 1899–1901

b. dnk, Egerton, Bolton, England **d.** nk • **Clubs** Wigan County; NH; Halliwell Rovers Aug 1895; NH **SU** Apr 1895 **UD** v Chesterfield Town (h) 28.4.1900, scored 1 **FL** 11/gls 3 **T** 11/gls 3

Gyves: William GK 1890–1891

b. 1867, Manchester, England **d.** nk **Clubs** Newton Heath LYR **UD** v Bootle Reserves (a) FAC 2Q, 4.10.1890 **FAC** 1/gls 0 **T** 1/gls 0

Hacking: Jack GK 1933–1935

b. 22.12.1897, Blackburn, England **d.** 1.6.1955 • *5ft 11in* • *12st 10lb* • **Clubs** Grimshaw Park Co-operative (Blackburn), Blackpool Jan 1919, Fleetwood cs. 1925, Oldham Athletic May 1926; UTD; Accrington Stanley (player-manager) May–Dec 1935 (manager) Dec 1935, Barrow (manager) May 1949 until his death **SU** Mar 1934 **UD** v Fulham (h) 17.3.1934 **FL** 32/gls 0 **FAC** 2/gls 0 **T** 34/gls 0

Hall: Jack F 1925–1926

b. 1905, Bolton, England • *5ft 9in* • *10st 4lb* • **Clubs** Lincoln City Aug 1923, Accrington Stanley Jul 1924; UTD **SU** May 1925 **UD** v Burnley (a) 6.2.1926 **FL** 3/gls 0 **T** 3/gls 0

Hall: Jack GK 1932–1936

b. 23.10.1912, Failsworth, Manchester, England • *5ft 10.5in* • *11st* • **Clubs** Failsworth FC, NH Loco; UTD; Tottenham Hotspur Jun 1936 (WW2: Blackburn Rovers, Hartlepools Utd, Nottingham Forest, Stockport County, Bolton Wanderers, Oldham Athletic, Rochdale), Stalybridge Celtic, Runcorn 1946, Stalybridge Celtic **SU** Sep 1932 **UD** v Oldham Athletic (a) 30.9.1933 **FL** 67/gls 0 **FAC** 6/gls 0 **T** 73/gls 0

Hall: Proctor F 1903–1904

b. 1884, Blackburn, England **d.** nk • *5ft 8.5in* • *10.8st* • **Clubs** Oswaldtwistle Rovers; UTD; Brighton & Hove Albion cs. 1905, Aston Villa May 1906, Bradford City Oct 1906, Luton Town May 1907, Chesterfield Town Jan 1908, Hyde FC cs. 1909, Newport County cs. 1912, Mardy FC cs. 1913 **SU** Sep 1903 **UD** v Grimsby Town (h) 26.3.1904 **FL** 8/gls 2 **T** 8/gls 2

Halse: Harold F 1907–1912

b. 1.1.1886, Stratford, London, England **d.** 25.3.1949 • *5ft 6.5in* • *10st 10lb* • **Clubs** Newportians FC (Leyton), Wanstead FC, Barking Town, Clapton Orient am. Aug 1905, Southend Utd Jun 1906; UTD; Aston Villa Jul 1912, Chelsea May 1913 (WW1: Clapton Orient), Charlton Athletic Jul 1921–cs. 1923, (scout) 1923–1925 **SU** Mar 1908 **TF** £350 **UD** v Sheffield Wednesday (h) 28.3.1908, scored 1 **FL** 109/gls 41 **FAC** 15/gls 9 **T** 124/gls 50 **INT** (England) 1/gls 2

Halse joined the club towards the end of the 1907/08 championship-winning season and scored in the first minute of his debut. Although he was never the most blindingly skilful of players, there was no doubting Halse's prowess in front of goal. He had demonstrated his ability to hit the target from all manner of angles at his previous club, Southend United, scoring more than 200 goals from them in two seasons. He managed 14 goals in his first full season for Manchester United, which ended with a 1-0 triumph in the 1909 FA Cup Final. Sandy Turnbull scored the winner after Halse's shot rebounded off the cross bar. En route to the final, Halse had scored four times, including the only goal of the semi-final against Newcastle United. This form earned him his one and only England cap in June 1909, an honour he celebrated with two goals in an 8-1 thrashing of Austria.

In 1911, he helped United to another League championship, scoring two goals in their crucial 5-1 win over Sunderland in the last match of the season. In that year's Charity Shield final, he rattled in a remarkable six in a row as United beat Swindon Town 8-4. Joining Villa for £1,200 in July 1912, Halse won the FA Cup with them in 1913 and then completed a rare hat-trick of Cup Final appearances as a runner-up with Chelsea in 1915.

Halton: Reg F 1936-1937

b. 11.7.1916, Buxton, England d. 1988 • 5ft 11in • 11st 4lb • Clubs Cheddington Mental Hospital; UTD; Notts County Jun 1937, Bury Nov 1937 (WW2: Rochdale, Portsmouth, Fulham, Arsenal), Chesterfield Dec 1948, Leicester City Sep 1950, Scarborough Town (player-manager) Feb 1953, Goole Town cs. 1954 SU Oct 1936 UD v Middlesbrough (a) 12.12.1936, scored 1 FL 4/gls 1 T 4/gls 1

Hamill: Mickey F 1911-1914

b. 19.1.1885, Belfast, Ireland d. 1943 • 5ft 7.5in • 11st • Clubs Belfast Rangers, Belfast Celtic; UTD; Belfast Celtic cs. 1914, Manchester City Sep 1920, Fall River Boston (USA) Aug 1924, Coats FC Rhode Island (USA) Nov 1925, Belfast Celtic Oct 1926, Belfast Distillery (manager), Belfast Celtic (manager) Jul 1934 SU Jan 1911 UD v West Bromwich Albion (a) 16.9.1911 FL 57/gls 2 FAC 2/gls 0 T 59/gls 2 INT (Ireland) 7/gls 1

Hanlon: Jimmy F 1938-1948

b. 12.10.1917, Manchester, England • 5ft 7.5in • 10st • Clubs UTD; Bury Oct 1948, Northwich Victoria cs. 1950, Rhyl 1953 SU Nov 1934 (am.), Nov 1935 (pro.) UD v Huddersfield Town (h) 26.11.1938, scored 1 FL 64/gls 20 FAC 6/gls 2 T 70/gls 22

Hannaford: Charlie F 1925-1927

b. 8.1.1896, Finsbury Park, London, England d. 1970 • 5ft 8in • 10st 7lb • Clubs Tufnell Park 1912, Maidstone Utd cs. 1920, Millwall Mar 1921, Charlton Athletic Jul 1923, Clapton Orient Mar 1924; UTD; Clapton Orient Sep 1928-cs. 1929 SU Dec 1925 UD v Leicester City (a) 28.12.1925 FL 11/gls 0 FAC 1/gls 0 T 12/gls 0

Hanson: Jimmy F 1924-1930

b. 6.11.1904, Manchester, England • 5ft 7.5in • 10st 8lb • Clubs Bradford Parish FC, Stalybridge Celtic, Manchester North End; UTD SU May 1924 UD v Hull City (h) 15.11.1924, scored 1 FL 138/gls 47 FAC 9/gls 5 T 147/gls 52

Former England Schoolboys player James (Jimmy) Hanson scored goals for fun in Manchester United's Reserve team, notching up five in one game against Stoke and six in another against Burnley. Slowly adjusting to the first team, he found his form in 1928/29 when he was the top scorer with 19 goals. Hanson's career was ended by a broken leg, sustained in a game against Birmingham City on Christmas Day, 1929.

Hardman: Harold F 1908-1909

b. 4.4.1882, Kirkmanshulme, Manchester, England d. 9.6.1965 • 5ft 6.5in • 10st 4lb • Clubs Blackpool am. Jul 1900, Everton am. May 1903; UTD; Bradford City am. Jan 1909, Stoke am. Feb 1910; UTD SU Aug 1908 (am.) UD v Manchester City (a) 19.8.1908 FL 4/gls 0 T 4/gls 0 INT (England) 4/gls 1

Harold Hardman was involved with Manchester United more as a director and chairman than as a player. Playing for Everton, from 1903-08, he won an FA Cup and four England caps. He also won gold with Great Britain in the London Olympics of 1908. Hardman played for United only four times, in 1908, before moving on, but in 1912 he was back, soon becoming a director. He was chairman from 1951 until his death in 1965.

Harris: Frank HB 1920-1922

b. 1.12.1899, Urmston, Manchester, England d. nk • 5ft 8.5in • 11st 3lb • Clubs Urmston Old Boys; UTD SU Feb 1920 (am.), May 1920 (pro.) UD v Sunderland (h) 14.2.1920, scored 1 FL 46/gls 2 FAC 3/gls 0 T 49/gls 2

Harris: Tom F 1926-1927

b. 18.9.1905, Ince-in-Makerfield, nr. Wigan, England • 5ft 9in • 11st 6lb • Clubs Skelmersdale Utd; UTD; Wigan Borough Jul 1928, Rotherham Utd Jun 1929, Crewe Alexandra Nov 1929, Chorley Jul 1931, Burton Town, Prescot Cables Aug 1933 SU May 1926 UD v West Ham Utd (a) 30.10.1926 FL 4/gls 1 T 4/gls 1

Harrison: Charlie FB 1889-1890

b. nk d. nk • Clubs Newton Heath LYR SU 1889 UD v Preston North End (a) FAC 1, 18.1.1890 FAC 1/gls 0 T 1/gls 0

Harrison: William F 1920-1922

b. 27.12.1886, Wybunbury, Crewe, England d. nk • 5ft 4.5in • 11st 2lb • Clubs Hough Utd, Crewe South End, Willaston White Star, Crewe Alexandra Apr 1905, Wolverhampton Wanderers May 1907 (WW1: Stoke); UTD; Port Vale Sep 1922, Wrexham Jun 1923-cs. 1924 SU Oct 1920 UD v Preston North End (h) 23.10.1920 FL 44/gls 5 FAC 2/gls 0 T 46/gls 5

Harrop: Bobby HB 1957-1959

b. 25.8.1936, Manchester, England • 5ft 10in • 12st 4lb • Clubs UTD; Tranmere Rovers Nov 1959-Jun 1961, Ramsgate FC SU 1953 (am.), May 1954 (pro.) UD v West Bromwich Albion (h) FAC 6 replay, scored 5.3.1958 FL 10/gls 0 FAC 1/gls 0 T 11/gls 0

Hartwell: William F 1903-1905

b. 1885 d. nk • 5ft 6in • 10st 6lb • Clubs Kettering Town; UTD; Northampton Town cs. 1905 SU Apr 1904 UD v Leicester Fosse (h) 30.4.1904 FL 3/gls 0 FAC 1/gls 0 T 4/gls 0

Haslam: "Tiny" (George) HB 1921-1928

b. 1898, Turton, nr. Bolton, England d. nk • 6ft 0.5in • 13st 4lb • Clubs Darwen; UTD; Portsmouth Nov 1927, Ashton National 1928, Whitchurch Nov 1928, Lancaster Town Aug 1929, Chorley Aug 1930, Burscough Rangers Apr 1931, Northwich Victoria May 1921 TF £750 (combined player fee) UD v Birmingham (h) 25.2.1922 FL 25/gls 0 FAC 2/gls 0 T 27/gls 0

Hawksworth: Tony GK 1956-1956

b. 15.1.1938, Sheffield, England • 5ft 9in • 10st 12lb • Clubs UTD SU May 1953 (am.), Apr 1955 (pro.) UD v Blackpool (a) 27.10.1956 FL 1/gls 0 T 1/gls 0

Haworth: Ronald F 1926-1927

b. 10.3.1901, Lower Darwen, nr. Blackburn, England d. 1973 • 5ft 9.5in • 11st 6lb • Clubs Blackburn Rovers am. Mar 1921, Hull City Jun 1924; UTD; Darwen Aug 1927 SU May 1926 TF £750 (combined player fee) UD v Liverpool (a) 28.8.1926 FL 2/gls 0 T 2/gls 0

Hay: Tom GK 1889-1890

b. 1858, Staveley, Chesterfield, England d. nk • 5ft 7.5in • 11st 10lb • Clubs Staveley FC 1882, Bolton Wanderers Oct 1883, Great Lever FC 1885, Halliwell FC 1886, Burslem FC; Newton Heath LYR; Accrington 1890, Burton Swifts Oct 1893

Herd: David F 1961-1968

Overshadowed

Despite playing for United during a glorious decade and having one of the finest scoring records, David Herd was always overshadowed by the presence of Law, Best and Charlton.

b. 15.4.1934, Hamilton, Scotland • 6ft • 13st • Clubs Stockport County am. Sep 1949, pro. Apr 1951, Arsenal Aug 1954; UTD; Stoke City Jul 1968, Waterford Dec 1970, Lincoln City (manager) Mar 1971-Dec 1972 SU Jul 1961 (pro.) TF £35,000 UD v West Ham Utd (a) 19.8.1961 FL 201(1)/gls 114 FAC 35/gls 15 FLC 1/gls 1 EUR 25/gls 14 T 262(1)/gls 144 INT (Scotland) 5/gls 4

In his seven years at United during the '60s, Herd made 262 (1) appearances in the red shirt and scored an incredible 144 goals. Only four Manchester United players have a better post-war ratio of goals to games: Tommy Taylor, Denis Law, Dennis Viollet and Andy Cole.

Born a stone's throw from Sir Matt Busby's birthplace in Lanarkshire, Scotland, Herd grew up in Moss Side, Manchester. His father, Alec, played for Manchester City in the 1930s. Alec Herd was a highly rated inside-right, and after the war, as his own illustrious career was coming to a close, his son David was making a name for himself as an up and coming inside-right, and joined his father at Stockport County. Alec and David Herd played together for Stockport in the final game of the 1950/51 season, only the second time that father and son had played in the same League team. David Herd went on to spend five years at Edgeley Park before Arsenal, one of many clubs impressed with his constant running, strength on the ball and ferocious shot, signed him in 1954.

In 1961 Herd finished second to Jimmy Greaves as Division One's leading scorer and Matt Busby paid £35,000 for the forward's services. After seven years playing for the Gunners, Herd made the move back north.

United's team was still being rebuilt following the Munich air crash. Despite Herd's 14 goals from 27 starts in his first season, 1961/62, United finished in a lowly 15th position. The struggle continued in the following season as the Reds skirted relegation, and it was only in the FA Cup that they saw a change in fortune. In 1963, United lifted the trophy at Wembley, with Herd scoring twice in a 3-1 win over Leicester City.

> 66 *David Herd was one of the most under-rated players ever to play for Manchester United.* 99
> **Pat Crerand**

United's recovery was finally under way by season 1963/64, and Herd's striking partnership with European Footballer of the Year, Denis Law, yielded 50 goals as United finished second in the League. United were crowned champions a year later and in the following season, 1965/66, Herd's name was on the score sheet 32 times. United won the championship again in 1966/67, but in November 1966 Herd broke his leg in an injury which would ultimately limit his future first-team chances. Herd and Law both missed the European Cup Final victory, although they

were awarded medals for their part. In 1968, with Brian Kidd developing into a ferocious attacker at the age of 19 and Herd pushing 35, Busby accepted an offer for Herd from Stoke City. He later played briefly for the League of Ireland side, Waterford, in 1970, but three months later he became manager of Lincoln City, where he stayed for 21 months.

After his footballing career ended, Herd ran a garage in Urmston, close to Old Trafford, where he still holds a season ticket and plays an active role in the Association of Former Manchester United Players.

Fact file

• **Quick start**
Herd scored on his United debuts in the FA Cup, the FL Cup, and all three European competitions.

• **Ball speed**
The velocity of Herd's shot was once calculated and registered to be 72.5 m.p.h.

• **Triple victory**
In 1966, Herd got an unusual hat-trick for United when he scored past three different goalkeepers in a 5-0 demolition of Sunderland.

• **Other interests**
A keen cricketer, David Herd opened the batting for one of Cheshire's top club sides, Cheadle Hulme, when his football career was over.

SU Sep 1888 **UD** v Preston North End (a) FAC 1, 18.1.1890 **FAC** 1/gls 0 **T** 1/gls 0

Haydock: Frank HB 1960–1963

b. 29.11.1940, Eccles, Manchester, England • *6ft 0.5in* • *12st 2lb* • **Clubs** Blackpool am. Jun 1956; UTD; Charlton Athletic Aug 1963, Portsmouth Dec 1965, Southend Utd Feb 1969 **SU** 1957–1958 (am.), Dec 1959 (pro.) **UD** v Blackburn Rovers (h) 20.8.1960 **FL** 6/gls 0 **T** 6/gls 0

Hayes: Vince FB 1900–1905; 1908–1911

b. 1879, Miles Platting, Manchester, England **d.** nk • *5ft 7.5in* • *11st 8lb* • **Clubs** Newton Heath Athletic; NH; Brentford May 1907; UTD; Bradford Nov 1910, Norwegian Olympic team (coach) Apr 1912, Wiener SV (Austria, coach) Aug 1912, Rochdale (player-manager) Aug 1913, Preston North End (secretary-manager) Mar 1919–Feb 1923, Madrid (Spain, manager) 1923 **SU** Feb 1901 and Jun 1908 **UD** v Walsall (a) 25.2.1901 **FL** 115/gls 2 **FAC** 13/gls 0 **T** 128/gls 2

Haywood: Joe HB 1913–1915

b. c. 1893, Wednesbury, West Bromwich, England **d.** nk • *5ft 6in* • *10st 8lb* • **Clubs** Hindley Central; UTD **SU** May 1913 **TF** £50 **UD** v Sheffield Utd (a) 22.11.1913 **FL** 26/gls 0 **T** 26/gls 0

Healy: David F 1999–2001

b. 5.8.1979, Downpatrick, Northern Ireland • *5ft 9in* • *9st 6lb* • **Clubs** UTD (on loan to Port Vale Feb–May 2000, Preston North End Dec 2000–Jan 2001); Preston North End Jan 2001 **SU** 8.7.1996 (appr.), 24.11.1997 (pro.) **UD** v Aston Villa (sub) (a) FLC (3), 13.10.1999 **FL** (1)/gls 0 **FLC** (2)/gls **T** (3)**INT** (Northern Ireland) 7/gls 5

Heathcote: Joe F 1899–1902

b. nk **d.** nk • **Clubs** Berry's Association FC; NH **SU** Apr 1899 **UD** v Middlesbrough (h) 16.12.1899 **FL** 7/gls 0 **FAC** 1/gls 0 **T** 8/gls 0

Henderson: William F 1921–1925

b. 1898, Edinburgh, Scotland **d.** 1964 • *5ft 10.5in* • *11st 10lb* • **Clubs** Airdreonians May 1920; UTD; Preston North End Jan 1925, Clapton Orient Jul 1925, Heart of Midlothian 1926–1927, Morton cs. 1927, Torquay Utd Aug 1928, Exeter City Jun 1929–1930 **SU** Nov 1921 **TF** £1,750 **UD** v Aston Villa (h) 26.11.1921, scored 1 **FL** 34/gls 17 **FAC** 2/gls 0 **T** 36/gls 17

Hendry: James F 1892–1893

b. nk **d.** nk • **Clubs** Alloa Athletic; NH **SU** Sep 1892 **UD** v Wolverhampton Wanderers (h) 15.10.1892, scored 1 **FL** 2/gls 1 **T** 2/gls 1

Henrys: Arthur HB 1892–1893

b. nk **d.** nk • **Clubs** NH cs. 1891 (registered as FL player May 1892); Notts Jardines; NH Oct 1892; Leicester Fosse Mar 1893, Notts County Jun 1896–cs. 1897 **SU** May 1892, Oct 1892 **UD** v Ardwick (h) FAC 1Q, 3.10.1891 **FL** 3/gls 0 **FAC** 3/gls 0 **T** 6/gls 0

Herd: David F 1961–1968

See p.90.

Heron: Tommy F 1957–1961

b. 31.3.1936, Irvine, nr. Kilmarnock, Scotland • *5ft 8.5in* • *11st 6lb* • **Clubs** Queen's Park, Kilmarnock, Portadown; UTD; York City May 1961, Altrincham Jun 1966, Droylsden 1969–1970 **SU** Mar 1958 (pro.) **UD** v Preston North End (a) 5.4.1958 **FL** 3/gls 0 **T** 3/gls 0

Heywood: Herbert F 1932–1934

b. dnk, Little Hulton, Bolton, England • **Clubs** Turton FC, Oldham Athletic am., Northwich Victoria; UTD; Tranmere Rovers Dec 1934, Altrincham 1935, Wigan Athletic, Astley & Tyldesley Colliery am. Jul 1936 **SU** Apr 1933 (am.), May 1933 (pro.) **UD** v Swansea Town (h) 6.5.1933 **FL** 4/gls 2 **T** 4/gls 2

Higginbotham: Danny D 1997–1999

b. 29.12.1978, Manchester, England • *6ft 1in* • *12st 3lb* • **Clubs** UTD; Royal Antwerp, Derby County **SU** 10.7.1995 (appr.), 1.7.1997 (pro.) **UD** v Barnsley (sub) (a) 10.5.1998 **FL** 3(1)/gls 0 **FLC** 1/gls **EUR** (1)/gls **CWC** 1/gls 0 **T** 4(2)/gls 0

Higgins: Mark D 1985–1986

b. 29.9.1958, Buxton, England • *6ft 1in* • *13st 3lb* • **Clubs** Everton appr. 1975, pro. Aug 1976–cs. 1984; UTD (on loan to Bury Jan 1987); Bury Feb 1987, Stoke City Sep 1988–Dec 1990 **SU** Dec 1985 (pro.) **TF** £60,000 **UD** v Rochdale FAC 3, 9.1.1986 **FL** 6/gls 0 **FAC** 2/gls 0 **T** 8/gls 0

Higgins: "Sandy" (Alexander) HB 1901–1902

b. 1870, Smethwick, West Bromwich, England **d.** nk • *5ft 10in* • *12st* • **Clubs** Woodfield FC, Albion Swifts, Birmingham St. George's, Grimsby Town Jun 1892, Bristol City May 1897, Newcastle Utd May 1898, Middlesbrough May 1900; NH **SU** Oct 1901 **UD** v Burton Utd (a) 12.10.1901 **FL** 10/gls 0 **T** 10/gls 0

Higson: James F 1901–1902

b. nk **d.** nk • **Clubs** Manchester Wednesday; NH **SU** Feb 1902 **UD** v Lincoln City (h) 1.3.1902 **FL** 5/gls 1 **T** 5/gls 1

Hilditch: "Lal" (Clarence) HB 1919–1932

b. 22.6.1894, Hartford, Northwich, England **d.** nk • *5ft 10in* • *11st 3lb* • **Clubs** Hartford FC, Witton Albion, Altrincham; UTD (player-manager Oct 1926–Apr 1927); Colts Team (manager) 1932–1933 **SU** Jan 1916 (pro.) **UD** v Derby County (a) 30.8.1919 **FL** 301/gls 7 **FAC** 21/gls 0 **T** 322/gls 7

Clarence Hilditch, known as both "Clarrie" and "Lal", commenced his Manchester United career in the regional wartime league, and had to wait until 30th August, 1919 to make his Football League debut in a 1-1 draw at Derby County. Hilditch established himself at half-back, having previously been a centre-forward with Witton Albion. He rarely committed fouls, which was unusual for a player in the middle line, and he quickly developed a reputation as one of the cleanest players in the game. In short, he was a gentleman and, in the FA's eyes, an ideal representative of English football, hence his inclusion in the squad that travelled to South Africa in 1920. In the previous year, he had played at centre half-back for England, winning against Wales in Cardiff. But international caps were hard to come by for a player from a mediocre club side, and United's League form was steadily deteriorating towards relegation in 1921/22.

Hilditch was limited by injury to just four appearances in 1924/25 when United won promotion back to Division One, but he returned to the fore in the top flight and was appointed player-manager in October 1926, a position unique in the history of the club. Relinquishing control to new manager Herbert Bamlett in April 1927, Hilditch remained on the playing staff for another four seasons. He made his final League appearance aged 37 on 30th January, 1932 in a 3-2 win over Nottingham Forest at Old Trafford. Sadly, Clarence Hilditch retired from football without ever winning any medals.

Hill: Gordon F 1975–1978

b. 1.4.1954, Sunbury-on-Thames, England • *5ft 7in* • *10st 12lb* • **Clubs** Staines Town, Slough Town, Southall, Millwall Jan 1973 (on loan to Chicago Sting, Apr–Aug 1975); UTD; Derby County Apr 1978, Queen's Park Rangers Nov 1979, Montreal Manic (Canada) Apr 1981, Chicago Sting (USA) May 1982, New York Arrows (USA), Kansas Comets (USA), Tacoma Stars (USA), HJK Helsinki (Finland), Twente Enschede, Northwich Victoria Sep 1986 (caretaker-manager) Dec 1986, Stafford Rangers Aug 1987, Northwich Victoria Jan 1988 (player-manager) May 1988 (player-coach) to Oct 1988, Radcliffe Borough Mar 1990, Chester City (manager) Jun 2001 **SU** Nov 1975 (pro.) **TF** £70,000 + clause **UD** v Aston Villa (h) 15.11.1975 **FL** 100(1)/gls 39 **FAC** 17/gls 6 **FLC** 7/gls 4 **EUR** 8/gls 2 **T** 132(1)/gls 51 **INT** (England) 6/gls 0

The Stretford End loved him. "Gordon Hill, King of all Cockneys," the supporters would sing from the terraces in appreciation of the little winger. Hill epitomized Manchester United's attacking spirit under their manager Tommy Docherty, who brought him to Old Trafford as part of his grand plan to rejuvenate the squad.

Hill came to Old Trafford from Millwall in 1975, for a £70,000 fee and a clause stating that a further £10,000 should be paid if he was selected for England. Six months later, Hill earned his first international cap against Italy.

At Old Trafford, Gordon Hill struck up an exciting pairing with Steve Coppell on the opposite wing, as United's attacking formation thrilled huge crowds all over the country. Hill's quick instincts, tricky footwork and ability to scorch past full-backs gave him one of the best scoring records ever achieved by a United winger: 51 goals in 132 (1) appearances. At Hillsborough on 3rd April, 1976, Hill distinguished himself by scoring twice in the FA Cup semi-final against Derby County, qualifying for the final against Southampton.

Hill's magical footballing skills, for which his team mates had nicknamed him "Merlin," shone brightly under Tommy Docherty, but when "the Doc" left the club in a blaze of publicity in 1977, Hill sensed that his days were numbered.

In April 1978, Hill went to Derby County, but the move turned out to be a bad one, and in November 1979, Tommy Docherty, who was now manager of Queen's Park Rangers, signed Gordon Hill for the third time. Fifteen months later, in the twilight of his career, Hill set off to play for a series of clubs across North America and Europe.

Hillam: Charlie GK 1933–1934

b. 6.10.1908, Burnley, England • *5ft 11in* • *11st 8lb* • **Clubs** Clitheroe, Nelson am. Mar 1930–Jan 1931, Clitheroe, Burnley May 1932; UTD; Clapton Orient May 1934, Southend Utd Jun 1938, post WW2: Chingford Town, trainer 1948–1949 **SU** May 1933 **UD** v Plymouth Argyle (a) 26.8.1933 **FL** 8/gls 0 **T** 8/gls 0

Hine: Ernie F 1932–1934

b. 9.4.1901, Smithy Cross, Barnsley, England **d.** 1974 • *5ft 9in* • *12st* • **Clubs** New Mills FC, Staincross Station, Barnsley am. Apr 1921, pro. Jan 1922, Leicester City Jan 1926, Huddersfield Town May 1932; UTD; Barnsley Dec 1934–May 1938, (coach) May 1939 **SU** Feb 1933 **TF** £10,000 (combined player fee) **UD** v Preston North End (a) 11.2.1933 **FL** 51/gls 12 **FAC** 2/gls 0 **T** 53/gls 12 **INT** (England) 6/gls 4

Hodge: James D 1910–1920

b. 5.7.1891, Stenhousemuir, nr. Falkirk, Scotland **d.** 2.9.1970 • *5ft 8in* • *10st 10lb* • **Clubs** Stenhousemuir; UTD; Millwall Athletic Dec 1919, Norwich City Jan 1922, Southend Utd Sep 1923–1924 **SU** May 1910 **UD** v Sheffield Wednesday (a) 17.4.1911 **FL** 79/gls 2 **FAC** 7/gls 0 **T** 86/gls 2

James Hodge could play anywhere, even in goal. He was best known at United as a right full-back until the 1914/15 season when he was dropped to make way for younger brother John, who'd previously played in front of him as a centre-half. After serving in the war with the Royal Field Artillery, James was sold to Millwall for £1,500.

Hodge: John D 1913–1915

b. dnk, Stenhousemuir, Scotland **d.** nk • *5ft 10in* • *11st 9lb* • **Clubs** Stenhousemuir; UTD **SU** Jun 1913 **UD** v Sheffield Wednesday (h) 27.12.1913 **FL** 30/gls 0 **T** 30/gls 0

Hodges: Frank F 1919–1921

b. 26.1.1891, Nechells Green, Birmingham, England **d.** 5.6.1985 • **Clubs** Alum Roch All Souls, Birmingham City Gas, Birmingham May 1912 (WW1: St. Mirren); UTD; Wigan Borough Jun 1921, Crewe Alexandra Aug 1922, Winsford Utd Aug 1926 **SU** Aug 1919 **TF** £100 **UD** v Manchester City (h) 18.10.1919 **FL** 20/gls 4 **T** 20/gls 4

Hofton: Leslie FB 1910–1913; 1919–1921

b. 1888, Sheffield, England **d.** nk • *5ft 9in* • *12st* • **Clubs** Kiveton Park FC, Worksop Town, Denaby Utd, Glossop Apr 1908; UTD; Denaby Main Feb 1922 **SU** Jul 1910 (pro.) **TF** £1,000 **UD** v Bristol City (h) 11.2.1911 **FL** 17/gls 0 **FAC** 1/gls 0 **T** 18/gls 0

Hogg: Graeme D 1984–1988

b. 17.6.1964, Aberdeen, Scotland • *6ft 1in* • *13st 3lb* • **Clubs** UTD (on loan to West Bromwich Albion Nov–Dec 1987); Portsmouth Aug 1988, Heart of Midlothian Aug 1991, Notts County Jan 1995, Brentford Jan–May 1998 **SU** Jul 1980 (appr.), Jun 1982 (pro.) **UD** v AFC Bournemouth (a) FAC 3, 7.1.1984 **FL** 82(1)/gls 1 **FAC** 8/gls 0 **FLC** 7(1)/gls 0 **EUR** 10/gls 0 **T** 107(2)/gls 1

Graeme Hogg's United career began badly, with the team being knocked out of the FA Cup by Third Division club Bournemouth. Good in the air but sluggish on the ground, Hogg lost out to the Kevin Moran-Paul McGrath partnership and his own injury problems, which forced him to miss the 1985 FA Cup Final and perhaps denied him international caps at senior level.

Holden: Dick FB 1904–1913

b. 12.6.1885, Middleton, Manchester, England **d.** nk • *5ft 10in* • *11st 11lb* • **Clubs** Parkfield Central, Tonge FC 1903–1904; UTD **SU** May 1904 (am.), Sep 1904 (pro.) **UD** v Blackpool (h) 24.4.1905 **FL** 106/gls 0 **FAC** 11/gls 0 **T** 117/gls 0

Converted by Tonge FC from a forward to a full-back, Richard (Dick) Holden earned a championship medal with United in 1907/08. A knee injury then caused him to lose his place in the side to George Stacey and reduced him to the role of spectator as the club won the 1909 FA Cup and another championship in 1910/11.

Holt: Edward F 1899–1900

b. nk **d.** nk • **Clubs** Newton Heath Athletic; NH **SU** Mar 1899 **UD** v Chesterfield (h) 28.4.1900, scored 1 **FL** 1/gls 1 **T** 1/gls 1

Holton: Jim HB 1972–1975

b. 11.4.1951, Lesmahagow, nr. Lanark, Scotland **d.** 5.10.1993 • *6ft 1in* • *13st 5lb* • **Clubs** Celtic ground staff, West Bromwich Albion Apr 1968, Shrewsbury Town Jun 1971; UTD (on loan to Miami Toros, USA, Jun–Aug 1976 and to Sunderland Sep 1976); Sunderland Oct 1976, Coventry City Mar 1977 (on loan to Detroit Express, USA, May–Aug 1980), Sheffield Wednesday May 1981–cs. 1982 **SU** Jan 1973 (pro.) **TF** £80,000 **UD** v West Ham Utd (h) 20.1.1973 **FL** 63/gls 5 **FAC** 2/gls 0 **FLC** 4/gls 0 **T** 69/gls 5 **INT** (Scotland) 15/gls 2

Homer: Tom F 1909–1912

b. 1886, Winson Green, Birmingham England **d.** nk • *5ft 10in* • *11st 12lb* • **Clubs** Soho Caledonians, Erdington FC, Aston Villa am. Jun 1904 (on loan to Stourbridge), Kidderminster Harriers; UTD **SU** Oct 1909 **UD** v Woolwich Arsenal (h) 30.10.1909 **FL** 25/gls 14 **T** 25/gls 14

Hood: Billy F 1892–1894

b. nk **d.** nk • **Clubs** NH 1891–1892 (Jul 1892 registered with FL) **SU** Jul 1892 **UD** v West Bromwich Albion (a) 1.10.1892 **FL** 33/gls 6 **TM** 2/gls 0 **FAC** 3/gls 0 **T** 38/gls 6

Hooper: Arthur F 1909–1914

b. 1889, Brierley Hill, nr. Stourbridge, England **d.** nk • *5ft 7in* • *10st 12lb* • **Clubs** Kidderminster Harriers; UTD; Crystal Palace Jun 1914–cs. 1915 **SU** Oct 1909 **UD** v Tottenham Hotspur (h) 22.1.1910, scored 1 **FL** 7/gls 1 **T** 7/gls 1

Hopkin: Fred F 1919–1921

b. 23.9.1895, Dewsbury, England **d.** 1970 • *5ft 8.5in* • *11st 6lb* • **Clubs** Darlington (WW1: UTD, Tottenham Hotspur); UTD (registered for FL matches May 1919); Liverpool May 1921, Darlington Aug 1931–cs. 1932, Redcar Borough FC (trainer) 1933–1934, Leeds Utd (asst. trainer) late 1930s **SU** Feb 1919 **UD** v Derby County (a) 30.8.1919 **FL** 70/gls 8 **FAC** 4/gls 0 **T** 74/gls 8

Key: a=away am.=amateur appr.=apprentice b.=born c.=circa cs.=close season CWC=Club World Championship D=Defender d.=died dnk=date not known EUR=European competitions F=Forward FAC=FA Cup FB=Full-back (defender) FL=Football League FLC=Football League Cup GK=Goalkeeper gls=goals h=home HB=Half-back (midfield) INT=International matches M=Midfield NH=Newton Heath Newton Heath LYR=Newton Heath Lancashire & Yorkshire Railway nk=not known pro.=professional Q=qualifying round SU=signed for United sub=substitute; substitute apps are in brackets after appearances T=total TF=transfer fee TM=Test match U=Utility UD=United debut UTD=Manchester United v=versus CWC=Club World Cup

Hughes: Mark F 1983–1986; 1988–1995

b. 1.11.1963, Wrexham, Wales • *5ft 9.5in* • *13st 5lb*
• **Clubs** <u>UTD</u>; Barcelona Aug 1986 (on loan to Bayern Munich Nov 1987); <u>UTD</u> Jul 1988; Chelsea Jul 1995, Southampton July 1998, Wales (manager) Dec 1999, Everton Mar 2000, Blackburn Oct 2000 **SU** Jun 1980 (appr.), 1.11.1980 (pro.) **TF** £1.5 million (1988) **UD** v Oxford Utd (a) FLC 4, 30.11.1983, scored 1 **FL** 336(9)/gls 120 **FAC** 45(1)/gls 18 **FLC** 37(1)/gls 16 **EUR** 30(3)/gls 9 **T** 448(14)/gls 163 **INT** (Wales) 72/gls 16

In his two periods at Old Trafford Mark Hughes established himself as one of Manchester United's finest-ever players. His manager Alex Ferguson called him "a warrior you could trust with your life", while in the dressing room, his awe-inspired team mates christened him "the Legend". Supporters adored Hughes for his flamboyant style of play and commitment to the cause, and managers valued him for his sense of occasion and ability to win matches. For 10 seasons at Old Trafford, he led the forward line with his unique ability to shield the ball and bring others into the game. Hughes will be remembered for a set of spectacular and important goals that are without equal in the modern game. In Cup finals, European finals, title clashes and semi-finals Hughes always delivered, as his collection of awards and medals testifies. As Alex Ferguson once said, "Hughes was the best big game player I have known."

Flying high
Season 1984/85 was a great one for Hughes, shown above after scoring the winner in the 1985 FA Cup semi-final replay against Liverpool. United went on to win the Cup against Double-chasing Everton.

In partnership with Eric
Hughes had lacked an effective partnership until the arrival of Eric Cantona in November 1992. "I know that the Frenchman changed my footballing life," Hughes said in his autobiography. Together, Hughes and Cantona helped United to their first League title for 26 years. It was therefore apt that Cantona should provide the chip for Hughes to volley in the goal that effectively sealed the title at Crystal Palace in April 1993.

> *" He was brilliant at holding the ball up and always scored spectacular goals. I think he left Old Trafford too early. "*
> **Alex Ferguson**

The call-up

At his home in North Wales, the young Hughes had been receiving Christmas cards from United encouraging him to come to Old Trafford for a couple of years before he signed schoolboy forms for them in 1978. Hughes was originally a midfielder but, in a masterstroke by United's youth coach Syd Owen, he was converted into a centre-forward. Dave Sexton lured Mark Hughes to Manchester, but Ron Atkinson gave the Welshman his first-team debut, in November 1983. He scored that night and by the end of the season he had an impressive record of four goals in seven starts. He had also scored in his debut for Wales against England. The following season, 1984/85, Hughes was a first-team regular, and by the end of it he had scored 24 goals, won the FA Cup and been voted PFA Young Player of the Year.

Surprise sale

Hughes began 1985/86 in sensational form, scoring 10 goals in his first 13 games. Then Ron Atkinson received an inquiry about him from Terry Venables, at Barcelona. Atkinson offered Hughes the chance to leave. For months he dithered, eventually signing for Barcelona in January 1986, but he could not join up with his new team until the summer. Hughes returned to play for United, sworn to secrecy about his transfer. Unsurprisingly his form suffered. From the moment news of the move was leaked, Hughes scored only one goal in 17 games. As former United manager, Tommy Docherty claimed:

"The day United sold Mark Hughes was the day the title went out of the window." United, who had once had a seemingly unassailable lead, finished fourth and Hughes headed for Barcelona. He never settled there, and scored only four times in 28 games. The Catalan fans waved white handkerchiefs from the stands, the local sign of impatience with a matador. Hughes later said: "It was horrible. I remember looking up at the stadium and everywhere you looked you just saw white. But it was my fault. I was out of my depth, a mixed-up lonely Welsh boy who didn't want to be there in the first place."

Did you know?

- *Mark Hughes played the violin in the school orchestra.*
- *Hughes was also known as "Sparky".*
- *Hughes scored United's first-ever goal in the Premier League.*
- *United decided not to sign the legendary Peter Beardsley based solely on Mark Hughes' potential, while he was in the Reserves.*
- *On 21st April, 1993, Hughes became the 10th United player to score 100 League goals for the club.*
- *In June 1999, Hughes and former Everton goalkeeper Neville Southall took temporary charge of the Welsh national team following the resignation of Bobby Gould. Their first match as co-managers ended in a 2-0 defeat by Denmark at Anfield, Liverpool.*

Mark Hughes: Career timeline

June 1980 Signs as an apprentice with United

| 1978 | 1979 | 1980 | 1981 | 1982 | 1983 | 1984 |

March 1978 Signs schoolboy forms with United

1st November, 1980 Signs as a professional with United

30th November, 1983 Debut for United v Oxford United in League Cup

Proving himself
In the 1991 Cup Winners' Cup Final, United met Hughes' old club, Barcelona. On a night of personal triumph, Hughes' two goals led

Coming home

Hughes was loaned to Bayern Munich, and away from the claustrophobic Nou Camp stadium he started to enjoy his football again. A return to England seemed inevitable. Ron Atkinson, never forgiven for selling Hughes, had been replaced by Alex Ferguson in the autumn of 1986. Hughes was exactly what Ferguson needed to keep United in the Premiership, and he signed him for £1.5 million in the summer of 1988. Hughes inspired United during the dark days of the late '80s. In April 1989, at the end of his first season back in England, he was voted Player of the Year. He would later celebrate Cup Final wins, but his goal at Millwall in March 1990 to keep United out of the relegation zone was just as important. In 1991 he became the first player to win the PFA Player of the Year award twice.

Hughes won his second FA Cup winners' medal in 1990, scoring twice against Crystal Palace in the first game to force a replay, and United had a passage back to Europe. They reached the final of the European Cup Winners' Cup in Rotterdam, where they beat Hughes' former club, Barcelona. In 1992, the United side brought home the League Cup, and Hughes had now won three Cups since his return. However, the League championship was proving to be elusive. One reason for this was that Hughes never formed an effective partnership up front with anyone, until the arrival of Eric Cantona in 1992. They

United to a 2-1 win against the Catalans. "I wanted to show everyone there what I was capable of" he said, "because I felt I'd never done myself justice over there."

immediately gelled and helped United to their first League title for 26 years.

Their partnership grew better and the 1993/94 season saw Hughes at his best. He scored 21 goals as United charged towards success in all three domestic competitions. In the spring of 1994, though, United began to falter. Blackburn had cut their lead in the League, and

100th goal
Hughes' 100th League goal for United, against Crystal Palace in April 1993. The goal practically confirmed United's League title that season.

Equalizer
In the 1994 FA Cup semi-final on 10th April at Wembley, with just 40 seconds of the game to go, Hughes volleyed home a goal to equalize 1-1 against Oldham. As Oldham's manager, Joe Royle, reflected: "It would have gone over the stand with most players. But unfortunately for us it fell to Mark Hughes."

they had lost the League Cup Final to Aston Villa. Hughes revived the club's fortunes with a last-minute equalizer against Oldham in the FA Cup semi-final at Wembley. United went on to retain the Premiership and win the Double, beating Chelsea in the FA Cup Final 4-0, with Hughes scoring the third goal.

Moving on

Andrew Cole's arrival in January 1995 signalled the end of Hughes' 15 years at Old Trafford, although several dramatic

events delayed his departure for a while. During what was supposed to be his last game for United, Hughes injured himself. While he was recuperating, Eric Cantona took his infamous jump into the crowd at Crystal Palace and was subsequently banned, so Hughes was retained until the end of the season.

Chelsea were alerted to the fact that Hughes hadn't actually signed a new contract, and in a shock deal signed him for £1.5 million in July 1995. First under Glenn Hoddle, then Ruud Gullit, Hughes enjoyed renewed success at the Stamford Bridge club and picked up his fourth FA Cup winners' medal in 1997.

A reliable test of an ex-player's standing among fans is how he is received when he comes back to Old Trafford with his new club. Some players are booed, but each time Mark Hughes has returned with other teams, he has been given a hero's welcome.

Fact file

- **FA Cup star**
Hughes is the only player in the history of the game to win four FA Cup winners' medals.

- **Goals and games**
Hughes is United's eighth leading appearance maker with 448(14) games and Manchester United's seventh leading goal scorer with 163 goals.

- **Four in one season**
In 1994 Mark Hughes became the first-ever player to score at Wembley in four different club matches in one season; the Charity Shield, the League Cup Final, the FA Cup Final and the FA Cup semi-final.

- **Twice as nice**
Hughes has won two European Cup Winners' Cup winners' medals, with United in 1991 and with Chelsea in 1998.

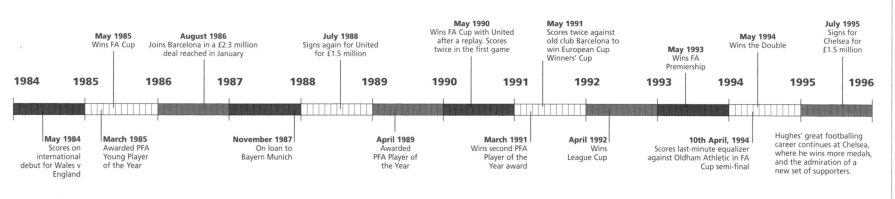

Timeline

May 1985 Wins FA Cup	
August 1986 Joins Barcelona in a £2.3 million deal reached in January	
July 1988 Signs again for United for £1.5 million	
May 1990 Wins FA Cup with United after a replay. Scores twice in the first game	
May 1991 Scores twice against old club Barcelona to win European Cup Winners' Cup	
May 1993 Wins FA Premiership	
May 1994 Wins the Double	
July 1995 Signs for Chelsea for £1.5 million	

1984 | 1985 | 1986 | 1987 | 1988 | 1989 | 1990 | 1991 | 1992 | 1993 | 1994 | 1995 | 1996

May 1984 Scores on international debut for Wales v England	
March 1985 Awarded PFA Young Player of the Year	
November 1987 On loan to Bayern Munich	
April 1989 Awarded PFA Player of the Year	
March 1991 Wins second PFA Player of the Year award	
April 1992 Wins League Cup	
10th April, 1994 Scores last-minute equalizer against Oldham Athletic in FA Cup semi-final	
Hughes' great footballing career continues at Chelsea, where he wins more medals, and the admiration of a new set of supporters.	

KEY: a=away **am.**=amateur **appr.**=apprentice **b.**=born **c.**=circa **cs.**=close season **D**=Defender **d.**=died **dnk**=date not known **EUR**=European competitions **F**=Forward **FAC**=FA Cup **FB**=Full-back (defender) **FL**=Football League **FLC**=Football League Cup **GK**=Goalkeeper **gls**=goals **h**=home **HB**=Half-back (midfield) **INT**=International matches **M**=Midfield **NH**=Newton Heath **Newton Heath LYR**=Newton Heath Lancashire & Yorkshire Railway **nk**=not known **pro.**=professional **Q**=qualifying round **SU**=signed for United **sub**=substitute; substitute apps are in brackets after appearances **T**=total **TF**=transfer fee **TM**=Test match **U**=Utility **UD**=United debut **UTD**=Manchester United **v**=versus

93

Ince: Paul M 1989–1995

b. 21.10.1967, Ilford, London, England • *5ft 10in* • *11st 13lb* • **Clubs** West Ham Utd pro. Jul 1985; UTD; Inter Milan (Italy) Jul 1995, Liverpool 1997, Middlesbrough Jul 1999 **SU** Sep 1989 (pro.) **TF** £2 million **UD** v Millwall (h) 16.9.1989 **FL** 203(3)/gls 25 **FAC** 26(1)/gls 1 **FLC** 23(1)/gls 2 **EUR** 20/gls 0 **T** 272(5)/gls 28 **INT** (England) 42/gls 2

Paul Ince's decision to join Manchester United's traditional rivals, Liverpool, in July 1997 brought him some criticism among United's faithful fans, but his contribution to United's return to greatness should never be underestimated.

It was Paul Ince's ability to win the ball and distribute it in midfield that gave the Manchester United side its driving force in the first half of the '90s. His kind of play won trophies for United, and it was only in Ince's final season that he finished a campaign without a winners' medal.

In September 1989 Ince arrived at United from West Ham United for around £2 million. He was a 21-year-old with raw talent and a suspect temperament. During his six seasons at Old Trafford he developed into a great player, one mature enough to be trusted with the England captaincy.

Ince, an East End boy, took time to settle at Old Trafford and did not immediately fulfil his potential. The turning point came in the 1990 FA Cup Final replay, a game which Alex Ferguson said "marked his breakthrough as a player of heroic quality". Ince's Cup winners' medal on that night was followed by two more, for the European Cup Winners' Cup and the League Cup. As Ferguson said: "The emergence of Paul Ince was really a mirror image of Manchester United's own improvement".

By 1992/93, with Bryan Robson no longer the force he once was, Ince was playing the best football of his career, as United ended their 26-year wait for the championship. He was now the self-styled "Guv'nor" of United's midfield. He finished as runner-up to Paul McGrath in the PFA Player of the Year award, but the greatest mark of his rise was when he was made England's captain against the USA in June 1993. In just one season he had gone from England debutant to captain. Like so many of his team mates, Ince, now partnered by Roy Keane in midfield, maintained his brilliant form to be part of the team that won the Double in 1994.

Ince's departure from Old Trafford in June 1995 was a shock to many. To most observers he had enjoyed another fine season, but this was not a view that was shared by Alex Ferguson, who thought Ince had under-performed. Ferguson believed that in Ince, Butt and Keane he had three midfielders of similar ability, so when Inter Milan offered £7 million for Ince, he decided to let him go.

> *"The man of a thousand faces, all of them snarling."*
> **Jimmy Greaves**

> *"Probably the best midfielder in the world, certainly the best in Europe."*
> **Eric Cantona**

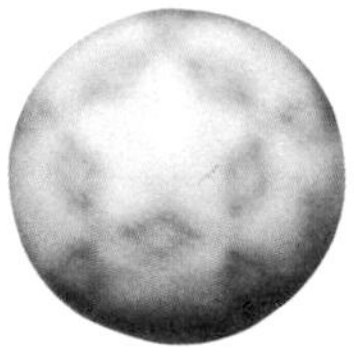

Influential
Ince's style of play strongly influenced United's success in the early '90s. His runs set up their attacks, while his back-tracking and tackling stopped those of the opposition.

Fact file

• Captain Paul
In June 1993, Paul Ince became the first black player to captain England, in a match against the United States.

• One in four
Only four United players have captained England: Bobby Charlton, Ray Wilkins, Bryan Robson and Paul Ince.

• High price
Ince became United's most expensive outgoing transfer when he joined Inter Milan in June 1995 for £7 million.

• Patience
Ince scored twice in his second game for United, away at Portsmouth, but he had to wait 70 games for his next goal.

Hopkins: James F 1898–1899

b. dnk, Manchester, England **d.** nk • **Clubs** Berry's Association; NH **SU** Mar 1899 **UD** v New Brighton Tower (h) 18.3.1899 **FL** 1/gls 0 **T** 1/gls 0

Hopkinson: Samuel F 1930–1934

b. 9.2.1902, Killamarsh, nr. Sheffield, England **d.** nk • *5ft 7.5in* • *11st 1lb* • **Clubs** Shirebrook 1921, Valley Road BC Sep 1922, Chesterfield May 1924, Shirebrook Jun 1927, Ashton National Jun 1928; UTD; Tranmere Rovers May 1935 **SU** May 1929 **UD** v Newcastle Utd (a) 17.1.1931 **FL** 55/gls 10 **FAC** 2/gls 2 **T** 57/gls 12

Houston: Stewart FB 1973–1980

b. 20.8.1949, Dunoon, Scotland • *5ft 11in* • *11st 9lb* • **Clubs** Port Glasgow Rangers, Chelsea Aug 1969, Brentford Mar 1972; UTD; Sheffield Utd Jul 1980, Colchester Utd (player-coach) Aug 1983, Plymouth Argyle (coach), Arsenal (asst. manager), Queen's Park Rangers (manager) Sep 1996-Nov 1997, Tottenham Hotspur (assistant manager) Feb 1999 **SU** Dec 1973 (pro.) **TF** £55,000 **UD** v Queen's Park Rangers (a) 1.1.1974 **FL** 204(1)/gls 13 **FAC** 22/gls 1 **FLC** 16/gls 2 **EUR** 6(1)/gls 0 **T** 248(2)/gls 16 **INT** (Scotland) 1/gls 0

Stewart Houston made his United debut in 1974, and quickly established himself as a first-team regular. His consistency, athleticism and accuracy made him an important part of United's 1975 Second Division championship side. He played in the 1976 FA Cup Final, but missed United's 1977 victory due to a broken ankle. Houston lost his place to Arthur Albiston before he was transferred to Sheffield United in 1980.

Howarth: John FB 1921–1922

b. 1899, Darwen, nr. Blackburn, England **d.** nk • *5ft 8.5in* • *11st 8lb* • **Clubs** Darwen; UTD **SU** May 1921 **TF** £750 (combined player fee) **UD** v Sheffield Utd (a) 2.1.1922 **FL** 4/gls 0 **T** 4/gls 0

Howells: E. HB 1886–1887

b. nk **d.** nk • **Clubs** Newton Heath LYR **SU** 1885 **UD** v Fleetwood Rangers (a) FAC 1, 30.10.1886 **FAC** 1/gls 0 **T** 1/gls 0

Hudson: Edward FB 1913–1915

b. 1887, Bolton, England **d.** nk • *5ft 10in* • *11st 6lb* • **Clubs** Walkden Central; UTD; Stockport County Aug 1919, Aberdare cs. 1920–1921 **SU** Jan 1912 **TF** £75 **UD** v Oldham Athletic (a) 24.1.1914 **FL** 11/gls 0 **T** 11/gls 0

Hughes: Mark F 1983–1986; 1988–1995

See p.92.

Hulme: Aaron FB 1907–1909

b. 1883, Manchester, England **d.** 1933 • **Clubs** Newton Heath Athletic, Colne FC cs. 1904, Oldham Athletic Oct 1904; UTD; Nelson cs. 1909, Hyde FC Mar 1910, St. Helens Recs Aug 1912, Newton Heath Athletic Aug 1913 **SU** May 1906 **UD** v Preston North End (h) 25.4.1908 **FL** 4/gls 0 **T** 4/gls 0

Hunter: "Cocky" (George) HB 1913–1915

b. 1885, Peshawar, Pakistan **d.** 1934 • *5ft 7in* • *12st 5lb* • **Clubs** Maidstone, Croydon Common cs. 1907, Aston Villa Mar 1908, Oldham Athletic Jan 1912, Chelsea Mar 1913; UTD (WW1: Croydon Common, Brentford, Birmingham); Portsmouth Aug 1919–1922 **SU** Mar 1914 **TF** £1,300 **UD** v Aston Villa (h) 14.3.1914 **FL** 22/gls 2 **FAC** 1/gls 0 **T** 23/gls 2

Hunter: Reg F 1958–1959

b. 25.10.1938, Colwyn Bay, Wales • *5ft 8.5in* • *10st 10lb* • **Clubs** Colwyn Bay; UTD; Wrexham Feb 1960, Bangor City Feb 1962 **SU** Nov 1956 (pro.) **UD** v Aston Villa (a) 27.12.1958 **FL** 1/gls 0 **T** 1/gls 0

Hunter: William F 1912–1913

b. dnk, Sunderland, England **d.** nk • *5ft 10.5in* • *12st 2lb* • **Clubs** Sunderland West End, Liverpool Dec 1908, Sunderland May 1909, Lincoln City Nov 1909, South Shields 1911–1912, Barnsley Aug 1912; UTD; Clapton Orient Jul 1913, Exeter City May 1914–1915 **SU** Mar 1913 **UD** v Liverpool (a) 29.3.1913 **FL** 3/gls 2 **T** 3/gls 2

Hurst: Daniel F 1902–1903

b. 1876, Cockermouth, England **d.** nk • **Clubs** Black Diamonds FC, Blackburn Rovers Oct 1897, Workington Mar 1900, Manchester City May 1901; UTD **SU** May 1902 **UD** v Gainsborough Trinity (a) 6.9.1902 **FL** 16/gls 4 **FAC** 5/gls 0 **T** 21/gls 4

Iddon: Richard F 1925–1927

b. 22.6.1901, Tarleton, nr. Southport, England • *5ft 8in* • *11st* • **Clubs** Tarleton FC, Leyland Dec 1921, Preston North End am. Aug 1921, pro. Oct 1921, Chorley 1923; UTD; Chorley cs. 1927, Morecambe 1927, New Brighton May 1928, Lancaster Town Dec 1929, Horwich RMI, Altrincham Jan 1933 **SU** May 1925 (pro.) **UD** v West Ham Utd (a) 29.8.1925 **FL** 2/gls 0 **T** 2/gls 0

Ince: Paul M 1989–1995

See left.

Inglis: Bill FB 1925–1929

b. 2.3.1894, Kirkaldy, Scotland **d.** 20.1.1968 • *5ft 10in* • *12st* • **Clubs** Kirkcaldy Utd, Raith Rovers, Sheffield Wednesday Jun 1924; UTD; Northampton Town Jun 1930; UTD (asst. trainer) Aug 1934–cs. 1961 **SU** May 1925 **UD** v Everton (h) 20.3.1926 **FL** 14/gls 1 **T** 14/gls 1

Irwin: Denis FB 1990–

b. 31.10.1965, Cork, Rep. of Ireland • *5ft 8in* • *10st 8lb* • **Clubs** Leeds Utd appr. Mar 1982, pro. Nov 1983, Oldham Athletic May 1986; UTD **SU** 8.6.1990 (pro.) **TF** £625,000 **UD** v Coventry City (h) 25.8.1990 **FL** 346(10)/gls 22 **FAC** 42(1)/gls 7 **FLC** 28(3)/gls 0 **EUR** 65/gls 4 **CWC** 2/gls 0 **T** 482(14)/gls 33 **INT** (Rep. of Ireland) 56/gls 4

Denis Irwin probably rates with Roger Byrne as United's greatest ever left-back. For eleven seasons, as United swept aside all before them, Irwin showed remarkable consistency on the left side of defence. "Denis Irwin is one of those players who always gives you a nine out of ten game," says Alex Ferguson, "I never have to worry about him". Denis Irwin is quick, strong in the tackle and excellent at supporting the attack with his overlapping runs and superb crosses. A free-kick specialist, he has scored more than 30 goals for United.

The Cork-born defender joined United in 1990. Irwin played his first season as a right-back, but after the arrival of Paul Parker a year later he switched to the left side.

At United Irwin has collected winners' medals for seven championships, three FA Cup wins, one League Cup win, one European Cup Winners' Cup win, one European Cup win, plus 56 caps for the Republic of Ireland. This haul makes Irwin the most successful player in United's history.

In the 1993/94 season Denis Irwin was United's only player to start every League and Cup game. At the end of the season the PFA recognized him as the Premiership's best left-back.

Alex Ferguson has been ruthless in allowing United legends to leave to give his youngsters the chance they deserve: Ince for Butt, Kanchelskis for Beckham, Parker for Gary Neville. It is a testament to Denis Irwin's qualities that he continues to restrict Phil Neville's first-team appearances. He was forced to make way in the 1999 FA Cup Final, however, after being sent off in a League match at Liverpool. Denis then returned to the team for the Champions League Final.

KEY: **a**=away **am.**=amateur **appr.**=apprentice **b.**=born **c.**=circa **cs.**=close season **CWC**=Club World Championship **D**=Defender **d.**=died **dnk**=date not known **EUR**=European competitions **F**=Forward **FAC**=FA Cup **FB**=Full-back (defender) **FL**=Football League **FLC**=Football League Cup **GK**=Goalkeeper **gls**=goals **h**=home **HB**=Half-back (midfield) **INT**=International matches **M**=Midfield **NH**=Newton Heath **Newton Heath LYR**=Newton Heath Lancashire & Yorkshire Railway **nk**=not known **pro.**=professional **Q**=qualifying round **SU**=signed for United **sub**=substitute; substitute apps are in brackets after appearances **T**=total **TF**=transfer fee **TM**=Test match **U**=Utility **UD**=United debut **UTD**=Manchester United **v**=versus

Keane: Roy M 1993–

b. 10.8.1971, Cork, Rep. of Ireland • *5ft 10in* • *11st 3lb* • **Clubs** Cobh Ramblers, Nottingham Forest Jun 1990; UTD **SU** 19.7.1993 (pro.) **TF** £3.75 million **UD** v Norwich City (a) 15.8.1993 **FL** 205(8)/gls 26 **FAC** 31(1)/gls 1 **FLC** 9(2)/gls 0 **EUR** 53/gls 14 **CWC** 2/gls 0 **T** 300(11)/gls 41 **INT** (Rep. of Ireland) 52/gls 8

As a teenager in Ireland, Roy Keane wrote to most English clubs asking for a trial, but decided not to write to Manchester United, as he thought he wasn't good enough. Today he is a United legend. "Roy Keane is a marvellous player," Ferguson has eulogized. "He has a superb knowledge of the game, awareness, vision, passing ability, an incredible engine and is a great competitor." Keane has a real presence on the field, and other players often seem wary of him. He is also versatile enough to play comfortably in either defence or midfield. The one weak link in Keane's game is his temper, which tends to boil over, and this has led to several dismissals during his Old Trafford career.

At the same age that United's current crop of youngsters were on the fringes of the first-team squad, Keane was playing part-time for Cobh Ramblers for £25 a game. In June 1990 he was spotted by Nottingham Forest and taken to England by Brian Clough for £10,000.

Keane quickly adjusted to the English First Division, and finished his inaugural season with an FA Cup losers' medal and an international debut for the Republic of Ireland against Chile. At Forest, he developed a reputation as the finest young midfielder in the game, so when the club was relegated in 1993, there was no shortage of clubs queueing up for his signature.

Keane signed for United in a deal worth a British record £3.75 million. After three years, Alex Ferguson had got his man: "Since I saw him on his Forest debut I said to myself, 'Manchester United must have him'".

Roy Keane walked into a team of champions and helped them to go one better by winning the Double in 1993/94. Rarely have United had such a formidable midfield pairing as Roy Keane and Paul Ince. In the summer of 1994, Keane represented the Republic of Ireland in the World Cup Finals in the USA.

Keane's Man of the Match performance against Liverpool in the 1996 FA Cup Final was responsible for making the game such an anti-climax. Playing in front of the back four, Keane snuffed out any Liverpool threat by tight marking, and so delivered United the second part of the double Double.

During the 1996/97 season Keane began to be recognized as the most complete player in Britain. Ferguson gave him the United captaincy after Eric Cantona retired in the summer of 1997, but just as Keane was at the height of his powers, he injured his knee, snapping his cruciate ligament at Elland Road in September 1997 and missed the rest of the 1997/98 season.

Roy made a triumphant return to action in 1998/99 and regained the captaincy from Peter Schmeichel, the only man who made more appearances than him in the Treble-winning season. As well as motivating and driving the team with typical aggression, Roy scored a handful of important goals, including a deft header against Juventus which set United up for an amazing 3-2 win in the second leg of the Champions League semi-final. The only real setbacks were his suspension from the Champions League Final and an injury which restricted him to just eight minutes of play in the FA Cup Final.

Roy Keane's enormous influence on Manchester United increased in the following seasons as they regained the Premiership title in 2000 and 2001 under his captaincy. In December 1999, Roy ended months of speculation by signing a new, four-year contract at United. The club was greatly relieved as Keane proved to be in the form of his life during the 1999/2000 season. In May 2000 he was voted both the Football Writer's Footballer of the Year and the PFA's Player of the Year.

Despite a slow start in the 2000/01 season, Keane regained his form and drove United to yet another Premiership title. However, the club's failure to perform in the Champions League provoked an angry outburst from Keane, in which he predicted that the success enjoyed by Manchester United could be coming to an abrupt end.

Fact file

- **Britain's best**
  Roy Keane was voted Britain's best footballer in a Match of the Day *magazine poll in April 1997.*
- **Sendings off**
  Over the course of just 14 games during the 1995/96 season, Roy Keane was sent off three times. He was also sent off in his first game as captain of the Republic of Ireland.
- **Treble Double**
  Roy Keane is one of only four players to win the League and FA Cup Double on three occasions.
- **Five finals**
  Roy played in more FA Cup Finals than any other player during the 1990s. He appeared in four for Manchester United, and one for Nottingham Forest in 1991.

Respect
Roy Keane's constant awareness of the ball and of other players gives him a commanding presence on the pitch, and has earned him great respect among his team mates.

Irwin continued to serve United with distinction in the following seasons, but lost his starting place at left-back to Mikael Silvestre in the 2000/01 season.

Jackson: Tommy M 1975–1978

b. 3.11.1946, Belfast, N. Ireland • *5ft 7in* • *11st 3lb* • **Clubs** Glentoran, Everton Feb 1968, Nottingham Forest Oct 1970; UTD; Waterford **SU** Jul 1975 (pro.) **UD** v Wolverhampton Wanderers (a) 16.8.1975 **FL** 18(1)/gls 0 **FAC** 4/gls 0 **T** 22(1)/gls 0 **INT** (N. Ireland) 35/gls 0

Jackson: William F 1899–1901

b. 27.1.1876, Flint, Wales **d.** 25.3.1954 • *5ft 8in* • *11st 12lb* • **Clubs** Flint, Rhyl 1897–1898, Flint 1898–1899, St. Helens Recreation 1898–1899; NH; Barrow 1902–1903, Burnley Jul 1903, Flint 1905, Wigan County **SU** Jul 1899 **UD** v Gainsborough Trinity (h) 2.9.1899 **FL** 61/gls 12 **FAC** 3/gls 2 **T** 64/gls 14

James: Steve HB 1968–1975

b. 29.11.1949, Coseley, Wolverhampton, England • *5ft 11in* • *10st 10lb* • **Clubs** UTD; York City Jan 1976, Kidderminster Harriers May 1980, Tipton Town 1982 **SU** Jul 1965 (appr.), Dec 1966 (pro.) **UD** v Liverpool (a) 2.10.1968 **FL** 129/gls 4 **FAC** 12/gls 0 **FLC** 17(1)/gls 0 **EUR** 2/gls 0 **T** 160(1)/gls 4

Much was expected of England Youth player Steve James when he emerged from United's Reserves. However, James found the retired European Cup hero Bill Foulkes a hard act to replace, and his confidence suffered in the spotlight. Although James was a good tackler and header of the ball, he never commanded a regular place and left United after helping them to win Division Two in 1974/75.

Jenkyns: Caesar HB 1896–1898

b. 24.8.1866, Builth, nr. Llandrindod, Wales **d.** 23.7.1941 • *5ft 10in* • *14st 4lb* • **Clubs** Small Heath St. Andrews, Walsall Swifts, Unity Gas FC, Small Heath Jul 1888, Woolwich Arsenal May 1895; NH; Walsall Nov 1897, Coventry City 1902–1903, Unity Gas FC, Saltney Wednesday FC 1904–cs. 1905 **SU** May 1896 **UD** v Gainsborough Trinity (h) 1.9.1896 **FL** 35/gls 5 **TM** 4/gls 1 **FAC** 8/gls 0 **T** 47/gls 6 **INT** (Wales) 8/gls 1

John: Roy GK 1936–1937

b. 29.1.1911, Briton Ferry, Neath, Wales **d.** 12.7.1973 • *5ft 11in* • *11st 10lb* • **Clubs** Briton Ferry Athletic, Swansea Town am. Feb 1927, Walsall May 1928, Stoke Apr 1932, Preston North End Jun 1934, Sheffield Utd Dec 1934; UTD; Newport County Mar 1937, Swansea Town Jul 1937 (WW2: Southport, Blackburn Rovers, Burnley, Bolton Wanderers) **SU** Jun 1936 **UD** v Wolverhampton Wanderers (h) 29.8.1936 **FL** 15/gls 0 **T** 15/gls 0 **INT** (Wales) 12/gls 0

Johnsen: Ronny D 1996–

b. 10.6.1969, Sandefjord, Norway • *6ft 2in* • *13st* • **Clubs** IF ELK-Tonsberg 1991-1992, Lyn Oslo 1992-1994, Lillestrom 1994-1995, (all in Norway), Besiktas (Turkey) 1995-1996; UTD **SU** 10.7.1996 (pro.) **TF** £1.6 million **UD** v Wimbledon (a) 17.8.1996 **FL** 76(13)/gls 6 **FAC** 8(2)/gls 1 **FLC** 3/gls 0 **EUR** 24(2)/gls 2 **T** 111(17)/gls 9 **INT** (Norway) 43/gls 2

In the summer of 1996, Norwegian international defender, Ronny Johnsen, was signed for United from Turkish club Besiktas for around £1.6 million, which made him Norway's most expensive player at the time. Like fellow countryman Ole Gunnar Solskjaer, who arrived at the same time, Johnsen settled in immediately at Old Trafford, making 37 appearances in the championship-winning season of 1996/97.

In Norway, up to the age of 24, Johnsen had played as a striker before switching to a central defensive role for club and country. His versatility was to prove invaluable to United as he shifted easily between defence and midfield roles. Johnsen's pace, excellent sense of positioning and composure on the ball have won him many admirers. While playing for Norway in the 1998 World Cup Finals, he was described by Brazil coach Mario Zagallo as 'the king' for the way he marked Ronaldo out of the game. The following League season was interrupted for Ronny by injuries, but he still collected three winners' medals, including his first in the FA and European Cups. However, his injury problems soon returned, and he only played in 20 games in the two seasons after the Champions League Final. He failed to play enough games to claim a Premiership winner's medal in 2000, but managed to do so in the next season.

Johnson: Samuel F 1900–1901

b. nk **d.** nk • **Clubs** Tonge FC; NH; Heywood FC Nov 1902 **SU** Jan 1901 **UD** v Leicester Fosse (h) 20.3.1901 **FL** 1/gls 0 **T** 1/gls 0

Johnston: Billy F 1927–1929; 1931–1932

b. 16.1.1901, Edinburgh, Scotland **d.** nk • *5ft 8in* • *11st 2lb* • **Clubs** Dalkeith Thistle, Selby Town Dec 1918, Huddersfield Town Nov 1920, Stockport County Dec 1924; UTD; Macclesfield Jun 1929; UTD; Oldham Athletic May 1932, Frickley Colliery (player-manager) Jun 1935–late 1936 **SU** Oct 1927 and May 1931 **TF** £3,000 **UD** v Cardiff City (h) 15.10.1927 **FL** 71/gls 24 **FAC** 6/gls 3 **T** 77/gls 27

Jones: "Chorley" (Owen) F 1898–1899

b. 1871, Bangor, Wales **d.** 1955 • **Clubs** Bangor, Crewe Alexandra Oct 1894, Chorley Sep 1897; NH; Bangor, Earlestown, Stalybridge Rovers Nov 1901 **SU** May 1898 **UD** v Gainsborough Trinity (a) 3.9.1898 **FL** 2/gls 0 **T** 2/gls 0 **INT** (Wales) 2/gls 1

Jones: David HB 1937–1938

b. 23.11.1914, Ynysddu, Monmouth, Wales **d.** 30.5.1988 • *5ft 11in* • *12st 6lb* • **Clubs** Ynysddu, Tottenham Hotspur 1932 (on loan to Northfleet), Cardiff City Jul 1934, Newport County Jun 1935, Wigan Athletic Jul 1936; UTD; Swindon Town Jun 1938, Cheltenham Town 1946–1947 **SU** Dec 1937 **UD** v Bradford (a) 11.12.1937 **FL** 1/gls 0 **T** 1/gls 0

Jones: Mark HB 1950–1958

b. 15.6.1933, Barnsley, England **d.** 6.2.1958 • *6ft 1in* • *12st 12lb* • **Clubs** UTD until his death **SU** Jun 1948 (appr.), Jul 1950 (pro.) **UD** v Sheffield Wednesday (h) 7.10.1950 **FL** 103/gls 1 **FAC** 7/gls 0 **EUR** 10/gls 0 **T** 120/gls 1

Mark Jones was only 17 when he made his first team debut in 1950, and 24 when he was killed at Munich. Yet there was a maturity about him that made him seem much older. As deputy to the captain, Allenby Chilton, Jones often had to wait for a chance to play, but he joined the first team in 1954/55. From his centre-half spot Jones presented a formidable barrier to the enemy, and maintained the supply line to his forwards. Playing simple and effective football, Jones would keep the ball moving, passing it on quickly. Many considered the Colman, Jones and Edwards half-back line to be as strong as the earlier trio of Duckworth, Roberts and Bell.

Jones' toughness and foresight were assets much valued by Matt Busby, and only the talents of his friend Jackie Blanchflower kept him from sole possession of the centre-half position. Both Jones and Blanchflower were products of United's youth programme, and it is a measure of that programme's success that Matt Busby could afford to choose between two such powerful young players. The two were good friends, and Blanchflower was even the best man at James' wedding. Off the field, Mark was notable for smoking pipes and for his interest in budgerigars.

Mark Jones' death at Munich robbed the team of one of its mainstays, a gritty, instinctive foil to the more exuberant players among the Busby Babes.

Kidd: Brian F 1967–1974

b. 29.5.1949, Collyhurst, Manchester, England • *5ft 10in* • *11st 6lb* • **Clubs** UTD; Arsenal Aug 1974, Manchester City Jul 1976, Everton Mar 1979, Bolton Wanderers May 1980 (on loan to Atlanta Chiefs, USA, Apr–Aug 1981), Fort Lauderdale Strikers (USA) Jan 1982, Minnesota Strikers (USA) May 1984, Barrow (manager) 1984, Swindon Town (asst. manager) Apr 1985, Preston North End (asst. manager, later manager), Blackburn Rovers (manager) Dec 1998 Jan–Mar 1986; UTD (junior coach, director of School of Excellence) May 1988, (youth development officer) Oct 1990 (later asst. manager), Blackburn Rovers (manager) Dec 1998, Leeds United (Youth Development Director) May 2000, (First team coach) Mar 2001 **SU** Aug 1964 (appr.), Jun 1966 (pro.) **UD** v Everton (a) 19.8.1967 **FL** 195(8)/gls 52 **FAC** 24(1)/gls 8 **FLC** 20/gls 7 **EUR** 16/gls 3 **T** 255(9)/gls 70 **INT** (England) 2/gls 1

Born and bred in Collyhurst, just a couple of hundred yards from Manchester city centre, Brian Kidd attended the same school as United stars Nobby Stiles and Wilf McGuinness. Kidd was a keen United supporter and his childhood dream came true when, aged 14, he signed schoolboy forms for the club, going on to sign apprenticeship, then professional forms in what was to be a fine career. Kidd showed excellent form in United's Reserve side, and Matt Busby rewarded him with a debut at the start of the 1967/68 season, in the Charity Shield, when he went on as a substitute for the injured David Herd. Kidd was sufficiently impressive to secure himself a regular first-team place, missing just four matches during his glorious first season at United.

On his 19th birthday, Kidd played in United's European Cup Final victory over Benfica, scoring the third of United's four goals. He was a big hero with the supporters, and the Stretford End adopted the Beatles classic *Hello, Goodbye* as a tribute to him prior to the European Cup Final, with the chorus changed to: "Eusebio, and I say Kiddo".

Kidd was privileged to play alongside Law, Best and Charlton, and he was capped twice for England. However, a European Cup winners' medal was to be Kidd's only honour at United. Despite making over 250 appearances for the Reds, Kidd was playing for an ageing side in transition and, in 1974, after United had been relegated to the Second Division, he moved to Arsenal for £110,000. The move to Highbury rejuvenated Kidd's career and he figured in three more six-figure transfers over the next five years.

In 1988 Kidd rejoined Manchester United after working on a Professional Footballers' Association initiative to get clubs closer to the community supporting them. He went on to manage the "B" team on a part-time basis, before being given a full-time brief to concentrate on the youth development project. In 1991, manager Alex Ferguson asked Kidd to become his assistant, a role Kidd performed with great success. Seemingly content with his coaching work at the club, Kidd said in 1996: "I want to work for Manchester United until I retire." Highly surprising, then, was his decision in December 1998 to leave and become a manager in his own right at Blackburn Rovers. The decision looked a poor one at the end of the season when, in the cruellest of ironies, Treble-chasing United relegated Rovers from the Premiership with a 0-0 draw at Ewood Park. Kidd was sacked six months later, but he returned to the game as Youth Development Director at Leeds United in May 2000. In March 2001, he became their first team coach.

Did you know?

- *Kidd's most celebrated goal was undoubtedly the one he scored in the 1968 European Cup Final victory on his 19th birthday.*
- *In 1980, Kidd became only the second player since World War Two to be dismissed in an FA Cup semi-final, when he was sent off playing for Everton against West Ham.*
- *Kidd's appointment as assistant manager was hardly a formal affair; boss Alex Ferguson simply said: "Give us a hand with the first team, will you Kiddo?"*

Big shot
A big, strong centre-forward who possessed a ferocious shot and neat ball control.

Jones: Peter FB 1957–1958

b. 30.11.1937, Salford, Manchester, England • *5ft 10.5in* • *12st 4lb* • **Clubs** UTD (ground staff) Dec 1952; Wolverhampton Wanderers am. 1953–1954; UTD; Wrexham Mar 1960, Stockport County Jul 1966–Jun 1968, Altrincham **SU** 1954 (am.), Apr 1955 (pro.) **UD** v Portsmouth (h) 19.10.1957 **FL** 1/gls 0 **T** 1/gls 0

Jones: Tom FB 1924–1937

b. 6.12.1899, Penycae, Wrexham, Wales **d.** 20.2.1978 • *5ft 8in* • *10st 7lb* • **Clubs** Acrefair, Druids, Oswestry Town cs. 1922; UTD; Scunthorpe & Lindsay Utd (player-manager) Jul 1937–1939, (WW2: Chirk), Druids (coach) early 1950s **SU** May 1924 (pro.) **UD** v Portsmouth (a) 8.11.1924 **FL** 189/gls 0 **FAC** 11/gls 0 **T** 200/gls 0 **INT** (Wales) 4/gls 0

Thomas Jones signed for Manchester United after winning the North Wales Charity Cup and the Welsh National League title in two highly successful seasons, 1922/23 and 1923/24, at Oswestry Town. His move to Old Trafford mocked Everton's earlier assessment that he wasn't big enough to make the grade in professional football. In fact, Tom Jones compensated for any lack of strength with sound judgement, consistency and courage, and he became a more than useful squad player for United.

Serving mainly as cover for Jack Silcock and Charlie Moore, Tom Jones had to wait until 1927/28 for an extended run in the team. Playing 33 League games that season, he was unlucky enough to sustain an injury on the tennis court, which forced him to miss all of 1928/29. He became a regular again in 1933/34, but moved on to Scunthorpe and Lindsay United after making just one appearance in 1936/37.

In only his second season as player-manager of Scunthorpe and Lindsay United, Jones led them to the Midland League title with the club.

Jones: Tommy F 1934–1935

b. 6.12.1909, Tonypandy, nr. Pontypridd, Wales • *5ft 8in* • *11st* • **Clubs** Mid Rhondda, Tranmere Rovers Mar 1926, Sheffield Wednesday Jun 1929; UTD; Watford May 1935, Guildford City Jun 1946, Tranmere Rovers (trainer-coach) Aug 1946, Workington (trainer-coach) Aug 1953, Birmingham City (asst. trainer) Aug 1958, West Bromwich Albion (physiotherapist) 1966–1968 **SU** Jun 1934 **UD** v Bradford City (h) 25.8.1934 **FL** 20/gls 4 **FAC** 2/gls 0 **T** 22/gls 4 **INT** (Wales) 2/gls 0

Jordan: Joe F 1977–1981

b. 15.12.1951, Carluke, nr. Motherwell, Scotland • *5ft 11in* • *12st 4lb* • **Clubs** Blantyre Victoria, Morton Oct 1968, Leeds Utd Oct 1970; UTD; AC Milan (Italy) Jul 1981, Verona (Italy) 1983, Southampton Aug 1984, Bristol City Feb 1987, (player-asst. manager) Nov 1987, (manager) Mar 1988, Heart of Midlothian (manager) Sep 1990, Celtic (asst. manager) Jun 1993, Stoke City (manager) Nov 1993, Bristol City (manager) 1994–1997, N. Ireland (asst. manager) 1998 **SU** Jan 1978 (pro.) **TF** £350,000 **UD** v Bristol City (h) 8.2.1978 **FL** 109/gls 37 **FAC** 11(1)/gls 2 **FLC** 4/gls 2 **EUR** 1/gls 0 **T** 125(1)/gls 41 **INT** (Scotland) 52/gls 11

Joseph "Jaws" Jordan intimidated opposing defenders with his direct and physical approach to the game. He proved a useful target man for United, using his aerial prowess to set up attack partners, such as Macari and Greenhoff. United's top marksman in his last two seasons, he became the first Scotsman to score in three World Cup Final tournaments in Spain, in 1982.

Jovanovic: Nikki D 1979–1981

b. 18.9.1952, Cetinje, Yugoslavia • *6ft 3in* • *13st 10lb* • **Clubs** Red Star Belgrade, Yugoslavia; UTD (on loan to FC Buducnost, Yugoslavia, Dec 1981–Jul 1982); FC Buducnost **SU** Jan 1980 (pro.) **TF** £300,000 **UD** v Derby County (a) 2.2.1980 **FL** 20(1)/gls 4 **FAC** 1/gls 0 **FLC** 2/gls 0 **EUR** 2/gls 0 **T** 25(1)/gls 4 **INT** (Yugoslavia)

Kanchelskis: Andrei F 1990–1995

b. 23.1.1969, Kirovograd, Ukraine • *5ft 10in* • *12st 11lb* • **Clubs** Dynamo Kiev Aug 89, Shakhytor Donetsk (Ukraine) Jan 90; UTD; Everton Aug 1995, Fiorentina (Italy) Jan 1997, Glasgow Rangers Jul 1998 (on loan to Manchester City Jan–May 2001) **SU** Mar 1991 (non-contract) May 1991 (pro.) **UD** v Crystal Palace (a) 11.5.1991 **FL** 96(27)/gls 28 **FAC** 11(1)/gls 4 **FLC** 15(1)/gls 3 **EUR** 7/gls 1 **T** 129(29)/gls 36 **INT** (USSR, CIS)

When Andrei Kanchelskis arrived in Manchester in 1991, few United fans had ever heard of him. He played a trial for United and was signed in the summer, enjoying his first taste of first-team football in a 3-0 away defeat by Crystal Palace. The following season, Kanchelskis became a first-team regular for United and won a League Cup winner's medal in 1992. but, his form was inconsistent and his game wasn't yet complete.

Season 1992/93 saw Kanchelskis in and out of the side that won the League, and it wasn't until 1993/94 that the dashing winger really made his mark. Kanchelskis could turn a game with his long, lightning-fast runs down the right wing, usually ending in a first-class low cross to Cantona or Hughes. With Giggs on the opposite wing, United played superb football. In the summer of 1995, just when Andrei Kanchelskis had become a firm favourite with United fans, he left for Everton under acrimonious circumstances. By the time he moved to Glasgow, via Fiorentina in Italy, his various transfer deals had cost a total of £18.5 million. In his first season in Scotland, he helped Rangers win all three domestic trophies.

Keane: Roy M 1993–

See p.95.

Kelly: Jimmy M 1975–1976

b. 2.5.1957, Carlisle, England • *5ft 7in* • *10st* • **Clubs** UTD (on loan to Chicago Sting, USA, Apr–Aug 1976); Chicago Sting Apr 1977, Los Angeles Aztecs (USA) Jul 1978, Tulsa Roughnecks (USA) Apr 1980, Toronto Blizzard (Canada) Jul 1981 **SU** Apr 1972 (am.), Jul 1972 (appr.), May 1974 (pro.) **UD** v Wolverhampton Wanderers (sub) (h) 20.12.1975 **FL** (1)/gls 0 **T** (1)/gls 0

Kennedy: Fred F 1923–1925

b. 1902, Bury, England **d.** 1963 • *5ft 6in* • *10st* • **Clubs** Rossendale Utd 1920; UTD; Everton Mar 1925, Middlesbrough May 1927, Reading May 1929, Oldham Athletic Nov 1930, Rossendale Utd Sep 1931, Northwich Victoria Dec 1931, Racing Club de Paris (France) Sep 1932, Blackburn Rovers Aug 1933, Racing Club de Paris Jun 1934, Stockport County Jul 1937 **SU** May 1923 **UD** v Oldham Athletic (a) 6.10.1923 **FL** 17/gls 4 **FAC** 1/gls 0 **T** 18/gls 4

Kennedy: "Paddy" (Patrick) FB 1954–1955

b. 9.10.1934, Dublin, Rep. of Ireland • *5ft 11in* • *12st* • **Clubs** Johnville; UTD; Blackburn Rovers Aug 1956, Southampton Jul 1959, Oldham Athletic Jul 1960–Jun 1961 **SU** Feb 1952 (am.), Feb 1953 (pro.) **UD** v Wolverhampton Wanderers (a) 2.10.1954 **FL** 1/gls 0 **T** 1/gls 0

Kennedy: William F 1895–1897

b. nk **d.** nk • **Clubs** Ayr Parkhouse; NH; Stockport County Dec 1896, Greenock Morton am. Aug 1899 **SU** Jun 1895 (pro.) **UD** v Crewe Alexandra (h) 7.9.1895, scored 1 **FL** 30/gls 11 **FAC** 3/gls 1 **T** 33/gls 12

Kerr: Hugh F 1903–1904

b. 1882, **d.** nk • *5ft 6in* • *11st 6lb* • **Clubs** Ayr FC; UTD **SU** Jan 1904 **UD** v Blackpool (a) 9.3.1904 **FL** 2/gls 0 **T** 2/gls 0

Kidd: Brian F 1967–1974

See above.

Kinloch: Joe F 1892–1893

b. nk **d.** nk • **Clubs** NH **SU** Oct 1892 **UD** v Nottingham Forest (a) 29.10.1892 **FL** 1/gls 0 **T** 1/gls 0

Kinsey: Albert F 1964–1965

b. 19.9.1945, Liverpool, England • *5ft 9.5in* • *11st 5lb* • **Clubs** UTD; Wrexham Mar 1966, Crewe Alexandra Mar 1973–Nov 1974, Wigan Athletic **SU** Jun 1961 (appr.), Oct 1962 (pro.) **UD** v Chester (h) **FAC** 3, 9.1.1965, scored 1 **FAC** 1/gls 1 **T** 1/gls 1

Knowles: Frank HB 1911–1915

b. 1891, Hyde, Manchester, England **d.** nk

KEY: a=away am.=amateur appr.=apprentice b.=born c.=circa cs.=close season CWC=Club World Championship D=Defender d.=died dnk=date not known EUR=European competitions F=Forward FAC=FA Cup FB=Full-back (defender) FL=Football League FLC=Football League Cup GK=Goalkeeper gls=goals h=home HB=Half-back (midfield) INT=International matches M=Midfield NH=Newton Heath **Newton Heath LYR**=Newton Heath Lancashire & Yorkshire Railway nk=not known pro.=professional Q=qualifying round SU=signed for United sub=substitute; substitute apps are in brackets after appearances T=total TF=transfer fee TM=Test match U=Utility UD=United debut UTD=Manchester United v=versus

• *5ft 11in* • *11st 12lb* • **Clubs** Hyde FC, Stalybridge Celtic cs. 1911; UTD (WW1: Hyde, Arsenal, Oldham Athletic); Hartlepools Utd cs. 1919, Manchester City Oct 1919, Stalybridge Celtic 1919–1920, Ashington Aug 1921, Stockport County May 1922, Newport County Jun 1923, Queen's Park Rangers Feb 1924–Jun 1925, Ashton National Aug 1926, Macclesfield Oct 1926 **SU** Dec 1911 (pro.) **UD** v Aston Villa (a) 30.3.1912 **FL** 46/gls 1 **FAC** 1/gls 0 **T** 47/gls 1

Kopel: Frank FB 1967–1969

b. 28.3.1949, Falkirk, Scotland • *5ft 8.5in* • *11st* • **Clubs** UTD; Blackburn Rovers Mar 1969, Dundee Utd Feb 1972–cs. 1982, Arbroath (asst. manager) until Oct 1983, Forfar Athletic (asst. manager) 1991–1992 **SU** Sep 1964 (am.), Apr 1966 (pro.) **UD** v Nottingham Forest (a) 28.10.1967 **FL** 8(2)/gls 0 **FAC** 1/gls 0 **EUR** 1/gls 0 **T** 10(2)/gls 0

Lancaster: Joe GK 1949–1950

b. 28.4.1926, Stockport, England • *5ft 10in* • *11st 6lb* • **Clubs** UTD; Accrington Stanley Nov 1950, Northwich Victoria Aug 1951–1954 **SU** May 1949 (am.), Feb 1950 (pro.) **UD** v Chelsea (h) 14.1.1950 **FL** 2/gls 0 **FAC** 2/gls 0 **T** 4/gls 0

Lang: Tommy F 1935–1937

b. 3.4.1906, Larkhall, Motherwell, Scotland • *5ft 7in* • *10st 6lb* • **Clubs** Larkhall Thistle, Newcastle Utd Oct 1926, Huddersfield Town Dec 1934; UTD; Swansea Town Apr 1937, Queen of the South cs. 1938, Ipswich Town Oct 1946–Jun 1947 **SU** Dec 1935 **UD** v Bradford (h) 11.4.1936 **FL** 12/gls 1 **FAC** 1/gls 0 **T** 13/gls 1

Langford: Len GK 1934–1936

b. 30.5.1899, Sheffield, England **d.** 26.12.1973 • *6ft 0.5in* • *12st 9lb* • **Clubs** Attercliffe Victory, Rossington Colliery, Nottingham Forest Nov 1924, Manchester City Jun 1930; UTD **SU** Jun 1934 **UD** v Norwich City (h) 22.9.1934 **FL** 15/gls 0 **T** 15/gls 0

Lappin: Harry F 1900–1903

b. 1879, Manchester, England **d.** 1925 • *5ft 7.5in* • *10st 5lb* • **Clubs** Springfield FC (Failsworth), Oldham Athletic Oct 1900; NH; Grimsby Town Aug 1903, Rossendale Utd Aug 1904, Clapton Orient Aug 1906, Chester 1907, Birmingham Aug 1909, Chirk 1910, Hurst FC, Macclesfield FC **SU** Apr 1901 (pro.) **UD** v Chesterfield (h) 27.4.1901 **FL** 27/gls 4 **T** 27/gls 4

Law: Denis F 1962–1973

See p.98.

Lawson: Reg F 1900–1901

b. 1880, Bolton, England **d.** nk • **Clubs** Halliwell St. Paul's, Cheshire College; NH; Bolton Wanderers am. 1901–1902, pro. Sep 1902, Southport Central cs. 1903 **SU** Jun 1900 **UD** v Glossop (a) 1.9.1900 **FL** 3/gls 0 **T** 3/gls 0

Lawton: "Nobby" (Norbert) HB 1959–1963

b. 25.3.1940, Newton Heath, Manchester, England • *5ft 9.5in* • *11st 8lb* • **Clubs** UTD; Preston North End Mar 1963, Brighton & Hove Albion Sep 1967, Lincoln City Feb 1971–Jul 1972 **SU** 1956 (am.), 1958 (pro.) **UD** v Luton Town (a) 9.4.1960 **FL** 36/gls 6 **FAC** 7/gls 0 **FLC** 1/gls 0 **T** 44/gls 6

Lee: "Neddy" (Edwin) F 1898–1900

b. nk **d.** nk • **Clubs** Hurst Ramblers; NH; Hyde St. George's (coach) Sep 1903 **SU** May 1898 **UD** v Lincoln City (a) 25.3.1899 **FL** 11/gls 5 **T** 11/gls 5

Leigh: Tom F 1899–1901

b. nk **d.** nk • **Clubs** Derby County (reserves), Burton Swifts Aug 1896, New Brighton Tower Jan 1899; NH **SU** Mar 1900 **UD** v Barnsley (h) 17.3.1900, scored 1 **FL** 43/gls 15 **FAC** 3/gls 0 **T** 46/gls 15

Leighton MBE: Jim GK 1988–1990

b. 24.7.1958, Johnstone, nr. Paisley, Scotland • *6ft 1.5in* • *12st 3lb* • **Clubs** Dairy Thistle, Aberdeen 1977 (on loan to Deveronvale 1977–1978); UTD (on loan to Arsenal Mar–May 1991 and to Reading Nov 1991–Feb 1992); Dundee Feb 1992 Hibernian Jul 1993, Aberdeen Jun 1997 **SU** Jun 1988 (pro.) **TF** £450,000 **UD** v Queen's Park Rangers (h) 27.8.1988 **FL** 73/gls 0 **FAC** 14/gls 0 **FLC** 7/gls 0 **T** 94/gls 0 **INT** (Scotland) 91/gls 0

James (Jim) Leighton became Britain's most expensive goalkeeper when Alex Ferguson brought him to Old Trafford for £450,000. Leighton demonstrated his shot-stopping skills for two solid seasons at United but lost his confidence in the 1990 FA Cup Final, and was dropped for the replay. He later rediscovered his international form with Hibernian and was awarded the MBE in the 1998 New Year's Honours List.

Leonard: Harry F 1920–1921

b. 1886, Sunderland, England **d.** 3.11.1951 • *5ft 9.5in* • *11st 9lb* • **Clubs** Sunderland North End, Southwick FC, Newcastle Utd Nov 1907, Grimsby Town May 1908, Middlesbrough Mar 1911, Derby County Oct 1911; UTD; Heanor Town Jun 1921 **SU** Sep 1920 **UD** v Chelsea (h) 11.9.1920, scored 1 **FL** 10/gls 5 **T** 10/gls 5

Lewis: Eddie F 1952–1956

b. 3.1.1935, Manchester, England • *5ft 11in* • *11st 9lb* • **Clubs** UTD; Preston North End Dec 1955; West Ham Utd Nov 1956, Leyton Orient Jun 1958, Folkestone Town 1964, Ford Sports (manager), Wits FC (South Africa, manager) **SU** 1949–1950 (am.), Jan 1952 (pro.) **UD** v West Bromwich Albion (a) 29.11.1952, scored 1 **FL** 20/gls 9 **FAC** 4/gls 2 **T** 24/gls 11

Lievesley: Leslie HB 1931–1932

b. 1911, Staveley, England **d.** 4.5.1949 • *5ft 10in* • *12st* • **Clubs** Rossington Main Colliery, Doncaster Rovers Jul 1929; UTD; Chesterfield Mar 1933, Torquay Utd Jun 1933, Crystal Palace Apr 1937–1940, post-WW2: Holland and Spain as coach, and Turin, Italy 1947 until his death **SU** Feb 1932 **UD** v Charlton Athletic (h) 25.3.1932 **FL** 2/gls 0 **T** 2/gls 0

Lievesley: Wilfred F 1922–1923

b. 6.10.1902, Netlerthorpe, nr. Staveley, England **d.** nk • *5ft 10in* • *10st 6lb* • **Clubs** Derby County May 1920; UTD; Exeter City Aug 1923, Wigan Borough May 1928, Cardiff City May 1929–1930 **SU** Oct 1922 **UD** v Leeds Utd (h) 20.1.1923 **FL** 2/gls 0 **FAC** 1/gls 0 **T** 3/gls 0

Linkson: Oscar FB 1908–1913

b. 1888, New Barnet, London, England **d.** 1916 • *5ft 9.5in* • *11st 10lb* • **Clubs** Barnet & Alston, The Pirates FC; UTD; Shelbourne Aug 1913 (WW1: Queen's Park Rangers 1915–1916) **SU** Jul 1908 **UD** v Nottingham Forest (h) 24.10.1908 **FL** 55/gls 0 **FAC** 4/gls 0 **T** 59/gls 0

Livingstone: George F 1908–1914

b. 5.5.1876, Dumbarton, Scotland **d.** 15.1.1950 • *5ft 10.5in* • *11st 6lb* • **Clubs** Sinclair Swifts, Artizan Thistle, Heart of Midlothian Jun 1896, Sunderland Jun 1900, Celtic May 1901, Liverpool May 1902, Manchester City May 1903, Rangers Nov 1906; UTD (player-manager to Reserve XI Aug 1911, retired WW1); Dumbarton (manager) 1919, Clydebank (manager) Aug 1919, Rangers (trainer) Jul 1920–1927, Bradford City (trainer) Jul 1928 until his retirement in May 1935 **SU** Jan 1909 **UD** v Manchester City (h) 23.1.1909, scored 2 **FL** 43/gls 4 **FAC** 3/gls 0 **T** 46/gls 4 **INT** (Scotland) 2/gls 0

Lochhead: Arthur F 1921–1926

b. 8.12.1897, Busby, E. Kilbride, Scotland • *5ft 9in* • *11st 7lb* • **Clubs** Army football, Heart of Midlothian Mar 1919; UTD; Leicester City Oct 1925, (manager) Aug 1934–Jan 1936 **SU** Jul 1921 **UD** v Everton (a) 27.8.1921 **FL** 147/gls 50 **FAC** 6/gls 0 **T** 153/gls 50

Former engineering student Arthur Lochhead had a miserable first season with United, beaten 5–0 on his debut and relegated at the end. He demonstrated his goal-scoring prowess in Division Two, netting 13 in 37 appearances to help United win promotion in 1924–25. The skilful player then left for Leicester where he scored an impressive 106 goals in 303 League games.

Longair: William HB 1894–1895

b. 19.7.1870, Dundee, Scotland **d.** 28.11.1926 • **Clubs** Rockwell FC (Dundee), Dundee East End 1893; NH; Dundee Jun 1895, Sunderland Feb 1896, Burnley Nov 1896, Dundee May 1897, Brighton Utd May 1898, Dundee May 1899, (trainer) Aug 1900–1922, (groundsman) Sep 1924–1926 **SU** Feb 1895 **UD** v Notts County (h) 20.4.1895 **FL** 1/gls 0 **T** 1/gls 0 **INT** (Scotland) 1/gls 0

Longton: (no inital known) F 1886–1887

b. nk **d.** nk • **Clubs** Newton Heath LYR **SU** Mar 1885 **UD** v Fleetwood Rangers (a) FAC 1, 30.10.1886 **FAC** 1/gls 0 **T** 1/gls 0

Lowrie: Tommy HB 1947–1950

b. 14.1.1928, Glasgow, Scotland • *5ft 8.5in* • *10st 12lb* • **Clubs** Troon Athletic; UTD; Aberdeen Mar 1951, Oldham Athletic Aug 1952–Jun 1955 **SU** Aug 1947 **UD** v Manchester City (a) 7.4.1948 **FL** 13/gls 0 **FAC** 1/gls 0 **T** 14/gls 0

Lydon: George HB 1930–1932

b. 24.6.1902, Newton Heath, Manchester, England **d.** 12.8.1953 • *5ft 7in* • *10st 2lb* • **Clubs** Nelson Utd, Mossley; UTD; Southport Jan 1933, Burton Town cs. 1933, Hurst Aug 1934, Great Harwood Aug 1935 **SU** May 1928 **UD** v Bolton Wanderers (a) 25.12.1930 **FL** 3/gls 0 **T** 3/gls 0

Lyner: David F 1922–1923

b. dnk, Belfast, Ireland **d.** nk • *5ft 9in* • *11st* • **Clubs** Owen O'Cork FC, Glentoran, Belfast Distillery, Glentoran; UTD; Kilmarnock Dec 1922, Queen's Island cs. 1924, Clydebank Jan 1925, Mid Rhondda 1925–1926, New Brighton Sep 1926–Jun 1927 **SU** Aug 1922 **UD** v Coventry City (a) 23.9.1922 **FL** 3/gls 0 **T** 3/gls 0 **INT** (Ireland) 6/gls 0

Lynn: Sammy HB 1947–1950

b. 25.12.1920, St. Helens, England **d.** nk • *5ft 10in* • *11st 4lb* • **Clubs** UTD; Bradford Feb 1951–Jun 1955 **SU** 1935 (am.), Jan 1938 (pro.) **UD** v Charlton Athletic (a) 3.1.1948 **FL** 13/gls 0 **T** 13/gls 0

Lyons: George F 1903–1906

b. nk **d.** nk • *5ft 7in* • *11st 6lb* • **Clubs** Black Lane Temperance; UTD; Oldham Athletic Jul 1906, Rossendale Utd Nov 1906, Salford Utd Oct 1907 **SU** Apr 1904 **UD** v Burton Utd (a) 23.4.1904 **FL** 4/gls 0 **FAC** 1/gls 0 **T** 5/gls 0

Macari: Lou F 1972–1984

b. 4.6.1949, Edinburgh, Scotland • *5ft 6in* • *10st 9lb* • **Clubs** Kilwinning Amateurs, Celtic Jul 1966; UTD; Swindon Town (player-manager) Jul 1984, West Ham Utd (manager) Jul 1989–Feb 1990, Birmingham City (manager) Feb 1991, Stoke City (manager) Jun 1991, Celtic (manager) Oct 1993–Jun 1994, Stoke City 1994–1997, Sheffield United (chief scout) Jul 1998, Huddersfield Town (manager) Oct 2000 **SU** Jan 1973 (pro.) **TF** £200,000 **UD** v West Ham Utd (h) 20.1.1973, scored 1 **FL** 311(18)/gls 78 **FAC** 31(3)/gls 8 **FLC** 22(5)/gls 10 **EUR** 9(1)/gls 1 **T** 373(27)/gls 97 **INT** (Scotland) 24/gls 5

An impressive inside-forward, Luigi (Lou) Macari began his career with Glasgow Celtic, winning the Scottish League in 1970 and 1972, and the Scottish Cup in 1971 and 1972. In January 1973, as a guest of Bill Shankly, Lou Macari watched Liverpool beat Burnley in an FA Cup tie. But instead of signing for Liverpool as expected, Macari changed his mind and five days later he signed for United for the enormous fee of £200,000. On his debut Macari scored in a 2–2 draw with West Ham at Old Trafford.

In the late '70s Tommy Docherty thought that Macari would be better suited to a midfield role, and his game improved dramatically. Although his only honour with United was an FA Cup winners' medal in 1977, he did pick up two FA Cup losers' medals and one League Cup losers' medal.

Macari's career at Manchester United spanned 11 years and during that time he made 400 appearances, scoring 97 goals. The popular Scotsman was also capped 24 times. At the end of the 1983/84 season he became player-manager at Swindon Town, the first of many clubs he was to manage.

MacDonald: Ken F 1922–1924

b. 24.4.1898, Llanrwst, nr. Betws-y-Coed, Wales **d.** nk • *5ft 10in* • *11st 1lb* • **Clubs** Inverness Citadel, Inverness Clachnacuddin, Aberdeen cs. 1919, Caerau (Welsh League), Cardiff City Dec 1921; UTD; Bradford Oct 1923, Hull City Jun 1928, Halifax Town Mar 1930, Coleraine Dec 1930, Walker Celtic Jan 1931, Spennymoor Utd Jun 1931, Walker Celtic Oct 1931, Blyth Spartans **SU** Feb 1923 **UD** v Southampton (h) 3.3.1923 **FL** 9/gls 2 **T** 9/gls 2

MacDougall: Ted F 1972–1973

b. 8.1.1947, Inverness, Scotland • *5ft 10in* • *11st 11lb* • **Clubs** ICI Recs (Widnes), Liverpool am. 1964, pro. Jan 1966, York City Jul 1967, Bournemouth & Boscombe Athletic Jul 1969; UTD; West Ham Utd Mar 1973, Norwich City Dec 1973, South African football Jun–Jul 1975, Southampton Sep 1976, AFC Bournemouth Nov 1978, Detroit Express (USA) May–Jul 1979, Blackpool (player-coach/asst. manager) Feb–Oct 1980, Salisbury Aug 1981, Poole Town Dec 1981, Totton Jan 1982, Gosport Borough 1982, Athena (Australia) cs. 1982, Totton Oct–Dec 1982, Andover (coach) Oct–Dec 1983 **SU** Sep 1972 (pro.) **TF** £200,000 + clause **UD** v West Bromwich Albion (a) 7.10.1972 **FL** 18/gls 5 **T** 18/gls 5 **INT** (Scotland) 7/gls 1

Mackie: Charlie F 1904–1905

b. nk **d.** nk • *5ft 11in* • *12st 8lb* • **Clubs** Aberdeen; UTD; West Ham Utd cs. 1905, Aberdeen Dec 1905, Lochgelly Utd cs. 1906 **SU** May 1904 **UD** v Burslem Port Vale (a) 3.9.1904 **FL** 5/gls 3 **FAC** 2/gls 1 **T** 7/gls 4

Maiorana: Jules F 1988–1994

b. 18.4.1969, Cambridge, England • *5ft 9in* • *11st 8lb* • **Clubs** Histon FC; UTD **SU** Dec 1988 (pro.) **TF** £30,000 + clause **UD** v Millwall (sub) (h) 14.1.1989 **FL** 2(5)/gls 0 **FAC** 0(1)/gls 0 **T** 2(6)/gls 0

Manley: Tom HB 1931–1939

b. 7.10.1912, Northwich, England • *6ft 1in* • *12st 5lb* • **Clubs** Brunner Mods FC, Norley Utd, Northwich Victoria Apr 1930; UTD; Brentford Jul 1939 (WW2: UTD) until his retirement in May 1952, Northwich Victoria (manager) Mar–Oct 1954 **SU** Sep 1930 (am.), May 1931 (pro.) **UD** v Millwall (h) 5.12.1931 **FL** 188/gls 40 **FAC** 7/gls 1 **T** 195/gls 41

Starting out with Manchester United as a half-back, Tom Manley could also play in defence and attack. As a left-winger, he contributed 14 League goals in the Second Division championship-winning season of 1935/36, including four in a 7–2 win over Port Vale. Tom Manley also scored two goals in the 3–2 win over Bury that clinched the title that season.

Mann: Frank HB 1922–1930

b. 1891, Newark-on-Trent, England **d.** nk • *5ft 8in* • *11st 6lb* • **Clubs** Newark Castle Utd Apr 1905, Newark Castle Rovers Aug 1906, Newark Town Sep 1908, Leeds City am. Feb 1909, Lincoln City am. 1909, Aston Villa am. Dec 1909, pro. May 1911, Huddersfield Town Jul 1912; UTD; Mossley FC Aug 1930, Meltham Mills FC am. Oct 1931 **SU** Mar 1923 (pro.) **TF** £1,750 **UD** v Bradford City (a) 17.3.1923 **FL** 180/gls 5 **FAC** 17/gls 0 **T** 197/gls 5

Mann: Herbert F 1931–1932

b. 30.12.1907, Nuneaton, England • *5ft 8in* • *11st* • **Clubs** Griff Colliery, Derby County Feb 1926, Grantham Town Aug 1929; UTD; Ripley Town Nov 1933 **SU** May 1931 **UD** v Bradford (a) 29.8.1931 **FL** 13/gls 2 **T** 13/gls 2

Manns: Tom M 1933–1934

b. dnk, Rotherham, England **d.** nk • *5ft 10in* • *11st 3lb* • **Clubs** Eastwood Utd WMC, Rotherham Utd am. Dec 1930, Burnley May 1931; UTD; Clapton Orient Jun 1934, Carlisle Utd Jul 1935, Yeovil & Petters Utd Jul 1936 **SU** Jun 1933 **UD** v Burnley (a) 3.2.1934 **FL** 2/gls 0 **T** 2/gls 0

Law: Denis F 1962-1973

b. 24.2.1940, Aberdeen, Scotland • *5ft 9.5in* • *10st 5lb* • **Clubs** Huddersfield Town appr. Apr 1955, pro. Feb 1957, Manchester City 15.3.1960, Torino (Italy) 9.6.1961; <u>UTD</u>; Manchester City Jul 1973–Aug 1974 **SU** Aug 1962 (pro.) **UD** v West Bromwich Albion (h) 18.8.1962, scored 1 **FL** 305(4)/gls 171 **FAC** 44(2)/gls 34 **FLC** 11/gls 3 **EUR** 33/gls 28 **T** 393(6)/gls 236 **INT** (Scotland) 55/gls 30

Denis Law was hailed by supporters as "The King", the people's champion, the warrior footballer who held a particular sway over the terrace fans packed into the Stretford End of Old Trafford. They found it easy to identify with a player whose aggression was so obvious. He was slightly built, but the venom in his play frequently brought him into confrontation with referees as well as with opponents. The fans liked the streak of villainy which ran through Denis Law's football and which earnt him two four-week suspensions in the course of his career. They loved his willingness to fly into the action with few holds barred.

Law was a daring, cocky, impudent and abrasive player. These qualities, together with his lightning football, his flair for being in the right place at the right time and his prolific goal scoring, were an explosive mix which made him a popular hero.

Winning the championship
Law was top scorer in season 1964/65, when United won the championship. Unusually, on 3rd April, 1965, none of the five United goals against Blackburn were Law's. David Herd and Connelly scored one each, and Bobby Charlton the others.

Marksman

Law flourished especially in front of goal. He celebrated his goals by punching the air, wheeling away with his arm raised, his hand clutching his sleeve, and one finger pointing to the sky.

The young Law played for Aberdeen Schoolboys. His slim build worked against him and his squint, for which he wore glasses from the age of five, might explain his aggressive style; he admits that the handicap made him tougher. He couldn't wear glasses for football so he played with his right eye shut.

Despite his problem, he had enough ability to attract the attention of Archie Beattie in Scotland, whose brother Andy was manager of Huddersfield Town. He arranged a trial for Law. Bill Shankly, then in charge of Huddersfield's Reserves, said later: "He looked like a skinned rabbit. My first reaction was to say get him on the next train home." But Huddersfield took Law on as an apprentice in April 1955, and a few months later he had an operation to repair his squint. This was a success, though vision in his right eye remains slightly blurred. Denis describes it: "I could now open both eyes without having to look in two directions at once. I've been told I had a bit of a swagger on the football field and if that is so, that was the day it started. That operation changed my life. I strutted out of the hospital with my chest stuck out."

League debut

Law was soon in Huddersfield's Youth team, and caught the eye of Matt Busby in an FA Youth Cup tie against

Manchester United. Busby offered the club £10,000 for the 16-year-old; a remarkably big offer for such a young player, but it was rejected. On Christmas Eve, 1956, Law made his League debut, at 16 years and 10 months, the youngest player Huddersfield have ever fielded. They won 2-1 and Law went on to make 13 League appearances in the season.

Razor sharp

In February 1957 Bill Shankly, now Huddersfield's manager, signed Law as a full professional. He was still thin, but he made up for it with his aggression and razor-sharp reactions. Matt Busby, manager of Scotland, capped him against Wales in 1958, and he scored in a 3-0 win. It was a bizarre goal; the ball hit the

The Law and Herd combination

United's 1963 FA Cup Final victory against Leicester City gave Law a starring role, in his first season at the club. The exciting partnership between Denis Law and David Herd was to achieve all three goals in the 3-1 win, with Law scoring the first goal after 30 minutes, and Herd adding two more to win the cup for unfancied United.

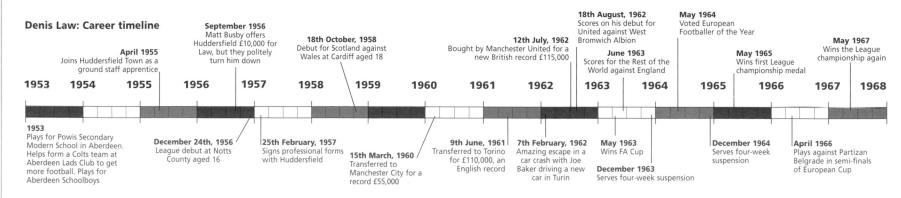

Denis Law: Career timeline

April 1955
Joins Huddersfield Town as a ground staff apprentice

September 1956
Matt Busby offers Huddersfield £10,000 for Law, but they politely turn him down

18th October, 1958
Debut for Scotland against Wales at Cardiff aged 18

12th July, 1962
Bought by Manchester United for a new British record £115,000

18th August, 1962
Scores on his debut for United against West Bromwich Albion

June 1963
Scores for the Rest of the World against England

May 1964
Voted European Footballer of the Year

May 1965
Wins first League championship medal

May 1967
Wins the League championship again

1953	1954	1955	1956	1957	1958	1959	1960	1961	1962	1963	1964	1965	1966	1967	1968

1953
Plays for Powis Secondary Modern School in Aberdeen. Helps form a Colts team at Aberdeen Lads Club to get more football. Plays for Aberdeen Schoolboys

December 24th, 1956
League debut at Notts County aged 16

25th February, 1957
Signs professional forms with Huddersfield

15th March, 1960
Transferred to Manchester City for a record £55,000

9th June, 1961
Transferred to Torino for £110,000, an English record

7th February, 1962
Amazing escape in a car crash with Joe Baker driving a new car in Turin

May 1963
Wins FA Cup

December 1963
Serves four-week suspension

December 1964
Serves four-week suspension

April 1966
Plays against Partizan Belgrade in semi-finals of European Cup

KEY: a=away **am.**=amateur **appr.**=apprentice **b.**=born **c.**=circa **cs.**=close season **D**=Defender **d.**=died **dnk**=date not known **EUR**=European competitions **F**=Forward **FAC**=FA Cup **FB**=Full-back (defender) **FL**=Football League **FLC**=Football League Cup **GK**=Goalkeeper **gls**=goals **h**=home **HB**=Half-back (midfield) **INT**=International matches **M**=Midfield **NH**=Newton Heath **Newton Heath LYR**=Newton Heath Lancashire & Yorkshire Railway **nk**=not known **pro.**=professional **Q**=qualifying round **SU**=signed for United **sub**=substitute; substitute apps are in brackets after appearances **T**=total **TF**=transfer fee **TM**=Test match **U**=Utility **UD**=United debut **UTD**=Manchester United **v**=versus

Two out of six
United won the championship again in season 1966/67, with this game against West Ham on 6th May effectively clinching the title. Denis Law scored twice in the game, here from the penalty spot, and was top scorer in the side again that season.

back of his head and rebounded into the net, but it marked the start of a long international career.

On 15th March, 1960, Manchester City paid a British record transfer fee for Law. City were a struggling team, and Law wondered what he was joining.

Torino transfer

Persuading Law to leave City in 1961 was easy. Torino offered him a £5,000 signing-on fee, plus bonuses such as £200 for a win, when the English maximum wage was £20 a week. However, the move was a disaster. Law didn't like the defensive game, the media attention or the training camps, and he was frequently in trouble. He longed to return to English football, and in July 1962 he arrived at Manchester United.

The first United season

During Law's first season, 1962/63, United flirted with relegation, though they won the FA Cup. Law made his mark in the final, taking a pass from Pat Crerand to beat Gordon Banks from

close range. It was his sixth Cup goal of the season and it prompted fluent football from the Reds, particularly David Herd. Law describes it as one of the best games he played for United.

Law's real break came the following season, with newly signed Crerand coming into his own to give improved support and help Law score 30 League goals from 41 games in 1963/64. At the end of the season he was voted European Footballer of the Year.

Honours then came thick and fast for United's '60s super side. They won the 1964/65 championship, with Law scoring 28, and in 1965/66 they reached the semi-finals of the European Cup, having beaten Benfica 5-1 in Lisbon.

Their finest hour

George Best grabbed the headlines in Lisbon. Law did not score, but his mere presence was a threat and he made gaps which were exploited by the others.

Law top-scored again, in 1966/67, helping United to win the League, then the European Cup in 1968, although

they did the latter without Law. He was in Manchester having a cartilage operation as United beat Benfica in the final.

After his operation, Law made 30 League appearances (14 goals) in 1968/69, but he had peaked. Best had taken over as the star and Docherty, the new manager, gave Law a free transfer at the end of 1972/73. It was a sad end to his United career.

He moved back to Manchester City, scoring a goal against United at the end of the season that seemed to be sending his old club down to Division Two. In fact United would have gone down anyway because their relegation rivals both won that day. In the 1974 World Cup he played for Scotland, but a few weeks later, at 34, he retired.

In all, Law made 55 appearances for Scotland and scored 30 goals, both records. For United he played 305(4) League games and scored 171 goals. In his career with all his clubs he scored 40 goals in the FA Cup, a record that was only beaten by Ian Rush in 1996. But what made him so lionized by the fans was the way he scored with spectacular overhead and scissors kicks, his style of pouncing on a loose ball quicker than anyone else, and the whiplash headers. Today he is paying the price for these, with neck problems. He has cut down on broadcasting work but is often called on to speak at sports functions.

29th May, 1968
Misses the final of the European Cup at Wembley against Benfica to have a knee operation, but still gets a winners' medal

July 1973
Given a free transfer at Manchester United by Tommy Docherty. Joins Manchester City

| 1968 | 1969 | 1970 | 1971 | 1972 | 1973 | 1974 |

In 1973/74, Law helped City to the final of the League Cup where they lost to Wolves. On 14th June, 1974, he won his 55th and last cap for Scotland, playing against Zaire in the World Cup in Germany. Law retired from football in August 1974. In 1975, he was presented with a Merit Award by the PFA in recognition of his great contribution to the game.

" *Up there with the all-time greats. Electric. He'd snap up any half chance. As a bloke and as a pal, he's a different class. Nobody has a bad word about Denis.* "
George Best

Famous trio
Charlton, Law and Best were all stars in their own right in that great '60s side. Bobby Charlton was admired, George Best was feted, but Law was worshipped because he brought together flair and fire.

Marshall: Arthur **FB** 1902-1903

b. 1881, Liverpool, England **d.** nk • *5ft 11in • 12st 6lb* • **Clubs** Crewe Alexandra, Leicester Fosse May 1901, Stockport County Jan 1902; UTD; Portsmouth May 1903-cs. 1904 **SU** May 1902 **UD** v Woolwich Arsenal (h) 9.3.1903 **FL** 6/gls 0 **T** 6/gls 0

Martin: Lee **D** 1988-1994

b. 5.2.1968, Hyde, Manchester, England • *5ft 11in • 11st 10lb* • **Clubs** UTD; Celtic Jan 1994, Bristol Rovers 1996 (on loan to Huddersfield Town Sep 1997) **SU** Jun 1985 (appr.), May 1986 (pro.) **UD** v Wimbledon (sub) (h) 9.5.1988 **FL** 56(17)/gls 1 **FAC** 13(1)/gls 1 **FLC** 8(2)/gls 0 **EUR** 6(5)/gls 0 **T** 83(25)/gls 2

Lee Martin first appeared for Manchester United as a substitute, in a 2–1 victory over Wimbledon. Two years later he struck United's winning goal in the FA Cup Final replay. Comfortable on the ball and capable in the air, he unfortunately injured his back in 1990/91 and subsequently lost his place to the newly signed Paul Parker and Denis Irwin.

Martin: Mick **M** 1972-1975

b. 9.8.1951, Dublin, Rep. of Ireland • *5ft 9in • 10st 11lb* • **Clubs** Home Farm FC, Bohemians; UTD (on loan to West Bromwich Albion Oct 1975); West Bromwich Albion Dec 1975, Newcastle Utd Dec 1978, Vancouver Whitecaps (Canada) May 1984, Willingdon FC, Cardiff City Nov 1984, Peterborough Utd Jan 1985, Rotherham Utd Aug 1985, Preston North End Sep 1985-cs. 1986, Newcastle Utd (scout, asst. manager) 1988, Celtic (coaching staff) until Jun 1993 **SU** Jan 1973 (pro.) **TF** £25,000 **UD** v Everton (h) 24.1.1973 **FL** 33(7)/gls 2 **FAC** 2/gls 0 **FLC** 1/gls 0 **T** 36(7)/gls 2 **INT** (Rep. of Ireland) 51/gls 4

Mathieson: William **F** 1892-1894

b. nk **d.** nk • **Clubs** Clydeside FC; NH; Rotherham Town Dec 1895-cs. 1896 **SU** Jun 1892 **UD** v Blackburn Rovers (a) 3.9.1892 **FL** 10/gls 2 **T** 10/gls 2

May: David **D** 1994-

b. 24.6.1970, Oldham, England • *6ft • 12st 10lb* • **Clubs** Blackburn Rovers; UTD **SU** 1.7.1994 (pro.) **TF** £1.25 million **UD** v Queen's Park Rangers (h) 20.8.1994 **FL** 66(16)/gls 6 **FAC** 6/gls 0 **FLC** 7/gls 1 **EUR** 12(1)/gls 1 **T** 91(17)/gls 8

David May had a difficult first season, struggling out of his natural position at right-back. But in 1995/96 he replaced the injured centre-half Steve Bruce and helped United to clinch the side's second League and FA Cup Double. May was first choice alongside Gary Pallister in the 1996/97 championship side, but injury hampered his chances in 1997/98. May's problems continued during 1998/99 when he didn't start a League match until 25th April at Leeds. However, he then retained his place in the team for the FA Cup Final and duly collected another winners medal. But his injury problems returned and he has only played in five games since that final.

McBain: Neil **HB** 1921-1923

b. 15.11.1895, Campbeltown, Scotland **d.** 13.5.1974 • *5ft 8in • 12st 3lb* • **Clubs** Campbeltown Academicals, Ayr Utd cs. 1914 (WW1: Portsmouth, Southampton); UTD; Everton Jan 1923, St. Johnstone Jul 1926, Liverpool Mar 1928, Watford Nov 1928 (player-manager: May 1929-1931, manager until Aug 1937), Ayr Utd (manager) season 1937-1938, Luton Town (manager) Jun 1938-Jun 1939, New Brighton (secretary-manager) Jun 1946, Leyton Orient (asst. manager) Feb 1948, (manager) Apr 1948, Estudiantes de la Plata (Argentina, coach) Aug 1949, Ayr Utd (manager) 1955-1956, Watford (manager) Aug 1956-Feb 1959, Ayr Utd (manager) Jan 1963 **SU** Nov 1921 **UD** v Aston Villa (h) 26.11.1921 **FL** 42/gls 2 **FAC** 1/gls 0 **T** 43/gls 2 **INT** (Scotland) 3/gls 0

McCalliog: Jim **M** 1973-1975

b. 23.9.1946, Glasgow, Scotland • *5ft 9in • 10st 5lb* • **Clubs** Leeds Utd am. May 1963, Chelsea Sep 1963, Sheffield Wednesday Oct 1965, Wolverhampton Wanderers Jul 1969; UTD; Southampton Feb 1975, Chicago Sting (USA) Apr-Aug 1977, played in Norway 1977-1978, Lincoln City (player-coach) Sep 1978-Mar 1979, Runcorn (player-manager) cs. 1979, Halifax Town (caretaker-manager) Mar 1990, (manager) May 1990-Oct 1991 **SU** Mar 1974 (pro.) **UD** v Birmingham City (a) 16.3.1974 **FL** 31/gls 7 **FAC** 1/gls 0 **FLC** 5(1)/gls 0 **T** 37(1)/gls 7 **INT** (Scotland) 5/gls 1

McCarthy: Pat **F** 1911-1912

b. 1888 **d.** nk • *5ft 11in • 11st 8lb* • **Clubs** Chester, Skelmersdale Utd cs. 1911; UTD; Skelmersdale Utd, Tranmere Rovers Oct 1912, Chester Aug 1913 **SU** Jan 1912 **UD** v West Bromwich Albion (h) 20.1.1912 **FL** 1/gls 0 **T** 1/gls 0

McCartney: John **FB** 1894-1895

b. dnk, Glasgow, Scotland **d.** 18.1.1933 • **Clubs** Cartvale FC, Thistle FC, Glasgow Rangers 1886, Cowlairs FC 1888; NH; Luton Town Apr 1895, Barnsley Aug 1898, (trainer) Aug 1900 (secretary-manager) Apr 1901, St. Mirren (secretary-manager) Aug 1904, Heart of Midlothian (secretary-manager) Jan 1910-Oct 1919, Portsmouth (secretary-manager) May 1920-May 1927, Luton Town (secretary-manager) Sep 1927-1929 **SU** Aug 1894 **UD** v Burton Wanderers (a) 8.9.1894 **FL** 18/gls 1 **TM** 1/gls 0 **FAC** 1/gls 0 **T** 20/gls 1

McCartney: William **F** 1903-1904

b. dnk, Newmilns, nr. Kilmarnock, Scotland **d.** nk • **Clubs** Rutherglen Glencairn, Ayr FC 1898, Hibernian Jan 1900; UTD; West Ham Utd cs. 1904, Broxburn, Lochgelly Utd 1905-1906, Clyde Sep 1906, Broxburn, Clyde-cs. 1913 **SU** May 1903 **UD** v Bristol City (a) 5.9.1903 **FL** 13/gls 1 **T** 13/gls 1

McClair: Brian **F** 1987-1998

b. 8.12.1963, Airdrie, nr. Coatbridge, Scotland • *5ft 10in • 12st 2lb* • **Clubs** Aston Villa appr. Jun 1980, Motherwell Aug 1981, Celtic Jun 1983; UTD; Motherwell Jul 1998, Blackburn Rovers (coach) Dec 1998, Manchester United (reserve team coach) Jul 2001 **SU** 1.7. 1987 (pro.) **TF** £850,000 **UD** v Southampton (a) 15.8.1987 **FL** 296(59)/gls 88 **FAC** 38(7)/gls 14 **FLC** 44(1)/gls 19 **EUR** 17(6)/gls 5 **T** 395(73)/gls 126 **INT** (Scotland) 30/gls 2

Affectionately known as "Choccy", Brian McClair loyally served United for over a decade, not only on the field, but off it as well, writing a popular diary feature in the club's official magazine. A prolific goal scorer for Celtic, with 99 goals in 145 games, Brian McClair was voted Scottish Player of the Year in 1987. He became Alex Ferguson's first major signing in July of that year. In his first season, McClair scored 31 goals, including 24 in the League. This made him the first player since George Best, 20 years earlier, to score 20 or more League goals in a season for United.

McClair never broke the 20 League goals barrier again, but his goals helped United to three Cup successes in the early 1990s. He scored three times en route to the FA Cup Final that United won in 1990, and scored in every round before the Final when they won the Cup Winners' Cup in 1991. His 100th goal for United won the League Cup in 1992.

When Eric Cantona arrived in November 1992 McClair moved back into midfield, partnering Paul Ince and scoring nine times in United's successful League campaign. Roy Keane's arrival in 1993 meant he was no longer guaranteed a first-team place. In the 1993/94 Double-winning season McClair started as many games on the bench as he did on the pitch, but he managed to score the last goal of the season to finish off Chelsea 4–0 in the FA Cup Final.

In the latter stages of his career, McClair became a valuable "squad" player and a father figure to United's emerging youngsters. He was given a free transfer, to Motherwell, in July 1998. Later that year, when Brian Kidd vacated his post at Old Trafford, McClair joined him as a member of the coaching staff at Blackburn Rovers. He then rejoined United as reserve team coach in July 2001.

McClelland: Jimmy **F** 1936-1937

b. 11.5.1902, Dysart, Kirkcaldy, Scotland **d.** nk • **Clubs** Rosslyn, Raith Rovers Oct 1922, Southend Utd Aug 1923, Middlesbrough Mar 1925, Bolton Wanderers Mar 1928, Preston North End Oct 1929, Blackpool Feb 1931, Bradford Jun 1933; UTD **SU** Jun 1936 **UD** v Huddersfield Town (a) 2.9.1936 **FL** 5/gls 1 **T** 5/gls 1

McCrae: James **HB** 1925-1926

b. 8.3.1897, Bridge of Weir, nr. Paisley, Scotland **d.** nk • *5ft 11in • 11st 12lb* • **Clubs** Clyde FC, West Ham Utd Jun 1919, Bury Dec 1920, Wigan Borough Sep 1923, New Brighton Nov 1924; UTD; Watford Aug 1926 (on loan to Third Lanark season 1926-1927) **SU** Aug 1925 **UD** v Arsenal (a) 16.1.1926 **FL** 9/gls 0 **FAC** 4/gls 0 **T** 13/gls 0

McCreery: David **M** 1975-1979

b. 16.9.1957, Belfast, N. Ireland • *5ft 7in • 10st 8lb* • **Clubs** UTD; Queen's Park Rangers Aug 1979, Tulsa Roughnecks (NASL) Mar 1981, Newcastle Utd Oct 1982, Heart of Midlothian Sep 1989, Hartlepool Utd (asst. player-manager) Aug 1991-Jun 1992, Coleraine, Carlisle Utd (player-coach) Sep 1992 **SU** Sep 1972 (am.), Apr 1974 (appr.), Oct 1974 (pro.) **UD** v Portsmouth (sub) (a) 15.10.1974 **FL** 48(39)/gls 7 **FAC** 1(6)/gls 0 **FLC** 4(4)/gls 1 **EUR** 4(3)/gls 0 **T** 57(52)/gls 8 **INT** (N. Ireland) 67/gls 0

Nicknamed "Roadrunner" for his speed and stamina, David McCreery was invariably the 12th man in Manchester United's exciting sides of the '70s. Called on as substitute in both the 1976 and 1977 FA Cup Finals, McCreery never claimed a regular place. He ultimately saw more action with Newcastle United and Northern Ireland, appearing for the latter in the 1982 World Cup Finals.

McDonald: Willie **F** 1931-1934

b. dnk, Coatbridge, Scotland • *5ft 9in • 11st 8lb* • **Clubs** Coatbridge FC, Dundee 1925-1926, Broxburn Utd cs. 1926, Laws Scotia FC, Airdrieonians 1927-1928; UTD; Tranmere Rovers Aug 1934, Coventry City Jun 1936, Plymouth Argyle Jun 1939 **SU** Apr 1932 **UD** v Bradford City (h) 23.4.1932 **FL** 27/gls 4 **T** 27/gls 4

McFarlane: Bob **FB** 1891-1892

b. dnk, Airdrie, nr. Coatbridge, Scotland **d.** 1898 • **Clubs** Airdrieonians, Bootle 1888, Sunderland Albion 1890-1891; NH; Airdrieonians am. Aug 1892 **SU** 1891 **UD** v South Shore (a) FAC 3Q, 14.11.1891 **FAC** 3/gls 0 **T** 3/gls 0

McFarlane: Noel **F** 1954-1955

b. 20.12.1934, Bray, Rep. of Ireland • *5ft 8in • 10st 4lb* • **Clubs** UTD; Waterford Jun 1956 **SU** Apr 1952 **UD** v Tottenham Hotspur (h) 13.2.1954 **FL** 1/gls 0 **T** 1/gls 0

McFetteridge: David **F** 1894-1895

b. nk **d.** nk • **Clubs** Bolton Wanderers Jun 1892, Cowlairs FC Aug 1893; NH, Stockport County 1896-1897 **SU** Jul 1894 **UD** v Newcastle Utd (a) 13.4.1895 **FL** 1/gls 0 **T** 1/gls 0

McGarvey: Scott **F** 1981-1983

b. 22.4.1963, Glasgow, Scotland • *5ft 11in • 11st 9lb* • **Clubs** UTD (on loan to Wolverhampton Wanderers Mar-May 1984); Portsmouth Jul 1984 (on loan to Carlisle Utd Jan 1986), Carlisle Utd Aug 1986, Grimsby Town Mar 1987, Bristol City Sep 1988, Oldham Athletic May 1989 (on loan to Wigan Athletic Sep-Oct 1989), Mazda (Japan) Jun 1990, Aris (Cyprus) Sep 1992, Derry City (player-coach), Witton Albion Feb 1994, Barrow 1993-1994 **SU** Jun 1979 (appr.), Apr 1980 (pro.) **UD** v Leicester City (sub) (h) 13.9.1980 **FL** 13(12)/gls 3 **T** 13(12)/gls 3

McGibbon: Pat **D** 1992-1997

b. 6.9.1973, Lurgan, N. Ireland • *6ft 1in • 13st 2lb* • **Clubs** Portadown; UTD (on loan to Swansea City and to Wigan Athletic 1996-1997), Wigan Athletic Jul 1997 **SU** 1.8.1992 (pro.) **TF** £500,000 **UD** v York City (h) FLC 2, 1st leg, 20.9.1995 **FLC** 1/gls 0 **T** 1/gls 0 **INT** (Ireland) 6/gls 0

McGillivray: Charlie **F** 1933-1934

b. 5.7.1912, East Whitburn, nr. Livingston, Scotland **d.** 7.11.1986 • *5ft 8in • 11st 6lb* • **Clubs** Ayr Utd Feb 1930, Celtic May 1932; UTD; Motherwell Apr 1934, Dundee Oct 1938 (on loan to Heart of Midlothian Aug 1940, Albion Rovers Sep 1940, Morton Aug 1941, Dunfermline Athletic 1942, Dundee Utd May 1942, Hibernian Feb 1943), Dundee Utd Jan 1944, (manager) Dec 1944-Oct 1945, Stirling Albion Nov 1945, Arbroath 1946, Downfield FC (coach) Sep 1947, LA Scots 1949 **SU** May 1933 **UD** v Plymouth Argyle (a) 26.8.1933 **FL** 8/gls 0 **FAC** 1/gls 0 **T** 9/gls 0

McGillivray: John **HB** 1907-1909

b. dnk, Broughton, nr. Preston, England **d.** nk • *5ft 10in • 11st 1lb* • **Clubs** Berry's Association; UTD; Southport Central cs. 1910, Stoke cs. 1911, Dartford cs. 1912 **SU** Jan 1907 (am.), Feb 1907 (pro.) **UD** v Blackpool (a) FAC 1, 11.1.1908 **FL** 3/gls 0 **FAC** 1/gls 0 **T** 4/gls 0

McGlen: Billy **HB** 1946-1952

b. 27.4.1921, Bedlington, nr. Ashington, England • *5ft 8in • 11st* • **Clubs** Blyth Spartans; UTD; Lincoln City Jul 1952, Oldham Athletic Feb 1953, Lincoln City (trainer) 1956-1957, Skegness Town (coach-manager) Jun 1967 **SU** Jan 1946 (am.), May 1946 (pro.) **UD** v Grimsby Town (h) 31.8.1946 **FL** 110/gls 2 **FAC** 12/gls 0 **T** 122/gls 2

William (Billy) McGlen was playing football for the forces in Italy during World War Two when he caught Matt Busby's eye, and he was one of Manchester United's first signings when League football resumed after the war in 1946/47.

A tenacious ball-winner, Billy McGlen was a versatile player who played in every position on the left. A cartilage injury in 1946/47 disrupted his career and when Manchester United won the title in 1951/52 McGlen was a frustrated reserve, having spent much of the season on the benches.

McGrath: Chris **M** 1976-1981

b. 29.11.1954, Belfast, N. Ireland • *5ft 9in • 10st 11lb* • **Clubs** Tottenham Hotspur appr. Jul 1970, pro. Jan 1972 (on loan to Millwall Feb-Apr 1976); UTD; Tulsa Roughnecks (NASL) Feb 1981-Sep 1982, South China (Hong Kong) **SU** Oct 1976 (pro.) **TF** £30,000 **UD** v Aston Villa (a) 6.11.1976 **FL** 12(16)/gls 1 **FLC** 0(2)/gls 0 **EUR** 3(1)/gls 0 **T** 15(19)/gls 1 **INT** (N. Ireland) 21/gls 4

McGrath: Paul **D** 1982-1989

b. 4.12.1959, Ealing, London, England • *6ft 2in • 13st 6lb* • **Clubs** St. Patrick's Athletic (Dublin); UTD; Aston Villa Aug 1989, Derby County Oct 1996, Sheffield United Aug 1997-May 1998 **SU** Apr 1982 (pro.) **TF** £30,000 **UD** v Tottenham Hotspur (h) 13.11.1982 **FL** 159(4)/gls 12 **FAC** 15(3)/gls 2 **FLC** 13/gls 2 **EUR** 4/gls 0 **T** 191(7)/gls 16 **INT** (Rep. of Ireland) 83/gls 8

Costing just £30,000 from Irish club St. Patrick's Athletic, the tall and powerful defender Paul McGrath was one of Ron Atkinson's finest buys. Competent in the air, McGrath established himself in the first team in 1984/85, a season that culminated with a heroic FA Cup victory over champions Everton.

Paul McGrath developed into an outstanding defender and the supporters' chant of "Ooh Aah Paul McGrath," was the forerunner to the Eric Cantona song of the same ilk in later years. Although he turned in good performances, McGrath was consistently plagued by knee injuries, and his off-the-field social problems were sensationalized in tabloid newspapers.

In August 1989, Alex Ferguson lost patience, and reluctantly let the Republic of Ireland international leave for a bargain £450,000 fee to Aston Villa, where he proved once again that he was a defender of

KEY: a=away **am.**=amateur **appr.**=apprentice **b.**=born **c.**=circa **cs.**=close season **CWC**=Club World Championship **D**=Defender **d.**=died **dnk**=date not known **EUR**=European competitions **F**=Forward **FAC**=FA Cup **FB**=Full-back (defender) **FL**=Football League **FLC**=Football League Cup **GK**=Goalkeeper **gls**=goals **h**=home **HB**=Half-back (midfield) **INT**=International matches **M**=Midfield **NH**=Newton Heath **Newton Heath LYR**=Newton Heath Lancashire & Yorkshire Railway **nk**=not known **pro.**=professional **Q**=qualifying round **SU**=signed for United **sub**=substitute; substitute apps are in brackets after appearances **T**=total **TF**=transfer fee **TM**=Test match **U**=Utility **UD**=United debut **UTD**=Manchester United **v**=versus

international pedigree. McGrath played in the final stages of both the 1990 and 1994 World Cups, and in 1996, he moved to Derby County where he played Premiership football until the age of 38.

McGuinness: Wilf HB 1955–1960

b. 25.10.1937, Manchester, England • *5ft 8in • 10st 6lb* • Clubs UTD 1961 (Reserve and Youth team trainer), 1963–1969 (England Youth team trainer), Jun 1969 (senior coach), Jun 1970 (manager), Dec 1970–Feb 1971 (Reserve team coach); Aris Salonica (Greece, manager) 1971, Panachaiki Patras (Greece, manager) 1973–1974, York City (manager) Jun 1975–Oct 1977, Hull City (coach) 1978–1979, Bury Reserve team (coach-physiotherapist) Aug 1980–1991 **SU** Jan 1953 (am.), Nov 1954 (pro.) **UD** v Wolverhampton Wanderers (h) 8.10.1955 **FL** 81/gls 2 **FAC** 2/gls 0 **EUR** 2/gls 0 **T** 85/gls 2 **INT** (England) 2/gls 0

After captaining Manchester, Lancashire and England Schoolboys, Wilfred McGuinness joined United in January 1953. Whatever he lacked in skill, he made up for in hard work, earning himself a League championship medal in 1955/56. A cartilage injury kept McGuinness out of the fateful Belgrade trip in 1958. After the tragedy, McGuinness established himself at left-half and was capped by England. A broken leg terminated his career at 22, and he went into coaching.

McIlroy MBE: Sammy M 1971–1982

See below.

McIlvenny: Eddie HB 1950–1951

b. 21.10.1924, Greenock, Scotland • *5ft 9in • 10st 10lb* • Clubs Morton, Wrexham Mar 1947, Fairhill Club Inc (USA) cs. 1948, Philadelphia Nationals (USA); UTD; Waterford (player-manager) Jul 1953 **SU** Aug 1950 **UD** v Fulham (h) 19.8.1950 **FL** 2/gls 0 **T** 2/gls 0

McKay: Bill HB 1933–1940

b. dnk, West Benhar, Scotland • *5ft 7in • 10st 8lb* • Clubs Shotts Battlefield FC, East Stirlingshire 1925, Hamilton Academical 1927, Bolton Wanderers Dec 1929; UTD (WW2: Stockport County, Port Vale); Stalybridge Celtic 1946 **SU** Mar 1934 **UD** v Fulham (h) 17.3.1934 **FL** 171/gls 15 **FAC** 13/gls 0 **T** 184/gls 15

William (Bill) McKay joined Manchester United when the club was at one of its lowest ebbs. Narrowly avoiding relegation to Division Three, United recovered to win Division Two in 1935/36, when McKay missed just seven games. A reliable left-half, he sometimes played in the forward line. In 1937/38, McKay scored four goals in the last four games to help clinch United's promotion to Division One.

McKee: Colin F 1993–1994

b. 22.8.1974, Glasgow, Scotland • *5ft 10in • 10st 11lb* • Clubs UTD (on loan to Bury 1992–1993); Kilmarnock 1994–1997, Falkirk Jun-Oct 1998, Ross County Feb 1999 **SU** Jun 1989 (appr.), May 1991 (pro.) **UD** v Coventry City (h) 8.5.1994 **FL** 1/gls 0 **T** 1/gls 0

McLachlan: George F 1929–1933

b. 21.9.1902, Glasgow, Scotland • *5ft 11in • 11st 8lb* • Clubs Clyde Oct 1922–Jul 1923 (on loan to King's Park Strollers), Cardiff City Nov 1925; UTD; Chester (player-coach) Jun 1933–cs. 1934, Le Havre (France, manager), Queen of the South (manager) Jun 1935 **SU** Dec 1929 **UD** v Leeds Utd (h) 21.12.1929 **FL** 110/gls 4 **FAC** 6/gls 0 **T** 116/gls 4

George McLachlan helped Cardiff City to become the first non-English winners of the FA Cup, beating Arsenal in 1927. Signed for Manchester United as a speedy winger, the well-built Scot moved back into midfield when United dropped into Division Two in 1931. After captaining the side for one season, George left Old Trafford to play for, and coach Chester City.

McLenahan: Hugh HB 1927–1937

b. 23.3.1909, West Gorton, Manchester, England d. 1988 • *5ft 10in • 11st 4lb* • Clubs Ambrose FC, Longsight "A" Team, Ashton Brothers, Stalybridge Celtic, Stockport County am. Feb 1927; UTD; Notts County Dec 1936–1939 **SU** May 1927 **UD** v Tottenham Hotspur (a) 4.2.1928 **FL** 112/gls 11 **FAC** 4/gls 1 **T** 116/gls 12

Twice capped by England Schoolboys, Hugh McLenahan signed for United in 1927. His transfer fee from Stockport County was reported to be a freezerful of ice cream! McLenahan helped Manchester United to avoid relegation in 1928, but missed the following season with a broken leg. Scoring six goals in five games in 1929/30, McLenahan was a versatile squad member for several years.

McMillan: Sammy F 1961–1963

b. 29.9.1941, Belfast, N. Ireland • *5ft 9in • 11st 8lb* • Clubs UTD; Wrexham Dec 1963, Southend Utd Sep 1967, Chester Dec 1969, Stockport County Jul 1970–cs. 1972, Oswestry Town **SU** 1957 (am.), Nov 1959 (pro.) **UD** v Sheffield Wednesday (a) 4.11.1961 **FL** 15/gls 6 **T** 15/gls 6 **INT** (N. Ireland) 2/gls 0

McMillen: Walter HB 1933–1935

b. 24.11.1913, Belfast, N. Ireland • *6ft • 12st 4lb* • Clubs Carrickfergus, Cliftonville 1932; UTD; Chesterfield Dec 1936; Millwall May 1939 (WW2: Glentoran, Linfield, Belfast Celtic), Tonbridge FC 1950 **SU** Aug 1933 **UD** v Brentford (a) 16.9.1933 **FL** 27/gls 2 **FAC** 2/gls 0 **T** 29/gls 2 **INT** (N. Ireland) 4/gls 0

McNaught: James HB 1893–1898

b. 8.6.1870, Dumbarton, Scotland d. 1919 • *5ft 6in • 10st 3lb* • Clubs Dumbarton, Linfield; NH; Tottenham Hotspur May 1898, Maidstone Apr 1907–1909 **SU** Feb 1893 (pro.) **UD** v Burnley (h) 2.9.1893 **FL** 140/gls 12 **TM** 5/gls 0 **FAC** 17/gls 0 **T** 162/gls 12

Nicknamed "Little Wonder" for his skill and size, James McNaught had to wait six months to make his League debut for Newton Heath, having dislocated his elbow in a friendly in March 1893. The club was relegated in his first season, losing a play-off to Liverpool. Newton Heath were still in Division Two when the forward-turned-half-back joined Tottenham Hotspur for a pay rise.

McNulty: Thomas FB 1949–1954

b. 30.12.1929, Salford, Manchester, England • *5ft 9in • 11st 1lb* • Clubs UTD; Liverpool Feb 1954–Jun 1958, Hyde Utd Aug 1963 **SU** May 1945 (am.), Jun 1947 (pro.) **UD** v Portsmouth (h) 15.4.1960 **FL** 57/gls 0 **FAC** 2/gls 0 **T** 59/gls 0

McPherson: Frank F 1923–1928

b. 14.5.1901, Barrow in Furness, England d. 5.3.1953 • *5ft 8.5in • 10st 9lb* • Clubs Barrow Shipbuilders FC, Partick Thistle am. Apr 1919, Chesterfield Municipal 1919, Barrow Feb 1921; UTD; Manchester Central Jul 1928, Watford Sep 1928, Reading Feb 1930, Watford Jun 1933, Barrow Mar 1937 **SU** May 1922 **UD** v Bristol City (a) 25.8.1923 **FL** 159/gls 45 **FAC** 16/gls 8 **T** 175/gls 52

McQueen: Gordon D 1978–1985

b. 26.6.1952, Kilbirnie, Scotland • *6ft 4in • 13st 8lb* • Clubs Largs Thistle, St. Mirren 1970, Leeds Utd Sep 1972; UTD; Seiko (Hong Kong, player-coach) Aug 1985, Airdrieonians (manager) Jun 1987–May 1989, St. Mirren (coach) Jun 1989, Middlesbrough (coach) 1994–Jun 2001 **SU** Feb 1978 (pro.) **TF** £495,000 **UD** v Liverpool (a) 25.2.1978 **FL** 184/gls 20 **FAC** 21/gls 2 **FLC** 16/gls 4 **EUR** 7/gls 0 **T** 228/gls 26 **INT** (Scotland) 30/gls 5

continued on p.103

McIlroy MBE: Sammy M 1971–1982

b. 2.8.1954, Belfast, N. Ireland • *5ft 10in • 10st 9lb* • Clubs UTD; Stoke City Feb 1982, Manchester City Aug 1985 (on loan to Orgryte IS, Sweden), Bury Mar 1987, VFB Modling (Austria) Jan-Aug 1988, Preston North End (player-coach) Feb 1990, Northwich Victoria (manager) Jul 1991–Oct 1992, Ashton Utd (team manager) Dec 1992, Macclesfield Town (manager) May 1993, Northern Ireland (manager) Jan 2000 **SU** Aug 1969 (appr.), Aug 1971 (pro.) **UD** v Manchester City (a) 6.11.1971, scored 1 **FL** 320(22)/gls 57 **FAC** 35(3)/gls 5 **FLC** 25(3)/gls 6 **EUR** 10/gls 2 **T** 390(28)/gls 70 **INT** (N. Ireland) 88/gls 5

Samuel Baxter McIlroy was Matt Busby's final signing, in September 1969. McIlroy had supported United as a youngster, and fellow Belfast boy George Best was his hero. When McIlroy came over from Ireland at the age of 15 comparisons with Best were inevitable and McIlroy later said: "It was a great honour for me just to play with George but as my father told me, there's only one George Best and there always will be."

Three months after signing as a professional, McIlroy made a dramatic first-team debut for United, against Manchester City at Maine Road. In front of 63,000 people, McIlroy scored one goal and had a hand in the other two in a thrilling 3–3 draw. For the remainder of that season McIlroy spent many games as a substitute, but still enjoyed the distinction of becoming the third youngest British player to win an international cap when, at just 17 years and 198 days, he played for Northern Ireland against Spain. Seriously injured in a car crash in January 1973, McIlroy

missed many of the later games of 1972/73, but in 1973/74, he managed to establish himself as a first-team regular.

Unfortunately, the club was relegated that season, but not for long. McIlroy was an ever-present in the United side that won the Second Division championship in 1974/75, and by that time he was also playing regularly for Northern Ireland.

A resourceful midfielder with an impressive goal-scoring record, McIlroy appeared in three FA Cup Finals for United. In the 1976 defeat by Southampton, his glancing header might have swung the game United's way had it not hit the crossbar. McIlroy did collect a winners' medal a year later, when United defeated the reigning champions, Liverpool, at Wembley.

In 1979, McIlroy made his third FA Cup Final appearance, scoring a memorable goal against Arsenal when he made a weaving run through a packed Gunners penalty area before curling a shot past his international team mate, Pat Jennings. Unfortunately the goal wasn't enough to prevent United from slipping to a 3–2 defeat.

In October 1981 McIlroy was dropped from the first team to make way for Manchester United's record new signing, Bryan Robson. McIlroy responded by scoring a hat-trick against Wolverhampton Wanderers after Robson had signed on the Old Trafford pitch.

After clocking up over 400 appearances for United, McIlroy was sold to Stoke City in 1982, where he played for three years before moving back to Manchester

to join City. After a short spell at Bury, Sammy McIlroy spent time in Austria and Preston before concluding a playing career that had included 88 Northern Ireland caps. McIlroy then embarked on a managerial career, where he took non-League Macclesfield Town into the Football League in 1997. The Silkmen earned promotion to Division Two in their first season but were then relegated back to Division Three at the end of 1998/99.

Honoured

Sammy McIlroy's career spanned many years and several clubs, as well as international appearances. In 1986 he was awarded the MBE for his services to football.

Did you know?

- *McIlroy was frequently labelled "the last Busby Babe", and later, when he played for Manchester City, the supporters of his new club disliked his United connections so much that they booed him.*

- *When McIlroy played at Stoke City, the 1984/85 side set the worst First Division record of all time and were promptly relegated.*

- *As manager of Macclesfield Town, McIlroy achieved a remarkable feat, assembling a side that won two Conference titles and one FA Trophy, despite having extremely limited resources.*

Meredith: Billy F 1906–1921

b. 30.7.1874, Black Park, Chirk, Wales
d. 19.4.1958 • 5ft 9in • 11st 4lb • **Clubs** Black Park (Chirk) 1890, Northwich Victoria am. 1892, pro. Sep 1893, Manchester City Oct 1894; UTD (WW1: Stalybridge Celtic 1915–1919); Manchester City (player-coach) Jul 1921–1924; UTD (coach) Sep 1931 SU Oct 1906 (pro.) UD v Aston Villa (h) 1.1.1907 FL 303/gls 35 FAC 29/gls 0 T 332/gls 35 INT (Wales) 48/gls 11

William Henry Meredith was one of the most talented footballers ever to put on a shirt for Manchester United. He was a giant of the game during the late 1890s and early 1900s, and a celebrity long before superstardom became common. An unlikely looking player with a slim frame, Meredith's skill and appetite for the game more than compensated for his lack of stature.

Meredith began playing for local clubs, winning a Welsh Cup winners' medal with Chirk in 1894. After a brief period with Northwich Victoria, and occasional outings for Wrexham, he signed for Manchester City.

In only his third appearance for the side, Meredith played in the "Derby" match against Newton Heath. City lost 5–2, but Meredith scored both goals. Six months later he was selected to play for Wales. Billy Meredith helped City to win two Second Division championships, in 1899 and 1903. In 1904 City won the FA Cup, with Meredith, the captain, scoring the only goal of the game.

It seemed that Meredith had the world at his feet, but in 1905 he was suspended by the FA, accused of bribing an Aston Villa player. Meredith denied the charge, but it brought to light other financial irregularities at Hyde Road. The FA dismissed several City directors and banned all the players for a year.

Did you know?

- *Meredith's trademark was that he played with a toothpick sticking out of his mouth. He said it helped him to concentrate.*
- *In 1904, Meredith became a partner in a well-known Manchester sports outfitters. The shop became known as Pilling, Briggs and Meredith.*
- *An accusation of bribery against Meredith, in 1905, led to a close investigation of Manchester City's finances, which resulted in the whole team being suspended from playing for a year.*
- *Billy Meredith was the oldest international of all time when he played for Wales for the 48th time, eight months after his 45th birthday.*

Meredith's suspension was quashed on 31st December, 1906, but he had already been transferred to Manchester United.

Billy Meredith played a big part in Manchester United's conversion into one of football's top clubs. The side won the Football League championship in 1908 and 1911, and the club's first FA Cup in 1909. It was the first great United side and Meredith was the star, mesmerizing opposing defenders with bursts of speed and accurate crossing to his fellow forwards.

During 1909 Meredith and other players suffered the FA's wrath after they refused to dissociate themselves from the Players' Union, formed in 1907. Many players bowed to pressure, but Meredith, who had been a prime mover in the Union's instigation, stuck to his principles, along with a group of mainly

> " *He cannot play football without that toothpick ...* "
>
> **Report on the 1909 FA Cup Final, from an unknown newspaper cutting**

Superstar
This early publicity photograph shows Billy Meredith, the first footballing superstar, surrounded by his numerous trophies and medals. The photograph was autographed by the player in 1911.

Manchester United players. The group started training independently for the 1909/10 season as "The Outcasts". Support for the Union gradually returned and, just before the start of the season, the FA relented. An agreement was reached and the Union was acknowledged. It was one of Billy Meredith's finest victories.

After another disagreement over finances with United officials, Meredith became steadily disenchanted with the club and, in July 1921, at the age of 47, he re-signed for Manchester City as player/coach. Meredith continued to play for another three years, appearing in an FA Cup semi-final against Newcastle United at the age of 49.

Welsh wizard
Meredith stands shoulder to shoulder with all the other great Welsh players. Arguably, Meredith was the original "Welsh wizard", the greatest of them all, a football genius with spindly, bowed legs and magic in his boots.

Fact file

- **Family fame**
Billy's younger brother, Ray, was also a Welsh international. He won eight caps between 1900 and 1907.

- **Lean and mean**
Meredith was nicknamed "Old Skinny" for his lean, slender body shape.

- **Golden oldie**
When he played in the 1924 FA Cup semi-final for Manchester City, Meredith was 49 years and 8 months old.

Billy Meredith: Career timeline

25th March, 1894
Welsh Cup winners' medal

16th March, 1895
International debut v Ireland

April 1903
Second Division championship medal

August 1905
Suspended by FA, following alleged bribe

31st December, 1906
Suspension terminated

April 1908
League championship medal

April 1911
League championship medal

15th March, 1920
Final international appearance v England

1893 1895 1897 1899 1901 1903 1905 1907 1909 1911 1913 1915 1917 1919 1921

October 1894
Transfers to Manchester City from Northwich Victoria

27th October, 1894
League debut v Newcastle United

April 1899
Second Division championship medal

23rd April, 1904
FA Cup winners' medal

October 1906
Signs for Manchester United

1st January, 1907
League debut v Aston Villa

24th April, 1909
FA Cup winners' medal

1914–1918
Britain entered World War One in August 1914, and only local League matches were played until the 1919/20 season, when the war was over

July 1921
Meredith re-signs for Manchester City as a player/coach.

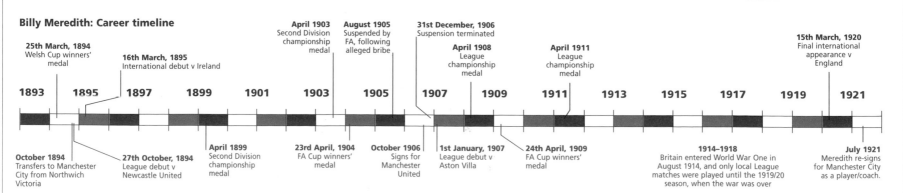

KEY: **a**=away **am.**=amateur **appr.**=apprentice **b.**=born **c.**=circa **cs.**=close season **D**=Defender **d.**=died **dnk**=date not known **EUR**=European competitions **F**=Forward **FAC**=FA Cup **FB**=Full-back (defender) **FL**=Football League **FLC**=Football League Cup **GK**=Goalkeeper **gls**=goals **h**=home **HB**=Half-back (midfield) **INT**=International matches **M**=Midfield **NH**=Newton Heath **Newton Heath LYR**=Newton Heath Lancashire & Yorkshire Railway **nk**=not known **pro.**=professional **Q**=Qualifying round **SU**=signed for United **sub**=substitute; substitute apps are in brackets after appearances **T**=Total **TF**=transfer fee **TM**=Test match **U**=Utility **UD**=United debut **UTD**="Manchester United" **v**=versus

McQueen: Gordon **D** 1978–1985 *continued*

Gordon McQueen left Leeds to become a Manchester United hero. Fearsome in the air at both ends of the pitch, he headed in his fair share of goals, including one in the 1979 FA Cup Final. He formed a good partnership with Martin Buchan, although McQueen was sometimes caught out of position. Having won the 1983 FA Cup, a bad knee injury in 1984 ended his playing career.

McShane: Harry **F** 1950–1954

b. 8.4.1920, Holytown, nr. Motherwell, Scotland • *5ft 8in* • *11st* • **Clubs** Bellshill Athletic, Blackburn Rovers am. Jan, pro. Feb 1937, Huddersfield Town Sep 1946, Bolton Wanderers Jul 1947; UTD; Oldham Athletic Feb 1954, Chorley (player-coach) 1955–1956, Wellington Town 1956–1957, Droylsden Sep 1958, Stalybridge Celtic (coach) Oct 1961 **SU** Sep 1950 (pro.) **UD** v Aston Villa (h) 13.9.1950 **FL** 56/gls 8 **FAC** 1/gls 0 **T** 57/gls 8

Meehan: Tommy **HB** 1919–1921

b. 1896, Harpurhey, Manchester, England **d.** 18.8.1924 • *5ft 6in* • *10st 6lb* • **Clubs** Newton FC, Walkden Central, Rochdale Jan 1917; UTD (on loan to Atherton, WW1: Rochdale); Chelsea Dec 1920 until his death **SU** Jun 1917 **UD** v Sheffield Wednesday (h) 1.9.1919 **FL** 51/gls 6 **FAC** 2/gls 0 **T** 53/gls 6 **INT** (England) 1/gls 0

Mellor: Jack **FB** 1930–1937

b. dnk, Oldham, England **d.** nk • *5ft 8in* • *11st 8lb* • **Clubs** Failsworth Trinity, Witton Albion; UTD; Cardiff City Jan 1937–May 1938 **SU** May 1929 **UD** v Huddersfield Town (a) 15.9.1930 **FL** 116/gls 0 **FAC** 6/gls 0 **T** 122/gls 0

Menzies: Alex **F** 1906–1908

b. 25.11.1882, Blantyre, Hamilton, Scotland **d.** nk • *5ft 10in* • *11st 10lb* • **Clubs** Blantyre Victoria, Heart of Midlothian Dec 1902 (on loan to Motherwell 1903), Arthurlie Aug 1904, Heart of Midlothian May 1905; UTD; Luton Town Sep 1907, Dundee cs. 1909–1910 **SU** Nov 1906 **UD** v Sheffield Wednesday (a) 17.11.1906, scored 1 **FL** 23/gls 4 **FAC** 2/gls 0 **T** 25/gls 4 **INT** (Scotland) 1/gls 0

Meredith: Billy **F** 1906–1921

See left.

Mew: Jack **GK** 1912–1926

b. 30.3.1889, Sunderland, England **d.** 1963 • *5ft 8in* • *12st 2lb* • **Clubs** Blaydon Utd, Marley Hill Utd; UTD; Barrow Sep 1926, Lyra FC (Belgium, trainer-coach) Oct 1927, Lima FC (Peru, coach) Jun 1928 **SU** Jul 1912 (am.), Sep 1912 (pro.) **UD** v Middlesbrough (h) 1.3.1913 **FL** 186/gls 0 **FAC** 13/gls 0 **T** 199/gls 0 **INT** (England) 1/gls 0

John (Jack) Mew made just four appearances for United before the First World War, as Robert Beale's goalkeeping deputy. Mew then dominated the position from 1919 to 1924. In his only appearance for England, in October 1923, Mew kept a clean sheet against Ireland. Later that year he received a gold watch from Manchester United for making 500 appearances in all competitions (including wartime) for the club. He added this to a Central League Championship medal won in 1913.

Milarvie: Bob **F** 1890–1891

b. nk **d.** 1912 • **Clubs** Pollokshields, Stoke cs. 1888, Burslem Port Vale cs. 1889, Derby County Nov 1889; NH; Ardwick cs. 1891–cs. 1896 **SU** 1890 **UD** v Higher Walton (h) FAC 1Q, 18.1.1891 **FAC** 1/gls 0 **T** 1/gls 0

Millar: George **F** 1894–1895

b. nk **d.** nk • **Clubs** Glasgow Perthshire; NH; Chatham 1895–1996 **SU** Dec 1894 **UD** v Lincoln City (h) 22.12.1894, scored 1 **FL** 6/gls 5 **FAC** 1/gls 0 **T** 7/gls 5

Miller: "Jock" (James) **F** 1923–1924

b. dnk, Greenock, Scotland **d.** nk • *5ft 7in* • *11st* • **Clubs** Port Glasgow Athletic, St. Mirren, Greenock Morton Oct 1920, Grimsby Town Jun 1921; UTD; York City cs. 1924, Boston Town Jul 1925, Shirebrook Aug 1927 **SU** Mar 1924 **TF** £500 **UD** v Hull City (h) 15.3.1924 **FL** 4/gls 1 **T** 4/gls 1

Miller: Tom **F** 1920–1921

b. 29.6.1890, Motherwell, Scotland **d.** 3.9.1958 • *5ft 9in* • *11st 5lb* • **Clubs** Larkhall Hearts, Glenview, Larkhall Utd, Hamilton Academical 1910, Liverpool Feb 1912; UTD; Heart of Midlothian Jul 1921, Torquay Utd 1922–1923, Hamilton Academical 1923, Raith Rovers Dec 1926–1927 **SU** Sep 1920 **TF** £2,000 **UD** v Tottenham Hotspur (h) 25.9.1920 **FL** 25/gls 7 **FAC** 2/gls 1 **T** 27/gls 8 **INT** (Scotland) 3/gls 2

Milne: Ralph **F** 1988–1990

b. 13.5.1961, Dundee, Scotland • *5ft 8in* • *12st 3lb* • **Clubs** Dundee Utd pro. May 1977, Charlton Athletic Jan 1987, Bristol City Feb 1988; UTD (on loan to West Ham Utd Jan–Feb 1990); Sing Tao FC (Hong Kong) **SU** Nov 1988 (pro.) **TF** £175,000 **UD** v Southampton (h) 19.11.1988 **FL** 19(4)/gls 3 **FAC** 7/gls 0 **T** 26(4)/gls 3

As one of Alex Ferguson's least successful buys, Ralph Milne seemed to leave his best form behind him at Dundee United, with whom he'd won the Scottish League championship in 1982/83. Although he was steady enough on the wing, the former Scotland Youth and Under-21s international's lack of flair did not endear him to Manchester United's fans, who missed his more skilful predecessor, Jesper Olsen.

Mitchell: Andrew **FB** 1892–1894

b. nk **d.** nk • **Clubs** Airdrieonians; NH; Burton Swifts Jun 1894–1895 **SU** Sept 1892 **UD** v Burnley (h) 10.9.1892 **FL** 54/gls 0 **TM** 3/gls 0 **FAC** 4/gls 0 **T** 61/gls 0

Mitchell: Andrew **F** 1932–1933

b. 20.4.1907, Coxhoe, England **d.** 3.12.1971 • *5ft 8in* • *11st 3lb* • **Clubs** Crook Town, Sunderland Dec 1927, Notts County Aug 1928, Darlington June 1929; UTD; Hull City Jun 1933, Northampton Town Dec 1933, Rossendale Utd Jul 1934 **SU** Apr 1932 **TF** £600 **UD** v Notts County (a) 18.3.1933 **FL** 1/gls 0 **T** 1/gls 0

Mitchell: J. **FB** 1885–1888; 1888–1891

b. nk **d.** nk • **Clubs** Newton Heath LYR; Bolton Wanderers cs. 1888; Newton Heath LYR **SU** Feb 1885 and Oct 1888 **UD** v Fleetwood Rangers (a) FAC 1, 30.10.1886 **FAC** 3/gls 0 **T** 3/gls 0

Mitten: Charlie **F** 1946–1950

b. 17.1.1921, Rangoon, Burma • *5ft 8in* • *11st* • **Clubs** Dunblane Rovers, Strathallan Hawthorn; UTD (WW2: Tranmere Rovers, Cardiff City, Southampton, Chelsea, Wolverhampton Wanderers); Santa Fe (Bogotá) cs. 1950–Jun 1951, Fulham Jan 1952, Mansfield Town (player-manager) Feb 1956, Newcastle Utd (manager) Jun 1958–Oct 1961, Altrincham (player-manager) cs. 1962 **SU** Aug 1936 (am.), Jan 1938 (pro.) **UD** v Grimsby Town (h) 31.8.1946 **FL** 142/gls 50 **FAC** 19/gls 11 **T** 161/gls 61

Charles Mitten had been with Manchester United for almost a decade by the time he made his full League debut. Almost immediately after he signed, the Second World War began, and he worked as an RAF Physical Training instructor touring Britain's aerodromes. The war years also saw him guesting for several clubs, including Chelsea and Tranmere Rovers.

Mitten made his debut for United in August 1946, as part of the first team assembled by new manager Matt Busby. Solidly occupying the left-wing position, Charlie was one of the pillars around whom Busby built his classic post-war side, and he played an important part in the FA Cup triumph of 1948. Charlie Mitten's speed and shooting ability were particularly in evidence the following season, when he scored a total of 23 goals in his League and Cup games for United.

During a tour of the USA and Canada in 1950 a number of United players were approached by Colombian sides, offering them lucrative contracts in South America. Mitten succumbed and, since Colombia was not at that time a member of FIFA, there was nothing to stop him joining Santa Fe FC in Bogotá. Within the year, however, his new mother-nation had joined FIFA, and Charlie was obliged to return home to an unforgiving Matt Busby. He was fined £250 and suspended for six months, at the end of which time he was unceremoniously transferred to Fulham for £20,000.

Moger: Harry **GK** 1903–1912

b. 1879, Southampton, England **d.** 1927 • *6ft 3in* • *12st 12lb* • **Clubs** Forest Swifts, Freemantle 1898, Southampton cs. 1900; UTD **SU** May 1903 **UD** v Barnsley (h) 10.10.1903 **FL** 242/gls 0 **FAC** 22/gls 0 **T** 264/gls 0

Henry Herbert Moger was the Peter Schmeichel of United's pre-First World War side. Just as tall and reliable, though slimmer in build than his counterpart of 80 years on, Harry Moger provided the last line of Manchester United's defence for seven seasons, during the club's first major brush with success.

Born in Southampton, Harry Moger spent three seasons with the Saints, most of the time as understudy to England international keeper, John (Jack) Robinson.

Moger could see that his opportunities were limited with the Saints, so in May 1903 he accepted an offer from Manchester United. It was a move that would see him become one of the top goalkeepers of his day and he played a huge part in securing a hat-trick of major trophies in the years before the outbreak of the First World War. During his first season at the club, Moger shared the goalkeeping duties with John Sutcliffe, who had won five England caps while at Bolton Wanderers and Millwall. When Sutcliffe left at the end of the 1903/04 season Moger took over as first-choice keeper. In 1905/06 United won promotion to the First Division. Harry Moger was firmly established as Manchester United's number one custodian and there he remained as the club carried off the League championship in 1908 and 1911, and the FA Cup in 1909. Harry Moger was widely looked upon as one of the country's top goalkeepers although, unlike his former colleagues, Jack Robinson and John Sutcliffe, he never won a place in the England team.

Moir: Ian **F** 1960–1965

b. 30.6.1943, Aberdeen, Scotland • *5ft 11in* • *11st 3lb* • **Clubs** UTD; Blackpool Feb 1965, Chester May 1967, Wrexham Jan 1968, Shrewsbury Town Mar 1972, Wrexham Jul 1973–1975, South African football **SU** 1958 (am.), Jul 1960 (pro.) **UD** v Bolton Wanderers (h) 1.10.1960 **FL** 45/gls 5 **T** 45/gls 5

Montgomery: Archie **GK** 1905–1906

b. 1871, Chryston, Scotland **d.** 1922 • *5ft 8in* • *11st 3lb* • **Clubs** Chryston Athletic, Glasgow Rangers Apr 1894, Bury Mar 1895; UTD; Bury cs. 1906, Feb 1907 (team manager), Feb 1914–Apr 1915 (secretary-manager), Jun 1920 (manager) **SU** May 1905 **UD** v Glossop (a) 16.9.1905 **FL** 3/gls 0 **T** 3/gls 0

Montgomery: James **HB** 1914–1921

b. dnk, Craghead, nr. Durham, England **d.** nk • *5ft 9in* • *12st 4lb* • **Clubs** Glossop Feb 1913; UTD (junior coach from Oct 1921); Crewe Alexandra **SU** Mar 1915 **UD** v Bradford City (h) 13.3.1915 **FL** 27/gls 1 **T** 27/gls 1

Moody: John **GK** 1931–1933

b. 1.11.1903, Heeley, Sheffield, England • *5ft 10in* • *11st 4lb* • **Clubs** Hathersage FC, Arsenal Aug 1925, Bradford May 1928, Doncaster Rovers Aug 1930; UTD; Chesterfield Aug 1933–cs. 1939 **SU** Feb 1932 **UD** v Oldham Athletic (h) 26.3.1932 **FL** 50/gls 0 **FAC** 1/gls 0 **T** 51/gls 0

Moore: Charlie **FB** 1919–1930

b. 3.6.1898, Cheslyn Hay, nr. Cannock, England **d.** nk • *5ft 8in* • *11st 8lb* • **Clubs** Hednesford Town; UTD (released cs. 1921 due to injury, re-registered Sep 1922) **SU** May 1919 **UD** v Derby County (a) 30.8.1919 **FL** 309/gls 0 **FAC** 19/gls 0 **T** 328/gls 0

It seemed that Charlie Moore's career was over in 1921 when, after two seasons, he was released with a serious ankle injury. But he returned to full fitness in 1922/23, and was first choice full-back for eight seasons, usually alongside Jack Silcock. Dependable and fair, Charlie was sent off only once, in 1929, after great provocation.

Moore: Graham **F** 1963–1964

b. 7.3.1941, Hengoed, nr. Caerphilly, Wales • *6ft* • *13st 2lb* • **Clubs** Cardiff City (ground staff) pro. May 1958, Chelsea Dec 1961; UTD; Northampton Town Dec 1965, Charlton Athletic May 1967, Doncaster Rovers Sep 1971–cs. 1974 **SU** Nov 1963 (pro.) **TF** £35,000 **UD** v Tottenham Hotspur (h) 9.11.1963 **FL** 18/gls 4 **FAC** 1/gls 1 **T** 19/gls 5 **INT** (Wales) 21/gls 1

Moran: Kevin **D** 1978–1988

b. 29.4.1956, Dublin, Rep. of Ireland • *5ft 10in* • *12st 8lb* • **Clubs** UTD; Sporting Gijon (Spain) Aug 1988, Blackburn Rovers Jan 1990 **SU** Feb 1978 (pro.) **UD** v Southampton (a) 30.4.1979 **FL** 228(3)/gls 21 **FAC** 18/gls 1 **FLC** 24(1)/gls 2 **EUR** 13(1)/gls 0 **T** 283(5)/gls 24 **INT** (Rep. of Ireland) 71/gls 6

An uncompromising defender who regularly required stitches in the line of duty, Kevin Moran was the first player to be sent off in an FA Cup Final, in 1985. Following his conversion from Gaelic football, Moran became a highly respected player both for Manchester United and for the Republic of Ireland. Over the years, Moran's passing skills developed to match his formidable heading and ball-winning ability.

Morgan: Billy **HB** 1896–1903

b. nk **d.** nk • *5ft 9in* • *12st* • **Clubs** Horwich FC; NH; Bolton Wanderers Mar 1903, Watford cs. 1903, Leicester Fosse Aug 1904, New Brompton cs. 1906, Newton Heath Athletic Mar 1910 **SU** Jan 1896 **UD** v Darwen (h) 2.3.1897 **FL** 143/gls 6 **FAC** 9/gls 1 **T** 152/gls 7

William (Billy) Morgan joined Newton Heath towards the end of their fifth year in the League, when they finished second and lost to Sunderland in the play-off for promotion to the First Division. Once described in the club programme as an "india-rubber doll", the resilient Morgan was a first choice half-back until Alex Downie was signed from Swindon Town in 1902.

Morgan: Hugh **F** 1900–1901

b. dnk, Lanarkshire, Scotland **d.** nk • **Clubs** Harthill Thistle, Airdrieonians Aug 1896, Sunderland Dec 1896, Bolton Wanderers Feb 1899; NH; Manchester City Jul 1901, Accrington Stanley cs. 1902, Blackpool May 1904–cs. 1905 **SU** Dec 1900 **UD** v Lincoln City (h) 15.2.1900 **FL** 20/gls 4 **FAC** 3/gls 0 **T** 23/gls 4

Morgan: Willie **F** 1968–1975

b. 2.10.1944, Sauchie, nr. Alloa, Scotland • *5ft 9in* • *10st 8lb* • **Clubs** Burnley am. May 1960, pro. Oct 1961; UTD; Burnley Jun 1975, Bolton Wanderers Mar 1976 (on loan to Chicago Sting, USA, May–Aug 1977 and to Minnesota Kicks, USA, May–Aug 1978, May–Aug 1979, Apr–Aug 1980), Blackpool Sep 1980–May 1982 **SU** Aug 1968 (pro.) **TF** £100,000 **UD** v Tottenham Hotspur (h) 28.8.1968 **FL** 236(2)/gls 25 **FAC** 27/gls 4 **FLC** 24(1)/gls 3 **EUR** 4/gls 1 **T** 291(3)/gls 33 **INT** (Scotland) 21/gls 1

Stepney: Alex GK 1966-1978

b. 18.9.1942, Mitcham, London, England • *6ft •
11st 9lb* • **Clubs** Achilles FC, Tooting & Mitcham
1958, Millwall am. Mar, pro. May 1963, Chelsea May
1966; UTD; Dallas Tornado (NASL) Feb 1979,
Altrincham (player-coach) Sep 1979, Dallas
Tornado Apr–Aug 1980, Southampton (scout),
Exeter City (scout), Manchester City (coach) 1997
SU Sep 1966 (pro.) **TF** £55,000 **UD** v Manchester
City (h) 17.9.1966 **FL** 433/gls 2 **FAC** 44/gls 0
FLC 35/gls 0 **EUR** 23/gls 0 **T** 535/gls 2
INT (England) 1/gls 0

Alex Stepney was
United's goalkeeper
during one of the club's
most successful periods,
culminating in the
European Cup triumph
of 1968, in which he
played a major part.
In 1966, when he was
transferred to Chelsea for £50,000, Stepney
had already won three England Under-23s
caps, and was regarded as the most
promising young keeper in the game, but at
the start of the season he found himself
playing a reserve game.

At the time, Matt Busby needed to
strengthen his goalkeeping position. He made
an inquiry for either Alex Stepney or Peter
Bonetti, and Chelsea manager Tommy
Docherty chose to let his newcomer move
on. Stepney had only been at Chelsea for five
months, with one League appearance, but
Docherty put on a £5,000 mark-up, selling
him for £55,000, a record fee for a goalkeeper.

Alex Stepney played a key part in United's
victory in the 1966/67 League championship,
playing every game, and Matt Busby named
him as a major force behind their title win.
League success brought entry into the
European Cup for 1967/68, and Stepney made

an outstanding contribution to United
becoming the first English club to win the
Cup, beating Benfica.

Although Stepney was chosen 20 times as a
substitute for England, Sir Alf Ramsey gave
him his only full cap against Sweden at
Wembley, the week before the European Cup
final. "Perhaps he did it to give me the feel of
Wembley ready for the European game," says
Stepney. It was a dramatic week, with an
international debut capped by a European
Cup win that saw him hailed as a hero for a
save against Eusebio.

That save is still discussed. Stepney says: "I
think the save stands out in people's minds

Did you know?

- *Stepney is United's top-scoring
  goalkeeper, having successfully
  converted two penalties in the
  relegation season of 1973/74.*
- *After retiring, Stepney returned to
  football as a scout for Southampton
  and Exeter City.*
- *Former United team mates still refer
  to Stepney as "Big Al".*
- *Stepney has run a pub and has also
  done commercial work for Stockport
  County and Rochdale.*
- *Alex Stepney now lives in Rochdale,
  Lancashire.*
- *In 1997, Stepney took up a post as
  goalkeeping coach for Alan Ball at
  Manchester City.*

because of the time of it in the game,
near the end with the score 1-1. Actually,
he hit it straight at me. He did hit it
hard but I remember standing there
holding the ball and thinking 'thank
you'". United went safely through to
extra time, and a long kick
downfield from Stepney led to a
goal from George Best. United
eventually won the game 4-1.

Following Busby's
retirement, Stepney played
under Wilf McGuinness,
Frank O'Farrell, Tommy
Docherty and Dave Sexton.
Coming to terms with
relegation in 1974, the side
came roaring back at the first
attempt in season 1974/75.
There were two FA Cup Final
appearances, too, with United
losing to Southampton in 1976,
but beating Liverpool in 1977.

Alex Stepney retired from
United at the end of the 1977/78
season and went to play in the
USA with Dallas Tornado for a
season before rounding off his
playing career with a short spell
for non-League Altrincham.

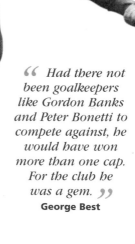

*" Had there not
been goalkeepers
like Gordon Banks
and Peter Bonetti to
compete against, he
would have won
more than one cap.
For the club he
was a gem. "*
George Best

*" The single most
important factor behind
our championship success
in 1967 was signing
Alex Stepney. "*
Matt Busby

Steady as a rock
*Stepney was rarely spectacular but
he was reliable, steady and efficient,
and he had a great sense of
anticipation and positioning. He
was also a rarity at Old Trafford, a
Londoner born and bred.*

In his three seasons at
Old Trafford, Jaap Stam
has established himself
as the world's best
defender. If proof was
required, UEFA voted
him Europe's best
defender in 1999 and
2000, while
Premiership managers have voted him as the
player they would most like to sign. A former
trainee electrician, Stam became the world's
most expensive defender when Manchester
United paid PSV Eindhoven £10.75 million
for his services in the summer of 1998. Stam
had a slow, and at times, unconvincing start
to his Old Trafford career, but within a month
he began to show his true form, and has been
regarded as a United legend ever since.

More skilful on the ball than his size might
suggest, Stam's colossal frame thwarted some
of the world's greatest strikers in the Treble-
winning season. Sometimes his mere
presence was enough to force an opponent
to retreat with the ball into his own half.
The Dutch international was eventually so
important that alarm bells started ringing at
the club when he missed a few League games
with an ankle injury. Happily, Jaap recovered
in time to play as a substitute at Wembley and
a full 90 minutes in the European Cup Final.

Stapleton: Frank F 1981-1987

b. 10.7.1956, Dublin, Rep. of Ireland • *5ft 11in •
13st 2lb* • **Clubs** St. Martins, Bolton Athletic
(Dublin); UTD; Ajax (Holland) trial 1972; Arsenal appr. Jun 1972,
pro. Sep 1973; UTD; Ajax (Holland) Aug 1987 (on
loan to Derby County Mar 1988), Le Havre (France)
Oct 1988, Blackburn Rovers Aug 1989, Aldershot
(non-contract) Sep 1991, Huddersfield Town (player-
coach) Oct 1991, Bradford City (player-manager)
Dec 1991–May 1994, New England Revolution
(USA) 1996–97 **SU** Aug 1981 (pro.) **TF** £900,000
UD v Coventry City (a) 29.8.1981 **FL** 204(19)/gls 60
FAC 21/gls 7 **FLC** 26(1)/gls 6 **EUR** 14(1)/gls 5
T 265(21)/gls 78 **INT** (Rep. of Ireland) 70/gls 20

As a 15-year-old
schoolboy, Frank
Stapleton went to
Old Trafford for an
unsuccessful trial. He
then signed for Arsenal,
who developed him
into one of the First
Division's best centre-
forwards. During his time at Highbury,
Stapleton scored 108 goals in 299 games and
won an FA Cup winners' medal, scoring
against United in the 1979 final.

In August 1981, nine years after Stapleton's
first trial, United paid £900,000 for him. A
big, strong forward, Stapleton was an
excellent header of the ball. While never a
prolific goal scorer at United, he was the
club's leading scorer in his first three
seasons. He won two FA Cup winners' medals
and, with his goal for United in the 1983 final
against Brighton, became the first player to
score for two different clubs in two Wembley
finals. In August 1987, after six years at Old
Trafford, Stapleton left for Ajax of Amsterdam.
For the Republic of Ireland he won 71 caps
and, with 20 goals, he is their all-time
leading goal scorer.

Stephenson: R. F 1895-1896

b. nk **d.** nk • **Clubs** Talbot FC; NH; Northern
Nomads **SU** Dec 1895 (am.); **UD** v Rotherham
Town (h) 11.1.1896, scored 1 **FL** 1/gls 1 **T** 1/gls 1

Stepney: Alex GK 1966-1978

See above.

Steward: Alfred GK 1920-1932

b. dnk, Manchester, England **d.** nk • *5ft 11in •
11st 13lb* • **Clubs** Army football, Stalybridge
Celtic; UTD (am.); Heaton Park FC; UTD;
Manchester North End (player-manager) Jun

1932, Altrincham May 1933 (player-manager), Sep
1936 (secretary-manager), Torquay Utd (manager)
1938–1940 **SU** 1919 (am.), Jan 1920 (pro.) **UD** v
Preston North End (h) 23.10.1920 **FL** 309/gls 0
TM 2/gls 0 **FAC** 17/gls 0 **T** 328/gls 0

Alfred (Alf) Steward was United's first-choice
goalkeeper for nine seasons. With the
Reserves, he won the Central League in
1920/21. After saving six penalties for the
Reserves, he helped the first team to keep
the best defensive record in 1924/25, with
25 clean sheets and only 23 goals conceded.

Stewart: Michael M 2000-

b. 26.2.1981, Edinburgh, Scotland • *5ft 11in •
11st 11lb* • **SU** 30.6.1997 (appr.), 13.3.1998
(pro.) **UD** v Watford (sub) (a) FLC (3), 31.10.2000
FL 3/gls 0 **FLC** (2)/gls 0 **T** 3(2)/gls 0

Stewart: William F 1932-1934

b. dnk, Glasgow, Scotland **d.** nk • *5ft 5.5in •
10st 6lb* • **Clubs** Cowdenbeath 1931–1932; UTD;
Motherwell Mar 1934–1937 **SU** Nov 1932 **TF**
£2,350 **UD** v Fulham (h) 19.11.1932 **FL** 46/gls 7
FAC 3/gls 0 **T** 49/gls 7

Stewart: Willie HB 1890-1895

b. 11.2.1872, Coupar Angus, Scotland **d.** 1945 •
5ft 11in • 13st • **Clubs** Warwick County, NH;
Luton Town May 1895, Millwall Athletic May
1898, Luton Town May 1899, Thames Ironworks
Jan 1900, Dundee Dec 1900 **SU** 1899 **UD** v
Higher Walton (h) FAC 1Q, 4.10.1890 **FL** 76/gls 5
TM 2/gls 0 **FAC** 9/gls 0 **T** 87/gls 5

Stiles: "Nobby" (Norbert) HB 1960-1971

See p.118.

Stone: Herbert HB 1893-1895

b. 1873, St. Albans, England **d.** nk • **Clubs** NH;
Ashton North End cs. 1895 **SU** Jul 1893 **UD** v
Blackburn Rovers (a) 26.3.1894 **FL** 6/gls 0
TM 1/gls 0 **T** 7/gls 0

Storey-Moore: Ian F 1971-1974

b. 17.1.1945, Ipswich, England • *5ft 10in • 11st
13lb* • **Clubs** Nottingham Forest am. Aug 1961,
pro. May 1962; UTD; Burton Albion Sep 1974,
Chicago Sting (NASL) May–Aug 1975, Shepshed
Charterhouse (manager) **SU** Mar 1972 (pro.) **TF**
£200,000 **UD** v Huddersfield Town (h) 11.3.1972,
scored 1 **FL** 39/gls 11 **FAC** 4/gls 1 **T** 43/gls 12
INT (England) 1/gls 0

Derby County claimed Ian Storey-Moore as
their new signing in February 1972, only to
have the transfer ruled invalid. United then
quickly snatched him up. Storey-Moore was a
skilful winger, and he made an impressive
start at United with a goal in each of his first
three games. Sadly, his career was cut short
two seasons later by an ankle injury.

Strachan OBE: Gordon M 1984-1989

b. 9.2.1957, Edinburgh, Scotland • *5ft 5.5in •
10st 4lb* • **Clubs** Dundee Oct 1971, Aberdeen
Nov 1977; UTD; Leeds Utd Mar 1989, Coventry
City Mar 1995, (player-manager) Nov 1996,
(manager) May 1997 **SU** Aug 1984 (pro.) **TF**
£600,000 **UD** v Watford (h) 25.8.1984, scored 1
FL 155(5)/gls 33 **FAC** 22/gls 2 **FLC** 12(1)/gls 1
EUR 6/gls 2 **T** 195(6)/gls 38 **INT** (Scotland)
50/gls 5

In his first season at
United, Gordon Strachan
added the 1985 FA Cup
to the many trophies he
won with Aberdeen. An
intelligent, impish
player, he could score
goals and set up others
with his incisive passes.
The fans were stunned in 1989 when Alex
Ferguson sold him for £300,000 to Leeds.

Street: Ernest F 1902-1903

b. dnk, Manchester, England **d.** nk • **Clubs** Sale
Holmfield; UTD (on loan to Sale Holmfield
Apr–Oct 1903) **SU** May 1902 **UD** v Liverpool (h)
FAC 1, 7.2.1903 **FL** 1/gls 0 **FAC** 2/gls 0 **T** 3/gls 0

Stiles: "Nobby" (Norbert) HB 1960–1971

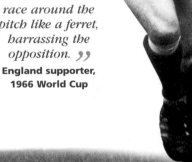

b. 18.5.1942, Collyhurst, Manchester, England • *5ft 6in* • *10st 12lb* • **Clubs** UTD; Middlesbrough May 1971, Preston North End Aug 1973, Aug 1975 (chief coach); Jul 1977–Jun 1981 (manager); Vancouver Whitecaps (Canada, coach), West Bromwich Albion 1984 (asst. manager), Oct 1985 (manager), Feb 1986 (coach); UTD (Youth team coach) Jul 1989–1993 **SU** Sep 1957 (am.), Jun 1959 (pro.) **UD** v Bolton Wanderers (a) 1.10.1960 **FL** 311/gls 17 **FAC** 38/gls 0 **FLC** 7/gls 0 **EUR** 36/gls 2 **T** 392/gls 19 **INT** (England) 28/gls 1

Many people remember Nobby Stiles dancing around the Wembley pitch after England's 1966 World Cup win, but Manchester United fans have many more memories of his 14 years and nearly 400 appearances for the club.

As a boy, Norbert Peter Stiles had walked to Old Trafford with his father, dreaming of hearing his name read out over the public address system. When he signed schoolboy forms in 1957 he moved one step towards realizing his dream, and a step further two years later, when he became a professional.

Thrown into first-team action a little earlier than expected, due to the void left by the tragedy of the Munich air crash, Stiles made his first-team debut against Bolton Wanderers in October 1960, at the age of 18. The aggressive little local lad soon established himself as a regular and made 31 appearances in that first season.

As Busby rebuilt his decimated squad and moulded a team capable of winning the championship and ultimately the European Cup, the fierce-tackling Stiles became a permanent fixture in the United midfield. Playing in a deep role Stiles could act as an extra defender, but such was his fitness that

he could still weigh in with the goals when it was necessary.

Despite missing out on an FA Cup winners' medal in 1963, Stiles, the renowned hard man and ball-winner of the team, picked up a championship winners' medal in 1965. Now a vital component of the United team, he began attracting the interest of the English national side's scouts.

Having been picked for England Schoolboys and the England Youth team in previous years, by 1964 Stiles had also been picked by the England Under-23 side. His full England debut followed soon afterwards against Scotland, and he won a further eight caps that year. International recognition came just at the right time for the determined Stiles and he played in all of England's World Cup

Fact file

- **28 caps**
  Capped by England at Schoolboy, Youth, and Under-23 levels, Stiles went on to earn no less than 28 full England caps.

- **League medals**
  In 1965 and 1967, Stiles won League championship winners' medals.

- **Rare treasures**
  Stiles has the rare distinction of owning two of the most treasured medals in football, a World Cup winners' medal from 1966 and a European Cup winners' medal from 1968.

- **TV star**
  In 1991, Stiles was chosen as the subject of This is Your Life.

matches before they lifted the Jules Rimet trophy. It was after the 4-2 win over West Germany that he went on his renowned joyful jig around Wembley.

In 1967 Stiles picked up his second championship medal, but the high point of his United career arrived 12 months later at the scene of Stiles' greatest triumph to date. Winning the European Cup was the pinnacle of his United career and for this local boy it was a very special night. The team beat Benfica 4–1 and the emotional embrace between Busby and Stiles showed how much it meant to the club and to Manchester. Stiles played on for the club until 1971 before joining Middlesbrough for £20,000. His heart was still at Old Trafford, though, and after spells in management at Preston and West Bromwich Albion he returned to United as a Youth-team coach in 1989, a role he occupied until the early 1990s.

A will to win

An active, aggressive defender, Stiles had great enthusiasm and a strong will to win. He was often seen shouting and encouraging fellow players to greater efforts on the pitch.

> **"** *He used to race around the pitch like a ferret, harrassing the opposition.* **"**
> **England supporter, 1966 World Cup**

Sutcliffe: John GK 1903–1904

b. 14.4.1868, Shibden, nr. Halifax, England • **d.** 7.7.1947 • *6ft* • *12st 10lb* • **Clubs** Bolton Wanderers Jun 1889, Millwall Athletic Apr 1902; UTD; Plymouth Argyle Jan 1905, Southend Utd (coach) 1911–1912, Heckmondwike AFC Feb 1913, Arnhem (Holland, coach) 1914, Bradford City (trainer) May 1919 **SU** May 1903 (pro.) **UD** v Bristol City (h) 5.9.1903 **FL** 21/gls 0 **FAC** 7/gls 0 **T** 28/gls 0 **INT** (England) 5/gls 0

Sweeney: Eric F 1925–1930

b. 3.10.1905, Rock Ferry, Birkenhead, England • *5ft 10in* • *10st 10lb* • **Clubs** Flint Town; UTD; Charlton Athletic Jun 1930, Crewe Alexandra Aug 1931, Carlisle Utd Jul 1932 **SU** Apr 1925 (am.), May 1925 (pro.) **UD** v Leeds Utd (h) 13.2.1926, scored 1 **FL** 27/gls 6 **FAC** 5/gls 1 **T** 32/gls 7

Taibi: Massimo GK 1999–2000

b. 18.2.1970, Palermo, Italy • *6ft 3in* • *12st 13lb* • **Clubs** Licata 1988–89, Trento 1989–90, AC Milan 1991–92, Como 1992–93, Piacenza 1993–1997, AC Milan 1997–98, Venezia 1998-2000 (all in Italy); UTD (on loan to Reggina Calcio Jan–Jun 2000); Reggina Calcio Jul 2000, Atalanta Jul 2001 **SU** 11.9.1999 (pro.) **TF** £4.4 million **FL** 4 **T** 4

Tapken: Norman GK 1938–1939

b. 21.1.1914, Wallsend, Newcastle upon Tyne, England • **Clubs** Wallsend Thermal Welfare, Newcastle Utd May 1933; UTD (WW2: Newcastle Utd, Sunderland, Darlington, Aldershot, Brighton & Hove Albion, Chester); Darlington Apr 1947, Shelborne 1948–1949, Stoke City (asst. trainer) Jul 1952 **SU** Dec 1938 **TF** £850 **UD** v Leicester City (h) 26.12.1938 **FL** 14/gls 0 **FAC** 2/gls 0 **T** 16/gls 0

Taylor: Chris F/HB 1924–1930

b. 1904, Small Heath, Birmingham, England • *5ft 10in* • *11st 4lb* • **Clubs** Canadian football, Evesham Town, Redditch FC; UTD; Hyde Utd Sep 1931 until his retirement in 1932 **SU** Feb 1924 **TF** £300 **UD** v Coventry City (a) 17.1.1925 **FL** 28/gls 6 **FAC** 2/gls 1 **T** 30/gls 7

Taylor: Ernie F 1957–1959

b. 2.9.1925, Sunderland, England **d.** 9.4.1985 • *5ft 4in* • *10st 2lb* • **Clubs** Newcastle Utd Sep 1942 (WW2) Plymouth Argyle, Blackpool Oct 1951; UTD; Sunderland Dec 1958, Altrincham Aug 1961, Derry City Nov 1961–Feb 1962, New Brighton FC (New Zealand, player) Feb 1964–1965 **SU** Feb 1958 **TF** £8,000 **UD** v Sheffield Wednesday (h) **FAC** 5, 19.2.1958 **FL** 22/gls 2 **FAC** 6/gls 1 **EUR** 2/gls 1 **T** 30/gls 4 **INT** (England) 1/gls 0

In a ten-month stay after the Munich crash, emergency signing Ernest Taylor helped to stabilize the United team and encourage the shell-shocked youngsters around him. The 32-year-old expert passer also lifted the fans with his entertaining back-heels and cheeky flicks. Twice an FA Cup winner with Newcastle and Blackpool, Taylor earned his only England cap in 1953, against Hungary.

Taylor: Tommy F 1953–1958

See right.

Taylor: Walter F 1921–1922

b. 1901 **d.** nk • **Clubs** New Mills FC; UTD **SU** Dec 1921 **TF** £25 **UD** v Sheffield Utd (a) 2.1.1922 **FL** 1/gls 0 **T** 1/gls 0

Thomas: Harry F 1921–1930

b. 28.2.1901, Swansea, Wales **d.** nk • *5ft 6in* • *10st 4lb* • **Clubs** Swansea Town 1919–1920, Porth FC 1920; UTD; Merthyr Town Oct 1930, Abercarn FC Apr 1932 **SU** Apr 1922 **UD** v Oldham Athletic (a) 22.4.22 **FL** 128/gls 12 **FAC** 7/gls 1 **T** 135/gls 13 **INT** (Wales) 1/gls 0

For most of his eight seasons at United, Henry (Harry) Thomas played second fiddle to the more prolific Teddy Partridge and Frank McPherson, who dominated his preferred left-wing position. Thomas' best spell in the side came in 1925/26, when he

played 29 games in Division One, and six in the FA Cup run which ended with a semi-final defeat by Manchester City.

Thomas: Mickey M 1978–1981

b. 7.7.1954, Mochdre, Colwyn Bay, Wales • *5ft 6in* • *10st 6lb* • **Clubs** Wrexham am. 1969, appr. 1971, pro. Apr 1972; UTD; Everton Aug 1981, Brighton & Hove Albion Nov 1981, Stoke City Aug 1982, Chelsea Jan 1984, West Bromwich Albion Sep 1985 (on loan to Derby County Apr–May 1986), Wichita Wings (US Indoor League) Aug 1986, Shrewsbury Town Aug 1988, Leeds Utd Aug 1989 (on loan to Stoke City Mar–May 1990), Stoke City Aug 1990, Wrexham Aug 1991, Conway Utd Jul–Aug 1993 **SU** Nov 1978 (pro.) **TF** £300,000 **UD** v Chelsea (a) 25.11.1978 **FL** 90/gls 11 **FAC** 13/gls 2 **FLC** 5/gls 2 **EUR** 2/gls 0 **T** 110/gls 15 **INT** (Wales) 51/gls 4

Michael (Mickey) Thomas was different from Gordon Hill, his entertaining predecessor on United's left wing. But whatever Mickey Thomas lacked in flair, he compensated for with tenacity and industry. He was a regular in Dave Sexton's side, but was traded in by Ron Atkinson for Everton's John Gidman. In 1993 Thomas went to jail for his part in a counterfeit money scam.

Thompson: John F 1936–1938

b. 1909, Newbiggin, nr. Ashington, England • **Clubs** Stakeford Utd, Carlisle Utd am. Aug, pro. Sep 1928, Bristol City Jun 1929, Bath City Feb 1930, Blackburn Rovers Apr 1931; UTD; Gateshead Mar 1938, York City cs. 1939 **SU** Nov 1936 (pro.) **TF** £4,500 **UD** v Liverpool (h) 21.11.1936, scored 1 **FL** 3/gls 1 **T** 3/gls 1

Thompson: William F 1893–1894

b. nk **d.** nk • **Clubs** Dumbarton, Aston Villa Apr 1893; NH **SU** Oct 1893 **UD** v Burnley (a) 21.10.1893 **FL** 3/gls 0 **T** 3/gls 0

Thomson: Arthur F 1929–1931

b. 1903, West Stanley, England • *5ft 9.5in* • *11st 4lb* • **Clubs** West Stanley FC 1925, Morecambe FC Oct 1927; UTD; Southend Utd Aug 1931, Tranmere Rovers 1933–1934 **SU** May 1928 **UD** v Bury (h) **FAC** 4, 26.1.1929 **FL** 3/gls 1 **FAC** 2/gls 0 **T** 5/gls 1

Thomson: Ernest HB 1907–1909

b. 1884 **d.** nk • *5ft 10in* • *11st 10lb* • **Clubs** Darwen; UTD; Nelson cs. 1909, Cardiff City 1911–1912, Nelson cs. 1912–1914 **SU** May 1906 **UD** v Middlesbrough (a) 14.9.1907 **FL** 4/gls 0 **T** 4/gls 0

Thomson: James F 1913–1914

b. nk **d.** nk • *5ft 9in* • *10st 9lb* • **Clubs** Clydebank, Renton FC; UTD; Dumbarton Harp, St. Mirren 1918–cs. 1928 **SU** May 1913 **UD** v Bradford City (h) 13.12.1913 **FL** 6/gls 0 **T** 6/gls 1

Thornley: Ben F 1993–1998

b. 21.4.1975, Bury, England • *5ft 9in* • *11st 12lb* • **Clubs** UTD (on loan to Stockport County 1995 and to Huddersfield Town 1995); Huddersfield Town Jul 1998 **SU** 8.7.1991 (appr.), 23.1.1993 (pro.) **UD** v West Ham Utd (sub) (a) 26.2.1994 **FL** 1(8)/gls 0 **FAC** 2/gls 0 **FLC** 3/gls 0 **T** 6(8)/gls 0

Tomlinson: Graeme F 1994–1998

b. 10.12.1975, Watford, England • *5ft 10in* • *12st 7lb* • **Clubs** Bradford City 1993; UTD (on loan to Wimbledon Sep-Oct 1994, to Luton Town Mar-Apr 1996, Bournemouth Aug-Oct 1997 and to Millwall Mar-Apr 1998), Macclesfield Town Jul 1998, Exeter City summer 2000 **SU** 12.7.1994 **UD** v Port Vale (sub) (h) **FLC** 2, 2nd leg, 5.10.94 **FLC** 0(2)/gls 0 **T** 0(2)/gls 0

Taylor: Tommy F 1953-1958

b. 29.1.1932, Barnsley, England **d.** 6.2.1958 • *5ft 11in • 12st 6lb* • **Clubs** Smithies Utd, Barnsley Jul 1949; <u>UTD</u> **SU** Mar 1953 (pro.) **TF** £29,999 **UD** v Preston North End (h) 7.3.1953, scored 2 **FL** 166/gls 112 **FAC** 9/gls 5 **EUR** 14/gls 11 **T** 189/gls 128 **INT** (England) 19/gls 16

England international and "Busby Babe" Thomas (Tommy) Taylor was one of United's greatest goal scorers and most memorable players. He played at left-back for his school team, moving into the forward line only when they were short of players. At 14, he started work, and played no football for nearly two seasons. At 16, however, Taylor deputized for his uncle at centre-forward in a local pub team, scoring once and making an impression on those watching. He soon attracted the notice of local scouts. In February 1948 Tommy Taylor signed amateur forms at Barnsley. A professional a year later, he made his first-team debut in the Paisley Charity Football Cup on 2nd May, 1950 at St. Mirren. His first League game was against Grimsby later that year.

During his national service, Taylor's football career was nearly cut short when, in a regiment game, he suffered a cracked bone, torn ligaments and severe cartilage damage. Another year out of the game and two operations later, Taylor returned to Barnsley, where he produced a string of outstanding performances. As an inside-forward he scored 26 goals in his 44 appearances for the club, and First Division managers began to show interest. Barnsley were at the bottom of Division Two, and in financial need. They would have to sell him.

Matt Busby tracked Tommy Taylor for seven months, finally signing him in March, 1953. Although Cardiff City offered more money, Taylor chose United because of Manchester's proximity to his Barnsley home. Busby had no trouble persuading the board to find the £30,000 to finance the deal but, aware that such a price tag could burden the youngster, he paid £29,999. Although far from being a complete player, Taylor's lightning speed, thunderbolt shot, powerful heading and excellent positioning made him a useful addition to the already successful forward line of Pegg, Berry and Viollet.

Tommy Taylor made his debut at Old Trafford against Preston North End in front of 52,590 people. Taylor scored the first two of seven goals in his first season, and immediately became a crowd favourite.

Just 10 weeks after signing for United, Taylor was selected to tour South America with England. His international debut against Argentina was abandoned, but a week later, he played and scored against Chile. Despite a huge choice of quality centre-forwards available at the time, Taylor won a regular place. In his last England game he scored both goals in the 2-0 victory over France, taking his tally to 16 goals in 19 international starts.

By 1954, Busby's ageing team needed new life, and he decided to use players from the Youth team in the same team as the recently signed Taylor. The gamble paid off, and in 1955/56 the club won the League once more, with Taylor netting 25 goals in his 33 appearances.

Busby had dreams of European glory, and despite the scepticism of others, he took his young side proudly into virgin territory. In their first European Cup game, United defeated Belgian champions Anderlecht 10-0 at Maine Road. Tommy Taylor contributed a hat-trick. United progressed to the semi-final stage before going out to the great Real Madrid side.

Twelve months on, the same team were even better equipped for a European Cup assault, but the challenge was knocked off course by the Munich air disaster on the return home from the quarter-final victory over Red Star Belgrade.

By the time Tommy Taylor died at Munich, his goal-scoring exploits had won the hearts of all who had seen him play, and to those lucky enough to remember him, there has never been a greater centre-forward.

> " *He was a brilliant player with bags of old-fashioned guts.* "
> **Jimmy Greaves**

Almost there
Tommy Taylor beats Aston Villa's goalkeeper, Nigel Simms, to score the only United goal in the 1957 FA Cup Final. United lost 1-2.

> " *There is only one word necessary to describe Tommy Taylor – Magnifico.* "
> **Alfredo di Stefano, Real Madrid player**

Timing
Despite his size, Tommy Taylor's timing was precise and he was able to combine power and accuracy when heading the ball. His stamina and neat passing created many openings for other players.

Fact file

- **Top scorer**
Tommy Taylor holds the highest goals-per-game ratio of all who have played more than 50 games for United. His 128 goals in only 189 games include 34 in 1956/57.

- **Finest 90 minutes**
Tommy Taylor's finest overall performance for Manchester United was probably the 3-0 win against Atletico Bilbao in the 1956/57 European Cup quarter-final.

- **Serving his country**
During his national service, Tommy Taylor played football for the British Army, the Football Association and the Football League.

Tommy Taylor: Career timeline

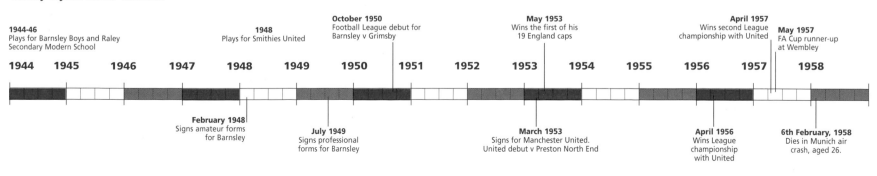

1944-46 Plays for Barnsley Boys and Raley Secondary Modern School

1948 Plays for Smithies United

October 1950 Football League debut for Barnsley v Grimsby

May 1953 Wins the first of his 19 England caps

April 1957 Wins second League championship with United

May 1957 FA Cup runner-up at Wembley

1944 1945 1946 1947 1948 1949 1950 1951 1952 1953 1954 1955 1956 1957 1958

February 1948 Signs amateur forms for Barnsley

July 1949 Signs professional forms for Barnsley

March 1953 Signs for Manchester United. United debut v Preston North End

April 1956 Wins League championship with United

6th February, 1958 Dies in Munich air crash, aged 26.

Viollet: Dennis **F** 1952–1962

b. 20.9.1933, Manchester, England • **d.** 6.3.1999 • *5ft 8in* • *10st 10lb* • **Clubs** UTD (on trial for one month Oct 1947); Stoke City Jan 1962, Baltimore Bays (NASL) Apr 1967–Sep 1968, Witton Albion Jan 1969, Linfield (player-coach) Aug 1969, Preston North End (coach) 1970, Crewe Alexandra Feb 1971 (coach), Aug–Nov 1971 (manager), Washington Diplomats (NASL, coach) 1974–Jun 1977, Jackson University (coach), Richmond (Virginia, coach) 1995 **SU** 1949 (am.), Sep 1950 (pro.) **UD** v Newcastle Utd (a) 11.4.1953 **FL** 259/gls 159 **FAC** 18/gls 5 **FLC** 2/gls 1 **EUR** 12/gls 13 **T** 291/gls 178 **INT** (England) 2/gls 1

There have been some outstanding strikers at Manchester United over the years, but none of them has matched Dennis Viollet's tally of 32 League goals in season 1959/60. This still stands as a United record, and is all the more remarkable considering that, just two seasons earlier, Viollet had been through the harrowing experience of the Munich air crash.

Despite growing up in the shadow of Manchester City in Moss Side, Viollet joined Matt Busby's burgeoning youth scheme on leaving school. Slightly built, slim and always pale faced, Dennis Viollet had a surprising strength, which brought him his first-team debut at Newcastle, aged 19, alongside Tommy Taylor. Viollet's silky, stealthy approach made him the perfect foil for the more robust Taylor, who scored twice that day in a 2–1 win. Together they won League championship medals in 1956 and 1957.

The Munich disaster in February 1958, which killed eight of his fellow players and three of the club's officials, left Dennis with head injuries that prevented him from playing again until near the end of the season, as a warm-up for his appearance in the FA Cup Final against Bolton Wanderers.

Dennis was just a shadow of his former self, and United lost 2–0 to Bolton, but the following season saw him score 21 League goals to help United finish second in the First Division.

Viollet went on to make 291 appearances in League and Cup competitions for United, scoring a total of 178 goals. He played three times for the Football League but was capped only twice for England, playing against Hungary and Luxembourg in 1960.

In January, 1962, Viollet left Old Trafford in a £25,000 transfer, making way for Denis Law.

> *"I consider Dennis Viollet as never quite the same player after the Munich air crash, even though he escaped with relatively minor injuries."*
> **Jimmy Murphy**

Viollet played more than 200 games and scored 66 goals for Tony Waddington at Stoke City before leaving in April 1967, to play in the North American Soccer League with Baltimore Bays. He came home 18 months later for a season with Linfield in Northern Ireland, and played non-League football at Witton Albion for several months.

As a coach, Viollet had spells at Preston and Crewe in 1971 before returning to America, to work with Washington Diplomats from 1974 to 1977. He continued coaching at Jacksonville University, then Richmond in Virginia in 1995.

Shortly after attending the 1997 European Cup Final in Munich as a guest of UEFA, along with the other Munich survivors, Dennis Viollet underwent surgery for a brain tumour. Less than two years later, in the spring of 1999 the illness sadly claimed his life.

Lightning striker
Viollet's lightning runs in the penalty box, his quick reflexes, intelligent positioning and accurate finishing in front of goal were the fulfilment of the early promise he showed as captain of Manchester Boys at the age of 15.

> *"He would always be in my best all-time United team. His lack of England caps was an insult."*
> **John Doherty**

Did you know?

- *Dennis Viollet captained Manchester United at the FA Cup Final in 1958 and in season 1959/60.*
- *For more than 20 years, Viollet lived in America, where he continued to coach.*
- *Dennis and his wife Helen have a tennis-playing daughter, Rachel, who has competed at Junior Wimbledon.*

Toms: Billy **F** 1919–1921

b. 19.5.1896, Manchester, England **d.** nk • *5ft 9in* • *12st* • **Clubs** Altrincham, Eccles Borough cs. 1914 (WW1: Southport Vulcan); UTD; Plymouth Argyle Sep 1920, Oldham Athletic Jul 1921, Coventry City Jul 1922, Stockport County Jun 1923, Wrexham Oct 1923, Crewe Alexandra Dec 1924, Great Harwood until Jan 1926, Winsford Utd Aug 1926, CWS Margarine Works (Manchester) am. Aug 1929 **SU** Sep 1919 (am.), Oct 1919 (pro.) **UD** v Middlesbrough (h) 4.10.1919 **FL** 13/gls 3 **FAC** 1/gls 1 **T** 14/gls 4

Topping: Henry **FB** 1932–1935

b. 1908, Manchester, England • *5ft 10in* • *12st 10lb* • **Clubs** UTD; Barnsley May 1935, Macclesfield Jul 1936 **SU** Dec 1932 **UD** v Bradford (a) 5.4.1933 **FL** 12/gls 1 **T** 12/gls 1

Tranter: Wilf **HB** 1963–1964

b. 5.3.1945, Pendlebury, Manchester, England • **Clubs** UTD (ground staff) May 1961; Brighton & Hove Albion May 1966 (on loan to Baltimore Bays, NASL, Apr–Aug 1968), Fulham Jan 1969, St. Louis Stars (NASL) Apr–Aug 1972 **SU** Sep 1961 (appr.), Apr 1962 (pro.) **UD** v West Ham Utd (a) 7.3.1964 **FL** 1/gls 0 **T** 1/gls 0

Travers: George **F** 1913–1915

b. 1888, Newtown, Birmingham, England **d.** 31.8.1946 • *5ft 8in* • *11st 6lb* • **Clubs** Bilston Utd 1904, Rowley Utd 1905, Wolverhampton Wanderers Jul 1906, Birmingham Aug 1907, Aston Villa Dec 1908, Queen's Park Rangers May 1909, Leicester Fosse Aug 1910, Barnsley Jan 1911; UTD (WW1: Tottenham Hotspur); Swindon Town cs. 1919, Millwall Athletic Jun 1920, Norwich City Oct 1920, Gillingham Jun 1921, Nuneaton Town Sep 1921, Cradley St. Luke's Nov 1922, Bilston Utd1929–1931 **SU** Feb 1914 **UD** v Tottenham Hotspur (a) 7.2.1914 **FL** 21/gls 4 **T** 21/gls 4

Turnbull: Jimmy **F** 1907–1910

b. 23.5.1884, East Plain, Bannockburn, Scotland **d.** nk • *5ft 10.5in* • *12st 3lb* • **Clubs** East Stirlingshire, Dundee cs. 1901; Falkirk 1903–1904, Rangers 1904, Preston North End Jan 1905, Leyton FC May 1906; UTD; Bradford Sep 1910, Chelsea Jun 1912; UTD (on trial for 1 month) Sep 1914; Hurst FC Oct 1914 **SU** May 1907 **UD** v Chelsea (a) 28.9.1907 **FL** 67/gls 36 **FAC** 9/gls 6 **T** 76/gls 42

Turnbull: Sandy **F** 1906–1915

b. 1884, Hurlford, Kilmarnock, Scotland **d.** 3.5.1917 • *5ft 7in* • *12st* • **Clubs** Hurlford Thistle, Manchester City Jul 1902; UTD (WW1: Rochdale and Clapton Orient) **SU** Dec 1906 **UD** v Aston Villa (h) 1.1.1907, scored 1 **FL** 220/gls 90 **FAC** 25/gls 10 **T** 245/gls 100

A cultured, precise and polished inside-forward, Alexander (Sandy) Turnbull occupies a special place in United's history. He will be forever remembered as the scorer of the only goal of the game when United won the FA Cup in 1909.

It was United's first success in the competition and it was sandwiched between the 1908 and 1911 Football League championships won by the side that included such illustrious players as Billy Meredith, Charlie Roberts and Harry Moger.

Turnbull signed for Manchester City in 1902 to begin a career that would bring him both fame and notoriety. His first full season at City brought him a Second Division championship medal and the following season he was in the line-up that won the FA Cup.

In 1905 City were found guilty of malpractice regarding payments to players. A number of officials were sacked and all the players were suspended. By the time the ban was lifted, on 31st December, 1906, Turnbull, Meredith, Herbert Burgess and Jimmy Bannister had moved to United, where they made their debut on 1st January, 1907. Turnbull was a regular in United's front line until just before the war, when he and several other players were accused of rigging a match between United and Liverpool. Several stars, including Turnbull, were found guilty and suspended from football for life.

Sadly, the ban was of little consequence, for on 3rd May, 1917, Sandy Turnbull, a member of the "Footballers' Battalion", was killed in action in Arras, France.

Turner: (no initial known) **F** 1890–1891

b. nk **d.** nk • **Clubs** Newton Heath LYR **SU** 1890 **UD** v Bootle Reserves (a) FAC 2Q, 25.10.1890 **FAC** 1/gls 0 **T** 1/gls 0

Turner: Chris **GK** 1985–1988

b. 15.9.1958, Sheffield, England • *5ft 10.5in* • *12st 2lb* • **Clubs** Sheffield Wednesday Mar 1975, pro. Aug 1976 (on loan to Lincoln City Oct 1978), Sunderland Jul 1979; UTD; Sheffield Wednesday Sep 1988 (on loan to Leeds Utd Nov 1989), Leyton Orient Oct 1991, (manager) Aug 1994-Apr 1995, Hartlepool (manager) Feb 1999 **SU** Aug 1985 (pro.) **TF** £275,000 **UD** v Aston Villa (a) 14.12.1985 **FL** 64/gls 0 **FAC** 8/gls 0 **FLC** 7/gls 0 **T** 79/gls 0

Turner: John **HB** 1898–1899

b. nk **d.** nk • **Clubs** Gravesend Utd; NH **SU** Sep 1898 **UD** v Loughborough Town (h) 22.10.1898 **FL** 3/gls 0 **FAC** 1/gls 0 **T** 4/gls 0

Turner: Robert **D** 1898–1899

b. dnk **d.** nk • **Clubs** NH; Brighton Utd Aug 1899–Feb 1900, Fulham 1900–1901, Glentoran 1901–1902 **SU** May 1898 **UD** v Burslem Port Vale (h) 8.10.1898 **FL** 2/gls 0 **T** 2/gls 0

Twiss: Michael **M** 1997–2000

b. 26.12.1977, Salford, Manchester, England • *5ft 11in* • *12st 13lb* • **Clubs** UTD (on loan to Sheffield Utd Aug 1998–May 1999), Port Vale Jul 2000–Jun 2001 **SU** 11.7.1994 (appr.), 1.7.1996 (pro.) **UD** v Barnsley (a) FAC 5 replay, 25.2.1998 **FAC** (1)/gls 0 **T** (1)/gls 0

Tyler: Sidney **FB** 1923–1924

b. 7.12.1904, Wolverhampton, England **d.** 25.1.1971 • *5ft 10.5in* • *12st 6lb* • **Clubs** Stourbridge FC; UTD; Wolverhampton Wanderers May 1924, Gillingham May 1927, Millwall Apr 1929, Colwyn Bay Utd Jun 1931, Chamberlain & Hookham (Birmingham) am. Sep 1933 **SU** May 1922 (pro.) **UD** v Leicester City (h) 10.11.1923 **FL** 1/gls 0 **T** 1/gls 0

Ure: Ian **D** 1969–1971

b. 7.12.1939, Ayr, Scotland • *6ft 0.5in* • *12st 10lb* • **Clubs** Ayr Albion, Dalry Thistle, Dundee Aug 1969, Arsenal Aug 1963; UTD; St. Mirren Aug 1972–Mar 1973, Cumnock FC (coach), East Stirlingshire (manager) Nov 1974–Nov 1975, Icelandic football (coach) Mar 1976–Jan 1977 **SU** Aug 1969 (pro.) **TF** £80,000 **UD** v Wolverhampton Wanderers (a) 23.8.1969 **FL** 47/gls 1 **FAC** 8/gls 0 **FLC** 10/gls 0 **T** 65/gls 1 **INT** (Scotland) 11/gls 0

Valentine: Bob **GK** 1904–1906

b. nk **d.** nk • **Clubs** Swinton (Rugby League) FC; UTD; Swinton (Rugby League) FC cs. 1907 **SU** May 1903 **UD** v Blackpool (a) 25.3.1905 **FL** 10/gls 0 **T** 10/gls 0

Vance: James **F** 1895–1897

b. 1877 **d.** nk • *5ft 10.5in* • *11st 9lb* • **Clubs** Annbank FC; NH; Fairfield FC Dec 1896, Annbank FC Mar 1897 **SU** Jan 1896 **UD** v Leicester Fosse (h) 3.2.1896 **FL** 11/gls 1 **T** 11/gls 1

Verón: Sebastián **M** 2001–

b. 9.2.1975, La Plata, Argentina • *6ft 1in* • *12st 3lb* • **Clubs** Estudiantes de la Plata 1993–1995, CA Boca Juniors 1995–1996 (both in Argentina), Sampdoria UC 1996–1998, Parma AC 1998–1999, SS Lazio 1999–2001 (all in Italy); UTD **SU** July 2001 **INT** (Argentina) 41/gls 6

Vincent: Ernest **HB** 1931–1934

b. 28.10.1907, Seaham Harbour, nr. Sunderland, England **d.** 2.6.1978 • *5ft 9.5in* • *11st 6lb* • **Clubs** Dawdon Colliery 1923–1925, Hyhope Colliery 1925–1926, Seaham Harbour, Washington Colliery 1929–1930, Southport Jul 1930; UTD; Queen's Park Rangers Jun 1935, Doncaster Rovers

KEY: **a**=away **am.**=amateur **appr.**=apprentice **b.**=born **c.**=circa **cs.**=close season **CWC**=Club World Championship **D**=Defender **d.**=died **dnk**=date not known **EUR**=European competitions **F**=Forward **FAC**=FA Cup **FB**=Full-back (defender) **FL**=Football League **FLC**=Football League Cup **GK**=Goalkeeper **gls**=goals **h**=home **HB**=Half-back (midfield) **INT**=International matches **M**=Midfield **NH**=Newton Heath **Newton Heath LYR**=Newton Heath Lancashire & Yorkshire Railway **nk**=not known **pro.**=professional **Q**=qualifying round **SU**=signed for United **sub**=substitute; substitute apps are in brackets after appearances **T**=total **TF**=transfer fee **TM**=Test match **U**=Utility **UD**=United debut **UTD**=Manchester United **v**=versus

May 1937–cs. 1939 **SU** Feb 1932 **TF** £1,000 **UD** v Chesterfield (a) 6.2.1932 **FL** 64/gls 1 **FAC** 1/gls 0 **T** 65/gls 1

Viollet: Dennis F 1952–1962

See opposite.

Vose: George HB 1933–1940

b. 4.10.1911, St. Helens, England **d.** 20.6.1981 • *5ft 10in* • *10st 6lb* • **Clubs** Peasley Cross Athletic; UTD (WW2: Chester, Manchester City, Stockport County, Derby County); Runcorn 1946–1947 **SU** Sep 1932 **UD** v Plymouth Argyle (a) 26.8.1933 **FL** 197/gls 1 **FAC** 14/gls 0 **T** 211/gls 1

George Vose was a dependable centre-half in a United team that flitted between Divisions One and Two. An effective passer of the ball, he scored his one League goal for United on Christmas Day, 1933, in a 3–1 home defeat by Grimsby Town. In 1938/39, his last full season at United, George had a trial with England but remained uncapped.

Waldron: Colin D 1976–1977

b. 22.6.1948, Bristol, England • *6ft* • *13st 13lb* • **Clubs** Bury appr., pro. May 1966, Chelsea Jun 1967, Burnley Oct 1967; UTD (on loan to Sunderland Feb–May 1977); Tulsa Roughnecks (NASL) Apr 1978, Philadelphia Fury (NASL) Jun 1978, Atlanta Chiefs (NASL) Apr 1979, Rochdale Oct 1979–cs. 1980 **SU** May 1976 (pro.) **UD** v Sunderland (a) FLC 3 replay, 4.10.1976 **FL** 3/gls 0 **FLC** 1/gls 0 **T** 4/gls 0

Walker: Dennis F 1962–1963

b. 26.10.1944, Northwich, England • *5ft 9in* • *11st 10lb* • **Clubs** UTD (ground staff, Mar 1960); York City Apr 1964, Cambridge Utd cs. 1968, Poole Town **SU** Sep 1960 (appr.), Nov 1961 (pro.) **UD** v Nottingham Forest (a) 20.5.1963 **FL** 1/gls 0 **T** 1/gls 0

Walker: Robert D 1898–1899

b. nk **d.** nk • **Clubs** NH (on trial for one month) **SU** Jan 1899 **UD** v Glossop North End (h) 14.1.1899 **FL** 2/gls 0 **T** 2/gls 0

Wall: George F 1905–1915

b. 20.2.1885, Boldon Colliery, England **d.** 1962 • *5ft 7in* • *10st 10lb* • **Clubs** Boldon Royal Rovers, Whitburn cs. 1901, Jarrow Sep 1903, Barnsley Nov 1903; UTD; Oldham Athletic Mar 1919, Hamilton Academical Jun 1921, Rochdale Jun 1922, Ashton National Sep 1923, Manchester Ship Canal FC 1926–1927 **SU** Apr 1906 **TF** £175 **UD** v Clapton Orient (a) 7.4.1906, scored 1 **FL** 287/gls 89 **FAC** 29/gls 9 **T** 316/gls 98 **INT** (England) 7/gls 2

During nine years as a regular player for United, George Wall built up a reputation as a goal-scoring winger of the very highest calibre. A north-easterner, Wall played for several local clubs before joining Barnsley in 1903. During his two-and-a-half years there, he all but made the number 11 shirt his sole property.

Wall moved to United in April 1906. His arrival coincided with the team's run-in to a successful promotion campaign. In his debut match, Wall scored the only goal of the game, an appropriate beginning to a career which would see him become an integral part of United's first great era.

The following season, 1906/07, Wall became the team's regular left-winger. In his first complete season he was ever-present in the side and finished as the club's leading scorer, with 11 goals.In 1907/08 United won the Football League championship. Wall had another outstanding season, missing just two of the 38 fixtures and scoring 19 goals – a remarkable total for a wing player. He also scored one of the goals when United defeated Queen's Park Rangers 4–0 to win the first FA Charity Shield. FA Cup victory followed in April, 1909 and two years later, in 1911, Wall picked up his second League championship medal. He continued on Manchester United's left flank for another four seasons before the First World War brought his career at the club to a close.

An England international with seven caps, George Wall later played for Oldham Athletic, Hamilton Academicals and Rochdale.

Wallace: Danny F 1989–1993

b. 21.1.1964, Greenwich, London, England • *5ft 5in* • *10st 5lb* • **Clubs** Southampton appr. Jul 1980, pro. Jan 1982; UTD (on loan to Millwall Mar 1993); Birmingham City Oct 1993, Wycombe Wanderers 1995, playing in Saudi Arabia 1998-99 **SU** Sep 1989 (pro.) **UD** v Portsmouth (a) FLC 2, 1st leg, 20.9.1989, scored 1 **FL** 36(11)/gls 6 **FAC** 7(2)/gls 2 **FLC** 4(3)/gls 3 **EUR** 5(2)/gls 0 **T** 52(18)/gls 11 **INT** (England) 1/gls 1

Danny Wallace was a skilful striker at Southampton, where his brothers Ray and Rod were team mates. Sadly his form at United was hindered by injury, although he still managed to score some great goals. An FA Cup winner in 1990, he was eventually replaced in the first team by Lee Sharpe.

Wallwork: Ronnie D 1997–1999

b. 10.9.1977, Manchester, England • *5ft 10in* • *13st 1lb* • **Clubs** UTD (on loan to Carlisle United Dec 1997–Feb 1998, Stockport County Mar–May 1998, Royal Antwerp, Belgium, Jan–May 1999) **SU** 11.7.1994 (appr.), 17.3.1995 (pro.) **UD** v Barnsley (sub) (h) 25.10.97 **FL** 4(14)/gls 0 **FAC** 0(1)/gls 0 **FLC** 3(1)/gls 0 **EUR** 0(1)/gls 0 **CWC** 1/gls 0 **T** 8(17)/gls 0

In August 1999, following an alleged assault on a referee in the tunnel after a game for Royal Antwerp, Wallwork was banned from the game for life pending a FIFA decision. The suspension was later lifted, and he has since amassed a total of 23 first team appearances for Manchester United.

Walsh: Gary GK 1986–1995

b. 21.3.1968, Wigan, England • *6ft 3in* • *14st 13lb* • **Clubs** UTD (on one month's loan to Airdrieonians Aug 1988, and to Oldham Athletic Nov–Dec 1993); Middlesbrough Aug 1995, Bradford City Oct 1997 **SU** Jun 1983 (appr.), Apr 1985 (pro.) **UD** v Aston Villa (a) 13.12.1986 **FL** 49(1)/gls 0 **FLC** 7/gls 0 **EUR** 6/gls 0 **T** 62(1)/gls 0

Gary Walsh was a courageous and acrobatic goalkeeper who could have played for years at the highest level for club and country. He was first choice at the start of the 1987/88 season, but injuries took him off the field. On his return to fitness, he had to settle for the role of deputy to Jim Leighton and then to Peter Schmeichel. Departing for Middlesbrough, Walsh later helped Bradford City to earn promotion to the Premier League in 1998/99.

Walton: Joe FB 1945–1948

b. 5.6.1925, Manchester, England • *5ft 7in* • *10st 9lb* • **Clubs** UTD (on loan to Goslings FC); Preston North End Mar 1948, Accrington Stanley Feb–Mar 1962 **SU** Apr 1940 (am.), Oct 1943 (pro.) **UD** v Preston North End (h) FAC 4, 1st leg, 26.1.1946 **FL** 21/gls 0 **FAC** 2/gls 0 **T** 23/gls 0

Walton: John F 1951–1952

b. 21.3.1928, Horwich, England • **Clubs** Army football (whilst in army: Plymouth Argyle am., Saltash Utd am.), Bury May 1949; UTD; Bury am. Jul 1953, pro. Feb 1954, Burnley Feb 1954, Coventry City Oct 1956, Kettering Town 1958, Chester Jul 1959 **SU** Jul 1951 (am.), **UD** v Preston North End (h) 29.9.1951 **FL** 2/gls 0 **T** 2/gls 0

Warburton: Arthur F 1929–1933

b. 30.10.1903, Whitefield, nr. Bury, England **d.** 21.4.1978 • *5ft 8in* • *10st 7lb* • **Clubs** Sedgley Park; UTD; Burnley Dec 1933, Nelson May 1934, Fulham Oct 1934, Queen's Park Rangers Jun 1938–1939 (WW2: Rochdale, Middlesbrough, Bradford, Lincoln City, Southport) **SU** Feb 1929 (am.), May 1929 (pro.) **UD** v Aston Villa (h) 8.3.1930, scored 1 **FL** 35/gls 10 **FAC** 4/gls 0 **T** 39/gls 10

Warner: Jack HB 1938–1950

b. 21.9.1911, Trelaw, nr. Pontypridd, Wales **d.** 4.10.1980 • *5ft 7in* • *10st 7lb* • **Clubs** Aberaman 1932, Swansea Town Jan 1934; UTD; Oldham Athletic (player-coach) Jun 1951, Rochdale (player-manager) Jul 1952–May 1953 **SU** Jun 1938 **UD** v Aston Villa (a) 5.11.1938 **FL** 105/gls 1 **FAC** 13/gls 1 **T** 118/gls 2 **INT** (Wales) 2/gls 0

John (Jack) Warner was signed two months after scoring a great goal against United for Swansea, and broke into United's first team in 1938. An effective passer, Jack Warner became United's oldest post-war League player when he faced Newcastle on 22nd April, 1950, aged 38. In his last few seasons at the club, Warner captained the United Reserves.

Warner: Jimmy GK 1892–1893

b. 1865, Lozells, Birmingham, England **d.** nk • **Clubs** Milton FC, Aston Villa May 1886; NH; Walsall Town Swifts Sep 1893–1894 **SU** Jul 1892 **UD** v Blackburn Rovers (a) 3.9.1892 **FL** 22/gls 0 **T** 22/gls 0

Wassall: Jackie F 1935–1940

b. 11.2.1917, Shrewsbury, England • *5ft 8in* • *10st 9lb* • **Clubs** Wellington Town; UTD (WW2: Brighton & Hove Albion); Stockport County Oct 1946–1947 **SU** Feb 1935 **UD** v Swansea Town (a) 9.11.1935 **FL** 46/gls 6 **FAC** 2/gls 0 **T** 48/gls 6

Watson: Willie FB 1970–1973

b. 4.12.1949, Motherwell, Scotland • *5ft 10in* • *11st 7lb* • **Clubs** UTD (on loan to Huddersfield Town Mar–Apr 1970); Miami Toros (NASL) May 1973, Motherwell Sep 1973 **SU** Jun 1965 (am.), Dec 1966 (pro.) **UD** v Blackpool (h) 26.9.1970 **FL** 11/gls 0 **FLC** 3/gls 0 **T** 14/gls 0

Wealands: Jeffrey GK 1982–1984

b. 26.8.1951, Darlington, England • *6ft* • *12st 9lb* • **Clubs** Darlington Cleveland Bridge FC, Wolverhampton Wanderers appr. Jun 1968, pro. Oct 1968 (on loan to Northampton Town 1970), Darlington Jul 1970, Hull City Mar 1972, Birmingham City Jul 1979 (on loan to UTD Feb 1983); UTD Aug 1983 (on loan to Oldham Athletic Mar–May 1984, to Preston North End Dec 1984–Jan 1985); Altrincham May 1985, Barrow Aug 1987, Altrincham 1988–Mar 1992 **SU** Aug 1983 (pro.) **UD** v Coventry City (h) 2.4.1983 **FL** 7/gls 0 **FLC** 1/gls 0 **T** 8/gls 0

Webb: Neil M 1989–1993

b. 30.7.1963, Reading, England • *6ft* • *13st 7lb* • **Clubs** Reading appr. Jun 1979, pro. Nov 1980, Portsmouth Jun 1982, Nottingham Forest Jun 1985; UTD; Nottingham Forest Nov 1992 (on loan to Swindon Town Oct 1994), Grimsby Town 1996 **SU** Jul 1989 (pro.) **TF** £1.5 million **UD** v Arsenal (h) 19.8.1989, scored 1 **FL** 70(5)/gls 8 **FAC** 9/gls 1 **FLC** 14/gls 1 **EUR** 11/gls 1 **T** 104(5)/gls 11 **INT** (England) 26/gls 4

During his first spell with Nottingham Forest, Neil Webb helped the side win the 1989 League Cup, and became the 1,000th player to be capped for England. After only four games for United, he ruptured an Achilles tendon playing for England in September 1989. Webb never fully regained his form, although he did set up Lee Martin's FA Cup-winning goal in May 1990.

Webber: Danny F 2000–

b. 28.12.1981, Manchester, England • *5ft 9in* • *10st 8lb* • **SU** 6.7.1998 (appr.), 1998 (am.), **UD** v Sunderland (a) FLC (4), 28.11.2000 **FLC** (1)/gls 0 **T** (1)/gls 0

Webster: Colin F 1953–1959

b. 17.8.1932, Cardiff, Wales • *5ft 9in* • *11st 2lb* • **Clubs** Avenue Villa, Cardiff Nomads, Cardiff City May 1950; UTD; Swansea Town Oct 1958, Newport County Mar 1963, Worcester City Jul 1964, Merthyr Tydfil, Portmadoc 1965 **SU** May 1952 (pro.) **UD** v Portsmouth (a) 28.11.1953 **FL** 65/gls 26 **FAC** 9/gls 4 **EUR** 5/gls 1 **T** 79/gls 31 **INT** (Wales) 4/gls 0

Colin Webster was recommended to United by Dennis Viollet, one of the forwards whose form frequently kept the quick-footed and quick-tempered Welshman on the sidelines. However, both of them played in the 1958 FA Cup Final, with Webster on the left-wing for the 2–0 defeat by Bolton. Colin Webster also represented Wales three times in that summer's World Cup Finals.

Wedge: Frank F 1897–1898

b. 1876, Dudley, Birmingham, England **d.** nk • **Clubs** Manchester Talbot FC; NH; Chorlton-cum-Hardy FC **SU** Dec 1896 **UD** v Leicester Fosse (a) 20.11.1897, scored 1 **FL** 2/gls 2 **T** 2/gls 2

Wellens: Richard M 1997–2000

b. 26.3.1980, Manchester, England • *5ft 10in* • *10st 11lb* • **Clubs** UTD; Blackpool **SU** 8.7.96 (appr.), 12.5.97 (pro.) **UD** v Aston Villa FLC (3), 13.10.1999 **FLC** (1)/gls 0 **T** (1)/gls 0

West: Enoch F 1910–1915

b. 31.3.1886, Hucknall Torkard, nr. Nottingham, England • *5ft 8in* • *12st 6lb* • **Clubs** Sheffield Utd Nov 1903, Hucknall Constitutional 1904, Nottingham Forest Jun 1905; UTD **SU** Jun 1910 **UD** v Woolwich Arsenal (a) 1.9.1910, scored 1 **FL** 166/gls 72 **FAC** 15/gls 8 **T** 181/gls 80

Enoch "Knocker" West scored 100 League and Cup goals for Nottingham Forest, and he was the First Division's top scorer in 1907/08. Playing in partnership with Sandy Turnbull, Enoch West scored 19 goals to help United win the 1910/11 championship, and he was the club's leading marksman in his first three seasons. West was banned from football in December 1915 for allegedly fixing a match against Liverpool on 2nd April, 1915.

Wetherell: Joe GK 1896–1897

b. nk **d.** nk • *5ft 10in* • *12st* • **Clubs** NH **SU** Jun 1896 **UD** v Walsall (a) 21.9.1896 **FL** 2/gls 0 **T** 2/gls 0

Whalley: Arthur HB 1909–1920

b. 17.2.1886, Rainford, nr. St. Helens, England **d.** 23.11.1952 • *5ft 8in* • *11st 10lb* • **Clubs** Brynn Central, Blackpool Mar 1908; UTD (WW1: Clapton Orient); Southend Utd Sep 1920, Charlton Athletic Aug 1921, Millwall Oct 1924, Barrow (trainer-coach) Dec 1926 **SU** Jun 1909 **TF** £50 **UD** v Sheffield Wednesday (a) 27.12.1909 **FL** 97/gls 6 **FAC** 9/gls 0 **T** 106/gls 6

Well-built Arthur Whalley was an excellent deputy for Duckworth, Roberts or Bell in midfield, where he used his close ball control to good effect. A championship-winner in 1910/11, he was hampered by a knee injury in 1913/14. Whalley recovered from war wounds to play again in 1919, but in 1920 he rejected a new contract with Manchester United when the board failed to guarantee him a benefit match.

Whalley: Bert HB 1935–1947

b. 6.8.1912, Ashton-under-Lyne, Manchester, England **d.** 6.2.1958 • *5ft 10in* • *11st 6lb* • **Clubs** Ferguson & Pailins FC, Stalybridge Celtic Dec 1933; UTD (WW2: Oldham Athletic, Bolton Wanderers, Liverpool), re-registered Apr 1946, later became coach **SU** May 1934 **UD** v Doncaster Rovers (h) 30.11.1935 **FL** 33/gls 0 **FAC** 6/gls 0 **T** 39/gls 0

Whiteside: Norman **F/M** 1981–1989

b. 7.5.1965, Belfast, N. Ireland • *6ft 1in* • *13st 7lb* • **Clubs** UTD; Everton Aug 1989-Jun 1991, Northwich Victoria (asst. manager) Oct 1991-Mar 1992 **SU** Jun 1981 (appr.), Jul 1982 (pro.) **UD** v Brighton & Hove Albion (a) (sub) 24.4.1982 **FL** 193(13)/gls 47 **FAC** 24/gls 10 **FLC** 26(3)/gls 9 **EUR** 11(2)/gls 1 **T** 254(18)/gls 67 **INT** (N. Ireland) 38/gls 9

Norman Whiteside was a rare and prodigious talent. By the time he was 20, he had achieved more than most players do in their whole career, by playing in the World Cup Finals and winning the FA Cup twice. Whiteside was discovered by Bob Bishop, the same Manchester United scout who had found George Best 15 years earlier. Whiteside was brought over to Old Trafford from west Belfast as a 13-year-old schoolboy in September 1978. In April 1982, at just 16 years old, Whiteside made his debut as a substitute for United at Brighton. That summer he deposed Pelé as the youngest-ever player to appear in the World Cup finals when he played for Northern Ireland in Spain, aged 17 years and 41 days.

The following season was just as momentous for Whiteside. He began to command a regular place in the United side and scored in both the FA Cup and League Cup Finals, becoming the youngest player to do so. Whiteside's greatest moment came in the 1985 FA Cup Final, when he charged down the Wembley turf deep into extra time and curled a stunning shot from an impossible angle beyond Neville Southall to win the Cup.

An extremely competitive footballer, Norman Whiteside's temper often got the better of him, and led to several dismissals and suspensions. For a time the press gave him the nickname "Nasty Norman".

Fact file

- **Good score**
  At the age of 10, Whiteside scored over 100 goals in one season for his west Belfast school.
- **Just seventeen**
  Whiteside was the youngest-ever player to score for United, in a match against Stoke City in May 1982, aged 17 years and 7 days old.
- **Youngest finalist**
  In 1983, Whiteside became the youngest player to score in a League Cup Final at 17 years and 323 days old and the youngest player to score in an FA Cup Final at 18 years and 18 days old.
- **Youngest again**
  Whiteside became the youngest-ever player to appear in a World Cup game, when he played for Northern Ireland aged 17 years and 41 days old.

In 1986 Whiteside played again in the World Cup finals. But back at Old Trafford his game was suffering, becoming even more physical and less skilful. He struggled with both form and fitness before being sold to Everton in 1989 for £750,000. After just two years at Goodison Park, a knee injury forced him to retire at the age of 26, a premature loss to football. Whiteside went on to become assistant manager to Sammy McIlroy at Northwich Victoria in October 1991, but left before completing the season to develop his career as a podiatrist.

> *"He was a man well before his time. We used to joke that he was nine before he was born."*
> **Sammy McIlroy**

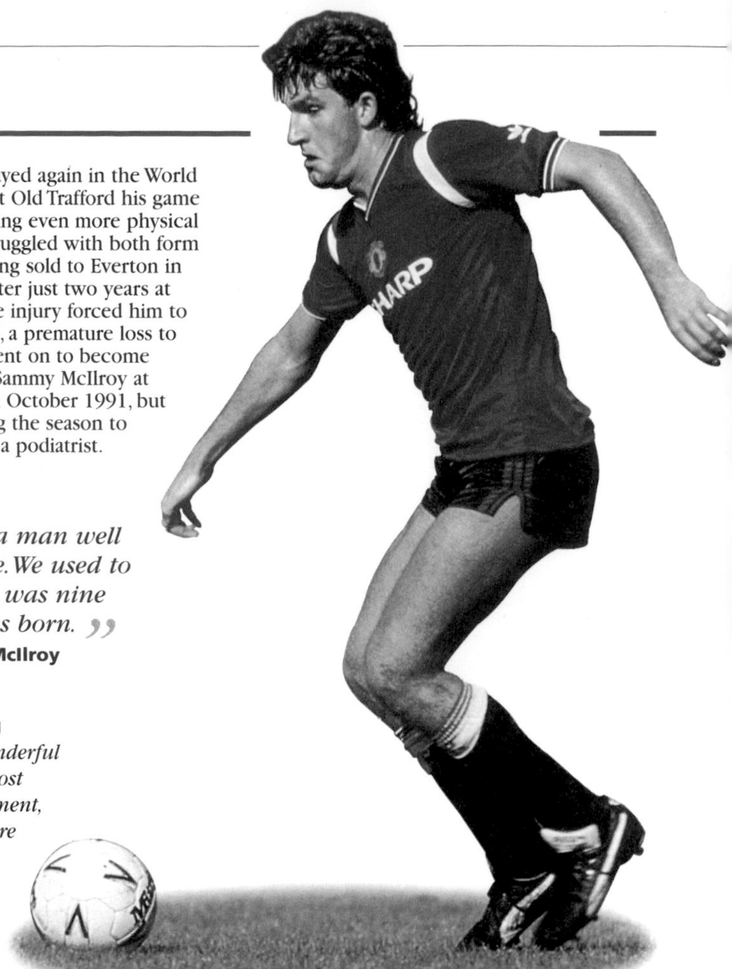

Almost everything
Whiteside was a wonderful player who had almost everything: temperament, awareness, composure and the ability to score great goals. With just a little more pace he would have been a complete player.

Whelan: Anthony **D** 1980–1981

b. 23.11.1959, Dublin, Rep. of Ireland • *6ft* • *12st* • **Clubs** Bohemians; UTD; Shamrock Rovers, Cork, Shamrock Rovers, Bray Wanderers, Shelbourne **SU** Aug 1980 (pro.) **TF** £30,000 **UD** v Southampton (sub) (h) 29.11.1980 **FL** 0(1)/gls 0 **T** 0(1)/gls 0

Whelan: "Liam"/"Billy" (William) **F** 1954–1958

b. 1.4.1935, Dublin, Rep.of Ireland **d.** 6.2.1958 • *5ft 10in* • *11st 11lb* • **Clubs** Home Farm FC; UTD until his death **SU** May 1953 **UD** v Preston North End (a) 26.3.1955 **FL** 79/gls 43 **FAC** 6/gls 4 **EUR** 11/gls 5 **T** 96/gls 52 **INT** (Rep. of Ireland) 4/gls 0

In 1953 Bert Whalley spotted William A. Whelan, otherwise known as Liam or Billy, playing with Home Farm FC, a famous Dublin nursery. At just 18, Whelan already exhibited a quiet grace, combining tremendous ball control with a sudden shot that left defenders dazed. Whalley was highly impressed.

Whelan's first engagement for United was the 1953 FA Youth Cup Final, which they won against Wolverhampton Wanderers. His full debut came in March 1955.

Matt Busby's only concern for the young Irishman was his lack of confidence. Amid the larger-than-life personalities of the Busby Babes, Whelan seemed unsure of his talents and was engagingly modest. Yet he earned championship medals in 1956 and 1957, and four caps for the Republic of Ireland. In 1956/57, he was United's leading League scorer, with 26 goals in 39 matches. Whelan died at Munich in February 1958, aged 22. He had recently lost his position at inside-forward to Bobby Charlton, but travelled nonetheless with the team party. Whelan's gentleness and skill would long be missed by many.

Whitefoot: Jeff **HB** 1949–1956

b. 31.12.1933, Cheadle, England • *5ft 7in* • *11st 4lb* • **Clubs** Stockport Schoolboys; UTD (ground staff 1949-1950); Grimsby Town Nov 1957, Nottingham Forest Jul 1958 **SU** Jan 1951 (pro.) **UD** v Portsmouth (h) 15.4.1950 **FL** 93/gls 0 **FAC** 2/gls 0 **T** 95/gls 0

Capped four times by England Schoolboys, Jeffrey Whitefoot started work at United as an office junior, then graduated to the first team at the age of 16. A talented passer, he lost his regular midfield place to fellow Busby Babe Eddie Colman during the championship season of 1955/56. Jeff Whitefoot still earned a medal, though, and another in 1959 for an FA Cup win at Nottingham Forest.

Whitehouse: Jimmy **GK** 1900–1903

b. 1873, Birmingham, England **d.** 7.2.1934 • *5ft 11in* • *11st 7lb* • **Clubs** Albion Swifts, Birmingham St. George 1890, Grimsby Town Jun 1892, Aston Villa Jul 1896, Bedminster May 1898, Grimsby Town May 1899; NH; Manchester City Feb 1903, Third Lanark Sep 1903, Hull City Jul 1904, Southend Utd Jul 1905-1907 **SU** Sep 1900 **UD** v Burnley (a) 15.9.1900 **FL** 59/gls 0 **FAC** 5/gls 0 **T** 64/gls 0

Whitehurst: Walter **HB** 1955–1956

b. 7.6.1934, Manchester, England • *5ft 11in* • *10st 10lb* • **Clubs** UTD; Chesterfield Nov 1956, Crewe Alexandra Jul 1960, Macclesfield Town, Mossley Nov 1961 **SU** Aug 1950 (am.), May 1952 (pro.) **UD** v Everton (a) 14.9.1955 **FL** 1/gls 0 **T** 1/gls 0

Whiteside: Kerr **HB** 1907–1908

b. 1887, Scotland **d.** nk • *5ft 6in* • *10st 9lb* • **Clubs** Irvine Victoria; UTD; Hurst FC cs. 1910-1915 **SU** May 1907 **UD** v Sheffield Utd (a) 18.1.1908 **FL** 1/gls 0 **T** 1/gls 0

Whiteside: Norman **F/M** 1981–1989

See above.

Whitney: John **HB** 1895–1896; 1900–1901

b. nk **d.** nk • **Clubs** NH **SU** Oct 1895 and cs. 1900 **UD** v Rotherham Town (a) 7.3.1896 **FL** 3/gls 0 **T** 3/gls 0

Whittaker: Walter **GK** 1895–1896

b. 20.9.1878, Manchester, England **d.** 2.6.1917 • *6ft 1in* • *13st 6lb* • **Clubs** Molyneaux FC (Manchester League), Buxton FC, Molyneaux FC; NH; Fairfield FC 1896-1897, Grimsby Town May 1897, Reading May 1898, Blackburn Rovers Feb 1900, Grimsby Town Dec 1901, Derby County Apr 1903, Brentford May 1904, Reading May 1906, Clapton Orient Jul 1907, Exeter City Jul 1910, Swansea Town (player-manager) Jul 1912, Llanelly (player-manager) Jun-Nov 1914 **SU** Feb 1896 **UD** v Grimsby Town (a) 14.3.1896 **FL** 3/gls 0 **T** 3/gls 0

Whittle: John **F** 1931–1932

b. dnk, Leigh, Manchester, England **d.** nk • **Clubs** Hindsford FC; UTD; Rossendale United Jul 1932, Hindsford FC am. Nov 1933 **SU** Oct 1931 (am.), Dec 1931 (pro.) **UD** v Swansea Town (a) 16.1.1932 **FL** 1/gls 0 **T** 1/gls 0

Whitworth: Neil **D** 1990–1991

b. 12.4.1972, Wigan, England • *6ft 2in* • *12st 6lb* • **Clubs** Wigan Athletic appr. Jul 1988, UTD (on loan to Preston North End Jan 1992, to Barnsley Feb 1992 and to Rotherham Utd Aug 1993); Blackpool Dec 1993, Kilmarnock Sep 1994, Wigan Athletic Mar 1998, Hull City Jun 1998 **SU** Jun 1990 (pro.) **TF** £45,000 **UD** v Southampton (a) 13.3.1991 **FL** 1/gls 0 **T** 1/gls 0

Wilcox: Tom **GK** 1908–1909

b. 1879, at sea between USA and UK **d.** 1962 • *5ft 10in* • *11st 8lb* • **Clubs** Millwall Athletic Reserves, Cray Wanderers, Woolwich Arsenal Reserves, Norwich City Oct 1905, Blackpool May 1906; UTD; Carlisle Utd cs. 1909, Goole Town Aug 1912, Abergavenny FC **SU** Aug 1907 **UD** v Nottingham Forest (h) 24.10.1908 **FL** 2/gls 0 **T** 2/gls 0

Wilkins MBE: Ray **M** 1979–1984

b. 14.9.1956, Hillingdon, London, England • *5ft 8in* • *10st 12lb* • **Clubs** Chelsea appr. 1971, pro. Oct 1973; UTD; AC Milan (Italy) Jun 1984, Paris St. Germain (France) Jul 1987, Glasgow Rangers Nov 1987, Queen's Park Rangers Nov 1989, Crystal Palace May 1994, Queen's Park Rangers (player-manager) 1994-1996, Wycombe Wanderers Sep 1996, Hibernian Sep 1996, Millwall Jan 1997, Leyton Orient Feb 1997, Fulham (manager) Sep 1997-May 1998, Chelsea (coach) Jul 1998, Watford (coach) 2001 **SU** Aug 1979 (pro.) **TF** £825,000 **UD** v Southampton (a) 18.8.1979 **FL** 158(2)/gls 7 **FAC** 10/gls 1 **FLC** 14(1)/gls 1 **EUR** 8/gls 1 **T** 190(3)/gls 10 **INT** (England) 84/gls 3

"A bald bloke who played too many square balls" was how Raymond Wilkins modestly expected to be remembered, but Michael Parkinson was closer to the truth when he said: "If football needed an ideal image with which to promote the game it would have to invent something like Ray Wilkins".

Wilkins was widely acknowledged as one of football's gentlemen. In 25 years, he earned 84 England caps, including 10 as captain. He arrived at Old Trafford from Chelsea for a club record fee of £825,000. A classy midfielder, he had captained Chelsea aged only 18, and went on to win United and England captaincies too.

Season 1983/84 was Wilkins' best for United, reaching the European Cup Winners' Cup semi-final before being knocked out by Juventus. In 1984, he moved to AC Milan and later played for the biggest clubs in France and Scotland. In 1993, he was awarded the MBE for 20 years' service to football.

Wilkinson: Harry **F** 1903–1904; 1906

b. 1883, Bury, England **d.** nk • *5ft 7in* • *10st 12lb* • **Clubs** Newton Heath Athletic 1902-1903; UTD; Hull City cs. 1904, West Ham Utd cs. 1905; UTD; Haslingden FC cs. 1906, St. Helens Recreation FC Mar 1907, Bury May 1907, Oswaldtwistle Rovers Oct 1908, Rochdale Dec 1908 **SU** Oct 1902 (am.), Dec 1903 (pro.) **UD** v Burton Utd (a) 26.12.1903 **FL** 8/gls 0 **FAC** 1/gls 0 **T** 9/gls 0

Wilkinson: Ian **GK** 1991–1992

b. 2.7.1973, Warrington, England • *6ft* • *13st* • **Clubs** UTD; Stockport County Jul 1993, Crewe Alexandra Oct 1993 (on loan to Doncaster Rovers

KEY: **a**=away **am.**=amateur **appr.**=apprentice **b.**=born **c.**=circa **cs.**=close season **CWC**=Club World Championship **D**=Defender **d.**=died **dnk**=date not known **EUR**=European competitions **F**=Forward **FAC**=FA Cup **FB**=Full-back (defender) **FL**=Football League **FLC**=Football League Cup **GK**=Goalkeeper **gls**=goals **h**=home **HB**=Half-back (midfield) **INT**=International matches **M**=Midfield **NH**=Newton Heath **Newton Heath LYR**=Newton Heath Lancashire & Yorkshire Railway **nk**=not known **pro.**=professional **Q**=qualifying round **SU**=signed for United **sub**=substitute; substitute apps are in brackets after appearances **T**=total **TF**=transfer fee **TM**=Test match **U**=Utility **UD**=United debut **UTD**=Manchester United **v**=versus

1994–1995) **SU** Jun 1989 (appr.), May 1991 (pro.) **UD** v Cambridge Utd (a) FLC 2, 2nd leg, 9.10.1991 **FL** 1/gls 0 **T** 1/gls 0

Williams: Bill **F** 1901–1902

b. nk **d.** nk • **Clubs** Everton Jan 1894, Blackburn Rovers May 1898, Bristol Rovers 1900–1901; NH **SU** Aug 1901 **UD** v Gainsborough Trinity (h) 7.9.1901 **FL** 4/gls 0 **T** 4/gls 0

Williams: Frank **HB** 1930–1931

b. 1908, Kearsley, nr. Bolton, England • *5ft 9in* • *10st 12lb* • **Clubs** Stalybridge Celtic; UTD; Stalybridge Celtic cs. 1927; UTD; Altrincham **SU** Apr 1927 and Sep 1929 (am.), May 1928 (pro.) **UD** v Newcastle Utd (h) 13.9.1930 **FL** 3/gls 0 **T** 3/gls 0

Williams: Fred **F** 1902–1903

b. 1902, Manchester, England **d.** 1903 • **Clubs** Hanley Swifts, South Shore Blackpool, Manchester City Nov 1896; UTD **SU** Jun 1902 **UD** v Gainsborough Trinity (a) 6.9.1902 **FL** 8/gls 0 **FAC** 2/gls 4 **T** 10/gls 4

Williams: Harry **F** 1904–1906

b. 1883, Farnworth, Widnes, England **d.** nk • *5ft 10in* • *11st 6lb* • **Clubs** Walkden St. Mary's, Turton FC, Bury am. 1900–1901, Bolton Wanderers Nov 1901, Burnley Jul 1903; UTD; Leeds City Aug 1908 **SU** May 1904 **UD** v Bristol City (h) 10.9.1904, scored 1 **FL** 32/gls 7 **FAC** 4/gls 1 **T** 36/gls 8

Williams: Harry **F** 1922–1923

b. 1899, Hucknall Torkard, nr. Nottingham, England **d.** nk • *5ft 10in* • *11st 10lb* • **Clubs** Hucknall Olympic, Sunderland am. May 1920, pro. Aug 1920, Chesterfield Aug 1921; UTD; Brentford Sep 1923–cs. 1925 **SU** May 1922 (pro.) **UD** v Sheffield Wednesday (a) 28.8.1922 **FL** 5/gls 2 **T** 5/gls 2

Williams: Joe **F** 1906–1907

b. dnk, Crewe, England **d.** nk • **Clubs** Macclesfield FC; UTD **SU** Nov 1905 **UD** v Sunderland (h) 25.3.1907, scored 1 **FL** 3/gls 1 **T** 3/gls 1

Williams: Rees **F** 1927–1929

b. 1900, Abercanaid, Merthyr Tydfil, Wales **d.** 30.12.1963 • *5ft 7in* • *11st* • **Clubs** Pentrebach FC, Merthyr Town Apr 1919, Sheffield Wednesday Jun 1922; UTD; Thames Association Aug 1929, Aldershot cs. 1930, Merthyr Town Aug 1931, Glenavon 1933 **SU** Oct 1927 **UD** v Everton (a) 8.10.1927 **FL** 31/gls 2 **FAC** 4/gls 0 **T** 35/gls 2 **INT** (Wales) 8/gls 0

Williamson: John **HB** 1919–1920

b. dnk, Manchester, England **d.** nk • *5ft 9in* • *11st* • **Clubs** Army football (WW1: St. Mirren); UTD (on trial for one month Sep 1919); Bury May 1921, Crewe Alexandra Aug 1922–cs. 1923, British Dyestuffs am. Aug 1927 **SU** Oct 1919 (pro.) **UD** v Blackburn Rovers (h) 17.4.1920 **FL** 2/gls 0 **T** 2/gls 0

Wilson: David **M** 1988–1989

b. 20.3.1969, Burnley, England • *5ft 10in* • *11st* • **Clubs** UTD (on loan to Lincoln City Oct–Nov 1990 and to Charlton Athletic Mar–May 1991); Bristol Rovers Jul 1991–cs. 1993 **SU** Jun 1985 (appr.), Mar 1987 (pro.) **UD** v Sheffield Wednesday (sub) (h) 23.11.1988 **FL** 0(4)/gls 0 **FAC** 0(2)/gls 0 **T** 0(6)/gls 0

Wilson: E. **F** 1889–1890

b. nk **d.** nk • **Clubs** Newton Heath LYR **SU** 1889 **UD** v Preston North End (a) FAC 1, 18.1.1890 **FAC** 1/gls 0 **T** 1/gls 0

Wilson: Jack **HB** 1926–1932

b. 8.3.1897, Leadgate, nr. Newcastle upon Tyne, England **d.** nk • *5ft 9in* • *11st 7lb* • **Clubs** Leadgate St. Ives, Leadgate Utd, Newcastle Utd May 1919, Leadgate Park (player-manager) cs. 1920, Durham City Feb 1922, Stockport County Jun 1922; UTD; Bristol City Jun 1932–May 1933 **SU** Sep 1926 **TF** £500 **UD** v Leeds Utd (h) 4.9.1926 **FL** 130/gls 3 **FAC** 10/gls 0 **T** 140/gls 3

Initially a forward, John (Jack) Wilson's natural strength and stamina made him an ideal midfielder, the position that he adopted at Stockport. He became United's regular left-half in 1926/27, despite a two-month ban following his dismissal in a Reserve match. After six seasons as a regular, Wilson moved on to Bristol City, where he spent his last season in League football.

Wilson: Mark **M** 1998–

b. 9.2.1979, Scunthorpe, England • *6ft* • *13st 1lb* • **Clubs** UTD (on loan to Wrexham Feb–May 1998) **SU** 10.7.1995 (appr.), 9.2.1996 (pro.) **UD** v Brondby, Denmark (sub) (a) Champions League group stage, 21.10.1998 **FL** 1(2)/gls 0 **FLC** 2/gls 0 **EUR** 2(2)/gls 0 **CWC** 1/gls 0 **T** 6(4)/gls 0

Wilson: Tommy **F** 1907–1908

b. 20.10.1877, Preston, England **d.** 30.8.1940 • *5ft 6in* • *11st 6lb* • **Clubs** Fishwick Ramblers, Ashton-in-Makerfield FC, West Manchester FC, Ashton Town, Ashton North End, Oldham County cs. 1896, Swindon Town May 1897, Blackburn Rovers May 1898, Swindon Town May 1899, Millwall Athletic May 1900, Aston Villa Apr 1901, Queen's Park Rangers cs. 1902, Bolton Wanderers May 1904, Leeds City Dec 1906; UTD; Chorley (manager) cs. 1912, Rochdale (chairman) Oct 1919, manager until Feb 1923 **SU** Feb 1908 **UD** v Blackburn Rovers (h) 15.2.1908 **FL** 1/gls 0 **T** 1/gls 0

Winterbottom: Sir Walter **HB** 1936–1938

b. 1914, Oldham, England • **Clubs** Royton Amateurs FC, Manchester City am., Mossley FC; UTD; (WW2: Chelsea guest-player), Mossley FC (player-manager), England (national team manager) 1946–1962 **SU** May 1936 **UD** v Leeds Utd (a) 28.11.1936 **FL** 25/gls 0 **FAC** 2/gls 0 **T** 27/gls 0

Good at reading the game and passing the ball, Walter Winterbottom unfortunately had to retire with a back injury in only his second season with Manchester United. Happily he found new fame in the game after the war, in which he served as an RAF Wing Commander. England's manager from 1946 to 1962, Walter Winterbottom was awarded the CBE in 1963 and a knighthood in 1978, in which year he also became vice-president of the FA Council.

Wombwell: Dick **F** 1904–1907

b. 1877, Nottingham, England **d.** nk • *5ft 7in* • *11st 6lb* • **Clubs** Bulwell FC, Ilkeston Town Dec 1898, Derby County May 1899, Bristol City Jul 1902; UTD; Heart of Midlothian Jan 1907, Brighton & Hove Albion Jun 1907, Blackburn Rovers Feb 1908, Ilkeston Utd Aug 1910 **SU** Mar 1905 **UD** v Grimsby Town (h) 18.3.1905 **FL** 47/gls 3 **FAC** 4/gls 0 **T** 51/gls 3

Wood: John **F** 1922–1923

b. dnk, Leven, nr. Kircaldy, Scotland **d.** nk • *5ft 9in* • *11st* • **Clubs** Hibernian, Dunfermline Athletic cs. 1920, Lochgelly Utd, Dumbarton Jun 1921; UTD; Lochgelly Utd cs. 1923, St. Mirren Dec 1923–cs. 1925, East Stirlingshire **SU** May 1922 **UD** v Crystal Palace (h) 28.8.1922, scored 1 **FL** 15/gls 1 **FAC** 1/gls 0 **T** 16/gls 1

Wood: Nicky **F** 1985–1987

b. 11.1.1966, Oldham, England • *5ft 11in* • *11st 5lb* • **Clubs** UTD until his retirement in 1989 **SU** Jun 1981 (appr.), May 1983 (pro.) **UD** v Everton (sub) (a) 26.12.1986 **FL** 2(1)/gls 0 **FLC** 0(1)/gls 0 **T** 2(2)/gls 0

Wood: Ray **GK** 1949–1959

b. 11.6.1931, Hebburn, Newcastle upon Tyne, England • *5ft 11in* • *11st 12lb* • **Clubs** Newcastle Utd am. May 1948, Darlington Sep 1949; UTD; Huddersfield Town Dec 1958, Bradford City Oct 1965, Barnsley Aug 1966–1967 **SU** Dec 1949 **TF** £5,000 **UD** v Newcastle Utd (h) 3.12.1949 **FL** 178/gls 0 **FAC** 15/gls 0 **EUR** 12/gls 0 **T** 205/gls 0 **INT** (England) 3/gls 0

Raymond Wood will probably be best remembered, not for his most glorious save, but for an incident that left him semi-conscious. A sickening collision with Aston Villa's Peter McParland in the 1957 FA Cup Final put Ray Wood out of the game after only six minutes with a shattered cheekbone and concussion. In that era before substitute goalkeepers, this incident is generally believed to have cost United the Cup.

Wood arrived at Manchester United in 1949 as an 18-year-old with only 12 League games under his belt. Matt Busby paid £5,000 for him and Wood made his debut in December. However, he had to wait until 1953/54 for a regular first-team place. Ray Wood earned championship medals in 1956 and 1957, twice played in European Cup semi-finals, and gained three England caps. He was a reliable keeper, but he was loath to venture from his own line.

Ray Wood travelled to Munich in 1958 with the team party, although by then he had lost his place to Harry Gregg. Both players survived the Munich air crash. Once Ray Wood had recovered his fitness, he transferred to Huddersfield Town in the December of that same year.

Woodcock: Wilf **F** 1913–1920

b. 1892, Ashton-under-Lyne, Manchester, England **d.** nk • *5ft 8in* • *10st 6lb* • **Clubs** Abbey Hey FC, Stalybridge Celtic; UTD; Manchester City May 1920, Stockport County Mar 1922, Wigan Borough Aug 1924–cs. 1925 **SU** May 1912 **UD** v Liverpool (h) 1.11.1913 **FL** 58/gls 20 **FAC** 3/gls 1 **T** 61/gls 21

Worrall: Harry **FB** 1946–1948

b. 19.11.1918, Northwich, England • **Clubs** Winsford Utd; UTD (re-registered Apr 1946); Swindon Town Jun 1948–Jul 1949 **SU** Oct 1937 **UD** v Wolverhampton Wanderers (a) 30.11.1946 **FL** 6/gls 0 **T** 6/gls 0

Wratten: Paul **M** 1990–1991

b. 29.11.1970, Middlesbrough, England, • *5ft 9in* • *12st 3lb* • **Clubs** UTD; Hartlepool Utd Jun 1992, York City 1995 **SU** Jun 1987 (appr.), Dec 1988 (pro.) **UD** v Wimbledon (sub) (h) 2.4.1991 **FL** 0(2)/gls 0 **T** 0(2)/gls 0

Wrigglesworth: Billy **F** 1936–1947

b. 12.11.1912, South Elmsall, nr. Barnsley, England • *5ft 4in* • *9st 7lb* • **Clubs** Frickley Colliery, Chesterfield May 1932, Wolverhampton Wanderers Dec 1934; UTD (WW2: Brentford, Cardiff City, York City, Walsall, Chelsea, Arsenal); Bolton Wanderers Jan 1947, Southampton Oct 1947, Reading Jun 1948, Burton Albion (player-manager) 1949, Scarborough Dec 1949–1950, Accrington Stanley (trainer) Jul 1952 **SU** Jan 1937 **UD** v Sheffield Wednesday (a) 23.1.1937 **FL** 30/gls 8 **FAC** 7/gls 2 **T** 37/gls 10

Yates: William **F** 1906–1907

b. 1883, Birmingham, England **d.** nk • *5ft 9in* • *11st 5lb* • **Clubs** Aston Villa Mar 1903, Brighton & Hove Albion cs. 1905; UTD; Heart of Midlothian Jan 1907, Portsmouth 1908, Coventry City Jun 1911 until his retirement cs. 1914 **SU** June 1906 **UD** v Sheffield Utd (a) 15.9.1906 **FL** 3/gls 0 **T** 3/gls 0

Yorke: Dwight 1998–

b. 3.11.1971, • *5ft 10in* • *12st 4lb* • **Clubs** Signal Hill (Tobago) Aug 1988-Dec 1989, Aston Villa Dec 1989-Aug 1998; UTD **SU** 20.8.1998 (pro.) **TF** £12.6 million **UD** v West Ham United (a) 22.8.1998 **FL** 76(10)/gls 47 **FAC** 6(4)/gls 3 **FLC** 2/gls 2 **EUR** 27(6)/gls 11 **CWC** 2/gls 1 **T** 113(20)/gls 63 **INT** (Trinidad & Tobago) appearance information is unavailable

Dwight Yorke achieved a boyhood dream when he joined United for a club record transfer fee of £12.6 million. He arrived after nine years at Aston Villa. Villa spotted his potential in 1989, whilst on a pre-season tour of Yorke's native West Indies, and paid just £120,000 for him. Ironically, Dwight made his Villa debut against United on 29th December, 1990, in a 1-1 draw at Old Trafford. Former United boss Tommy Docherty said at the time, "If that lad makes it, my name is Mao-Tse Tung." The Doc was made to eat his words as Dwight soon became one of the Premiership's top strikers, helping Villa to win the League Cup in 1994 and 1996. In 1996/97, he became the first man since 1981 to score more than 20 League goals in one season for the Midlands club. The chance to win more trophies at Manchester United was too good to resist and he signed for the club in August 1998, to the chagrin of Aston Villa manager John Gregory.

Dwight's close ball control and quick thinking suited United perfectly and helped them to win an historic Treble in 1998/99, when he was the club's top scorer with 29 goals. He was also the joint top scorer in the Champions League with eight goals, including two in Barcelona's Nou Camp stadium and two headers against Inter Milan in the quarter-final. All of his goals were accompanied by a broad grin, revealing something of Yorke's sunny personality and great love for the game.

In 1999 Yorke was the recipient of the Carling Player of the Year award.

Yorke's fortunes changed the following year when, despite finishing the season as United's top scorer with 23 goals, he failed to reproduce his previous stunning form.

During 2000/2001 Yorke found himself out of favour and on the substitutes' bench. However, there were highlights during this frustrating campaign, notably his hat-trick in the 6-1 win over Arsenal in February 2001.

Young: Arthur **F** 1906–1907

b. dnk, Scotland **d.** nk • **Clubs** Hurlford Thistle; UTD **SU** Oct 1906 **UD** v Birmingham (h) 27.10.1906 **FL** 2/gls 0 **T** 2/gls 0

Young: Tony **M/D** 1971–1976

b. 24.12.1952, Urmston, Manchester, England • *5ft 10in* • *10st 13lb* • **Clubs** UTD; Charlton Athletic Jan 1976, York City Sep 1976–Nov 1978, Bangor City (Alliance Premier League) Feb 1980 **SU** Aug 1968 (appr.), May 1968 (am.), Dec 1969 (pro.) **UD** v Liverpool (sub) (h) 3.4.1972 **FL** 69(14)/gls 1 **FAC** 5/gls 0 **FLC** 5(4)/gls 0 **T** 79(18)/gls 1

Results

The 1880s

1880/81
Friendly Matches

20 Nov	Bolton Wanderers XI	A	L	0–6
4 Dec	Manchester Arcadians	A	D	0–0
22 Jan	Bolton Wanderers XI	H	L	0–6
5 Feb	Bootle Reserves	H	W	2–0
15 Feb	Hurst	H	L	0–1

1881/82
Friendly Matches

15 Oct	Manchester Arcadians	H	W	3–0
22 Oct	Blackburn Olympic XI	A	L	0–4
12 Nov	West Gorton St Marks	H	W	3–0
4 Mar	West Gorton St Marks	A	L	1–2

1882/83
Friendly Matches

25 Nov	Bentfield	H	D	3–3
2 Dec	Middleton	H	W	4–3
13 Dec	Astley Bridge Res.	A	D	1–1
20 Dec	Bentfield	A	L	2–4
10 Feb	Manchester Arcadians	A	D	0–0

1883/84
Friendlies and Minor Competitions

6 Oct	Pendleton Olympic Res.	A	L	1–4
13 Oct	Haughton Dale	H	D	2–2
27 Oct	Blackburn Olympic	H	L	2–7
1 Dec	Manchester Arcadians	H	W	4–0
8 Dec	Earlestown	A	L	0–8
5 Jan	Bootle Wanderers	H	W	6–0
12 Jan	Bentfield	A	D	1–1
19 Jan	St Helen's	H	W	3–1
2 Feb	Greenheys	H	W	1–0
9 Feb	Bootle Wanderers	A	D	1–1
23 Feb	Blackburn Olympic XI	H	D	0–0
8 Mar	Manchester Arcadians	H	W	4–0
15 Mar	Astley Bridge Res.	A	D	0–0
29 Mar	Greenheys	A	L	1–5

1884/85
Friendlies and Minor Competitions

20 Sep	Haydock Temperance	H	W	4–0
4 Oct	Earlestown Res.	H	W	2–1
11 Oct	Haughton Dale Res.	A	W	7–0
25 Oct	Baxenden	A	L	1–4
8 Nov	Greenheys	A	W	3–1
15 Nov	Pendleton Olympic	H	W	3–1
22 Nov	Oughtrington Park	A	W	4–2
29 Nov	Heywood	H	W	5–1
13 Dec	Dalton Hall Owens Coll.	H	W	4–1
20 Dec	Levenshulme	A	W	4–0
27 Dec	Heywood	A	D	1–1
3 Jan	Eccles	H	D	0–0
10 Jan	Oughtrington Park	H	W	3–2
17 Jan	Gorton Association	H	W	2–1
24 Jan	Stretford	H	W	12–0
31 Jan	Eccles	A	W	3–1
7 Feb	Doncaster Rovers	A	D	2–2
14 Feb	Eccles	A	W	3–0
21 Feb	Gorton Association	H	W	6–0
7 Mar	Manchester	A	W	3–0
14 Mar	Greenhays	H	W	3–1
21 Mar	West Manchester	H	W	5–3
28 Mar	Earlestown	H	L	0–2
4 Apr	Blackburn Olympic XI	H	L	0–1
11 Apr	Stretford	A	D	0–0
18 Apr	Dalton Hall Owens Coll.	A	W	4–3
25 Apr	Hurst	A	L	0–3

1885/86
Friendlies and Minor Competitions

29 Aug	Crewe Alexandra	H	L	1–3
12 Sep	Kearsley	A	W	11–2
19 Sep	Blackburn Olympic XI	H	L	3–4
26 Sep	Bolton Wan. Swifts	H	L	0–3
3 Oct	Lytham	A	L	3–6
10 Oct	Macclesfield	A	W	4–3
17 Oct	Baxenden	A	D	2–2
24 Oct	Blackpool St. John	A	W	2–1
31 Oct	Crewe Britannia	H	W	3–1
7 Nov	Darwen & District	H	D	1–1
14 Nov	Crewe Britannia	A	W	3–0
21 Nov	Darwen Hibernian	A	W	2–1
28 Nov	Furness Vale Rovers	H	W	2–0
5 Dec	Greenheys	H	W	4–1
12 Dec	West Manchester	H	W	1–0
19 Dec	Eccles	H	W	2–0
2 Jan	Pendleton Olympic	H	W	5–0
16 Jan	Macclesfield	H	D	3–3
23 Jan	Gorton Villa	H	W	5–0
30 Jan	Southport Central	H	W	6–0
6 Feb	Lower Hurst	H	L	2–3
13 Feb	Thornham	H	W	10–0
20 Feb	Blackburn Olympic XI	H	W	3–1
27 Feb	Irwell Springs	H	W	2–0
6 Mar	West Manchester	A	L	1–2
13 Mar	Hurst	A	W	3–1
20 Mar	Baxenden	H	W	4–3
27 Mar	Pendleton Olympic	A	D	2–2
29 Mar	Blackburn Olympic	A	L	0–3
3 Apr	Manchester	A	W	2–1
10 Apr	Furness Vale Rovers	A	W	2–1
17 Apr	Accrington Res.	H	W	2–1
23 Apr	Bell's Temperance	A	D	1–1
24 Apr	Darwen & District	H	W	2–1
26 Apr	West Brom. Alb. Res.	H	W	1–0
8 May	Manchester Casuals	H	L	2–3
15 May	Salford & District	A	W	2–0
22 May	South Shore	H	D	1–1

1886/87
Friendlies and Minor Competitions

4 Sep	Northwich Victoria	A	L	0–5
11 Sep	Oswaldtwistle Rov.	H	L	2–4
18 Sep	Stanley	A	W	2–0
25 Sep	Hurst	A	L	1–3
2 Oct	Manchester	H	W	8–1
9 Oct	Oswaldtwistle Rov.	A	W	2–1
16 Oct	Rawtenstall	A	D	3–3
23 Oct	Burslem Port Vale	H	W	4–1
6 Nov	Blackburn Olympic	H	W	4–2
13 Nov	Irwell Springs	A	L	0–3
20 Nov	Rawtenstall	H	D	0–0
27 Nov	Macclesfield	H	W	1–0
4 Dec	Manchester	A	W	3–2
11 Dec	Hurst	H	W	5–0
18 Dec	Bury	A	D	0–0
25 Dec	Burton Wanderers	H	D	0–0
27 Dec	Notts Rangers	H	L	0–1
1 Jan	Crewe Alexandra	A	L	0–2
15 Jan	Irwell Springs	H	W	1–0
22 Jan	Witton	H	D	0–0
29 Jan	Stanley	H	W	2–0
5 Feb	Macclesfield	A	W	4–1
12 Feb	Hooley Hill	H	W	7–0
19 Feb	Gorton Association	H	W	11–1
26 Feb	Hurst	A	W	3–1
5 Mar	Derby Midland	H	W	3–1
12 Mar	Nottm Jardines	H	D	2–2
19 Mar	Gorton Villa	H	W	8–0
26 Mar	Blackburn Olympic	A	L	1–3
4 Apr	Ten Acres	A	W	1–0
8 Apr	Halliwell	H	D	0–0
9 Apr	Gainsborough Trin.	A	W	4–0
11 Apr	Accrington	H	L	0–3
16 Apr	Crewe Alexandra	H	L	2–3
23 Apr	West Manchester	A	L	1–2
30 Apr	Bolton Wanderers	H	L	0–5
14 May	Blackburn Rovers	H	W	1–0

FA Cup

30 Oct	Fleetwood Rangers	A	D	2–2

1887/88
Friendlies and Minor Competitions

3 Sep	Accrington	H	W	2–1
10 Sep	Bell's Temperance	A	L	1–2
17 Sep	Earlestown	H	W	7–0
24 Sep	West Manchester	H	W	6–0
1 Oct	Derby Midland	A	W	3–0
8 Oct	Hurst	H	W	3–1
15 Oct	Padiham	H	W	3–0
22 Oct	Accrington	A	L	1–2
29 Oct	Burnley	H	D	0–0
5 Nov	Ten Acres	H	W	9–0
12 Nov	Hurst	A	W	2–1
19 Nov	Nottm Jardines	H	W	8–0
26 Nov	Crewe Alexandra	H	W	1–0
3 Dec	Ten Acres	A	W	1–0
10 Dec	West Manchester	A	D	2–2
17 Dec	Astley Bridge	A	L	0–1
24 Dec	Leek	H	W	3–0
26 Dec	Burslem Port Vale	H	D	0–0
31 Dec	Casuals	H	W	2–1
2 Jan	Burton Wanderers	H	W	2–1
7 Jan	Bolton Wanderers	H	L	0–1
14 Jan	Astley Bridge	H	W	3–0
21 Jan	Gorton Villa	H	W	8–1
28 Jan	Oswaldtwistle Rov.	H	W	1–0
4 Feb	Bell's Temperance	H	W	4–2
11 Feb	Crewe Alexandra	A	D	0–0
18 Feb	Oswaldtwistle Rov.	A	L	0–6
25 Feb	Bootle	A	L	0–1
3 Mar	Blackburn Olympic	H	L	1–2
17 Mar	Hooley Hill	A	W	7–0
24 Mar	Rawtenstall	H	W	7–0
30 Mar	Halliwell	H	L	0–1
31 Mar	Mitchell St Georges	H	D	2–2
2 Apr	Accrington	H	L	0–1
7 Apr	Burnley	A	L	1–7
14 Apr	Hurst	A	W	2–0
21 Apr	Derby Midland	H	W	6–1
23 Apr	Bolton Wanderers	H	D	3–3
28 Apr	Denton	A	W	7–1
30 Apr	Hyde	A	D	1–1
5 May	Preston North End	H	D	1–1
12 May	Denton	A	W	4–1
21 May	Aston Villa XI	H	W	1–0

1888/89
Friendlies and Minor Competitions

1 Sep	Bolton Wanderers	H	W	1–0
8 Sep	Blackburn Rovers	H	W	2–1
15 Sep	Walsall Town Swifts	H	W	2–1
22 Sep	Darwen	H	W	4–3
29 Sep	Gainsborough Trinity	A	W	5–1
6 Oct	Canadian XI	H	L	0–2
13 Oct	Derby Midland	A	D	1–1
20 Oct	Leek	H	W	4–1
27 Oct	Witton	H	D	2–2
3 Nov	Leek	A	W	5–0
3 Nov	Bury	A	L	0–9
10 Nov	Burslem Port Vale	A	D	1–1
17 Nov	West Manchester	H	W	5–0
24 Nov	Halliwell	H	W	2–0
1 Dec	Bootle	A	W	1–0
8 Dec	West Manchester	A	L	1–2
15 Dec	West Manchester	A	W	2–1
22 Dec	Darwen Old Wan.	H	W	4–0
24 Dec	Davenham	H	W	13–1
25 Dec	West Manchester	H	W	4–0
26 Dec	Wolverhampton Wan.	A	L	1–6
29 Dec	Corinthians	H	L	0–4
31 Dec	3rd Lanark Rifle Volun.	A	L	1–2
1 Jan	Heart Of Midlothian	A	L	1–2
2 Jan	Casuals	H	W	1–0
5 Jan	Darwen	A	L	0–6
12 Jan	Sheffield Wednesday	A	L	1–2
19 Jan	Burslem Port Vale	H	W	3–0
26 Jan	Bootle	H	W	4–0
2 Feb	Bolton Wanderers	A	L	1–3
16 Feb	Rotherham Town	H	W	7–2
23 Feb	Preston North End	H	W	1–0
26 Feb	Ardwick & District	H	W	3–2
2 Mar	Derby Midland	H	W	2–0
9 Mar	Nottingham Forest	A	D	2–2
16 Mar	Ardwick	H	W	4–1
18 Mar	Bootle	A	L	1–2
23 Mar	Nottingham Forest	H	W	3–1
30 Mar	South Shore	H	L	0–1
6 Apr	Manchester Welsh XI	A	W	1–0
13 Apr	South Shore	A	D	2–2
19 Apr	Small Heath	H	W	1–0
20 Apr	Sheffield Wednesday	H	L	1–2
22 Apr	West Bromwich Alb.	H	L	1–3
27 Apr	Hooley Hill	A	W	7–0
4 May	Grimsby Town	H	L	0–3
11 May	Preston North End	H	L	1–2
18 May	Derby St. Luke's	H	W	2–1
20 May	Ardwick	A	L	1–2
25 May	Darwen	H	W	3–2

The 1890s

1889/90
Football Alliance

21 Sep	Sunderland Albion	H	W	4–1
23 Sep	Bootle	A	L	1–4
28 Sep	Crewe Alexandra	A	D	2–2
19 Oct	Walsall Town Swifts	A	L	0–4
26 Oct	Birmingham St Georges	A	L	1–5
9 Nov	Long Eaton Rangers	H	W	3–0
30 Nov	Sheffield Wednesday	A	L	1–3
7 Dec	Bootle	H	W	3–0
28 Dec	Darwen	A	L	1–4
25 Jan	Sunderland Albion	A	L	0–2
8 Feb	Grimsby Town	A	L	0–7
15 Feb	Nottingham Forest	A	W	3–1
1 Mar	Crewe Alexandra	H	L	1–2
15 Mar	Small Heath	A	D	1–1
22 Mar	Long Eaton Rangers	A	W	3–0
29 Mar	Darwen	H	W	2–1
5 Apr	Nottingham Forest	H	L	0–1
7 Apr	Small Heath	H	W	9–1
12 Apr	Grimsby Town	H	L	0–1
19 Apr	Birmingham St Georges	H	W	2–1
21 Apr	Walsall Town Swifts	H	W	2–1
26 Apr	Sheffield Wednesday	H	L	1–2

FA Cup

18 Jan	Preston North End	A	L	1–6

Football Alliance
P22 • W9 • D2 • L11 • F40 • A44 • PTS20
Position: 8

1890/91
Football Alliance

6 Sep	Darwen	H	W	4–2
13 Sep	Grimsby Town	A	L	1–3
20 Sep	Nottingham Forest	H	D	1–1
27 Sep	Stoke	A	L	1–2
11 Oct	Bootle	A	L	0–5
18 Oct	Grimsby Town	H	W	3–1
1 Nov	Crewe Alexandra	H	W	6–3
8 Nov	Walsall Town Swifts	A	L	1–2
22 Nov	Nottingham Forest	A	L	2–8
29 Nov	Sunderland Albion	H	L	1–5
13 Dec	Small Heath	H	W	3–1
27 Dec	Bootle	H	W	2–1
3 Jan	Stoke	H	L	0–1
10 Jan	Birmingham St Georges	A	L	1–6
17 Jan	Walsall Town Swifts	H	D	3–3
24 Jan	Sheffield Wednesday	A	W	2–1
14 Feb	Crewe Alexandra	A	W	1–0
21 Feb	Sheffield Wednesday	H	D	1–1
7 Mar	Small Heath	A	L	1–2
14 Mar	Birmingham St Georges	H	L	1–3
28 Mar	Darwen	A	L	1–2
11 Apr	Sunderland Albion	A	L	1–2

FA Cup

4 Oct	Higher Walton	H	W	2–0
25 Oct	Bootle	A	L	0–1

Football Alliance
P22 • W7 • D3 • L12 • F37 • A55 • PTS17
Position: 9

1891/92
Football Alliance

12 Sep	Burton Swifts	A	L	2–3
19 Sep	Bootle	H	W	4–0
26 Sep	Birmingham St Georges	A	W	3–1
10 Oct	Ardwick	H	W	3–1
17 Oct	Grimsby Town	A	D	2–2
31 Oct	Burton Swifts	H	W	3–1
7 Nov	Crewe Alexandra	A	W	2–0
21 Nov	Lincoln City	H	W	10–1
28 Nov	Walsall Town Swifts	A	W	4–1
12 Dec	Sheffield Wednesday	A	W	4–2
19 Dec	Ardwick	A	D	2–2
26 Dec	Small Heath	H	D	3–3
1 Jan	Nottingham Forest	H	D	1–1
9 Jan	Bootle	A	D	1–1
30 Jan	Crewe Alexandra	H	W	5–3
20 Feb	Sheffield Wednesday	H	D	1–1
27 Feb	Small Heath	A	L	2–3
5 Mar	Walsall Town Swifts	H	W	5–0
19 Mar	Nottingham Forest	A	L	0–3
26 Mar	Grimsby Town	H	D	3–3
2 Apr	Lincoln City	A	W	6–1
9 Apr	Birmingham St Georges	H	W	3–0

FA Cup

3 Oct	Ardwick	H	W	5–1
24 Oct	Heywood		W	w/o
14 Nov	South Shore	A	W	2–0
5 Dec	Blackpool	H	L	3–4

Football Alliance
P22 • W12 • D7 • L3 • F69 • A33 • PTS31
Position: 2

1892/93
Football League

3 Sep	Blackburn Rovers	A	L	3–4
10 Sep	Burnley	H	D	1–1
17 Sep	Burnley	A	L	1–4
24 Sep	Everton	A	L	0–6
1 Oct	West Bromwich Alb.	A	D	0–0
8 Oct	West Bromwich Alb.	H	L	2–4
15 Oct	Wolverhampton Wan.	H	W	10–1
19 Oct	Everton	H	L	3–4
22 Oct	Sheffield Wed.	A	L	0–1
29 Oct	Nottingham Forest	A	D	1–1
5 Nov	Blackburn Rovers	H	D	4–4
12 Nov	Notts County	H	L	1–3
19 Nov	Aston Villa	H	W	2–0
26 Nov	Accrington	A	D	2–2
3 Dec	Bolton Wanderers	A	L	1–4
10 Dec	Bolton Wanderers	H	W	1–0
17 Dec	Wolverhampton Wan.	A	L	0–2
24 Dec	Sheffield Wed.	H	L	1–5
26 Dec	Preston North End	A	L	1–2
31 Dec	Derby County	H	W	7–1
7 Jan	Stoke	A	L	1–7
14 Jan	Nottingham Forest	H	L	1–3
26 Jan	Notts County	A	L	0–4
11 Feb	Derby County	A	L	1–5
4 Mar	Sunderland	H	L	0–5
6 Mar	Aston Villa	A	L	0–2
31 Mar	Stoke	H	W	1–0
1 Apr	Preston North End	H	W	2–1
4 Apr	Sunderland	A	L	0–6
8 Apr	Accrington	H	D	3–3

Test Matches

22 Apr	Small Heath	A	D	1–1
27 Apr	Small Heath	A	W	5–2

FA Cup

21 Jan	Blackburn Rovers	A	L	0–4

Football League Division 1
P30 • W6 • D6 • L18 • F50 • A85 • PTS18
Position: 16

1893/94
Football League

2 Sep	Burnley	H	W	3–2
9 Sep	West Bromwich Alb.	A	L	1–3
16 Sep	Sheffield Wed.	A	W	1–0
23 Sep	Nottingham Forest	H	D	1–1
30 Sep	Darwen	A	L	0–1
7 Oct	Derby County	A	L	0–2
14 Oct	West Bromwich Alb.	H	W	4–1
21 Oct	Burnley	A	L	1–4
28 Oct	Wolverhampton Wan.	A	L	0–2
4 Nov	Darwen	H	L	0–1
11 Nov	Wolverhampton Wan.	H	W	1–0
25 Nov	Sheffield United	A	L	1–3
2 Dec	Everton	H	L	0–3
6 Dec	Sunderland	A	L	1–4
9 Dec	Bolton Wanderers	A	L	0–2
16 Dec	Aston Villa	H	L	1–3
23 Dec	Preston North End	A	L	0–2
6 Jan	Everton	A	L	0–2
13 Jan	Sheffield Wed.	H	L	1–2
3 Feb	Aston Villa	H	L	1–5
10 Feb	Sunderland	H	L	2–4
3 Mar	Sheffield United	H	L	0–2
12 Mar	Blackburn Rovers	H	W	5–1
17 Mar	Derby County	A	L	2–6
23 Mar	Stoke	H	W	6–2
24 Mar	Bolton Wanderers	H	D	2–2
26 Mar	Blackburn Rovers	A	L	0–4
31 Mar	Stoke	A	L	1–3
7 Apr	Nottingham Forest	A	L	0–2
14 Apr	Preston North End	H	L	1–3

Test Match

28 Apr	Liverpool	A	L	0–2

FA Cup

27 Jan	Middlesbrough	H	W	4–0
10 Feb	Blackburn Rovers	H	D	0–0
17 Feb	Blackburn Rovers	A	L	1–5

Football League Division 1
P30 • W6 • D2 • L22 • F36 • A72 • PTS14
Position: 16

1894/95
Football League

8 Sep	Burton Wanderers	A	L	0–1
15 Sep	Crewe Alexandra	H	W	6–1
22 Sep	Leicester Fosse	A	W	3–2
6 Oct	Darwen	A	D	1–1
13 Oct	Woolwich Arsenal	H	D	3–3
20 Oct	Burton Swifts	A	W	2–1
27 Oct	Leicester Fosse	H	D	2–2
3 Nov	Manchester City	A	W	5–2
10 Nov	Rotherham Town	H	W	3–2
17 Nov	Grimsby Town	A	L	1–2
24 Nov	Darwen	H	D	1–1
1 Dec	Crewe Alexandra	A	W	2–0
8 Dec	Burton Swifts	H	W	5–1
15 Dec	Notts County	A	D	1–1
22 Dec	Lincoln City	H	W	3–0
24 Dec	Burslem Port Vale	A	W	5–2
26 Dec	Walsall Town Swifts	A	W	2–1
29 Dec	Lincoln City	A	L	0–3
1 Jan	Burslem Port Vale	H	W	3–0
5 Jan	Manchester City	H	W	4–1
12 Jan	Rotherham Town	A	L	1–2
2 Mar	Burton Wanderers	H	D	1–1
23 Mar	Grimsby Town	H	W	2–0
30 Mar	Woolwich Arsenal	A	L	2–3
3 Apr	Walsall Town Swifts	H	W	9–0
6 Apr	Newcastle United	H	W	5–1
12 Apr	Bury	H	D	2–2
13 Apr	Newcastle United	A	L	0–3
15 Apr	Bury	A	L	1–2
20 Apr	Notts County	H	D	3–3

Test Match

27 Apr	Stoke	A	L	0–3

FA Cup

2 Feb	Stoke	H	L	2–3

Football League Division 2
P30 • W15 • D8 • L7 • F78 • A44 • PTS38
Position: 3

1895/96
Football League

7 Sep	Crewe Alexandra	H	W	5–0
14 Sep	Loughborough	A	D	3–3
21 Sep	Burton Swifts	H	W	5–0
28 Sep	Crewe Alexandra	A	W	2–0
5 Oct	Manchester City	H	D	1–1
12 Oct	Liverpool	A	L	1–7
19 Oct	Newcastle United	H	W	2–1
26 Oct	Newcastle United	A	L	1–2
2 Nov	Liverpool	H	W	5–2
9 Nov	Woolwich Arsenal	A	L	1–2
16 Nov	Lincoln City	H	D	5–5
23 Nov	Notts County	A	W	2–0
30 Nov	Woolwich Arsenal	H	W	5–1
7 Dec	Manchester City	A	L	1–2
14 Dec	Notts County	H	W	3–0
21 Dec	Darwen	A	L	0–3
1 Jan	Grimsby Town	H	W	3–2
4 Jan	Leicester Fosse	A	L	0–3
11 Jan	Rotherham Town	H	W	3–0
3 Feb	Leicester Fosse	H	W	2–0
8 Feb	Burton Swifts	A	L	1–4
29 Feb	Burton Wanderers	H	L	1–2
7 Mar	Rotherham Town	A	W	3–2
14 Mar	Grimsby Town	A	L	2–4
18 Mar	Burton Wanderers	A	L	1–5
23 Mar	Burslem Port Vale	A	L	0–3
3 Apr	Darwen	H	W	4–0
4 Apr	Loughborough	H	W	2–0
6 Apr	Burslem Port Vale	H	W	2–1
11 Apr	Lincoln City	A	L	0–2

FA Cup

1 Feb	Kettering	H	W	2–1
15 Feb	Derby County	H	D	1–1
19 Feb	Derby County	A	L	1–5

Football League Division 2
P30 • W15 • D3 • L12 • F66 • A57 • PTS33
Position: 6

1896/97
Football League

1 Sep	Gainsborough Trin.	H	W	2–0
5 Sep	Burton Swifts	A	W	5–3
7 Sep	Walsall	H	W	2–0
12 Sep	Lincoln City	H	W	3–1
19 Sep	Grimsby Town	A	L	0–2
21 Sep	Walsall	A	W	3–2
26 Sep	Newcastle United	H	W	4–0
3 Oct	Manchester City	A	D	0–0
10 Oct	Small Heath	H	D	1–1
17 Oct	Blackpool	A	L	2–4
21 Oct	Gainsborough Trin.	A	L	0–2
24 Oct	Burton Wanderers	H	W	3–0
7 Nov	Grimsby Town	H	W	4–2
28 Nov	Small Heath	A	L	0–1
19 Dec	Notts County	A	L	0–3
25 Dec	Manchester City	H	W	2–1
26 Dec	Blackpool	H	W	2–0
28 Dec	Leicester Fosse	A	L	0–1
1 Jan	Newcastle United	A	L	0–2
9 Jan	Burton Swifts	H	D	1–1
6 Feb	Loughborough	H	W	6–0
20 Feb	Leicester Fosse	H	W	2–1
2 Mar	Darwen	H	W	3–1
13 Mar	Darwen	A	W	2–0
20 Mar	Burton Wanderers	A	W	2–1
22 Mar	Woolwich Arsenal	H	D	1–1
27 Mar	Notts County	H	D	1–1
1 Apr	Lincoln City	A	W	3–1
3 Apr	Woolwich Arsenal	A	W	2–0
10 Apr	Loughborough	A	L	0–2

Test Matches

19 Apr	Burnley	A	L	0–2
21 Apr	Burnley	H	W	2–0
24 Apr	Sunderland	H	D	1–1
26 Apr	Sunderland	A	L	0–2

FA Cup

12 Dec	West Manchester	H	W	7–0
2 Jan	Nelson	H	W	3–0
16 Jan	Blackpool	H	D	2–2
20 Jan	Blackpool	A	W	2–1
30 Jan	Kettering	H	W	5–1
13 Feb	Southampton	A	D	1–1
17 Feb	Southampton	H	W	3–1
27 Feb	Derby County	A	L	0–2

Football League Division 2
P30 • W17 • D5 • L8 • F56 • A34 • PTS39
Position: 2

1897/98
Football League

4 Sep	Lincoln City	H	W	5–0
11 Sep	Burton Swifts	A	W	4–0
18 Sep	Luton Town	H	L	1–2
25 Sep	Blackpool	A	W	1–0
2 Oct	Leicester Fosse	H	W	2–0
9 Oct	Newcastle United	A	L	0–2
16 Oct	Manchester City	H	D	1–1
23 Oct	Small Heath	A	L	1–2
30 Oct	Walsall	H	W	6–0
6 Nov	Lincoln City	A	L	0–1
13 Nov	Newcastle United	H	L	0–1
20 Nov	Leicester Fosse	A	D	1–1
27 Nov	Grimsby Town	H	W	2–1
11 Dec	Walsall	A	D	1–1
25 Dec	Manchester City	A	W	1–0
27 Dec	Gainsborough Trin.	A	L	1–2
1 Jan	Burton Swifts	H	W	4–0
8 Jan	Woolwich Arsenal	A	L	1–5
12 Jan	Burnley	H	D	0–0
15 Jan	Blackpool	H	W	4–0
26 Feb	Woolwich Arsenal	H	W	5–1
7 Mar	Burnley	A	L	3–6
19 Mar	Darwen	A	W	3–2
21 Mar	Luton Town	A	D	2–2
29 Mar	Loughborough	H	W	5–1
2 Apr	Grimsby Town	A	W	3–1
8 Apr	Gainsborough Trin.	H	W	1–0
9 Apr	Small Heath	H	W	3–1
16 Apr	Loughborough	A	D	0–0
23 Apr	Darwen	H	W	3–2

FA Cup

29 Jan	Walsall	H	W	1–0
12 Feb	Liverpool	H	D	0–0
16 Feb	Liverpool	A	L	1–2

Football League Division 2
P30 • W16 • D6 • L8 • F64 • A35 • PTS38
Position: 4

1898/99
Football League

3 Sep	Gainsborough Trin.	A	W	2–0
10 Sep	Manchester City	H	W	3–0
17 Sep	Glossop	A	W	2–1
24 Sep	Walsall	H	W	1–0
1 Oct	Burton Swifts	A	L	1–5
8 Oct	Burslem Port Vale	H	W	2–1
15 Oct	Small Heath	A	L	1–4
22 Oct	Loughborough	H	W	6–1
5 Nov	Grimsby Town	H	W	3–2
12 Nov	Barnsley	H	D	0–0
19 Nov	New Brighton Tower	A	W	3–0
26 Nov	Lincoln City	H	W	1–0
3 Dec	Woolwich Arsenal	A	L	1–5
10 Dec	Blackpool	H	W	3–1
17 Dec	Leicester Fosse	A	L	0–1
24 Dec	Darwen	H	W	9–0
26 Dec	Manchester City	A	L	0–4
31 Dec	Gainsborough Trin.	H	W	6–1
2 Jan	Burton Swifts	H	D	2–2
7 Jan	Glossop	H	W	3–0
14 Jan	Walsall	A	L	0–2
21 Jan	Burslem Port Vale	A	L	0–1
4 Feb	Loughborough	A	W	1–0
18 Feb	Grimsby Town	A	W	2–0
25 Feb	Small Heath	H	D	3–3
4 Mar	Barnsley	A	L	0–3
18 Mar	New Brighton Tower	H	L	1–2
25 Mar	Lincoln City	A	L	0–2
1 Apr	Woolwich Arsenal	H	D	2–2
3 Apr	Blackpool	A	W	1–0
4 Apr	Barnsley	A	W	2–0
8 Apr	Luton Town	A	W	1–0
12 Apr	Luton Town	H	W	5–0
15 Apr	Leicester Fosse	H	D	2–2
22 Apr	Darwen	A	D	1–1

FA Cup

28 Jan	Tottenham Hotspur	A	D	1–1
1 Feb	Tottenham Hotspur	H	L	3–5

Football League Division 2
P34 • W19 • D5 • L10 • F67 • A43 • PTS43
Position: 4

The 1900s

1899/1900
Football League

2 Sep	Gainsborough Trin.	H	D	2–2
9 Sep	Bolton Wanderers	A	L	1–2
16 Sep	Loughborough	H	W	4–0
23 Sep	Burton Swifts	A	D	0–0
30 Sep	Sheffield Wed.	A	L	1–2
7 Oct	Lincoln City	H	W	1–0
14 Oct	Small Heath	A	L	0–1
21 Oct	New Brighton Tower	H	W	2–1
4 Nov	Woolwich Arsenal	H	W	2–0
11 Nov	Barnsley	A	D	0–0
25 Nov	Luton Town	A	W	1–0
2 Dec	Burslem Port Vale	H	W	3–0
16 Dec	Middlesbrough	H	W	2–1
23 Dec	Chesterfield	A	L	1–2
26 Dec	Grimsby Town	A	W	7–0
30 Dec	Gainsborough Trin.	A	W	1–0
6 Jan	Bolton Wanderers	H	L	1–2
13 Jan	Loughborough	A	W	2–0
20 Jan	Burton Swifts	H	W	4–0
3 Feb	Sheffield Wed.	H	W	1–0
10 Feb	Lincoln City	A	L	0–1
17 Feb	Small Heath	H	W	3–2
24 Feb	New Brighton Tower	A	W	4–1
3 Mar	Grimsby Town	H	W	1–0
10 Mar	Woolwich Arsenal	A	L	1–2
17 Mar	Barnsley	H	W	3–0
24 Mar	Leicester Fosse	A	L	0–2
31 Mar	Luton Town	H	W	5–0
7 Apr	Burslem Port Vale	A	L	0–1
13 Apr	Leicester Fosse	H	W	3–2
14 Apr	Walsall	H	W	5–0
17 Apr	Walsall	A	D	0–0
21 Apr	Middlesbrough	A	L	0–2
28 Apr	Chesterfield	H	W	2–1

FA Cup

28 Oct	South Shore	A	L	1–3

Football League Division 2
P34 • W20 • D4 • L10 • F63 • A27 • PTS44
Position: 4

1900/01
Football League

1 Sep	Glossop	A	L	0–1
8 Sep	Middlesbrough	H	W	4–0
15 Sep	Burnley	A	L	0–1
22 Sep	Burslem Port Vale	H	W	4–0
29 Sep	Leicester Fosse	A	L	0–1
6 Oct	New Brighton Tower	H	W	1–0
13 Oct	Gainsborough Trin.	A	W	1–0
20 Oct	Walsall	H	D	1–1
27 Oct	Burton Swifts	A	L	1–3
10 Nov	Woolwich Arsenal	A	L	1–2
24 Nov	Stockport County	A	L	0–1
1 Dec	Small Heath	A	L	0–1
8 Dec	Grimsby Town	A	L	0–2
15 Dec	Lincoln City	H	W	4–1
22 Dec	Chesterfield	A	L	1–2
26 Dec	Blackpool	H	W	4–0
29 Dec	Glossop	H	W	3–0
1 Jan	Middlesbrough	A	W	2–1
12 Jan	Burnley	H	L	0–1
19 Jan	Burslem Port Vale	A	L	0–2
16 Feb	Gainsborough Trin.	H	D	0–0
19 Feb	New Brighton Tower	H	L	0–2
25 Feb	Walsall	A	D	1–1
2 Mar	Burton Swifts	H	D	1–1
13 Mar	Barnsley	H	W	1–0
16 Mar	Woolwich Arsenal	H	W	1–0
20 Mar	Leicester Fosse	H	L	2–3
23 Mar	Blackpool	A	W	2–1
30 Mar	Stockport County	H	W	3–1
5 Apr	Lincoln City	A	L	0–2
6 Apr	Small Heath	A	L	0–1
9 Apr	Barnsley	A	L	2–6
13 Apr	Grimsby Town	H	W	1–0
27 Apr	Chesterfield	H	W	1–0

FA Cup

5 Jan	Portsmouth	H	W	3–0
9 Feb	Burnley	H	D	0–0
13 Feb	Burnley	A	L	1–7

Football League Division 2
P34 • W14 • D4 • L16 • F42 • A38 • PTS32
Position: 10

1901/02
Football League

7 Sep	Gainsborough Trin.	H	W	3–0
14 Sep	Middlesbrough	A	L	0–5
21 Sep	Bristol City	H	W	1–0
28 Sep	Blackpool	A	W	4–2
5 Oct	Stockport County	H	D	3–3
12 Oct	Burton United	A	D	0–0
19 Oct	Glossop	A	D	0–0
26 Oct	Doncaster Rovers	H	W	6–0
9 Nov	West Bromwich Alb.	H	L	1–2
16 Nov	Woolwich Arsenal	A	L	0–2
23 Nov	Barnsley	H	W	1–0
30 Nov	Leicester Fosse	A	L	2–3
7 Dec	Preston North End	A	L	1–5
21 Dec	Burslem Port Vale	H	W	1–0
26 Dec	Lincoln City	H	L	0–2
1 Jan	Preston North End	H	L	0–2
4 Jan	Gainsborough Trin.	A	D	1–1
18 Jan	Bristol City	A	L	0–4
25 Jan	Blackpool	H	L	0–1
1 Feb	Stockport County	A	L	0–1
11 Feb	Burnley	H	W	2–0
15 Feb	Glossop	H	W	1–0
22 Feb	Doncaster Rovers	A	L	0–4
1 Mar	Lincoln City	H	D	0–0
8 Mar	West Bromwich Alb.	A	L	0–4
15 Mar	Woolwich Arsenal	H	L	0–1
17 Mar	Chesterfield	A	L	0–3
22 Mar	Barnsley	A	L	2–3
28 Mar	Burnley	A	L	0–1
29 Mar	Leicester Fosse	H	W	2–0
7 Apr	Middlesbrough	H	L	1–2
19 Apr	Burslem Port Vale	A	D	1–1
21 Apr	Burton United	H	W	3–1
23 Apr	Chesterfield	H	W	2–0

FA Cup

14 Dec	Lincoln City	H	L	1–2

Football League Division 2
P34 • W11 • D6 • L17 • F38 • A53 • PTS28
Position: 15

Key

- H : Home
- A : Away
- P : Total games played
- W : Games won
- D : Games drawn
- L : Games lost
- F : Goals for United
- A : Goals against United
- PTS: Total points
- • : Own goals by opposition
- w/o: Walk over

1902/03

Football League

6 Sep	Gainsborough Trin.	A	W	1–0
13 Sep	Burton United	H	W	1–0
20 Sep	Bristol City	A	L	1–3
27 Sep	Glossop	H	D	1–1
4 Oct	Chesterfield	H	W	2–1
11 Oct	Stockport County	A	L	1–2
25 Oct	Woolwich Arsenal	A	W	1–0
8 Nov	Lincoln City	A	W	3–1
15 Nov	Small Heath	H	L	0–1
22 Nov	Leicester Fosse	A	D	1–1
6 Dec	Burnley	A	W	2–0
20 Dec	Burslem Port Vale	A	D	1–1
25 Dec	Manchester City	H	D	1–1
26 Dec	Blackpool	H	D	2–2
27 Dec	Barnsley	H	W	2–1
3 Jan	Gainsborough Trin.	H	W	3–1
10 Jan	Burton United	A	L	1–3
17 Jan	Bristol City	H	L	1–2
24 Jan	Glossop	A	W	3–1
31 Jan	Chesterfield	A	L	0–2
14 Feb	Blackpool	A	L	0–2
28 Feb	Doncaster Rovers	A	D	2–2
7 Mar	Lincoln City	H	L	1–2
9 Mar	Woolwich Arsenal	H	W	3–0
21 Mar	Leicester Fosse	H	W	5–1
23 Mar	Stockport County	H	D	0–0
30 Mar	Preston North End	H	L	0–1
4 Apr	Burnley	H	W	4–0
10 Apr	Manchester City	A	W	2–0
11 Apr	Preston North End	A	L	1–3
13 Apr	Doncaster Rovers	H	W	4–0
18 Apr	Burslem Port Vale	H	W	2–1
20 Apr	Small Heath	A	L	1–2
25 Apr	Barnsley	A	D	0–0

FA Cup

1 Nov	Accrington Stanley	H	W	7–0
13 Nov	Oswaldtwistle Rov.	H	W	3–2
29 Nov	Southport Central	H	W	4–1
13 Dec	Burton United	H	D	1–1
17 Dec	Burton United	H	W	3–1
7 Feb	Liverpool	H	W	2–1
21 Feb	Everton	A	L	1–3

Football League Division 2
P34 • W15 • D8 • L11 • F53 • A38 • PTS38
Position: 5

1903/04

Football League

5 Sep	Bristol City	H	D	2–2
7 Sep	Burnley	A	L	0–2
12 Sep	Burslem Port Vale	A	L	0–1
19 Sep	Glossop	A	W	5–0
26 Sep	Bradford City	H	W	3–1
3 Oct	Woolwich Arsenal	A	L	0–4
10 Oct	Barnsley	H	W	4–0
17 Oct	Lincoln City	A	D	0–0
24 Oct	Stockport County	H	W	3–1
7 Nov	Bolton Wanderers	H	D	0–0
21 Nov	Preston North End	H	L	0–2
19 Dec	Gainsborough Trin.	H	W	4–2
25 Dec	Chesterfield	H	W	3–1
26 Dec	Burton United	A	D	2–2
2 Jan	Bristol City	A	D	1–1
9 Jan	Burslem Port Vale	H	W	2–0
16 Jan	Glossop	H	W	3–1
23 Jan	Bradford City	A	D	3–3
30 Jan	Woolwich Arsenal	H	W	1–0
13 Feb	Lincoln City	H	W	2–0
9 Mar	Blackpool	A	L	1–2
12 Mar	Burnley	H	W	3–1
19 Mar	Preston North End	A	D	1–1
26 Mar	Grimsby Town	H	W	2–0
28 Mar	Stockport County	A	W	3–0
1 Apr	Chesterfield	A	W	2–0
2 Apr	Leicester Fosse	A	W	1–0
5 Apr	Barnsley	A	W	2–0
9 Apr	Blackpool	H	W	3–1
12 Apr	Grimsby Town	A	L	1–3
16 Apr	Gainsborough Trin.	A	W	1–0
23 Apr	Burton United	H	W	2–0
25 Apr	Bolton Wanderers	A	D	0–0
30 Apr	Leicester Fosse	H	W	5–2

FA Cup

12 Dec	Small Heath	H	D	1–1
16 Dec	Small Heath	A	D	1–1
21 Dec	Small Heath	A	D	1–1
11 Jan	Small Heath	A	W	3–1
6 Feb	Notts County	A	D	3–3
10 Feb	Notts County	H	W	2–1
20 Feb	Sheffield Wed.	A	L	0–6

Football League Division 2
P34 • W20 • D8 • L6 • F65 • A33 • PTS48
Position: 3

1904/05

Football League

3 Sep	Burslem Port Vale	A	D	2–2
10 Sep	Bristol City	H	W	4–1
17 Sep	Bolton Wanderers	H	L	1–2
24 Sep	Glossop	A	W	2–1
8 Oct	Bradford City	A	D	1–1
15 Oct	Lincoln City	H	W	2–0
22 Oct	Leicester Fosse	A	W	3–0
29 Oct	Barnsley	H	W	4–0
5 Nov	West Bromwich Alb.	A	W	2–0
12 Nov	Burnley	H	W	1–0
19 Nov	Grimsby Town	A	W	1–0
3 Dec	Doncaster Rovers	A	W	1–0
10 Dec	Gainsborough Trin.	H	W	3–1
17 Dec	Burton United	A	W	3–2
24 Dec	Liverpool	H	W	3–1
26 Dec	Chesterfield	H	W	3–0
31 Dec	Burslem Port Vale	H	W	6–1
2 Jan	Bradford City	H	W	7–0
3 Jan	Bolton Wanderers	A	W	4–2
7 Jan	Bristol City	A	D	1–1
21 Jan	Glossop	H	W	4–1
11 Feb	Lincoln City	A	L	0–3
18 Feb	Leicester Fosse	H	W	4–1
25 Feb	Barnsley	A	D	0–0
4 Mar	West Bromwich Alb.	H	W	2–0
11 Mar	Burnley	A	L	0–2
18 Mar	Grimsby Town	H	W	2–1
25 Mar	Blackpool	A	W	1–0
1 Apr	Doncaster Rovers	H	W	6–0
8 Apr	Gainsborough Trin.	A	D	0–0
15 Apr	Burton United	H	W	5–0
21 Apr	Chesterfield	A	L	0–2
22 Apr	Liverpool	A	L	0–4
24 Apr	Blackpool	H	W	3–1

FA Cup

14 Jan	Fulham	H	D	2–2
18 Jan	Fulham	A	D	0–0
23 Jan	Fulham	A	L	0–1

Football League Division 2
P34 • W24 • D5 • L5 • F81 • A30 • PTS53
Position: 3

1905/06

Football League

2 Sep	Bristol City	H	W	5–1
4 Sep	Blackpool	H	W	2–1
9 Sep	Grimsby Town	A	W	1–0
16 Sep	Glossop	A	W	2–1
23 Sep	Stockport County	H	W	3–1
30 Sep	Blackpool	A	W	1–0
7 Oct	Bradford City	H	D	0–0
14 Oct	West Bromwich Alb.	A	L	0–1
21 Oct	Leicester Fosse	H	W	3–2
25 Oct	Gainsborough Trin.	A	D	2–2
28 Oct	Hull City	A	W	1–0
4 Nov	Lincoln City	H	W	2–1
11 Nov	Chesterfield	A	L	0–1
18 Nov	Burslem Port Vale	H	W	3–0
25 Nov	Barnsley	A	W	3–0
2 Dec	Clapton Orient	H	W	4–0
9 Dec	Burnley	A	W	3–1
23 Dec	Burton United	A	W	2–0
25 Dec	Chelsea	H	D	0–0
30 Dec	Bristol City	A	D	1–1
6 Jan	Grimsby Town	H	W	5–0
15 Jan	Leeds City	H	L	0–3
20 Jan	Glossop	H	W	5–2
27 Jan	Stockport County	A	W	1–0
10 Feb	Bradford City	A	W	5–1
17 Feb	West Bromwich Alb.	H	D	0–0
3 Mar	Hull City	H	W	5–0
17 Mar	Chesterfield	H	W	4–1
24 Mar	Burslem Port Vale	A	L	0–1
29 Mar	Leicester Fosse	A	W	5–2
31 Mar	Barnsley	H	W	5–1
7 Apr	Clapton Orient	A	W	1–0
13 Apr	Chelsea	A	D	1–1
14 Apr	Burnley	H	W	1–0
16 Apr	Gainsborough Trin.	H	W	2–0
21 Apr	Leeds City	A	W	3–1
25 Apr	Lincoln City	A	W	3–2
28 Apr	Burton United	H	W	6–0

FA Cup

13 Jan	Staple Hill	H	W	7–2
3 Feb	Norwich City	H	W	3–0
24 Feb	Aston Villa	H	W	5–1
10 Mar	Woolwich Arsenal	H	L	2–3

Football League Division 2
P38 • W28 • D6 • L4 • F90 • A28 • PTS62
Position: 2

1906/07

Football League

1 Sep	Bristol City	A	W	2–1
3 Sep	Derby County	A	D	2–2
8 Sep	Notts County	H	D	0–0
15 Sep	Sheffield United	A	W	2–0
22 Sep	Bolton Wanderers	H	L	1–2
29 Sep	Derby County	H	D	1–1
6 Oct	Stoke	A	W	2–1
13 Oct	Blackburn Rovers	H	D	1–1
20 Oct	Sunderland	A	L	1–4
27 Oct	Birmingham	H	W	2–1
3 Nov	Everton	A	L	0–3
10 Nov	Woolwich Arsenal	H	W	1–0
17 Nov	Sheffield Wed.	A	L	2–5
24 Nov	Bury	H	L	2–4
1 Dec	Manchester City	A	L	0–3
8 Dec	Middlesbrough	H	W	3–1
15 Dec	Preston North End	A	L	0–2
22 Dec	Newcastle United	H	L	1–3
25 Dec	Liverpool	H	D	0–0
26 Dec	Aston Villa	A	L	0–2
29 Dec	Bristol City	H	D	0–0
1 Jan	Aston Villa	H	W	1–0
5 Jan	Notts County	A	L	0–3
19 Jan	Sheffield United	H	W	2–0
26 Jan	Bolton Wanderers	A	W	1–0
2 Feb	Newcastle United	A	L	0–5
9 Feb	Stoke	H	W	4–1
16 Feb	Blackburn Rovers	A	W	4–2
23 Feb	Preston North End	H	W	3–0
2 Mar	Birmingham	A	D	1–1
16 Mar	Woolwich Arsenal	A	L	0–4
25 Mar	Sunderland	H	W	2–0
30 Mar	Bury	A	W	2–1
1 Apr	Liverpool	A	W	1–0
6 Apr	Manchester City	H	D	1–1
10 Apr	Sheffield Wed.	H	W	5–0
13 Apr	Middlesbrough	A	L	0–2
22 Apr	Everton	H	W	3–0

FA Cup

12 Jan	Portsmouth	A	D	2–2
16 Jan	Portsmouth	H	L	1–2

Football League Division 1
P38 • W17 • D8 • L13 • F53 • A56 • PTS42
Position: 8

1907/08

Football League

2 Sep	Aston Villa	A	W	4–1
7 Sep	Liverpool	H	W	4–0
9 Sep	Middlesbrough	H	W	2–1
14 Sep	Middlesbrough	A	L	1–2
21 Sep	Sheffield United	H	W	2–1
28 Sep	Chelsea	A	W	4–1
5 Oct	Nottingham Forest	H	W	4–0
12 Oct	Newcastle United	A	W	6–1
19 Oct	Blackburn Rovers	A	W	5–1
26 Oct	Bolton Wanderers	H	W	2–1
2 Nov	Birmingham	A	W	4–3
9 Nov	Everton	H	W	4–3
16 Nov	Sunderland	A	W	2–1
23 Nov	Woolwich Arsenal	H	W	4–2
30 Nov	Sheffield Wed.	A	L	0–2
7 Dec	Bristol City	H	W	2–1
14 Dec	Notts County	A	D	1–1
21 Dec	Manchester City	H	W	3–1
25 Dec	Bury	H	W	2–1
28 Dec	Preston North End	A	D	0–0
1 Jan	Bury	A	W	1–0
18 Jan	Sheffield United	A	L	0–2
25 Jan	Chelsea	H	W	1–0
8 Feb	Newcastle United	H	D	1–1
15 Feb	Blackburn Rovers	H	L	1–2
29 Feb	Birmingham	H	W	1–0
14 Mar	Sunderland	H	W	3–0
21 Mar	Woolwich Arsenal	A	L	0–1
25 Mar	Liverpool	A	L	4–7
28 Mar	Sheffield Wed.	H	W	4–1
4 Apr	Bristol City	A	D	1–1
8 Apr	Everton	A	W	3–1
11 Apr	Notts County	H	L	0–1
17 Apr	Nottingham Forest	A	L	0–2
18 Apr	Manchester City	A	D	0–0
20 Apr	Aston Villa	H	L	1–2
22 Apr	Bolton Wanderers	A	D	2–2
25 Apr	Preston North End	H	W	2–1

FA Cup

11 Jan	Blackpool	H	W	3–1
1 Feb	Chelsea	H	W	1–0
22 Feb	Aston Villa	A	W	2–0
7 Mar	Fulham	A	L	1–2

Football League Division 1
P38 • W23 • D6 • L9 • F81 • A48 • PTS52
Position: 1

1908/09

Football League

5 Sep	Preston North End	A	W	3–0
7 Sep	Bury	H	W	2–1
12 Sep	Middlesbrough	H	W	6–3
19 Sep	Manchester City	A	W	2–1
26 Sep	Liverpool	H	W	3–2
3 Oct	Bury	A	D	2–2
10 Oct	Sheffield United	H	W	2–1
17 Oct	Aston Villa	A	L	1–3
24 Oct	Nottingham Forest	H	D	2–2
31 Oct	Sunderland	A	L	1–6
7 Nov	Chelsea	H	L	0–1
14 Nov	Blackburn Rovers	A	W	3–1
21 Nov	Bradford City	H	W	2–0
28 Nov	Sheffield Wed.	H	W	3–1
5 Dec	Everton	A	L	2–3
12 Dec	Leicester Fosse	H	W	4–2
19 Dec	Woolwich Arsenal	A	W	1–0
25 Dec	Newcastle United	A	L	1–2
26 Dec	Newcastle United	H	W	1–0
1 Jan	Notts County	H	W	4–3
2 Jan	Preston North End	H	L	0–2
9 Jan	Middlesbrough	A	L	0–5
23 Jan	Manchester City	H	W	3–1
30 Jan	Liverpool	A	L	1–3
13 Feb	Sheffield United	A	D	0–0
27 Feb	Nottingham Forest	A	L	0–2
13 Mar	Chelsea	A	D	1–1
15 Mar	Sunderland	H	D	2–2
20 Mar	Blackburn Rovers	H	L	0–3
31 Mar	Aston Villa	H	L	0–2
3 Apr	Sheffield Wed.	A	L	0–2
9 Apr	Bristol City	H	L	0–1
10 Apr	Everton	H	D	2–2
12 Apr	Bristol City	A	D	0–0
13 Apr	Notts County	A	W	1–0
17 Apr	Leicester Fosse	A	L	2–3
27 Apr	Woolwich Arsenal	H	L	1–4
29 Apr	Bradford City	A	L	0–1

FA Cup

16 Jan	Brighton & Hove Alb.	H	W	1–0
6 Feb	Everton	H	W	1–0
20 Feb	Blackburn Rovers	H	W	6–1
10 Mar	Burnley	A	W	3–2
27 Mar	Newcastle United	A	W	1–0
24 Apr	Bristol City	A	W	1–0

Football League Division 1
P38 • W15 • D7 • L16 • F58 • A68 • PTS37
Position: 13

The 1910s

1909/10

Football League

1 Sep	Bradford City	H	W	1–0
4 Sep	Bury	H	W	2–0
6 Sep	Notts County	H	W	2–1
11 Sep	Tottenham Hotspur	A	D	2–2
18 Sep	Preston North End	H	D	1–1
25 Sep	Notts County	A	L	2–3
2 Oct	Newcastle United	H	D	1–1
9 Oct	Liverpool	A	L	2–3
16 Oct	Aston Villa	H	W	2–0
23 Oct	Sheffield United	A	W	1–0
30 Oct	Woolwich Arsenal	H	W	1–0
6 Nov	Bolton Wanderers	A	W	3–2
13 Nov	Chelsea	H	W	2–0
20 Nov	Blackburn Rovers	A	L	2–3
27 Nov	Nottingham Forest	H	L	2–6
4 Dec	Sunderland	A	L	0–3
18 Dec	Middlesbrough	A	W	2–1
25 Dec	Sheffield Wed.	H	L	0–3
27 Dec	Sheffield Wed.	A	L	1–4
1 Jan	Bradford City	A	W	2–0
8 Jan	Bury	A	D	1–1
22 Jan	Tottenham Hotspur	H	W	5–0
5 Feb	Preston North End	A	L	0–1
12 Feb	Newcastle United	A	W	4–3
19 Feb	Liverpool	H	L	3–4
26 Feb	Aston Villa	A	L	1–7
5 Mar	Sheffield United	H	W	1–0
12 Mar	Woolwich Arsenal	A	D	0–0
19 Mar	Bolton Wanderers	H	W	5–0
25 Mar	Bristol City	H	W	2–1
26 Mar	Chelsea	A	D	1–1
28 Mar	Bristol City	A	L	1–2
2 Apr	Blackburn Rovers	H	W	2–0
6 Apr	Everton	H	W	3–2
9 Apr	Nottingham Forest	A	L	0–2
16 Apr	Sunderland	H	W	2–0
23 Apr	Everton	A	D	3–3
30 Apr	Middlesbrough	H	W	4–1

FA Cup

15 Jan	Burnley	A	L	0–2

Football League Division 1
P38 • W19 • D7 • L12 • F69 • A61 • PTS45
Position: 5

1910/11

Football League

1 Sep	Woolwich Arsenal	A	W	2–1
3 Sep	Blackburn Rovers	H	W	3–2
10 Sep	Nottingham Forest	A	L	1–2
17 Sep	Manchester City	H	W	2–1
24 Sep	Everton	A	W	1–0
1 Oct	Sheffield Wed.	H	W	3–2
8 Oct	Bristol City	A	W	1–0
15 Oct	Newcastle United	H	W	2–0
22 Oct	Tottenham Hotspur	A	D	2–2
29 Oct	Middlesbrough	H	L	1–2
5 Nov	Preston North End	A	W	2–0
12 Nov	Notts County	H	D	0–0
19 Nov	Oldham Athletic	A	W	3–1
26 Nov	Liverpool	A	L	2–3
3 Dec	Bury	H	W	3–2
10 Dec	Sheffield United	A	L	0–2
17 Dec	Aston Villa	H	W	2–0
24 Dec	Sunderland	A	W	2–1
26 Dec	Woolwich Arsenal	H	W	5–0
27 Dec	Bradford City	A	L	0–1
31 Dec	Blackburn Rovers	A	L	0–1
2 Jan	Bradford City	H	W	1–0
7 Jan	Nottingham Forest	H	W	4–2
21 Jan	Manchester City	A	D	1–1
28 Jan	Everton	H	D	2–2
11 Feb	Bristol City	H	W	3–1
18 Feb	Newcastle United	A	W	1–0
4 Mar	Middlesbrough	A	D	2–2
11 Mar	Preston North End	H	W	5–0
15 Mar	Tottenham Hotspur	H	W	3–2
18 Mar	Notts County	A	L	0–1
25 Mar	Oldham Athletic	H	D	0–0
1 Apr	Liverpool	H	W	2–0
8 Apr	Bury	A	W	3–0
15 Apr	Sheffield United	H	D	1–1
17 Apr	Sheffield Wed.	A	D	0–0
22 Apr	Aston Villa	A	L	2–4
29 Apr	Sunderland	H	W	5–1

FA Cup

14 Jan	Blackpool	A	W	2–1
4 Feb	Aston Villa	H	W	2–1
25 Feb	West Ham United	A	L	1–2

Football League Division 1
P38 • W22 • D8 • L8 • F72 • A40 • PTS52
Position: 1

1911/12

Football League

2 Sep	Manchester City	A	D	0–0
9 Sep	Everton	H	W	2–1
16 Sep	West Bromwich Alb.	A	L	0–1
23 Sep	Sunderland	H	D	2–2
30 Sep	Blackburn Rovers	A	D	2–2
7 Oct	Sheffield Wed.	H	W	3–1
14 Oct	Bury	A	W	1–0
21 Oct	Middlesbrough	H	L	3–4
28 Oct	Notts County	A	W	1–0
4 Nov	Tottenham Hotspur	H	L	1–2
11 Nov	Preston North End	H	D	0–0
18 Nov	Liverpool	A	L	2–3
25 Nov	Aston Villa	H	W	3–1
2 Dec	Newcastle United	A	W	3–2
9 Dec	Sheffield United	H	W	1–0
16 Dec	Oldham Athletic	A	D	2–2
23 Dec	Bolton Wanderers	H	W	2–0
25 Dec	Bradford City	H	L	0–1
26 Dec	Bradford City	A	W	1–0
30 Dec	Manchester City	H	D	0–0
1 Jan	Woolwich Arsenal	H	W	2–0
6 Jan	Everton	A	L	0–4
20 Jan	West Bromwich Alb.	H	L	1–2
27 Jan	Sunderland	A	L	0–5
10 Feb	Sheffield Wed.	A	L	0–3
17 Feb	Bury	H	D	0–0
2 Mar	Notts County	H	W	2–0
16 Mar	Preston North End	A	D	0–0
23 Mar	Liverpool	H	D	1–1
30 Mar	Aston Villa	A	L	0–6
5 Apr	Woolwich Arsenal	A	L	1–2
6 Apr	Newcastle United	H	L	0–2
9 Apr	Tottenham Hotspur	A	D	1–1
13 Apr	Sheffield United	A	L	1–6
17 Apr	Middlesbrough	A	L	0–3
20 Apr	Oldham Athletic	H	W	3–1
27 Apr	Bolton Wanderers	A	D	1–1
29 Apr	Blackburn Rovers	H	W	3–1

FA Cup

13 Jan	Huddersfield Town	H	W	3–1
3 Feb	Coventry City	A	W	5–1
24 Feb	Reading	A	D	1–1
29 Feb	Reading	H	W	3–0
9 Mar	Blackburn Rovers	H	D	1–1
14 Mar	Blackburn Rovers	A	L	2–4

Football League Division 1
P38 • W13 • D11 • L14 • F45 • A60 • PTS37
Position: 13

1912/13

Football League

2 Sep	Woolwich Arsenal	A	D	0–0
7 Sep	Manchester City	H	L	0–1
14 Sep	West Bromwich Alb.	A	W	2–1
21 Sep	Everton	H	W	2–0
28 Sep	Sheffield Wed.	A	D	3–3
5 Oct	Blackburn Rovers	H	D	1–1
12 Oct	Derby County	A	L	1–2
19 Oct	Tottenham Hotspur	H	W	2–0
26 Oct	Middlesbrough	A	L	2–3
2 Nov	Notts County	H	W	2–1
9 Nov	Sunderland	A	L	1–3
16 Nov	Aston Villa	A	L	2–4
23 Nov	Liverpool	H	W	3–1
30 Nov	Bolton Wanderers	A	L	1–2
7 Dec	Sheffield United	H	W	4–0
14 Dec	Newcastle United	A	W	3–1
21 Dec	Oldham Athletic	H	D	0–0
25 Dec	Chelsea	A	W	4–1
26 Dec	Chelsea	H	W	4–2
28 Dec	Manchester City	A	W	2–0
1 Jan	Bradford City	H	W	2–0
4 Jan	West Bromwich Alb.	H	D	1–1
18 Jan	Everton	A	L	1–4
25 Jan	Sheffield Wed.	H	W	2–0
8 Feb	Blackburn Rovers	A	D	0–0
15 Feb	Derby County	H	W	4–0
1 Mar	Middlesbrough	H	L	2–3
8 Mar	Notts County	A	W	2–1
15 Mar	Sunderland	H	L	1–3
21 Mar	Woolwich Arsenal	H	W	2–0
22 Mar	Aston Villa	H	W	4–0
25 Mar	Bradford City	A	L	0–1
29 Mar	Liverpool	A	W	2–0
31 Mar	Tottenham Hotspur	A	D	1–1
5 Apr	Bolton Wanderers	H	W	2–1
12 Apr	Sheffield United	A	L	1–2
19 Apr	Newcastle United	H	W	3–0
26 Apr	Oldham Athletic	A	D	0–0

FA Cup

11 Jan	Coventry City	H	D	1–1
16 Jan	Coventry City	A	W	2–1
1 Feb	Plymouth Argyle	A	W	2–0
22 Feb	Oldham Athletic	A	D	0–0
26 Feb	Oldham Athletic	H	L	1–2

Football League Division 1
P38 • W19 • D8 • L11 • F69 • A43 • PTS46
Position: 4

1913/14

Football League

6 Sep	Sheffield Wed.	A	W	3–1
8 Sep	Sunderland	H	W	3–1
13 Sep	Bolton Wanderers	H	L	0–1
20 Sep	Chelsea	A	W	2–0
27 Sep	Oldham Athletic	H	W	4–1
4 Oct	Tottenham Hotspur	H	W	3–1
11 Oct	Burnley	A	W	2–1
18 Oct	Preston North End	H	W	3–0
25 Oct	Newcastle United	A	W	1–0
1 Nov	Liverpool	H	W	3–0
8 Nov	Aston Villa	A	L	1–3
15 Nov	Middlesbrough	H	L	0–1
22 Nov	Sheffield United	A	L	0–2
29 Nov	Derby County	H	D	3–3
6 Dec	Manchester City	A	W	2–0
13 Dec	Bradford City	H	D	1–1
20 Dec	Blackburn Rovers	A	W	1–0
25 Dec	Everton	H	L	0–1
26 Dec	Everton	A	L	0–5
27 Dec	Sheffield Wed.	H	W	2–1
1 Jan	West Bromwich Alb.	H	W	1–0
3 Jan	Bolton Wanderers	A	L	1–6
17 Jan	Chelsea	H	L	0–1
24 Jan	Oldham Athletic	A	D	2–2
7 Feb	Tottenham Hotspur	A	L	1–2
14 Feb	Burnley	H	L	0–1
21 Feb	Middlesbrough	A	L	1–3
28 Feb	Newcastle United	H	D	2–2
5 Mar	Preston North End	A	L	2–4
14 Mar	Aston Villa	H	L	0–6
4 Apr	Derby County	A	L	2–4
10 Apr	Sunderland	A	L	0–2
11 Apr	Manchester City	H	L	0–1
13 Apr	West Bromwich Alb.	A	L	1–2
15 Apr	Liverpool	A	W	2–1
18 Apr	Bradford City	A	D	1–1
22 Apr	Sheffield United	H	W	2–1
25 Apr	Blackburn Rovers	H	D	0–0

FA Cup

10 Jan	Swindon Town	A	L	0–1

Football League Division 1
P38 • W15 • D6 • L17 • F52 • A62 • PTS36
Position: 14

1914/15

Football League

2 Sep	Oldham Athletic	H	L	1–3
5 Sep	Manchester City	H	D	0–0
12 Sep	Bolton Wanderers	A	L	0–3
19 Sep	Blackburn Rovers	H	W	2–0
26 Sep	Notts County	A	L	2–4
3 Oct	Sunderland	H	W	3–0
10 Oct	Sheffield Wed.	A	L	0–1
17 Oct	West Bromwich Alb.	H	D	0–0
24 Oct	Everton	A	L	2–4
31 Oct	Chelsea	H	D	2–2
7 Nov	Bradford City	A	L	2–4
14 Nov	Burnley	H	L	0–2
21 Nov	Tottenham Hotspur	A	L	0–2
28 Nov	Newcastle United	H	W	1–0
5 Dec	Middlesbrough	A	D	1–1
12 Dec	Sheffield United	H	L	1–2
19 Dec	Aston Villa	A	D	3–3
26 Dec	Liverpool	A	D	1–1
1 Jan	Bradford Park Ave.	H	L	1–2
2 Jan	Manchester City	A	D	1–1
16 Jan	Bolton Wanderers	H	W	4–1
23 Jan	Blackburn Rovers	A	D	3–3
30 Jan	Notts County	H	D	2–2
6 Feb	Sunderland	A	L	0–1
13 Feb	Sheffield Wed.	H	W	2–0
20 Feb	West Bromwich Alb.	A	D	0–0
27 Feb	Everton	H	L	1–2
13 Mar	Bradford City	H	W	1–0
20 Mar	Burnley	A	L	0–3
27 Mar	Tottenham Hotspur	H	D	1–1
2 Apr	Liverpool	H	W	2–0
3 Apr	Newcastle United	A	L	0–2
5 Apr	Bradford Park Ave.	A	L	0–5
6 Apr	Oldham Athletic	A	L	0–1
10 Apr	Middlesbrough	H	D	2–2
17 Apr	Sheffield United	A	L	1–3
19 Apr	Chelsea	A	W	3–1
26 Apr	Aston Villa	H	W	1–0

FA Cup

9 Jan	Sheffield Wednesday	A	L	0–1

Football League Division 1
P38 • W9 • D12 • L17 • F46 • A62 • PTS30
Position: 18

1915/16

Lancashire Section Principal Tournament

4 Sep	Oldham Athletic	A	L	2–3
11 Sep	Everton	H	L	2–4
18 Sep	Bolton Wanderers	A	W	5–3
25 Sep	Manchester City	H	D	1–1
2 Oct	Stoke	A	D	0–0
9 Oct	Burnley	H	L	3–7
16 Oct	Preston North End	A	D	0–0
23 Oct	Stockport County	H	W	3–0
30 Oct	Liverpool	A	W	2–0
6 Nov	Bury	H	D	1–1
13 Nov	Rochdale	H	W	2–0
20 Nov	Blackpool	A	L	1–5
27 Nov	Southport	H	D	0–0
4 Dec	Oldham Athletic	H	W	2–0
11 Dec	Everton	A	L	0–2
18 Dec	Bolton Wanderers	H	W	1–0
25 Dec	Manchester City	A	L	1–2
1 Jan	Stoke	H	L	1–2
8 Jan	Burnley	A	L	4–7
15 Jan	Preston North End	H	W	4–0
22 Jan	Stockport County	A	L	1–3
29 Jan	Liverpool	H	D	1–1
5 Feb	Bury	A	L	1–2
12 Feb	Rochdale	A	D	2–2
19 Feb	Blackpool	H	D	1–1
26 Feb	Southport	A	L	0–5

P26 • W7 • D8 • L11 • F41 • A51 • PTS22
Position: 11

Lancashire Section Subsidiary (Southern) Tournament

4 Mar	Everton	H	L	0–2
11 Mar	Oldham Athletic	A	L	0–1
18 Mar	Liverpool	H	D	0–0
25 Mar	Manchester City	H	L	0–2
1 Apr	Stockport County	A	L	3–5
8 Apr	Everton	A	L	1–3
15 Apr	Oldham Athletic	H	W	3–0
21 Apr	Stockport County	H	W	3–2
22 Apr	Liverpool	A	L	1–7
29 Apr	Manchester City	A	L	1–2

P10 • W2 • D1 • L7 • F12 • A24 • PTS5
Position: 6

1916/17

Lancashire Section Principal Tournament

2 Sep	Port Vale	H	D	2–2
9 Sep	Oldham Athletic	A	W	2–0
16 Sep	Preston North End	H	W	2–1
23 Sep	Burnley	A	L	1–7
30 Sep	Blackpool	A	D	2–2
7 Oct	Liverpool	H	D	0–0
14 Oct	Stockport County	A	L	0–1
21 Oct	Bury	H	W	3–1
28 Oct	Stoke	A	L	0–3
4 Nov	Southport	H	W	1–0
11 Nov	Blackburn Rovers	A	W	2–1
18 Nov	Manchester City	H	W	2–1
25 Nov	Everton	A	L	2–3
2 Dec	Rochdale	H	D	1–1
9 Dec	Bolton Wanderers	A	L	1–5
23 Dec	Oldham Athletic	H	W	3–2
30 Dec	Preston North End	A	L	2–3
6 Jan	Burnley	H	W	3–1
13 Jan	Blackpool	H	W	3–2
20 Jan	Liverpool	A	D	3–3
27 Jan	Stockport County	H	L	0–1
3 Feb	Bury	A	D	1–1
10 Feb	Stoke	H	W	4–2
17 Feb	Southport	A	W	1–0
24 Feb	Blackburn Rovers	H	W	1–0
3 Mar	Manchester City	A	L	0–1
10 Mar	Everton	H	L	0–2
17 Mar	Rochdale	A	L	0–2
24 Mar	Bolton Wanderers	H	W	6–3
6 Apr	Port Vale	A	L	0–3

P30 • W13 • D6 • L11 • F48 • A54 • PTS33
Position: 7

Lancashire Section Subsidiary Tournament

31 Mar	Stoke	A	L	1–2
7 Apr	Manchester City	H	W	5–1
9 Apr	Port Vale	H	W	5–1
14 Apr	Stoke	H	W	1–0
21 Apr	Manchester City	A	W	1–0
28 Apr	Port Vale	A	L	2–5

P6 • W4 • D0 • L2 • F15 • A9 • PTS8
Position: 4

1917/18

Lancashire Section Principal Tournament

1 Sep	Blackburn Rovers	A	W	5–0
8 Sep	Blackburn Rovers	H	W	6–1
15 Sep	Rochdale	A	L	0–1
22 Sep	Rochdale	H	D	1–1
29 Sep	Manchester City	H	L	1–3
6 Oct	Manchester City	A	D	1–1
13 Oct	Everton	A	L	0–3
20 Oct	Everton	H	D	0–0
27 Oct	Port Vale	H	D	3–3
3 Nov	Port Vale	A	D	2–2
10 Nov	Bolton Wanderers	H	L	1–3
17 Nov	Bolton Wanderers	A	L	2–4
24 Nov	Preston North End	H	W	2–1
1 Dec	Preston North End	A	D	0–0
8 Dec	Blackpool	H	W	1–0
15 Dec	Blackpool	A	W	3–2
22 Dec	Burnley	A	W	5–0
29 Dec	Burnley	H	W	1–0
5 Jan	Southport	A	L	0–3
12 Jan	Southport	H	D	0–0
19 Jan	Liverpool	A	L	1–5
26 Jan	Liverpool	H	L	0–2
2 Feb	Stoke	A	L	1–5
9 Feb	Stoke	H	W	2–1
16 Feb	Bury	H	D	0–0
23 Feb	Bury	A	W	2–1
2 Mar	Oldham Athletic	H	W	2–1
9 Mar	Oldham Athletic	A	L	0–2
16 Mar	Stockport County	H	W	2–0
23 Mar	Stockport County	A	L	1–2

P30 • W11 • D8 • L11 • F45 • A39 • PTS30
Position: 8

Lancashire Section Subsidiary Tournament

29 Mar	Manchester City	A	L	0–3
30 Mar	Stoke	H	W	2–1
1 Apr	Manchester City	H	W	2–0
6 Apr	Stoke	A	D	0–0
13 Apr	Port Vale	H	W	2–0
20 Apr	Port Vale	A	L	0–3

P6 • W3 • D1 • L2 • F6 • A7 • PTS7
Position: 8

1918/19

Lancashire Section Principal Tournament

7 Sep	Oldham Athletic	H	L	1–4
14 Sep	Oldham Athletic	A	W	2–0
21 Sep	Blackburn Rovers	H	W	1–0
28 Sep	Blackburn Rovers	A	D	1–1
5 Oct	Manchester City	H	L	0–2
12 Oct	Manchester City	A	D	0–0
19 Oct	Everton	H	D	1–1
26 Oct	Everton	A	L	2–6
2 Nov	Rochdale	H	W	3–1
9 Nov	Rochdale	A	L	0–1
16 Nov	Preston North End	A	L	2–4
23 Nov	Preston North End	H	L	1–2
30 Nov	Bolton Wanderers	A	L	1–3
7 Dec	Bolton Wanderers	H	W	1–0
14 Dec	Port Vale	A	L	1–3
21 Dec	Port Vale	H	W	5–1
28 Dec	Blackpool	A	D	2–2
11 Jan	Stockport County	A	L	1–2
18 Jan	Stockport County	H	L	0–2
25 Jan	Liverpool	A	D	1–1
1 Feb	Liverpool	H	L	0–1
8 Feb	Southport	A	L	1–2
15 Feb	Southport	H	L	1–3
22 Feb	Burnley	A	L	2–4
1 Mar	Burnley	H	W	4–0
8 Mar	Stoke	A	W	2–1
15 Mar	Stoke	H	W	3–1
22 Mar	Bury	A	W	2–0
29 Mar	Bury	H	W	5–1
30 Apr	Blackpool	H	W	5–1

P30 • W11 • D5 • L14 • F51 • A47 • PTS27
Position: 9

Lancashire Section Subsidiary Tournament (Section C)

5 Apr	Port Vale	A	W	3–1
12 Apr	Port Vale	H	W	2–1
18 Apr	Manchester City	A	L	0–3
19 Apr	Stoke	H	L	0–1
21 Apr	Manchester City	H	L	2–4
26 Apr	Stoke	A	L	2 4

P6 • W2 • D0 • L4 • F9 • A14 • PTS4
Position: 3

The 1920s

1919/20

Football League

30 Aug	Derby County	A	D	1–1
1 Sep	Sheffield Wed.	H	D	0–0
6 Sep	Derby County	H	L	0–2
8 Sep	Sheffield Wed.	A	W	3–1
13 Sep	Preston North End	A	W	3–2
20 Sep	Preston North End	H	W	5–1
27 Sep	Middlesbrough	A	D	1–1
4 Oct	Middlesbrough	H	D	1–1
11 Oct	Manchester City	A	D	3–3
18 Oct	Manchester City	H	W	1–0
25 Oct	Sheffield United	A	D	2–2
1 Nov	Sheffield United	H	W	3–0
8 Nov	Burnley	A	L	1–2
15 Nov	Burnley	H	L	0–1
22 Nov	Oldham Athletic	A	W	3–0
6 Dec	Aston Villa	A	L	0–2
13 Dec	Aston Villa	H	L	1–2
20 Dec	Newcastle United	H	W	2–1
26 Dec	Liverpool	H	D	0–0
27 Dec	Newcastle United	A	L	1–2
1 Jan	Liverpool	A	D	0–0
3 Jan	Chelsea	H	L	0–2
17 Jan	Chelsea	A	L	0–1
24 Jan	West Bromwich Alb.	A	L	1–2
7 Feb	Sunderland	A	L	0–3
11 Feb	Oldham Athletic	H	D	1–1
14 Feb	Sunderland	H	W	2–0
21 Feb	Arsenal	A	W	3–0
25 Feb	West Bromwich Alb.	H	L	1–2
28 Feb	Arsenal	H	L	0–1

1919/20 continued
Football League continued
- 6 Mar Everton H W 1–0
- 13 Mar Everton A D 0–0
- 20 Mar Bradford City H D 0–0
- 27 Mar Bradford City A L 1–2
- 2 Apr Bradford Park Ave. A L 0–1
- 3 Apr Bolton Wanderers H D 1–1
- 6 Apr Bradford Park Ave. A W 4–1
- 10 Apr Bolton Wanderers A W 5–3
- 17 Apr Blackburn Rovers H D 1–1
- 24 Apr Blackburn Rovers A L 0–5
- 26 Apr Notts County H D 0–0
- 1 May Notts County A W 2–0

FA Cup
- 10 Jan Port Vale A W 1–0
- 31 Jan Aston Villa H L 1–2

Football League Division 1
P42 • W13 • D14 • L15 • F54 • A50 • PTS40
Position: 12

1920/21
Football League
- 28 Aug Bolton Wanderers H L 2–3
- 30 Aug Arsenal A L 0–2
- 4 Sep Bolton Wanderers A D 1–1
- 6 Sep Arsenal H D 1–1
- 11 Sep Chelsea H W 3–1
- 18 Sep Chelsea A W 2–1
- 25 Sep Tottenham Hotspur H L 0–1
- 2 Oct Tottenham Hotspur A L 1–4
- 9 Oct Oldham Athletic H W 4–1
- 16 Oct Oldham Athletic A D 2–2
- 23 Oct Preston North End H W 1–0
- 30 Oct Preston North End A D 0–0
- 6 Nov Sheffield United H W 2–1
- 13 Nov Sheffield United A D 0–0
- 20 Nov Manchester City H D 1–1
- 27 Nov Manchester City A L 0–3
- 4 Dec Bradford Park Ave. H W 5–1
- 11 Dec Bradford Park Ave. A W 4–2
- 18 Dec Newcastle United H W 2–0
- 25 Dec Aston Villa A W 4–3
- 27 Dec Aston Villa H L 1–3
- 1 Jan Newcastle United A L 3–6
- 15 Jan West Bromwich Alb. H L 1–4
- 22 Jan West Bromwich Alb. A W 2–0
- 5 Feb Liverpool H D 1–1
- 9 Feb Liverpool A L 0–2
- 12 Feb Everton H L 1–2
- 26 Feb Sunderland H W 3–0
- 5 Mar Sunderland A W 3–2
- 9 Mar Everton A L 0–2
- 12 Mar Bradford City H D 1–1
- 19 Mar Bradford City A D 1–1
- 25 Mar Burnley A L 0–1
- 26 Mar Huddersfield Town A L 2–5
- 28 Mar Burnley H L 0–3
- 2 Apr Huddersfield Town H W 2–0
- 9 Apr Middlesbrough A W 4–2
- 16 Apr Middlesbrough H L 0–1
- 23 Apr Blackburn Rovers A L 0–2
- 30 Apr Blackburn Rovers H L 0–1
- 2 May Derby County A D 1–1
- 7 May Derby County H W 3–0

FA Cup
- 8 Jan Liverpool A D 1–1
- 12 Jan Liverpool H L 1–2

Football League Division 1
P42 • W15 • D10 • L17 • F64 • A68 • PTS40
Position: 13

1921/22
Football League
- 27 Aug Everton A L 0–5
- 29 Aug West Bromwich Alb. H L 2–3
- 3 Sep Everton H W 2–1
- 7 Sep West Bromwich Alb. A D 0–0
- 10 Sep Chelsea A D 0–0
- 17 Sep Chelsea H D 0–0
- 24 Sep Preston North End A L 2–3
- 1 Oct Preston North End H D 1–1
- 8 Oct Tottenham Hotspur A D 2–2
- 15 Oct Tottenham Hotspur H W 2–1
- 22 Oct Manchester City A L 1–4
- 29 Oct Manchester City H W 3–1
- 5 Nov Middlesbrough H L 3–5
- 12 Nov Middlesbrough A L 0–2
- 19 Nov Aston Villa A L 1–3
- 26 Nov Aston Villa H W 1–0
- 3 Dec Bradford City A L 1–2
- 10 Dec Bradford City H D 1–1
- 17 Dec Liverpool A L 1–2
- 24 Dec Liverpool H D 0–0
- 26 Dec Burnley H L 0–1
- 27 Dec Burnley A L 2–4
- 31 Dec Newcastle United A L 0–3
- 2 Jan Sheffield United A L 0–3
- 14 Jan Newcastle United H L 0–1
- 21 Jan Sunderland A L 1–2
- 28 Jan Sunderland H W 3–1
- 11 Feb Huddersfield Town H D 1–1
- 18 Feb Birmingham A W 1–0
- 25 Feb Birmingham H D 1–1
- 27 Feb Huddersfield Town A D 1–1
- 11 Mar Arsenal H W 1–0
- 18 Mar Blackburn Rovers H L 0–1
- 25 Mar Blackburn Rovers A L 0–3
- 1 Apr Bolton Wanderers H L 0–1
- 5 Apr Arsenal A L 1–3
- 8 Apr Bolton Wanderers A L 0–1
- 15 Apr Oldham Athletic H L 1–3
- 17 Apr Sheffield United H W 3–2
- 22 Apr Oldham Athletic A D 1–1
- 29 Apr Cardiff City H D 1–1
- 6 May Cardiff City A L 1–3

FA Cup
- 7 Jan Cardiff City H L 1–4

Football League Division 1
P42 • W8 • D12 • L22 • F41 • A73 • PTS28
Position: 22

1922/23
Football League
- 26 Aug Crystal Palace H W 2–1
- 28 Aug Sheffield Wed. A L 0–1
- 2 Sep Crystal Palace A W 3–2
- 4 Sep Sheffield Wed. H W 1–0
- 9 Sep Wolverhampton Wan. A W 1–0
- 16 Sep Wolverhampton Wan. H W 1–0
- 23 Sep Coventry City A L 0–2
- 30 Sep Coventry City H W 2–1
- 7 Oct Port Vale H L 1–2
- 14 Oct Port Vale A L 0–1
- 21 Oct Fulham H D 1–1
- 28 Oct Fulham A D 0–0
- 4 Nov Clapton Orient H D 0–0
- 11 Nov Clapton Orient A D 1–1
- 18 Nov Bury A D 2–2
- 25 Nov Bury H L 0–1
- 2 Dec Rotherham County H W 3–0
- 9 Dec Rotherham County A D 1–1
- 16 Dec Stockport County H W 1–0
- 23 Dec Stockport County A L 0–1
- 25 Dec West Ham United H L 1–2
- 26 Dec West Ham United A W 2–0
- 30 Dec Hull City A L 1–2
- 1 Jan Barnsley H W 1–0
- 6 Jan Hull City H W 3–2
- 20 Jan Leeds United A D 0–0
- 27 Jan Leeds United A W 1–0
- 10 Feb Notts County A W 6–1
- 17 Feb Derby County H D 0–0
- 21 Feb Notts County H D 1–1
- 3 Mar Southampton H L 1–2
- 14 Mar Derby County A D 1–1
- 17 Mar Bradford City A D 1–1
- 21 Mar Bradford City H D 1–1
- 30 Mar South Shields H W 3–0
- 31 Mar Blackpool A L 0–1
- 2 Apr South Shields A W 3–0
- 7 Apr Blackpool H W 2–1
- 11 Apr Southampton A D 0–0
- 14 Apr Leicester City A W 1–0
- 21 Apr Leicester City H L 0–2
- 28 Apr Barnsley A D 2–2

FA Cup
- 13 Jan Bradford City A D 1–1
- 17 Jan Bradford City H W 2–0
- 3 Feb Tottenham Hotspur H L 0–4

Football League Division 2
P42 • W17 • D14 • L11 • F51 • A36 • PTS48
Position: 4

1923/24
Football League
- 25 Aug Bristol City A W 2–1
- 27 Aug Southampton H W 1–0
- 1 Sep Bristol City H W 2–1
- 3 Sep Southampton A D 0–0
- 8 Sep Bury A L 0–2
- 15 Sep Bury H L 0–1
- 22 Sep South Shields A L 0–1
- 29 Sep South Shields H D 1–1
- 6 Oct Oldham Athletic A L 2–3
- 13 Oct Oldham Athletic H W 2–0
- 20 Oct Stockport County H W 3–0
- 27 Oct Stockport County A L 2–3
- 3 Nov Leicester City A D 2–2
- 10 Nov Leicester City H W 3–0
- 17 Nov Coventry City A D 1–1
- 1 Dec Leeds United A D 0–0
- 8 Dec Leeds United H W 3–1
- 15 Dec Port Vale A W 1–0
- 22 Dec Port Vale H W 5–0
- 25 Dec Barnsley H L 1–2
- 26 Dec Barnsley A L 0–1
- 29 Dec Bradford City A D 0–0
- 2 Jan Coventry City H L 1–2
- 5 Jan Bradford City H W 3–0
- 19 Jan Fulham A L 1–3
- 26 Jan Fulham H D 0–0
- 6 Feb Blackpool A L 0–1
- 9 Feb Blackpool H D 0–0
- 16 Feb Derby County A L 0–3
- 23 Feb Derby County H D 0–0
- 1 Mar Nelson A W 2–0
- 8 Mar Nelson H L 0–1
- 15 Mar Hull City H D 1–1
- 22 Mar Hull City A D 1–1
- 29 Mar Stoke H D 2–2
- 5 Apr Stoke A L 0–3
- 12 Apr Crystal Palace H W 5–1
- 18 Apr Clapton Orient A L 0–1
- 19 Apr Crystal Palace A D 1–1
- 21 Apr Clapton Orient H D 2–2
- 26 Apr Sheffield Wed. H W 2–0
- 3 May Sheffield Wed. A L 0–2

FA Cup
- 12 Jan Plymouth Argyle H W 1–0
- 2 Feb Huddersfield Town H L 0–3

Football League Division 2
P42 • W13 • D14 • L15 • F52 • A44 • PTS40
Position: 14

1924/25
Football League
- 30 Aug Leicester City H W 1–0
- 1 Sep Stockport County A L 1–2
- 6 Sep Stoke A D 0–0
- 8 Sep Barnsley H W 1–0
- 13 Sep Coventry City H W 5–1
- 20 Sep Oldham Athletic A W 3–0
- 27 Sep Sheffield Wed. H W 2–0
- 4 Oct Clapton Orient A W 1–0
- 11 Oct Crystal Palace H W 1–0
- 18 Oct Southampton A W 2–0
- 25 Oct Wolverhampton Wan. A D 0–0
- 1 Nov Fulham H W 2–0
- 8 Nov Portsmouth A D 1–1
- 15 Nov Hull City H W 2–0
- 22 Nov Blackpool A D 1–1
- 29 Nov Derby County H D 1–1
- 6 Dec South Shields A W 2–1
- 13 Dec Bradford City H W 3–0
- 20 Dec Port Vale A L 1–2
- 25 Dec Middlesbrough A D 1–1
- 26 Dec Middlesbrough H W 2–0
- 27 Dec Leicester City A L 0–3
- 1 Jan Chelsea H W 1–0
- 3 Jan Stoke H W 2–0
- 17 Jan Coventry City A L 0–1
- 24 Jan Oldham Athletic H L 0–1
- 7 Feb Clapton Orient H W 4–2
- 14 Feb Crystal Palace A L 1–2
- 23 Feb Sheffield Wed. A D 1–1
- 28 Feb Wolverhampton Wan. H W 3–0
- 7 Mar Fulham A L 0–1
- 14 Mar Portsmouth H W 2–0
- 21 Mar Hull City A W 1–0
- 28 Mar Blackpool H D 0–0
- 4 Apr Derby County A L 0–1
- 10 Apr Stockport County H W 2–0
- 11 Apr South Shields H W 1–0
- 13 Apr Chelsea A D 0–0
- 18 Apr Bradford City A W 1–0
- 22 Apr Southampton H D 1–1
- 25 Apr Port Vale H W 4–0
- 2 May Barnsley A D 0–0

FA Cup
- 10 Jan Sheffield Wednesday A L 0–2

Football League Division 2
P42 • W23 • D11 • L8 • F57 • A23 • PTS57
Position: 2

1925/26
Football League
- 29 Aug West Ham United A L 0–1
- 2 Sep Aston Villa H W 3–0
- 5 Sep Arsenal H L 0–1
- 7 Sep Aston Villa A D 2–2
- 12 Sep Manchester City A D 1–1
- 16 Sep Leicester City H W 3–2
- 19 Sep Liverpool A L 0–5
- 26 Sep Burnley H W 6–1
- 3 Oct Leeds United A L 0–2
- 10 Oct Newcastle United H W 2–1
- 17 Oct Tottenham Hotspur H D 0–0
- 24 Oct Cardiff City A W 2–0
- 31 Oct Huddersfield Town H D 1–1
- 7 Nov Everton A W 3–1
- 14 Nov Birmingham H W 3–1
- 21 Nov Bury A W 3–1
- 28 Nov Blackburn Rovers H W 2–0
- 5 Dec Sunderland A L 1–2
- 12 Dec Sheffield United H L 1–2
- 19 Dec West Bromwich Alb. A L 1–5
- 25 Dec Bolton Wanderers H W 2–1
- 28 Dec Leicester City A W 3–1
- 2 Jan West Ham United H W 2–1
- 16 Jan Arsenal A L 2–3
- 23 Jan Manchester City H L 1–6
- 6 Feb Burnley A W 1–0
- 13 Feb Leeds United H W 2–1
- 27 Feb Tottenham Hotspur A W 1–0
- 10 Mar Liverpool H D 3–3
- 13 Mar Huddersfield Town A L 0–5
- 17 Mar Bolton Wanderers A L 1–3
- 20 Mar Everton H D 0–0
- 2 Apr Notts County A W 3–0
- 3 Apr Bury H L 0–1
- 5 Apr Notts County H L 0–1
- 10 Apr Blackburn Rovers A L 0–7
- 14 Apr Newcastle United A L 1–4
- 19 Apr Birmingham A L 1–2
- 21 Apr Sunderland H W 5–1
- 24 Apr Sheffield United A L 0–2
- 28 Apr Cardiff City H W 1–0
- 1 May West Bromwich Alb. H W 3–2

FA Cup
- 9 Jan Port Vale A W 3–2
- 30 Jan Tottenham Hotspur A D 2–2
- 3 Feb Tottenham Hotspur H W 2–0
- 20 Feb Sunderland A D 3–3
- 24 Feb Sunderland H W 2–1
- 6 Mar Fulham A W 2–1
- 27 Mar Manchester City H L 0–3

Football League Division 1
P42 • W19 • D6 • L17 • F66 • A73 • PTS44
Position: 9

1926/27
Football League
- 28 Aug Liverpool A L 2–4
- 30 Aug Sheffield United A D 2–2
- 4 Sep Leeds United H D 2–2
- 11 Sep Newcastle United A L 2–4
- 15 Sep Arsenal H D 2–2
- 18 Sep Burnley H W 2–1
- 25 Sep Cardiff City A W 2–0
- 2 Oct Aston Villa H W 2–1
- 9 Oct Bolton Wanderers A L 0–4
- 16 Oct Bury A W 3–0
- 23 Oct Birmingham H L 0–1
- 30 Oct West Ham United A L 0–4
- 6 Nov Sheffield Wed. H D 0–0
- 13 Nov Leicester City A W 3–2
- 20 Nov Everton H W 2–1
- 27 Nov Blackburn Rovers A L 1–2
- 4 Dec Huddersfield Town H D 0–0
- 11 Dec Sunderland A L 0–6
- 18 Dec West Bromwich Alb. H W 2–0
- 25 Dec Tottenham Hotspur H D 1–1
- 27 Dec Tottenham Hotspur A W 2–1
- 28 Dec Arsenal A L 0–1
- 1 Jan Sheffield United H W 5–0
- 15 Jan Liverpool H L 0–1
- 22 Jan Leeds United A W 3–2
- 5 Feb Burnley A L 0–1
- 9 Feb Newcastle United A W 3–1
- 12 Feb Cardiff City H D 1–1
- 19 Feb Aston Villa A L 0–2
- 26 Feb Bolton Wanderers H D 0–0
- 5 Mar Bury H L 1–2
- 12 Mar Birmingham A L 0–4
- 19 Mar West Ham United H L 0–3
- 26 Mar Sheffield Wed. A L 0–2
- 2 Apr Leicester City H W 1–0
- 9 Apr Everton A D 0–0
- 15 Apr Derby County H D 2–2
- 16 Apr Blackburn Rovers H W 2–0
- 18 Apr Derby County A D 2–2
- 23 Apr Huddersfield Town A D 0–0
- 30 Apr Sunderland H D 0–0
- 7 May West Bromwich Alb. A D 2–2

FA Cup
- 8 Jan Reading A D 1–1
- 12 Jan Reading H D 2–2
- 17 Jan Reading A L 1–2

Football League Division 1
P42 • W13 • D14 • L15 • F52 • A64 • PTS40
Position: 15

1927/28
Football League
- 27 Aug Middlesbrough H W 3–0
- 29 Aug Sheffield Wed. A W 2–0
- 3 Sep Birmingham A D 0–0
- 7 Sep Sheffield Wed. H D 1–1
- 10 Sep Newcastle United H L 1–7
- 17 Sep Huddersfield Town A L 2–4
- 19 Sep Blackburn Rovers A L 0–3
- 24 Sep Tottenham Hotspur H W 3–0
- 1 Oct Leicester City A L 0–1
- 8 Oct Everton A L 2–5
- 15 Oct Cardiff City H D 2–2
- 22 Oct Derby County H W 5–0
- 29 Oct West Ham United A W 2–1
- 5 Nov Portsmouth H W 2–0
- 12 Nov Sunderland A L 1–4
- 19 Nov Aston Villa H W 5–1
- 26 Nov Burnley A L 0–4
- 3 Dec Bury H L 0–1
- 10 Dec Sheffield United A L 1–2
- 17 Dec Arsenal H W 4–1
- 24 Dec Liverpool A L 0–2
- 26 Dec Blackburn Rovers H D 1–1
- 31 Dec Middlesbrough A W 2–1
- 7 Jan Birmingham H D 1–1
- 21 Jan Newcastle United A L 1–4
- 4 Feb Tottenham Hotspur A L 1–4
- 11 Feb Leicester City H W 5–2
- 25 Feb Cardiff City A L 0–2
- 7 Mar Huddersfield Town H D 0–0
- 10 Mar West Ham United H D 1–1
- 14 Mar Everton H W 1–0
- 17 Mar Portsmouth A L 0–1
- 28 Mar Derby County A L 0–5
- 31 Mar Aston Villa A L 1–3
- 6 Apr Bolton Wanderers A L 2–3
- 7 Apr Burnley H W 4–3
- 9 Apr Bolton Wanderers H W 2–1
- 14 Apr Bury A L 3–4
- 21 Apr Sheffield United H L 2–3
- 25 Apr Sunderland H W 2–1
- 28 Apr Arsenal A W 1–0
- 5 May Liverpool H W 6–1

FA Cup
- 14 Jan Brentford H W 7–1
- 28 Jan Bury A D 1–1
- 1 Feb Bury H W 1–0
- 18 Feb Birmingham H W 1–0
- 3 Mar Blackburn Rovers A L 0–2

Football League Division 1
P42 • W16 • D7 • L19 • F72 • A80 • PTS39
Position: 18

1928/29
Football League
- 25 Aug Leicester City H D 1–1
- 27 Aug Aston Villa A D 0–0
- 1 Sep Manchester City A D 2–2
- 8 Sep Leeds United A L 2–3
- 15 Sep Liverpool H D 2–2
- 22 Sep West Ham United A L 1–3
- 29 Sep Newcastle United H W 5–0
- 6 Oct Burnley A W 4–3
- 13 Oct Cardiff City H D 1–1
- 20 Oct Birmingham H W 1–0
- 27 Oct Huddersfield Town A W 2–1
- 3 Nov Bolton Wanderers H D 1–1
- 10 Nov Sheffield Wed. A L 1–2
- 17 Nov Derby County H L 0–1
- 24 Nov Sunderland A L 1–5
- 1 Dec Blackburn Rovers H L 1–4
- 8 Dec Arsenal A L 1–3
- 15 Dec Everton H D 1–1
- 22 Dec Portsmouth A L 0–3
- 25 Dec Sheffield United A D 1–1
- 26 Dec Sheffield United H L 1–6
- 29 Dec Leicester City A L 1–2
- 1 Jan Aston Villa H D 2–2
- 5 Jan Manchester City H L 1–2
- 19 Jan Leeds United H L 1–2
- 2 Feb West Ham United H L 2–3
- 9 Feb Newcastle United A L 0–5
- 13 Feb Liverpool A W 3–2
- 16 Feb Burnley H W 1–0
- 23 Feb Cardiff City A D 2–2
- 2 Mar Birmingham A D 1–1
- 9 Mar Huddersfield Town H W 1–0
- 16 Mar Bolton Wanderers A D 1–1
- 23 Mar Sheffield Wed. H W 2–1
- 29 Mar Bury A W 3–1
- 30 Mar Derby County A L 1–6
- 1 Apr Bury H W 1–0
- 6 Apr Sunderland H W 3–0
- 13 Apr Blackburn Rovers A W 3–0
- 20 Apr Arsenal H W 4–1
- 27 Apr Everton A W 4–2
- 4 May Portsmouth H D 0–0

FA Cup
- 12 Jan Port Vale A W 3–0
- 26 Jan Bury H L 0–1

Football League Division 1
P42 • W16 • D13 • L15 • F66 • A76 • PTS41
Position: 12

The 1930s

1929/30
Football League
- 31 Aug Newcastle United A L 1–4
- 2 Sep Leicester City A L 1–4
- 7 Sep Blackburn Rovers H W 1–0
- 11 Sep Leicester City H W 2–1
- 14 Sep Middlesbrough A W 3–2
- 21 Sep Liverpool H L 1–2
- 28 Sep West Ham United A L 1–2
- 5 Oct Manchester City H L 1–3
- 7 Oct Sheffield United A L 1–3
- 12 Oct Grimsby Town H L 2–5
- 19 Oct Portsmouth A L 0–3
- 26 Oct Arsenal H W 1–0
- 2 Nov Aston Villa A L 0–1
- 9 Nov Derby County H W 3–2
- 16 Nov Sheffield Wed. A L 2–7
- 23 Nov Burnley H W 1–0
- 30 Nov Sunderland A W 4–2
- 7 Dec Bolton Wanderers H D 1–1
- 14 Dec Everton A D 0–0
- 21 Dec Leeds United H W 3–1
- 25 Dec Birmingham H D 0–0
- 26 Dec Birmingham A W 1–0
- 28 Dec Newcastle United H W 5–0
- 4 Jan Blackburn Rovers A L 4–5
- 18 Jan Middlesbrough A L 0–3
- 25 Jan Liverpool A L 0–1
- 1 Feb West Ham United H W 4–2
- 8 Feb Manchester City A W 1–0
- 15 Feb Grimsby Town A D 2–2
- 22 Feb Portsmouth H W 3–0
- 1 Mar Bolton Wanderers A L 1–4
- 8 Mar Aston Villa H L 2–3
- 12 Mar Arsenal A L 2–4
- 15 Mar Derby County A D 1–1
- 29 Mar Burnley A L 0–4
- 5 Apr Sunderland H W 2–1
- 14 Apr Sheffield Wed. H D 2–2
- 18 Apr Huddersfield Town H W 1–0
- 19 Apr Everton H D 3–3
- 22 Apr Huddersfield Town A D 2–2
- 26 Apr Leeds United A L 1–3
- 3 May Sheffield United H L 1–5

FA Cup
- 11 Jan Swindon Town H L 0–2

Football League Division 1
P42 • W15 • D8 • L19 • F67 • A88 • PTS38
Position:17

1930/31
Football League
- 30 Aug Aston Villa H L 3–4
- 3 Sep Middlesbrough A L 1–3
- 6 Sep Chelsea A L 2–6
- 10 Sep Huddersfield Town H L 0–6
- 13 Sep Newcastle United H L 4–7
- 15 Sep Huddersfield Town A L 0–3
- 20 Sep Sheffield Wed. A L 0–3
- 27 Sep Grimsby Town H L 0–2
- 4 Oct Manchester City A L 1–4
- 11 Oct West Ham United A L 1–5
- 18 Oct Arsenal H L 1–2
- 25 Oct Portsmouth A L 1–4
- 1 Nov Birmingham H W 2–0
- 8 Nov Leicester City A L 4–5
- 15 Nov Blackpool H D 0–0
- 22 Nov Sheffield United A L 1–3
- 29 Nov Sunderland H D 1–1
- 6 Dec Blackburn Rovers A L 1–4
- 13 Dec Derby County H W 2–1
- 20 Dec Leeds United A L 0–5
- 25 Dec Bolton Wanderers A L 1–3
- 26 Dec Bolton Wanderers H D 1–1
- 27 Dec Aston Villa A L 0–7
- 1 Jan Leeds United H D 0–0
- 3 Jan Chelsea H W 1–0
- 17 Jan Newcastle United A L 3–4
- 28 Jan Sheffield Wed. H W 4–1
- 31 Jan Grimsby Town A L 1–2
- 7 Feb Manchester City H L 1–3
- 14 Feb West Ham United H W 1–0
- 21 Feb Arsenal A L 1–4
- 7 Mar Birmingham A D 0–0
- 16 Mar Portsmouth H L 0–1
- 21 Mar Blackpool A L 1–5
- 25 Mar Leicester City H D 0–0
- 28 Mar Sheffield United H L 1–2
- 3 Apr Liverpool A D 1–1
- 4 Apr Sunderland A W 2–1
- 6 Apr Liverpool H W 4–1
- 11 Apr Blackburn Rovers H L 0–1
- 18 Apr Derby County A L 1–6
- 2 May Middlesbrough H D 4–4

FA Cup
- 10 Jan Stoke City A D 3–3
- 14 Jan Stoke City H D 0–0
- 19 Jan Stoke City A W 4–2
- 24 Jan Grimsby Town A L 0–1

Football League Division 1
P42 • W7 • D8 • L27 • F53 • A115 • PTS22
Position: 22

1931/32
Football League
- 29 Aug Bradford Park Ave. A L 1–3
- 2 Sep Southampton H L 2–3
- 5 Sep Swansea Town H W 2–1
- 7 Sep Stoke City A L 0–3
- 12 Sep Tottenham Hotspur H D 1–1
- 16 Sep Stoke City H D 1–1
- 19 Sep Nottingham Forest A L 1–2
- 26 Sep Chesterfield H W 3–1
- 3 Oct Burnley A L 0–2
- 10 Oct Preston North End H W 3–2
- 17 Oct Barnsley A D 0–0
- 24 Oct Notts County H D 3–3
- 31 Oct Plymouth Argyle A L 1–3
- 7 Nov Leeds United H L 2–5
- 14 Nov Oldham Athletic A W 5–1
- 21 Nov Bury H L 1–2
- 28 Nov Port Vale A W 2–1
- 5 Dec Millwall H W 2–0
- 12 Dec Bradford City A L 3–4
- 19 Dec Bristol City H L 0–1
- 25 Dec Wolverhampton Wan. H W 3–2
- 26 Dec Wolverhampton Wan. A L 0–7
- 2 Jan Bradford Park Ave. H L 0–2
- 16 Jan Swansea Town A L 1–3
- 23 Jan Tottenham Hotspur A L 1–4
- 30 Jan Nottingham Forest H W 3–2
- 6 Feb Chesterfield A W 3–1
- 17 Feb Burnley H W 5–1
- 20 Feb Preston North End A D 0–0
- 27 Feb Barnsley H W 3–0
- 5 Mar Notts County A W 2–1
- 12 Mar Plymouth Argyle H W 2–1
- 19 Mar Leeds United A W 4–1
- 25 Mar Charlton Athletic H L 0–2
- 26 Mar Oldham Athletic H W 5–1
- 28 Mar Charlton Athletic A L 0–1
- 2 Apr Bury A D 0–0
- 9 Apr Port Vale H W 2–0
- 16 Apr Millwall A D 1–1
- 23 Apr Bradford City H W 1–0
- 30 Apr Bristol City A L 1–2
- 7 May Southampton A D 1–1

FA Cup
- 9 Jan Plymouth Argyle A L 1–4

Football League Division 2
P42 • W17 • D8 • L17 • F71 • A72 • PTS42
Position: 12

1932/33
Football League
- 27 Aug Stoke City H L 0–2
- 29 Aug Charlton Athletic A W 1–0
- 3 Sep Southampton A L 2–4
- 7 Sep Charlton Athletic H D 1–1
- 10 Sep Tottenham Hotspur H L 1–6
- 17 Sep Grimsby Town H D 1–1
- 24 Sep Oldham Athletic A D 1–1
- 1 Oct Preston North End H D 0–0
- 8 Oct Burnley A W 3–2
- 15 Oct Bradford Park Ave. H W 2–1
- 22 Oct Millwall H W 7–1
- 29 Oct Port Vale A D 3–3
- 5 Nov Notts County H W 2–0
- 12 Nov Bury A D 2–2
- 19 Nov Fulham H W 4–3
- 26 Nov Chesterfield A D 1–1
- 3 Dec Bradford City H L 0–1
- 10 Dec West Ham United A L 1–3
- 17 Dec Lincoln City H W 4–1
- 24 Dec Swansea Town A L 1–2
- 26 Dec Plymouth Argyle A W 3–2
- 31 Dec Stoke City A D 0–0
- 2 Jan Plymouth Argyle H W 4–0
- 7 Jan Southampton H L 1–2
- 21 Jan Tottenham Hotspur A W 2–1
- 31 Jan Grimsby Town A D 1–1
- 4 Feb Oldham Athletic H W 2–0
- 11 Feb Preston North End A D 3–3
- 22 Feb Burnley H W 2–1
- 4 Mar Millwall A L 0–2
- 11 Mar Port Vale H D 1–1
- 18 Mar Notts County A L 0–1
- 25 Mar Bury H L 1–3
- 1 Apr Fulham A L 1–3
- 5 Apr Bradford Park Ave. A D 1–1
- 8 Apr Chesterfield H W 2–1
- 14 Apr Nottingham Forest A L 2–3
- 15 Apr Bradford City A W 2–1
- 17 Apr Nottingham Forest H W 2–1
- 22 Apr West Ham United H L 1–2
- 29 Apr Lincoln City A L 2–3
- 6 May Swansea Town H D 1–1

FA Cup
- 14 Jan Middlesbrough H L 1–4

Football League Division 2
P42 • W15 • D13 • L14 • F71 • A68 • PTS43
Position: 6

1933/34
Football League
- 26 Aug Plymouth Argyle A L 0–4
- 30 Aug Nottingham Forest H L 0–1
- 2 Sep Lincoln City H D 1–1
- 7 Sep Nottingham Forest A D 1–1
- 9 Sep Bolton Wanderers A L 1–5
- 16 Sep Brentford H L 3–4
- 23 Sep Burnley A W 5–2
- 30 Sep Oldham Athletic H L 0–2
- 7 Oct Preston North End A W 1–0
- 14 Oct Bradford Park Ave. H L 1–6
- 21 Oct Bury A L 1–2
- 28 Oct Hull City H W 4–1
- 4 Nov Fulham A W 2–0
- 11 Nov Southampton H W 1–0
- 18 Nov Blackpool A L 1–3
- 25 Nov Bradford City H W 2–1
- 2 Dec Port Vale A W 3–2
- 9 Dec Notts County H L 1–2
- 16 Dec Swansea Town A L 1–2
- 23 Dec Millwall H D 1–1
- 25 Dec Grimsby Town H L 1–3
- 26 Dec Grimsby Town A L 3–7
- 30 Dec Plymouth Argyle H L 0–3
- 6 Jan Lincoln City A L 1–5
- 20 Jan Bolton Wanderers H L 1–3
- 27 Jan Brentford A L 1–3
- 3 Feb Burnley A W 4–1
- 10 Feb Oldham Athletic H L 2–3
- 21 Feb Preston North End A L 2–3
- 24 Feb Bradford Park Ave. A L 0–4
- 3 Mar Bury H W 2–1
- 10 Mar Hull City A L 1–4
- 17 Mar Fulham H W 1–0
- 24 Mar Southampton A L 0–1
- 30 Mar West Ham United H L 0–1
- 31 Mar Blackpool H W 2–0
- 2 Apr West Ham United A L 1–2
- 7 Apr Bradford City A D 1–1
- 14 Apr Port Vale H W 2–0
- 21 Apr Notts County A D 0–0
- 28 Apr Swansea Town H D 1–1
- 5 May Millwall A W 2–0

FA Cup
- 13 Jan Portsmouth H D 1–1
- 17 Jan Portsmouth A L 1–4

Football League Division 2
P42 • W14 • D6 • L22 • F59 • A85 • PTS34
Position: 20

1934/35
Football League
- 25 Aug Bradford City H W 2–0
- 1 Sep Sheffield United A L 2–3
- 3 Sep Bolton Wanderers A L 1–3
- 8 Sep Barnsley H W 4–1
- 12 Sep Bolton Wanderers H L 0–3
- 15 Sep Port Vale A L 2–3
- 22 Sep Norwich City H W 5–0
- 29 Sep Swansea Town H W 3–1
- 6 Oct Burnley A W 2–1
- 13 Oct Oldham Athletic H W 4–0
- 20 Oct Newcastle United A W 1–0
- 27 Oct West Ham United H W 3–1
- 3 Nov Blackpool A W 2–1
- 10 Nov Bury H W 1–0
- 17 Nov Hull City A L 2–3
- 24 Nov Nottingham Forest H W 3–2
- 1 Dec Brentford A L 1–3
- 8 Dec Fulham H W 1–0
- 15 Dec Bradford Park Ave. A W 2–1
- 22 Dec Plymouth Argyle H W 3–1
- 25 Dec Notts County H W 2–1
- 26 Dec Notts County A L 0–1
- 29 Dec Bradford City A L 0–2
- 1 Jan Southampton H W 3–0
- 5 Jan Sheffield United H D 3–3
- 19 Jan Barnsley A W 2–0
- 2 Feb Norwich City A L 2–3
- 6 Feb Port Vale H W 2–1
- 9 Feb Swansea Town A L 0–1
- 23 Feb Oldham Athletic A L 1–3
- 2 Mar Newcastle United H L 0–1
- 9 Mar West Ham United A D 0–0
- 16 Mar Blackpool H W 3–2
- 23 Mar Bury A W 1–0
- 27 Mar Burnley H L 3–4
- 30 Mar Hull City H W 3–0
- 6 Apr Nottingham Forest A D 2–2
- 13 Apr Brentford H D 0–0
- 20 Apr Fulham A L 1–3
- 22 Apr Southampton A L 0–1
- 27 Apr Bradford Park Ave. H W 2–0
- 4 May Plymouth Argyle A W 2–0

FA Cup
- 12 Jan Bristol Rovers A W 3–1
- 26 Jan Nottingham Forest A D 0–0
- 30 Jan Nottingham Forest H L 0–3

Football League Division 2
P42 • W23 • D4 • L15 • F76 • A55 • PTS50
Position: 5

1935/36
Football League
- 31 Aug Plymouth Argyle A L 1–3
- 4 Sep Charlton Athletic H W 3–0
- 7 Sep Bradford City H W 3–1
- 9 Sep Charlton Athletic A D 0–0
- 14 Sep Newcastle United A W 2–0
- 18 Sep Hull City A W 2–0
- 21 Sep Tottenham Hotspur H D 0–0
- 28 Sep Southampton A L 1–2
- 5 Oct Port Vale A W 3–0
- 12 Oct Fulham H W 1–0
- 19 Oct Sheffield United H W 3–1
- 26 Oct Bradford Park Ave. A L 0–1
- 2 Nov Leicester City H L 0–1
- 9 Nov Swansea Town A L 1–2
- 16 Nov West Ham United H L 2–3
- 23 Nov Norwich City A W 5–3
- 30 Nov Doncaster Rovers H D 0–0
- 7 Dec Blackpool A L 1–4
- 14 Dec Nottingham Forest H W 5–0
- 26 Dec Barnsley H D 1–1
- 28 Dec Plymouth Argyle H W 3–2
- 1 Jan Barnsley A W 3–0
- 4 Jan Bradford City A L 0–1
- 18 Jan Newcastle United H W 3–1
- 1 Feb Southampton H W 4–0
- 5 Feb Tottenham Hotspur A D 0–0
- 8 Feb Port Vale A W 7–2
- 22 Feb Sheffield United A D 1–1
- 29 Feb Blackpool H W 3–2
- 7 Mar West Ham United A W 2–1
- 14 Mar Swansea Town H W 3–0
- 21 Mar Leicester City A D 1–1
- 28 Mar Norwich City H W 2–1
- 1 Apr Fulham A D 2–2
- 4 Apr Doncaster Rovers A D 0–0
- 10 Apr Burnley A D 2–2
- 11 Apr Bradford Park Ave. H W 4–0
- 13 Apr Burnley H W 4–0
- 18 Apr Nottingham Forest A D 1–1
- 25 Apr Bury H W 2–1
- 29 Apr Bury A W 3–2
- 2 May Hull City A D 1–1

FA Cup
- 11 Jan Reading A W 3–1
- 25 Jan Stoke City A D 0–0
- 29 Jan Stoke City H L 0–2

Football League Division 2
P42 • W22 • D12 • L8 • F85 • A43 • PTS56
Position: 1

1936/37
Football League
- 29 Aug Wolverhampton Wan. H D 1–1
- 2 Sep Huddersfield Town A L 1–3
- 5 Sep Derby County A L 4–5

9 Sep	Huddersfield Town	H W	3–1
12 Sep	Manchester City	H W	3–2
19 Sep	Sheffield Wed.	H D	1–1
26 Sep	Preston North End	A L	1–3
3 Oct	Arsenal	H W	2–0
10 Oct	Brentford	A L	0–4
17 Oct	Portsmouth	A L	1–2
24 Oct	Chelsea	H D	0–0
31 Oct	Stoke City	A L	0–3
7 Nov	Charlton Athletic	H D	0–0
14 Nov	Grimsby Town	A L	2–6
21 Nov	Liverpool	H L	2–5
28 Nov	Leeds United	A L	1–2
5 Dec	Birmingham	H L	1–2
12 Dec	Middlesbrough	A L	2–3
19 Dec	West Bromwich Alb.	H D	2–2
25 Dec	Bolton Wanderers	H W	1–0
26 Dec	Wolverhampton Wan.	A L	1–3
28 Dec	Bolton Wanderers	A W	4–0
1 Jan	Sunderland	H W	2–1
2 Jan	Derby County	H D	2–2
9 Jan	Manchester City	A L	0–1
23 Jan	Sheffield Wed.	A L	0–1
3 Feb	Preston North End	H D	1–1
6 Feb	Arsenal	A D	1–1
13 Feb	Brentford	H L	1–3
20 Feb	Portsmouth	H L	0–1
27 Feb	Chelsea	A L	2–4
6 Mar	Stoke City	H W	2–1
13 Mar	Charlton Athletic	A L	0–3
20 Mar	Grimsby Town	H D	1–1
26 Mar	Everton	H W	2–1
27 Mar	Liverpool	A L	0–2
29 Mar	Everton	A W	3–2
3 Apr	Leeds United	H D	0–0
10 Apr	Birmingham	A D	2–2
17 Apr	Middlesbrough	H W	2–1
21 Apr	Sunderland	A D	1–1
24 Apr	West Bromwich Alb.	A L	0–1

FA CUP

16 Jan	Reading	H W	1–0
30 Jan	Arsenal	A L	0–5

FOOTBALL LEAGUE DIVISION 1
P42 • W10 • D12 • L20 • F55 • A78 • PTS32
POSITION: 21

1937/38
FOOTBALL LEAGUE

28 Aug	Newcastle United	H W	3–0
30 Aug	Coventry City	A L	0–1
4 Sep	Luton Town	A L	0–1
8 Sep	Coventry City	H D	2–2
11 Sep	Barnsley	H W	4–1
13 Sep	Bury	A W	2–1
18 Sep	Stockport County	A L	0–1
25 Sep	Southampton	H L	1–2
2 Oct	Sheffield United	H L	0–1
9 Oct	Tottenham Hotspur	A W	1–0
16 Oct	Blackburn Rovers	A D	1–1
23 Oct	Sheffield Wed.	H W	1–0
30 Oct	Fulham	A L	0–1
6 Nov	Plymouth Argyle	H D	0–0
13 Nov	Chesterfield	A W	7–1
20 Nov	Aston Villa	H W	3–1
27 Nov	Norwich City	A W	3–2
4 Dec	Swansea Town	H W	5–1
11 Dec	Bradford Park Ave.	A L	0–4
27 Dec	Nottingham Forest	H W	4–3
28 Dec	Nottingham Forest	A W	3–2
1 Jan	Newcastle United	A D	2–2
15 Jan	Luton Town	H W	4–2
29 Jan	Stockport County	H W	3–1
2 Feb	Barnsley	A D	2–2
5 Feb	Southampton	A D	3–3
17 Feb	Sheffield United	A W	2–1
19 Feb	Tottenham Hotspur	H L	0–1
23 Feb	West Ham United	H W	4–0
26 Feb	Blackburn Rovers	H W	2–1
5 Mar	Sheffield Wed.	A W	3–1
12 Mar	Fulham	H W	1–0
19 Mar	Plymouth Argyle	A D	1–1
26 Mar	Chesterfield	H W	4–1
2 Apr	Aston Villa	A L	0–3
9 Apr	Norwich City	H D	0–0
15 Apr	Burnley	A L	0–1
16 Apr	Swansea Town	A D	2–2
18 Apr	Burnley	H W	4–0
23 Apr	Bradford Park Ave.	H W	3–1
30 Apr	West Ham United	A L	0–1
7 May	Bury	H W	2–0

FA CUP

8 Jan	Yeovil Town	H W	3–0
22 Jan	Barnsley	A D	2–2
26 Jan	Barnsley	H W	1–0
12 Feb	Brentford	A L	0–2

FOOTBALL LEAGUE DIVISION 2
P42 • W22 • D9 • L11 • F82 • A50 • PTS53
POSITION: 2

1938/39
FOOTBALL LEAGUE

27 Aug	Middlesbrough	A L	1–3
31 Aug	Bolton Wanderers	H D	2–2
3 Sep	Birmingham	H W	4–1
7 Sep	Liverpool	A L	0–1
10 Sep	Grimsby Town	A L	0–1
17 Sep	Stoke City	A D	1–1
24 Sep	Chelsea	H W	5–1
1 Oct	Preston North End	A D	1–1
8 Oct	Charlton Athletic	H L	0–2
15 Oct	Blackpool	H D	0–0
22 Oct	Derby County	A L	1–5
29 Oct	Sunderland	H L	0–1
5 Nov	Aston Villa	A W	2–0
12 Nov	Wolverhampton Wan.	H L	1–3
19 Nov	Everton	A L	0–3
26 Nov	Huddersfield Town	H D	1–1
3 Dec	Portsmouth	A D	0–0
10 Dec	Arsenal	H W	1–0
17 Dec	Brentford	A W	5–2
24 Dec	Middlesbrough	H D	1–1
26 Dec	Leicester City	H W	3–0
27 Dec	Leicester City	A D	1–1
31 Dec	Birmingham	A D	3–3
14 Jan	Grimsby Town	H W	3–1
21 Jan	Stoke City	H L	0–1
28 Jan	Chelsea	A W	1–0
4 Feb	Preston North End	H D	1–1
11 Feb	Charlton Athletic	A L	1–7
18 Feb	Blackpool	A W	5–3
25 Feb	Derby County	H D	1–1
4 Mar	Sunderland	A L	2–5
11 Mar	Aston Villa	H D	1–1
18 Mar	Wolverhampton Wan.	A L	0–3
29 Mar	Everton	H L	0–2
1 Apr	Huddersfield Town	A D	1–1
7 Apr	Leeds United	H D	0–0
8 Apr	Portsmouth	H D	1–1
10 Apr	Leeds United	A L	1–3
15 Apr	Arsenal	A L	1–2
22 Apr	Brentford	H W	3–0
29 Apr	Bolton Wanderers	A D	0–0
6 May	Liverpool	H W	2–0

FA CUP

7 Jan	West Bromwich Alb.	A D	0–0
11 Jan	West Bromwich Alb.	H L	1–5

FOOTBALL LEAGUE DIVISION 1
P42 • W11 • D16 • L15 • F57 • A65 • PTS38
POSITION: 14

The 1940s

1939/40
FOOTBALL LEAGUE DIVISION ONE

26 Aug	Grimsby T	H W	4–0
30 Aug	Chelsea	A D	1–1
2 Sep	Charlton Ath.	A L	0–2

COMPETITION CANCELLED
BECAUSE OF WAR

WAR LEAGUE
WESTERN DIVISION

21 Oct	Manchester City	H L	0–4
28 Oct	Chester	A W	4–0
11 Nov	Crewe Alex.	H W	5–1
18 Nov	Liverpool	A L	0–1
25 Nov	Port Vale	H W	8–1
2 Dec	Tranmere Rovers	A W	4–2
9 Dec	Stockport County	A W	7–4
23 Dec	Wrexham	H W	5–1
6 Jan	Everton	A L	2–3
20 Jan	Stoke City	H W	4–3
10 Feb	Manchester City	A L	0–1
24 Feb	Chester	H W	5–1
9 Mar	Crewe Alex.	A W	4–1
16 Mar	Liverpool	H W	1–0
23 Mar	Port Vale	A W	3–1
30 Mar	Tranmere Rovers	H W	6–1
6 Apr	Stockport County	H W	6–1
6 May	New Brighton	H W	6–0
13 May	Wrexham	A L	2–3
18 May	New Brighton	A L	0–6
25 May	Stoke City	A L	2–3
1 Jun	Everton	H L	0–3

P22 • W14 • D0 • L8 • F74 • A41 • PTS28
POSITION: 4

LEAGUE WAR CUP

20 Apr	Manchester City	H L	0–1
27 Apr	Manchester City	A W	2–0
4 May	Blackburn Rovers	A W	2–1
11 May	Blackburn Rovers	H L	1–3

1940/41
NORTH
REGIONAL LEAGUE

31 Aug	Rochdale	A W	3–1
7 Sep	Bury	H D	0–0
14 Sep	Oldham Athletic	A L	1–2
21 Sep	Oldham Athletic	H L	2–3
28 Sep	Manchester City	A L	1–4
5 Oct	Manchester City	H L	0–2
12 Oct	Burnley	A W	1–0
19 Oct	Preston North End	H W	4–1
26 Oct	Preston North End	A L	1–3
2 Nov	Burnley	H W	4–1
9 Nov	Everton	A L	2–5
16 Nov	Everton	H D	0–0
23 Nov	Liverpool	A D	2–2
30 Nov	Liverpool	H W	2–0
7 Dec	Blackburn Rovers	A D	5–5
14 Dec	Rochdale	H L	3–4
21 Dec	Bury	A L	1–4
25 Dec	Stockport County	A W	3–1
28 Dec	Blackburn Rovers	H W	9–0
4 Jan	Blackburn Rovers	A W	2–0
11 Jan	Blackburn Rovers	H D	0–0
18 Jan	Bolton Wanderers	A L	2–3
25 Jan	Bolton Wanderers	H W	4–1
1 Mar	Chesterfield	A D	1–1
8 Mar	Bury	H W	7–3
22 Mar	Oldham Athletic	A W	1–0
29 Mar	Blackpool	A L	0–2
5 Apr	Blackpool	H L	2–3
12 Apr	Everton	A W	2–1
14 Apr	Manchester City	A W	7–1
19 Apr	Chester	A W	6–4
26 Apr	Liverpool	A L	1–2
3 May	Liverpool	H D	1–1
10 May	Bury	A L	1–5
17 May	Burnley	H W	1–0

P35 • W15 • D7 • L13 • F82 • A65
POSITION: 7

LEAGUE WAR CUP

15 Feb	Everton	H D	2–2
22 Feb	Everton	A L	1–2

1941/42
FOOTBALL LEAGUE
NORTHERN SECTION
FIRST CHAMPIONSHIP

30 Aug	New Brighton	H W	13–1
6 Sep	New Brighton	A D	3–3
13 Sep	Stockport County	A W	5–1
20 Sep	Stockport County	H W	7–1
27 Sep	Everton	H L	2–3
4 Oct	Everton	A W	3–1
11 Oct	Chester	A W	7–0
18 Oct	Chester	H W	8–1
25 Oct	Stoke City	A D	1–1
1 Nov	Stoke City	H W	3–0
8 Nov	Tranmere Rovers	H W	6–1
15 Nov	Tranmere Rovers	A D	1–1
22 Nov	Liverpool	A D	1–1
29 Nov	Liverpool	H D	2–2
6 Dec	Wrexham	H W	10–3
13 Dec	Wrexham	A W	4–3
20 Dec	Manchester City	A L	1–2
25 Dec	Manchester City	H D	2–2

P18 • W10 • D6 • L2 • F79 • A27 • PTS26
POSITION: 4

FOOTBALL LEAGUE
NORTHERN SECTION
SECOND CHAMPIONSHIP

27 Dec	Bolton Wanderers	H W	3–1
3 Jan	Bolton Wanderers	A D	2–2
10 Jan	Oldham Athletic	H D	1–1
17 Jan	Oldham Athletic	A W	3–1
31 Jan	Southport	A W	3–1
14 Feb	Sheffield United	A W	2–0
21 Feb	Preston North End	H L	0–2
28 Feb	Preston North End	A W	3–1
21 Mar	Sheffield United	H D	2–2
28 Mar	Southport	H W	4–2
4 Apr	Blackburn Rovers	A W	2–1
6 Apr	Blackburn Rovers	H W	3–1
11 Apr	Wolves	H W	5–4
18 Apr	Wolves	A L	0–2
25 Apr	Oldham Athletic	H W	5–1
2 May	Oldham Athletic	A W	2–1
9 May	Blackburn Rovers	A D	1–1
16 May	Blackburn Rovers	H L	0–1
23 May	Manchester City	A W	3–1

P19 • W12 • D4 • L3 • F44 • A25 • PTS28
POSITION: 1

1942/43
FOOTBALL LEAGUE NORTHERN
SECTION FIRST CHAMPIONSHIP

29 Aug	Everton	A D	2–2
5 Sep	Everton	H W	2–1
12 Sep	Chester	H L	0–2
19 Sep	Chester	A D	2–2
26 Sep	Blackburn Rovers	A L	2–4
3 Oct	Blackburn Rovers	H W	5–2
10 Oct	Liverpool	H L	3–4
17 Oct	Liverpool	A L	1–2
24 Oct	Stockport County	A W	4–1
31 Oct	Stockport County	H W	3–1
7 Nov	Manchester City	H W	2–1
14 Nov	Manchester City	A W	5–0
21 Nov	Tranmere Rovers	A W	5–0
28 Nov	Tranmere Rovers	H W	5–1
5 Dec	Wrexham	H W	6–1
12 Dec	Wrexham	A W	5–2
19 Dec	Bolton Wanderers	A W	2–0
25 Dec	Bolton Wanderers	H W	4–0

P18 • W12 • D2 • L4 • F58 • A26 • PTS26
POSITION: 4

FOOTBALL LEAGUE NORTHERN
SECTION SECOND CHAMPIONSHIP

26 Dec	Chester	H W	3–0
2 Jan	Chester	A L	1–4
9 Jan	Blackpool	A D	1–1
16 Jan	Blackpool	H W	5–3
23 Jan	Everton	H L	1–4
30 Jan	Everton	A W	5–0
6 Feb	Manchester City	A D	0–0
13 Feb	Manchester City	H D	1–1
20 Feb	Crewe Alexandra	H W	7–0
27 Feb	Crewe Alexandra	A W	3–2
6 Mar	Manchester City	H L	0–1
13 Mar	Manchester City	A L	0–2
20 Mar	Bury	H W	4–1
27 Mar	Bury	A W	5–3
3 Apr	Crewe Alexandra	H W	4–1
10 Apr	Crewe Alexandra	A W	6–0
17 Apr	Oldham Athletic	H W	3–0
24 Apr	Oldham Athletic	A L	1–3
1 May	Sheffield United	H W	2–0
8 May	Liverpool	A W	3–1
15 May	Liverpool	H D	3–3

P19 • W11 • D3 • L5 • F52 • A26 • PTS25
POSITION: 6

1943/44
FOOTBALL LEAGUE NORTHERN
SECTION FIRST CHAMPIONSHIP

28 Aug	Stockport County	H W	6–0
4 Sep	Stockport County	A D	3–3
11 Sep	Everton	H W	4–1
18 Sep	Everton	A L	1–6
25 Sep	Blackburn Rovers	H W	2–1
2 Oct	Blackburn Rovers	A L	1–2
9 Oct	Chester	H W	3–1
16 Oct	Chester	A L	4–5
23 Oct	Liverpool	A W	4–3
30 Oct	Liverpool	H W	1–0
6 Nov	Manchester City	A D	2–2
13 Nov	Manchester City	H W	3–0
20 Nov	Tranmere Rovers	H W	6–3
27 Nov	Tranmere Rovers	A W	1–0
4 Dec	Wrexham	A W	4–1
11 Dec	Wrexham	H W	5–0
18 Dec	Bolton Wanderers	H W	3–1
25 Dec	Bolton Wanderers	A W	3–1

P18 • W13 • D2 • L3 • F56 • A30 • PTS28
POSITION: 2

FOOTBALL LEAGUE NORTHERN
SECTION SECOND CHAMPIONSHIP

27 Dec	Halifax Town	H W	6–2
1 Jan	Halifax Town	A D	1–1
8 Jan	Stockport County	A W	3–2
15 Jan	Stockport County	H W	4–2
22 Jan	Manchester City	H L	1–3
29 Jan	Manchester City	A W	3–2
5 Feb	Bury	A W	3–0
12 Feb	Bury	H D	3–3
19 Feb	Oldham Athletic	H W	3–2
26 Feb	Oldham Athletic	A D	1–1
4 Mar	Wrexham	A W	4–1
11 Mar	Wrexham	H D	2–2
18 Mar	Birmingham	A L	1–3
25 Mar	Birmingham	H D	1–1
1 Apr	Bolton Wanderers	A L	0–3
8 Apr	Bolton Wanderers	H W	3–2
10 Apr	Manchester City	A L	1–4
15 Apr	Burnley	H W	9–0
22 Apr	Burnley	A D	3–3
29 Apr	Oldham Athletic	H D	0–0
6 May	Oldham Athletic	A W	3–1

P21 • W10 • D7 • L4 • F55 • A38 • PTS27
POSITION: 9

1944/45
FOOTBALL LEAGUE NORTH
FIRST CHAMPIONSHIP

26 Aug	Everton	A W	2–1
2 Sep	Everton	H L	1–3
9 Sep	Stockport County	H L	3–4
16 Sep	Stockport County	A D	4–4
23 Sep	Bury	H D	2–2
30 Sep	Bury	A L	2–4
7 Oct	Chester	A L	0–2
14 Oct	Chester	H W	1–0
21 Oct	Tranmere Rovers	H W	6–1
28 Oct	Tranmere Rovers	A W	4–2
4 Nov	Liverpool	A L	2–3
11 Nov	Liverpool	H L	2–5
18 Nov	Manchester City	H W	3–2
25 Nov	Manchester City	A L	0–4
2 Dec	Crewe Alexandra	A W	4–1
9 Dec	Crewe Alexandra	H W	2–0
16 Dec	Wrexham	H W	1–0
23 Dec	Wrexham	A L	1–2

P18 • W8 • D2 • L8 • F40 • A40 • PTS18
POSITION: 30

FOOTBALL LEAGUE
NORTH SECOND
CHAMPIONSHIP

26 Dec	Sheffield United	A W	4–3
30 Dec	Oldham Athletic	A W	4–3
6 Jan	Huddersfield Town	H W	1–0
13 Jan	Huddersfield Town	A D	2–2
3 Feb	Manchester City	H L	1–3
10 Feb	Manchester City	A L	0–2
17 Feb	Bury	H W	2–0
24 Feb	Bury	A L	1–3
3 Mar	Oldham Athletic	H W	3–2
10 Mar	Halifax Town	A L	0–1
17 Mar	Halifax Town	H W	2–0
24 Mar	Burnley	A W	3–2
31 Mar	Burnley	H W	4–0
2 Apr	Blackpool	A L	1–4
7 Apr	Stoke City	H W	6–1
14 Apr	Stoke City	A W	4–1
21 Apr	Doncaster Rovers	A W	2–1
28 Apr	Doncaster Rovers	H W	3–1
5 May	Chesterfield	H D	1–1
12 May	Chesterfield	A W	1–0
19 May	Bolton Wanderers	A L	0–1
26 May	Bolton Wanderers	H D	2–2

P22 • W13 • D3 • L6 • F47 • A33 • PTS29
POSITION: 9

1945/46
FOOTBALL LEAGUE
NORTH

25 Aug	Huddersfield Town	A L	2–3
1 Sep	Huddersfield Town	H L	2–3
8 Sep	Chesterfield	H L	0–2
12 Sep	Middlesbrough	A L	1–2
15 Sep	Chesterfield	A D	1–1
20 Sep	Stoke City	A W	2–1
22 Sep	Barnsley	A D	2–2
29 Sep	Barnsley	H D	1–1
6 Oct	Everton	H D	0–0
13 Oct	Everton	A L	0–3
20 Oct	Bolton Wanderers	A D	1–1
27 Oct	Bolton Wanderers	H W	2–1
3 Nov	Preston North End	H W	6–1
10 Nov	Preston North End	A D	2–2
17 Nov	Leeds United	A D	3–3
24 Nov	Leeds United	H W	6–1
1 Dec	Burnley	H D	3–3
8 Dec	Burnley	A D	2–2
15 Dec	Sunderland	H W	2–1
22 Dec	Sunderland	A L	2–4
25 Dec	Sheffield United	A L	0–1
26 Dec	Sheffield United	H L	2–3
29 Dec	Middlesbrough	H W	4–1
12 Jan	Grimsby Town	H W	5–0
19 Jan	Grimsby Town	A L	0–1
2 Feb	Blackpool	H W	4–2
9 Feb	Liverpool	H W	2–1
16 Feb	Liverpool	A W	5–0
23 Feb	Bury	A D	1–1
2 Mar	Bury	H D	1–1
9 Mar	Blackburn Rovers	H W	0–2
16 Mar	Blackburn Rovers	A W	3–1
23 Mar	Bradford	A L	1–2
27 Mar	Blackpool	A W	5–1
30 Mar	Bradford	H W	4–0
6 Apr	Manchester City	H L	1–4
13 Apr	Manchester City	A W	3–1
19 Apr	Newcastle United	A W	1–0
20 Apr	Sheffield Wed.	H W	4–0
22 Apr	Newcastle United	H W	4–1
27 Apr	Sheffield Wed.	A L	0–1
4 May	Stoke City	H W	2–1

P42 • W19 • D11 • L12 • F98 • A62 • PTS49
POSITION: 4

FA CUP

5 Jan	Accrington Stanley	A D	2–2
9 Jan	Accrington Stanley	H W	5–1
26 Jan	Preston North End	H W	1–0
30 Jan	Preston North End	A L	1–3

1946/47
FOOTBALL LEAGUE

SUBSTITUTIONS: NOT INTRODUCED UNTIL 1965/66

Date	Opponent	Attendances	Venue			Players and Scores											Substitutions
31 Aug	Grimsby Town	41,025	Maine Road	H W	2–1	Crompton	Carey	McGlen	Warner J	Chilton	Cockburn	Delaney	Pearson SC	Hanlon	Rowley J 1	Mitten 1	
4 Sep	Chelsea	27,750	Stamford Bridge	A W	3–0	Crompton	Carey	McGlen	Warner J	Chilton	Cockburn	Delaney	Pearson SC 1	Hanlon	Rowley J 1	Mitten 1	
7 Sep	Charlton Athletic	44,088	The Valley	A W	•3–1	Crompton	Carey	McGlen	Warner J	Chilton	Cockburn	Delaney	Pearson SC	Hanlon 1	Rowley J 1	Mitten	
11 Sep	Liverpool	41,657	Maine Road	H W	5–0	Crompton	Carey	McGlen	Warner J	Chilton	Cockburn	Delaney	Pearson SC 3	Hanlon	Rowley J 1	Mitten 1	
14 Sep	Middlesbrough	65,112	Maine Road	H W	1–0	Crompton	Carey	McGlen	Warner J	Chilton	Cockburn	Delaney	Pearson SC	Hanlon	Rowley J 1	Mitten	
18 Sep	Chelsea	30,275	Maine Road	H D	1–1	Crompton	Carey	Chilton 1	Warner J	Whalley H	Cockburn	Delaney	Aston (Snr.)	Hanlon	Pearson SC	Mitten	
21 Sep	Stoke City	41,699	Victoria Ground	A L	2–3	Crompton	Carey	McGlen	Warner J	Chilton	Cockburn	Delaney 1	Pearson SC	Hanlon 1	Rowley J	Mitten	
28 Sep	Arsenal	62,718	Maine Road	H W	5–2	Crompton	Walton JW	McGlen	Warner J	Chilton	Aston (Snr.)	Delaney	Pearson SC	Hanlon 2	Rowley J 2	Wrigglesworth 1	
5 Oct	Preston North End	55,395	Maine Road	H D	1–1	Crompton	Carey	McGlen	Warner J	Chilton	Cockburn	Delaney	Pearson SC	Hanlon	Rowley J	Wrigglesworth 1	
12 Oct	Sheffield United	35,543	Bramall Lane	A D	2–2	Crompton	Walton JW	McGlen	Warner J	Chilton	Carey	Delaney	Pearson SC	Hanlon	Rowley J 2	Wrigglesworth	
19 Oct	Blackpool	26,307	Bloomfield Road	A L	1–3	Crompton	Walton JW	McGlen	Carey	Chilton	Cockburn	Delaney 1	Pearson SC	Hanlon	Rowley J	Wrigglesworth	
26 Oct	Sunderland	48,385	Maine Road	H L	0–3	Crompton	Walton JW	McGlen	Warner J	Chilton	Cockburn	Delaney	Morris	Burke R	Pearson SC	Rowley J	
2 Nov	Aston Villa	53,668	Villa Park	A D	0–0	Collinson C	Walton JW	McGlen	Warner J	Chilton	Cockburn	Delaney	Morris	Rowley J	Pearson SC	Mitten	
9 Nov	Derby County	57,340	Maine Road	H W	4–1	Collinson C	Walton JW	McGlen	Warner J	Chilton	Cockburn	Delaney	Morris	Rowley J 1	Pearson SC 2	Mitten 1	
16 Nov	Everton	45,832	Goodison Park	A D	2–2	Collinson C	Walton JW	McGlen	Warner J	Chilton	Cockburn	Delaney	Morris	Rowley J 1	Pearson SC 1	Mitten	
23 Nov	Huddersfield Town	39,216	Maine Road	H W	5–2	Collinson C	Walton JW	McGlen	Carey	Chilton	Cockburn	Delaney	Morris 2	Rowley J 1	Pearson SC	Mitten 2	
30 Nov	Wolverhampton Wan.	46,704	Molineux	A L	2–3	Collinson C	Worrall	McGlen	Carey	Chilton	Cockburn	Delaney 1	Morris	Hanlon 1	Pearson SC	Mitten	
7 Dec	Brentford	31,962	Maine Road	H W	4–1	Collinson C	Carey	McGlen	Warner J	Chilton	Cockburn	Hanlon	Morris	Rowley J 3	Pearson SC	Mitten 1	
14 Dec	Blackburn Rovers	21,455	Ewood Park	A L	1–2	Collinson C	Carey	McGlen	Warner J	Chilton	Cockburn	Hanlon	Morris 1	Rowley J	Pearson SC	Mitten	
25 Dec	Bolton Wanderers	28,505	Burnden Park	A D	2–2	Crompton	Carey	McGlen	Warner J	Chilton	Cockburn	Delaney	Morris	Rowley J 2	Pearson SC	Mitten	
26 Dec	Bolton Wanderers	57,186	Maine Road	H W	1–0	Crompton	Carey	McGlen	Warner J	Chilton	Cockburn	Delaney	Morris	Rowley J	Pearson SC 1	Mitten	
28 Dec	Grimsby Town	17,183	Blundell Park	A D	0–0	Crompton	Whalley H	Aston (Snr.)	Warner J	Chilton	Cockburn	Delaney	Morris	Rowley J	Pearson SC	Mitten	
4 Jan	Charlton Athletic	43,406	Maine Road	H W	4–1	Crompton	Aston (Snr.)	McGlen	Warner J	Chilton	Cockburn	Delaney	Morris	Burke R 2	Pearson SC 1	Buckle 1	
18 Jan	Middlesbrough	37,435	Ayresome Park	A W	4–2	Crompton	Aston (Snr.)	McGlen	Warner J	Chilton	Carey	Delaney	Morris 1	Rowley J	Pearson SC 2	Buckle 1	
1 Feb	Arsenal	29,415	Highbury	A L	2–6	Fielding	Aston (Snr.)	McGlen	Warner J	Chilton	Cockburn	Delaney	Morris 1	Hanlon	Pearson SC 1	Buckle	
5 Feb	Stoke City	8,456	Maine Road	H D	1–1	Fielding	Aston (Snr.)	Walton JW	Warner J	Chilton	Cockburn	Delaney	Morris	Hanlon	Pearson SC	Buckle 1	
22 Feb	Blackpool	29,993	Maine Road	H W	3–0	Fielding	Aston (Snr.)	Walton JW	Warner J	Chilton	Carey	Delaney	Morris	Hanlon 1	Pearson SC	Rowley J 2	
1 Mar	Sunderland	25,038	Roker Park	A D	1–1	Fielding	Aston (Snr.)	Walton JW	Warner J	Chilton	Cockburn	Delaney 1	Morris	Hanlon	Pearson SC	Rowley J	
8 Mar	Aston Villa	36,965	Maine Road	H W	2–1	Fielding	Aston (Snr.)	Walton JW	Warner J	Chilton	Carey	Delaney	Morris	Burke R 1	Pearson SC 1	Rowley J	
15 Mar	Derby County	19,579	Baseball Ground	A L	3–4	Fielding	Walton JW	McGlen	Warner J	Chilton	Carey	Delaney	Morris	Burke R 2	Pearson SC 1	Rowley J	
22 Mar	Everton	43,441	Maine Road	H W	3–0	Crompton	Carey	McGlen	Warner J 1	Chilton	Cockburn	Delaney 1	Morris	Burke R 1	Pearson SC	Rowley J	
29 Mar	Huddersfield Town	18,509	Leeds Road	A D	2–2	Crompton	Carey	Aston (Snr.)	Cockburn	Chilton	McGlen	Delaney 1	Hanlon	Burke R	Pearson SC 1	Rowley J	
5 Apr	Wolverhampton Wan.	66,967	Maine Road	H W	3–1	Crompton	Carey	Aston (Snr.)	Cockburn	Chilton	McGlen	Delaney	Hanlon 1	Burke R	Pearson SC	Rowley J 2	
7 Apr	Leeds United	41,772	Maine Road	H W	3–1	Crompton	Carey	Aston (Snr.)	Cockburn	Chilton	McGlen	Delaney 1	Hanlon	Burke R 2	Pearson SC	Rowley J	
8 Apr	Leeds United	15,528	Elland Road	A W	2–0	Crompton	Carey	Aston (Snr.)	Cockburn	Chilton	McGlen 1	Delaney	Hanlon	Burke R 1	Pearson SC	Rowley J	
12 Apr	Brentford	21,714	Griffin Park	A D	0–0	Crompton	Carey	Aston (Snr.)	Warner J	Chilton	Cockburn	Rowley J	Hanlon	Burke R	Pearson SC	Mitten	
19 Apr	Blackburn Rovers	46,196	Maine Road	H W	•4–0	Crompton	Carey	Aston (Snr.)	Warner J	Whalley H	Cockburn	Delaney	Morris	Hanlon	Pearson SC 2	Rowley J 1	
26 Apr	Portsmouth	30,623	Fratton Park	A W	1–0	Crompton	Carey	Aston (Snr.)	Cockburn	Chilton	McGlen	Delaney 1	Hanlon	Burke R	Pearson SC	Rowley J	
3 May	Liverpool	48,800	Anfield	A L	0–1	Crompton	Carey	Aston (Snr.)	Warner J	Chilton	McGlen	Delaney	Hanlon	Burke R	Pearson SC	Rowley J	
10 May	Preston North End	23,278	Deepdale	A D	1–1	Crompton	Walton JW	Aston (Snr.)	Warner J	Chilton	McGlen	Delaney	Morris	Burke R	Pearson SC 1	Rowley J	
17 May	Portsmouth	37,614	Maine Road	H W	3–0	Crompton	Walton JW	Aston (Snr.)	Warner J	Chilton	Carey	Buckle	Morris 1	Rowley J 1	Pearson SC	Mitten 1	
26 May	Sheffield United	34,059	Maine Road	H W	6–2	Crompton	Carey	Aston (Snr.)	Warner J	Chilton	McGlen	Hanlon	Morris 2	Rowley J 3	Pearson SC 1	Mitten	

FA CUP

11 Jan	Bradford Park Ave.	26,990	Park Avenue	A W	3–0	Crompton	Aston (Snr.)	McGlen	Warner J	Chilton	Carey	Delaney	Morris	Rowley J 2	Pearson SC	Buckle 1	
25 Jan	Nottingham Forest	58,641	Maine Road	H L	0–2	Fielding	Aston (Snr.)	McGlen	Warner J	Chilton	Carey	Delaney	Morris	Rowley J	Pearson SC	Buckle	

FOOTBALL LEAGUE DIVISION 1
P42 • W22 • D12 • L 8 • F95 • A54 • PTS56
POSITION: 2

1947/48

Football League		Attendances	Venue				Players and Scores											Substitutions: not introduced until 1965/66
23 Aug	Middlesbrough	39,554	Ayresome Park	A	D	2–2	Crompton	Carey	Aston (Snr.)	Warner J	Chilton	McGlen	Delaney	Morris	Rowley J 2	Pearson SC	Mitten	
27 Aug	Liverpool	52,385	Maine Road	H	W	2–0	Crompton	Carey	Aston (Snr.)	Warner J	Chilton	McGlen	Delaney	Morris 1	Rowley J	Pearson SC 1	Mitten	
30 Aug	Charlton Athletic	52,659	Maine Road	H	W	6–2	Crompton	Carey	Aston (Snr.)	Warner J	Chilton	McGlen	Delaney	Morris 1	Rowley J 4	Pearson SC 1	Mitten	
3 Sep	Liverpool	48,081	Anfield	A	D	2–2	Crompton	Carey	Aston (Snr.)	Warner J	Chilton	McGlen	Delaney	Morris	Rowley J	Pearson SC 1	Mitten 1	
6 Sep	Arsenal	64,905	Highbury	A	L	1–2	Crompton	Carey	Aston (Snr.)	Warner J	Chilton	McGlen	Delaney	Morris 1	Rowley J	Pearson SC	Mitten	
8 Sep	Burnley	37,517	Turf Moor	A	D	0–0	Crompton	Carey	Aston (Snr.)	Warner J	Chilton	McGlen	Delaney	Morris	Rowley J	Pearson SC	Mitten	
13 Sep	Sheffield United	49,808	Maine Road	H	L	0–1	Crompton	Carey	Aston (Snr.)	Warner J	Chilton	McGlen	Delaney	Morris	Burke R	Pearson SC	Rowley J	
20 Sep	Manchester City	71,364	Maine Road	A	D	0–0	Crompton	Carey	Aston (Snr.)	Warner J	Chilton	McGlen	Delaney	Morris	Rowley J	Pearson SC	Mitten	
27 Sep	Preston North End	34,372	Deepdale	A	L	1–2	Crompton	Aston (Snr.)	McGlen	Warner J	Chilton	Cockburn	Dale J	Morris 1	Hanlon	Pearson SC	Rowley J	
4 Oct	Stoke City	45,745	Maine Road	H	D	1–1	Crompton	Aston (Snr.)	McGlen	Warner J	Chilton	Cockburn	Dale J	Morris	Hanlon 1	Pearson SC	Rowley J	
11 Oct	Grimsby Town	40,035	Maine Road	H	L	3–4	Crompton	Aston (Snr.)	McGlen	Warner J	Chilton	Pearson SC	Delaney	Morris 1	Hanlon	Rowley J 1	Mitten 1	
18 Oct	Sunderland	37,148	Roker Park	A	L	0–1	Crompton	Walton JW	Aston (Snr.)	Carey	Chilton	McGlen	Delaney	Pearson SC	Hanlon	Rowley J	Mitten	
25 Oct	Aston Villa	47,078	Maine Road	H	W	2–0	Crompton	Aston (Snr.)	Worrall	Carey	Chilton	Cockburn	Delaney 1	Morris	Rowley J 1	Pearson SC	Mitten	
1 Nov	Wolverhampton Wan.	44,309	Molineux	A	W	6–2	Crompton	Aston (Snr.)	Worrall	Carey	Chilton	Cockburn	Delaney 1	Morris 2	Rowley J	Pearson SC 2	Mitten 1	
8 Nov	Huddersfield Town	59,772	Maine Road	H	D	4–4	Crompton	Aston (Snr.)	Worrall	Carey	Chilton	Cockburn	Delaney	Morris	Rowley J 4	Pearson SC	Mitten	
15 Nov	Derby County	32,990	Baseball Ground	A	D	1–1	Pegg J	Aston (Snr.)	Worrall	Carey 1	Chilton	Cockburn	Delaney	Morris	Rowley J	Pearson SC	Mitten	
22 Nov	Everton	35,509	Maine Road	H	D	2–2	Pegg J	Aston (Snr.)	Worrall	Carey	Chilton	Cockburn 1	Delaney	Morris 1	Rowley J	Pearson SC	Mitten	
29 Nov	Chelsea	43,617	Stamford Bridge	A	W	4–0	Crompton	Aston (Snr.)	Walton JW	Carey	Chilton	Cockburn	Delaney	Morris 3	Rowley J 1	Pearson SC	Mitten	
6 Dec	Blackpool	63,683	Maine Road	H	D	1–1	Crompton	Walton JW	Aston (Snr.)	Carey	Chilton	Cockburn	Delaney	Morris	Rowley J	Pearson SC 1	Mitten	
13 Dec	Blackburn Rovers	22,784	Ewood Park	A	D	1–1	Crompton	Walton JW	Aston (Snr.)	Carey	Chilton	Cockburn	Delaney	Morris 1	Rowley J	Pearson SC	Mitten	
20 Dec	Middlesbrough	46,666	Maine Road	H	W	2–1	Crompton	Walton JW	Aston (Snr.)	Anderson J	Chilton	Cockburn	Delaney	Morris	Rowley J	Pearson SC 2	Mitten	
25 Dec	Portsmouth	42,776	Maine Road	H	W	3–2	Crompton	Walton JW	Aston (Snr.)	Carey	Chilton	Cockburn	Delaney	Morris 2	Rowley J 1	Pearson SC	Mitten	
27 Dec	Portsmouth	27,674	Fratton Park	A	W	3–1	Crompton	Carey	Aston (Snr.)	Anderson J	Chilton	Cockburn	Delaney 1	Morris 2	Rowley J	Pearson SC	Mitten	
1 Jan	Burnley	59,838	Maine Road	H	W	5–0	Crompton	Carey	Aston (Snr.)	Anderson J	Chilton	Cockburn	Delaney	Morris	Rowley J 3	Pearson SC	Mitten 2	
3 Jan	Charlton Athletic	40,484	The Valley	A	W	2–1	Crompton	Carey	Aston (Snr.)	Warner J	Chilton	Lynn	Delaney	Morris 1	Rowley J	Pearson SC 1	Mitten	
17 Jan	Arsenal	81,962	Maine Road	H	D	1–1	Crompton	Carey	Aston (Snr.)	Anderson J	Chilton	Cockburn	Delaney	Morris	Rowley J 1	Pearson SC	Mitten	
31 Jan	Sheffield United	45,189	Bramall Lane	A	L	1–2	Brown R	Carey	Aston (Snr.)	Anderson J	Chilton	Cockburn	Delaney	Morris	Rowley J 1	Pearson SC	Mitten	
14 Feb	Preston North End	61,765	Maine Road	H	D	1–1	Crompton	Carey	Aston (Snr.)	Warner J	Chilton	Cockburn	Delaney 1	Morris	Rowley J	Pearson SC	Mitten	
21 Feb	Stoke City	36,794	Victoria Ground	A	W	2–0	Crompton	Carey	Aston (Snr.)	Anderson J	Chilton	Cockburn	Delaney	Morris	Rowley J	Pearson SC 1	Buckle 1	
6 Mar	Sunderland	55,160	Maine Road	H	W	3–1	Crompton	Carey	Aston (Snr.)	Anderson J	Chilton	Cockburn	Delaney 1	Morris	Rowley J 1	Pearson SC	Mitten 1	
17 Mar	Grimsby Town	12,284	Blundell Park	A	D	1–1	Crompton	Carey	Aston (Snr.)	Anderson J	Chilton	Cockburn	Delaney	Hanlon	Rowley J 1	Pearson SC	Mitten	
20 Mar	Wolverhampton Wan.	50,667	Maine Road	H	W	3–2	Crompton	Carey	Aston (Snr.)	Warner J	Chilton	Anderson J	Delaney 1	Morris 1	Rowley J	Pearson SC	Mitten 1	
22 Mar	Aston Villa	52,368	Villa Park	A	W	1–0	Crompton	Carey	Aston (Snr.)	Anderson J	Chilton	Lynn	Delaney	Morris	Rowley J	Pearson SC 1	Mitten	
26 Mar	Bolton Wanderers	71,623	Maine Road	H	L	0–2	Crompton	Carey	Aston (Snr.)	Anderson J	Chilton	Lynn	Delaney	Morris	Rowley J	Pearson SC	Mitten	
27 Mar	Huddersfield Town	38,266	Leeds Road	A	W	2–0	Brown R	Carey	Aston (Snr.)	Warner J	McGlen	Cockburn	Delaney	Morris	Burke R 1	Pearson SC 1	Mitten	
29 Mar	Bolton Wanderers	44,225	Burnden Park	A	W	1–0	Brown R	Carey	Aston (Snr.)	Anderson J 1	Chilton	Cockburn	Hanlon	Morris	Burke R	Pearson SC	Mitten	
3 Apr	Derby County	49,609	Maine Road	H	W	1–0	Crompton	Carey	Aston (Snr.)	Anderson J	Chilton	Cockburn	Delaney	Morris	Rowley J	Pearson SC 1	Mitten	
7 Apr	Manchester City	71,690	Maine Road	H	D	1–1	Crompton	Carey	Aston (Snr.)	Anderson J	Chilton	Lowrie	Hanlon	Morris	Burke R	Rowley J 1	Mitten	
10 Apr	Everton	44,198	Goodison Park	A	L	0–2	Crompton	Ball J	Aston (Snr.)	Anderson J	Chilton	Lowrie	Buckle	Morris	Burke R	Cassidy L	Mitten	
17 Apr	Chelsea	43,225	Maine Road	H	W	5–0	Crompton	Carey	Aston (Snr.)	Anderson J	Chilton	Cockburn	Delaney 1	Morris	Rowley J 1	Pearson SC 2	Mitten 1	
28 Apr	Blackpool	32,236	Bloomfield Road	A	L	0–1	Crompton	Carey	Aston (Snr.)	Anderson J	Chilton	Cockburn	Buckle	Hanlon	Rowley J	Pearson SC	Mitten	
1 May	Blackburn Rovers	44,439	Maine Road	H	W	4–1	Crompton	Carey	Aston (Snr.)	Anderson J	Chilton	Cockburn	Delaney 1	Burke R	Rowley J	Pearson SC 3	Mitten	

FA Cup

10 Jan	Aston Villa	58,683	Villa Park	A	W	6–4	Crompton	Carey	Aston (Snr.)	Anderson J	Chilton	Cockburn	Delaney 1	Morris 2	Rowley J 1	Pearson SC 2	Mitten	
24 Jan	Liverpool	74,000	Goodison Park	H	W	3–0	Crompton	Carey	Aston (Snr.)	Anderson J	Chilton	Cockburn	Delaney	Morris 1	Rowley J 1	Pearson SC	Mitten 1	
7 Feb	Charlton Athletic	33,312	Leeds Road	H	W	2–0	Crompton	Carey	Aston (Snr.)	Warner J 1	Chilton	Cockburn	Delaney	Morris	Rowley J	Pearson SC	Mitten 1	
28 Feb	Preston North End	74,213	Maine Road	H	W	4–2	Crompton	Carey	Aston (Snr.)	Anderson J	Chilton	Cockburn	Delaney	Morris	Rowley J 1	Pearson SC 2	Mitten 1	
13 Mar	Derby County	60,000	Hillsborough	A	W	3–1	Crompton	Carey	Aston (Snr.)	Anderson J	Chilton	Cockburn	Delaney	Morris	Rowley J	Pearson SC 3	Mitten	
24 Apr	Blackpool	99,000	Wembley	A	W	4–2	Crompton	Carey	Aston (Snr.)	Anderson J 1	Chilton	Cockburn	Delaney	Morris	Rowley J 2	Pearson SC 1	Mitten	

Football League Division 1
P42 • W19 • D14 • L9 • F81 • A48 • PTS52
Position: 2

1948/49

Football League		Attendances	Venue				Players and Scores											Substitutions: not introduced until 1965/66
21 Aug	Derby County	52,620	Maine Road	H	L	1–2	Crompton	Carey	Aston (Snr.)	Anderson J	Chilton	Cockburn	Delaney	Morris	Rowley J	Pearson SC 1	Mitten	
23 Aug	Blackpool	36,880	Bloomfield Road	A	W	3–0	Crompton	Ball J	Carey	Anderson J	Chilton	McGlen	Delaney	Morris	Rowley J 2	Pearson SC	Mitten 1	
28 Aug	Arsenal	64,150	Highbury	A	W	1–0	Crompton	Carey	Aston (Snr.)	Anderson J	Chilton	Cockburn	Delaney	Morris	Rowley J	Pearson SC	Mitten 1	
1 Sep	Blackpool	51,187	Maine Road	H	L	3–4	Brown R	Carey	Aston (Snr.)	Anderson J	Chilton	Cockburn	Delaney 1	Morris 1	Rowley J	Pearson SC	Mitten 1	
4 Sep	Huddersfield Town	57,714	Maine Road	H	W	4–1	Crompton	Carey	Aston (Snr.)	Anderson J	Chilton	McGlen	Delaney 1	Morris	Rowley J	Pearson SC 2	Mitten 1	
8 Sep	Wolverhampton Wan.	42,617	Molineux	A	L	2–3	Crompton	Carey	Aston (Snr.)	Anderson J	Chilton	McGlen	Delaney	Morris 1	Rowley J 1	Pearson SC	Mitten	
11 Sep	Manchester City	64,502	Maine Road	A	D	0–0	Crompton	Carey	Aston (Snr.)	Cockburn	Chilton	McGlen	Delaney	Morris	Rowley J	Pearson SC	Mitten	
15 Sep	Wolverhampton Wan.	33,871	Maine Road	H	W	2–0	Crompton	Carey	Aston (Snr.)	Anderson J	Chilton	Cockburn	Buckle 1	Morris	Rowley J	Pearson SC 1	Mitten	
18 Sep	Sheffield United	36,880	Bramall Lane	A	D	2–2	Crompton	Carey	Aston (Snr.)	Cockburn	Chilton	McGlen	Buckle 1	Morris	Rowley J	Pearson SC 1	Mitten	
25 Sep	Aston Villa	53,820	Maine Road	H	W	3–1	Crompton	Carey	Aston (Snr.)	Cockburn	Chilton	McGlen	Delaney	Hanlon	Rowley J	Pearson SC 1	Mitten 2	
2 Oct	Sunderland	54,419	Roker Park	A	L	1–2	Crompton	Carey	Aston (Snr.)	Cockburn	Chilton	McGlen	Delaney	Buckle	Rowley J 1	Pearson SC	Mitten	
9 Oct	Charlton Athletic	46,964	Maine Road	H	D	1–1	Crompton	Ball J	Aston (Snr.)	Anderson J	Chilton	Warner J	Delaney	Morris	Burke R 1	Rowley J	Mitten	
16 Oct	Stoke City	45,830	Victoria Ground	A	L	1–2	Crompton	Carey	Aston (Snr.)	Anderson J	Chilton	Cockburn	Delaney	Morris 1	Rowley J	Pearson SC	Mitten	
23 Oct	Burnley	47,093	Maine Road	H	D	1–1	Crompton	Carey	Aston (Snr.)	Anderson J	Chilton	Cockburn	Delaney	Morris	Rowley J	Pearson SC	Mitten 1	
30 Oct	Preston North End	37,372	Deepdale	A	W	6–1	Crompton	Carey	Aston (Snr.)	Warner J	Chilton	Cockburn	Delaney	Morris 1	Rowley J 1	Pearson SC 2	Mitten 2	
6 Nov	Everton	42,789	Maine Road	H	W	2–0	Crompton	Carey	Aston (Snr.)	Warner J	Chilton	Cockburn	Delaney 1	Morris 1	Rowley J	Pearson SC	Mitten	
13 Nov	Chelsea	62,542	Stamford Bridge	A	D	1–1	Crompton	Carey	Aston (Snr.)	Anderson J	Chilton	Cockburn	Delaney	Morris	Rowley J 1	Pearson SC	Mitten	
20 Nov	Birmingham City	45,482	Maine Road	H	W	3–0	Crompton	Carey	Aston (Snr.)	Cockburn	Chilton	McGlen	Delaney	Morris 1	Rowley J 1	Pearson SC 1	Mitten	
27 Nov	Middlesbrough	31,331	Ayresome Park	A	W	4–1	Crompton	Carey	Aston (Snr.)	Cockburn	Chilton	McGlen	Delaney 1	Morris	Rowley J 3	Pearson SC	Mitten	
4 Dec	Newcastle United	70,787	Maine Road	H	D	1–1	Crompton	Carey	Aston (Snr.)	Cockburn	Chilton	McGlen	Delaney	Morris	Rowley J	Pearson SC	Mitten 1	
11 Dec	Portsmouth	29,966	Fratton Park	A	D	2–2	Crompton	Carey	Aston (Snr.)	Cockburn	Chilton	McGlen 1	Delaney	Morris	Rowley J	Pearson SC	Mitten 1	
18 Dec	Derby County	31,498	Baseball Ground	A	W	3–1	Crompton	Carey	Aston (Snr.)	Cockburn	Chilton	McGlen	Delaney	Pearson SC 1	Burke R 2	Rowley J	Mitten	
25 Dec	Liverpool	47,788	Maine Road	H	D	0–0	Crompton	Carey	Aston (Snr.)	Cockburn	Chilton	McGlen	Delaney	Pearson SC	Burke R	Rowley J	Mitten	
27 Dec	Liverpool	53,325	Anfield	A	W	2–0	Crompton	Carey	Aston (Snr.)	Cockburn	Chilton	McGlen	Buckle	Pearson SC 1	Burke R 1	Rowley J	Mitten	
1 Jan	Arsenal	58,688	Maine Road	H	W	2–0	Crompton	Carey	Aston (Snr.)	Cockburn	Chilton	McGlen	Delaney	Morris	Burke R 1	Pearson SC	Mitten 1	
22 Jan	Manchester City	66,485	Maine Road	H	D	0–0	Crompton	Carey	Aston (Snr.)	Cockburn	Chilton	McGlen	Delaney	Morris	Rowley J	Pearson SC	Mitten	
19 Feb	Aston Villa	68,354	Villa Park	A	L	1–2	Crompton	Carey	Aston (Snr.)	Cockburn	Chilton	McGlen	Delaney	Pearson SC	Burke R	Rowley J 1	Mitten	
5 Mar	Charlton Athletic	55,291	The Valley	A	W	3–2	Crompton	Carey	Aston (Snr.)	Cockburn	Chilton	McGlen	Delaney	Downie J 1	Rowley J	Pearson SC 2	Mitten	
12 Mar	Stoke City	55,949	Maine Road	H	W	3–0	Crompton	Carey	Aston (Snr.)	Cockburn	Chilton	McGlen	Delaney	Downie J 1	Rowley J 1	Pearson SC	Mitten 1	
19 Mar	Birmingham City	46,819	St Andrews	A	L	0–1	Crompton	Carey	Aston (Snr.)	Cockburn	Chilton	McGlen	Delaney	Anderson J	Rowley J	Pearson SC	Mitten	
6 Apr	Huddersfield Town	17,256	Leeds Road	A	L	1–2	Crompton	Carey	Ball J	Anderson J	Chilton	McGlen	Delaney	Downie J	Burke R	Rowley J 1	Mitten	
9 Apr	Chelsea	27,304	Maine Road	H	D	1–1	Crompton	Carey	Ball J	Anderson J	Chilton	McGlen	Buckle	Downie J	Burke R	Rowley J	Mitten 1	
15 Apr	Bolton Wanderers	44,999	Burnden Park	A	W	1–0	Crompton	Ball J	Aston (Snr.)	Lowrie	Chilton	Cockburn	Carey 1	Downie J	Rowley J	Pearson SC	Mitten	
16 Apr	Burnley	37,722	Turf Moor	A	W	2–0	Crompton	Ball J	Aston (Snr.)	Lowrie	Chilton	Cockburn	Carey	Downie J	Rowley J 2	Pearson SC	Mitten	
18 Apr	Bolton Wanderers	47,653	Maine Road	H	W	3–0	Crompton	Ball J	Aston (Snr.)	Lowrie	Chilton	Cockburn	Delaney	Carey	Rowley J 2	Pearson SC	Mitten 1	
21 Apr	Sunderland	30,640	Maine Road	H	L	1–2	Crompton	Ball J	Aston (Snr.)	Lowrie	Chilton	Cockburn	Delaney	Carey	Rowley J	Pearson SC	Mitten 1	
23 Apr	Preston North End	43,214	Maine Road	H	D	2–2	Crompton	Carey	Aston (Snr.)	Lowrie	Chilton	Cockburn	Delaney	Downie J 2	Rowley J	Pearson SC	Mitten	
27 Apr	Everton	39,106	Goodison Park	A	L	0–2	Crompton	Carey	Aston (Snr.)	Lowrie	Chilton	Cockburn	Delaney	Downie J	Cassidy L	Pearson SC	Mitten	
30 Apr	Newcastle United	38,266	St James' Park	A	W	1–0	Crompton	Carey	Aston (Snr.)	Lowrie	Chilton	Cockburn	Delaney	Downie J	Burke R 1	Pearson SC	Mitten	
2 May	Middlesbrough	20,158	Maine Road	H	W	1–0	Crompton	Carey	Aston (Snr.)	Lowrie	Chilton	Cockburn	Delaney	Downie J	Rowley J 1	Pearson SC	Mitten	
4 May	Sheffield United	20,880	Maine Road	H	W	3–2	Crompton	Carey	Aston (Snr.)	Cockburn	Chilton	McGlen	Delaney	Downie J 1	Rowley J	Pearson SC 1	Mitten 1	
7 May	Portsmouth	49,808	Maine Road	H	W	3–2	Crompton	Carey	Aston (Snr.)	Anderson J	Chilton	Cockburn	Delaney	Downie J	Rowley J 2	Pearson SC	Mitten 1	

FA Cup

8 Jan	Bournemouth	55,012	Maine Road	H	W	6–0	Crompton	Carey	Aston (Snr.)	Cockburn	Chilton	McGlen	Delaney	Pearson SC 1	Burke R 2	Rowley J 2	Mitten 1	
29 Jan	Bradford Park Ave.	82,771	Maine Road	H	D	1–1	Crompton	Carey	Aston (Snr.)	Cockburn	Chilton	McGlen	Delaney	Morris	Rowley J	Pearson SC	Mitten 1	
5 Feb	Bradford Park Ave.	30,000	Park Avenue	A	D	1–1	Crompton	Carey	Aston (Snr.)	Cockburn	Chilton	McGlen	Buckle	Pearson SC	Burke R	Rowley J	Mitten 1	
7 Feb	Bradford Park Ave.	70,434	Maine Road	H	W	5–0	Crompton	Carey	Aston (Snr.)	Cockburn	Chilton	McGlen	Buckle	Pearson SC 1	Burke R 2	Rowley J 2	Mitten	
12 Feb	Yeovil Town	81,565	Maine Road	H	W	8–0	Crompton	Carey	Aston (Snr.)	Cockburn	Chilton	McGlen	Delaney	Pearson SC	Burke R 2	Rowley J 5	Mitten 1	
26 Feb	Hull City	55,000	Boothferry Park	A	W	1–0	Crompton	Ball J	Aston (Snr.)	Cockburn	Chilton	McGlen	Delaney	Pearson SC 1	Burke R	Rowley J	Mitten	
26 Mar	Wolverhampton Wan.	62,250	Hillsborough	A	D	1–1	Crompton	Carey	Aston (Snr.)	Cockburn	Chilton	McGlen	Delaney	Anderson J	Rowley J	Pearson SC	Mitten 1	
2 Apr	Wolverhampton Wan.	73,000	Goodison Park	A	L	0–1	Crompton	Carey	Aston (Snr.)	Cockburn	Chilton	McGlen	Delaney	Pearson SC	Burke R	Rowley J	Mitten	

Football League Division 1
P42 • W21 • D11 • L10 • F77 • A44 • PTS53
Position: 2

RESULTS

The 1950s

1949/50

FOOTBALL LEAGUE		ATTENDANCES	VENUE				PLAYERS AND SCORES											SUBSTITUTIONS: NOT INTRODUCED UNTIL 1965/66
20 Aug	Derby County	35,687	Baseball Ground	A	W	1–0	Crompton	Carey	Aston (Snr.)	Warner J	Lynn	Cockburn	Delaney	Downie J	Rowley J 1	Pearson SC	Mitten	
24 Aug	Bolton Wanderers	41,748	Old Trafford	H	W	•3–0	Crompton	Carey	Aston (Snr.)	Warner J	Lynn	Cockburn	Delaney	Downie J	Rowley J 1	Pearson SC	Mitten 1	
27 Aug	West Bromwich Alb.	44,655	Old Trafford	H	D	1–1	Crompton	Carey	Aston (Snr.)	Warner J	Lynn	Cockburn	Delaney	Pearson SC 1	Rowley J	Birch	Mitten	
31 Aug	Bolton Wanderers	36,277	Burnden Park	A	W	2–1	Crompton	Carey	Aston (Snr.)	Warner J	Lynn	Cockburn	Delaney	Pearson SC 1	Rowley J	Buckle	Mitten 1	
3 Sep	Manchester City	47,760	Old Trafford	H	W	2–1	Crompton	Carey	Aston (Snr.)	Warner J	Lynn	Cockburn	Delaney	Pearson SC 2	Rowley J	Buckle	Mitten	
7 Sep	Liverpool	51,587	Anfield	A	D	1–1	Crompton	Carey	Aston (Snr.)	Lowrie	Lynn	Chilton	Delaney	Pearson SC	Rowley J	Buckle	Mitten 1	
10 Sep	Chelsea	61,357	Stamford Bridge	A	D	1–1	Crompton	Carey	Aston (Snr.)	Lowrie	Lynn	Chilton	Delaney	Pearson SC	Rowley J 1	Buckle	Mitten	
17 Sep	Stoke City	43,522	Old Trafford	H	D	2–2	Crompton	Carey	Aston (Snr.)	Chilton	Lynn	Cockburn	Delaney	Pearson SC	Rowley J 2	Buckle	Mitten	
24 Sep	Burnley	41,072	Turf Moor	A	L	0–1	Crompton	Carey	Aston (Snr.)	Chilton	Lynn	Cockburn	Delaney	Pearson SC	Rowley J	Buckle	Mitten	
1 Oct	Sunderland	49,260	Old Trafford	H	L	1–3	Crompton	Carey	Aston (Snr.)	Lowrie	Chilton	Cockburn	Delaney	Pearson SC 1	Rowley J	Buckle	Mitten	
8 Oct	Charlton Athletic	43,809	Old Trafford	H	W	3–2	Crompton	Ball J	Aston (Snr.)	Warner J	Chilton	McGlen	Delaney	Bogan	Rowley J 1	Pearson SC	Mitten 2	
15 Oct	Aston Villa	47,483	Villa Park	A	W	4–0	Crompton	Ball J	Carey	Warner J	Lynn	Cockburn	Delaney	Bogan 1	Rowley J 1	Pearson SC	Mitten 2	
22 Oct	Wolverhampton Wan.	51,427	Old Trafford	H	W	3–0	Crompton	Carey	Aston (Snr.)	Warner J	Chilton	Cockburn	Delaney	Bogan 1	Rowley J	Pearson SC 2	Mitten	
29 Oct	Portsmouth	41,098	Fratton Park	A	D	0–0	Crompton	Carey	Aston (Snr.)	Warner J	Chilton	Cockburn	Delaney	Bogan	Rowley J	Pearson SC	Mitten	
5 Nov	Huddersfield Town	40,295	Old Trafford	H	W	6–0	Feehan	Carey	Aston (Snr.)	Cockburn	Chilton	McGlen	Delaney 1	Bogan	Rowley J 2	Pearson SC 2	Mitten 1	
12 Nov	Everton	46,672	Goodison Park	A	D	0–0	Crompton	Carey	Aston (Snr.)	Warner J	Chilton	Cockburn	Delaney	Bogan	Rowley J	Pearson SC	Mitten	
19 Nov	Middlesbrough	42,626	Old Trafford	H	W	2–0	Crompton	Carey	Aston (Snr.)	Cockburn	Chilton	McGlen	Delaney	Bogan	Rowley J 1	Pearson SC 1	Mitten	
26 Nov	Blackpool	27,742	Bloomfield Road	A	D	3–3	Feehan	Carey	Aston (Snr.)	Cockburn	Chilton	McGlen	Delaney	Rowley J	Bogan 1	Pearson SC 2	Mitten	
3 Dec	Newcastle United	30,343	Old Trafford	H	D	1–1	Wood R	Carey	Aston (Snr.)	Cockburn	Chilton	McGlen	Delaney	Downie J	Bogan	Pearson SC	Mitten 1	
10 Dec	Fulham	35,362	Craven Cottage	A	L	0–1	Feehan	Carey	Aston (Snr.)	Cockburn	Chilton	McGlen	Delaney	Bogan	Rowley J	Pearson SC	Mitten	
17 Dec	Derby County	33,753	Old Trafford	H	L	0–1	Feehan	Carey	Aston (Snr.)	Cockburn	Chilton	McGlen	Delaney	Bogan	Rowley J	Pearson SC	Mitten	
24 Dec	West Bromwich Alb.	46,973	The Hawthorns	A	W	2–1	Feehan	Carey	Aston (Snr.)	Cockburn	Chilton	McGlen	Delaney	Bogan 1	Rowley J 1	Pearson SC	Mitten	
26 Dec	Arsenal	53,928	Old Trafford	H	W	2–0	Feehan	Carey	Aston (Snr.)	Warner J	Chilton	McGlen	Delaney	Bogan	Rowley J	Pearson SC 2	Mitten	
27 Dec	Arsenal	65,133	Highbury	A	D	0–0	Feehan	Carey	Aston (Snr.)	Warner J	Chilton	McGlen	Delaney	Bogan	Rowley J	Pearson SC	Mitten	
31 Dec	Manchester City	63,704	Maine Road	A	W	2–1	Feehan	Carey	Aston (Snr.)	Warner J	Chilton	McGlen	Delaney 1	Bogan	Rowley J	Pearson SC 1	Mitten	
14 Jan	Chelsea	46,954	Old Trafford	H	W	1–0	Lancaster	Carey	Aston (Snr.)	Cockburn	Chilton	McGlen	Delaney	Downie J	Rowley J	Pearson SC	Mitten 1	
21 Jan	Stoke City	38,877	Victoria Ground	A	L	1–3	Feehan	Carey	Aston (Snr.)	Cockburn	Chilton	McGlen	Delaney	Bogan	Rowley J	Pearson SC	Mitten 1	
4 Feb	Burnley	46,702	Old Trafford	H	W	3–2	Lancaster	Carey	Aston (Snr.)	Warner J	Chilton	Cockburn	Delaney	Bogan	Rowley J 2	Pearson SC	Mitten 1	
18 Feb	Sunderland	63,251	Roker Park	A	D	2–2	Feehan	Carey	Aston (Snr.)	Warner J	Chilton 1	Cockburn	Delaney	Clempson	Rowley J 1	Downie J	Mitten	
25 Feb	Charlton Athletic	44,920	The Valley	A	W	2–1	Crompton	Ball J	Aston (Snr.)	Carey 1	Chilton	Cockburn	Delaney	Downie J	Rowley J 1	Pearson SC	Mitten	
8 Mar	Aston Villa	22,149	Old Trafford	H	W	7–0	Crompton	Ball J	Aston (Snr.)	Warner J	Carey	Cockburn	Delaney	Downie J 2	Rowley J 1	Pearson SC	Mitten 4	
11 Mar	Middlesbrough	46,702	Ayresome Park	A	W	3–2	Crompton	Ball J	Aston (Snr.)	Warner J	Chilton	Carey	Delaney	Downie J 2	Rowley J 1	Pearson SC	Mitten	
15 Mar	Liverpool	43,456	Old Trafford	H	D	0–0	Crompton	Carey	Aston (Snr.)	Warner J	Chilton	Cockburn	Delaney	Downie J	Rowley J	Pearson SC	Mitten	
18 Mar	Blackpool	53,688	Old Trafford	H	L	1–2	Crompton	Carey	Aston (Snr.)	Warner J	Chilton	Cockburn	Bogan	Downie J	Delaney 1	Pearson SC	Mitten	
25 Mar	Huddersfield Town	34,348	Leeds Road	A	L	1–3	Crompton	Ball J	Aston (Snr.)	Warner J	Chilton	Cockburn	Delaney	Downie J 1	Carey	Pearson SC	Mitten	
1 Apr	Everton	35,381	Old Trafford	H	D	1–1	Feehan	Ball J	Aston (Snr.)	Carey	Chilton	Cockburn	Delaney 1	Downie J	Rowley J	Pearson SC	Mitten	
7 Apr	Birmingham City	47,170	Old Trafford	H	L	0–2	Feehan	Ball J	Aston (Snr.)	Carey	Chilton	Cockburn	Delaney	Pearson SC	Rowley J	Downie J	Mitten	
8 Apr	Wolverhampton Wan.	54,296	Molineux	A	D	1–1	Crompton	Ball J	Aston (Snr.)	Carey	Chilton	Cockburn	Delaney	Pearson SC	Rowley J 1	Downie J	Mitten	
10 Apr	Birmingham City	35,863	St Andrews	A	D	0–0	Crompton	Ball J	Aston (Snr.)	Carey	Chilton	Cockburn	Delaney	Pearson SC	Rowley J	Downie J	Mitten	
15 Apr	Portsmouth	44,908	Old Trafford	H	L	0–2	Crompton	McNulty	Ball J	Whitefoot	Chilton	Cockburn	Delaney	Pearson SC	Rowley J	Downie J	Mitten	
22 Apr	Newcastle United	52,203	St James' Park	A	L	1–2	Crompton	Ball J	Aston (Snr.)	Warner J	Chilton	Cockburn	Delaney	Pearson SC	Rowley J	Downie J 1	Mitten	
29 Apr	Fulham	11,968	Old Trafford	H	W	3–0	Crompton	McNulty	Ball J	Aston (Snr.)	Chilton	Cockburn 1	Delaney	Pearson SC	Rowley J 2	Downie J	Mitten	

FA CUP

7 Jan	Weymouth Town	38,284	Old Trafford	H	W	4–0	Feehan	Carey	Aston (Snr.)	Cockburn	Chilton	McGlen	Delaney 1	Bogan	Rowley J 2	Pearson SC 1	Mitten	
28 Jan	Watford	32,800	Vicarage Road	A	W	1–0	Lancaster	Carey	Aston (Snr.)	Warner J	Chilton	Cockburn	Delaney	Bogan	Rowley J 1	Pearson SC	Mitten	
11 Feb	Portsmouth	53,688	Old Trafford	H	D	3–3	Lancaster	Carey	Aston (Snr.)	Warner J	Chilton	Cockburn	Delaney	Bogan	Rowley J	Pearson SC 1	Mitten 2	
15 Feb	Portsmouth	49,962	Fratton Park	A	W	3–1	Feehan	Carey	Aston (Snr.)	Warner J	Chilton	Cockburn	Delaney 1	Bogan	Rowley J	Downie J 1	Mitten 1	
4 Mar	Chelsea	70,362	Stamford Bridge	A	L	0–2	Crompton	Carey	Aston (Snr.)	Warner J	Chilton	Cockburn	Delaney	Downie J	Rowley J	Pearson SC	Mitten	

FOOTBALL LEAGUE DIVISION 1
P42 • W18 • D14 • L10 • F69 • A44 • PTS50
POSITION: 4

1950/51

FOOTBALL LEAGUE		ATTENDANCES	VENUE				PLAYERS AND SCORES											SUBSTITUTIONS: NOT INTRODUCED UNTIL 1965/66
19 Aug	Fulham	44,042	Old Trafford	H	W	1–0	Allen	Carey	Aston (Snr.)	McIlvenny	Chilton	Cockburn	Delaney	Downie J	Rowley J	Pearson SC 1	McGlen	
23 Aug	Liverpool	30,211	Anfield	A	L	1–2	Allen	Carey	Aston (Snr.)	McIlvenny	Chilton	Cockburn	Delaney	Downie J	Rowley J 1	Pearson SC	McGlen	
26 Aug	Bolton Wanderers	40,431	Burnden Park	A	L	0–1	Allen	Carey	Aston (Snr.)	Gibson D	Chilton	Cockburn	Delaney	Downie J	Rowley J	Pearson SC	McGlen	
30 Aug	Liverpool	34,835	Old Trafford	H	W	1–0	Allen	Carey	Aston (Snr.)	Gibson D	Chilton	Cockburn	Bogan	Downie J 1	Rowley J	Pearson SC	McGlen	
2 Sep	Blackpool	53,260	Old Trafford	H	W	1–0	Allen	Carey	Aston (Snr.)	Gibson D	Chilton	Cockburn	Bogan 1	Downie J	Rowley J	Pearson SC	McGlen	
4 Sep	Aston Villa	42,724	Villa Park	A	W	3–1	Allen	Carey	Aston (Snr.)	Gibson D	Chilton	Cockburn	Bogan	Downie J	Rowley J 2	Pearson SC 1	McGlen	
9 Sep	Tottenham Hotspur	60,621	White Hart Lane	A	L	0–1	Allen	Carey	Aston (Snr.)	Gibson D	Chilton	Cockburn	Bogan	Downie J	Rowley J	Pearson SC	McGlen	
13 Sep	Aston Villa	33,021	Old Trafford	H	D	0–0	Allen	Carey	Aston (Snr.)	Gibson D	Chilton	Cockburn	Delaney	Bogan	Rowley J	Cassidy L	McShane	
16 Sep	Charlton Athletic	36,619	Old Trafford	H	W	3–0	Allen	Carey	Aston (Snr.)	Gibson D	Chilton	Cockburn	Delaney 1	Downie J	Rowley J 1	Pearson SC 1	McShane	
23 Sep	Middlesbrough	48,051	Ayresome Park	A	W	2–1	Allen	Carey	Aston (Snr.)	Gibson D	Chilton	Cockburn	Delaney	Downie J	Rowley J	Pearson SC 2	McShane	
30 Sep	Wolverhampton Wan.	45,898	Molineux	A	D	0–0	Allen	Carey	Aston (Snr.)	Gibson D	Chilton	Cockburn	Delaney	Downie J	Rowley J	Pearson SC	McShane	
7 Oct	Sheffield Wednesday	40,651	Old Trafford	H	W	3–1	Allen	Carey	Redman	Gibson D	Jones M	McGlen	Delaney	Downie J 1	Rowley J 1	Pearson SC	McShane 1	
14 Oct	Arsenal	66,150	Highbury	A	L	0–3	Allen	Carey	Aston (Snr.)	Gibson D	Chilton	Cockburn	Delaney	Downie J	Rowley J	Pearson SC	McShane	
21 Oct	Portsmouth	41,842	Old Trafford	H	D	0–0	Allen	Carey	Aston (Snr.)	Gibson D	Chilton	McGlen	Delaney	Downie J	Rowley J	Pearson SC	McShane	
28 Oct	Everton	51,142	Goodison Park	A	W	4–1	Crompton	Carey	Aston (Snr.) 1	Gibson D	Jones M	Cockburn	Delaney	Bogan	Rowley J 2	Pearson SC 1	McShane	
4 Nov	Burnley	39,454	Old Trafford	H	D	1–1	Allen	Carey	Aston (Snr.)	Gibson D	Chilton	Cockburn	Delaney	Bogan	Rowley J	Pearson SC	McShane 1	
11 Nov	Chelsea	51,882	Stamford Bridge	A	L	0–1	Allen	Carey	Aston (Snr.)	Gibson D	Chilton	Cockburn	Delaney	Pearson SC	Rowley J	Downie J	McShane	
18 Nov	Stoke City	30,031	Old Trafford	H	D	0–0	Allen	Carey	Aston (Snr.)	Gibson D	Chilton	Cockburn	Bogan	Pearson SC	Rowley J	Birch	McShane	
25 Nov	West Bromwich Alb.	28,146	The Hawthorns	A	W	1–0	Allen	McNulty	Aston (Snr.)	Gibson D	Chilton	Cockburn	Bogan	Pearson SC	Rowley J	Birch 1	McShane	
2 Dec	Newcastle United	34,502	Old Trafford	H	L	1–2	Allen	Carey	Aston (Snr.)	Gibson D	Chilton	Cockburn	Birkett	Pearson SC	Rowley J	Birch 1	McShane	
9 Dec	Huddersfield Town	26,713	Leeds Road	A	W	3–2	Allen	McNulty	McGlen	Gibson D	Chilton	Cockburn	Birkett 1	Pearson SC	Aston (Snr.) 2	Birch	McShane	
16 Dec	Fulham	19,649	Craven Cottage	A	D	2–2	Allen	McNulty	McGlen	Gibson D	Chilton	Cockburn	Birkett	Pearson SC 2	Aston (Snr.)	Downie J	McShane	
23 Dec	Bolton Wanderers	35,382	Old Trafford	H	L	2–3	Allen	Carey	McGlen	Gibson D	Chilton	Cockburn	Birkett	Pearson SC 1	Aston (Snr.) 1	Downie J	McShane	
25 Dec	Sunderland	41,215	Roker Park	A	L	1–2	Allen	Carey	McGlen	Gibson D	Chilton	Cockburn	Birkett	Pearson SC	Aston (Snr.) 1	Birch	Rowley J	
26 Dec	Sunderland	35,176	Old Trafford	H	L	3–5	Allen	Carey	McGlen	Gibson D	Chilton	Cockburn	McShane	Pearson SC	Aston (Snr.) 1	Bogan 2	Rowley J	
13 Jan	Tottenham Hotspur	43,283	Old Trafford	H	W	2–1	Allen	Carey	Redman	Gibson D	Chilton	Cockburn	Birkett	Birch 1	Aston (Snr.)	Pearson SC	Rowley J 1	
20 Jan	Charlton Athletic	31,978	The Valley	A	W	2–1	Crompton	Carey	Redman	Gibson D	Chilton	Cockburn	Birkett 1	Birch	Aston (Snr.) 1	Pearson SC	Rowley J	
3 Feb	Middlesbrough	44,633	Old Trafford	H	W	1–0	Allen	Carey	Redman	Gibson D	Chilton	Cockburn	Birkett	Bogan	Aston (Snr.)	Pearson SC 1	Rowley J	
17 Feb	Wolverhampton Wan.	42,022	Old Trafford	H	W	2–1	Allen	McNulty	Carey	Gibson D	Chilton	Cockburn	Birkett	Pearson SC	Aston (Snr.)	Birch 1	Rowley J 1	
26 Feb	Sheffield Wednesday	25,693	Hillsborough	A	W	4–0	Allen	Carey	McGlen	Gibson D	Jones M	Cockburn	McShane 1	Pearson SC 1	Aston (Snr.)	Downie J 1	Rowley J 1	
3 Mar	Arsenal	46,202	Old Trafford	H	W	3–1	Allen	Carey	Redman	Whitefoot	Jones M	Cockburn	McShane	Pearson SC	Aston (Snr.) 2	Downie J 1	Rowley J	
10 Mar	Portsmouth	33,148	Fratton Park	A	D	0–0	Allen	Carey	Redman	Whitefoot	Chilton	McGlen	McShane	Pearson SC	Aston (Snr.)	Downie J	Rowley J	
17 Mar	Everton	29,317	Old Trafford	H	W	3–0	Allen	Carey	Redman	Gibson D	Chilton	McGlen	McShane	Pearson SC 1	Aston (Snr.) 1	Downie J 1	Rowley J	
23 Mar	Derby County	42,009	Old Trafford	H	W	2–0	Allen	Carey	Redman	Gibson D	Chilton	McGlen	McShane	Clempson	Aston (Snr.) 1	Downie J 1	Rowley J	
24 Mar	Burnley	36,656	Turf Moor	A	W	2–1	Allen	Carey	Redman	Gibson D	Chilton	McGlen	McShane 1	Clempson	Aston (Snr.) 1	Downie J	Rowley J	
26 Mar	Derby County	25,860	Baseball Ground	A	W	4–2	Allen	Carey	Redman	Cockburn	Chilton	McGlen	McShane	Pearson SC 1	Aston (Snr.) 1	Downie J 1	Rowley J 1	
31 Mar	Chelsea	25,779	Old Trafford	H	W	4–1	Allen	Carey	Redman	Cockburn	Chilton	McGlen	McShane 1	Pearson SC 3	Aston (Snr.)	Downie J	Rowley J	
7 Apr	Stoke City	25,690	Victoria Ground	A	L	0–2	Allen	Carey	Redman	Cockburn	Chilton	McGlen	McShane	Pearson SC	Aston (Snr.)	Downie J	Rowley J	
14 Apr	West Bromwich Alb.	24,764	Old Trafford	H	W	3–0	Allen	Carey	Redman	Gibson D	Chilton	McGlen	McShane	Pearson SC 1	Aston (Snr.)	Downie J 1	Rowley J 1	
21 Apr	Newcastle United	45,209	St James' Park	A	W	2–0	Allen	Carey	Redman	Cockburn	Chilton	McGlen	McShane	Pearson SC 1	Aston (Snr.)	Downie J	Rowley J 1	
28 Apr	Huddersfield Town	25,560	Old Trafford	H	W	6–0	Allen	Carey	Redman	Cockburn	Chilton	McGlen	McShane 2	Pearson SC	Aston (Snr.) 2	Downie J 1	Rowley J 1	
5 May	Blackpool	22,864	Bloomfield Road	A	D	1–1	Allen	Carey	Redman	Cockburn	Chilton	McGlen	McShane	Pearson SC	Aston (Snr.)	Downie J 1	Rowley J	

FA CUP

6 Jan	Oldham Athletic	37,161	Old Trafford	H	W	•4–1	Allen	Carey	McGlen	Lowrie	Chilton	Cockburn	Birkett	Pearson SC 1	Aston (Snr.) 1	Birch 1	McShane	
27 Jan	Leeds United	55,434	Old Trafford	H	W	4–0	Allen	Carey	Redman	Gibson D	Chilton	Cockburn	Birkett	Pearson SC 3	Aston (Snr.)	Birch	Rowley J 1	
10 Feb	Arsenal	55,058	Old Trafford	H	W	1–0	Allen	Carey	Redman	Gibson D	Chilton	Cockburn	Birkett	Pearson SC 1	Aston (Snr.)	Birch	Rowley J	
24 Feb	Birmingham City	50,000	St Andrews	A	L	0–1	Allen	McNulty	Carey	Gibson D	Chilton	Cockburn	Birkett	Pearson SC	Aston (Snr.)	Birch	Rowley J	

FOOTBALL LEAGUE DIVISION 1
P42 • W24 • D8 • L10 • F74 • A40 • PTS56
POSITION: 2

1951/52

Football League — Substitutions: not introduced until 1965/66

		Attendances	Venue			Players and Scores										
18 Aug	West Bromwich Alb.	27,486	The Hawthorns	A D	3–3	Allen	Carey	Redman	Cockburn	Chilton	McGlen	McShane	Pearson SC	Rowley J 3	Downie J	Bond
22 Aug	Middlesbrough	37,339	Old Trafford	H W	4–2	Allen	Carey	Redman	Gibson D	Chilton	Cockburn	McShane	Pearson SC 1	Rowley J 3	Downie J	Bond
25 Aug	Newcastle United	51,850	Old Trafford	H W	2–1	Allen	Carey	Redman	Gibson D	Chilton	Cockburn	McShane	Pearson SC	Rowley J 1	Downie J 1	Bond
29 Aug	Middlesbrough	44,212	Ayresome Park	A W	4–1	Allen	Carey	Redman	Gibson D	Chilton	Cockburn	McShane	Pearson SC 2	Rowley J 2	Downie J	Bond
1 Sep	Bolton Wanderers	52,239	Burnden Park	A L	0–1	Allen	Carey	Redman	Gibson D	Chilton	Cockburn	Berry J	Pearson SC	Rowley J	Downie J	Bond
5 Sep	Charlton Athletic	26,773	Old Trafford	H W	3–2	Allen	Carey	Redman	Gibson D	Chilton	Cockburn	Berry J	Pearson SC	Rowley J 2	Downie J 1	Bond
8 Sep	Stoke City	43,660	Old Trafford	H W	4–0	Allen	Carey	Redman	Gibson D	Chilton	Cockburn	Berry J	Pearson SC 1	Rowley J 3	Downie J	McShane
12 Sep	Charlton Athletic	28,806	The Valley	A D	2–2	Allen	Carey	Redman	Gibson D	Chilton	Cockburn	Berry J	Pearson SC	Rowley J	Downie J 2	McShane
15 Sep	Manchester City	52,571	Maine Road	A W	2–1	Allen	Carey	Redman	Gibson D	Chilton	Cockburn	Berry J 1	Pearson SC	Cassidy L	Downie J	McShane 1
22 Sep	Tottenham Hotspur	70,882	White Hart Lane	A L	0–2	Allen	Carey	Redman	Gibson D	Chilton	Cockburn	Berry J	Pearson SC	Rowley J	Downie J	McShane
29 Sep	Preston North End	53,454	Old Trafford	H L	1–2	Allen	Carey	Redman	Gibson D	Chilton	Cockburn	Berry J	Walton JA	Aston (Snr.) 1	Pearson SC	Rowley J
6 Oct	Derby County	39,767	Old Trafford	H W	2–1	Allen	Carey	Redman	Gibson D	Chilton	Cockburn	Berry J 1	Walton JA	Rowley J	Pearson SC 1	McShane
13 Oct	Aston Villa	47,795	Villa Park	A W	5–2	Allen	McNulty	Redman	Gibson D	Chilton	Cockburn	Berry J	Pearson SC 2	Rowley J 2	Downie J	Bond 1
20 Oct	Sunderland	40,915	Old Trafford	H L	0–1	Allen	Carey	Redman	Gibson D	Chilton	McGlen	Berry J	Downie J	Rowley J	Pearson SC	McShane
27 Oct	Wolverhampton Wan.	46,167	Molineux	A W	2–0	Allen	Carey	Redman	Gibson D	Chilton	Cockburn	McShane	Pearson SC 1	Rowley J 1	Birch	Bond
3 Nov	Huddersfield Town	25,616	Old Trafford	H D	1–1	Allen	Carey	Redman	Gibson D	Chilton	Cockburn	McShane	Pearson SC 1	Rowley J	Birch	Bond
10 Nov	Chelsea	48,960	Stamford Bridge	A L	2–4	Allen	Carey	Redman	Gibson D	Chilton	Cockburn	Berry J	Pearson SC 1	Aston (Snr.)	Downie J	Rowley J 1
17 Nov	Portsmouth	35,914	Old Trafford	H L	1–3	Allen	Carey	Redman	Gibson D	Chilton	Cockburn	Berry J	Pearson SC	Aston (Snr.)	Downie J 1	Rowley J
24 Nov	Liverpool	42,378	Anfield	A D	0–0	Crompton	Carey	Byrne R	Blanchflower	Chilton	Cockburn	Berry J	Pearson SC	Rowley J	Downie J	Bond
1 Dec	Blackpool	34,154	Old Trafford	H W	3–1	Crompton	McNulty	Byrne R	Carey	Chilton	Cockburn	Berry J	Pearson SC	Rowley J 1	Downie J 2	Bond
8 Dec	Arsenal	55,451	Highbury	A W	•3–1	Crompton	McNulty	Byrne R	Carey	Chilton	Cockburn	Berry J	Pearson SC 1	Rowley J 1	Downie J	Bond
15 Dec	West Bromwich Alb.	27,584	Old Trafford	H W	5–1	Allen	McNulty	Byrne R	Carey	Chilton	Cockburn	Berry J 1	Pearson SC 2	Rowley J	Downie J 2	Bond
22 Dec	Newcastle United	45,414	St James' Park	A D	2–2	Allen	McNulty	Byrne R	Carey	Chilton	Cockburn 1	Berry J	Pearson SC	Rowley J	Downie J	Bond 1
25 Dec	Fulham	33,802	Old Trafford	H W	3–2	Allen	McNulty	Byrne R	Chilton	Jones M	Cockburn	Berry J 1	Pearson SC	Rowley J 1	Downie J	Bond 1
26 Dec	Fulham	32,671	Craven Cottage	A D	3–3	Allen	McNulty	Byrne R	Chilton	Jones M	Cockburn	Berry J	Pearson SC 1	Rowley J 1	Downie J	Bond 1
29 Dec	Bolton Wanderers	53,205	Old Trafford	H W	1–0	Allen	McNulty	Byrne R	Chilton	Jones M	Cockburn	Berry J	Pearson SC 1	Rowley J	Downie J	Bond
5 Jan	Stoke City	36,389	Victoria Ground	A D	0–0	Allen	McNulty	Byrne R	Carey	Chilton	Cockburn	Berry J	Pearson SC	Rowley J	Downie J	Bond
19 Jan	Manchester City	54,245	Old Trafford	H D	1–1	Allen	McNulty	Byrne R	Carey 1	Chilton	Cockburn	Berry J	Pearson SC	Aston (Snr.)	Downie J	Rowley J
26 Jan	Tottenham Hotspur	40,845	Old Trafford	H W	•2–0	Allen	McNulty	Byrne R	Carey	Chilton	Cockburn	Berry J	Clempson	Aston (Snr.)	Pearson SC 1	Rowley J
9 Feb	Preston North End	38,792	Deepdale	A W	2–1	Allen	McNulty	Byrne R	Carey	Chilton	Cockburn	Berry J 1	Clempson	Aston (Snr.) 1	Pearson SC	Rowley J
16 Feb	Derby County	27,693	Baseball Ground	A W	3–0	Crompton	McNulty	Byrne R	Carey	Chilton	Cockburn	Berry J	Clempson	Aston (Snr.) 1	Pearson SC 1	Rowley J 1
1 Mar	Aston Villa	39,910	Old Trafford	H D	1–1	Crompton	McNulty	Byrne R	Carey	Chilton	Cockburn	Berry J 1	Clempson	Aston (Snr.)	Pearson SC	Rowley J
8 Mar	Sunderland	48,078	Roker Park	A W	2–1	Crompton	McNulty	Byrne R	Carey	Chilton	Cockburn 1	Berry J	Clempson	Aston (Snr.)	Pearson SC	Rowley J 1
15 Mar	Wolverhampton Wan.	45,109	Old Trafford	H W	2–0	Crompton	McNulty	Byrne R	Carey	Chilton	Cockburn	Berry J	Clempson 1	Aston (Snr.) 1	Pearson SC	Rowley J
22 Mar	Huddersfield Town	30,316	Leeds Road	A L	2–3	Crompton	McNulty	Byrne R	Carey	Chilton	Cockburn	Berry J	Clempson 1	Aston (Snr.)	Pearson SC 1	Rowley J
5 Apr	Portsmouth	25,522	Fratton Park	A L	0–1	Crompton	McNulty	Byrne R	Carey	Chilton	Whitefoot	Berry J	Clempson	Aston (Snr.)	Downie J	Bond
11 Apr	Burnley	38,907	Turf Moor	A D	1–1	Allen	McNulty	Aston (Snr.)	Carey	Chilton	Cockburn	Berry J	Downie J	Rowley J	Pearson SC	Byrne R 1
12 Apr	Liverpool	42,970	Old Trafford	H W	4–0	Allen	McNulty	Aston (Snr.)	Carey	Chilton	Whitefoot	Berry J	Downie J 1	Rowley J 1	Pearson SC	Byrne R 2
14 Apr	Burnley	44,508	Old Trafford	H W	6–1	Allen	McNulty	Aston (Snr.)	Carey 1	Chilton	Whitefoot	Berry J	Downie J 1	Rowley J 1	Pearson SC 1	Byrne R 2
19 Apr	Blackpool	29,118	Bloomfield Road	A D	2–2	Allen	McNulty	Aston (Snr.)	Carey	Chilton	Cockburn	Berry J	Downie J	Rowley J 1	Pearson SC	Byrne R 1
21 Apr	Chelsea	37,436	Old Trafford	H W	•3–0	Allen	McNulty	Aston (Snr.)	Carey 1	Chilton	Cockburn	Berry J	Downie J	Rowley J	Pearson SC 1	Byrne R
26 Apr	Arsenal	53,651	Old Trafford	H W	6–1	Allen	McNulty	Aston (Snr.)	Carey	Chilton	Cockburn	Berry J	Downie J	Rowley J 3	Pearson SC 2	Byrne R 1

FA Cup

12 Jan	Hull City	43,517	Old Trafford	H L	0–2	Allen	McNulty	Byrne R	Carey	Chilton	Cockburn	Berry J	Pearson SC	Rowley J	Downie J	Bond

Football League Division 1
P42 • W23 • D11 • L8 • F95 • A52 • PTS57
Position: 1

1952/53

Football League — Substitutions: not introduced until 1965/66

		Attendances	Venue			Players and Scores										
23 Aug	Chelsea	43,629	Old Trafford	H W	2–0	Wood R	McNulty	Aston (Snr.)	Carey	Chilton	Gibson D	Berry J 1	Downie J 1	Rowley J	Pearson SC	Byrne R
27 Aug	Arsenal	58,831	Highbury	A L	1–2	Crompton	McNulty	Aston (Snr.)	Carey	Chilton	Cockburn	Berry J	Downie J	Rowley J 1	Pearson SC	Byrne R
30 Aug	Manchester City	56,140	Maine Road	A L	1–2	Crompton	McNulty	Aston (Snr.)	Carey	Chilton	Cockburn	Berry J	Downie J 1	Rowley J	Pearson SC	Byrne R
3 Sep	Arsenal	39,193	Old Trafford	H D	0–0	Crompton	Carey	Byrne R	Gibson D	Chilton	Cockburn	Berry J	Clempson	Aston (Snr.)	Pearson SC	Bond
6 Sep	Portsmouth	37,278	Fratton Park	A L	0–2	Crompton	McNulty	Byrne R	Gibson D	Chilton	Cockburn	Berry J	Clempson	Aston (Snr.)	Pearson SC	Rowley J
10 Sep	Derby County	20,226	Baseball Ground	A W	3–2	Crompton	McNulty	Aston (Snr.)	Carey	Chilton	Gibson D	Berry J	Downie J	Rowley J	Pearson SC 3	Byrne R
13 Sep	Bolton Wanderers	40,531	Old Trafford	H W	1–0	Allen	McNulty	Aston (Snr.)	Carey	Chilton	Gibson D	Berry J 1	Downie J	Rowley J	Pearson SC	Byrne R
20 Sep	Aston Villa	43,490	Villa Park	A D	3–3	Wood R	McNulty	Aston (Snr.)	Carey	Chilton	Gibson D	Berry J	Downie J 1	Rowley J 2	Pearson SC	Byrne R
27 Sep	Sunderland	28,967	Old Trafford	H L	0–1	Wood R	McNulty	Aston (Snr.)	Jones M	Chilton	Gibson D	Berry J	Downie J	Clempson	Pearson SC	Byrne R
4 Oct	Wolverhampton Wan.	40,132	Molineux	A L	2–6	Allen	McNulty	Aston (Snr.)	Carey	Chilton	Gibson D	Berry J	Downie J	Rowley J 2	Pearson SC	Scott J
11 Oct	Stoke City	28,968	Old Trafford	H L	0–2	Wood R	McNulty	Aston (Snr.)	Carey	Chilton	Gibson D	Berry J	Clempson	Rowley J	Downie J	Scott J
18 Oct	Preston North End	33,502	Deepdale	A W	5–0	Crompton	Carey	Byrne R	Whitefoot	Chilton	Gibson D	Berry J	Downie J	Aston (Snr.) 2	Pearson SC 2	Rowley J 1
25 Oct	Burnley	36,913	Old Trafford	H L	1–3	Crompton	Carey	Byrne R	Whitefoot	Chilton	Gibson D	Berry J	Downie J	Aston (Snr.) 1	Pearson SC	Rowley J
1 Nov	Tottenham Hotspur	44,300	White Hart Lane	A W	2–1	Crompton	McNulty	Byrne R	Whitefoot	Chilton	Gibson D	Berry J 2	Downie J	Aston (Snr.)	Pearson SC	McShane
8 Nov	Sheffield Wednesday	48,571	Old Trafford	H D	1–1	Crompton	McNulty	Byrne R	Whitefoot	Chilton	Gibson D	Berry J	Downie J	Aston (Snr.)	Pearson SC 1	McShane
15 Nov	Cardiff City	40,096	Ninian Park	A W	2–1	Crompton	McNulty	Byrne R	Cockburn	Chilton	Gibson D	Berry J	Downie J	Aston (Snr.) 1	Pearson SC 1	McShane
22 Nov	Newcastle United	33,528	Old Trafford	H D	2–2	Crompton	McNulty	Byrne R	Cockburn	Chilton	Gibson D	Berry J	Downie J	Aston (Snr.) 1	Pearson SC 1	McShane
29 Nov	West Bromwich Alb.	23,499	The Hawthorns	A L	1–3	Crompton	McNulty	Byrne R	Cockburn	Chilton	Gibson D	Berry J	Downie J	Lewis 1	Pearson SC	McShane
6 Dec	Middlesbrough	27,617	Old Trafford	H W	3–2	Crompton	McNulty	Byrne R	Carey	Chilton	Cockburn	Berry J	Doherty	Aston (Snr.) 1	Pearson SC 2	Pegg D
13 Dec	Liverpool	34,450	Anfield	A W	2–1	Crompton	Foulkes	Byrne R	Carey	Chilton	Cockburn	Berry J	Doherty	Aston (Snr.) 1	Pearson SC 1	Pegg D
20 Dec	Chelsea	23,261	Stamford Bridge	A W	3–2	Crompton	Foulkes	Byrne R	Carey	Chilton	Cockburn	Berry J	Doherty 2	Aston (Snr.) 1	Pearson SC	Pegg D
25 Dec	Blackpool	27,778	Bloomfield Road	A D	0–0	Wood R	McNulty	Byrne R	Carey	Chilton	Cockburn	Berry J	Doherty	Aston (Snr.)	Pearson SC	Pegg D
26 Dec	Blackpool	48,077	Old Trafford	H W	2–1	Wood R	McNulty	Byrne R	Carey 1	Chilton	Cockburn	Berry J	Lewis 1	Aston (Snr.)	Pearson SC	Pegg D
1 Jan	Derby County	34,813	Old Trafford	H W	1–0	Wood R	Redman	Byrne R	Carey	Chilton	Cockburn	Berry J	Aston (Snr.)	Lewis 1	Pearson SC	Pegg D
3 Jan	Manchester City	47,883	Old Trafford	H D	1–1	Wood R	Aston (Snr.)	Byrne R	Carey	Chilton	Whitefoot	Berry J	Doherty	Lewis	Pearson SC 1	Pegg D
17 Jan	Portsmouth	32,341	Old Trafford	H W	1–0	Wood R	Aston (Snr.)	Byrne R	Carey	Chilton	Cockburn	Berry J	Downie J	Lewis 1	Pearson SC	Pegg D
24 Jan	Bolton Wanderers	43,638	Burnden Park	A L	1–2	Wood R	Aston (Snr.)	Byrne R	Carey	Chilton	Cockburn	Berry J	Downie J	Lewis 1	Pearson SC	Pegg D
7 Feb	Aston Villa	34,339	Old Trafford	H W	3–1	Wood R	Aston (Snr.)	Byrne R	Carey	Chilton	Cockburn	Berry J	Lewis 1	Rowley J 2	Pearson SC	Pegg D
18 Feb	Sunderland	24,263	Roker Park	A D	2–2	Carey	Aston (Snr.)	Byrne R	Gibson D	Chilton	Cockburn	Berry J	Lewis 1	Rowley J	Pearson SC	Pegg D 1
21 Feb	Wolverhampton Wan.	38,269	Old Trafford	H L	0–3	Wood R	Aston (Snr.)	Byrne R	Carey	Chilton	Cockburn	Berry J	Lewis	Rowley J	Pearson SC	Pegg D
28 Feb	Stoke City	30,219	Victoria Ground	A L	1–3	Crompton	McNulty	Byrne R	Chilton	Jones M	Gibson D	Berry J 1	Aston (Snr.)	Rowley J	Downie J	Pegg D
7 Mar	Preston North End	52,590	Old Trafford	H W	5–2	Crompton	Aston (Snr.)	Byrne R	Carey	Chilton	Cockburn	Berry J	Rowley J 1	Taylor T 2	Pearson SC	Pegg D 2
14 Mar	Burnley	45,682	Turf Moor	A L	1–2	Crompton	Aston (Snr.)	Byrne R 1	Carey	Chilton	Cockburn	Berry J	Rowley J	Taylor T	Pearson SC	Pegg D
25 Mar	Tottenham Hotspur	18,384	Old Trafford	H W	3–2	Crompton	Aston (Snr.)	Byrne R	Gibson D	Chilton	Cockburn	Berry J	Rowley J	Taylor T	Pearson SC 2	Pegg D 1
28 Mar	Sheffield Wednesday	36,509	Hillsborough	A D	0–0	Crompton	Aston (Snr.)	Byrne R	Carey	Chilton	Cockburn	Berry J	Rowley J	Taylor T	Pearson SC	Pegg D
3 Apr	Charlton Athletic	41,814	The Valley	A D	2–2	Crompton	Aston (Snr.)	Byrne R	Carey	Chilton	Blanchflower	Berry J 1	Rowley J	Taylor T 1	Pearson SC	Pegg D
4 Apr	Cardiff City	37,163	Old Trafford	H L	1–4	Crompton	Aston (Snr.)	Byrne R 1	Gibson D	Chilton	Edwards D	Berry J	Rowley J	Taylor T	Pearson SC	Pegg D
6 Apr	Charlton Athletic	30,105	Old Trafford	H W	3–2	Crompton	McNulty	Byrne R	Carey	Chilton	Whitefoot	Berry J	Lewis	Taylor T 2	Pearson SC	Rowley J 1
11 Apr	Newcastle United	38,970	St James' Park	A W	2–1	Olive	McNulty	Byrne R	Carey	Chilton	Whitefoot	Viollet	Pearson SC	Aston (Snr.)	Taylor T 2	Rowley J
18 Apr	West Bromwich Alb.	31,380	Old Trafford	H D	2–2	Olive	McNulty	Byrne R	Carey	Chilton	Whitefoot	Viollet 1	Pearson SC 1	Aston (Snr.)	Taylor T	Rowley J
20 Apr	Liverpool	20,869	Old Trafford	H W	3–1	Crompton	Aston (Snr.)	Byrne R	Carey	Chilton	Whitefoot	Berry J 1	Downie J	Taylor T	Pearson SC 1	Rowley J 1
25 Apr	Middlesbrough	34,344	Ayresome Park	A L	0–5	Crompton	McNulty	Byrne R	Carey	Chilton	Whitefoot	Berry J	Viollet	Aston (Snr.)	Taylor T	Rowley J

FA Cup

10 Jan	Millwall	35,652	The Den	A W	1–0	Wood R	Aston (Snr.)	Byrne R	Carey	Chilton	Cockburn	Berry J	Downie J	Lewis	Pearson SC 1	Rowley J
31 Jan	Walthamstow Ave.	34,748	Old Trafford	H D	1–1	Wood R	Aston (Snr.)	Byrne R	Carey	Chilton	Cockburn	Berry J	Downie J	Lewis 1	Pearson SC	Rowley J
5 Feb	Walthamstow Ave.	49,119	Highbury	A W	5–2	Wood R	Aston (Snr.)	Byrne R 1	Carey	Chilton	Cockburn	Berry J	Lewis 1	Rowley J 2	Pearson SC 1	Pegg D
14 Feb	Everton	77,920	Goodison Park	A L	1–2	Wood R	Aston (Snr.)	Byrne R	Carey	Chilton	Cockburn	Berry J	Lewis	Rowley J 1	Pearson SC	Pegg D

Football League Division 1
P42 • W18 • D10 • L14 • F69 • A72 • PTS46
Position: 8

1953/54

Football League		Attendances	Venue				Players and Scores											Substitutions: not introduced until 1965/66
19 Aug	Chelsea	28,936	Old Trafford	H	D	1–1	Crompton	Aston (Snr.)	Byrne R	Gibson D	Chilton	Cockburn	Berry J	Rowley J	Taylor T	Pearson SC 1	Pegg D	
22 Aug	Liverpool	48,422	Anfield	A	D	4–4	Crompton	Aston (Snr.)	Byrne R 1	Gibson D	Chilton	Cockburn	Berry J	Rowley J 1	Taylor T 1	Lewis 1	Pegg D	
26 Aug	West Bromwich Alb.	31,806	Old Trafford	H	L	1–3	Crompton	Aston (Snr.)	Byrne R	Gibson D	Chilton	Cockburn	Berry J	Rowley J	Taylor T 1	Lewis	Pegg D	
29 Aug	Newcastle United	27,837	Old Trafford	H	D	1–1	Wood R	McNulty	Aston (Snr.)	Whitefoot	Chilton 1	Cockburn	Berry J	Byrne R	Taylor T	Lewis	Rowley J	
2 Sep	West Bromwich Alb.	28,892	The Hawthorns	A	L	0–2	Wood R	Aston (Snr.)	Byrne R	Whitefoot	Chilton	Cockburn	Berry J	Lewis	Taylor T	Viollet	Rowley J	
5 Sep	Manchester City	53,097	Maine Road	A	L	0–2	Wood R	Aston (Snr.)	Byrne R	Whitefoot	Chilton	Cockburn	Berry J	Viollet	Taylor T	Pearson SC	Rowley J	
9 Sep	Middlesbrough	18,161	Old Trafford	H	D	2–2	Wood R	McNulty	Byrne R	Whitefoot	Chilton	Cockburn	Berry J	Lewis	Rowley J 2	Pearson SC	McShane	
12 Sep	Bolton Wanderers	43,544	Burnden Park	A	D	0–0	Wood R	McNulty	Byrne R	Whitefoot	Chilton	Cockburn	Berry J	Taylor T	Rowley J	Pearson SC	McShane	
16 Sep	Middlesbrough	23,607	Ayresome Park	A	W	4–1	Wood R	McNulty	Byrne R 1	Whitefoot	Chilton	Cockburn	Berry J	Taylor T 2	Rowley J 1	Pearson SC	McShane	
19 Sep	Preston North End	41,171	Old Trafford	H	W	1–0	Wood R	Foulkes	Byrne R 1	Whitefoot	Chilton	Cockburn	Berry J	Taylor T	Rowley J	Pearson SC	McShane	
26 Sep	Tottenham Hotspur	52,837	White Hart Lane	A	D	1–1	Wood R	Foulkes	Byrne R	Whitefoot	Chilton	Cockburn	Berry J	Taylor T	Rowley J 1	Pearson SC	McShane	
3 Oct	Burnley	37,696	Old Trafford	H	L	1–2	Wood R	Foulkes	Byrne R	Whitefoot	Chilton	Cockburn	Berry J	Taylor T	Rowley J	Pearson SC 1	McShane	
10 Oct	Sunderland	34,617	Old Trafford	H	W	1–0	Wood R	Aston (Snr.)	Byrne R	Whitefoot	Chilton	Cockburn	Berry J	Taylor T	Rowley J 1	Pearson SC	McShane	
17 Oct	Wolverhampton Wan.	40,084	Molineux	A	L	1–3	Wood R	Foulkes	Byrne R	Whitefoot	Chilton	Cockburn	Berry J	Pearson SC	Taylor T 1	Rowley J	McShane	
24 Oct	Aston Villa	30,266	Old Trafford	H	W	1–0	Wood R	Foulkes	Byrne R	Whitefoot	Chilton	Cockburn	Berry J 1	Pearson SC	Taylor T	Rowley J	McShane	
31 Oct	Huddersfield Town	34,175	Leeds Road	A	D	0–0	Wood R	Foulkes	Byrne R	Whitefoot	Chilton	Edwards D	Berry J	Blanchflower	Taylor T	Viollet	Rowley J	
7 Nov	Arsenal	28,141	Old Trafford	H	D	2–2	Wood R	Foulkes	Byrne R	Whitefoot	Chilton	Edwards D	Berry J	Blanchflower 1	Taylor T	Viollet	Rowley J 1	
14 Nov	Cardiff City	26,844	Ninian Park	A	W	6–1	Wood R	Foulkes	Byrne R	Whitefoot	Chilton	Edwards D	Berry J 1	Blanchflower 1	Taylor T 1	Viollet 2	Rowley J 1	
21 Nov	Blackpool	49,853	Old Trafford	H	W	4–1	Wood R	Foulkes	Byrne R	Whitefoot	Chilton	Edwards D	Berry J	Blanchflower	Taylor T 3	Viollet 1	Rowley J	
28 Nov	Portsmouth	29,233	Fratton Park	A	D	1–1	Wood R	Foulkes	Byrne R	Whitefoot	Chilton	Edwards D	Webster	Blanchflower	Taylor T 1	Viollet	Rowley J	
5 Dec	Sheffield United	31,693	Old Trafford	H	D	2–2	Wood R	Foulkes	Byrne R	Whitefoot	Chilton	Edwards D	Berry J	Blanchflower 2	Taylor T	Viollet	Rowley J	
12 Dec	Chelsea	37,153	Stamford Bridge	A	L	1–3	Wood R	Foulkes	Byrne R	Whitefoot	Chilton	Edwards D	Berry J 1	Blanchflower	Taylor T	Viollet	Rowley J	
19 Dec	Liverpool	26,074	Old Trafford	H	W	5–1	Wood R	Foulkes	Byrne R	Whitefoot	Chilton	Edwards D	Berry J	Blanchflower 2	Taylor T 2	Viollet 1	Rowley J	
25 Dec	Sheffield Wednesday	27,123	Old Trafford	H	W	5–2	Wood R	Foulkes	Byrne R	Whitefoot	Chilton	Edwards D	Berry J	Blanchflower 1	Taylor T 3	Viollet 1	Rowley J	
26 Dec	Sheffield Wednesday	44,196	Hillsborough	A	W	1–0	Wood R	Foulkes	Byrne R	Whitefoot	Chilton	Edwards D	Berry J	Blanchflower	Taylor T	Viollet 1	Rowley J	
2 Jan	Newcastle United	55,780	St James' Park	A	W	2–1	Wood R	Foulkes 1	Byrne R	Whitefoot	Chilton	Edwards D	Berry J	Blanchflower 1	Taylor T	Viollet	Rowley J	
16 Jan	Manchester City	46,379	Old Trafford	H	D	1–1	Wood R	Foulkes	Byrne R	Whitefoot	Chilton	Edwards D	Berry J 1	Blanchflower	Taylor T	Viollet	Pegg D	
23 Jan	Bolton Wanderers	46,663	Old Trafford	H	L	1–5	Wood R	Foulkes	Byrne R	Whitefoot	Chilton	Edwards D	Berry J	Blanchflower	Taylor T 1	Viollet	Pegg D	
6 Feb	Preston North End	30,064	Deepdale	A	W	3–1	Crompton	Foulkes	Byrne R	Whitefoot	Chilton	Edwards D	Berry J	Blanchflower 1	Taylor T 1	Viollet	Rowley J 1	
13 Feb	Tottenham Hotspur	35,485	Old Trafford	H	W	2–0	Crompton	Foulkes	Byrne R	Whitefoot	Chilton	Edwards D	McFarlane N	Blanchflower	Taylor T 1	Viollet	Rowley J 1	
20 Feb	Burnley	29,576	Turf Moor	A	L	0–2	Crompton	Foulkes	Byrne R	Whitefoot	Chilton	Edwards D	Berry J	Blanchflower	Taylor T	Viollet	Pegg D	
27 Feb	Sunderland	58,440	Roker Park	A	W	2–0	Wood R	Foulkes	Byrne R	Whitefoot	Chilton	Edwards D	Berry J	Blanchflower 1	Taylor T 1	Viollet	Rowley J	
6 Mar	Wolverhampton Wan.	38,939	Old Trafford	H	W	1–0	Wood R	Foulkes	Byrne R	Whitefoot	Chilton	Edwards D	Berry J 1	Blanchflower	Taylor T	Viollet	Rowley J	
13 Mar	Aston Villa	26,023	Villa Park	A	D	2–2	Crompton	Foulkes	Byrne R	Whitefoot	Chilton	Cockburn	Berry J	Blanchflower	Taylor T 2	Viollet	Rowley J	
20 Mar	Huddersfield Town	40,181	Old Trafford	H	W	3–1	Crompton	Foulkes	Byrne R	Whitefoot	Chilton	Edwards D	Berry J	Blanchflower 1	Taylor T	Viollet 1	Rowley J 1	
27 Mar	Arsenal	42,753	Highbury	A	L	1–3	Crompton	Foulkes	Byrne R	Gibson D	Chilton	Edwards D	Berry J	Blanchflower	Taylor T 1	Viollet	Rowley J	
3 Apr	Cardiff City	22,832	Old Trafford	H	L	2–3	Crompton	Foulkes	Redman	Whitefoot	Chilton	Edwards D	Berry J	Blanchflower	Lewis	Viollet 1	Rowley J 1	
10 Apr	Blackpool	25,996	Bloomfield Road	A	L	0–2	Crompton	Foulkes	Byrne R	Whitefoot	Chilton	Edwards D	Berry J	Blanchflower	Aston (Snr.)	Viollet	Rowley J	
16 Apr	Charlton Athletic	31,876	Old Trafford	H	W	2–0	Crompton	Foulkes	Byrne R	Whitefoot	Chilton	Edwards D	Gibson D	Blanchflower	Aston (Snr.) 1	Viollet 1	Pegg D	
17 Apr	Portsmouth	29,663	Old Trafford	H	W	2–0	Crompton	Foulkes	Byrne R	Whitefoot	Chilton	Edwards D	Gibson D	Blanchflower 1	Aston (Snr.)	Viollet 1	Pegg D	
19 Apr	Charlton Athletic	19,111	The Valley	A	L	0–1	Crompton	Foulkes	Byrne R	Whitefoot	Chilton	Cockburn	Gibson D	Blanchflower	Aston (Snr.)	Viollet	Pegg D	
24 Apr	Sheffield United	29,189	Bramall Lane	A	W	3–1	Crompton	Foulkes	Byrne R	Whitefoot	Chilton	Cockburn	Berry J	Blanchflower 1	Aston (Snr.) 1	Viollet 1	Rowley J	

FA Cup

9 Jan	Burnley	54,000	Turf Moor	A	L	3–5	Wood R	Foulkes	Byrne R	Whitefoot	Chilton	Edwards D	Berry J	Blanchflower 1	Taylor T 1	Viollet 1	Rowley J	

Football League Division 1
P42 • W18 • D12 • L12 • F73 • A58 • PTS48
Position: 4

1954/55

Football League		Attendances	Venue				Players and Scores											Substitutions: not introduced until 1965/66
21 Aug	Portsmouth	38,203	Old Trafford	H	L	1–3	Wood R	Foulkes	Byrne R	Whitefoot	Chilton	Edwards D	Berry J	Blanchflower	Webster	Viollet	Rowley J 1	
23 Aug	Sheffield Wednesday	38,118	Hillsborough	A	W	4–2	Wood R	Foulkes	Byrne R	Whitefoot	Chilton	Edwards D	Berry J	Blanchflower 2	Webster	Viollet 2	Rowley J	
28 Aug	Blackpool	31,855	Bloomfield Road	A	W	4–2	Wood R	Foulkes	Byrne R	Whitefoot	Chilton	Edwards D	Berry J	Blanchflower 1	Webster 2	Viollet 1	Rowley J	
1 Sep	Sheffield Wednesday	31,371	Old Trafford	H	W	2–0	Wood R	Foulkes	Byrne R	Whitefoot	Chilton	Edwards D	Berry J	Blanchflower	Webster	Viollet 2	Rowley J	
4 Sep	Charlton Athletic	38,105	Old Trafford	H	W	3–1	Wood R	Foulkes	Byrne R	Whitefoot	Chilton	Edwards D	Berry J	Blanchflower	Taylor T 1	Viollet	Rowley J 2	
8 Sep	Tottenham Hotspur	35,162	White Hart Lane	A	W	2–0	Wood R	Foulkes	Byrne R	Whitefoot	Chilton	Edwards D	Berry J 1	Blanchflower	Webster 1	Viollet	Rowley J	
11 Sep	Bolton Wanderers	44,661	Burnden Park	A	D	1–1	Wood R	Foulkes	Byrne R	Whitefoot	Chilton	Edwards D	Berry J	Blanchflower	Webster 1	Viollet	Rowley J	
15 Sep	Tottenham Hotspur	29,212	Old Trafford	H	W	2–1	Wood R	Foulkes	Byrne R	Whitefoot	Chilton	Edwards D	Berry J	Blanchflower	Taylor T	Viollet 1	Rowley J 1	
18 Sep	Huddersfield Town	45,648	Old Trafford	H	D	1–1	Wood R	Foulkes	Byrne R	Whitefoot	Chilton	Edwards D	Berry J	Blanchflower	Taylor T	Viollet 1	Rowley J	
25 Sep	Manchester City	54,105	Maine Road	A	L	2–3	Wood R	Foulkes	Byrne R	Gibson D	Chilton	Edwards D	Berry J	Blanchflower 1	Taylor T 1	Viollet	Rowley J	
2 Oct	Wolverhampton Wan.	39,617	Molineux	A	L	2–4	Crompton	Greaves	Kennedy P	Gibson D	Chilton	Cockburn	Berry J	Edwards D	Taylor T	Viollet 1	Rowley J 1	
9 Oct	Cardiff City	39,378	Old Trafford	H	W	5–2	Wood R	Foulkes	Byrne R	Gibson D	Chilton	Edwards D	Berry J	Blanchflower	Taylor T 4	Viollet 1	Rowley J	
16 Oct	Chelsea	55,966	Stamford Bridge	A	W	6–5	Wood R	Foulkes	Byrne R	Gibson D	Chilton	Edwards D	Berry J	Blanchflower 1	Taylor T 2	Viollet 3	Rowley J	
23 Oct	Newcastle United	29,217	Old Trafford	H	D	•2–2	Wood R	Foulkes	Byrne R	Gibson D	Chilton	Edwards D	Berry J	Blanchflower	Taylor T 1	Viollet	Rowley J	
30 Oct	Everton	63,021	Goodison Park	A	L	2–4	Wood R	Foulkes	Byrne R	Gibson D	Chilton	Edwards D	Berry J	Blanchflower	Taylor T 1	Viollet	Rowley J 1	
6 Nov	Preston North End	30,063	Old Trafford	H	W	2–1	Wood R	Foulkes	Byrne R	Gibson D	Chilton	Edwards D	Berry J	Blanchflower	Taylor T	Viollet 2	Rowley J	
13 Nov	Sheffield United	26,257	Bramall Lane	A	L	0–3	Wood R	Foulkes	Byrne R	Gibson D	Chilton	Edwards D	Berry J	Blanchflower	Taylor T	Viollet	Rowley J	
20 Nov	Arsenal	33,373	Old Trafford	H	W	2–1	Wood R	Foulkes	Byrne R	Gibson D	Chilton	Goodwin F	Berry J	Blanchflower 1	Taylor T 1	Viollet	Scanlon	
27 Nov	West Bromwich Alb.	33,931	The Hawthorns	A	L	0–2	Wood R	Foulkes	Byrne R	Gibson D	Chilton	Edwards D	Berry J	Blanchflower	Taylor T	Viollet	Scanlon	
4 Dec	Leicester City	19,369	Old Trafford	H	W	3–1	Wood R	Foulkes	Byrne R	Gibson D	Chilton	Whitefoot	Berry J	Blanchflower	Webster 1	Viollet 1	Rowley J 1	
11 Dec	Burnley	24,977	Turf Moor	A	W	4–2	Wood R	Foulkes	Bent	Gibson D	Chilton	Whitefoot	Berry J	Blanchflower	Webster 3	Viollet 1	Rowley J	
18 Dec	Portsmouth	26,019	Fratton Park	A	D	0–0	Wood R	Foulkes	Byrne R	Gibson D	Chilton	Edwards D	Berry J	Blanchflower	Webster	Viollet	Rowley J	
27 Dec	Aston Villa	49,136	Old Trafford	H	L	0–1	Wood R	Foulkes	Byrne R	Gibson D	Chilton	Edwards D	Berry J	Blanchflower	Webster	Viollet	Rowley J	
28 Dec	Aston Villa	48,718	Villa Park	A	L	1–2	Wood R	Foulkes	Byrne R	Gibson D	Chilton	Edwards D	Berry J	Webster	Taylor T 1	Viollet	Pegg D	
1 Jan	Blackpool	51,918	Old Trafford	H	W	4–1	Wood R	Foulkes	Byrne R	Gibson D	Chilton	Edwards D 1	Berry J	Blanchflower 2	Taylor T	Viollet 1	Pegg D	
22 Jan	Bolton Wanderers	39,873	Old Trafford	H	D	1–1	Wood R	Foulkes	Byrne R	Gibson D	Chilton	Edwards D	Berry J	Blanchflower	Taylor T 1	Viollet	Rowley J	
5 Feb	Huddersfield Town	31,408	Leeds Road	A	W	3–1	Wood R	Foulkes	Byrne R	Gibson D	Chilton	Whitefoot	Berry J 1	Blanchflower	Webster	Edwards D 1	Pegg D 1	
12 Feb	Manchester City	47,914	Old Trafford	H	L	0–5	Wood R	Foulkes	Byrne R	Gibson D	Chilton	Whitefoot	Berry J	Blanchflower	Webster	Edwards D	Pegg D	
23 Feb	Wolverhampton Wan.	15,679	Old Trafford	H	L	2–4	Wood R	Foulkes	Byrne R	Gibson D	Chilton	Whitefoot	Webster	Viollet	Taylor T 1	Edwards D 1	Pegg D	
26 Feb	Cardiff City	16,329	Ninian Park	A	L	0–3	Wood R	Foulkes	Byrne R	Gibson D	Jones M	Whitefoot	Webster	Viollet	Taylor T	Edwards D	Pegg D	
5 Mar	Burnley	31,729	Old Trafford	H	W	1–0	Wood R	Foulkes	Byrne R	Gibson D	Jones M	Whitefoot	Berry J	Taylor T	Webster	Edwards D 1	Scanlon	
19 Mar	Everton	32,295	Old Trafford	H	L	1–2	Wood R	Foulkes	Byrne R	Gibson D	Jones M	Whitefoot	Berry J	Taylor T	Webster	Edwards D	Scanlon 1	
26 Mar	Preston North End	13,327	Deepdale	A	W	2–0	Wood R	Foulkes	Byrne R 1	Gibson D	Jones M	Whitefoot	Berry J	Whelan L	Taylor T	Edwards D	Scanlon 1	
2 Apr	Sheffield United	21,158	Old Trafford	H	W	5–0	Wood R	Foulkes	Bent	Gibson D	Jones M	Whitefoot	Berry J 1	Whelan L 1	Taylor T 2	Viollet 1	Scanlon	
8 Apr	Sunderland	43,882	Roker Park	A	L	3–4	Wood R	Foulkes	Byrne R	Gibson D	Jones M	Whitefoot	Berry J	Whelan L	Taylor T	Edwards D 2	Scanlon 1	
9 Apr	Leicester City	34,362	Filbert Street	A	L	0–1	Crompton	Foulkes	Byrne R	Gibson D	Jones M	Whitefoot	Berry J	Whelan L	Taylor T	Edwards D	Scanlon	
11 Apr	Sunderland	36,013	Old Trafford	H	D	2–2	Crompton	Foulkes	Byrne R 1	Gibson D	Jones M	Whitefoot	Berry J	Whelan L	Taylor T 1	Edwards D	Scanlon	
16 Apr	West Bromwich Alb.	24,765	Old Trafford	H	W	3–0	Crompton	Foulkes	Byrne R	Goodwin F	Jones M	Whitefoot	Berry J	Whelan L	Taylor T 2	Viollet 1	Scanlon	
18 Apr	Newcastle United	35,540	St James' Park	A	L	0–2	Crompton	Foulkes	Byrne R	Gibson D	Jones M	Whitefoot	Berry J	Whelan L	Taylor T	Viollet	Scanlon	
23 Apr	Arsenal	42,754	Highbury	A	W	•3–2	Wood R	Foulkes	Byrne R	Gibson D	Jones M	Goodwin F	Berry J	Blanchflower 2	Taylor T	Viollet	Scanlon	
26 Apr	Charlton Athletic	13,149	The Valley	A	D	1–1	Wood R	Foulkes	Byrne R	Gibson D	Jones M	Goodwin F	Berry J	Blanchflower	Taylor T	Viollet 1	Scanlon	
30 Apr	Chelsea	34,933	Old Trafford	H	W	2–1	Wood R	Foulkes	Byrne R	Gibson D	Jones M	Goodwin F	Berry J	Blanchflower	Taylor T 1	Viollet	Scanlon 1	

FA Cup

8 Jan	Reading	26,000	Elm Park	A	D	1–1	Wood R	Foulkes	Byrne R	Gibson D	Chilton	Edwards D	Berry J	Blanchflower	Webster 1	Viollet	Rowley J	
12 Jan	Reading	24,578	Old Trafford	H	W	4–1	Wood R	Foulkes	Byrne R	Gibson D	Chilton	Edwards D	Berry J	Blanchflower	Webster 2	Viollet 1	Rowley J 1	
29 Jan	Manchester City	75,000	Maine Road	H	L	0–2	Wood R	Foulkes	Byrne R	Gibson D	Chilton	Edwards D	Berry J	Blanchflower	Taylor T	Viollet	Rowley J	

Football League Division 1
P42 • W20 • D7 • L15 • F84 • A74 • PTS47
Position: 5

1955/56

Football League		Attendances	Venue			Players and Scores											Substitutions: not introduced until 1965/66
20 Aug	Birmingham City	37,994	St Andrews	A D	2–2	Wood R	Foulkes	Byrne R	Whitefoot	Jones M	Edwards D	Webster	Blanchflower	Taylor T	Viollet 2	Scanlon	
24 Aug	Tottenham Hotspur	25,406	Old Trafford	H D	2–2	Wood R	Foulkes	Byrne R	Whitefoot	Jones M	Edwards D	Berry J 1	Blanchflower	Webster 1	Viollet	Scanlon	
27 Aug	West Bromwich Alb.	31,996	Old Trafford	H W	3–1	Wood R	Foulkes	Byrne R	Whitefoot	Jones M	Edwards D	Webster	Blanchflower	Lewis 1	Viollet 1	Scanlon 1	
31 Aug	Tottenham Hotspur	27,453	White Hart Lane	A W	2–1	Wood R	Foulkes	Byrne R	Whitefoot	Jones M	Edwards D 2	Webster	Blanchflower	Lewis	Viollet	Scanlon	
3 Sep	Manchester City	59,162	Maine Road	A L	0–1	Wood R	Foulkes	Byrne R	Whitefoot	Jones M	Goodwin F	Webster	Blanchflower	Lewis	Edwards D	Scanlon	
7 Sep	Everton	27,843	Old Trafford	H W	2–1	Wood R	Foulkes	Byrne R	Whitefoot	Jones M	Goodwin F	Webster	Blanchflower 1	Lewis	Edwards D 1	Scanlon	
10 Sep	Sheffield United	28,241	Bramall Lane	A L	0–1	Wood R	Foulkes	Byrne R	Whitefoot	Jones M	Goodwin F	Berry J	Whelan L	Webster	Blanchflower	Pegg D	
14 Sep	Everton	34,897	Goodison Park	A L	2–4	Wood R	Foulkes	Byrne R	Whitehurst	Jones M	Goodwin F	Webster 1	Whelan L	Blanchflower 1	Doherty	Berry J	
17 Sep	Preston North End	33,078	Old Trafford	H W	3–2	Wood R	Foulkes	Byrne R	Whitefoot	Jones M	Goodwin F	Webster	Blanchflower	Taylor T 1	Viollet 1	Pegg D 1	
24 Sep	Burnley	26,873	Turf Moor	A D	0–0	Wood R	Foulkes	Byrne R	Whitefoot	Jones M	Goodwin F	Webster	Blanchflower	Taylor T	Viollet	Pegg D	
1 Oct	Luton Town	34,409	Old Trafford	H W	3–1	Wood R	Foulkes	Bent	Whitefoot	Jones M	Goodwin F	Berry J	Blanchflower	Taylor T 2	Webster 1	Pegg D	
8 Oct	Wolverhampton Wan.	48,638	Old Trafford	H W	4–3	Wood R	Byrne R	Bent	Whitefoot	Jones M	McGuinness	Berry J	Doherty 1	Taylor T 2	Webster	Pegg D 1	
15 Oct	Aston Villa	29,478	Villa Park	A D	4–4	Wood R	Foulkes	Byrne R	Whitefoot	Jones M	McGuinness	Berry J	Blanchflower 1	Taylor T	Webster 1	Pegg D 2	
22 Oct	Huddersfield Town	34,150	Old Trafford	H W	3–0	Crompton	Foulkes	Bent	Whitefoot	Jones M	Edwards D	Berry J 1	Blanchflower	Taylor T 1	Viollet	Pegg D 1	
29 Oct	Cardiff City	27,795	Ninian Park	A W	1–0	Wood R	Foulkes	Byrne R	Whitefoot	Jones M	Edwards D	Berry J	Blanchflower	Taylor T 1	Viollet	Pegg D	
5 Nov	Arsenal	41,586	Old Trafford	H D	1–1	Wood R	Foulkes	Byrne R	Whitefoot	Jones M	Edwards D	Berry J	Blanchflower	Taylor T 1	Viollet	Pegg D	
12 Nov	Bolton Wanderers	38,109	Burnden Park	A L	1–3	Wood R	Foulkes	Byrne R	Colman	Jones M	Edwards D	Berry J	Blanchflower	Taylor T 1	Webster	Pegg D	
19 Nov	Chelsea	22,192	Old Trafford	H W	3–0	Wood R	Foulkes	Byrne R 1	Colman	Jones M	Edwards D	Berry J	Doherty	Taylor T 2	Viollet	Pegg D	
26 Nov	Blackpool	26,240	Bloomfield Road	A D	0–0	Wood R	Greaves	Byrne R	Colman	Jones M	Edwards D	Berry J	Doherty	Taylor T	Viollet	Pegg D	
3 Dec	Sunderland	39,901	Old Trafford	H W	2–1	Wood R	Foulkes	Byrne R	Colman	Jones M	Edwards D	Berry J	Doherty 1	Taylor T	Viollet 1	Pegg D	
10 Dec	Portsmouth	24,594	Fratton Park	A L	2–3	Wood R	Foulkes	Byrne R	Colman	Jones M	Edwards D	Berry J	Doherty	Taylor T 1	Viollet	Pegg D 1	
17 Dec	Birmingham City	27,704	Old Trafford	H W	2–1	Wood R	Foulkes	Byrne R	Colman	Jones M 1	Edwards D	Berry J	Doherty	Taylor T	Viollet 1	Pegg D	
24 Dec	West Bromwich Alb.	25,168	The Hawthorns	A W	4–1	Wood R	Foulkes	Byrne R	Colman	Jones M	Edwards D	Berry J	Doherty	Taylor T 1	Viollet 3	Pegg D	
26 Dec	Charlton Athletic	44,611	Old Trafford	H W	5–1	Wood R	Foulkes	Byrne R 1	Colman	Jones M	Edwards D	Berry J	Doherty 1	Taylor T 1	Viollet 2	Pegg D	
27 Dec	Charlton Athletic	42,040	The Valley	A L	0–3	Wood R	Foulkes	Byrne R	Colman	Jones M	Edwards D	Berry J	Doherty	Taylor T	Viollet	Pegg D	
31 Dec	Manchester City	60,956	Old Trafford	H W	2–1	Wood R	Foulkes	Byrne R	Colman	Jones M	Edwards D	Berry J	Doherty	Taylor T 1	Viollet 1	Pegg D	
14 Jan	Sheffield United	30,162	Old Trafford	H W	3–1	Wood R	Foulkes	Byrne R	Colman	Jones M	Edwards D	Berry J 1	Whelan L	Taylor T 1	Viollet	Pegg D 1	
21 Jan	Preston North End	28,047	Deepdale	A L	1–3	Wood R	Foulkes	Byrne R	Colman	Jones M	Edwards D	Scott J	Whelan L 1	Webster	Viollet	Pegg D	
4 Feb	Burnley	27,342	Old Trafford	H W	2–0	Wood R	Greaves	Byrne R	Colman	Jones M	Edwards D	Berry J	Whelan L	Taylor T 1	Viollet 1	Pegg D	
11 Feb	Luton Town	16,354	Kenilworth Road	A W	2–0	Wood R	Greaves	Byrne R	Goodwin F	Jones M	Blanchflower	Berry J	Whelan L 1	Taylor T	Viollet 1	Pegg D	
18 Feb	Wolverhampton Wan.	40,014	Molineux	A W	2–0	Wood R	Greaves	Byrne R	Colman	Jones M	Edwards D	Berry J	Whelan L	Taylor T 2	Viollet	Pegg D	
25 Feb	Aston Villa	36,277	Old Trafford	H W	1–0	Wood R	Greaves	Byrne R	Colman	Jones M	Edwards D	Berry J	Whelan L 1	Taylor T	Viollet	Pegg D	
3 Mar	Chelsea	32,050	Stamford Bridge	A W	4–2	Wood R	Greaves	Byrne R	Colman	Jones M	Edwards D	Berry J	Whelan L	Taylor T 1	Viollet 2	Pegg D 1	
10 Mar	Cardiff City	44,693	Old Trafford	H D	1–1	Wood R	Greaves	Byrne R 1	Colman	Jones M	Edwards D	Berry J	Whelan L	Taylor T	Viollet	Pegg D	
17 Mar	Arsenal	50,758	Highbury	A D	1–1	Wood R	Greaves	Byrne R	Colman	Jones M	Edwards D	Berry J	Whelan L	Taylor T	Viollet 1	Pegg D	
24 Mar	Bolton Wanderers	46,114	Old Trafford	H W	1–0	Wood R	Greaves	Byrne R	Colman	Jones M	Edwards D	Berry J	Whelan L	Taylor T 1	Viollet	Pegg D	
30 Mar	Newcastle United	58,994	Old Trafford	H W	5–2	Wood R	Greaves	Byrne R	Colman	Jones M	Edwards D	Berry J	Doherty 1	Taylor T 1	Viollet 2	Pegg D 1	
31 Mar	Huddersfield Town	37,780	Leeds Road	A W	2–0	Wood R	Greaves	Byrne R	Colman	Jones M	Edwards D	Berry J	Doherty	Taylor T 2	Viollet	Pegg D	
2 Apr	Newcastle United	37,395	St James' Park	A D	0–0	Wood R	Greaves	Byrne R	Colman	Jones M	Edwards D	Berry J	Doherty	Taylor T	Viollet	Pegg D	
7 Apr	Blackpool	62,277	Old Trafford	H W	2–1	Wood R	Greaves	Byrne R	Colman	Jones M	Edwards D	Berry J 1	Doherty	Taylor T 1	Viollet	Pegg D	
14 Apr	Sunderland	19,865	Roker Park	A D	2–2	Wood R	Greaves	Bent	Colman	Jones M	McGuinness 1	Berry J	Whelan L 1	Blanchflower	Viollet	Pegg D	
21 Apr	Portsmouth	38,417	Old Trafford	H W	1–0	Wood R	Greaves	Byrne R	Colman	Jones M	Edwards D	Berry J	Doherty	Taylor T	Viollet 1	Pegg D	

FA Cup

7 Jan	Bristol Rovers	35,872	Eastville	A L	0–4	Wood R	Foulkes	Byrne R	Colman	Jones M	Whitefoot	Berry J	Doherty	Taylor T	Viollet	Pegg D	

Football League Division 1
P42 • W25 • D10 • L7 • F83 • A51 • PTS60
Position: 1

1956/57

Football League		Attendances	Venue			Players and Scores											Substitutions: not introduced until 1965/66
18 Aug	Birmingham City	32,752	Old Trafford	H D	2–2	Wood R	Foulkes	Byrne R	Colman	Jones M	Edwards D	Berry J	Whelan L	Taylor T	Viollet 2	Pegg D	
20 Aug	Preston North End	32,569	Deepdale	A W	3–1	Wood R	Foulkes	Byrne R	Colman	Jones M	Edwards D	Berry J	Whelan L 1	Taylor T 2	Viollet	Pegg D	
25 Aug	West Bromwich Alb.	26,387	The Hawthorns	A W	3–2	Wood R	Foulkes	Byrne R	Colman	Jones M	Edwards D	Berry J	Whelan L 1	Taylor T 1	Viollet 1	Pegg D	
29 Aug	Preston North End	32,515	Old Trafford	H W	3–2	Wood R	Foulkes	Byrne R	Colman	Jones M	Edwards D	Berry J	Whelan L	Taylor T	Viollet 3	Pegg D	
1 Sep	Portsmouth	40,369	Old Trafford	H W	3–0	Wood R	Foulkes	Byrne R	Colman	Jones M	Edwards D	Berry J 1	Whelan L	Taylor T	Viollet 1	Pegg D 1	
5 Sep	Chelsea	29,082	Stamford Bridge	A W	2–1	Wood R	Foulkes	Byrne R	Colman	Jones M	Edwards D	Berry J	Whelan L 1	Taylor T 1	Viollet	Pegg D	
8 Sep	Newcastle United	50,130	St James' Park	A D	1–1	Wood R	Foulkes	Byrne R	Colman	Jones M	Edwards D	Berry J	Whelan L 1	Taylor T	Viollet	Pegg D	
15 Sep	Sheffield Wednesday	48,078	Old Trafford	H W	4–1	Wood R	Foulkes	Byrne R	Colman	Jones M	Edwards D	Berry J 1	Whelan L 1	Taylor T 1	Viollet 1	Pegg D	
22 Sep	Manchester City	53,525	Old Trafford	H W	2–0	Wood R	Foulkes	Byrne R	Colman	Jones M	Edwards D	Berry J	Whelan L 1	Taylor T	Viollet 1	Pegg D	
29 Sep	Arsenal	62,479	Highbury	A W	2–1	Wood R	Foulkes	Byrne R	Colman	Cope	Edwards D	Berry J 1	Whelan L 1	Taylor T	Viollet	Pegg D	
6 Oct	Charlton Athletic	41,439	Old Trafford	H W	4–2	Wood R	Foulkes	Bent	Colman	Jones M	McGuinness	Berry J 1	Whelan L 1	Charlton 2	Viollet	Pegg D	
13 Oct	Sunderland	49,487	Roker Park	A W	3–1	Wood R	Foulkes	Byrne R	Colman	Jones M	Edwards D	Berry J	Whelan L 1	Taylor T	Viollet 1	Pegg D	
20 Oct	Everton	43,451	Old Trafford	H L	2–5	Wood R	Foulkes	Byrne R	Colman	Jones M	Edwards D	Berry J	Whelan L 1	Taylor T	Charlton 1	Pegg D	
27 Oct	Blackpool	32,632	Bloomfield Road	A D	2–2	Hawksworth	Foulkes	Byrne R	Colman	Jones M	Edwards D	Berry J	Whelan L	Taylor T 2	Viollet	Pegg D	
3 Nov	Wolverhampton Wan.	59,835	Old Trafford	H W	3–0	Wood R	Foulkes	Byrne R	Colman	Jones M	Edwards D	Berry J	Whelan L 1	Taylor T 1	Charlton	Pegg D 1	
10 Nov	Bolton Wanderers	39,922	Burnden Park	A L	0–2	Wood R	Foulkes	Byrne R	Colman	Jones M	Edwards D	Berry J	Whelan L	Taylor T	Charlton	Pegg D	
17 Nov	Leeds United	51,131	Old Trafford	H W	3–2	Wood R	Foulkes	Byrne R	Colman	Jones M	McGuinness	Berry J	Whelan L 2	Taylor T	Charlton 1	Pegg D	
24 Nov	Tottenham Hotspur	57,724	White Hart Lane	A D	2–2	Wood R	Foulkes	Byrne R	Colman 1	Blanchflower	McGuinness	Berry J 1	Whelan L	Taylor T	Edwards D	Pegg D	
1 Dec	Luton Town	34,736	Old Trafford	H W	3–1	Wood R	Foulkes	Byrne R	Colman	Jones M	McGuinness	Berry J	Whelan L	Taylor T 1	Edwards D 1	Pegg D 1	
8 Dec	Aston Villa	42,530	Villa Park	A W	3–1	Wood R	Foulkes	Bent	Colman	Jones M	Edwards D	Berry J	Whelan L	Taylor T 2	Viollet 1	Pegg D	
15 Dec	Birmingham City	36,146	St Andrews	A L	1–3	Wood R	Foulkes	Bent	Colman	Jones M	Edwards D	Berry J	Whelan L 1	Taylor T	Viollet	Pegg D	
26 Dec	Cardiff City	28,607	Old Trafford	H W	3–1	Wood R	Foulkes	Byrne R	Colman	Jones M	Edwards D	Berry J	Whelan L 1	Taylor T 1	Viollet 1	Pegg D	
29 Dec	Portsmouth	32,147	Fratton Park	A W	3–1	Wood R	Foulkes	Byrne R	Colman	Jones M	McGuinness	Berry J	Whelan L	Edwards D 1	Viollet 1	Pegg D 1	
1 Jan	Chelsea	42,116	Old Trafford	H W	3–0	Wood R	Foulkes	Byrne R	Colman	Jones M	Edwards D	Berry J	Whelan L 1	Taylor T 2	Viollet	Pegg D	
12 Jan	Newcastle United	44,911	Old Trafford	H W	6–1	Wood R	Foulkes	Byrne R	Colman	Jones M	Edwards D	Berry J	Whelan L 2	Taylor T	Viollet 2	Pegg D 2	
19 Jan	Sheffield Wednesday	51,068	Hillsborough	A L	1–2	Wood R	Foulkes	Byrne R	Colman	Jones M	Edwards D	Berry J	Whelan L	Taylor T 1	Viollet	Pegg D	
2 Feb	Manchester City	63,872	Maine Road	A W	4–2	Wood R	Foulkes	Byrne R	Colman	Jones M	Edwards D 1	Berry J	Whelan L 1	Taylor T 1	Viollet 1	Pegg D	
9 Feb	Arsenal	60,384	Old Trafford	H W	6–2	Wood R	Foulkes	Byrne R	Colman	Jones M	Edwards D 1	Berry J 2	Whelan L 2	Taylor T 1	Viollet	Pegg D	
18 Feb	Charlton Athletic	16,308	The Valley	A W	5–1	Wood R	Byrne R	Bent	Colman	Jones M	McGuinness	Berry J	Whelan L	Taylor T 2	Charlton 3	Pegg D	
23 Feb	Blackpool	42,602	Old Trafford	H L	0–2	Wood R	Foulkes	Byrne R	Colman	Jones M	Edwards D	Berry J	Whelan L	Taylor T	Charlton	Pegg D	
6 Mar	Everton	34,029	Goodison Park	A W	2–1	Wood R	Byrne R	Bent	Goodwin F	Blanchflower	McGuinness	Berry J	Whelan L	Webster 2	Doherty	Pegg D	
9 Mar	Aston Villa	55,484	Old Trafford	H D	1–1	Wood R	Foulkes	Byrne R	Goodwin F	Blanchflower	McGuinness	Berry J	Whelan L	Edwards D	Charlton 1	Pegg D	
16 Mar	Wolverhampton Wan.	53,228	Molineux	A D	1–1	Clayton	Foulkes	Byrne R	Colman	Blanchflower	Edwards D	Berry J	Whelan L	Webster	Charlton 1	Pegg D	
25 Mar	Bolton Wanderers	60,862	Old Trafford	H L	0–2	Wood R	Foulkes	Byrne R	Colman	Blanchflower	McGuinness	Berry J	Whelan L	Edwards D	Charlton	Pegg D	
30 Mar	Leeds United	47,216	Elland Road	A W	2–1	Wood R	Foulkes	Byrne R	Colman	Blanchflower	Edwards D	Berry J 1	Whelan L	Webster	Charlton 1	Pegg D	
6 Apr	Tottenham Hotspur	60,349	Old Trafford	H D	0–0	Wood R	Foulkes	Bent	Colman	Blanchflower	McGuinness	Berry J	Whelan L	Taylor T	Viollet	Scanlon	
13 Apr	Luton Town	21,227	Kenilworth Road	A W	2–0	Wood R	Foulkes	Byrne R	Goodwin F	Blanchflower	Edwards D	Berry J	Viollet	Taylor T 2	Charlton	Scanlon	
19 Apr	Burnley	41,321	Turf Moor	A W	3–1	Wood R	Foulkes	Byrne R	Goodwin F	Blanchflower	Edwards D	Berry J	Whelan L 3	Taylor T	Charlton	Pegg D	
20 Apr	Sunderland	58,725	Old Trafford	H W	4–0	Wood R	Foulkes	Byrne R	Colman	Blanchflower	Edwards D 1	Berry J	Whelan L 2	Taylor T 1	Charlton	Pegg D	
22 Apr	Burnley	41,321	Old Trafford	H W	2–0	Wood R	Foulkes	Greaves	Goodwin F	Cope	McGuinness	Webster 1	Doherty	Dawson 1	Viollet	Scanlon	
27 Apr	Cardiff City	17,708	Ninian Park	A W	3–2	Wood R	Foulkes	Greaves	Colman	Blanchflower	McGuinness	Webster	Whelan L	Dawson 1	Viollet	Scanlon 2	
29 Apr	West Bromwich Alb.	20,357	Old Trafford	H D	1–1	Clayton	Greaves	Byrne R	Goodwin F	Jones M	McGuinness	Berry J	Doherty	Dawson 1	Viollet	Scanlon	

FA Cup

5 Jan	Hartlepools Utd	17,264	Victoria Ground	A W	4–3	Wood R	Foulkes	Byrne R	Colman	Jones M	Edwards D	Berry J 1	Whelan L 2	Taylor T 1	Viollet	Pegg D	
26 Jan	Wrexham	34,445	The Racecourse	A W	5–0	Wood R	Foulkes	Byrne R 1	Colman	Jones M	Edwards D	Webster	Whelan L 2	Taylor T 2	Viollet	Pegg D	
16 Feb	Everton	61,803	Old Trafford	H W	1–0	Wood R	Foulkes	Byrne R	Colman	Jones M	Edwards D 1	Berry J	Whelan L	Taylor T	Viollet	Pegg D	
2 Mar	Bournemouth	28,799	Dean Court	A W	2–1	Wood R	Foulkes	Byrne R	Colman	Jones M	McGuinness	Berry J 2	Whelan L	Edwards D	Viollet	Pegg D	
23 Mar	Birmingham City	65,107	Hillsborough	A W	2–0	Wood R	Foulkes	Byrne R	Colman	Blanchflower	Edwards D	Berry J 1	Whelan L	Charlton 1	Viollet	Pegg D	
4 May	Aston Villa	100,000	Wembley	A L	1–2	Wood R	Foulkes	Byrne R	Colman	Blanchflower	Edwards D	Berry J	Whelan L	Taylor T 1	Charlton	Pegg D	

European Cup

12 Sep	Anderlecht	35,000	Parc Astrid	A W	2–0	Wood R	Foulkes	Byrne R	Colman	Jones M	Blanchflower	Berry J	Whelan L	Taylor T 1	Viollet 1	Pegg D	
26 Sep	Anderlecht	40,000	Maine Road	A W	10–0	Wood R	Foulkes	Byrne R	Colman	Jones M	Edwards D	Berry J 1	Whelan L 2	Taylor T 3	Viollet 4	Pegg D	
17 Oct	Borussia Dortmund	75,598	Maine Road	A W	3–2	Wood R	Foulkes	Byrne R	Colman	Jones M	Edwards D	Berry J	Whelan L	Taylor T	Viollet 2	Pegg D 1	
21 Nov	Borussia Dortmund	44,570	Rote Erde Stadion	A D	0–0	Wood R	Foulkes	Byrne R	Colman	Jones M	McGuinness	Berry J	Whelan L	Taylor T	Edwards D	Pegg D	
16 Jan	Atletico Bilbao	60,000	Estadio San Mames	A L	3–5	Wood R	Foulkes	Byrne R	Colman	Jones M	Edwards D	Berry J	Whelan L 1	Taylor T 1	Viollet 1	Pegg D	
6 Feb	Atletico Bilbao	70,000	Maine Road	A W	3–0	Wood R	Foulkes	Byrne R	Colman	Jones M	Edwards D	Berry J 1	Whelan L	Taylor T 1	Viollet 1	Pegg D	
11 Apr	Real Madrid	135,000	Bernabeu	A L	1–3	Wood R	Foulkes	Byrne R	Colman	Blanchflower	Edwards D	Berry J	Whelan L	Taylor T 1	Viollet	Pegg D	
25 Apr	Real Madrid	65,000	Old Trafford	H D	2–2	Wood R	Foulkes	Byrne R	Colman	Blanchflower	Edwards D	Berry J	Whelan L	Taylor T 1	Charlton 1	Pegg D	

Football League Division 1
P42 • W28 • D8 • L6 • F103 • A54 • PTS64
Position: 1

Results

1957/58

Football League

Substitutions: not introduced until 1965/66

Date	Opponent	Attendances	Venue				Players and Scores										
24 Aug	Leicester City	40,214	Filbert Street	A	W	3–0	Wood R	Foulkes	Byrne R	Colman	Blanchflower	Edwards D	Berry J	Whelan L 3	Taylor T	Viollet	Pegg D
28 Aug	Everton	59,103	Old Trafford	H	W	•3–0	Wood R	Foulkes	Byrne R	Colman	Blanchflower	Edwards D	Berry J	Whelan L	Taylor T 1	Viollet 1	Pegg D
31 Aug	Manchester City	63,347	Old Trafford	H	W	4–1	Wood R	Foulkes	Byrne R	Colman	Blanchflower	Edwards D 1	Berry J 1	Whelan L	Taylor T 1	Viollet 1	Pegg D
4 Sep	Everton	72,077	Goodison Park	A	D	3–3	Wood R	Foulkes	Byrne R	Colman	Blanchflower	Edwards D	Berry J 1	Whelan L 1	Taylor T	Viollet 1	Pegg D
7 Sep	Leeds United	50,842	Old Trafford	H	W	5–0	Wood R	Foulkes	Byrne R	Colman	Blanchflower	Edwards D	Berry J 2	Whelan L	Taylor T 2	Viollet 1	Pegg D
9 Sep	Blackpool	34,181	Bloomfield Road	A	W	4–1	Wood R	Foulkes	Byrne R	Colman	Blanchflower	Edwards D	Berry J	Whelan L 2	Taylor T	Viollet 2	Pegg D
14 Sep	Bolton Wanderers	48,003	Burnden Park	A	L	0–4	Wood R	Foulkes	Byrne R	Colman	Blanchflower	Edwards D	Berry J	Whelan L	Taylor T	Viollet	Pegg D
18 Sep	Blackpool	40,763	Old Trafford	H	L	1–2	Wood R	Foulkes	Byrne R	Colman	Blanchflower	Edwards D 1	Berry J	Whelan L	Taylor T	Viollet	Pegg D
21 Sep	Arsenal	47,142	Old Trafford	H	W	4–2	Wood R	Foulkes	Byrne R	Colman	Blanchflower	Edwards D	Berry J	Whelan L 2	Taylor T 1	Viollet	Pegg D 1
28 Sep	Wolverhampton Wan.	48,825	Molineux	A	L	1–3	Wood R	Foulkes	McGuinness	Goodwin F	Blanchflower	Edwards D	Berry J	Doherty 1	Taylor T	Charlton	Pegg D
5 Oct	Aston Villa	43,102	Old Trafford	H	W	•4–1	Wood R	Foulkes	Byrne R	Colman	Jones M	McGuinness	Berry J	Whelan L	Taylor T 2	Charlton	Pegg D 1
12 Oct	Nottingham Forest	47,654	City Ground	A	W	2–1	Wood R	Foulkes	Byrne R	Colman	Blanchflower	Edwards D	Berry J	Whelan L 1	Taylor T	Viollet 1	Pegg D
19 Oct	Portsmouth	38,253	Old Trafford	H	L	0–3	Wood R	Foulkes	Jones P	Colman	Blanchflower	McGuinness	Berry J	Whelan L	Dawson	Viollet	Pegg D
26 Oct	West Bromwich Alb.	52,160	The Hawthorns	A	L	3–4	Wood R	Foulkes	Byrne R	Goodwin F	Blanchflower	Edwards D	Berry J	Whelan L 1	Taylor T 2	Charlton	Pegg D
2 Nov	Burnley	49,449	Old Trafford	H	W	1–0	Wood R	Foulkes	Byrne R	Goodwin F	Blanchflower	Edwards D	Berry J	Whelan L	Taylor T 1	Webster	Pegg D
9 Nov	Preston North End	39,063	Deepdale	A	D	1–1	Wood R	Foulkes	Byrne R	Goodwin F	Blanchflower	Edwards D	Berry J	Whelan L 1	Taylor T	Webster	Pegg D
16 Nov	Sheffield Wednesday	40,366	Old Trafford	H	W	2–1	Wood R	Foulkes	Byrne R	Colman	Blanchflower	Edwards D	Berry J	Whelan L	Taylor T	Webster 2	Pegg D
23 Nov	Newcastle United	53,890	St James' Park	A	W	2–1	Wood R	Foulkes	Byrne R	Colman	Blanchflower	Edwards D 1	Scanlon	Whelan L	Taylor T 1	Webster	Pegg D
30 Nov	Tottenham Hotspur	43,077	Old Trafford	H	L	3–4	Gaskell	Foulkes	Byrne R	Colman	Blanchflower	Edwards D	Scanlon	Whelan L 1	Webster	Charlton	Pegg D 2
7 Dec	Birmingham City	35,791	St Andrews	A	D	3–3	Wood R	Foulkes	Byrne R	Colman	Jones M	Edwards D	Berry J	Whelan L	Taylor T 1	Viollet 2	Pegg D
14 Dec	Chelsea	36,853	Old Trafford	H	L	0–1	Wood R	Foulkes	Byrne R	Colman	Jones M	Edwards D	Berry J	Whelan L	Taylor T	Viollet	Pegg D
21 Dec	Leicester City	41,631	Old Trafford	H	W	4–0	Gregg	Foulkes	Byrne R	Colman	Jones M	Edwards D	Morgans	Charlton 1	Taylor T	Viollet 2	Scanlon 1
25 Dec	Luton Town	39,444	Old Trafford	H	W	3–0	Gregg	Foulkes	Byrne R	Colman	Jones M	Edwards D 1	Morgans	Charlton 1	Taylor T 1	Viollet	Scanlon
26 Dec	Luton Town	26,458	Kenilworth Road	A	D	2–2	Gregg	Foulkes	Byrne R	Colman	Jones M	Edwards D	Berry J	Charlton	Taylor T 1	Viollet	Scanlon 1
28 Dec	Manchester City	70,483	Maine Road	A	D	2–2	Gregg	Foulkes	Byrne R	Colman	Jones M	Edwards D	Morgans	Charlton 1	Webster	Viollet 1	Scanlon
11 Jan	Leeds United	39,401	Elland Road	A	D	1–1	Gregg	Foulkes	Byrne R	Colman	Jones M	Edwards D	Morgans	Charlton	Taylor T	Viollet 1	Scanlon
18 Jan	Bolton Wanderers	41,141	Old Trafford	H	W	7–2	Gregg	Foulkes	Byrne R	Colman	Jones M	Edwards D 1	Morgans	Charlton 3	Taylor T	Viollet 2	Scanlon 1
1 Feb	Arsenal	63,578	Highbury	A	W	5–4	Gregg	Foulkes	Byrne R	Colman	Jones M	Edwards D 1	Morgans	Charlton 1	Taylor T 2	Viollet 1	Scanlon
22 Feb	Nottingham Forest	66,124	Old Trafford	H	D	1–1	Gregg	Foulkes	Greaves	Goodwin F	Cope	Crowther	Webster	Taylor E	Dawson 1	Pearson M	Brennan
8 Mar	West Bromwich Alb.	63,278	Old Trafford	H	L	0–4	Gregg	Foulkes	Greaves	Goodwin F	Cope	Harrop	Webster	Taylor E	Dawson	Pearson M	Charlton
15 Mar	Burnley	37,247	Turf Moor	A	L	0–3	Gregg	Foulkes	Greaves	Goodwin F	Cope	Crowther	Webster	Harrop	Dawson	Pearson M	Charlton
29 Mar	Sheffield Wednesday	35,608	Hillsborough	A	L	0–1	Gregg	Foulkes	Cope	Goodwin F	Harrop	Crowther	Webster	Taylor E	Dawson	Charlton	Brennan
31 Mar	Aston Villa	16,631	Villa Park	A	L	2–3	Gregg	Foulkes	Cope	Goodwin F	Harrop	Crowther	Webster 1	Pearson M	Dawson 1	Charlton	Brennan
4 Apr	Sunderland	47,421	Old Trafford	H	D	2–2	Gregg	Foulkes	Greaves	Goodwin F	Cope	Crowther	Webster	Taylor E	Dawson 1	Charlton 1	Brennan
5 Apr	Preston North End	47,816	Old Trafford	H	D	0–0	Gregg	Foulkes	Greaves	Goodwin F	Cope	Crowther	Morgans	Taylor E	Webster	Charlton	Heron
7 Apr	Sunderland	51,302	Roker Park	A	W	2–1	Gregg	Foulkes	Greaves	Goodwin F	Harrop	McGuinness	Morgans	Taylor E	Webster 2	Charlton	Pearson M
12 Apr	Tottenham Hotspur	59,836	White Hart Lane	A	L	0–1	Gregg	Foulkes	Greaves	Goodwin F	Cope	Crowther	Morgans	Taylor E	Webster	Charlton	Pearson M
16 Apr	Portsmouth	39,975	Fratton Park	A	D	3–3	Gaskell	Foulkes	Greaves	Crowther	Cope	McGuinness	Dawson 1	Taylor E 1	Webster 1	Pearson M	Morgans
19 Apr	Birmingham City	38,991	Old Trafford	H	L	0–2	Gregg	Foulkes	Greaves	Goodwin F	Cope	Crowther	Dawson	Taylor E	Webster	Pearson M	Morgans
21 Apr	Wolverhampton Wan.	33,267	Old Trafford	H	L	0–4	Gaskell	Foulkes	Greaves	Goodwin F	Cope	McGuinness	Dawson	Brennan	Webster	Viollet	Morgans
23 Apr	Newcastle United	28,393	Old Trafford	H	D	1–1	Gregg	Foulkes	Greaves	Crowther	Cope	McGuinness	Dawson 1	Taylor E	Webster	Charlton	Morgans
26 Apr	Chelsea	45,011	Stamford Bridge	A	L	1–2	Gregg	Foulkes	Greaves	Goodwin F	Cope	Crowther	Dawson	Taylor E 1	Charlton	Viollet	Webster

FA Cup

Date	Opponent	Attendances	Venue				Players and Scores										
4 Jan	Workington Town	21,000	Borough Park	A	W	3–1	Gregg	Foulkes	Byrne R	Colman	Jones M	Edwards D	Morgans	Charlton	Taylor T	Viollet 3	Scanlon
25 Jan	Ipswich Town	53,550	Old Trafford	H	W	2–0	Gregg	Foulkes	Byrne R	Colman	Jones M	Edwards D	Morgans	Charlton 2	Taylor T	Viollet	Scanlon
19 Feb	Sheffield Wednesday	59,848	Old Trafford	H	W	3–0	Gregg	Foulkes	Greaves	Goodwin F	Cope	Crowther	Webster	Taylor E	Dawson 1	Pearson M	Brennan 2
1 Mar	West Bromwich Alb.	58,250	The Hawthorns	A	D	2–2	Gregg	Foulkes	Greaves	Goodwin F	Cope	Crowther	Webster	Taylor E 1	Dawson 1	Pearson M	Charlton
5 Mar	West Bromwich Alb.	60,000	Old Trafford	H	W	1–0	Gregg	Foulkes	Greaves	Goodwin F	Cope	Harrop	Webster 1	Taylor E	Dawson	Pearson M	Charlton
22 Mar	Fulham	69,745	Villa Park	A	D	2–2	Gregg	Foulkes	Greaves	Goodwin F	Cope	Crowther	Webster	Taylor E	Dawson	Pearson M	Charlton 2
26 Mar	Fulham	38,000	Highbury	A	W	5–3	Gregg	Foulkes	Greaves	Goodwin F	Cope	Crowther	Webster	Taylor E	Dawson 3	Charlton 1	Brennan 1
3 May	Bolton Wanderers	100,000	Wembley	A	L	0–2	Gregg	Foulkes	Greaves	Goodwin F	Cope	Crowther	Dawson	Taylor E	Charlton	Viollet	Webster

European Cup

Date	Opponent	Attendances	Venue				Players and Scores										
25 Sep	Shamrock Rovers	45,000	Dalymount Park	A	W	6–0	Wood R	Foulkes	Byrne R	Goodwin F	Blanchflower	Edwards D	Berry J 1	Whelan L 2	Taylor T 2	Viollet	Pegg D 1
2 Oct	Shamrock Rovers	33,754	Old Trafford	H	W	3–2	Wood R	Foulkes	Byrne R	Colman	Jones M	McGuinness	Berry J	Webster	Taylor T	Viollet 2	Pegg D 1
20 Nov	Dukla Prague	60,000	Old Trafford	H	W	3–0	Wood R	Foulkes	Byrne R	Colman	Blanchflower	Edwards D	Berry J	Whelan L	Taylor T 1	Webster 1	Pegg D 1
4 Dec	Dukla Prague	35,000	Stadion Strahov	A	L	0–1	Wood R	Foulkes	Byrne R	Colman	Jones M	Edwards D	Scanlon	Whelan L	Taylor T	Webster	Pegg D
14 Jan	Red Star Belgrade	60,000	Old Trafford	H	W	2–1	Gregg	Foulkes	Byrne R	Colman 1	Jones M	Edwards D	Morgans	Charlton 1	Taylor T	Viollet	Scanlon
5 Feb	Red Star Belgrade	55,000	Stadion JNA	A	D	3–3	Gregg	Foulkes	Byrne R	Colman	Jones M	Edwards D	Morgans	Charlton 2	Taylor T	Viollet 1	Scanlon
8 May	AC Milan	44,880	Old Trafford	H	W	2–1	Gregg	Foulkes	Greaves	Goodwin F	Cope	Crowther	Morgans	Taylor E 1	Webster	Viollet 1	Pearson M
14 May	AC Milan	80,000	Stadio San Siro	A	L	0–4	Gregg	Foulkes	Greaves	Goodwin F	Cope	Crowther	Morgans	Taylor E	Webster	Viollet	Pearson M

Football League Division 1
P42 • W16 • D11 • L15 • F85 • A75 • PTS43
Position: 9

1958/59

Football League

Substitutions: not introduced until 1965/66

Date	Opponent	Attendances	Venue				Players and Scores										
23 Aug	Chelsea	52,382	Old Trafford	H	W	5–2	Gregg	Foulkes	Greaves	Goodwin F	Cope	McGuinness	Dawson 2	Taylor E	Viollet	Charlton 3	Scanlon
27 Aug	Nottingham Forest	44,971	City Ground	A	W	3–0	Gregg	Foulkes	Greaves	Goodwin F	Cope	McGuinness	Dawson	Taylor E	Viollet	Charlton 2	Scanlon 1
30 Aug	Blackpool	36,719	Bloomfield Road	A	L	1–2	Gregg	Foulkes	Greaves	Goodwin F	Cope	McGuinness	Dawson	Taylor E	Viollet 1	Charlton	Scanlon
3 Sep	Nottingham Forest	51,880	Old Trafford	H	D	1–1	Gregg	Foulkes	Greaves	Goodwin F	Cope	McGuinness	Dawson	Taylor E	Viollet	Charlton 1	Scanlon
6 Sep	Blackburn Rovers	65,187	Old Trafford	H	W	6–1	Gregg	Foulkes	Greaves	Goodwin F	Cope	McGuinness	Webster 1	Taylor E	Viollet 2	Charlton 2	Scanlon 1
8 Sep	West Ham United	35,672	Upton Park	A	L	2–3	Gregg	Foulkes	Greaves	Goodwin F	Cope	McGuinness 1	Webster 1	Taylor E	Viollet	Charlton	Scanlon
13 Sep	Newcastle United	60,670	St James' Park	A	D	1–1	Gregg	Foulkes	Greaves	Goodwin F	Cope	Crowther	Webster	Taylor E	Dawson	Charlton 1	Scanlon
17 Sep	West Ham United	53,276	Old Trafford	H	W	4–1	Gregg	Foulkes	Greaves	Goodwin F	Cope	McGuinness	Webster 1	Taylor E	Viollet	Charlton	Scanlon 3
20 Sep	Tottenham Hotspur	62,277	Old Trafford	H	D	2–2	Gregg	Foulkes	Greaves	Goodwin F	Cope	McGuinness	Webster 2	Quixall	Dawson	Charlton	Scanlon
27 Sep	Manchester City	62,912	Maine Road	A	D	1–1	Gregg	Foulkes	Greaves	Goodwin F	Cope	McGuinness	Viollet	Quixall	Webster	Charlton 1	Scanlon
4 Oct	Wolverhampton Wan.	36,840	Molineux	A	L	0–4	Wood R	Foulkes	Greaves	Goodwin F	Harrop	Crowther	Viollet	Quixall	Webster	Pearson M	Scanlon
8 Oct	Preston North End	46,163	Old Trafford	H	L	0–2	Gregg	Foulkes	Greaves	Goodwin F	Cope	McGuinness	Dawson	Taylor E	Viollet	Charlton	Scanlon
11 Oct	Arsenal	56,148	Old Trafford	H	D	1–1	Gregg	Foulkes	Greaves	Goodwin F	Cope	McGuinness	Viollet 1	Quixall	Charlton	Taylor E	Scanlon
18 Oct	Everton	64,079	Goodison Park	A	L	2–3	Gregg	Foulkes	Greaves	Goodwin F	Cope 2	McGuinness	Viollet	Quixall	Charlton	Taylor E	Scanlon
25 Oct	West Bromwich Alb.	51,721	Old Trafford	H	L	1–2	Gregg	Foulkes	Greaves	Goodwin F 1	Harrop	McGuinness	Viollet	Quixall	Dawson	Charlton	Scanlon
1 Nov	Leeds United	48,574	Elland Road	A	W	2–1	Gregg	Foulkes	Greaves	Goodwin F 1	Harrop	McGuinness	Morgans	Quixall	Dawson	Charlton	Scanlon 1
8 Nov	Burnley	48,509	Old Trafford	H	L	1–3	Gregg	Foulkes	Greaves	Goodwin F	Harrop	McGuinness	Morgans	Quixall 1	Dawson	Charlton	Scanlon
15 Nov	Bolton Wanderers	33,358	Burnden Park	A	L	3–6	Gregg	Foulkes	Greaves	Goodwin F	Cope	McGuinness	Bradley	Quixall	Dawson 2	Charlton 1	Scanlon
22 Nov	Luton Town	42,428	Old Trafford	H	W	2–1	Gregg	Foulkes	Carolan	Goodwin F	Cope	McGuinness	Bradley	Quixall	Viollet 1	Charlton 1	Scanlon
29 Nov	Birmingham City	28,658	St Andrews	A	W	4–0	Gregg	Foulkes	Carolan	Goodwin F	Cope	McGuinness	Bradley 1	Quixall	Viollet	Charlton 2	Scanlon 1
6 Dec	Leicester City	38,482	Old Trafford	H	W	4–1	Gregg	Foulkes	Carolan	Goodwin F	Cope	McGuinness	Bradley 1	Quixall	Viollet 1	Charlton 1	Scanlon 1
13 Dec	Preston North End	26,290	Deepdale	A	W	4–3	Gregg	Foulkes	Carolan	Goodwin F	Cope	McGuinness	Bradley 1	Quixall	Viollet 1	Charlton 1	Scanlon 1
20 Dec	Chelsea	48,550	Stamford Bridge	A	W	•3–2	Gregg	Foulkes	Carolan	Goodwin F 1	Cope	McGuinness	Bradley	Quixall	Viollet	Charlton 1	Scanlon
26 Dec	Aston Villa	63,098	Old Trafford	H	W	2–1	Gregg	Foulkes	Carolan	Goodwin F	Cope	McGuinness	Bradley	Quixall 1	Viollet 1	Pearson M	Scanlon
27 Dec	Aston Villa	56,450	Villa Park	A	W	2–0	Gregg	Foulkes	Greaves	Goodwin F	Cope	McGuinness	Hunter R	Quixall	Viollet 1	Pearson M 1	Scanlon
3 Jan	Blackpool	61,961	Old Trafford	H	W	3–1	Gregg	Foulkes	Carolan	Goodwin F	Cope	McGuinness	Bradley	Quixall	Viollet 1	Charlton 2	Scanlon
31 Jan	Newcastle United	49,008	Old Trafford	H	D	4–4	Gregg	Foulkes	Carolan	Harrop	Goodwin F	McGuinness	Bradley	Quixall 1	Viollet 1	Charlton 1	Scanlon 1
7 Feb	Tottenham Hotspur	48,401	White Hart Lane	A	W	3–1	Gregg	Greaves	Carolan	Goodwin F	Cope	McGuinness	Bradley	Quixall	Viollet	Charlton 2	Scanlon 1
14 Feb	Manchester City	59,846	Old Trafford	H	W	4–1	Gregg	Greaves	Carolan	Goodwin F 1	Cope	McGuinness	Bradley 2	Quixall	Viollet	Charlton	Scanlon 1
21 Feb	Wolverhampton Wan.	62,794	Old Trafford	H	W	2–1	Gregg	Greaves	Carolan	Goodwin F	Cope	McGuinness	Bradley	Quixall	Viollet 1	Charlton 1	Scanlon
28 Feb	Arsenal	67,162	Highbury	A	L	2–3	Gregg	Greaves	Carolan	Goodwin F	Cope	McGuinness	Bradley 1	Quixall	Viollet 1	Charlton	Scanlon
2 Mar	Blackburn Rovers	40,401	Ewood Park	A	W	3–1	Gregg	Greaves	Carolan	Goodwin F	Cope	McGuinness	Bradley 2	Quixall	Viollet	Charlton	Scanlon 1
7 Mar	Everton	51,254	Old Trafford	H	W	2–1	Gregg	Greaves	Carolan	Goodwin F 1	Cope	McGuinness	Bradley	Quixall	Viollet	Charlton	Scanlon 1
14 Mar	West Bromwich Alb.	35,463	The Hawthorns	A	W	3–1	Gregg	Greaves	Carolan	Goodwin F	Cope	McGuinness	Bradley 1	Quixall	Viollet 1	Charlton	Scanlon 1
21 Mar	Leeds United	45,473	Old Trafford	H	W	4–0	Gregg	Greaves	Carolan	Goodwin F	Cope	McGuinness	Bradley	Quixall	Viollet 3	Charlton 1	Scanlon
27 Mar	Portsmouth	52,004	Old Trafford	H	W	•6–1	Gregg	Greaves	Carolan	Goodwin F	Cope	McGuinness	Bradley 1	Quixall	Viollet 2	Charlton 2	Scanlon
28 Mar	Burnley	44,577	Turf Moor	A	L	2–4	Gregg	Greaves	Carolan	Goodwin F 1	Cope	McGuinness	Bradley	Quixall	Viollet 1	Charlton	Scanlon
30 Mar	Portsmouth	29,359	Fratton Park	A	W	3–1	Gregg	Greaves	Carolan	Goodwin F	Foulkes	McGuinness	Bradley 1	Quixall	Viollet	Charlton 2	Scanlon
4 Apr	Bolton Wanderers	61,528	Old Trafford	H	W	3–0	Gregg	Greaves	Carolan	Goodwin F	Foulkes	McGuinness	Bradley	Quixall	Viollet 1	Charlton 1	Scanlon 1
11 Apr	Luton Town	27,025	Kenilworth Road	A	D	0–0	Gregg	Greaves	Carolan	Goodwin F	Foulkes	McGuinness	Bradley	Quixall	Viollet	Pearson M	Scanlon
18 Apr	Birmingham City	43,006	Old Trafford	H	W	1–0	Gregg	Greaves	Carolan	Goodwin F	Foulkes	McGuinness	Bradley	Quixall 1	Viollet	Charlton	Scanlon
25 Apr	Leicester City	38,466	Filbert Street	A	L	1–2	Gregg	Greaves	Carolan	Goodwin F	Foulkes	Brennan	Bradley 1	Quixall	Viollet	Charlton	Scanlon

FA Cup

Date	Opponent	Attendances	Venue				Players and Scores										
10 Jan	Norwich City	38,000	Carrow Road	A	L	0–3	Gregg	Foulkes	Carolan	Goodwin F	Cope	McGuinness	Bradley	Quixall	Viollet	Charlton	Scanlon

Football League Division 1
P42 • W24 • D7 • L11 • F103 • A66 • PTS55
Position: 2

The 1960s

1959/60

Football League		Attendances	Venue				Players and Scores											Substitutions: not introduced until 1965/66
22 Aug	West Bromwich Alb.	40,076	The Hawthorns	A	L	2–3	Gregg	Greaves	Carolan	Goodwin F	Foulkes	McGuinness	Bradley	Quixall	Viollet 2	Charlton	Scanlon	
26 Aug	Chelsea	57,674	Old Trafford	H	L	0–1	Gregg	Greaves	Carolan	Goodwin F	Foulkes	McGuinness	Bradley	Quixall	Dawson	Viollet	Charlton	
29 Aug	Newcastle United	53,257	Old Trafford	H	W	3–2	Gregg	Cope	Carolan	Brennan	Foulkes	McGuinness	Bradley	Quixall	Viollet 2	Charlton 1	Scanlon	
2 Sep	Chelsea	66,579	Stamford Bridge	A	W	6–3	Gregg	Cope	Carolan	Brennan	Foulkes	McGuinness	Bradley 2	Quixall 1	Viollet 2	Charlton 1	Scanlon	
5 Sep	Birmingham City	38,220	St Andrews	A	D	1–1	Gregg	Cope	Carolan	Brennan	Foulkes	McGuinness	Bradley	Quixall 1	Viollet	Charlton	Scanlon	
9 Sep	Leeds United	48,407	Old Trafford	H	W	6–0	Gregg	Cope	Carolan	Brennan	Foulkes	McGuinness	Bradley 2	Quixall	Viollet 1	Charlton 2	Scanlon 1	
12 Sep	Tottenham Hotspur	55,402	Old Trafford	H	L	1–5	Gregg	Cope	Carolan	Goodwin F	Foulkes	McGuinness	Bradley	Giles	Viollet 1	Charlton	Scanlon	
16 Sep	Leeds United	34,048	Elland Road	A	D	•2–2	Gregg	Cope	Carolan	Brennan	Foulkes	McGuinness	Bradley	Quixall	Viollet	Charlton 1	Scanlon	
19 Sep	Manchester City	58,300	Maine Road	A	L	0–3	Gregg	Foulkes	Carolan	Brennan	Cope	McGuinness	Bradley	Quixall	Viollet	Charlton	Scanlon	
26 Sep	Preston North End	35,016	Deepdale	A	L	0–4	Gregg	Foulkes	Carolan	Viollet	Cope	McGuinness	Bradley	Quixall	Dawson	Charlton	Scanlon	
3 Oct	Leicester City	41,637	Old Trafford	H	W	4–1	Gaskell	Foulkes	Carolan	Goodwin F	Cope	McGuinness	Bradley	Quixall 1	Viollet 2	Charlton 1	Scanlon	
10 Oct	Arsenal	51,626	Old Trafford	H	W	•4–2	Gregg	Foulkes	Carolan	Goodwin F	Cope	McGuinness	Bradley	Quixall 1	Viollet 1	Charlton 1	Scanlon	
17 Oct	Wolverhampton Wan.	45,451	Molineux	A	L	•2–3	Gregg	Foulkes	Carolan	Goodwin F	Cope	McGuinness	Bradley	Giles	Viollet 1	Pearson M	Scanlon	
24 Oct	Sheffield Wednesday	39,259	Old Trafford	H	W	3–1	Gregg	Foulkes	Carolan	Goodwin F	Cope	McGuinness	Bradley 1	Quixall	Viollet 2	Charlton	Scanlon	
31 Oct	Blackburn Rovers	39,621	Ewood Park	A	D	1–1	Gregg	Foulkes	Carolan	Goodwin F	Cope	McGuinness	Bradley	Quixall 1	Viollet	Charlton	Scanlon	
7 Nov	Fulham	44,063	Old Trafford	H	D	3–3	Gregg	Foulkes	Carolan	Goodwin F	Cope	McGuinness	Bradley	Quixall	Viollet 1	Charlton 1	Scanlon 1	
14 Nov	Bolton Wanderers	37,892	Burnden Park	A	D	1–1	Gregg	Foulkes	Carolan	Goodwin F	Cope	McGuinness	Bradley	Quixall	Viollet	Charlton	Dawson 1	
21 Nov	Luton Town	40,572	Old Trafford	H	W	4–1	Gregg	Foulkes	Carolan	Goodwin F 1	Cope	McGuinness	Bradley	Quixall 1	Viollet 2	Charlton	Scanlon	
28 Nov	Everton	46,095	Goodison Park	A	L	1–2	Gregg	Foulkes	Carolan	Goodwin F	Cope	McGuinness	Bradley	Quixall	Viollet 1	Charlton	Scanlon	
5 Dec	Blackpool	45,558	Old Trafford	H	W	3–1	Gaskell	Foulkes	Carolan	Goodwin F	Cope	Brennan	Dawson	Quixall	Viollet 2	Pearson M 1	Scanlon	
12 Dec	Nottingham Forest	31,666	City Ground	A	W	5–1	Gaskell	Foulkes	Carolan	Goodwin F	Cope	Brennan	Dawson 1	Quixall	Viollet 3	Pearson M	Scanlon 1	
19 Dec	West Bromwich Alb.	33,677	Old Trafford	H	L	2–3	Gaskell	Foulkes	Carolan	Goodwin F	Cope	Brennan	Dawson 1	Quixall 1	Viollet	Pearson M	Scanlon	
26 Dec	Burnley	62,376	Old Trafford	H	L	1–2	Gaskell	Foulkes	Carolan	Goodwin F	Cope	Brennan	Dawson	Quixall 1	Viollet	Charlton	Scanlon	
28 Dec	Burnley	47,253	Turf Moor	A	W	4–1	Gaskell	Foulkes	Carolan	Goodwin F	Cope	Brennan	Dawson	Quixall	Viollet 2	Charlton	Scanlon 2	
2 Jan	Newcastle United	57,200	St James' Park	A	L	3–7	Gaskell	Foulkes	Carolan	Goodwin F	Cope	Brennan	Dawson 1	Quixall 2	Viollet	Charlton	Scanlon	
16 Jan	Birmingham City	47,361	Old Trafford	H	W	2–1	Gregg	Foulkes	Carolan	Setters	Cope	Brennan	Bradley	Quixall 1	Viollet 1	Charlton	Scanlon	
23 Jan	Tottenham Hotspur	62,602	White Hart Lane	A	L	1–2	Gregg	Foulkes	Carolan	Setters	Cope	Brennan	Bradley 1	Quixall	Viollet	Charlton	Scanlon	
6 Feb	Manchester City	59,450	Old Trafford	H	D	0–0	Gregg	Foulkes	Carolan	Setters	Cope	Brennan	Bradley	Quixall	Viollet	Charlton	Scanlon	
13 Feb	Preston North End	44,014	Old Trafford	H	D	1–1	Gregg	Foulkes	Carolan	Setters	Cope	Brennan	Bradley	Quixall	Viollet 1	Charlton	Scanlon	
24 Feb	Leicester City	33,191	Filbert Street	A	L	1–3	Gregg	Foulkes	Carolan	Setters	Cope	Brennan	Viollet	Quixall	Dawson	Charlton	Scanlon 1	
27 Feb	Blackpool	23,996	Bloomfield Road	A	W	6–0	Gregg	Foulkes	Carolan	Setters	Cope	Brennan	Viollet 2	Quixall	Dawson	Charlton 3	Scanlon 1	
5 Mar	Wolverhampton Wan.	60,560	Old Trafford	H	L	0–2	Gregg	Foulkes	Carolan	Setters	Cope	Brennan	Viollet	Quixall	Dawson	Charlton	Scanlon	
19 Mar	Nottingham Forest	35,269	Old Trafford	H	W	3–1	Gregg	Foulkes	Carolan	Setters	Cope	Brennan	Giles	Viollet	Dawson 1	Pearson M	Charlton 2	
26 Mar	Fulham	38,250	Craven Cottage	A	W	5–0	Gregg	Foulkes	Carolan	Setters	Cope	Brennan	Giles 1	Viollet 2	Dawson 1	Pearson M 1	Charlton	
30 Mar	Sheffield Wednesday	26,821	Hillsborough	A	L	2–4	Gaskell	Foulkes	Heron	Setters	Cope	Brennan	Bradley	Viollet 1	Dawson	Pearson M	Charlton 1	
2 Apr	Bolton Wanderers	45,298	Old Trafford	H	W	2–0	Gaskell	Foulkes	Carolan	Setters	Cope	Brennan	Bradley	Giles	Dawson	Pearson M	Charlton 2	
9 Apr	Luton Town	21,242	Kenilworth Road	A	W	3–2	Gregg	Foulkes	Carolan	Setters	Cope	Brennan	Bradley 1	Giles	Dawson 2	Lawton	Scanlon	
15 Apr	West Ham United	34,969	Upton Park	A	L	1–2	Gregg	Foulkes	Carolan	Setters	Cope	Brennan	Bradley	Giles	Dawson 1	Lawton	Charlton	
16 Apr	Blackburn Rovers	45,945	Old Trafford	H	W	1–0	Gregg	Foulkes	Carolan	Setters	Cope	Brennan	Bradley	Giles	Dawson 1	Lawton	Charlton	
18 Apr	West Ham United	34,676	Old Trafford	H	W	5–3	Gregg	Foulkes	Carolan	Setters	Cope	Brennan	Giles	Quixall 1	Dawson 2	Viollet	Charlton 2	
23 Apr	Arsenal	41,057	Highbury	A	L	2–5	Gregg	Foulkes	Carolan	Setters	Cope	Brennan	Giles 1	Quixall	Dawson	Pearson M 1	Charlton	
30 Apr	Everton	43,823	Old Trafford	H	W	5–0	Gregg	Foulkes	Carolan	Setters	Cope	Brennan	Bradley 1	Quixall 1	Dawson 3	Pearson M	Charlton	
FA Cup																		
9 Jan	Derby County	33,297	Baseball Ground	A	W	•4–2	Gregg	Foulkes	Carolan	Goodwin F 1	Cope	Brennan	Dawson	Quixall	Viollet	Charlton 1	Scanlon 1	
30 Jan	Liverpool	56,736	Anfield	A	W	3–1	Gregg	Foulkes	Carolan	Setters	Cope	Brennan	Bradley 1	Quixall	Viollet	Charlton 2	Scanlon	
20 Feb	Sheffield Wednesday	66,350	Old Trafford	H	L	0–1	Gregg	Foulkes	Carolan	Setters	Cope	Brennan	Bradley	Quixall	Viollet	Charlton	Scanlon	

Football League Division 1
P42 • W19 • D7 • L16 • F102 • A80 • PTS45
Position: 7

1960/61

Football League		Attendances	Venue				Players and Scores											Substitutions: not introduced until 1965/66
20 Aug	Blackburn Rovers	47,778	Old Trafford	H	L	1–3	Gregg	Cope	Carolan	Setters	Haydock	Brennan	Giles	Quixall	Viollet	Charlton 1	Scanlon	
24 Aug	Everton	51,602	Goodison Park	A	L	0–4	Gregg	Brennan	Carolan	Setters	Haydock	Nicholson	Giles	Quixall	Viollet	Charlton	Scanlon	
31 Aug	Everton	51,818	Old Trafford	H	W	4–0	Gregg	Foulkes	Brennan	Setters	Haydock	Nicholson 1	Quixall	Giles	Dawson 2	Viollet	Charlton 1	
3 Sep	Tottenham Hotspur	55,445	White Hart Lane	A	L	1–4	Gregg	Foulkes	Brennan	Setters	Haydock	Nicholson	Quixall	Giles	Dawson	Viollet 1	Charlton	
5 Sep	West Ham United	30,506	Upton Park	A	L	1–2	Gregg	Foulkes	Brennan	Setters	Cope	Nicholson	Quixall 1	Giles	Dawson	Viollet	Charlton	
10 Sep	Leicester City	35,493	Old Trafford	H	D	1–1	Gregg	Foulkes	Brennan	Setters	Cope	Nicholson	Quixall	Giles 1	Dawson	Viollet	Charlton	
14 Sep	West Ham United	33,695	Old Trafford	H	W	6–1	Gregg	Foulkes	Brennan	Setters	Cope	Nicholson	Quixall 1	Giles	Viollet 2	Charlton 2	Scanlon 1	
17 Sep	Aston Villa	43,593	Villa Park	A	L	1–3	Gregg	Foulkes	Brennan	Setters	Cope	Nicholson	Giles	Quixall	Viollet 1	Charlton	Scanlon	
24 Sep	Wolverhampton Wan.	44,458	Old Trafford	H	L	1–3	Gregg	Foulkes	Brennan	Setters	Cope	Nicholson	Giles	Quixall	Viollet	Charlton 1	Scanlon	
1 Oct	Bolton Wanderers	39,197	Burnden Park	A	D	1–1	Gregg	Setters	Brennan	Stiles	Foulkes	Nicholson	Moir	Giles 1	Dawson	Charlton	Scanlon	
15 Oct	Burnley	32,011	Turf Moor	A	L	3–5	Gregg	Setters	Dunne A	Stiles	Foulkes	Nicholson	Quixall	Giles	Viollet 3	Pearson M	Charlton	
22 Oct	Newcastle United	37,516	Old Trafford	H	W	3–2	Gregg	Setters 1	Brennan	Stiles 1	Foulkes	Nicholson	Dawson 1	Giles	Viollet	Charlton	Scanlon	
24 Oct	Nottingham Forest	23,628	Old Trafford	H	W	2–1	Gregg	Dunne A	Brennan	Stiles	Foulkes	Nicholson	Dawson	Giles	Viollet 2	Pearson M	Scanlon	
29 Oct	Arsenal	45,715	Highbury	A	L	1–2	Gregg	Brennan	Heron	Stiles	Foulkes	Nicholson	Dawson	Giles	Viollet	Quixall 1	Charlton	
5 Nov	Sheffield Wednesday	36,855	Old Trafford	H	D	0–0	Gregg	Setters	Brennan	Stiles	Foulkes	Nicholson	Dawson	Giles	Viollet	Quixall	Charlton	
12 Nov	Birmingham City	31,549	St Andrews	A	L	1–3	Gregg	Setters	Brennan	Stiles	Foulkes	Nicholson	Dawson	Giles	Viollet	Pearson M	Charlton 1	
19 Nov	West Bromwich Alb.	32,756	Old Trafford	H	W	3–0	Gregg	Setters	Brennan	Stiles	Foulkes	Nicholson	Bradley	Quixall 1	Dawson 1	Viollet 1	Charlton	
26 Nov	Cardiff City	21,122	Ninian Park	A	L	0–3	Gregg	Brennan	Cantwell	Setters	Foulkes	Nicholson	Bradley	Quixall	Dawson	Viollet	Charlton	
3 Dec	Preston North End	24,904	Old Trafford	H	W	1–0	Gregg	Brennan	Cantwell	Setters	Foulkes	Nicholson	Bradley	Quixall	Dawson 1	Pearson M	Charlton	
10 Dec	Fulham	23,625	Craven Cottage	A	D	4–4	Gregg	Brennan	Cantwell	Setters	Foulkes	Nicholson	Bradley	Quixall 2	Dawson 1	Pearson M	Charlton 1	
17 Dec	Blackburn Rovers	17,285	Ewood Park	A	W	2–1	Gregg	Brennan	Cantwell	Setters	Foulkes	Nicholson	Quixall	Stiles	Dawson	Pearson M 2	Charlton	
24 Dec	Chelsea	37,601	Stamford Bridge	A	W	2–1	Gregg	Brennan	Cantwell	Setters	Foulkes	Nicholson	Quixall	Stiles	Dawson 1	Pearson M	Charlton 1	
26 Dec	Chelsea	50,164	Old Trafford	H	W	6–0	Gregg	Brennan	Cantwell	Setters	Foulkes	Nicholson 2	Quixall	Stiles	Dawson 3	Pearson M	Charlton 1	
31 Dec	Manchester City	61,213	Old Trafford	H	W	5–1	Gregg	Brennan	Cantwell	Setters	Foulkes	Nicholson	Quixall	Stiles	Dawson 3	Pearson M	Charlton 2	
16 Jan	Tottenham Hotspur	65,295	Old Trafford	H	W	2–0	Gregg	Brennan	Cantwell	Setters	Foulkes	Nicholson	Quixall	Stiles 1	Dawson	Pearson M 1	Charlton	
21 Jan	Leicester City	31,308	Filbert Street	A	L	0–6	Briggs	Brennan	Cantwell	Setters	Foulkes	Nicholson	Quixall	Stiles	Dawson	Pearson M	Charlton	
4 Feb	Aston Villa	33,525	Old Trafford	H	D	1–1	Pinner	Brennan	Cantwell	Setters	Foulkes	Nicholson	Quixall	Stiles	Dawson	Pearson M	Charlton 1	
11 Feb	Wolverhampton Wan.	38,526	Molineux	A	L	1–2	Pinner	Brennan	Cantwell	Setters	Foulkes	Nicholson 1	Quixall	Stiles	Dawson	Pearson M	Charlton	
18 Feb	Bolton Wanderers	37,558	Old Trafford	H	W	3–1	Pinner	Brennan	Cantwell	Stiles	Foulkes	Setters	Morgans	Quixall 1	Dawson 2	Pearson M	Charlton	
25 Feb	Nottingham Forest	26,850	City Ground	A	L	2–3	Gregg	Brennan	Cantwell	Setters	Foulkes	Nicholson	Morgans	Quixall 1	Dawson	Pearson M	Charlton 1	
4 Mar	Manchester City	50,479	Maine Road	A	W	3–1	Gregg	Brennan	Cantwell	Setters	Foulkes	Stiles	Moir	Quixall	Dawson 1	Pearson M 1	Charlton 1	
11 Mar	Newcastle United	28,870	St James' Park	A	D	1–1	Pinner	Brennan	Cantwell	Setters	Foulkes	Stiles	Moir	Quixall	Lawton	Pearson M	Charlton 1	
18 Mar	Arsenal	29,732	Old Trafford	H	D	1–1	Gaskell	Brennan	Cantwell	Setters	Foulkes	Stiles	Moir 1	Quixall	Dawson	Pearson M	Charlton	
25 Mar	Sheffield Wednesday	35,901	Hillsborough	A	L	1–5	Gaskell	Brennan	Cantwell	Setters	Foulkes	Stiles	Moir	Quixall	Dawson	Pearson M	Charlton 1	
31 Mar	Blackpool	30,835	Bloomfield Road	A	L	0–2	Gaskell	Brennan	Cantwell	Setters	Foulkes	Stiles	Moir	Quixall	Dawson	Pearson M	Charlton	
1 Apr	Fulham	24,654	Old Trafford	H	W	3–1	Gaskell	Brennan	Cantwell	Setters	Foulkes	Nicholson	Giles	Quixall 1	Viollet 1	Pearson M	Charlton 1	
3 Apr	Blackpool	39,169	Old Trafford	H	W	•2–0	Gaskell	Brennan	Cantwell	Setters	Foulkes	Nicholson 1	Giles	Quixall	Viollet	Pearson M	Charlton	
8 Apr	West Bromwich Alb.	27,750	The Hawthorns	A	D	1–1	Gaskell	Brennan	Cantwell	Setters	Foulkes	Nicholson	Giles	Quixall	Viollet	Pearson M 1	Charlton	
12 Apr	Burnley	25,019	Old Trafford	H	W	6–0	Gaskell	Brennan	Cantwell	Setters	Foulkes	Stiles	Giles	Quixall 3	Viollet 3	Pearson M	Moir	
15 Apr	Birmingham City	28,376	Old Trafford	H	W	4–1	Gaskell	Brennan	Cantwell	Setters	Foulkes	Stiles	Giles	Quixall 1	Viollet 1	Pearson M 2	Moir	
22 Apr	Preston North End	21,252	Deepdale	A	W	4–2	Gaskell	Dunne A	Brennan	Setters 2	Foulkes	Stiles	Giles	Quixall	Viollet	Pearson M	Charlton 2	
29 Apr	Cardiff City	30,320	Old Trafford	H	D	3–3	Gaskell	Brennan	Cantwell	Setters 1	Foulkes	Stiles	Giles	Quixall	Viollet	Pearson M	Charlton 2	
FA Cup																		
7 Jan	Middlesbrough	49,184	Old Trafford	H	W	3–0	Gregg	Brennan	Cantwell 1	Setters	Foulkes	Nicholson	Quixall	Stiles	Dawson 2	Pearson M	Charlton	
28 Jan	Sheffield Wednesday	58,000	Hillsborough	A	D	1–1	Briggs	Brennan	Cantwell 1	Setters	Foulkes	Nicholson	Viollet	Stiles	Dawson	Pearson M	Charlton	
1 Feb	Sheffield Wednesday	65,243	Old Trafford	H	L	2–7	Briggs	Brennan	Cantwell	Setters	Foulkes	Nicholson	Quixall	Stiles	Dawson 1	Pearson M 1	Charlton	
FL Cup																		
19 Oct	Exeter City	14,494	St James's Park	A	D	1–1	Gregg	Setters	Brennan	Stiles	Foulkes	Nicholson	Dawson 1	Lawton	Viollet	Pearson M	Scanlon	
26 Oct	Exeter City	15,662	Old Trafford	H	W	4–1	Gaskell	Dunne A	Carolan	Stiles	Cope	Nicholson	Dawson	Giles 1	Quixall 2	Pearson M 1	Scanlon	
2 Nov	Bradford City	4,670	Valley Parade	A	L	1–2	Gregg	Setters	Brennan	Bratt	Foulkes	Nicholson	Dawson	Giles	Viollet 1	Pearson M	Scanlon	

Football League Division 1
P42 • W18 • D9 • L15 • F88 • A76 • PTS45
Position: 7

1961/62

FOOTBALL LEAGUE

Substitutions: not introduced until 1965/66

Date	Opponent	Attendances	Venue				Players and Scores										
19 Aug	West Ham United	32,628	Upton Park	A	D	1–1	Gregg	Brennan	Cantwell	Stiles 1	Foulkes	Setters	Quixall	Viollet	Herd	Pearson M	Charlton
23 Aug	Chelsea	45,847	Old Trafford	H	W	3–2	Gregg	Brennan	Cantwell	Stiles	Foulkes	Setters	Quixall	Viollet 1	Herd 1	Pearson M 1	Charlton
26 Aug	Blackburn Rovers	45,302	Old Trafford	H	W	6–1	Gregg	Brennan	Cantwell	Stiles	Foulkes	Setters 1	Quixall 2	Viollet	Herd 2	Pearson M	Charlton 1
30 Aug	Chelsea	42,248	Stamford Bridge	A	L	0–2	Gregg	Brennan	Cantwell	Stiles	Foulkes	Setters	Quixall	Viollet	Herd	Pearson M	Charlton
2 Sep	Blackpool	28,156	Bloomfield Road	A	W	3–2	Gregg	Brennan	Cantwell	Stiles	Foulkes	Setters	Bradley	Viollet 2	Herd	Pearson M	Charlton 1
9 Sep	Tottenham Hotspur	57,135	Old Trafford	H	W	1–0	Gregg	Brennan	Cantwell	Stiles	Foulkes	Setters	Quixall 1	Viollet	Herd	Pearson M	Charlton
16 Sep	Cardiff City	29,251	Ninian Park	A	W	2–1	Gregg	Brennan	Cantwell	Stiles	Foulkes	Setters	Quixall 1	Viollet	Dawson 1	Pearson M	Charlton
18 Sep	Aston Villa	38,837	Villa Park	A	D	1–1	Gaskell	Brennan	Dunne A	Stiles 1	Foulkes	Setters	Quixall	Viollet	Herd	Pearson M	Charlton
23 Sep	Manchester City	56,345	Old Trafford	H	W	•3–2	Gregg	Brennan	Dunne A	Stiles 1	Foulkes	Setters	Quixall	Viollet 1	Herd	Pearson M	Charlton
30 Sep	Wolverhampton Wan.	39,457	Old Trafford	H	L	0–2	Gregg	Brennan	Cantwell	Stiles	Foulkes	Lawton	Quixall	Giles	Dawson	Pearson M	Charlton
7 Oct	West Bromwich Alb.	25,645	The Hawthorns	A	D	1–1	Gaskell	Brennan	Cantwell	Stiles	Foulkes	Lawton	Moir	Quixall	Dawson 1	Giles	Charlton
14 Oct	Birmingham City	30,674	Old Trafford	H	L	0–2	Gregg	Brennan	Cantwell	Stiles	Haydock	Lawton	Bradley	Giles	Dawson	Herd	Moir
21 Oct	Arsenal	54,245	Highbury	A	L	1–5	Gregg	Brennan	Cantwell	Nicholson	Foulkes	Lawton	Moir	Giles	Herd	Viollet 1	Charlton
28 Oct	Bolton Wanderers	31,442	Old Trafford	H	L	0–3	Gregg	Brennan	Dunne A	Nicholson	Foulkes	Setters	Moir	Quixall	Herd	Viollet	Charlton
4 Nov	Sheffield Wednesday	35,998	Hillsborough	A	L	1–3	Gregg	Brennan	Cantwell	Stiles	Foulkes	Setters	Bradley	Giles	Viollet 1	Charlton	McMillan
11 Nov	Leicester City	21,567	Old Trafford	H	D	2–2	Gaskell	Brennan	Cantwell	Stiles	Foulkes	Setters	Bradley	Giles 1	Viollet 1	Charlton	McMillan
18 Nov	Ipswich Town	25,755	Portman Road	A	L	1–4	Gaskell	Brennan	Dunne A	Stiles	Foulkes	Setters	Bradley	Giles	Herd	Charlton	McMillan 1
25 Nov	Burnley	41,029	Old Trafford	H	L	1–4	Gaskell	Brennan	Dunne A	Stiles	Foulkes	Setters	Bradley	Giles	Herd 1	Quixall	Charlton
2 Dec	Everton	48,099	Goodison Park	A	L	1–5	Gaskell	Brennan	Dunne A	Nicholson	Foulkes	Setters	Chisnall	Giles	Herd 1	Lawton	Charlton
9 Dec	Fulham	22,193	Old Trafford	H	W	3–0	Gaskell	Brennan	Dunne A	Nicholson	Foulkes	Setters	Chisnall	Giles	Herd 2	Lawton 1	Charlton
16 Dec	West Ham United	29,472	Old Trafford	H	L	1–2	Gaskell	Brennan	Dunne A	Nicholson	Foulkes	Setters	Chisnall	Giles	Herd 1	Lawton	Charlton
26 Dec	Nottingham Forest	30,822	Old Trafford	H	W	6–3	Gaskell	Brennan 1	Dunne A	Nicholson	Foulkes	Setters	Chisnall	Giles	Herd 1	Lawton 3	Charlton 1
13 Jan	Blackpool	26,999	Old Trafford	H	L	0–1	Gaskell	Brennan	Dunne A	Nicholson	Foulkes	Setters	Chisnall	Giles	Herd	Lawton	Charlton
15 Jan	Aston Villa	20,807	Old Trafford	H	W	2–0	Gaskell	Brennan	Dunne A	Nicholson	Foulkes	Setters	Chisnall	Giles	Quixall 1	Lawton	Charlton 1
20 Jan	Tottenham Hotspur	55,225	White Hart Lane	A	D	2–2	Gaskell	Brennan	Dunne A	Nicholson	Foulkes	Setters	Chisnall	Stiles 1	Lawton	Giles	Charlton 1
3 Feb	Cardiff City	29,200	Old Trafford	H	W	3–0	Gaskell	Brennan	Dunne A	Nicholson	Foulkes	Setters	Chisnall	Stiles 1	Lawton 1	Giles 1	Charlton
10 Feb	Manchester City	49,959	Maine Road	A	W	2–0	Gaskell	Brennan	Dunne A	Stiles	Setters	Nicholson	Chisnall 1	Giles	Herd 1	Lawton	Charlton
24 Feb	West Bromwich Alb.	32,456	Old Trafford	H	W	4–1	Briggs	Brennan	Dunne A	Stiles	Foulkes	Setters 1	Quixall 1	Giles	Herd	Lawton	Charlton 2
28 Feb	Wolverhampton Wan.	27,565	Molineux	A	D	2–2	Briggs	Brennan	Dunne A	Setters	Foulkes	Nicholson	Quixall	Stiles	Herd 1	Lawton 1	Charlton
3 Mar	Birmingham City	25,817	St Andrews	A	D	1–1	Briggs	Brennan	Dunne A	Stiles	Foulkes	Setters	Quixall	Giles	Herd 1	Lawton	Charlton
17 Mar	Bolton Wanderers	34,366	Burnden Park	A	L	0–1	Briggs	Brennan	Dunne A	Nicholson	Foulkes	Setters	Quixall	Giles	Lawton	Stiles	Charlton
20 Mar	Nottingham Forest	27,833	City Ground	A	L	0–1	Briggs	Brennan	Dunne A	Nicholson	Foulkes	Setters	Quixall	Giles	Lawton	Stiles	Moir
24 Mar	Sheffield Wednesday	31,322	Old Trafford	H	D	1–1	Gaskell	Brennan	Dunne A	Stiles	Foulkes	Setters	Moir	Giles	Quixall	Lawton	Charlton 1
4 Apr	Leicester City	15,318	Filbert Street	A	L	3–4	Gaskell	Setters	Dunne A	Stiles	Foulkes	Nicholson	Moir	Quixall 1	Herd	Lawton	McMillan 2
7 Apr	Ipswich Town	24,976	Old Trafford	H	W	5–0	Briggs	Brennan	Dunne A	Stiles 1	Foulkes	Setters 1	Moir	Giles	Quixall 3	McMillan	Charlton
10 Apr	Blackburn Rovers	14,623	Ewood Park	A	L	0–3	Gaskell	Brennan	Dunne A	Stiles	Foulkes	Setters	Moir	Giles	Cantwell	Pearson M	McMillan
14 Apr	Burnley	36,240	Turf Moor	A	W	3–1	Briggs	Brennan 1	Dunne A	Stiles	Foulkes	Setters	Giles	Pearson M	Cantwell 1	Herd 1	McMillan
16 Apr	Arsenal	24,258	Old Trafford	H	L	2–3	Briggs	Brennan	Cantwell 1	Stiles	Foulkes	Setters	Giles	Pearson M	Herd	McMillan 1	Charlton
21 Apr	Everton	31,926	Old Trafford	H	D	1–1	Gaskell	Brennan	Dunne A	Stiles	Foulkes	Setters	Giles	Pearson M	Cantwell	Herd 1	Charlton
23 Apr	Sheffield United	30,073	Old Trafford	H	L	0–1	Gaskell	Brennan	Dunne A	Stiles	Foulkes	Setters	Giles	Pearson M	Herd	McMillan	Charlton
24 Apr	Sheffield United	25,324	Bramall Lane	A	W	3–2	Gaskell	Brennan	Dunne A	Nicholson	Foulkes	Setters	Giles	Pearson M	McMillan 2	Stiles 1	Charlton
28 Apr	Fulham	40,113	Craven Cottage	A	L	0–2	Gaskell	Brennan	Dunne A	Setters	Foulkes	Nicholson	Giles	Pearson M	McMillan	Stiles	Charlton

FA CUP

Date	Opponent	Attendances	Venue				Players and Scores										
6 Jan	Bolton Wanderers	42,202	Old Trafford	H	W	2–1	Gaskell	Brennan	Dunne A	Nicholson 1	Foulkes	Setters	Chisnall	Giles	Herd 1	Lawton	Charlton
31 Jan	Arsenal	54,082	Old Trafford	H	W	1–0	Gaskell	Brennan	Dunne A	Nicholson	Foulkes	Setters 1	Chisnall	Stiles	Lawton	Giles	Charlton
17 Feb	Sheffield Wednesday	59,553	Old Trafford	H	D	0–0	Gaskell	Brennan	Dunne A	Nicholson	Foulkes	Setters	Chisnall	Giles	Herd	Lawton	Charlton
21 Feb	Sheffield Wednesday	62,969	Hillsborough	A	W	2–0	Gaskell	Brennan	Dunne A	Stiles	Foulkes	Setters	Quixall	Giles 1	Herd	Lawton	Charlton 1
10 Mar	Preston North End	37,521	Deepdale	A	D	0–0	Gaskell	Brennan	Dunne A	Nicholson	Foulkes	Setters	Chisnall	Giles	Cantwell	Lawton	Charlton
14 Mar	Preston North End	63,468	Old Trafford	H	W	2–1	Gaskell	Brennan	Dunne A	Stiles	Foulkes	Setters	Quixall	Giles	Herd 1	Lawton	Charlton 1
31 Mar	Tottenham Hotspur	65,000	Hillsborough	A	L	1–3	Gaskell	Dunne A	Cantwell	Stiles	Foulkes	Setters	Quixall	Giles	Herd 1	Lawton	Charlton

Football League Division 1
P42 • W15 • D9 • L18 • F72 • A75 • PTS39
Position: 15

1962/63

FOOTBALL LEAGUE

Substitutions: not introduced until 1965/66

Date	Opponent	Attendances	Venue				Players and Scores										
18 Aug	West Bromwich Alb.	51,685	Old Trafford	H	D	2–2	Gaskell	Brennan	Dunne A	Stiles	Foulkes	Setters	Giles	Quixall	Herd 1	Law 1	Moir
22 Aug	Everton	69,501	Goodison Park	A	L	1–3	Gaskell	Brennan	Dunne A	Stiles	Foulkes	Setters	Giles	Pearson M	Herd	Law	Moir 1
25 Aug	Arsenal	62,308	Highbury	A	W	3–1	Gaskell	Brennan	Dunne A	Nicholson	Foulkes	Lawton	Giles	Chisnall 1	Herd 2	Law	Moir
29 Aug	Everton	63,437	Old Trafford	H	L	0–1	Gaskell	Brennan	Dunne A	Nicholson	Foulkes	Lawton	Giles	Chisnall	Herd	Law	Moir
1 Sep	Birmingham City	39,847	Old Trafford	H	W	2–0	Gaskell	Brennan	Dunne A	Nicholson	Foulkes	Lawton	Giles 1	Chisnall	Herd 1	Law	Moir
5 Sep	Bolton Wanderers	44,859	Burnden Park	A	L	0–3	Gaskell	Brennan	Dunne A	Nicholson	Foulkes	Lawton	Giles	Quixall	Herd	Law	Moir
8 Sep	Leyton Orient	24,901	Brisbane Road	A	L	0–1	Gaskell	Brennan	Dunne A	Nicholson	Foulkes	Lawton	Moir	Setters	Herd	Law	McMillan
12 Sep	Bolton Wanderers	37,721	Old Trafford	H	W	3–0	Gaskell	Brennan	Dunne A	Stiles	Foulkes	Setters	Giles	Lawton	Herd 2	Law	Cantwell 1
15 Sep	Manchester City	49,193	Old Trafford	H	L	2–3	Gaskell	Brennan	Dunne A	Stiles	Foulkes	Nicholson	Giles	Lawton	Herd	Law 2	Cantwell
22 Sep	Burnley	45,954	Old Trafford	H	L	2–5	Gaskell	Brennan	Dunne A	Stiles 1	Foulkes	Lawton	Giles	Law 1	Herd	Pearson M	Moir
29 Sep	Sheffield Wednesday	40,520	Hillsborough	A	L	0–1	Gregg	Brennan	Dunne A	Stiles	Foulkes	Lawton	Giles	Law	Quixall	Chisnall	McMillan
6 Oct	Blackpool	33,242	Bloomfield Road	A	D	2–2	Gregg	Brennan	Dunne A	Stiles	Foulkes	Nicholson	Giles	Law	Herd 2	Lawton	McMillan
13 Oct	Blackburn Rovers	42,252	Old Trafford	H	L	0–3	Gregg	Brennan	Dunne A	Stiles	Foulkes	Nicholson	Giles	Law	Herd	Charlton	McMillan
24 Oct	Tottenham Hotspur	51,314	White Hart Lane	A	L	2–6	Gregg	Brennan	Cantwell	Stiles	Foulkes	Setters	Giles	Quixall 1	Herd 1	Law	Charlton
27 Oct	West Ham United	29,204	Old Trafford	H	W	3–1	Gregg	Brennan	Cantwell	Stiles	Foulkes	Setters	Giles	Quixall 2	Herd	Law 1	Charlton
3 Nov	Ipswich Town	18,483	Portman Road	A	W	5–3	Gregg	Brennan	Cantwell	Stiles	Foulkes	Setters	Giles	Quixall	Herd 1	Law 4	Charlton
10 Nov	Liverpool	43,810	Old Trafford	H	D	3–3	Gregg	Brennan	Cantwell	Stiles	Foulkes	Setters	Giles 1	Quixall 1	Herd 1	Law	Charlton
17 Nov	Wolverhampton Wan.	27,305	Molineux	A	W	3–2	Gregg	Brennan	Cantwell	Stiles	Foulkes	Setters	Giles	Quixall	Herd 1	Law 2	Charlton
24 Nov	Aston Villa	36,852	Old Trafford	H	D	2–2	Gregg	Brennan	Cantwell	Stiles	Foulkes	Setters	Giles	Quixall 2	Herd	Law	Charlton
1 Dec	Sheffield United	25,173	Bramall Lane	A	D	1–1	Gregg	Brennan	Cantwell	Stiles	Foulkes	Setters	Giles	Quixall	Herd	Lawton	Charlton 1
8 Dec	Nottingham Forest	27,946	Old Trafford	H	W	5–1	Gregg	Brennan	Cantwell	Nicholson	Foulkes	Lawton	Giles 1	Quixall	Herd 2	Law 1	Charlton 1
15 Dec	West Bromwich Alb.	18,113	The Hawthorns	A	L	0–3	Gregg	Brennan	Cantwell	Stiles	Foulkes	Nicholson	Giles	Quixall	Herd	Law	Moir
26 Dec	Fulham	23,928	Craven Cottage	A	W	1–0	Gregg	Brennan	Cantwell	Stiles	Foulkes	Setters	Giles	Quixall	Herd	Law	Charlton 1
23 Feb	Blackpool	43,121	Old Trafford	H	D	1–1	Gregg	Brennan	Cantwell	Crerand	Foulkes	Setters	Giles	Quixall	Herd 1	Chisnall	Charlton
2 Mar	Blackburn Rovers	27,924	Ewood Park	A	D	2–2	Gregg	Brennan	Cantwell	Crerand	Foulkes	Setters	Giles	Quixall	Herd	Law 1	Charlton 1
9 Mar	Tottenham Hotspur	53,416	Old Trafford	H	L	0–2	Gregg	Brennan	Cantwell	Crerand	Foulkes	Stiles	Giles	Quixall	Herd	Law	Charlton
18 Mar	West Ham United	28,950	Upton Park	A	L	1–3	Gregg	Brennan	Cantwell	Crerand	Foulkes	Setters	Giles	Stiles	Herd 1	Law	Charlton
23 Mar	Ipswich Town	32,792	Old Trafford	H	L	0–1	Gregg	Brennan	Cantwell	Crerand	Foulkes	Setters	Giles	Quixall	Herd	Law	Charlton
1 Apr	Fulham	28,124	Old Trafford	H	L	0–2	Gregg	Brennan	Dunne A	Crerand	Foulkes	Setters	Giles	Chisnall	Quixall	Law	Charlton
9 Apr	Aston Villa	26,867	Villa Park	A	W	2–1	Gregg	Brennan	Cantwell	Crerand	Foulkes	Setters	Giles	Stiles 1	Herd	Quixall	Charlton 1
13 Apr	Liverpool	51,529	Anfield	A	L	0–1	Gregg	Brennan	Dunne A	Crerand	Foulkes	Setters	Giles	Stiles	Quixall	Law	Charlton
15 Apr	Leicester City	50,005	Old Trafford	H	D	2–2	Gregg	Brennan	Dunne A	Crerand	Foulkes	Setters	Quixall	Stiles	Herd 1	Law	Charlton 1
16 Apr	Leicester City	37,002	Filbert Street	A	L	3–4	Gregg	Brennan	Dunne A	Crerand	Foulkes	Setters	Quixall	Stiles	Herd	Law 3	Charlton
20 Apr	Sheffield United	31,179	Old Trafford	H	D	1–1	Gregg	Brennan	Dunne A	Crerand	Foulkes	Setters	Quixall	Stiles	Herd	Law 1	Charlton
22 Apr	Wolverhampton Wan.	36,147	Old Trafford	H	W	2–1	Gaskell	Brennan	Dunne A	Crerand	Foulkes	Setters	Quixall	Stiles	Herd 1	Law 1	Charlton
1 May	Sheffield Wednesday	31,878	Old Trafford	H	L	1–3	Gaskell	Brennan	Cantwell	Crerand	Foulkes	Setters 1	Quixall	Stiles	Herd	Law	Charlton
4 May	Burnley	30,266	Turf Moor	A	W	1–0	Gaskell	Dunne A	Cantwell	Crerand	Foulkes	Setters	Giles	Stiles	Quixall	Law 1	Charlton
6 May	Arsenal	35,999	Old Trafford	H	L	2–3	Gaskell	Dunne A	Cantwell	Crerand	Foulkes	Setters	Giles	Stiles	Quixall	Law 2	Charlton
10 May	Birmingham City	21,814	St Andrews	A	L	1–2	Gaskell	Dunne A	Cantwell	Crerand	Foulkes	Stiles	Quixall	Giles	Herd	Law 1	Charlton
15 May	Manchester City	52,424	Maine Road	A	D	1–1	Gaskell	Dunne A	Cantwell	Crerand	Foulkes	Stiles	Quixall 1	Giles	Herd	Law	Charlton
18 May	Leyton Orient	32,759	Old Trafford	H	W	•3–1	Gaskell	Dunne A	Cantwell	Crerand	Foulkes	Setters	Quixall	Giles	Herd	Law 1	Charlton 1
20 May	Nottingham Forest	16,130	City Ground	A	L	2–3	Gaskell	Dunne A	Cantwell	Crerand	Haydock	Brennan	Quixall	Stiles	Herd 1	Giles 1	Walker D

FA CUP

Date	Opponent	Attendances	Venue				Players and Scores										
4 Mar	Huddersfield Town	47,703	Old Trafford	H	W	5–0	Gregg	Brennan	Cantwell	Stiles	Foulkes	Setters	Giles 1	Quixall 1	Herd	Law 3	Charlton
11 Mar	Aston Villa	52,265	Old Trafford	H	W	1–0	Gregg	Brennan	Cantwell	Stiles	Foulkes	Setters	Giles	Quixall 1	Herd	Law	Charlton
16 Mar	Chelsea	48,298	Old Trafford	H	W	2–1	Gregg	Brennan	Cantwell	Stiles	Foulkes	Setters	Giles	Quixall 1	Herd	Law 1	Charlton
30 Mar	Coventry City	44,000	Highfield Road	A	W	3–1	Gregg	Brennan	Dunne A	Crerand	Foulkes	Setters	Giles	Quixall 1	Herd	Law	Charlton 2
27 Apr	Southampton	65,000	Villa Park	A	W	1–0	Gaskell	Dunne A	Cantwell	Crerand	Foulkes	Setters	Giles	Stiles	Herd	Law 1	Charlton
25 May	Leicester City	100,000	Wembley	A	W	3–1	Gaskell	Dunne A	Cantwell	Crerand	Foulkes	Setters	Giles	Quixall	Herd 2	Law 1	Charlton

Football League Division 1
P42 • W12 • D10 • L20 • F67 • A81 • PTS34
Position: 19

1963/64

FOOTBALL LEAGUE

Substitutions: not introduced until 1965/66

Date	Opponent	Attendances	Venue			Players and Scores										
24 Aug	Sheffield Wednesday	32,177	Hillsborough	A D	3–3	Gregg	Dunne A	Cantwell	Crerand	Foulkes	Setters	Moir 1	Chisnall	Sadler	Law	Charlton 2
28 Aug	Ipswich Town	39,921	Old Trafford	H W	2–0	Gregg	Dunne A	Cantwell	Crerand	Foulkes	Setters	Moir	Chisnall	Sadler	Law 2	Charlton
31 Aug	Everton	62,965	Old Trafford	H W	5–1	Gregg	Dunne A	Cantwell	Crerand	Foulkes	Stiles	Moir	Chisnall 2	Sadler 1	Law 2	Charlton
3 Sep	Ipswich Town	28,113	Portman Road	A W	7–2	Gregg	Dunne A	Cantwell	Crerand	Foulkes	Setters 1	Moir 1	Chisnall 1	Sadler 1	Law 3	Charlton
7 Sep	Birmingham City	36,874	St Andrews	A D	1–1	Gregg	Dunne A	Cantwell	Crerand	Foulkes	Setters	Moir	Chisnall 1	Sadler	Law	Charlton
11 Sep	Blackpool	47,400	Old Trafford	H W	3–0	Gregg	Dunne A	Cantwell	Crerand	Foulkes	Setters	Moir	Chisnall	Sadler	Law 1	Charlton 2
14 Sep	West Bromwich Alb.	50,453	Old Trafford	H W	1–0	Gregg	Dunne A	Cantwell	Crerand	Foulkes	Setters	Best	Stiles	Sadler 1	Chisnall	Charlton
16 Sep	Blackpool	29,806	Bloomfield Road	A L	0–1	Gregg	Dunne A	Cantwell	Crerand	Foulkes	Setters	Moir	Stiles	Sadler	Chisnall	Charlton
21 Sep	Arsenal	56,776	Highbury	A L	1–2	Gregg	Dunne A	Cantwell	Crerand	Foulkes	Setters	Herd 1	Chisnall	Sadler	Law	Charlton
28 Sep	Leicester City	41,374	Old Trafford	H W	3–1	Gregg	Dunne A	Cantwell	Crerand	Foulkes	Setters 1	Moir	Chisnall	Sadler	Herd 2	Charlton
2 Oct	Chelsea	45,351	Stamford Bridge	A D	1–1	Gregg	Dunne A	Cantwell	Crerand	Foulkes	Setters 1	Moir	Chisnall	Sadler	Herd	Charlton
5 Oct	Bolton Wanderers	35,872	Burnden Park	A W	1–0	Gregg	Dunne A	Cantwell	Crerand	Foulkes	Setters	Herd 1	Chisnall	Sadler	Stiles	Charlton
19 Oct	Nottingham Forest	41,426	City Ground	A W	2–1	Gregg	Dunne A	Cantwell	Crerand	Foulkes	Setters	Quixall 1	Chisnall 1	Herd	Law	Charlton
26 Oct	West Ham United	45,120	Old Trafford	H L	0–1	Gregg	Dunne A	Cantwell	Crerand	Foulkes	Setters	Moir	Chisnall	Herd	Law	Charlton
28 Oct	Blackburn Rovers	41,169	Old Trafford	H D	2–2	Gregg	Dunne A	Cantwell	Crerand	Foulkes	Stiles	Moir	Chisnall	Quixall 2	Law	Charlton
2 Nov	Wolverhampton Wan.	34,159	Molineux	A L	0–2	Gregg	Dunne A	Cantwell	Crerand	Foulkes	Setters	Moir	Chisnall	Quixall	Law	Charlton
9 Nov	Tottenham Hotspur	57,413	Old Trafford	H W	4–1	Gregg	Dunne A	Cantwell	Crerand	Foulkes	Setters	Quixall	Moore G	Herd 1	Law 3	Charlton
16 Nov	Aston Villa	36,276	Villa Park	A L	0–4	Gregg	Dunne A	Cantwell	Crerand	Foulkes	Setters	Quixall	Moore G	Herd	Law	Charlton
23 Nov	Liverpool	54,654	Old Trafford	H L	0–1	Gregg	Dunne A	Cantwell	Crerand	Foulkes	Setters	Quixall	Moore G	Herd	Law	Charlton
30 Nov	Sheffield United	30,615	Bramall Lane	A W	2–1	Gaskell	Dunne A	Cantwell	Crerand	Foulkes	Setters	Quixall	Moore G	Herd	Law 2	Charlton
7 Dec	Stoke City	52,232	Old Trafford	H W	5–2	Gaskell	Dunne A	Cantwell	Crerand	Foulkes	Setters	Quixall	Moore G	Herd 1	Law 4	Charlton
14 Dec	Sheffield Wednesday	35,139	Old Trafford	H W	3–1	Gaskell	Brennan	Dunne A	Crerand	Foulkes	Setters	Chisnall	Moore G	Sadler	Herd 3	Charlton
21 Dec	Everton	48,027	Goodison Park	A L	0–4	Gaskell	Dunne A	Cantwell	Crerand	Foulkes	Setters	Moir	Moore G	Sadler	Herd	Charlton
26 Dec	Burnley	35,764	Turf Moor	A L	1–6	Gaskell	Dunne A	Cantwell	Crerand	Foulkes	Setters	Quixall	Moore G	Charlton	Herd 1	Brennan
28 Dec	Burnley	47,834	Old Trafford	H W	5–1	Gaskell	Dunne A	Cantwell	Crerand	Foulkes	Setters	Anderson W	Moore G 2	Charlton	Herd 2	Best 1
11 Jan	Birmingham City	44,695	Old Trafford	H L	1–2	Gaskell	Dunne A	Cantwell	Crerand	Foulkes	Setters	Herd	Moore G	Sadler 1	Law	Best
18 Jan	West Bromwich Alb.	25,624	The Hawthorns	A W	4–1	Gaskell	Dunne A	Cantwell	Crerand	Foulkes	Setters	Herd	Moore G	Charlton 1	Law 2	Best 1
1 Feb	Arsenal	48,340	Old Trafford	H W	3–1	Gaskell	Brennan	Dunne A	Stiles	Foulkes	Setters 1	Herd 1	Moore G	Charlton	Law 1	Best
8 Feb	Leicester City	35,538	Filbert Street	A L	2–3	Gaskell	Brennan	Dunne A	Crerand	Foulkes	Setters	Herd 1	Moore G	Charlton	Law 1	Best
19 Feb	Bolton Wanderers	33,926	Old Trafford	H W	5–0	Gaskell	Brennan	Dunne A	Crerand	Foulkes	Setters	Herd 2	Stiles	Charlton 1	Law	Best 2
22 Feb	Blackburn Rovers	36,726	Ewood Park	A W	3–1	Gaskell	Brennan	Dunne A	Crerand	Foulkes	Setters	Herd	Chisnall 1	Charlton	Law 2	Best
7 Mar	West Ham United	27,027	Upton Park	A W	2–0	Gaskell	Brennan	Dunne A	Crerand	Tranter	Stiles	Anderson W	Chisnall	Sadler 1	Herd 1	Moir
21 Mar	Tottenham Hotspur	56,392	White Hart Lane	A W	3–2	Gaskell	Brennan	Dunne A	Crerand	Foulkes	Stiles	Best	Moore G 1	Sadler	Law 1	Charlton 1
23 Mar	Chelsea	42,931	Old Trafford	H D	1–1	Gaskell	Brennan	Dunne A	Crerand	Foulkes	Stiles	Best	Moore G	Sadler	Law 1	Charlton
27 Mar	Fulham	41,769	Craven Cottage	A D	2–2	Gaskell	Brennan	Dunne A	Crerand	Foulkes	Stiles	Best	Moore G	Herd 1	Law 1	Charlton
28 Mar	Wolverhampton Wan.	44,470	Old Trafford	H D	2–2	Gregg	Brennan	Cantwell	Crerand	Foulkes	Stiles	Best	Chisnall	Herd 1	Setters	Charlton 1
30 Mar	Fulham	42,279	Old Trafford	H W	3–0	Gregg	Brennan	Dunne A	Crerand 1	Foulkes 1	Stiles	Moir	Moore G	Herd 1	Law	Charlton
4 Apr	Liverpool	52,559	Anfield	A L	0–3	Gregg	Brennan	Dunne A	Crerand	Foulkes	Setters	Best	Stiles	Herd	Law	Charlton
6 Apr	Aston Villa	25,848	Old Trafford	H W	1–0	Gregg	Brennan	Dunne A	Crerand	Foulkes	Stiles	Best	Charlton	Herd	Law 1	Moir
13 Apr	Sheffield United	27,587	Old Trafford	H W	2–1	Gregg	Brennan	Cantwell	Crerand	Foulkes	Stiles	Best	Charlton	Herd	Law 1	Moir 1
18 Apr	Stoke City	45,670	Victoria Ground	A L	1–3	Gregg	Brennan	Dunne A	Crerand	Foulkes	Stiles	Best	Charlton 1	Sadler	Herd	Moir
25 Apr	Nottingham Forest	31,671	Old Trafford	H W	3–1	Gaskell	Brennan	Dunne A	Crerand	Foulkes	Setters	Best	Moore G 1	Herd	Law 2	Charlton

FA CUP

4 Jan	Southampton	29,164	The Dell	A W	3–2	Gaskell	Dunne A	Cantwell	Crerand 1	Foulkes	Setters	Anderson W	Moore G 1	Charlton	Herd 1	Best
25 Jan	Bristol Rovers	55,772	Old Trafford	H W	4–1	Gaskell	Dunne A	Cantwell	Crerand	Foulkes	Setters	Herd 1	Chisnall	Charlton	Law 3	Best
15 Feb	Barnsley	38,076	Oakwell	A W	4–0	Gaskell	Brennan	Dunne A	Crerand	Foulkes	Setters	Herd 1	Stiles	Charlton	Law 2	Best 1
29 Feb	Sunderland	63,700	Old Trafford	H D	•3–3	Gaskell	Brennan	Dunne A	Crerand	Foulkes	Setters	Herd	Stiles	Charlton 1	Law	Best 1
4 Mar	Sunderland	68,000	Roker Park	A D	2–2	Gaskell	Brennan	Dunne A	Crerand	Foulkes	Setters	Herd	Chisnall	Charlton 1	Law 1	Best
9 Mar	Sunderland	54,952	Leeds Road	A W	5–1	Gaskell	Brennan	Dunne A	Crerand	Foulkes	Setters	Herd 1	Chisnall 1	Charlton	Law 3	Best
14 Mar	West Ham United	65,000	Hillsborough	A L	1–3	Gaskell	Brennan	Dunne A	Crerand	Foulkes	Setters	Herd	Chisnall	Charlton	Law 1	Best

EUROPEAN CUP WINNERS' CUP

25 Sep	Willem II	20,000	Feyenoord Stadion	A D	1–1	Gregg	Dunne A	Cantwell	Crerand	Foulkes	Setters	Herd 1	Chisnall	Sadler	Law	Charlton
15 Oct	Willem II	46,272	Old Trafford	H W	6–1	Gregg	Dunne A	Cantwell	Crerand	Foulkes	Setters 1	Quixall	Chisnall 1	Herd	Law 3	Charlton 1
3 Dec	Tottenham Hotspur	57,447	White Hart Lane	A L	0–2	Gaskell	Dunne A	Cantwell	Crerand	Foulkes	Setters	Quixall	Stiles	Herd	Law	Charlton
10 Dec	Tottenham Hotspur	50,000	Old Trafford	H W	4–1	Gaskell	Dunne A	Cantwell	Crerand	Foulkes	Setters	Quixall	Chisnall	Sadler	Herd 2	Charlton 2
26 Feb	Sporting Lisbon	60,000	Old Trafford	H W	4–1	Gaskell	Brennan	Dunne A	Crerand	Foulkes	Setters	Herd	Stiles	Charlton 1	Law 3	Best
18 Mar	Sporting Lisbon	40,000	de Jose Alvalade	A L	0–5	Gaskell	Brennan	Dunne A	Crerand	Foulkes	Setters	Herd	Chisnall	Charlton	Law	Best

FOOTBALL LEAGUE DIVISION 1
P42 • W23 • D7 • L12 • F90 • A62 • PTS53
POSITION: 2

1964/65

FOOTBALL LEAGUE

Substitutions: not introduced until 1965/66

Date	Opponent	Attendances	Venue			Players and Scores										
22 Aug	West Bromwich Alb.	52,007	Old Trafford	H D	2–2	Gaskell	Brennan	Dunne A	Setters	Foulkes	Stiles	Connelly	Charlton 1	Herd	Law 1	Best
24 Aug	West Ham United	37,070	Upton Park	A L	1–3	Gaskell	Brennan	Dunne A	Setters	Foulkes	Stiles	Connelly	Charlton	Herd	Law 1	Best
29 Aug	Leicester City	32,373	Filbert Street	A D	2–2	Gaskell	Brennan	Dunne A	Crerand	Foulkes	Stiles	Connelly	Charlton	Sadler 1	Law 1	Best
2 Sep	West Ham United	45,123	Old Trafford	H W	3–1	Gaskell	Brennan	Dunne A	Crerand	Foulkes	Stiles	Connelly 1	Charlton	Sadler	Law 1	Best 1
5 Sep	Fulham	36,291	Craven Cottage	A L	1–2	Gaskell	Brennan	Dunne A	Crerand	Foulkes	Stiles	Connelly 1	Charlton	Sadler	Law	Best
8 Sep	Everton	63,024	Goodison Park	A D	3–3	Dunne P	Brennan	Dunne A	Crerand	Foulkes	Stiles	Connelly 1	Charlton	Herd 1	Law 1	Best
12 Sep	Nottingham Forest	45,012	Old Trafford	H W	3–0	Dunne P	Brennan	Dunne A	Crerand	Foulkes	Setters	Connelly 1	Charlton	Herd 2	Stiles	Best
16 Sep	Everton	49,968	Old Trafford	H W	2–1	Dunne P	Brennan	Dunne A	Crerand	Foulkes	Stiles	Connelly	Charlton	Herd	Law 1	Best 1
19 Sep	Stoke City	40,031	Victoria Ground	A W	2–1	Dunne P	Brennan	Dunne A	Crerand	Foulkes	Setters	Connelly 1	Charlton	Herd 1	Stiles	Best
26 Sep	Tottenham Hotspur	53,058	Old Trafford	H W	4–1	Dunne P	Brennan	Dunne A	Crerand 2	Foulkes	Stiles	Connelly	Charlton	Herd	Law 2	Best
30 Sep	Chelsea	60,769	Stamford Bridge	A W	2–0	Dunne P	Brennan	Dunne A	Crerand	Foulkes	Stiles	Connelly	Charlton	Herd	Law 1	Best 1
6 Oct	Burnley	30,761	Turf Moor	A D	0–0	Dunne P	Brennan	Dunne A	Crerand	Foulkes	Stiles	Connelly	Charlton	Herd	Law	Best
10 Oct	Sunderland	48,577	Old Trafford	H W	1–0	Dunne P	Brennan	Dunne A	Crerand	Foulkes	Stiles	Connelly	Charlton	Herd 1	Law	Best
17 Oct	Wolverhampton Wan.	26,763	Molineux	A W	•4–2	Dunne P	Brennan	Dunne A	Crerand	Foulkes	Stiles	Connelly	Charlton	Herd 1	Law 2	Best
24 Oct	Aston Villa	35,807	Old Trafford	H W	7–0	Dunne P	Brennan	Dunne A	Crerand	Foulkes	Setters	Connelly 1	Stiles	Herd 2	Law 4	Best
31 Oct	Liverpool	52,402	Anfield	A W	2–0	Dunne P	Brennan	Dunne A	Crerand 1	Foulkes	Stiles	Connelly	Charlton	Herd 1	Law	Best
7 Nov	Sheffield Wednesday	50,178	Old Trafford	H W	1–0	Dunne P	Brennan	Dunne A	Crerand	Foulkes	Stiles	Connelly	Charlton	Herd 1	Law	Best
14 Nov	Blackpool	31,129	Bloomfield Road	A W	2–1	Dunne P	Brennan	Dunne A	Crerand	Foulkes	Stiles	Connelly 1	Charlton	Herd 1	Law	Moir
21 Nov	Blackburn Rovers	49,633	Old Trafford	H W	3–0	Dunne P	Brennan	Dunne A	Crerand	Foulkes	Stiles	Connelly 1	Charlton	Herd 1	Law	Best 1
28 Nov	Arsenal	59,627	Highbury	A W	3–2	Dunne P	Brennan	Dunne A	Crerand	Foulkes	Stiles	Connelly 1	Charlton	Herd	Law 2	Best
5 Dec	Leeds United	53,374	Old Trafford	H L	0–1	Dunne P	Brennan	Dunne A	Crerand	Foulkes	Stiles	Connelly	Charlton	Herd	Law	Best
12 Dec	West Bromwich Alb.	28,126	The Hawthorns	A D	1–1	Dunne P	Brennan	Dunne A	Crerand	Foulkes	Stiles	Connelly	Charlton	Herd	Law 1	Best
16 Dec	Birmingham City	25,721	Old Trafford	H D	1–1	Dunne P	Brennan	Dunne A	Crerand	Foulkes	Stiles	Connelly	Charlton 1	Sadler	Herd	Best
26 Dec	Sheffield United	37,295	Bramall Lane	A W	1–0	Dunne P	Brennan	Dunne A	Crerand	Foulkes	Stiles	Connelly	Charlton	Sadler	Herd	Best 1
28 Dec	Sheffield United	42,219	Old Trafford	H D	1–1	Dunne P	Brennan	Dunne A	Crerand	Foulkes	Stiles	Connelly	Charlton	Sadler	Herd 1	Best
16 Jan	Nottingham Forest	43,009	City Ground	A D	2–2	Dunne P	Brennan	Dunne A	Crerand	Foulkes	Stiles	Connelly	Charlton	Herd	Law 2	Best
23 Jan	Stoke City	50,392	Old Trafford	H D	1–1	Dunne P	Brennan	Dunne A	Crerand	Foulkes	Stiles	Connelly	Charlton	Herd	Law 1	Best
6 Feb	Tottenham Hotspur	58,639	White Hart Lane	A L	0–1	Dunne P	Brennan	Dunne A	Crerand	Foulkes	Stiles	Connelly	Charlton	Herd	Law	Best
13 Feb	Burnley	38,865	Old Trafford	H W	3–2	Dunne P	Brennan	Dunne A	Crerand	Foulkes	Stiles	Connelly	Charlton 1	Herd 1	Law	Best 1
24 Feb	Sunderland	51,336	Roker Park	A L	0–1	Dunne P	Brennan	Dunne A	Crerand	Foulkes	Fitzpatrick	Connelly	Charlton	Herd	Law	Best
27 Feb	Wolverhampton Wan.	37,018	Old Trafford	H W	3–0	Dunne P	Brennan	Dunne A	Crerand	Foulkes	Stiles	Connelly 1	Charlton 2	Herd	Law	Best
13 Mar	Chelsea	56,261	Old Trafford	H W	4–0	Dunne P	Brennan	Dunne A	Crerand	Foulkes	Stiles	Connelly	Charlton	Herd 2	Law 1	Best 1
15 Mar	Fulham	45,402	Old Trafford	H W	4–1	Dunne P	Brennan	Dunne A	Crerand	Foulkes	Stiles	Connelly 2	Charlton	Herd 2	Law	Best
20 Mar	Sheffield Wednesday	33,549	Hillsborough	A L	0–1	Dunne P	Brennan	Dunne A	Crerand	Foulkes	Stiles	Connelly	Charlton	Herd	Law	Best
22 Mar	Blackpool	42,318	Old Trafford	H W	2–0	Dunne P	Brennan	Dunne A	Crerand	Foulkes	Stiles	Connelly	Charlton	Herd	Law 2	Best

continued on page 137

1964/65 continued

FOOTBALL LEAGUE continued

Date	Opponent	Attendances	Venue				Players and Scores											Substitutions: not introduced until 1965/66
3 Apr	Blackburn Rovers	29,363	Ewood Park	A	W	5–0	Dunne P	Brennan	Dunne A	Crerand	Foulkes	Stiles	Connelly 1	Charlton 3	Herd 1	Law	Best	
12 Apr	Leicester City	34,114	Old Trafford	H	W	1–0	Dunne P	Brennan	Dunne A	Crerand	Foulkes	Stiles	Connelly	Charlton	Herd 1	Best	Aston (Jnr.)	
17 Apr	Leeds United	52,368	Elland Road	A	W	1–0	Dunne P	Brennan	Dunne A	Crerand	Foulkes	Stiles	Connelly 1	Charlton	Herd	Law	Best	
19 Apr	Birmingham City	28,907	St Andrews	A	W	4–2	Dunne P	Brennan	Dunne A	Crerand	Foulkes	Stiles	Connelly	Charlton 1	Cantwell 1	Law	Best 2	
24 Apr	Liverpool	55,772	Old Trafford	H	W	3–0	Dunne P	Brennan	Dunne A	Crerand	Foulkes	Stiles	Connelly 1	Charlton	Cantwell	Law 2	Best	
26 Apr	Arsenal	51,625	Old Trafford	H	W	3–1	Dunne P	Brennan	Dunne A	Crerand	Foulkes	Stiles	Connelly	Charlton	Herd	Law 2	Best 1	
28 Apr	Aston Villa	36,081	Villa Park	A	L	1–2	Dunne P	Brennan	Dunne A	Fitzpatrick	Foulkes	Stiles	Connelly	Charlton 1	Herd	Law	Best	

FA CUP

Date	Opponent	Attendances	Venue				Players and Scores											Substitutions
9 Jan	Chester	40,000	Old Trafford	H	W	2–1	Dunne P	Brennan	Dunne A	Crerand	Foulkes	Stiles	Connelly	Charlton	Herd	Kinsey 1	Best 1	
30 Jan	Stoke City	53,009	Victoria Ground	A	D	0–0	Dunne P	Brennan	Dunne A	Crerand	Foulkes	Stiles	Connelly	Charlton	Herd	Law	Best	
3 Feb	Stoke City	50,814	Old Trafford	H	W	1–0	Dunne P	Brennan	Dunne A	Crerand	Foulkes	Stiles	Connelly	Charlton	Herd 1	Law	Best	
20 Feb	Burnley	54,000	Old Trafford	H	W	2–1	Dunne P	Brennan	Dunne A	Crerand 1	Foulkes	Stiles	Connelly	Charlton	Herd	Law 1	Best	
10 Mar	Wolverhampton Wan.	53,581	Molineux	A	W	5–3	Dunne P	Brennan	Dunne A	Crerand 1	Foulkes	Stiles	Connelly	Charlton	Herd 1	Law 2	Best 1	
27 Mar	Leeds United	65,000	Hillsborough	A	D	0–0	Dunne P	Brennan	Dunne A	Crerand	Foulkes	Stiles	Connelly	Charlton	Herd	Law	Best	
31 Mar	Leeds United	46,300	City Ground	A	L	0–1	Dunne P	Brennan	Dunne A	Crerand	Foulkes	Stiles	Connelly	Charlton	Herd	Law	Best	

INTER–CITY FAIRS CUP

Date	Opponent	Attendances	Venue				Players and Scores											Substitutions
23 Sep	Djurgaarden	6,537	Rasunda Stadion	A	D	1–1	Dunne P	Brennan	Dunne A	Crerand	Foulkes	Stiles	Connelly	Charlton	Herd 1	Setters	Best	
27 Oct	Djurgaarden	38,437	Old Trafford	H	W	6–1	Dunne P	Brennan	Dunne A	Crerand	Foulkes	Stiles	Connelly	Charlton 2	Herd	Law 3	Best 1	
11 Nov	Borussia Dortmund	25,000	Rote Erde Stadion	A	W	6–1	Dunne P	Brennan	Dunne A	Crerand	Foulkes	Stiles	Connelly	Charlton 3	Herd 1	Law 1	Best 1	
2 Dec	Borussia Dortmund	31,896	Old Trafford	H	W	4–0	Dunne P	Brennan	Dunne A	Crerand	Foulkes	Stiles	Connelly 1	Charlton 2	Herd	Law 1	Best	
20 Jan	Everton	50,000	Old Trafford	H	D	1–1	Dunne P	Brennan	Dunne A	Crerand	Foulkes	Stiles	Connelly 1	Charlton	Herd	Law	Best	
9 Feb	Everton	54,397	Goodison Park	A	W	2–1	Dunne P	Brennan	Dunne A	Crerand	Foulkes	Stiles	Connelly 1	Charlton	Herd 1	Law	Best	
12 May	Strasbourg	30,000	Stade de la Meinau	A	W	5–0	Dunne P	Brennan	Dunne A	Crerand	Foulkes	Stiles	Connelly 1	Charlton 1	Herd 1	Law 2	Best	
19 May	Strasbourg	34,188	Old Trafford	H	D	0–0	Dunne P	Brennan	Dunne A	Crerand	Foulkes	Stiles	Connelly	Charlton	Herd	Law	Best	
31 May	Ferencvaros	39,902	Old Trafford	H	W	3–2	Dunne P	Brennan	Dunne A	Crerand	Foulkes	Stiles	Connelly	Charlton	Herd 2	Law 1	Best	
6 Jun	Ferencvaros	50,000	Nep Stadion	A	L	0–1	Dunne P	Brennan	Dunne A	Crerand	Foulkes	Stiles	Connelly	Charlton	Herd	Law	Best	
16 Jun	Ferencvaros	60,000	Nep Stadion	A	L	1–2	Dunne P	Brennan	Dunne A	Crerand	Foulkes	Stiles	Connelly 1	Charlton	Herd	Law	Best	

FOOTBALL LEAGUE DIVISION 1
P42 • W26 • D9 • L7 • F89 • A39 • PTS61
POSITION: 1

1965/66

FOOTBALL LEAGUE

Date	Opponent	Attendances	Venue				Players and Scores											Substitutions
21 Aug	Sheffield Wednesday	37,524	Old Trafford	H	W	1–0	Dunne P	Brennan	Dunne A	Crerand	Foulkes	Stiles	Anderson W	Charlton	Herd 1	Best	Aston (Jnr.)	
24 Aug	Nottingham Forest	33,744	City Ground	A	L	2–4	Dunne P	Brennan	Dunne A	Crerand	Foulkes	Stiles	Connelly	Charlton	Herd	Best 1	Aston (Jnr.) 1	
28 Aug	Northampton Town	21,140	County Ground	A	D	1–1	Gaskell	Dunne A	Cantwell	Crerand	Foulkes	Stiles	Connelly 1	Charlton	Herd	Law	Best	
1 Sep	Nottingham Forest	38,777	Old Trafford	H	D	0–0	Gaskell	Brennan	Dunne A	Crerand	Foulkes	Stiles	Connelly	Charlton	Herd	Law	Best	
4 Sep	Stoke City	37,603	Old Trafford	H	D	1–1	Gaskell	Brennan	Dunne A	Crerand	Foulkes	Stiles	Connelly	Charlton	Herd 1	Law	Best	
8 Sep	Newcastle United	57,380	St James' Park	A	W	2–1	Gaskell	Brennan	Dunne A	Crerand	Foulkes	Stiles	Connelly	Charlton	Herd 1	Law 1	Best	
11 Sep	Burnley	30,235	Turf Moor	A	L	0–3	Gaskell	Brennan	Dunne A	Crerand	Foulkes	Stiles	Connelly	Charlton	Herd	Law	Best	
15 Sep	Newcastle United	30,401	Old Trafford	H	D	1–1	Gaskell	Brennan	Dunne A	Crerand	Foulkes	Stiles 1	Connelly	Charlton	Herd	Law	Best	
18 Sep	Chelsea	37,917	Old Trafford	H	W	4–1	Gaskell	Brennan	Dunne A	Crerand	Foulkes	Stiles	Connelly	Charlton 1	Herd	Law 3	Aston (Jnr.)	
25 Sep	Arsenal	56,757	Highbury	A	L	2–4	Dunne P	Brennan	Dunne A	Crerand	Foulkes	Stiles	Connelly	Charlton 1	Herd	Law	Aston (Jnr.) 1	
9 Oct	Liverpool	58,161	Old Trafford	H	W	2–0	Dunne P	Brennan	Dunne A	Crerand	Foulkes	Stiles	Connelly	Best 1	Charlton	Law 1	Aston (Jnr.)	
16 Oct	Tottenham Hotspur	58,051	White Hart Lane	A	L	1–5	Dunne P	Brennan	Dunne A	Crerand	Foulkes	Stiles	Connelly	Best	Charlton 1	Law	Aston (Jnr.)	Fitzpatrick replaced Law
23 Oct	Fulham	32,716	Old Trafford	H	W	4–1	Dunne P	Brennan	Dunne A	Crerand	Foulkes	Stiles	Connelly	Best	Charlton 1	Herd 3	Aston (Jnr.)	
30 Oct	Blackpool	24,703	Bloomfield Road	A	W	2–1	Gregg	Brennan	Dunne A	Crerand	Foulkes	Stiles	Connelly	Best	Charlton	Herd 2	Aston (Jnr.)	
6 Nov	Blackburn Rovers	38,823	Old Trafford	H	D	2–2	Gregg	Brennan	Dunne A	Crerand	Foulkes	Stiles	Best	Law 1	Charlton 1	Herd	Aston (Jnr.)	Connelly replaced Aston (Jnr.)
13 Nov	Leicester City	34,551	Filbert Street	A	W	5–0	Gregg	Dunne A	Cantwell	Crerand	Foulkes	Stiles	Best 1	Law	Charlton 1	Herd 2	Connelly 1	
20 Nov	Sheffield United	37,922	Old Trafford	H	W	3–1	Gregg	Dunne A	Cantwell	Crerand	Sadler	Stiles	Best 2	Law 1	Charlton	Herd	Connelly	
4 Dec	West Ham United	32,924	Old Trafford	H	D	0–0	Dunne P	Dunne A	Cantwell	Crerand	Foulkes	Stiles	Best	Law	Charlton	Herd	Connelly	
11 Dec	Sunderland	37,417	Roker Park	A	W	3–2	Dunne P	Dunne A	Cantwell	Crerand	Foulkes	Stiles	Best 2	Law	Charlton	Herd 1	Connelly	
15 Dec	Everton	32,624	Old Trafford	H	W	3–0	Gregg	Dunne A	Cantwell	Crerand	Foulkes	Stiles	Best 1	Law	Charlton 1	Herd 1	Connelly	
18 Dec	Tottenham Hotspur	39,270	Old Trafford	H	W	•5–1	Gregg	Dunne A	Cantwell	Crerand	Foulkes	Stiles	Best	Law 2	Charlton 1	Herd 1	Connelly	
27 Dec	West Bromwich Alb.	54,102	Old Trafford	H	D	1–1	Gregg	Dunne A	Cantwell	Crerand	Foulkes	Stiles	Best	Law 1	Charlton	Herd	Connelly	
1 Jan	Liverpool	53,790	Anfield	A	L	1–2	Gregg	Dunne A	Cantwell	Crerand	Foulkes	Stiles	Best	Law 1	Charlton	Herd	Connelly	
8 Jan	Sunderland	39,162	Old Trafford	H	D	1–1	Gregg	Dunne A	Cantwell	Crerand	Foulkes	Stiles	Best 1	Law	Charlton	Herd	Aston (Jnr.)	
12 Jan	Leeds United	49,672	Elland Road	A	D	1–1	Gregg	Dunne A	Cantwell	Crerand	Foulkes	Stiles	Best	Law	Charlton	Herd 1	Aston (Jnr.)	
15 Jan	Fulham	33,018	Craven Cottage	A	W	1–0	Gregg	Dunne A	Cantwell	Crerand	Foulkes	Stiles	Best	Law	Charlton 1	Herd	Aston (Jnr.)	
29 Jan	Sheffield Wednesday	39,281	Hillsborough	A	D	0–0	Gregg	Dunne A	Cantwell	Crerand	Foulkes	Stiles	Best	Law	Charlton	Herd	Aston (Jnr.)	
5 Feb	Northampton Town	34,986	Old Trafford	H	W	6–2	Gregg	Dunne A	Cantwell	Crerand	Foulkes	Stiles	Best	Law 2	Charlton 3	Herd	Connelly 1	
19 Feb	Stoke City	36,667	Victoria Ground	A	D	2–2	Gregg	Brennan	Dunne A	Crerand	Foulkes	Stiles	Connelly 1	Best	Charlton	Herd 1	Aston (Jnr.)	
26 Feb	Burnley	49,892	Old Trafford	H	W	4–2	Gregg	Brennan	Dunne A	Crerand	Foulkes	Stiles	Best	Law	Charlton 1	Herd 3	Connelly	
12 Mar	Chelsea	60,269	Stamford Bridge	A	L	0–2	Gregg	Brennan	Dunne A	Crerand	Foulkes	Stiles	Best	Law	Charlton	Herd	Connelly	
19 Mar	Arsenal	47,246	Old Trafford	H	W	2–1	Gregg	Brennan	Dunne A	Crerand	Foulkes	Stiles 1	Best	Law 1	Charlton	Herd	Connelly	
6 Apr	Aston Villa	28,211	Villa Park	A	D	1–1	Gaskell	Brennan	Dunne A	Crerand	Foulkes	Fitzpatrick	Connelly	Law	Anderson W	Cantwell 1	Aston (Jnr.)	
9 Apr	Leicester City	42,593	Old Trafford	H	L	1–2	Gregg	Brennan	Noble	Crerand	Sadler	Stiles	Best	Anderson W	Charlton	Herd	Connelly 1	
16 Apr	Sheffield United	22,330	Bramall Lane	A	L	1–3	Gregg	Brennan	Cantwell	Fitzpatrick	Foulkes	Stiles	Connelly	Anderson W	Sadler 1	Herd	Aston (Jnr.)	
25 Apr	Everton	50,843	Goodison Park	A	D	0–0	Gregg	Brennan	Dunne A	Crerand	Cantwell	Stiles	Anderson W	Law	Sadler	Charlton	Aston (Jnr.)	
27 Apr	Blackpool	26,953	Old Trafford	H	W	2–1	Gregg	Brennan	Dunne A	Crerand	Cantwell	Stiles	Connelly	Law 1	Sadler	Charlton 1	Aston (Jnr.)	
30 Apr	West Ham United	36,416	Upton Park	A	L	2–3	Gregg	Brennan	Dunne A	Crerand	Cantwell 1	Stiles	Connelly	Law	Sadler	Charlton	Aston (Jnr.) 1	Herd replaced Dunne A
4 May	West Bromwich Alb.	22,609	The Hawthorns	A	D	3–3	Gregg	Brennan	Dunne A 1	Crerand	Cantwell	Fitzpatrick	Ryan	Law	Sadler	Herd 1	Aston (Jnr.) 1	Anderson W replaced Fitzpatrick
7 May	Blackburn Rovers	14,513	Ewood Park	A	W	4–1	Gregg	Brennan	Dunne A	Crerand	Cantwell	Stiles	Ryan	Charlton 1	Sadler 1	Herd 2	Aston (Jnr.)	
9 May	Aston Villa	23,039	Old Trafford	H	W	6–1	Gregg	Brennan	Dunne A	Crerand	Cantwell	Stiles	Ryan 1	Herd 2	Sadler 2	Charlton 1	Aston (Jnr.)	
19 May	Leeds United	35,008	Old Trafford	H	D	1–1	Gregg	Brennan	Noble	Crerand	Cantwell	Dunne A	Ryan	Herd 1	Sadler	Law	Aston (Jnr.)	

FA CUP

Date	Opponent	Attendances	Venue				Players and Scores											Substitutions
22 Jan	Derby County	33,827	Baseball Ground	A	W	5–2	Gregg	Dunne A	Cantwell	Crerand	Foulkes	Stiles	Best 2	Law 2	Charlton	Herd 1	Aston (Jnr.)	
12 Feb	Rotherham United	54,263	Old Trafford	H	D	0–0	Gregg	Dunne A	Cantwell	Crerand	Foulkes	Stiles	Best	Law	Charlton	Herd	Connelly	
15 Feb	Rotherham United	23,500	Millmoor	A	W	1–0	Gregg	Brennan	Dunne A	Crerand	Foulkes	Stiles	Best	Law	Charlton	Herd	Connelly 1	
5 Mar	Wolverhampton Wan.	53,500	Molineux	A	W	4–2	Gregg	Brennan	Dunne A	Crerand	Foulkes	Stiles	Best 1	Law 2	Charlton	Herd 1	Connelly	
26 Mar	Preston North End	37,876	Deepdale	A	D	1–1	Gregg	Brennan	Dunne A	Crerand	Foulkes	Stiles	Best	Law	Charlton	Herd 1	Connelly	
30 Mar	Preston North End	60,433	Old Trafford	H	W	3–1	Gregg	Brennan	Dunne A	Crerand	Foulkes	Stiles	Connelly 1	Law 2	Charlton	Herd	Aston (Jnr.)	
23 Apr	Everton	60,000	Burnden Park	A	L	0–1	Gregg	Brennan	Dunne A	Crerand	Foulkes	Stiles	Anderson W	Law	Charlton	Herd	Connelly	

EUROPEAN CUP

Date	Opponent	Attendances	Venue				Players and Scores											Substitutions
22 Sep	HJK Helsinki	25,000	Olympiastadion	A	W	3–2	Gaskell	Brennan	Dunne A	Fitzpatrick	Foulkes	Stiles	Connelly 1	Charlton	Herd 1	Law 1	Aston (Jnr.)	
6 Oct	HJK Helsinki	30,388	Old Trafford	H	W	6–0	Dunne P	Brennan	Dunne A	Crerand	Foulkes	Stiles	Connelly 3	Best 2	Charlton 1	Law	Aston (Jnr.)	
17 Nov	ASK Vorwaerts	40,000	Walter Ulbrichrt	A	W	2–0	Gregg	Dunne A	Cantwell	Crerand	Foulkes	Stiles	Best	Law 1	Charlton	Herd	Connelly 1	
1 Dec	ASK Vorwaerts	30,082	Old Trafford	H	W	3–1	Dunne P	Dunne A	Cantwell	Crerand	Foulkes	Stiles	Best	Law	Charlton	Herd 3	Connelly	
2 Feb	Benfica	64,035	Old Trafford	H	W	3–2	Gregg	Dunne A	Cantwell	Crerand	Foulkes 1	Stiles	Best	Law 1	Charlton	Herd 1	Connelly	
9 Mar	Benfica	75,000	Estadio da Luz	A	W	5–1	Gregg	Brennan	Dunne A	Crerand 1	Foulkes	Stiles	Best 2	Law	Charlton 1	Herd	Connelly 1	
13 Apr	Partizan Belgrade	60,000	Stadion JNA	A	L	0–2	Gregg	Brennan	Dunne A	Crerand	Foulkes	Stiles	Best	Law	Charlton	Herd	Connelly	
20 Apr	Partizan Belgrade	62,500	Old Trafford	H	W	1–0	Gregg	Brennan	Dunne A	Crerand	Foulkes	Stiles 1	Anderson W	Law	Charlton	Herd	Connelly	

FOOTBALL LEAGUE DIVISION 1
P42 • W18 • D15 • L9 • F84 • A59 • PTS51
POSITION: 4

1966/67

Football League		Attendances	Venue				Players and Scores											Substitutions
20 Aug	West Bromwich Alb.	41,343	Old Trafford	H	W	5–3	Gaskell	Brennan	Dunne A	Fitzpatrick	Foulkes	Stiles 1	Best 1	Law 2	Charlton	Herd 1	Connelly	
23 Aug	Everton	60,657	Goodison Park	A	W	2–1	Gaskell	Brennan	Dunne A	Fitzpatrick	Foulkes	Stiles	Best	Law 2	Charlton	Herd	Connelly	
27 Aug	Leeds United	45,092	Elland Road	A	L	1–3	Gaskell	Brennan	Dunne A	Fitzpatrick	Foulkes	Stiles	Best 1	Law	Charlton	Herd	Connelly	
31 Aug	Everton	61,114	Old Trafford	H	W	3–0	Gaskell	Brennan	Dunne A	Crerand	Foulkes 1	Stiles	Connelly 1	Law 1	Charlton	Herd	Best	
3 Sep	Newcastle United	44,448	Old Trafford	H	W	3–2	Gregg	Brennan	Dunne A	Crerand	Foulkes	Stiles	Connelly 1	Law 1	Charlton	Herd 1	Best	
7 Sep	Stoke City	44,337	Victoria Ground	A	L	0–3	Gregg	Brennan	Dunne A	Crerand	Foulkes	Stiles	Connelly	Law	Charlton	Herd	Best	
10 Sep	Tottenham Hotspur	56,295	White Hart Lane	A	L	1–2	Gaskell	Brennan	Dunne A	Crerand	Foulkes	Stiles	Best	Law 1	Sadler	Herd	Charlton	Aston (Jnr.) replaced Sadler
17 Sep	Manchester City	62,085	Old Trafford	H	W	1–0	Stepney	Brennan	Dunne A	Crerand	Foulkes	Stiles	Best	Law 1	Sadler	Charlton	Aston (Jnr.)	
24 Sep	Burnley	52,697	Old Trafford	H	W	4–1	Stepney	Brennan	Dunne A	Crerand 1	Foulkes	Stiles	Herd 1	Law 1	Sadler 1	Charlton	Best	Aston (Jnr.) replaced Law
1 Oct	Nottingham Forest	41,854	City Ground	A	L	1–4	Stepney	Brennan	Dunne A	Crerand	Foulkes	Stiles	Best	Charlton 1	Sadler	Herd	Aston (Jnr.)	
8 Oct	Blackpool	33,555	Bloomfield Road	A	W	2–1	Stepney	Dunne A	Noble	Crerand	Cantwell	Stiles	Herd	Law 2	Sadler	Charlton	Best	
15 Oct	Chelsea	56,789	Old Trafford	H	D	1–1	Stepney	Dunne A	Noble	Crerand	Cantwell	Stiles	Herd	Law 1	Sadler	Charlton	Best	
29 Oct	Arsenal	45,387	Old Trafford	H	W	1–0	Stepney	Dunne A	Noble	Crerand	Cantwell	Stiles	Herd	Law	Sadler 1	Charlton	Best	
5 Nov	Chelsea	55,958	Stamford Bridge	A	W	3–1	Stepney	Brennan	Noble	Crerand	Foulkes	Stiles	Herd	Aston (Jnr.) 2	Sadler	Charlton	Best 1	
12 Nov	Sheffield Wednesday	46,942	Old Trafford	H	W	2–0	Stepney	Dunne A	Noble	Crerand	Foulkes	Stiles	Herd 1	Law	Sadler	Charlton 1	Best	Aston (Jnr.) replaced Foulkes
19 Nov	Southampton	29,458	The Dell	A	W	2–1	Stepney	Dunne A	Noble	Crerand	Cantwell	Stiles	Herd	Law	Sadler	Charlton 2	Best	Aston (Jnr.) replaced Cantwell
26 Nov	Sunderland	44,687	Old Trafford	H	W	5–0	Stepney	Dunne A	Noble	Crerand	Sadler	Stiles	Best	Law 1	Charlton	Herd 4	Aston (Jnr.)	
30 Nov	Leicester City	39,014	Filbert Street	A	W	2–1	Stepney	Dunne A	Noble	Crerand	Sadler	Stiles	Best 1	Law 1	Charlton	Herd	Aston (Jnr.)	
3 Dec	Aston Villa	39,937	Villa Park	A	L	1–2	Stepney	Dunne A	Noble	Crerand	Sadler	Stiles	Best	Law	Charlton	Herd 1	Aston (Jnr.)	
10 Dec	Liverpool	61,768	Old Trafford	H	D	2–2	Stepney	Brennan	Noble	Crerand	Sadler	Dunne A	Best 2	Ryan	Charlton	Herd	Aston (Jnr.)	Anderson W replaced Dunne A
17 Dec	West Bromwich Alb.	32,080	The Hawthorns	A	W	4–3	Stepney	Brennan	Noble	Crerand	Sadler	Stiles	Best	Law 1	Charlton	Herd 3	Aston (Jnr.)	
26 Dec	Sheffield United	42,752	Bramall Lane	A	L	1–2	Stepney	Dunne A	Noble	Crerand	Foulkes	Sadler	Best	Law	Charlton	Herd 1	Aston (Jnr.)	
27 Dec	Sheffield United	59,392	Old Trafford	H	W	2–0	Stepney	Dunne A	Noble	Crerand 1	Foulkes	Sadler	Best	Law	Charlton	Herd 1	Aston (Jnr.)	
31 Dec	Leeds United	53,486	Old Trafford	H	D	0–0	Stepney	Dunne A	Noble	Crerand	Foulkes	Sadler	Best	Law	Charlton	Herd	Aston (Jnr.)	
14 Jan	Tottenham Hotspur	57,366	Old Trafford	H	W	1–0	Stepney	Dunne A	Noble	Crerand	Foulkes	Sadler	Best	Ryan	Charlton	Herd 1	Aston (Jnr.)	
21 Jan	Manchester City	62,983	Maine Road	A	D	1–1	Stepney	Dunne A	Noble	Crerand	Foulkes 1	Stiles	Ryan	Charlton	Sadler	Herd	Best	
4 Feb	Burnley	40,165	Turf Moor	A	D	1–1	Stepney	Dunne A	Noble	Crerand	Foulkes	Stiles	Best	Law	Sadler 1	Herd	Charlton	
11 Feb	Nottingham Forest	62,727	Old Trafford	H	W	1–0	Stepney	Dunne A	Noble	Crerand	Foulkes	Stiles	Best	Law 1	Sadler	Herd	Charlton	Ryan replaced Foulkes
25 Feb	Blackpool	47,158	Old Trafford	H	W	•4–0	Stepney	Dunne A	Noble	Crerand	Foulkes	Stiles	Best	Law 1	Sadler	Charlton 2	Aston (Jnr.)	
3 Mar	Arsenal	63,363	Highbury	A	D	1–1	Stepney	Dunne A	Noble	Crerand	Foulkes	Stiles	Best	Law	Sadler	Charlton	Aston (Jnr.) 1	
11 Mar	Newcastle United	37,430	St James' Park	A	D	0–0	Stepney	Dunne A	Noble	Crerand	Foulkes	Stiles	Best	Law	Sadler	Charlton	Aston (Jnr.)	
18 Mar	Leicester City	50,281	Old Trafford	H	W	5–2	Stepney	Dunne A	Noble	Crerand	Foulkes	Stiles	Best	Law 1	Charlton 1	Herd 1	Aston (Jnr.) 1	Sadler 1 replaced Herd
25 Mar	Liverpool	53,813	Anfield	A	D	0–0	Stepney	Dunne A	Noble	Crerand	Foulkes	Stiles	Best	Law	Sadler	Charlton	Aston (Jnr.)	
27 Mar	Fulham	47,290	Craven Cottage	A	D	2–2	Stepney	Dunne A	Noble	Crerand	Foulkes	Stiles 1	Best 1	Law	Sadler	Charlton	Aston (Jnr.)	
28 Mar	Fulham	51,673	Old Trafford	H	W	2–1	Stepney	Dunne A	Noble	Crerand	Foulkes 1	Stiles 1	Best	Law	Sadler	Charlton	Aston (Jnr.)	
1 Apr	West Ham United	61,308	Old Trafford	H	W	3–0	Stepney	Dunne A	Noble	Crerand	Foulkes	Stiles	Best 1	Law 1	Sadler	Charlton 1	Aston (Jnr.)	
10 Apr	Sheffield Wednesday	51,101	Hillsborough	A	D	2–2	Stepney	Dunne A	Noble	Crerand	Foulkes	Stiles	Best	Law	Sadler	Charlton 2	Aston (Jnr.)	
18 Apr	Southampton	54,291	Old Trafford	H	W	3–0	Stepney	Dunne A	Noble	Crerand	Foulkes	Stiles	Best	Law 1	Sadler 1	Charlton 1	Aston (Jnr.)	
22 Apr	Sunderland	43,570	Roker Park	A	D	0–0	Stepney	Dunne A	Noble	Crerand	Foulkes	Stiles	Best	Law	Sadler	Charlton	Aston (Jnr.)	
29 Apr	Aston Villa	55,782	Old Trafford	H	W	3–1	Stepney	Brennan	Dunne A	Crerand	Foulkes	Stiles	Best 1	Law 1	Sadler	Charlton	Aston (Jnr.) 1	
6 May	West Ham United	38,424	Upton Park	A	W	6–1	Stepney	Brennan	Dunne A	Crerand 1	Foulkes 1	Stiles	Best 1	Law 2	Sadler	Charlton 1	Aston (Jnr.)	
13 May	Stoke City	61,071	Old Trafford	H	D	0–0	Stepney	Brennan	Dunne A	Crerand	Foulkes	Stiles	Best	Ryan	Sadler	Charlton	Aston (Jnr.)	

FA Cup																		
28 Jan	Stoke City	63,500	Old Trafford	H	W	2–0	Stepney	Dunne A	Noble	Crerand	Foulkes	Stiles	Best	Law 1	Sadler	Herd 1	Charlton	
18 Feb	Norwich City	63,409	Old Trafford	H	L	1–2	Stepney	Dunne A	Noble	Crerand	Sadler	Stiles	Ryan	Law 1	Charlton	Herd	Best	

FL Cup																		
14 Sep	Blackpool	15,570	Bloomfield Road	A	L	1–5	Dunne P	Brennan	Dunne A	Crerand	Foulkes	Stiles	Connelly	Best	Sadler	Herd 1	Aston (Jnr.)	

Football League Division 1
P42 • W24 • D12 • L6 • F84 • A45 • PTS60
Position: 1

1967/68

Football League		Attendances	Venue				Players and Scores											Substitutions
19 Aug	Everton	61,452	Goodison Park	A	L	1–3	Stepney	Brennan	Dunne A	Crerand	Foulkes	Stiles	Best	Law	Charlton 1	Kidd	Aston (Jnr.)	Sadler replaced Crerand
23 Aug	Leeds United	53,016	Old Trafford	H	W	1–0	Stepney	Brennan	Dunne A	Crerand	Foulkes	Stiles	Ryan	Law	Charlton 1	Kidd	Aston (Jnr.)	
26 Aug	Leicester City	51,256	Old Trafford	H	D	1–1	Stepney	Brennan	Dunne A	Sadler	Foulkes 1	Stiles	Best	Law	Charlton	Kidd	Aston (Jnr.)	
2 Sep	West Ham United	36,562	Upton Park	A	W	3–1	Stepney	Dunne A	Burns	Crerand	Foulkes	Stiles	Ryan 1	Sadler 1	Charlton	Kidd 1	Best	
6 Sep	Sunderland	51,527	Roker Park	A	D	1–1	Stepney	Dunne A	Burns	Crerand	Foulkes	Stiles	Ryan	Sadler	Charlton	Kidd 1	Best	Fitzpatrick replaced Stiles
9 Sep	Burnley	55,809	Old Trafford	H	D	2–2	Stepney	Dunne A	Burns 1	Crerand 1	Foulkes	Fitzpatrick	Ryan	Sadler	Charlton	Kidd	Best	Kopel replaced Fitzpatrick
16 Sep	Sheffield Wednesday	47,274	Hillsborough	A	D	1–1	Stepney	Dunne A	Burns	Crerand	Foulkes	Stiles	Best 1	Sadler	Charlton	Law	Kidd	
23 Sep	Tottenham Hotspur	58,779	Old Trafford	H	W	3–1	Stepney	Dunne A	Burns	Crerand	Foulkes	Stiles	Best 2	Sadler	Charlton	Law 1	Kidd	
30 Sep	Manchester City	62,942	Maine Road	A	W	2–1	Stepney	Dunne A	Burns	Crerand	Foulkes	Stiles	Best	Sadler	Charlton 2	Law	Kidd	Aston (Jnr.) replaced Foulkes
7 Oct	Arsenal	60,197	Old Trafford	H	W	1–0	Stepney	Dunne A	Burns	Crerand	Sadler	Stiles	Best	Kidd	Charlton	Law	Aston (Jnr.) 1	
14 Oct	Sheffield United	29,170	Bramall Lane	A	W	3–0	Stepney	Dunne A	Burns	Crerand	Sadler	Stiles	Best	Kidd 1	Charlton	Law 1	Aston (Jnr.) 1	Fitzpatrick replaced Stiles
25 Oct	Coventry City	54,253	Old Trafford	H	W	4–0	Stepney	Dunne A	Burns	Crerand	Sadler	Fitzpatrick	Best 1	Kidd	Charlton 1	Law	Aston (Jnr.) 2	
28 Oct	Nottingham Forest	49,946	City Ground	A	L	1–3	Stepney	Kopel	Burns	Crerand	Sadler	Fitzpatrick	Best 1	Kidd	Charlton	Law	Aston (Jnr.)	
4 Nov	Stoke City	51,041	Old Trafford	H	W	1–0	Stepney	Dunne A	Burns	Crerand	Foulkes	Sadler	Ryan	Kidd	Charlton 1	Best	Aston (Jnr.)	
8 Nov	Leeds United	43,999	Elland Road	A	L	0–1	Stepney	Dunne A	Burns	Crerand	Foulkes	Sadler	Ryan	Kidd	Charlton	Best	Aston (Jnr.)	Fitzpatrick replaced Ryan
11 Nov	Liverpool	54,515	Anfield	A	W	2–1	Stepney	Dunne A	Burns	Crerand	Foulkes	Sadler	Fitzpatrick	Kidd	Charlton	Best 2	Aston (Jnr.)	
18 Nov	Southampton	48,732	Old Trafford	H	W	3–2	Stepney	Dunne A	Burns	Crerand	Foulkes	Sadler	Fitzpatrick	Kidd 1	Charlton 1	Best	Aston (Jnr.) 1	
25 Nov	Chelsea	54,712	Stamford Bridge	A	D	1–1	Stepney	Brennan	Dunne A	Crerand	Foulkes	Sadler	Burns	Kidd 1	Charlton	Best	Aston (Jnr.)	
2 Dec	West Bromwich Alb.	52,568	Old Trafford	H	W	2–1	Stepney	Brennan	Dunne A	Crerand	Foulkes	Sadler	Burns	Kidd	Charlton	Best 2	Aston (Jnr.)	
9 Dec	Newcastle United	48,639	St James' Park	A	D	2–2	Stepney	Brennan	Dunne A 1	Crerand	Foulkes	Sadler	Burns	Kidd 1	Charlton	Best	Aston (Jnr.)	
16 Dec	Everton	60,736	Old Trafford	H	W	3–1	Stepney	Dunne A	Burns	Crerand	Foulkes	Sadler 1	Best	Kidd	Charlton	Law 1	Aston (Jnr.) 1	
23 Dec	Leicester City	40,104	Filbert Street	A	D	2–2	Stepney	Dunne A	Burns	Crerand	Foulkes	Sadler	Best	Kidd	Charlton 1	Law 1	Aston (Jnr.)	
26 Dec	Wolverhampton Wan.	63,450	Old Trafford	H	W	4–0	Stepney	Dunne A	Burns	Crerand	Foulkes	Sadler	Best 2	Kidd 1	Charlton 1	Law	Aston (Jnr.)	
30 Dec	Wolverhampton Wan.	53,940	Molineux	A	W	3–2	Stepney	Dunne A	Burns	Crerand	Foulkes	Sadler	Best	Kidd 1	Charlton 1	Law	Aston (Jnr.) 1	
6 Jan	West Ham United	54,498	Old Trafford	H	W	3–1	Stepney	Dunne A	Burns	Crerand	Sadler	Fitzpatrick	Best 1	Kidd	Charlton 1	Law	Aston (Jnr.) 1	
20 Jan	Sheffield Wednesday	55,254	Old Trafford	H	W	4–2	Stepney	Dunne A	Burns	Crerand	Sadler	Fitzpatrick	Best 2	Kidd 1	Charlton 1	Law	Aston (Jnr.)	
3 Feb	Tottenham Hotspur	57,790	White Hart Lane	A	W	2–1	Stepney	Dunne A	Burns	Crerand	Sadler	Fitzpatrick	Best 1	Kidd	Charlton 1	Herd	Aston (Jnr.)	
17 Feb	Burnley	31,965	Turf Moor	A	L	1–2	Stepney	Dunne A	Burns	Crerand	Sadler	Stiles	Best 1	Kidd	Charlton	Law	Aston (Jnr.)	
24 Feb	Arsenal	46,417	Highbury	A	W	•2–0	Stepney	Dunne A	Burns	Crerand	Sadler	Stiles	Best 1	Kidd	Fitzpatrick	Law	Aston (Jnr.)	
2 Mar	Chelsea	62,978	Old Trafford	H	L	1–3	Stepney	Dunne A	Burns	Crerand	Sadler	Stiles	Best	Kidd 1	Charlton	Ryan	Aston (Jnr.)	
16 Mar	Coventry City	47,110	Highfield Road	A	L	0–2	Stepney	Brennan	Burns	Crerand	Sadler	Stiles	Best	Kidd	Charlton	Fitzpatrick	Herd	Aston (Jnr.) replaced Kidd
23 Mar	Nottingham Forest	61,978	Old Trafford	H	W	3–0	Stepney	Brennan 1	Burns 1	Crerand	Sadler	Stiles	Fitzpatrick	Herd 1	Charlton	Best	Aston (Jnr.)	
27 Mar	Manchester City	63,004	Old Trafford	H	L	1–3	Stepney	Brennan	Burns	Crerand	Sadler	Stiles	Fitzpatrick	Law	Charlton	Best 1	Herd	Aston (Jnr.) replaced Herd
30 Mar	Stoke City	30,141	Victoria Ground	A	W	4–2	Stepney	Brennan	Burns	Crerand	Sadler	Fitzpatrick	Best 1	Gowling 1	Charlton	Herd	Aston (Jnr.) 1	Ryan 1 replaced Herd
6 Apr	Liverpool	63,059	Old Trafford	H	L	1–2	Stepney	Dunne A	Burns	Crerand	Sadler	Fitzpatrick	Best 1	Gowling	Charlton	Herd	Aston (Jnr.)	
12 Apr	Fulham	40,152	Craven Cottage	A	W	4–0	Stepney	Dunne A	Burns	Crerand	Sadler	Stiles	Best 2	Kidd 1	Charlton	Law 1	Aston (Jnr.)	
13 Apr	Southampton	30,079	The Dell	A	D	2–2	Stepney	Dunne A	Burns	Crerand	Foulkes	Sadler	Best 1	Kidd	Charlton 1	Gowling	Aston (Jnr.)	
15 Apr	Fulham	60,465	Old Trafford	H	W	3–0	Rimmer	Dunne A	Burns	Crerand	Foulkes	Sadler	Best 1	Kidd	Charlton 1	Law	Aston (Jnr.) 1	
20 Apr	Sheffield United	55,033	Old Trafford	H	W	1–0	Stepney	Brennan	Dunne A	Crerand	Sadler	Stiles	Best	Kidd	Charlton	Law 1	Aston (Jnr.)	
29 Apr	West Bromwich Alb.	43,412	The Hawthorns	A	L	3–6	Stepney	Dunne A	Burns	Crerand	Sadler	Stiles	Best	Kidd 2	Charlton	Law 1	Aston (Jnr.)	
4 May	Newcastle United	59,976	Old Trafford	H	W	6–0	Stepney	Brennan	Dunne A	Crerand	Foulkes	Sadler 1	Best 3	Kidd 2	Charlton	Gowling	Aston (Jnr.)	
11 May	Sunderland	62,963	Old Trafford	H	L	1–2	Stepney	Brennan	Dunne A	Crerand	Foulkes	Stiles	Best 1	Kidd	Charlton	Sadler	Aston (Jnr.)	Gowling replaced Foulkes

FA Cup																		
27 Jan	Tottenham Hotspur	63,500	Old Trafford	H	D	2–2	Stepney	Dunne A	Burns	Crerand	Sadler	Fitzpatrick	Best 1	Kidd	Charlton 1	Law	Aston (Jnr.)	
31 Jan	Tottenham Hotspur	57,200	White Hart Lane	A	L	0–1	Stepney	Dunne A	Burns	Crerand	Sadler	Fitzpatrick	Best	Kidd	Charlton	Herd	Aston (Jnr.)	

European Cup																		
20 Sep	Hibernian Malta	43,912	Old Trafford	H	W	4–0	Stepney	Dunne A	Burns	Crerand	Foulkes	Stiles	Best	Sadler 2	Charlton	Law 2	Kidd	
27 Sep	Hibernian Malta	25,000	Empire Stadium	A	D	0–0	Stepney	Dunne A	Burns	Crerand	Foulkes	Stiles	Best	Sadler	Charlton	Law	Kidd	
15 Nov	Sarajevo	45,000	Stadion Kosevo	A	D	0–0	Stepney	Dunne A	Burns	Crerand	Foulkes	Sadler	Fitzpatrick	Kidd	Charlton	Best	Aston (Jnr.)	
29 Nov	Sarajevo	62,801	Old Trafford	H	W	2–1	Stepney	Brennan	Dunne A	Crerand	Foulkes	Sadler	Burns	Kidd	Charlton	Best 1	Aston (Jnr.) 1	
28 Feb	Gornik Zabrze	63,456	Old Trafford	H	W	•2–0	Stepney	Dunne A	Burns	Crerand	Sadler	Stiles	Best	Kidd 1	Charlton	Ryan	Aston (Jnr.)	
13 Mar	Gornik Zabrze	105,000	Stadion Slaski	A	L	0–1	Stepney	Dunne A	Burns	Crerand	Sadler	Stiles	Fitzpatrick	Charlton	Herd	Kidd	Best	
24 Apr	Real Madrid	63,500	Old Trafford	H	W	1–0	Stepney	Dunne A	Burns	Crerand	Sadler	Stiles	Best 1	Kidd	Charlton	Law	Aston (Jnr.)	
15 May	Real Madrid	125,000	Bernabeu	A	D	•3–3	Stepney	Brennan	Dunne A	Crerand	Foulkes 1	Stiles	Best	Kidd	Charlton	Sadler 1	Aston (Jnr.)	
29 May	Benfica	100,000	Wembley	A	W	4–1	Stepney	Brennan	Dunne A	Crerand	Foulkes	Stiles	Best 1	Kidd 1	Charlton 2	Sadler	Aston (Jnr.)	

Football League Division 1
P42 • W24 • D8 • L10 • F89 • A55 • PTS56
Position: 2

1968/69

Football League		Attendances	Venue				Players and Scores											Substitutions
10 Aug	Everton	61,311	Old Trafford	H	W	2–1	Stepney	Brennan	Dunne A	Crerand	Foulkes	Stiles	Best 1	Kidd	Charlton 1	Law	Aston (Jnr.)	
14 Aug	West Bromwich Alb.	38,299	The Hawthorns	A	L	1–3	Stepney	Brennan	Dunne A	Crerand	Foulkes	Stiles	Best	Kidd	Charlton 1	Law	Aston (Jnr.)	Sadler replaced Foulkes
17 Aug	Manchester City	63,052	Maine Road	A	D	0–0	Stepney	Kopel	Dunne A	Fitzpatrick	Sadler	Stiles	Best	Gowling	Charlton	Kidd	Aston (Jnr.)	Burns replaced Aston (Jnr.)
21 Aug	Coventry City	51,201	Old Trafford	H	W	1–0	Stepney	Kopel	Dunne A	Fitzpatrick	Sadler	Stiles	Ryan 1	Kidd	Charlton	Burns	Best	
24 Aug	Chelsea	55,114	Old Trafford	H	L	0–4	Stepney	Kopel	Dunne A	Crerand	Sadler	Stiles	Ryan	Kidd	Charlton	Burns	Best	
28 Aug	Tottenham Hotspur	62,649	Old Trafford	H	W	•3–1	Stepney	Brennan	Dunne A	Fitzpatrick 2	Sadler	Stiles	Morgan W	Kidd	Charlton	Law	Best	
31 Aug	Sheffield Wednesday	50,490	Hillsborough	A	L	4–5	Stepney	Brennan	Dunne A	Fitzpatrick	Sadler	Stiles	Morgan W	Kidd	Charlton 1	Law 2	Best 1	Burns replaced Dunne A

continued on page 139

1968/69 continued

Football League continued

Date	Opponents	Attendances	Venue				Players and Scores											Substitutions
7 Sep	West Ham United	63,274	Old Trafford	H	D	1–1	Stepney	Dunne A	Burns	Fitzpatrick	Foulkes	Stiles	Morgan W	Sadler	Charlton	Law 1	Best	
14 Sep	Burnley	32,935	Turf Moor	A	L	0–1	Stepney	Dunne A	Burns	Fitzpatrick	Foulkes	Stiles	Morgan W	Sadler	Charlton	Law	Best	
21 Sep	Newcastle United	47,262	Old Trafford	H	W	3–1	Stepney	Dunne A	Burns	Crerand	Sadler	Stiles	Morgan W	Fitzpatrick	Charlton	Law 1	Best 2	Kidd replaced Crerand
5 Oct	Arsenal	61,843	Old Trafford	H	D	0–0	Stepney	Dunne A	Burns	Crerand	Foulkes	Stiles	Morgan W	Fitzpatrick	Charlton	Law	Best	
9 Oct	Tottenham Hotspur	56,205	White Hart Lane	A	D	2–2	Stepney	Dunne A	Burns	Crerand 1	Foulkes	Stiles	Morgan W	Fitzpatrick	Charlton	Law 1	Best	Sartori replaced Burns
12 Oct	Liverpool	53,392	Anfield	A	L	0–2	Stepney	Brennan	Kopel	Crerand	James	Stiles	Ryan	Fitzpatrick	Charlton	Gowling	Sartori	
19 Oct	Southampton	46,526	Old Trafford	H	L	1–2	Stepney	Kopel	Dunne A	Crerand	Foulkes	Stiles	Morgan W	Sadler	Charlton	Sartori	Best 1	Fitzpatrick replaced Foulkes
26 Oct	Queen's Park Rangers	31,138	Loftus Road	A	W	3–2	Stepney	Brennan	Dunne A	Crerand	Sadler	Stiles	Morgan W	Kidd	Charlton	Law 1	Best 2	
2 Nov	Leeds United	53,839	Old Trafford	H	D	0–0	Stepney	Brennan	Dunne A	Crerand	Sadler	Stiles	Morgan W	Kidd	Charlton	Law	Best	
9 Nov	Sunderland	33,151	Roker Park	A	D	•1–1	Stepney	Brennan	Dunne A	Crerand	Sadler	Stiles	Morgan W	Kidd	Charlton	Sartori	Best	
16 Nov	Ipswich Town	45,796	Old Trafford	H	D	0–0	Stepney	Brennan	Dunne A	Crerand	James	Stiles	Morgan W	Kidd	Charlton	Law	Best	Kopel replaced Kidd
23 Nov	Stoke City	30,562	Victoria Ground	A	D	0–0	Stepney	Kopel	Dunne A	Crerand	James	Stiles	Morgan W	Best	Charlton	Fitzpatrick	Sartori	
30 Nov	Wolverhampton Wan.	50,165	Old Trafford	H	W	2–0	Stepney	Kopel	Dunne A	Crerand	Sadler	Stiles	Morgan W	Sartori	Charlton	Law 1	Best 1	Fitzpatrick replaced Stiles
7 Dec	Leicester City	36,303	Filbert Street	A	L	1–2	Stepney	Dunne A	Burns	Crerand	Sadler	Stiles	Morgan W	Sartori	Charlton	Law 1	Best	
14 Dec	Liverpool	55,354	Old Trafford	H	W	1–0	Stepney	Dunne A	Burns	Crerand	James	Stiles	Best	Sadler	Charlton	Law 1	Sartori	
21 Dec	Southampton	26,194	The Dell	A	L	0–2	Stepney	Dunne A	Burns	Crerand	James	Stiles	Best	Sadler	Charlton	Law	Sartori	
26 Dec	Arsenal	62,300	Highbury	A	L	0–3	Stepney	Dunne A	Burns	Crerand	James	Stiles	Best	Sadler	Charlton	Law	Kidd	Sartori replaced Crerand
11 Jan	Leeds United	48,145	Elland Road	A	L	1–2	Stepney	Dunne A	Burns	Crerand	James	Stiles	Best	Fitzpatrick	Charlton 1	Law	Sartori	
18 Jan	Sunderland	45,670	Old Trafford	H	W	4–1	Rimmer	Dunne A	Burns	Fitzpatrick	James	Stiles	Morgan W	Sartori	Charlton	Law 3	Best 1	
1 Feb	Ipswich Town	30,837	Portman Road	A	L	0–1	Stepney	Fitzpatrick	Dunne A	Crerand	James	Stiles	Morgan W	Kidd	Charlton	Law	Best	
15 Feb	Wolverhampton Wan.	44,023	Molineux	A	D	2–2	Stepney	Fitzpatrick	Dunne A	Crerand	James	Sadler	Morgan W	Kidd	Charlton 1	Sartori	Best 1	Foulkes replaced Sartori
8 Mar	Manchester City	63,264	Old Trafford	H	L	0–1	Stepney	Brennan	Fitzpatrick	Crerand	Foulkes	Stiles	Morgan W	Kidd	Charlton	Sadler	Best	
10 Mar	Everton	57,514	Goodison Park	A	D	0–0	Stepney	Brennan	Dunne A	Crerand	James	Stiles	Best	Kidd	Fitzpatrick	Sadler	Aston (Jnr.)	Foulkes replaced Brennan
15 Mar	Chelsea	60,436	Stamford Bridge	A	L	2–3	Stepney	Fitzpatrick	Dunne A	Crerand	James 1	Stiles	Morgan W	Kidd	Sadler	Law 1	Best	
19 Mar	Queen's Park Rangers	36,638	Old Trafford	H	W	8–1	Stepney	Fitzpatrick	Dunne A	Crerand	James	Stiles 1	Morgan W 3	Kidd 1	Aston (Jnr.) 1	Law	Best 2	
22 Mar	Sheffield Wednesday	45,527	Old Trafford	H	W	1–0	Stepney	Fitzpatrick	Dunne A	Crerand	James	Stiles	Morgan W	Kidd	Best 1	Law	Aston (Jnr.)	
24 Mar	Stoke City	39,931	Old Trafford	H	D	1–1	Stepney	Fitzpatrick	Dunne A	Crerand	James	Stiles	Morgan W	Kidd	Aston (Jnr.) 1	Law	Best	Sadler replaced Morgan W
29 Mar	West Ham United	41,546	Upton Park	A	D	0–0	Stepney	Fitzpatrick	Dunne A	Crerand	James	Stiles	Ryan	Kidd	Aston (Jnr.)	Law	Best	Sadler replaced Dunne A
31 Mar	Nottingham Forest	41,892	City Ground	A	W	1–0	Stepney	Fitzpatrick	Stiles	Crerand	James	Sadler	Ryan	Kidd	Aston (Jnr.)	Law	Best 1	
2 Apr	West Bromwich Alb.	38,846	Old Trafford	H	W	2–1	Stepney	Fitzpatrick	Stiles	Crerand	James	Sadler	Morgan W	Ryan	Aston (Jnr.)	Kidd	Best 2	Foulkes replaced Ryan
5 Apr	Nottingham Forest	51,952	Old Trafford	H	W	3–1	Stepney	Fitzpatrick	Stiles	Crerand	James	Sadler	Morgan W 2	Kidd	Aston (Jnr.)	Law	Best 1	
8 Apr	Coventry City	45,402	Highfield Road	A	L	1–2	Stepney	Fitzpatrick 1	Stiles	Crerand	James	Sadler	Morgan W	Kidd	Aston (Jnr.)	Charlton	Best	
12 Apr	Newcastle United	46,379	St James' Park	A	L	0–2	Rimmer	Fitzpatrick	Stiles	Crerand	James	Sadler	Morgan W	Kidd	Charlton	Law	Best	
19 Apr	Burnley	52,626	Old Trafford	H	W	•2–0	Rimmer	Brennan	Fitzpatrick	Crerand	Foulkes	Stiles	Morgan W	Kidd	Aston (Jnr.)	Law	Best 1	
17 May	Leicester City	45,860	Old Trafford	H	W	3–2	Rimmer	Brennan	Burns	Crerand	Foulkes	Stiles	Morgan W 1	Kidd	Charlton	Law 1	Best 1	

FA Cup

Date	Opponents	Attendances	Venue				Players and Scores											Substitutions
4 Jan	Exeter City	18,500	St James' Park	A	W	•3–1	Stepney	Dunne A	Burns	Fitzpatrick 1	James	Stiles	Best	Kidd 1	Charlton	Law	Sartori	Sadler replaced Best
25 Jan	Watford	63,498	Old Trafford	H	D	1–1	Rimmer	Kopel	Dunne A	Fitzpatrick	James	Stiles	Morgan W	Best	Charlton	Law 1	Sartori	
3 Feb	Watford	34,000	Vicarage Road	A	W	2–0	Stepney	Fitzpatrick	Dunne A	Crerand	James	Stiles	Morgan W	Kidd	Charlton	Law 2	Best	
8 Feb	Birmingham City	52,500	St Andrews	A	D	2–2	Stepney	Fitzpatrick	Dunne A	Crerand	James	Stiles	Morgan W	Kidd	Charlton	Law 1	Best 1	
24 Feb	Birmingham City	61,932	Old Trafford	H	W	6–2	Stepney	Fitzpatrick	Dunne A	Crerand 1	James	Stiles	Morgan W 1	Kidd 1	Charlton	Law 3	Best	
1 Mar	Everton	63,464	Goodison Park	A	L	0–1	Stepney	Fitzpatrick	Dunne A	Crerand	James	Stiles	Morgan W	Kidd	Charlton	Law	Best	

European Cup

Date	Opponents	Attendances	Venue				Players and Scores											Substitutions
18 Sep	Waterford	48,000	Lansdowne Road	A	W	3–1	Stepney	Dunne A	Burns	Crerand	Foulkes	Stiles	Best	Law 3	Charlton	Sadler	Kidd	Rimmer replaced Stepney
2 Oct	Waterford	41,750	Old Trafford	H	W	7–1	Stepney	Dunne A	Burns 1	Crerand	Foulkes	Stiles 1	Best	Law 4	Charlton 1	Sadler	Kidd	
13 Nov	Anderlecht	51,000	Old Trafford	H	W	3–0	Stepney	Brennan	Dunne A	Crerand	Sadler	Stiles	Ryan	Kidd 1	Charlton	Law 2	Sartori	
27 Nov	Anderlecht	40,000	Parc Astrid	A	L	1–3	Stepney	Kopel	Dunne A	Crerand	Foulkes	Stiles	Fitzpatrick	Law	Charlton	Sadler	Sartori 1	
26 Feb	Rapid Vienna	61,932	Old Trafford	H	W	3–0	Stepney	Fitzpatrick	Dunne A	Crerand	James	Stiles	Morgan W 1	Kidd	Charlton	Law	Best 2	
5 Mar	Rapid Vienna	52,000	Wiener Stadion	A	D	0–0	Stepney	Fitzpatrick	Dunne A	Crerand	James	Stiles	Morgan W	Kidd	Charlton	Sadler	Best	
23 Apr	AC Milan	80,000	Stadio San Siro	A	L	0–2	Rimmer	Brennan	Fitzpatrick	Crerand	Foulkes	Stiles	Morgan W	Kidd	Charlton	Law	Best	Burns replaced Stiles
15 May	AC Milan	63,103	Old Trafford	H	W	1–0	Rimmer	Brennan	Burns	Crerand	Foulkes	Stiles	Morgan W	Kidd	Charlton 1	Law	Best	

Football League Division 1
P42 • W15 • D12 • L15 • F57 • A53 • PTS42
Position: 11

The 1970s

1969/70

Football League

Date	Opponents	Attendances	Venue				Players and Scores											Substitutions
9 Aug	Crystal Palace	48,610	Selhurst Park	A	D	2–2	Rimmer	Dunne A	Burns	Crerand	Foulkes	Sadler	Morgan W 1	Kidd	Charlton 1	Law	Best	Givens replaced Dunne A
13 Aug	Everton	57,752	Old Trafford	H	L	0–2	Rimmer	Brennan	Burns	Crerand	Foulkes	Sadler	Morgan W	Kidd	Charlton	Law	Best	Givens replaced Foulkes
16 Aug	Southampton	46,328	Old Trafford	H	L	1–4	Rimmer	Brennan	Burns	Crerand	Foulkes	Sadler	Morgan W 1	Kidd	Charlton	Law	Best	
19 Aug	Everton	53,185	Goodison Park	A	L	0–3	Stepney	Fitzpatrick	Burns	Crerand	Edwards P	Sadler	Morgan W	Kidd	Givens	Best	Aston (Jnr.)	
23 Aug	Wolverhampton Wan.	50,783	Molineux	A	D	0–0	Stepney	Fitzpatrick	Burns	Crerand	Ure	Sadler	Morgan W	Kidd	Charlton	Law	Best	Givens replaced Law
27 Aug	Newcastle United	52,774	Old Trafford	H	D	0–0	Stepney	Fitzpatrick	Dunne A	Crerand	Ure	Sadler	Morgan W	Kidd	Charlton	Givens	Best	
30 Aug	Sunderland	50,570	Old Trafford	H	W	3–1	Stepney	Fitzpatrick	Dunne A	Crerand	Ure	Sadler	Morgan W	Kidd 1	Charlton	Givens 1	Best 1	
6 Sep	Leeds United	44,271	Elland Road	A	D	2–2	Stepney	Fitzpatrick	Dunne A	Burns	Ure	Sadler	Morgan W	Givens	Charlton	Gowling	Best 2	
13 Sep	Liverpool	56,509	Old Trafford	H	W	1–0	Stepney	Fitzpatrick	Dunne A	Burns	Ure	Sadler	Morgan W 1	Kidd	Charlton	Gowling	Best	
17 Sep	Sheffield Wednesday	39,298	Hillsborough	A	W	3–1	Stepney	Fitzpatrick	Dunne A	Burns	Ure	Sadler	Morgan W	Kidd 1	Charlton	Gowling	Best 2	Aston (Jnr.) replaced Gowling
20 Sep	Arsenal	59,498	Highbury	A	D	2–2	Stepney	Fitzpatrick	Dunne A	Burns	Ure	Sadler 1	Morgan W	Kidd	Charlton	Aston (Jnr.)	Best 1	
27 Sep	West Ham United	58,579	Old Trafford	H	W	5–2	Stepney	Fitzpatrick	Dunne A	Burns 1	Ure	Sadler	Morgan W	Kidd 1	Charlton 1	Aston (Jnr.)	Best 2	
4 Oct	Derby County	40,724	Baseball Ground	A	L	0–2	Stepney	Fitzpatrick	Dunne A	Burns	Ure	Sadler	Morgan W	Kidd	Charlton	Aston (Jnr.)	Best	Sartori replaced Aston (Jnr.)
8 Oct	Southampton	31,044	The Dell	A	W	3–0	Stepney	Fitzpatrick	Dunne A	Burns 1	Ure	Sadler	Morgan W	Kidd 1	Charlton	Aston (Jnr.)	Best 1	
11 Oct	Ipswich Town	52,281	Old Trafford	H	W	2–1	Stepney	Fitzpatrick	Dunne A	Burns	Ure	Sadler	Morgan W	Kidd 1	Charlton	Aston (Jnr.)	Best 1	Brennan replaced Best
18 Oct	Nottingham Forest	53,702	Old Trafford	H	D	1–1	Stepney	Fitzpatrick	Dunne A	Burns	Ure	Sadler	Morgan W	Kidd	Charlton	Aston (Jnr.)	Best 1	
25 Oct	West Bromwich Alb.	45,120	The Hawthorns	A	L	1–2	Stepney	Brennan	Dunne A	Burns	Ure	Sadler	Sartori	Kidd 1	Charlton	Aston (Jnr.)	Best	Givens replaced Aston (Jnr.)
1 Nov	Stoke City	53,406	Old Trafford	H	D	1–1	Stepney	Brennan	Dunne A	Burns	Ure	Sadler	Law	Kidd	Charlton 1	Aston (Jnr.)	Best	
8 Nov	Coventry City	43,446	Highfield Road	A	W	2–1	Stepney	Brennan	Dunne A	Burns	Ure	Sadler	Sartori	Best	Charlton	Law 1	Aston (Jnr.) 1	
15 Nov	Manchester City	63,013	Maine Road	A	L	0–4	Stepney	Brennan	Dunne A	Burns	Ure	Sadler	Sartori	Best	Charlton	Law	Aston (Jnr.)	Kidd replaced Sartori
22 Nov	Tottenham Hotspur	50,003	Old Trafford	H	W	3–1	Stepney	Fitzpatrick	Dunne A	Burns 1	Ure	Sadler	Sartori	Kidd	Charlton 2	Best	Aston (Jnr.)	Edwards P replaced Fitzpatrick
29 Nov	Burnley	23,770	Turf Moor	A	D	1–1	Stepney	Edwards P	Dunne A	Burns	Ure	Sadler	Best 1	Kidd	Charlton	Stiles	Aston (Jnr.)	
6 Dec	Chelsea	49,344	Old Trafford	H	L	0–2	Stepney	Edwards P	Dunne A	Burns	Ure	Sadler	Best	Kidd	Charlton	Stiles	Aston (Jnr.)	Ryan replaced Kidd
13 Dec	Liverpool	47,682	Anfield	A	W	•4–1	Stepney	Brennan	Dunne A	Burns	Ure 1	Sadler	Morgan W 1	Best	Charlton 1	Crerand	Aston (Jnr.)	Sartori replaced Aston (Jnr.)
26 Dec	Wolverhampton Wan.	50,806	Old Trafford	H	D	0–0	Stepney	Edwards P	Dunne A	Burns	Ure	Sadler	Morgan W	Crerand	Charlton	Kidd	Best	
27 Dec	Sunderland	36,504	Roker Park	A	D	1–1	Stepney	Edwards P	Brennan	Burns	Ure	Sadler	Morgan W	Crerand	Charlton	Kidd 1	Best	
10 Jan	Arsenal	41,055	Old Trafford	H	W	2–1	Stepney	Edwards P	Dunne A	Burns	Ure	Sadler	Morgan W 1	Crerand	Charlton	Kidd	Aston (Jnr.)	Sartori 1 replaced Dunne A
17 Jan	West Ham United	41,643	Upton Park	A	D	0–0	Rimmer	Edwards P	Burns	Crerand	Ure	Sadler	Morgan W	Sartori	Charlton	Kidd	Aston (Jnr.)	
26 Jan	Leeds United	59,879	Old Trafford	H	D	2–2	Stepney	Edwards P	Burns	Crerand	Ure	Sadler 1	Morgan W	Sartori	Charlton	Kidd 1	Aston (Jnr.)	
31 Jan	Derby County	59,315	Old Trafford	H	W	1–0	Stepney	Edwards P	Burns	Crerand	Ure	Sadler	Morgan W	Sartori	Charlton 1	Kidd	Aston (Jnr.)	
10 Feb	Ipswich Town	29,755	Portman Road	A	W	1–0	Stepney	Edwards P	Dunne A	Crerand	Ure	Sadler	Morgan W	Sartori	Charlton	Kidd 1	Best	
14 Feb	Crystal Palace	54,711	Old Trafford	H	D	1–1	Stepney	Edwards P	Dunne A	Crerand	Ure	Sadler	Morgan W	Sartori	Charlton	Kidd 1	Best	
28 Feb	Stoke City	38,917	Victoria Ground	A	D	2–2	Stepney	Edwards P	Dunne A	Crerand	Ure	Sadler	Morgan W 1	Sartori 1	Charlton	Kidd	Best	Burns replaced Sadler
17 Mar	Burnley	38,377	Old Trafford	H	D	3–3	Rimmer	Edwards P	Dunne A	Crerand 1	Ure	Sadler	Morgan W	Sartori	Charlton	Law 1	Best 1	
21 Mar	Chelsea	61,479	Stamford Bridge	A	L	1–2	Stepney	Edwards P	Burns	Crerand	Ure	Stiles	Morgan W 1	Sartori	Charlton	Law	Best	
28 Mar	Manchester City	59,777	Old Trafford	H	L	1–2	Stepney	Edwards P	Dunne A	Crerand	Sadler	Burns	Morgan W	Sartori	Charlton	Kidd 1	Best	Law replaced Sartori
30 Mar	Coventry City	38,647	Old Trafford	H	D	1–1	Stepney	Edwards P	Dunne A	Fitzpatrick	Ure	Sadler	Morgan W	Best	Law	Kidd 1	Aston (Jnr.)	Burns replaced Kidd
31 Mar	Nottingham Forest	39,228	City Ground	A	W	2–1	Stepney	Stiles	Dunne A	Crerand	James	Sadler	Morgan W	Fitzpatrick	Charlton 1	Gowling 1	Best	
4 Apr	Newcastle United	43,094	St James' Park	A	L	1–5	Stepney	Fitzpatrick	Dunne A	Crerand	James	Sadler	Morgan W	Gowling	Charlton 1	Stiles	Aston (Jnr.)	Sartori replaced Aston (Jnr.)
8 Apr	West Bromwich Alb.	26,582	Old Trafford	H	W	7–0	Stepney	Stiles	Dunne A	Crerand	Ure	Sadler	Morgan W	Fitzpatrick 2	Charlton 2	Gowling 2	Best 1	
13 Apr	Tottenham Hotspur	41,808	White Hart Lane	A	L	1–2	Stepney	Edwards P	Dunne A	Crerand	Ure	Stiles	Morgan W	Fitzpatrick 1	Charlton	Kidd	Best	Gowling replaced Morgan W
15 Apr	Sheffield Wednesday	36,649	Old Trafford	H	D	2–2	Stepney	Edwards P	Dunne A	Crerand	Sadler	Stiles	Morgan W	Fitzpatrick	Charlton 1	Kidd	Best 1	

FA Cup

Date	Opponents	Attendances	Venue				Players and Scores											Substitutions
3 Jan	Ipswich Town	29,552	Portman Road	A	W	•1–0	Stepney	Edwards P	Brennan	Burns	Ure	Sadler	Morgan W	Crerand	Charlton	Kidd	Best	Aston (Jnr.) replaced Morgan W
24 Jan	Manchester City	63,417	Old Trafford	H	W	3–0	Stepney	Edwards P	Burns	Crerand	Ure	Sadler	Morgan W 1	Sartori	Charlton	Kidd 2	Aston (Jnr.)	
7 Feb	Northampton Town	21,771	County Ground	A	W	8–2	Stepney	Edwards P	Dunne A	Crerand	Ure	Sadler	Morgan W	Sartori	Charlton	Kidd 2	Best 6	Burns replaced Charlton
21 Feb	Middlesbrough	40,000	Ayresome Park	A	D	1–1	Stepney	Edwards P	Dunne A	Crerand	Ure	Sadler	Morgan W	Sartori 1	Charlton	Kidd	Best	
25 Feb	Middlesbrough	63,418	Old Trafford	H	W	2–1	Stepney	Dunne A	Burns	Crerand	Ure	Sadler	Morgan W 1	Sartori	Charlton 1	Kidd	Best	
14 Mar	Leeds United	55,000	Hillsborough	A	D	0–0	Stepney	Edwards P	Dunne A	Crerand	Ure	Sadler	Morgan W	Sartori	Charlton	Kidd	Best	
23 Mar	Leeds United	62,500	Villa Park	A	D	0–0	Stepney	Edwards P	Dunne A	Crerand	Sadler	Stiles	Morgan W	Sartori	Charlton	Kidd	Best	Law replaced Sartori
26 Mar	Leeds United	56,000	Burnden Park	A	L	0–1	Stepney	Edwards P	Dunne A	Crerand	Sadler	Stiles	Morgan W	Sartori	Charlton	Kidd	Best	Law replaced Sartori

FL Cup

Date	Opponents	Attendances	Venue				Players and Scores											Substitutions
3 Sep	Middlesbrough	38,939	Old Trafford	H	W	1–0	Stepney	Fitzpatrick	Dunne A	Crerand	James	Sadler 1	Morgan W	Kidd	Charlton	Givens	Best	Gowling replaced Kidd
23 Sep	Wrexham	48,347	Old Trafford	H	W	2–0	Stepney	Fitzpatrick	Dunne A	Burns	Ure	Sadler	Morgan W	Kidd 1	Charlton	Aston (Jnr.)	Best 1	
14 Oct	Burnley	27,959	Turf Moor	A	D	0–0	Stepney	Fitzpatrick	Dunne A	Burns	Ure	Sadler	Morgan W	Kidd	Charlton	Aston (Jnr.)	Best	
20 Oct	Burnley	50,275	Old Trafford	H	W	1–0	Stepney	Fitzpatrick	Dunne A	Burns	Ure	Sadler	Morgan W	Kidd	Charlton	Aston (Jnr.)	Best 1	Sartori replaced Fitzpatrick
12 Nov	Derby County	38,895	Baseball Ground	A	D	0–0	Stepney	Brennan	Dunne A	Burns	Ure	Sadler	Sartori	Best	Charlton	Law	Aston (Jnr.)	
19 Nov	Derby County	57,393	Old Trafford	H	W	1–0	Stepney	Fitzpatrick	Dunne A	Burns	Ure	Sadler	Best	Kidd 1	Charlton	Law	Aston (Jnr.)	Sartori replaced Law
3 Dec	Manchester City	55,799	Maine Road	A	L	1–2	Stepney	Edwards P	Dunne A	Burns	Ure	Sadler	Best	Kidd	Charlton 1	Stiles	Aston (Jnr.)	
17 Dec	Manchester City	63,418	Old Trafford	H	D	2–2	Stepney	Edwards P 1	Dunne A	Stiles	Ure	Sadler	Morgan W	Crerand	Charlton	Law 1	Best	

Football League Division 1
P42 • W14 • D17 • L11 • F66 • A61 • PTS45
Position: 8

1970/71

Football League	Attendances	Venue			Players and Scores											Substitutions
15 Aug Leeds United	59,365	Old Trafford	H L	0–1	Stepney	Edwards P	Dunne A	Crerand	Ure	Sadler	Fitzpatrick	Stiles	Charlton	Kidd	Best	Gowling for Stiles
19 Aug Chelsea	50,979	Old Trafford	H D	0–0	Stepney	Edwards P	Dunne A	Crerand	Ure	Sadler	Morgan W	Fitzpatrick	Charlton	Stiles	Best	
22 Aug Arsenal	54,117	Highbury	A L	0–4	Stepney	Stiles	Dunne A	Crerand	Ure	Sadler	Morgan W	Fitzpatrick	Charlton	Law	Best	Edwards P for Stepney
25 Aug Burnley	29,385	Turf Moor	A W	2–0	Rimmer	Edwards P	Dunne A	Fitzpatrick	Ure	Sadler	Morgan W	Law 2	Charlton	Stiles	Best	
29 Aug West Ham United	50,643	Old Trafford	H D	1–1	Rimmer	Edwards P	Dunne A	Fitzpatrick 1	Ure	Sadler	Morgan W	Law	Charlton	Stiles	Best	Gowling for Stiles
2 Sep Everton	51,346	Old Trafford	H W	2–0	Rimmer	Edwards P	Dunne A	Fitzpatrick	Ure	Sadler	Stiles	Law	Charlton 1	Kidd	Best 1	
5 Sep Liverpool	52,542	Anfield	A D	1–1	Rimmer	Edwards P	Dunne A	Fitzpatrick	Ure	Sadler	Stiles	Law	Charlton	Kidd 1	Best	
12 Sep Coventry City	48,939	Old Trafford	H W	2–0	Rimmer	Edwards P	Dunne A	Fitzpatrick	Ure	Sadler	Stiles	Law	Charlton 1	Kidd	Best 1	
19 Sep Ipswich Town	27,776	Portman Road	A L	0–4	Rimmer	Edwards P	Dunne A	Fitzpatrick	Ure	Sadler	Stiles	Law	Charlton	Gowling	Best	Young A for Dunne A
26 Sep Blackpool	46,647	Old Trafford	H D	1–1	Rimmer	Watson	Burns	Fitzpatrick	James	Sadler	Morgan W	Gowling	Charlton	Kidd	Best 1	
3 Oct Wolverhampton Wan.	38,629	Molineux	A L	2–3	Rimmer	Watson	Burns	Fitzpatrick	James	Sadler	Morgan W	Gowling 1	Charlton	Kidd 1	Best	Sartori for Watson
10 Oct Crystal Palace	42,979	Old Trafford	H L	0–1	Rimmer	Edwards P	Dunne A	Fitzpatrick	Ure	Stiles	Morgan W	Best	Charlton	Kidd	Aston (Jnr.)	
17 Oct Leeds United	50,190	Elland Road	A D	2–2	Rimmer	Edwards P	Dunne A	Fitzpatrick 1	Ure	Stiles	Burns	Best	Charlton 1	Kidd	Aston (Jnr.)	Sartori for Stiles
24 Oct West Bromwich Alb.	43,278	Old Trafford	H W	2–1	Rimmer	Edwards P	Dunne A	Fitzpatrick	Ure	Burns	Law 1	Best	Charlton	Kidd 1	Aston (Jnr.)	
31 Oct Newcastle United	45,140	St James' Park	A L	0–1	Rimmer	Edwards P	Dunne A	Fitzpatrick	James	Sadler	Burns	Best	Charlton	Kidd	Aston (Jnr.)	
7 Nov Stoke City	47,451	Old Trafford	H D	2–2	Rimmer	Edwards P	Burns	Fitzpatrick	James	Sadler 1	Law 1	Best	Charlton	Kidd	Aston (Jnr.)	
14 Nov Nottingham Forest	36,364	City Ground	A W	2–1	Rimmer	Watson	Dunne A	Fitzpatrick	James	Sadler	Law	Best	Charlton	Gowling 1	Sartori 1	
21 Nov Southampton	30,202	The Dell	A L	0–1	Rimmer	Watson	Dunne A	Fitzpatrick	James	Sadler	Law	Best	Charlton	Kidd	Aston (Jnr.)	Sartori for Fitzpatrick
28 Nov Huddersfield Town	45,306	Old Trafford	H D	1–1	Rimmer	Watson	Dunne A	Fitzpatrick	James	Sadler	Law	Best 1	Charlton	Kidd	Aston (Jnr.)	
5 Dec Tottenham Hotspur	55,693	White Hart Lane	A D	2–2	Rimmer	Watson	Dunne A	Fitzpatrick	James	Sadler	Law 1	Best 1	Charlton	Kidd	Aston (Jnr.)	
12 Dec Manchester City	52,636	Old Trafford	H L	1–4	Rimmer	Watson	Dunne A	Fitzpatrick	James	Stiles	Law	Best	Charlton	Kidd 1	Aston (Jnr.)	Sartori for Law
19 Dec Arsenal	33,182	Old Trafford	H L	1–3	Rimmer	Watson	Dunne A	Crerand	James	Fitzpatrick	Morgan W	Best	Charlton	Kidd	Sartori 1	
26 Dec Derby County	34,068	Baseball Ground	A D	4–4	Rimmer	Fitzpatrick	Dunne A	Crerand	Ure	Sadler	Morgan W	Best 1	Charlton	Kidd 1	Law 2	
9 Jan Chelsea	53,482	Stamford Bridge	A W	2–1	Stepney	Fitzpatrick	Dunne A	Crerand	Edwards P	Stiles	Morgan W 1	Law	Charlton	Gowling 1	Aston (Jnr.)	
16 Jan Burnley	40,135	Old Trafford	H D	1–1	Stepney	Fitzpatrick	Dunne A	Crerand	Edwards P	Stiles	Morgan W	Law	Charlton	Gowling	Aston (Jnr.) 1	
30 Jan Huddersfield Town	41,464	Leeds Road	A W	2–1	Stepney	Fitzpatrick	Burns	Crerand	Edwards P	Sadler	Morgan W	Law 1	Charlton	Gowling	Best	Aston (Jnr.) 1 for Law
6 Feb Tottenham Hotspur	48,965	Old Trafford	H W	2–1	Stepney	Fitzpatrick	Burns	Crerand	Edwards P	Sadler	Morgan W 1	Kidd	Charlton	Gowling	Best 1	
20 Feb Southampton	36,060	Old Trafford	H W	5–1	Stepney	Fitzpatrick	Burns	Crerand	Edwards P	Sadler	Morgan W 1	Best	Charlton	Gowling 4	Aston (Jnr.)	
23 Feb Everton	52,544	Goodison Park	A L	0–1	Stepney	Fitzpatrick	Dunne A	Crerand	Edwards P	Sadler	Morgan W	Best	Charlton	Gowling	Aston (Jnr.)	Burns for Gowling
27 Feb Newcastle United	41,902	Old Trafford	H W	1–0	Stepney	Fitzpatrick	Dunne A	Crerand	Edwards P	Sadler	Morgan W	Best	Charlton	Kidd 1	Aston (Jnr.)	
6 Mar West Bromwich Alb.	41,112	The Hawthorns	A L	3–4	Stepney	Fitzpatrick	Dunne A	Crerand	Edwards P	Sadler	Morgan W	Best 1	Charlton	Kidd 1	Aston (Jnr.) 1	
13 Mar Nottingham Forest	40,473	Old Trafford	H W	2–0	Stepney	Fitzpatrick	Dunne A	Crerand	Edwards P	Sadler	Morgan W	Best 1	Charlton	Law 1	Aston (Jnr.)	Burns for Aston (Jnr.)
20 Mar Stoke City	40,005	Victoria Ground	A W	2–1	Stepney	Fitzpatrick	Dunne A	Crerand	Edwards P	Sadler	Morgan W	Best 2	Charlton	Law	Aston (Jnr.)	
3 Apr West Ham United	38,507	Upton Park	A L	1–2	Stepney	Fitzpatrick	Dunne A	Crerand	Edwards P	Sadler	Morgan W	Best 1	Charlton	Law	Aston (Jnr.)	Burns for Sadler
10 Apr Derby County	45,691	Old Trafford	H L	1–2	Stepney	Dunne A	Burns	Crerand	Edwards P	Stiles	Morgan W	Best	Charlton	Law 1	Aston (Jnr.)	Gowling for Aston (Jnr.)
12 Apr Wolverhampton Wan.	41,886	Old Trafford	H W	1–0	Stepney	Dunne A	Burns	Crerand	Edwards P	Stiles	Best	Gowling 1	Charlton	Law	Morgan W	Kidd for Law
13 Apr Coventry City	33,818	Highfield Road	A L	1–2	Stepney	Dunne A	Burns	Crerand	Edwards P	Stiles	Best 1	Gowling	Charlton	Kidd	Morgan W	
17 Apr Crystal Palace	39,145	Selhurst Park	A W	5–3	Stepney	Fitzpatrick	Dunne A	Crerand	Edwards P	Sadler	Best 2	Gowling	Charlton	Law 3	Morgan W	
19 Apr Liverpool	44,004	Old Trafford	H L	0–2	Stepney	Dunne A	Burns	Crerand	Edwards P	Sadler	Best	Gowling	Charlton	Law	Morgan W	Burns for Crerand
24 Apr Ipswich Town	33,566	Old Trafford	H W	3–2	Stepney	Dunne A	Burns	Crerand	James	Sadler	Law	Gowling	Charlton 1	Kidd 1	Best 1	Sartori for Sadler
1 May Blackpool	29,857	Bloomfield Road	A D	1–1	Stepney	Dunne A	Burns	Crerand	James	Sadler	Law 1	Gowling	Charlton	Kidd	Best	
5 May Manchester City	43,626	Maine Road	A W	4–3	Stepney	O'Neill	Burns	Crerand	James	Sadler	Law 1	Gowling	Charlton 1	Kidd	Best 2	

FA Cup

2 Jan Middlesbrough	47,824	Old Trafford	H D	0–0	Rimmer	Fitzpatrick	Dunne A	Crerand	Ure	Sadler	Morgan W	Best	Charlton	Kidd	Law	
5 Jan Middlesbrough	41,000	Ayresome Park	A L	1–2	Rimmer	Fitzpatrick	Dunne A	Crerand	Edwards P	Sadler	Morgan W	Best 1	Charlton	Kidd	Law	Gowling for Kidd

FL Cup

9 Sep Aldershot	18,509	Recreation Ground	A W	3–1	Rimmer	Edwards P	Dunne A	Fitzpatrick	Ure	Sadler	Stiles	Law 1	Charlton	Kidd 1	Best 1	James for Dunne A
7 Oct Portsmouth	32,068	Old Trafford	H W	1–0	Rimmer	Donald	Burns	Fitzpatrick	Ure	Sadler	Morgan W	Gowling	Charlton 1	Kidd	Best	Aston (Jnr.) for Sadler
28 Oct Chelsea	47,565	Old Trafford	H W	2–1	Rimmer	Edwards P	Dunne A	Fitzpatrick	James	Sadler	Aston (Jnr.)	Best 1	Charlton 1	Kidd	Law	Burns for Law
18 Nov Crystal Palace	48,961	Old Trafford	H W	4–2	Rimmer	Watson	Dunne A	Fitzpatrick 1	James	Sadler	Law	Best	Charlton 1	Kidd 2	Aston (Jnr.)	
16 Dec Aston Villa	48,889	Old Trafford	H D	1–1	Rimmer	Watson	Dunne A	Fitzpatrick	James	Stiles	Sartori	Best	Charlton	Kidd 1	Aston (Jnr.)	
23 Dec Aston Villa	58,667	Villa Park	A L	1–2	Rimmer	Fitzpatrick	Dunne A	Crerand	Ure	Sadler	Morgan W	Best	Charlton	Kidd 1	Law	

Football League Division 1
P42 • W16 • D11 • L15 • F65 • A66 • PTS43
Position: 8

1971/72

Football League	Attendances	Venue			Players and Scores											Substitutions
14 Aug Derby County	35,886	Baseball Ground	A D	2–2	Stepney	O'Neill	Dunne A	Gowling 1	James	Sadler	Morgan W	Kidd	Charlton	Law 1	Best	
18 Aug Chelsea	54,763	Stamford Bridge	A W	3–2	Stepney	Fitzpatrick	Dunne A	Gowling	James	Sadler	Morgan W 1	Kidd 1	Charlton 1	Law	Best	
20 Aug Arsenal	27,649	Anfield	A W	3–1	Stepney	O'Neill	Dunne A	Gowling 1	James	Sadler	Morgan W	Kidd 1	Charlton 1	Law	Best	Aston (Jnr.) for Best
23 Aug West Bromwich Alb.	23,146	Victoria Ground	A W	3–1	Stepney	O'Neill	Dunne A	Gowling 1	James	Sadler	Morgan W	Kidd	Charlton	Best 2	Aston (Jnr.)	Burns for Charlton
28 Aug Wolverhampton Wan.	46,471	Molineux	A D	1–1	Stepney	O'Neill	Dunne A	Gowling	James	Sadler	Morgan W	Kidd	Charlton	Law	Best 1	
31 Aug Everton	52,151	Goodison Park	A L	0–1	Stepney	O'Neill	Dunne A	Gowling	James	Sadler	Morgan W	Kidd	Charlton	Law	Best	
4 Sep Ipswich Town	45,656	Old Trafford	H W	1–0	Stepney	O'Neill	Dunne A	Gowling	James	Sadler	Morgan W	Kidd	Charlton	Law	Best 1	Aston (Jnr.) for Law
11 Sep Crystal Palace	44,020	Selhurst Park	A W	3–1	Stepney	O'Neill	Dunne A	Gowling	James	Sadler	Morgan W	Kidd 1	Charlton	Law 2	Best	Aston (Jnr.) for Gowling
18 Sep West Ham United	55,339	Old Trafford	H W	4–2	Stepney	O'Neill	Dunne A	Gowling	James	Sadler	Morgan W	Kidd	Charlton 1	Law	Best 3	
25 Sep Liverpool	55,634	Anfield	A D	2–2	Stepney	O'Neill	Burns	Gowling	James	Sadler	Morgan W	Kidd	Charlton 1	Law 1	Best	
2 Oct Sheffield United	51,735	Old Trafford	H W	2–0	Stepney	O'Neill	Dunne A	Gowling 1	James	Sadler	Morgan W	Kidd	Charlton	Best 1	Aston (Jnr.)	Burns for Dunne A
9 Oct Huddersfield Town	33,458	Leeds Road	A W	3–0	Stepney	O'Neill	Dunne A	Gowling	James	Sadler	Morgan W	Kidd	Charlton 1	Law 1	Best 1	
16 Oct Derby County	53,247	Old Trafford	H W	1–0	Stepney	O'Neill	Dunne A	Gowling	James	Sadler	Morgan W	Kidd	Charlton	Law	Best 1	
23 Oct Newcastle United	52,411	St James' Park	A W	1–0	Stepney	O'Neill	Dunne A	Gowling	James	Sadler	Morgan W	Kidd	Charlton	Law	Best 1	Aston (Jnr.) for Gowling
30 Oct Leeds United	53,960	Old Trafford	H L	0–1	Stepney	O'Neill	Dunne A	Gowling	James	Sadler	Morgan W	Kidd	Charlton	Law	Best	Sartori for Kidd
6 Nov Manchester City	63,326	Maine Road	A D	3–3	Stepney	O'Neill	Dunne A	Gowling 1	James	Sadler	Morgan W	Kidd 1	Charlton	McIlroy 1	Best	Aston (Jnr.) for Dunne A
13 Nov Tottenham Hotspur	54,058	Old Trafford	H W	3–1	Stepney	O'Neill	Burns	Gowling	James	Sadler	Morgan W	McIlroy 1	Charlton	Law 2	Best	
20 Nov Leicester City	48,757	Old Trafford	H W	3–2	Stepney	O'Neill	Burns	Gowling	James	Edwards P	Morgan W	Kidd 1	Charlton	Law 2	Best	McIlroy for Law
27 Nov Southampton	30,323	The Dell	A W	5–2	Stepney	O'Neill	Burns	Gowling	James	Sadler	Morgan W	Kidd 1	Charlton	McIlroy 1	Best 3	Aston (Jnr.) for Best
4 Dec Nottingham Forest	45,411	Old Trafford	H W	3–2	Stepney	O'Neill	Burns	Gowling	James	Sadler	Morgan W	Kidd 2	Charlton	Law 1	Best	
11 Dec Stoke City	33,857	Victoria Ground	A D	1–1	Stepney	O'Neill	Burns	Gowling	James	Sadler	Morgan W	Kidd	Charlton	Law 1	Best	McIlroy for Kidd
18 Dec Ipswich Town	29,229	Portman Road	A D	0–0	Stepney	Dunne A	Burns	Gowling	James	Sadler	Morgan W	Kidd	Charlton	Law	Best	
27 Dec Coventry City	52,117	Old Trafford	H D	2–2	Stepney	Dunne A	Burns	Gowling	James 1	Sadler	Morgan W	Kidd	Charlton	Law 1	Best	McIlroy for James
1 Jan West Ham United	41,892	Upton Park	A L	0–3	Stepney	Dunne A	Burns	Gowling	Edwards P	Sadler	Morgan W	Kidd	Charlton	Law	Best	
8 Jan Wolverhampton Wan.	46,781	Old Trafford	H L	1–3	Stepney	Dunne A	Burns	Gowling	Edwards P	Sadler	Morgan W	Kidd	Charlton	Law	McIlroy 1	Sartori for Gowling
22 Jan Chelsea	55,927	Old Trafford	H L	0–1	Stepney	O'Neill	Burns	Gowling	Edwards P	Sadler	Morgan W	McIlroy	Charlton	Law	Best	Aston (Jnr.) for McIlroy
29 Jan West Bromwich Alb.	47,012	The Hawthorns	A L	1–2	Stepney	O'Neill	Dunne A	Burns	James	Sadler	Morgan W	Kidd 1	Charlton	Law	Best	
12 Feb Newcastle United	44,983	Old Trafford	H L	0–2	Stepney	O'Neill	Burns	Gowling	James	Sadler	Morgan W	Kidd	Charlton	Law	Best	
19 Feb Leeds United	45,399	Elland Road	A L	1–5	Stepney	O'Neill	Dunne A	Burns 1	James	Sadler	Morgan W	Kidd	Charlton	Gowling	Best	McIlroy for Kidd
4 Mar Tottenham Hotspur	54,814	White Hart Lane	A L	0–2	Stepney	O'Neill	Dunne A	Buchan M	James	Sadler	Morgan W	Gowling	Charlton	Law	Best	
8 Mar Everton	38,415	Old Trafford	H D	0–0	Stepney	O'Neill	Dunne A	Buchan M	James	Sadler	Burns	Gowling	Kidd	Law	Best	McIlroy for Gowling
11 Mar Huddersfield Town	53,581	Old Trafford	H W	2–0	Stepney	O'Neill	Dunne A	Buchan M	James	Sadler	Morgan W	Kidd	Charlton	Best 1	Storey-Moore 1	
25 Mar Crystal Palace	41,550	Old Trafford	H W	4–0	Stepney	O'Neill	Dunne A	Buchan M	James	Gowling 1	Best	Kidd	Charlton 1	Law 1	Storey-Moore 1	McIlroy for Kidd
1 Apr Coventry City	37,901	Highfield Road	A W	3–2	Stepney	O'Neill	Dunne A	Buchan M	James	Gowling	Morgan W	Best 1	Charlton 1	Law	Storey-Moore 1	
3 Apr Liverpool	53,826	Old Trafford	H L	0–3	Stepney	O'Neill	Dunne A	Buchan M	James	Gowling	Morgan W	Best	Charlton	Law	Storey-Moore	Young A for Law
4 Apr Sheffield United	45,045	Bramall Lane	A D	1–1	Connaughton	O'Neill	Dunne A	Buchan M	James	Sadler 1	Best	McIlroy	Charlton	Young A	Storey-Moore	
8 Apr Leicester City	35,970	Filbert Street	A L	0–2	Connaughton	O'Neill	Dunne A	Buchan M	Sadler	Morgan W	Best	McIlroy	Charlton	Young A	Storey-Moore	Gowling for McIlroy
12 Apr Manchester City	56,362	Old Trafford	H L	1–3	Connaughton	O'Neill	Dunne A	Buchan M 1	James	Sadler	Best	Gowling	Charlton	Kidd	Storey-Moore	Law for Gowling
15 Apr Southampton	38,437	Old Trafford	H W	3–2	Stepney	O'Neill	Dunne A	Buchan M	James	Sadler	Best 1	Young A	Kidd 1	Law	Storey-Moore 1	McIlroy for Kidd
22 Apr Nottingham Forest	35,063	City Ground	A D	0–0	Stepney	O'Neill	Dunne A	Buchan M	James	Sadler	Morgan W	Kidd	Charlton	Law	Storey-Moore	Young A for James
25 Apr Arsenal	49,125	Highbury	A L	0–3	Stepney	O'Neill	Dunne A	Buchan M	Sadler	Gowling	Best	Young A	Charlton	Kidd	Storey-Moore	McIlroy for Young A
29 Apr Stoke City	34,959	Old Trafford	H W	3–0	Stepney	O'Neill	Dunne A	Buchan M	James	Young A	Best 1	McIlroy	Charlton 1	Law	Storey-Moore 1	Gowling for Charlton

FA Cup

15 Jan Southampton	30,190	The Dell	A D	1–1	Stepney	O'Neill	Burns	Gowling	Edwards P	Sadler	Morgan W	Kidd	Charlton 1	Law	Best	McIlroy for Kidd
19 Jan Southampton	50,960	Old Trafford	H W	4–1	Stepney	O'Neill	Burns	Gowling	Edwards P	Sadler 1	Morgan W	McIlroy	Charlton	Law	Best 2	Aston (Jnr.) 1 for McIlroy
5 Feb Preston North End	27,025	Deepdale	A W	2–0	Stepney	O'Neill	Burns	Gowling 2	James	Sadler	Morgan W	Kidd	Charlton	Law	Best	
26 Feb Middlesbrough	53,850	Old Trafford	H D	0–0	Stepney	O'Neill	Dunne A	Burns	James	Sadler	Morgan W	Gowling	Charlton	Law	Best	
29 Feb Middlesbrough	39,683	Ayresome Park	A W	3–0	Stepney	O'Neill	Dunne A	Burns	James	Sadler	Morgan W 1	Gowling	Charlton 1	Law	Best 1	
18 Mar Stoke City	54,226	Old Trafford	H D	1–1	Stepney	O'Neill	Dunne A	Buchan M	James	Sadler	Morgan W	Kidd	Charlton	Law	Best 1	Gowling for Sadler
22 Mar Stoke City	49,192	Victoria Ground	A L	1–2	Stepney	O'Neill	Dunne A	Gowling	James	Buchan M	Morgan W	Kidd	Charlton	Law	Best 1	McIlroy for Morgan W

FL Cup

7 Sep Ipswich Town	28,143	Portman Road	A W	3–1	Stepney	O'Neill	Dunne A	Gowling	James	Sadler	Morgan W 1	Kidd	Charlton	Best 2	Aston (Jnr.)	
6 Oct Burnley	44,600	Old Trafford	H D	1–1	Stepney	O'Neill	Dunne A	Gowling	James	Sadler	Morgan W	Kidd	Charlton 1	Best	Aston (Jnr.)	
18 Oct Burnley	27,511	Turf Moor	A W	1–0	Stepney	O'Neill	Dunne A	Gowling	James	Sadler	Morgan W	Kidd	Charlton 1	Law	Best	
27 Oct Stoke City	47,062	Old Trafford	H D	1–1	Stepney	O'Neill	Burns	Gowling 1	James	Sadler	Morgan W	Kidd	Charlton	Law	Best	Aston (Jnr.) for Kidd
8 Nov Stoke City	40,805	Victoria Ground	A D	0–0	Stepney	O'Neill	Burns	Gowling	James	Sadler	Morgan W	Kidd	Charlton	McIlroy	Best	Aston (Jnr.) for Kidd
15 Nov Stoke City	42,249	Victoria Ground	A L	1–2	Stepney	O'Neill	Burns	Gowling	James	Sadler	Morgan W	McIlroy	Charlton	Sartori	Best 1	

Football League Division 1
P42 • W19 • D10 • L13 • F69 • A61 • PTS48
Position: 8

1972/73

Football League

Date	Opponent	Attendances	Venue				Players and Scores											Substitutions
12 Aug	Ipswich Town	51,459	Old Trafford	H	L	1–2	Stepney	O'Neill	Dunne A	Morgan W	James	Buchan M	Best	Kidd	Charlton	Law 1	Storey–Moore	McIlroy for Charlton
15 Aug	Liverpool	54,799	Anfield	A	L	0–2	Stepney	O'Neill	Dunne A	Young A	James	Buchan M	Morgan W	Kidd	Charlton	Best	Storey–Moore	McIlroy for Kidd
19 Aug	Everton	52,348	Goodison Park	A	L	0–2	Stepney	O'Neill	Dunne A	Buchan M	James	Sadler	Morgan W	Fitzpatrick	Kidd	Best	Storey–Moore	McIlroy for James
23 Aug	Leicester City	40,067	Old Trafford	H	D	1–1	Stepney	O'Neill	Dunne A	Buchan M	James	Sadler	Morgan W	Fitzpatrick	McIlroy	Best 1	Storey–Moore	Kidd for McIlroy
26 Aug	Arsenal	48,108	Old Trafford	H	D	0–0	Stepney	O'Neill	Dunne A	Buchan M	James	Sadler	Morgan W	Young A	McIlroy	Best	Storey–Moore	
30 Aug	Chelsea	44,482	Old Trafford	H	D	0–0	Stepney	O'Neill	Dunne A	Buchan M	James	Sadler	Morgan W	Fitzpatrick	Law	Best	Storey–Moore	Charlton for Storey–Moore
2 Sep	West Ham United	31,939	Upton Park	A	D	2–2	Stepney	O'Neill	Dunne A	Buchan M	James	Sadler	Morgan W	Law	Charlton	Best 1	Storey–Moore 1	McIlroy for Law
9 Sep	Coventry City	37,073	Old Trafford	H	L	0–1	Stepney	O'Neill	Buchan M	Fitzpatrick	James	Sadler	McIlroy	Law	Charlton	Best	Storey–Moore	Young A for Law
16 Sep	Wolverhampton Wan.	34,049	Molineux	A	L	0–2	Stepney	Buchan M	Dunne A	Fitzpatrick	James	Sadler	Young A	McIlroy	Charlton	Best	Storey–Moore	Kidd for Sadler
23 Sep	Derby County	48,255	Old Trafford	H	W	3–0	Stepney	Donald	Dunne A	Young A	James	Buchan M	Morgan W 1	Davies W 1	Charlton	Best	Storey–Moore 1	
30 Sep	Sheffield United	37,347	Bramall Lane	A	L	0–1	Stepney	Donald	Dunne A	Young A	James	Buchan M	Morgan W	Davies W	Charlton	Best	Storey–Moore	McIlroy for Storey–Moore
7 Oct	West Bromwich Alb.	32,909	The Hawthorns	A	D	2–2	Stepney	Donald	Dunne A	Young A	James	Buchan M	Morgan W	MacDougall	Davies W	Best 1	Storey–Moore 1	
14 Oct	Birmingham City	52,104	Old Trafford	H	W	1–0	Stepney	Watson	Dunne A	Young A	Sadler	Buchan M	Morgan W	MacDougall 1	Davies W	Best	Storey–Moore	
21 Oct	Newcastle United	38,170	St James' Park	A	L	1–2	Stepney	Watson	Dunne A	Young A	Sadler	Buchan M	Morgan W	MacDougall	Davies W	Best	Storey–Moore	Charlton 1 for Storey–Moore
28 Oct	Tottenham Hotspur	52,497	Old Trafford	H	L	1–4	Stepney	Watson	Dunne A	Law	Sadler	Buchan M	Morgan W	MacDougall	Davies W	Best	Charlton 1	
4 Nov	Leicester City	32,575	Filbert Street	A	D	2–2	Stepney	Donald	Dunne A	Morgan W	Sadler	Buchan M	Best 1	MacDougall	Davies W 1	Charlton	Storey–Moore	
11 Nov	Liverpool	53,944	Old Trafford	H	W	2–0	Stepney	O'Neill	Dunne A	Morgan W	Sadler	Buchan M	Best	MacDougall 1	Charlton	Davies W 1	Storey–Moore	McIlroy for Dunne A
18 Nov	Manchester City	52,050	Maine Road	A	L	0–3	Stepney	O'Neill	Dunne A	Morgan W	Sadler	Buchan M	Best	MacDougall	Charlton	Davies W	Storey–Moore	Kidd for Morgan W
25 Nov	Southampton	36,073	Old Trafford	H	W	2–1	Stepney	O'Neill	Dunne A	Morgan W	Edwards P	Buchan M	Best	MacDougall 1	Charlton	Davies W 1	Storey–Moore	
2 Dec	Norwich City	35,910	Carrow Road	A	W	2–0	Stepney	O'Neill	Dunne A	Morgan W	Sadler	Buchan M	Young A	MacDougall 1	Charlton	Davies W	Storey–Moore 1	
9 Dec	Stoke City	41,347	Old Trafford	H	L	0–2	Stepney	O'Neill	Dunne A	Young A	Sadler	Buchan M	Morgan W	MacDougall	Charlton	Davies W	Storey–Moore	Law for Young A
16 Dec	Crystal Palace	39,484	Selhurst Park	A	L	0–5	Stepney	O'Neill	Dunne A	Young A	Sadler	Buchan M	Morgan W	MacDougall	Kidd	Davies W	Storey–Moore	Law for Dunne A
23 Dec	Leeds United	46,382	Old Trafford	H	D	1–1	Stepney	O'Neill	Dunne A	Law	Sadler	Buchan M	Morgan W	MacDougall 1	Charlton	Davies W	Storey–Moore	Kidd for Law
26 Dec	Derby County	35,098	Baseball Ground	A	L	1–3	Stepney	O'Neill	Dunne A	Kidd	Sadler	Buchan M	Morgan W	MacDougall	Charlton	Davies W	Storey–Moore 1	Young A for Dunne A
6 Jan	Arsenal	51,194	Highbury	A	L	1–3	Stepney	Young A	Forsyth	Graham G	Sadler	Buchan M	Morgan W	Kidd 1	Charlton	Law	Storey–Moore	
20 Jan	West Ham United	50,878	Old Trafford	H	D	2–2	Stepney	Young A	Forsyth	Law	Holton	Buchan M	Morgan W	MacDougall	Charlton 1	Macari 1	Graham G	Davies W for Law
24 Jan	Everton	58,970	Old Trafford	H	D	0–0	Stepney	Young A	Forsyth	Martin M	Holton	Buchan M	Morgan W	MacDougall	Charlton	Macari	Graham G	Kidd for MacDougall
27 Jan	Coventry City	42,767	Highfield Road	A	D	1–1	Stepney	Young A	Forsyth	Graham G	Holton 1	Buchan M	Morgan W	MacDougall	Charlton	Macari	Martin M	
10 Feb	Wolverhampton Wan.	52,089	Old Trafford	H	W	2–1	Stepney	Young A	Forsyth	Graham G	Holton	Buchan M	Morgan W	MacDougall	Charlton 2	Macari	Martin M	
17 Feb	Ipswich Town	31,918	Portman Road	A	L	1–4	Stepney	Forsyth	Dunne A	Graham G	Holton	Buchan M	Martin M	MacDougall	Charlton	Macari 1	Kidd	
3 Mar	West Bromwich Alb.	46,735	Old Trafford	H	W	2–1	Stepney	Young A	Forsyth	Graham G	James	Buchan M	Morgan W	Kidd 1	Charlton	Macari 1	Storey–Moore	Martin M for Storey–Moore
10 Mar	Birmingham City	51,278	St Andrews	A	L	1–3	Rimmer	Young A	Forsyth	Graham G	James	Buchan M	Morgan W	Kidd	Charlton	Macari 1	Storey–Moore	Martin M for Storey–Moore
17 Mar	Newcastle United	48,426	Old Trafford	H	W	2–1	Rimmer	Young A	James	Graham G	Holton 1	Buchan M	Morgan W	Kidd	Charlton	Macari	Martin M 1	
24 Mar	Tottenham Hotspur	49,751	White Hart Lane	A	D	1–1	Rimmer	Young A	James	Graham G 1	Holton	Buchan M	Morgan W	Kidd	Charlton	Macari	Martin M	
31 Mar	Southampton	23,161	The Dell	A	W	2–0	Rimmer	Young A	James	Graham G	Holton 1	Buchan M	Morgan W	Kidd	Charlton 1	Macari	Martin M	Anderson T for Kidd
7 Apr	Norwich City	48,593	Old Trafford	H	W	1–0	Stepney	Young A	James	Graham G	Holton	Buchan M	Morgan W	Kidd	Charlton	Law	Martin M 1	Anderson T for Kidd
11 Apr	Crystal Palace	46,891	Old Trafford	H	W	2–0	Stepney	Young A	James	Graham G	Holton	Buchan M	Morgan W 1	Kidd 1	Charlton	Macari	Martin M	Anderson T for Kidd
14 Apr	Stoke City	37,051	Victoria Ground	A	D	2–2	Stepney	Young A	James	Graham G	Holton	Buchan M	Morgan W 1	Anderson T	Charlton	Macari 1	Martin M	Fletcher for Anderson T
18 Apr	Leeds United	45,450	Elland Road	A	W	1–0	Stepney	Young A	James	Graham G	Holton	Buchan M	Morgan W	Anderson T 1	Charlton	Macari	Martin M	Fletcher for Anderson T
21 Apr	Manchester City	61,676	Old Trafford	H	D	0–0	Stepney	Young A	James	Graham G	Holton	Buchan M	Morgan W	Kidd	Charlton	Macari	Martin M	Anderson T for James
23 Apr	Sheffield United	57,280	Old Trafford	H	L	1–2	Stepney	Young A	Sidebottom	Graham G	Holton	Buchan M	Morgan W	Kidd 1	Charlton	Macari	Martin M	
28 Apr	Chelsea	44,184	Stamford Bridge	A	L	0–1	Stepney	Young A	Sidebottom	Graham G	Holton	Buchan M	Morgan W	Kidd	Charlton	Macari	Martin M	Anderson T for Kidd

FA Cup

Date	Opponent	Attendances	Venue				Players and Scores											Substitutions
13 Jan	Wolverhampton Wan.	40,005	Molineux	A	L	0–1	Stepney	Young A	Forsyth	Law	Sadler	Buchan M	Morgan W	Kidd	Charlton	Davies W	Graham G	Dunne A for Kidd

FL Cup

Date	Opponent	Attendances	Venue				Players and Scores											Substitutions
6 Sep	Oxford United	16,560	Manor Ground	A	D	2–2	Stepney	O'Neill	Dunne A	Buchan M	James	Sadler	Morgan W	Law 1	Charlton 1	Best	Storey–Moore	McIlroy for Dunne A
12 Sep	Oxford United	21,486	Old Trafford	H	W	3–1	Stepney	Fitzpatrick	Buchan M	Young A	James	Sadler	Morgan W	Law	Charlton	Best 2	Storey–Moore 1	McIlroy for Law
3 Oct	Bristol Rovers	33,957	Eastville	A	D	1–1	Stepney	Donald	Dunne A	Young A	James	Buchan M	Morgan W 1	Kidd	Charlton	Best	Storey–Moore	
11 Oct	Bristol Rovers	29,349	Old Trafford	H	L	1–2	Stepney	Watson	Dunne A	Young A	James	Buchan M	Morgan W	Kidd	Charlton	Best	Storey–Moore	McIlroy 1 for Kidd

Football League Division 1
P42 • W12 • D13 • L17 • F44 • A60 • PTS37
Position: 18

1973/74

Football League

Date	Opponent	Attendances	Venue				Players and Scores											Substitutions
25 Aug	Arsenal	51,501	Highbury	A	L	0–3	Stepney	Young A	Buchan M	Daly	Holton	James	Morgan W	Anderson T	Macari	Graham G	Martin M	McIlroy for Daly
29 Aug	Stoke City	43,614	Old Trafford	H	W	1–0	Stepney	Young A	Buchan M	Martin M	Holton	James 1	Morgan W	Anderson T	Macari	Graham G	McIlroy	Fletcher for James
1 Sep	Queen's Park Rangers	44,156	Old Trafford	H	W	2–1	Stepney	Young A	Buchan M	Martin M	Holton 1	Sidebottom	Morgan W	Anderson T	Macari	Graham G	McIlroy 1	Fletcher for Martin M
5 Sep	Leicester City	29,152	Filbert Street	A	L	0–1	Stepney	Young A	Buchan M	Daly	Holton	Sadler	Morgan W	Anderson T	Kidd	Graham G	McIlroy	Martin M for Daly
8 Sep	Ipswich Town	22,023	Portman Road	A	L	1–2	Stepney	Young A	Buchan M	Daly	Sadler	Greenhoff B	Morgan W	Anderson T 1	Kidd	Graham G	McIlroy	Macari for Kidd
12 Sep	Leicester City	40,793	Old Trafford	H	L	1–2	Stepney 1	Buchan M	Young A	Martin M	Holton	James	Morgan W	Anderson T	Macari	Graham G	Storey–Moore	
15 Sep	West Ham United	44,757	Old Trafford	H	W	3–1	Stepney	Buchan M	Young A	Martin M	Holton	James	Morgan W	Kidd 2	Anderson T	Graham G	Storey–Moore 1	Buchan G for Holton
22 Sep	Leeds United	47,058	Elland Road	A	D	0–0	Stepney	Buchan M	Young A	Greenhoff B	Holton	James	Morgan W	Anderson T	Macari	Kidd	Graham G	Buchan G for Macari
29 Sep	Liverpool	53,882	Old Trafford	H	D	0–0	Stepney	Buchan M	Young A	Greenhoff B	Holton	James	Morgan W	Anderson T	Macari	Kidd	Graham G	Buchan G for Graham G
6 Oct	Wolverhampton Wan.	32,962	Molineux	A	L	1–2	Stepney	Buchan M	Young A	Greenhoff B	Holton	James	Morgan W	Anderson T	Macari	Kidd	Graham G	McIlroy 1 for Anderson T
13 Oct	Derby County	43,724	Old Trafford	H	L	0–1	Stepney	Buchan M	Forsyth	Greenhoff B	Holton	James	Morgan W	Young A	Kidd	Anderson T	Graham G	
20 Oct	Birmingham City	48,937	Old Trafford	H	W	1–0	Stepney 1	Buchan M	Young A	Greenhoff B	Holton	James	Morgan W	Kidd	Macari	Graham G	Best	Martin M for Best
27 Oct	Burnley	31,976	Turf Moor	A	D	0–0	Stepney	Buchan M	Young A	Greenhoff B	Holton	Griffiths C	Morgan W	Kidd	Macari	Graham G	Best	Sadler for Kidd
3 Nov	Chelsea	48,036	Old Trafford	H	D	2–2	Stepney	Buchan M	Young A 1	Greenhoff B 1	James	Griffiths C	Morgan W	Macari	Kidd	Graham G	Best	
10 Nov	Tottenham Hotspur	42,756	White Hart Lane	A	L	1–2	Stepney	Buchan M	Young A	Greenhoff B	Holton	James	Morgan W	Macari	Kidd	Graham G	Best 1	
17 Nov	Newcastle United	41,768	St James' Park	A	L	2–3	Stepney	Buchan M	Young A	Greenhoff B	Holton	James	Morgan W	Macari 1	Kidd	Graham G 1	Best	
24 Nov	Norwich City	36,338	Old Trafford	H	D	0–0	Stepney	Buchan M	Young A	Greenhoff B	Holton	James	Morgan W	Macari	Kidd	Graham G	Best	Fletcher for Morgan W
8 Dec	Southampton	31,648	Old Trafford	H	D	0–0	Stepney	Buchan M	Forsyth	Greenhoff B	James	Griffiths C	Morgan W	Young A	Kidd	McIlroy	Best	Anderson T for Kidd
15 Dec	Coventry City	28,589	Old Trafford	H	L	2–3	Stepney	Buchan M	Forsyth	Greenhoff B	Holton	Griffiths C	Morgan W 1	Macari	McIlroy	Young A	Best 1	Martin M for James
22 Dec	Liverpool	40,420	Anfield	A	L	0–2	Stepney	Buchan M	Young A	Greenhoff B	Sidebottom	Griffiths C	Morgan W	Macari	Kidd	Graham G	Best	McIlroy for Kidd
26 Dec	Sheffield United	38,653	Old Trafford	H	L	1–2	Stepney	Young A	Griffiths C	Greenhoff B	Holton	Buchan M	Morgan W	Macari 1	McIlroy	Graham G	Best	
29 Dec	Ipswich Town	36,365	Old Trafford	H	W	2–0	Stepney	Young A	Griffiths C	Greenhoff B	Holton	Buchan M	Morgan W	Macari 1	McIlroy 1	Graham G	Best	
1 Jan	Queen's Park Rangers	32,339	Loftus Road	A	L	0–3	Stepney	Young A	Houston	Greenhoff B	Holton	Buchan M	Morgan W	Macari	McIlroy	Graham G	Best	
12 Jan	West Ham United	34,147	Upton Park	A	L	1–2	Stepney	Forsyth	Houston	Greenhoff B	Holton	Buchan M	Morgan W	Macari	Kidd	Young A	Graham G	McIlroy 1 for Kidd
19 Jan	Arsenal	38,589	Old Trafford	H	D	1–1	Stepney	Buchan M	Houston	Greenhoff B	Holton	James 1	Morgan W	Macari	McIlroy	Young A	Martin M	
2 Feb	Coventry City	25,313	Highfield Road	A	L	0–1	Stepney	Buchan M	Houston	Greenhoff B	Holton	James	Morgan W	Macari	McIlroy	Kidd	Young A	Forsyth for McIlroy
9 Feb	Leeds United	60,025	Old Trafford	H	L	0–2	Stepney	Buchan M	Houston	Greenhoff B	Holton	James	Morgan W	Macari	Kidd	Young A	Forsyth	McIlroy for Forsyth
16 Feb	Derby County	29,987	Baseball Ground	A	D	2–2	Stepney	Forsyth	Houston 1	Greenhoff B 1	Holton	Buchan M	Morgan W	Fletcher	Kidd	Macari	McIlroy	Daly for Morgan W
23 Feb	Wolverhampton Wan.	39,260	Old Trafford	H	D	0–0	Stepney	Forsyth	Houston	Greenhoff B	Holton	Buchan M	Morgan W	Fletcher	Kidd	Macari	McIlroy	Daly for McIlroy
2 Mar	Sheffield United	29,203	Bramall Lane	A	W	1–0	Stepney	Forsyth	Houston	Greenhoff B	Holton	Buchan M	Morgan W	Macari 1	McIlroy	Daly	Martin M	
13 Mar	Manchester City	51,331	Maine Road	A	D	0–0	Stepney	Forsyth	Houston	Martin M	Holton	Buchan M	Morgan W	Macari	Greenhoff B	Daly	Bielby	Graham G for Martin M
16 Mar	Birmingham City	37,768	St Andrews	A	L	0–1	Stepney	Forsyth	Houston	Martin M	Holton	Buchan M	McCalliog	Macari	Greenhoff B	Graham G	Bielby	
23 Mar	Tottenham Hotspur	36,278	Old Trafford	H	L	0–1	Stepney	Forsyth	Houston	Greenhoff B	James	Buchan M	Morgan W	McIlroy	Kidd	McCalliog	Daly	Bielby for Kidd
30 Mar	Chelsea	29,602	Stamford Bridge	A	W	3–1	Stepney	Forsyth	Houston	Daly 1	James	Buchan M	Morgan W 1	McIlroy 1	Greenhoff B	McCalliog	Martin M	Bielby for James
3 Apr	Burnley	33,336	Old Trafford	H	D	3–3	Stepney	Forsyth 1	Houston	Daly	Holton 1	Buchan M	Morgan W	McIlroy 1	Greenhoff B	McCalliog	Martin M	
6 Apr	Norwich City	28,223	Carrow Road	A	W	2–0	Stepney	Forsyth	Houston	Greenhoff B 1	Holton	Buchan M	Morgan W	Macari 1	McIlroy	McCalliog	Daly	
13 Apr	Newcastle United	44,751	Old Trafford	H	W	1–0	Stepney	Forsyth	Houston	Greenhoff B	Holton	Buchan M	Morgan W	Daly	McCalliog 1	Macari	McIlroy	
15 Apr	Everton	48,424	Old Trafford	H	W	3–0	Stepney	Young A	Houston 1	Greenhoff B	Holton	Buchan M	Morgan W	Macari	McIlroy	McCalliog 2	Daly	Martin M for McIlroy
20 Apr	Southampton	30,789	The Dell	A	D	1–1	Stepney	Young A	Houston	Greenhoff B	Holton	Buchan M	Morgan W	Macari	McIlroy	McCalliog 1	Daly	
23 Apr	Everton	46,093	Goodison Park	A	L	0–1	Stepney	Forsyth	Houston	Greenhoff B	Holton	Buchan M	Morgan W	Macari	McIlroy	McCalliog	Daly	
27 Apr	Manchester City	56,996	Old Trafford	H	L	0–1	Stepney	Forsyth	Houston	Greenhoff B	Holton	Buchan M	Morgan W	Macari	McIlroy	McCalliog	Daly	
29 Apr	Stoke City	27,392	Victoria Ground	A	L	0–1	Stepney	Forsyth	Houston	Greenhoff B	Holton	Buchan M	Morgan W	Macari	McIlroy	McCalliog	Martin M	

FA Cup

Date	Opponent	Attendances	Venue				Players and Scores											Substitutions
5 Jan	Plymouth Argyle	31,810	Old Trafford	H	W	1–0	Stepney	Young A	Forsyth	Greenhoff B	Holton	Buchan M	Morgan W	Macari 1	Kidd	Graham G	Martin M	McIlroy for Martin M
26 Jan	Ipswich Town	37,177	Old Trafford	H	L	0–1	Stepney	Buchan M	Forsyth	Greenhoff B	Holton	James	Morgan W	Macari	McIlroy	Young A	Martin M	Kidd for Macari

FL Cup

Date	Opponent	Attendances	Venue				Players and Scores											Substitutions
8 Oct	Middlesbrough	23,906	Old Trafford	H	L	0–1	Stepney	Buchan M	Young A	Greenhoff B	Holton	James	Morgan W	Daly	Macari	Kidd	Graham G	Buchan G for Macari

Football League Division 1
P42 • W10 • D12 • L20 • F38 • A48 • PTS32
Position: 21

1974/75

Football League

Date	Opponent	Attendances	Venue				Players and Scores											Substitutions
17 Aug	Leyton Orient	17,772	Brisbane Road	A	W	2–0	Stepney	Forsyth	Houston 1	Greenhoff B	Holton	Buchan M	Morgan W 1	Macari	Pearson SJ	McCalliog	Daly	McIlroy replaced Macari
24 Aug	Millwall	44,756	Old Trafford	H	W	4–0	Stepney	Forsyth	Houston	Greenhoff B	Holton	Buchan M	Morgan W	McIlroy	Pearson SJ 1	Martin M	Daly 3	
28 Aug	Portsmouth	42,547	Old Trafford	H	W	2–1	Stepney	Forsyth	Houston	Greenhoff B	Holton	Buchan M	Morgan W	McIlroy 1	Pearson SJ	Martin M	Daly 1	
31 Aug	Cardiff City	22,344	Ninian Park	A	W	1–0	Stepney	Forsyth	Houston	Greenhoff B	Holton	Buchan M	Morgan W	McIlroy	Pearson SJ	Martin M	Daly 1	Young A replaced Pearson SJ
7 Sep	Nottingham Forest	40,671	Old Trafford	H	D	2–2	Stepney	Forsyth	Houston	Greenhoff B 1	Holton	Buchan M	Morgan W	McIlroy 1	Martin M	McCalliog	Daly	Macari replaced Greenhoff B
14 Sep	West Bromwich Alb.	23,721	The Hawthorns	A	D	1–1	Stepney	Forsyth	Houston	Martin M	Holton	Buchan M	Morgan W	McIlroy	Pearson SJ 1	McCalliog	Daly	Greenhoff B replaced Martin M
16 Sep	Millwall	16,988	The Den	A	W	1–0	Stepney	Forsyth	Houston	Greenhoff B	Sidebottom	Buchan M	Morgan W	McIlroy	Macari	McCalliog	Daly 1	Young A replaced Daly 1
21 Sep	Bristol Rovers	42,948	Old Trafford	H	W	•2–0	Stepney	Forsyth	Houston	Greenhoff B 1	Holton	Buchan M	Morgan W	McIlroy	Macari	McCalliog	Daly	Young A replaced McCalliog
25 Sep	Bolton Wanderers	47,084	Old Trafford	H	W	•3–0	Stepney	Forsyth	Houston 1	Greenhoff B	Sidebottom	Buchan M	Morgan W	McIlroy	Macari 1	McCalliog	Daly	
28 Sep	Norwich City	24,586	Carrow Road	A	L	0–2	Stepney	Forsyth	Houston	Greenhoff B	Sidebottom	Buchan M	Morgan W	McIlroy	Macari	McCalliog	Daly	Young A replaced Morgan W
5 Oct	Fulham	26,513	Craven Cottage	A	W	2–1	Stepney	Forsyth	Houston	Greenhoff B	Holton	Buchan M	Morgan W	McIlroy	Pearson SJ 2	McCalliog	Daly	Macari replaced Daly
12 Oct	Notts County	46,565	Old Trafford	H	W	1–0	Stepney	Forsyth	Houston	Greenhoff B	Holton	Buchan M	Morgan W	McIlroy 1	Macari	McCalliog	Daly	Young A replaced McCalliog
15 Oct	Portsmouth	25,608	Fratton Park	A	D	0–0	Stepney	Forsyth	Albiston	Greenhoff B	Holton	Buchan M	Morgan W	McIlroy	Macari	McCalliog	Daly	McCreery replaced Morgan W
19 Oct	Blackpool	25,370	Bloomfield Road	A	W	3–0	Stepney	Forsyth 1	Houston	Greenhoff B	Holton	Buchan M	Morgan W	McIlroy	Macari 1	McCalliog 1	Daly	McCreery replaced Daly
26 Oct	Southampton	48,724	Old Trafford	H	W	1–0	Stepney	Forsyth	Houston	Greenhoff B	Holton	Buchan M	Morgan W	McIlroy	Macari	McCalliog	Daly	Pearson SJ 1 replaced Morgan W
2 Nov	Oxford United	41,909	Old Trafford	H	W	4–0	Stepney	Forsyth	Houston	Greenhoff B	Sidebottom	Buchan M	Macari 1	McIlroy	Pearson SJ 3	McCalliog	Daly	Morgan W replaced Greenhoff B
9 Nov	Bristol City	28,104	Ashton Gate	A	L	0–1	Stepney	Forsyth	Houston	Greenhoff B	Sidebottom	Buchan M	Macari	McIlroy	Pearson SJ	McCalliog	Daly	Graham G replaced Daly
16 Nov	Aston Villa	55,615	Old Trafford	H	W	2–1	Stepney	Forsyth	Houston	Macari	Sidebottom	Buchan M	Morgan W	McIlroy	Pearson SJ	McCalliog	Daly 2	Greenhoff B replaced Pearson SJ
23 Nov	Hull City	23,287	Boothferry Park	A	L	0–2	Stepney	Forsyth	Houston	Macari	Sidebottom	Buchan M	Morgan W	McIlroy	Greenhoff B	McCalliog	Daly	
30 Nov	Sunderland	60,585	Old Trafford	H	W	3–2	Stepney	Forsyth	Houston	Greenhoff B	Holton	Buchan M	Morgan W 1	McIlroy 1	Pearson SJ 1	Macari	Daly	Davies R replaced Greenhoff B
7 Dec	Sheffield Wednesday	35,230	Hillsborough	A	D	4–4	Stepney	Forsyth	Houston 1	Greenhoff B	Holton	Buchan M	Morgan W	McIlroy	Pearson SJ 1	Macari 2	McCalliog	Davies R replaced Holton
14 Dec	Leyton Orient	41,200	Old Trafford	H	D	0–0	Stepney	Forsyth	Houston	Greenhoff B	Sidebottom	Buchan M	Morgan W	McIlroy	Pearson SJ	Macari	Daly	Davies R replaced Greenhoff B
21 Dec	York City	15,567	Bootham Crescent	A	W	1–0	Stepney	Young A	Houston	Greenhoff B	Sidebottom	Buchan M	Morgan W	McIlroy	Pearson SJ 1	Macari	Daly	Davies R replaced Sidebottom
26 Dec	West Bromwich Alb.	51,104	Old Trafford	H	W	2–1	Stepney	Young A	Houston	Greenhoff B	Sidebottom	Buchan M	Morgan W	McIlroy 1	Pearson SJ	Macari	Daly 1	
28 Dec	Oldham Athletic	26,384	Boundary Park	A	L	0–1	Stepney	Young A	Albiston	Greenhoff B	Sidebottom	Buchan M	Morgan W	McIlroy	Pearson SJ	Macari	Daly	Davies R replaced Greenhoff B
11 Jan	Sheffield Wednesday	45,662	Old Trafford	H	W	2–0	Stepney	Forsyth	Houston	Greenhoff B	James	Buchan M	Morgan W	McIlroy	Pearson SJ	Macari	McCalliog 2	Daly replaced Morgan W
18 Jan	Sunderland	45,976	Roker Park	A	D	0–0	Stepney	Forsyth	Houston	Greenhoff B	James	Buchan M	Morgan W	McIlroy	Baldwin	Macari	McCalliog	
1 Feb	Bristol City	47,118	Old Trafford	H	L	0–1	Stepney	Forsyth	Houston	Daly	James	Buchan M	Morgan W	McIlroy	Baldwin	Macari	McCalliog	Young A replaced Daly
8 Feb	Oxford United	15,959	Manor Ground	A	L	0–1	Roche	Forsyth	Houston	Greenhoff B	James	Buchan M	Morgan W	McIlroy	Pearson SJ	Macari	Young A	Davies R replaced Morgan W
15 Feb	Hull City	44,712	Old Trafford	H	W	2–0	Roche	Forsyth	Houston 1	Greenhoff B	James	Buchan M	Young A	McIlroy	Pearson SJ 1	Macari	Martin M	Davies R replaced James
22 Feb	Aston Villa	39,156	Villa Park	A	L	0–2	Stepney	Forsyth	Houston	Greenhoff B	Sidebottom	Buchan M	Young A	McIlroy	Pearson SJ	Macari	Martin M	Davies R replaced Martin M
1 Mar	Cardiff City	43,601	Old Trafford	H	W	4–0	Stepney	Forsyth	Houston 1	Greenhoff B	James	Buchan M	Morgan W	McIlroy 1	Pearson SJ 1	Macari 1	Daly	Coppell replaced Morgan W
8 Mar	Bolton Wanderers	38,152	Burnden Park	A	W	1–0	Stepney	Forsyth	Houston	Greenhoff B	James	Buchan M	Coppell	McIlroy	Pearson SJ 1	Macari	Daly	Young A replaced Houston
15 Mar	Norwich City	56,202	Old Trafford	H	D	1–1	Stepney	Forsyth	Houston	Greenhoff B	James	Buchan M	Coppell	McIlroy	Pearson SJ 1	Macari	Daly	Young A replaced Coppell
22 Mar	Nottingham Forest	21,893	City Ground	A	W	1–0	Stepney	Forsyth	Houston	Greenhoff B	James	Buchan M	Coppell	McIlroy	Pearson SJ	Macari	Daly 1	
28 Mar	Bristol Rovers	19,337	Eastville	A	D	1–1	Stepney	Forsyth	Houston	Greenhoff B	James	Buchan M	Coppell	McIlroy	Pearson SJ	Macari 1	Daly	Morgan W replaced James
29 Mar	York City	46,002	Old Trafford	H	W	2–1	Stepney	Forsyth	Houston	Morgan W 1	Greenhoff B	Buchan M	Coppell	McIlroy	Pearson SJ	Macari 1	Daly	
31 Mar	Oldham Athletic	56,618	Old Trafford	H	W	3–2	Stepney	Forsyth	Houston	Morgan W	Greenhoff B	Buchan M	Coppell 1	McIlroy 1	Pearson SJ	Macari 1	Daly	Martin M replaced Daly
5 Apr	Southampton	21,866	The Dell	A	W	1–0	Stepney	Forsyth	Houston	Young A	Greenhoff B	Buchan M	Morgan W	McIlroy	Pearson SJ	Macari 1	Daly	Nicholl replaced Buchan M
12 Apr	Fulham	52,971	Old Trafford	H	W	1–0	Stepney	Forsyth	Houston	Greenhoff B	James	Morgan W	Coppell	McIlroy	Pearson SJ	Macari	Daly 1	
19 Apr	Notts County	17,320	County Ground	A	D	2–2	Stepney	Forsyth	Houston 1	Greenhoff B 1	James	Buchan M	Coppell	McIlroy	Pearson SJ	Macari	Daly	
26 Apr	Blackpool	58,769	Old Trafford	H	W	4–0	Stepney	Forsyth	Houston	Greenhoff B 1	James	Buchan M	Coppell	McIlroy	Pearson SJ 2	Macari 1	Daly	

FA Cup

4 Jan	Walsall	43,353	Old Trafford	H	D	0–0	Stepney	Young A	Houston	Greenhoff B	Sidebottom	Buchan M	Morgan W	McIlroy	Pearson SJ	Macari	Daly	Davies R replaced Morgan W
7 Jan	Walsall	18,105	Fellows Park	A	L	2–3	Stepney	Young A	Houston	Greenhoff B	Sidebottom	Buchan M	McCalliog	McIlroy 1	Pearson SJ	Macari	Daly 1	Davies R replaced Daly

FL Cup

11 Sep	Charlton Athletic	21,616	Old Trafford	H	W	•5–1	Stepney	Forsyth	Houston 1	Martin M	Holton	Buchan M	Morgan W	McIlroy 1	Macari 2	McCalliog	Daly	Young A replaced Forsyth
9 Oct	Manchester City	55,159	Old Trafford	H	W	1–0	Stepney	Forsyth	Albiston	Greenhoff B	Holton	Buchan M	Morgan W	McIlroy	Pearson SJ	McCalliog	Daly 1	Macari replaced Pearson SJ
13 Nov	Burnley	46,275	Old Trafford	H	W	3–2	Stepney	Forsyth	Houston	Greenhoff B	Sidebottom	Buchan M	Macari 2	McIlroy	Pearson SJ	McCalliog	Daly	Morgan W 1 replaced Greenhoff B
4 Dec	Middlesbrough	36,005	Ayresome Park	A	D	0–0	Stepney	Forsyth	Houston	Greenhoff B	Holton	Buchan M	Morgan W	McIlroy	Pearson SJ	Macari	Daly	Young A replaced Morgan W
18 Dec	Middlesbrough	49,501	Old Trafford	H	W	3–0	Stepney	Young A	Houston	Greenhoff B	Sidebottom	Buchan M	Morgan W	McIlroy 1	Pearson SJ 1	Macari 1	Daly	McCalliog replaced Daly
15 Jan	Norwich City	58,010	Old Trafford	H	D	2–2	Stepney	Forsyth	Houston	Greenhoff B	James	Buchan M	Morgan W	McIlroy	Daly	Macari 2	McCalliog	Young A replaced Daly
22 Jan	Norwich City	31,621	Carrow Road	A	L	0–1	Stepney	Forsyth	Houston	Greenhoff B	James	Buchan M	Morgan W	McIlroy	Daly	Macari	McCalliog	Young A replaced James

Football League Division 2
P42 • W26 • D9 • L7 • F66 • A30 • PTS61
Position: 1

1975/76

Football League

Date	Opponent	Attendances	Venue				Players and Scores											Substitutions
16 Aug	Wolverhampton Wan.	32,348	Molineux	A	W	2–0	Stepney	Forsyth	Houston	Jackson T	Greenhoff B	Buchan M	Coppell	McIlroy	Pearson SJ	Macari 2	Daly	Nicholl replaced Pearson SJ
19 Aug	Birmingham City	33,177	St Andrews	A	W	2–0	Stepney	Forsyth	Houston	Jackson T	Greenhoff B	Buchan M	Coppell	McIlroy 2	McCreery	Macari	Daly	Nicholl replaced Greenhoff B
23 Aug	Sheffield United	55,949	Old Trafford	H	W	•5–1	Stepney	Forsyth	Houston	Jackson T	Greenhoff B	Buchan M	Coppell	McIlroy 1	Pearson SJ 2	Macari	Daly 1	Nicholl replaced Forsyth
27 Aug	Coventry City	52,169	Old Trafford	H	D	1–1	Stepney	Forsyth	Houston	Jackson T	Greenhoff B	Buchan M	Coppell	McIlroy	Pearson SJ 1	Macari	Daly	
30 Aug	Stoke City	33,092	Victoria Ground	A	W	•1–0	Stepney	Forsyth	Houston	Jackson T	Greenhoff B	Buchan M	Coppell	McIlroy	Pearson SJ	Macari	Daly	
6 Sep	Tottenham Hotspur	51,641	Old Trafford	H	W	•3–2	Stepney	Nicholl	Houston	Jackson T	Greenhoff B	Buchan M	Coppell	McIlroy	Pearson SJ	Macari	Daly 2	
13 Sep	Queen's Park Rangers	29,237	Loftus Road	A	L	0–1	Stepney	Nicholl	Houston	Jackson T	Albiston	Buchan M	Coppell	McIlroy	Pearson SJ	Macari	Daly	Young A replaced Jackson T
20 Sep	Ipswich Town	50,513	Old Trafford	H	W	1–0	Stepney	Nicholl	Houston 1	McCreery	Greenhoff B	Buchan M	Coppell	McIlroy	Pearson SJ	Macari	Daly	
24 Sep	Derby County	33,187	Baseball Ground	A	L	1–2	Stepney	Nicholl	Houston	McCreery	Greenhoff B	Buchan M	Coppell	McIlroy	Pearson SJ	Macari	Daly 1	
27 Sep	Manchester City	46,931	Maine Road	A	D	2–2	Stepney	Nicholl	Houston	McCreery 1	Greenhoff B	Buchan M	Coppell	McIlroy	Pearson SJ	Macari 1	Daly	
4 Oct	Leicester City	47,878	Old Trafford	H	D	0–0	Stepney	Nicholl	Houston	Jackson T	Greenhoff B	Buchan M	Coppell	McIlroy	Pearson SJ	Macari	Daly	McCreery replaced Jackson T
11 Oct	Leeds United	40,264	Elland Road	A	W	2–1	Stepney	Nicholl	Houston	Jackson T	Greenhoff B	Buchan M	Coppell	McIlroy 2	Pearson SJ	Macari	Daly	Grimshaw replaced Houston
18 Oct	Arsenal	53,885	Old Trafford	H	W	3–1	Stepney	Nicholl	Houston	Jackson T	Greenhoff B	Buchan M	Coppell 2	McIlroy	Pearson SJ 1	Macari	Daly	
25 Oct	West Ham United	38,528	Upton Park	A	L	1–2	Stepney	Nicholl	Houston	Jackson T	Greenhoff B	Buchan M	Coppell	McIlroy	Pearson SJ	Macari 1	Daly	McCreery replaced Daly
1 Nov	Norwich City	50,587	Old Trafford	H	W	1–0	Roche	Nicholl	Houston	Jackson T	Greenhoff B	Buchan M	Coppell	McIlroy	Pearson SJ 1	Macari	Daly	
8 Nov	Liverpool	49,136	Anfield	A	L	1–3	Roche	Nicholl	Houston	Jackson T	Greenhoff B	Buchan M	Coppell 1	McIlroy	Pearson SJ	Macari	Daly	McCreery replaced Jackson T
15 Nov	Aston Villa	51,682	Old Trafford	H	W	2–0	Roche	Nicholl	Houston	Daly	Greenhoff B	Buchan M	Coppell 1	McIlroy 1	Pearson SJ	Macari	Hill	McCreery replaced McIlroy
22 Nov	Arsenal	40,102	Highbury	A	L	1–3	Roche	Nicholl	Houston	Daly	Greenhoff B	Buchan M	Coppell	McIlroy	Pearson SJ 1	Macari	Hill	McCreery replaced McIlroy
29 Nov	Newcastle United	52,624	Old Trafford	H	W	1–0	Stepney	Nicholl	Houston	Daly 1	Greenhoff B	Buchan M	Coppell	McIlroy	Pearson SJ	Macari	Hill	McCreery replaced Pearson SJ
6 Dec	Middlesbrough	32,454	Ayresome Park	A	D	0–0	Stepney	Forsyth	Houston	Daly	Greenhoff B	Buchan M	Coppell	McIlroy	Pearson SJ	Macari	Hill	Nicholl replaced Forsyth
13 Dec	Sheffield United	31,741	Bramall Lane	A	W	4–1	Stepney	Forsyth	Houston	Daly	Greenhoff B	Buchan M	Coppell	McIlroy	Pearson SJ 2	Macari 1	Hill 1	McCreery replaced McIlroy
20 Dec	Wolverhampton Wan.	44,269	Old Trafford	H	W	1–0	Stepney	Forsyth	Houston	Daly	Greenhoff B	Buchan M	Coppell	McIlroy	Pearson SJ	Macari	Hill 1	Kelly replaced Greenhoff B
23 Dec	Everton	41,732	Goodison Park	A	D	1–1	Stepney	Forsyth	Houston	Daly	Greenhoff B	Buchan M	Coppell	McIlroy	Pearson SJ	Macari 1	Hill	
27 Dec	Burnley	59,726	Old Trafford	H	W	2–1	Stepney	Forsyth	Houston	Daly	Greenhoff B	Buchan M	Coppell	McIlroy 1	Pearson SJ	Macari 1	Hill	McCreery replaced Pearson SJ
10 Jan	Queen's Park Rangers	58,312	Old Trafford	H	W	2–1	Stepney	Forsyth	Houston	Daly	Greenhoff B	Buchan M	Coppell	McIlroy 1	Pearson SJ	Macari	Hill 1	
17 Jan	Tottenham Hotspur	49,189	White Hart Lane	A	D	1–1	Stepney	Forsyth	Houston	Daly	Greenhoff B	Buchan M	Coppell	McIlroy	Pearson SJ	Macari	Hill 1	McCreery replaced McIlroy
31 Jan	Birmingham City	50,724	Old Trafford	H	W	3–1	Stepney	Forsyth 1	Houston	Daly	Greenhoff B	Buchan M	Coppell	McIlroy 1	Pearson SJ	Macari 1	Hill	McCreery replaced Pearson SJ
7 Feb	Coventry City	33,922	Highfield Road	A	D	1–1	Stepney	Forsyth	Houston	Daly	Greenhoff B	Buchan M	Coppell	McIlroy	Pearson SJ	Macari 1	Hill	McCreery replaced Pearson SJ
18 Feb	Liverpool	59,709	Old Trafford	H	D	0–0	Stepney	Forsyth	Houston	Daly	Greenhoff B	Buchan M	Coppell	McIlroy	Pearson SJ	Macari	Hill	McCreery replaced McIlroy
21 Feb	Aston Villa	50,094	Villa Park	A	L	1–2	Stepney	Forsyth	Houston	Daly	Greenhoff B	Buchan M	Coppell	McIlroy	Pearson SJ	Macari 1	Hill	Coyne replaced Pearson SJ
25 Feb	Derby County	59,632	Old Trafford	H	D	1–1	Stepney	Forsyth	Houston	Daly	Greenhoff B	Buchan M	Coppell	McIlroy	Pearson SJ 1	Macari	Hill	McCreery replaced Hill
28 Feb	West Ham United	57,220	Old Trafford	H	W	4–0	Stepney	Forsyth 1	Houston	Daly	Greenhoff B	Buchan M	Coppell	McIlroy	Pearson SJ 1	Macari 1	Hill	McCreery 1 replaced McIlroy
13 Mar	Leeds United	59,429	Old Trafford	H	W	3–2	Stepney	Forsyth	Houston 1	Daly 1	Greenhoff B	Buchan M	Coppell	McIlroy	Pearson SJ 1	McCreery	Hill	
17 Mar	Norwich City	27,787	Carrow Road	A	D	1–1	Stepney	Forsyth	Houston	Daly	Greenhoff B	Buchan M	Coppell	McIlroy	Pearson SJ	McCreery	Hill 1	
20 Mar	Newcastle United	45,043	St James' Park	A	W	••4–3	Stepney	Forsyth	Houston	Daly	Greenhoff B	Buchan M	Coppell	McIlroy	Pearson SJ 2	McCreery	Hill	
27 Mar	Middlesbrough	58,527	Old Trafford	H	W	3–0	Stepney	Forsyth	Houston	Daly 1	Greenhoff B	Buchan M	Coppell	McIlroy	Pearson SJ	McCreery 1	Hill 1	
10 Apr	Ipswich Town	34,886	Portman Road	A	L	0–3	Stepney	Forsyth	Houston	Daly	Greenhoff B	Buchan M	Coppell	McIlroy	Pearson SJ	McCreery	Hill	
17 Apr	Everton	61,879	Old Trafford	H	W	•2–1	Stepney	Forsyth	Houston	Daly	Greenhoff B	Buchan M	Coppell	McIlroy	Pearson SJ	Macari	Hill	McCreery 1 replaced Coppell
19 Apr	Burnley	27,418	Turf Moor	A	W	1–0	Stepney	Forsyth	Houston	Daly	Greenhoff B	Buchan M	McCreery	McIlroy	Pearson SJ	Macari 1	Hill	Jackson T replaced Pearson SJ
21 Apr	Stoke City	53,879	Old Trafford	H	L	0–1	Stepney	Forsyth	Houston	Daly	Greenhoff B	Buchan M	Jackson T	McIlroy	McCreery	Macari	Hill	Nicholl replaced Jackson T
24 Apr	Leicester City	31,053	Filbert Street	A	L	1–2	Stepney	Forsyth	Houston	Nicholl	Greenhoff B	Buchan M	Jackson T	McCreery	Coyne 1	Macari	Hill	Albiston replaced Houston
4 May	Manchester City	59,517	Old Trafford	H	W	2–0	Stepney	Forsyth	Houston	Daly	Albiston	Buchan M	Coppell	McIlroy 1	Pearson SJ	Jackson T	Hill 1	McCreery replaced Pearson SJ

FA Cup

3 Jan	Oxford United	41,082	Old Trafford	H	W	2–1	Stepney	Forsyth	Houston	Daly 2	Greenhoff B	Buchan M	Coppell	McIlroy	Pearson SJ	Macari	Hill	Nicholl replaced Forsyth
24 Jan	Peterborough	56,352	Old Trafford	H	W	3–1	Stepney	Forsyth 1	Houston	Daly	Greenhoff B	Buchan M	Coppell	McIlroy 1	Pearson SJ	Macari	Hill 1	
14 Feb	Leicester City	34,000	Filbert Street	A	W	2–1	Stepney	Forsyth	Houston	Daly 1	Greenhoff B	Buchan M	Coppell	McIlroy	Pearson SJ	Macari 1	Hill	McCreery replaced Hill
6 Mar	Wolverhampton Wan.	59,433	Old Trafford	H	D	1–1	Stepney	Forsyth	Houston	Daly 1	Greenhoff B	Buchan M	Coppell	McIlroy	Pearson SJ	Macari	Hill	
9 Mar	Wolverhampton Wan.	44,373	Molineux	A	W	3–2	Stepney	Forsyth	Houston	Daly	Greenhoff B 1	Buchan M	Coppell	McIlroy 1	Pearson SJ 1	Macari	Hill	Nicholl replaced Macari
3 Apr	Derby County	55,000	Hillsborough	A	W	2–0	Stepney	Forsyth	Houston	Daly	Greenhoff B	Buchan M	Coppell	McIlroy	Pearson SJ	McCreery	Hill 2	
1 May	Southampton	100,000	Wembley	A	L	0–1	Stepney	Forsyth	Houston	Daly	Greenhoff B	Buchan M	Coppell	McIlroy	Pearson SJ	Macari	Hill	McCreery replaced Hill

FL Cup

10 Sep	Brentford	25,286	Old Trafford	H	W	2–1	Stepney	Nicholl	Houston	Jackson T	Greenhoff B	Buchan M	Coppell	McIlroy 1	Pearson SJ	Macari 1	Daly	Grimshaw replaced Jackson T
8 Oct	Aston Villa	41,447	Villa Park	A	W	2–1	Stepney	Nicholl	Houston	Jackson T	Greenhoff B	Buchan M	Coppell 1	McIlroy	Pearson SJ	Macari 1	Daly	
12 Nov	Manchester City	50,182	Maine Road	A	L	0–4	Roche	Nicholl	Houston	Jackson T	Greenhoff B	Buchan M	Coppell	McIlroy	Pearson SJ	Macari	Daly	McCreery replaced Jackson T

Football League Division 1
P42 • W23 • D10 • L9 • F68 • A42 • PTS56
Position: 3

1976/77

Football League

Date	Opponent	Attendances	Venue				Players and Scores											Substitutions
21 Aug	Birmingham City	58,898	Old Trafford	H	D	2–2	Stepney	Nicholl	Houston	Daly	Greenhoff B	Buchan M	Coppell 1	McIlroy	Pearson SJ 1	Macari	Hill	Foggon replaced Daly
24 Aug	Coventry City	26,775	Highfield Road	A	W	2–0	Stepney	Nicholl	Houston	Daly	Greenhoff B	Buchan M	Coppell	McIlroy	Pearson SJ	Macari 1	Hill 1	
28 Aug	Derby County	30,054	Baseball Ground	A	D	0–0	Stepney	Nicholl	Houston	Daly	Greenhoff B	Buchan M	Coppell	McIlroy	Pearson SJ	Macari	Hill	

continued on page 143

1976/77 continued

Football League continued

Date	Opponents	Attendances	Venue	H/A	Result	Score	Players and Scores											Substitutions
4 Sep	Tottenham Hotspur	60,723	Old Trafford	H	L	2–3	Stepney	Nicholl	Houston	Daly	Greenhoff B	Buchan M	Coppell 1	McIlroy	Pearson SJ 1	Macari	Hill	McCreery replaced McIlroy
11 Sep	Newcastle United	39,037	St James' Park	A	D	2–2	Stepney	Nicholl	Houston	Daly	Greenhoff B 1	Buchan M	Coppell	McIlroy	Pearson SJ 1	Macari	Hill	Foggon replaced Hill
18 Sep	Middlesbrough	56,712	Old Trafford	H	W	•2–0	Stepney	Nicholl	Houston	Daly	Greenhoff B	Buchan M	Coppell	McIlroy	Pearson SJ 1	Macari	Hill	Foggon replaced Daly
25 Sep	Manchester City	48,861	Maine Road	A	W	3–1	Stepney	Nicholl	Houston	Daly 1	Greenhoff B	Buchan M	Coppell 1	McIlroy	Pearson SJ	Macari	Hill	McCreery 1 replaced Pearson SJ
2 Oct	Leeds United	44,512	Elland Road	A	W	2–0	Stepney	Nicholl	Houston	Daly 1	Greenhoff B	Buchan M	Coppell 1	McIlroy	Pearson SJ	Macari	Hill	McCreery replaced Pearson SJ
16 Oct	West Bromwich Alb.	36,615	The Hawthorns	A	L	0–4	Stepney	Nicholl	Houston	Daly	Greenhoff B	Waldron	Coppell	McIlroy	Pearson SJ	Macari	Hill	McCreery replaced Macari
23 Oct	Norwich City	54,356	Old Trafford	H	D	2–2	Stepney	Nicholl	Houston	Daly 1	Greenhoff B	Waldron	Coppell	McIlroy	Pearson SJ	Macari	Hill 1	McGrath C replaced McIlroy
30 Oct	Ipswich Town	57,416	Old Trafford	H	L	0–1	Stepney	Nicholl	Albiston	Daly	Greenhoff B	Houston	Coppell	McIlroy	Pearson SJ	Macari	Hill	McCreery replaced Macari
6 Nov	Aston Villa	44,789	Villa Park	A	L	2–3	Stepney	Nicholl	Albiston	Daly	Greenhoff B	Houston	McGrath C	McIlroy	Pearson SJ 1	Coppell	Hill 1	
10 Nov	Sunderland	42,685	Old Trafford	H	D	3–3	Roche	Albiston	Houston	Daly	Paterson	Waldron	Coppell	Greenhoff B 1	Pearson SJ 1	Macari	Hill 1	Clark J replaced Waldron
20 Nov	Leicester City	26,421	Filbert Street	A	D	1–1	Stepney	Nicholl	Albiston	Daly 1	Greenhoff B	Paterson	Coppell	McIlroy	Pearson SJ	Greenhoff J	Hill	
27 Nov	West Ham United	55,366	Old Trafford	H	L	0–2	Stepney	Forsyth	Albiston	Daly	Greenhoff B	Houston	Coppell	McIlroy	Pearson SJ	Greenhoff J	Hill	
18 Dec	Arsenal	39,572	Highbury	A	L	1–3	Stepney	Forsyth	Houston	McIlroy 1	Greenhoff B	Buchan M	McCreery	Greenhoff J	Pearson SJ	Macari	Hill	McGrath C replaced Greenhoff B
27 Dec	Everton	56,786	Old Trafford	H	W	4–0	Stepney	Nicholl	Houston	McIlroy	Greenhoff B	Buchan M	Coppell	Greenhoff J 1	Pearson SJ 1	Macari 1	Hill 1	McCreery replaced Coppell
1 Jan	Aston Villa	55,446	Old Trafford	H	W	2–0	Stepney	Nicholl	Houston	McIlroy	Greenhoff B	Buchan M	Coppell	Greenhoff J	Pearson SJ 2	Macari	Hill	McCreery replaced Pearson SJ
3 Jan	Ipswich Town	30,105	Portman Road	A	L	1–2	Stepney	Nicholl	Albiston	McIlroy	Greenhoff B	Buchan M	McCreery	Greenhoff J	Pearson SJ 1	Macari	Hill	McGrath C replaced Pearson SJ
15 Jan	Coventry City	46,567	Old Trafford	H	W	2–0	Stepney	Nicholl	Houston	McIlroy	Greenhoff B	Buchan M	Coppell	Greenhoff J	Pearson SJ	Macari 2	Hill	McCreery replaced Hill
19 Jan	Bristol City	43,051	Old Trafford	H	W	2–1	Stepney	Nicholl	Houston	McIlroy	Greenhoff B 1	Buchan M	Coppell	Greenhoff J	Pearson SJ 1	Macari	Hill	
22 Jan	Birmingham City	35,316	St Andrews	A	W	3–2	Stepney	Nicholl	Houston 1	McIlroy	Greenhoff B	Buchan M	Coppell	Greenhoff J 1	Pearson SJ 1	Macari	Hill	Daly replaced Hill
5 Feb	Derby County	54,044	Old Trafford	H	W	•3–1	Stepney	Nicholl	Houston 1	McIlroy	Greenhoff B	Buchan M	Coppell	Greenhoff J	Pearson SJ	Macari 1	Daly	
12 Feb	Tottenham Hotspur	46,946	White Hart Lane	A	W	3–1	Stepney	Nicholl	Houston	McIlroy 1	Greenhoff B	Buchan M	Coppell	Greenhoff J	Pearson SJ	Macari 1	Hill 1	
16 Feb	Liverpool	57,487	Old Trafford	H	D	0–0	Stepney	Nicholl	Houston	McIlroy	Greenhoff B	Buchan M	Coppell	Greenhoff J	Pearson SJ	Macari	Hill	
19 Feb	Newcastle United	51,828	Old Trafford	H	W	3–1	Stepney	Nicholl	Houston	McIlroy	Greenhoff B	Buchan M	Coppell	Greenhoff J 3	Pearson SJ	Macari	Hill	Albiston replaced Hill
5 Mar	Manchester City	58,595	Old Trafford	H	W	3–1	Stepney	Nicholl	Houston	McIlroy	Greenhoff B	Buchan M	Coppell 1	Greenhoff J	Pearson SJ 1	Macari	Hill 1	McCreery replaced Hill
12 Mar	Leeds United	60,612	Old Trafford	H	W	•1–0	Stepney	Nicholl	Houston	McIlroy	Greenhoff B	Buchan M	Coppell	Greenhoff J	Pearson SJ	Macari	Hill	McCreery replaced Hill
23 Mar	West Bromwich Alb.	51,053	Old Trafford	H	D	2–2	Stepney	Nicholl	Albiston	McIlroy	Houston	Buchan M	Coppell 1	Greenhoff J	Pearson SJ	Macari	Hill 1	McCreery replaced McIlroy
2 Apr	Norwich City	24,161	Carrow Road	A	L	•1–2	Stepney	Nicholl	Houston	McIlroy	Greenhoff B	Buchan M	Coppell	Greenhoff J	McCreery	Macari	Hill	McGrath C replaced Hill
5 Apr	Everton	38,216	Goodison Park	A	W	2–1	Stepney	Nicholl	Houston	McIlroy	Greenhoff B	Buchan M	Coppell	Greenhoff J	Pearson SJ	McCreery	Hill 2	Albiston replaced Hill
9 Apr	Stoke City	53,102	Old Trafford	H	W	3–0	Stepney	Nicholl	Houston 1	McIlroy	Greenhoff B	Buchan M	Coppell	Greenhoff J	Pearson SJ 1	Macari 1	Hill	McCreery replaced Greenhoff J
11 Apr	Sunderland	38,785	Roker Park	A	L	1–2	Stepney	Nicholl	Houston	McIlroy	Greenhoff B	Buchan M	Coppell	McCreery	Pearson SJ	Macari	Hill 1	Albiston replaced Macari
16 Apr	Leicester City	49,161	Old Trafford	H	D	1–1	Stepney	Nicholl	Albiston	McIlroy	Greenhoff B	Buchan M	Coppell	Greenhoff J 1	Pearson SJ	Macari	McCreery	Hill replaced McCreery
19 Apr	Queen's Park Rangers	28,848	Loftus Road	A	L	0–4	Stepney	Nicholl	Albiston	McIlroy	Greenhoff B	Houston	Coppell	Greenhoff J	Pearson SJ	Macari	McCreery	Forsyth replaced Greenhoff B
26 Apr	Middlesbrough	21,744	Ayresome Park	A	L	0–3	Stepney	Nicholl	Houston	McIlroy	Greenhoff B	Buchan M	Coppell	Greenhoff J	Pearson SJ	Macari	Hill	
30 Apr	Queen's Park Rangers	50,788	Old Trafford	H	W	1–0	Stepney	Nicholl	Houston	McIlroy	Greenhoff B	Buchan M	Coppell	Greenhoff J	Pearson SJ	Macari 1	Hill	McCreery replaced Hill
3 May	Liverpool	53,046	Anfield	A	L	0–1	Stepney	Nicholl	Houston	McIlroy	Forsyth	Albiston	Coppell	Greenhoff J	Pearson SJ	Macari	Hill	McCreery replaced Greenhoff J
7 May	Bristol City	28,864	Ashton Gate	A	D	1–1	Stepney	Nicholl	Houston	Jackson T	Greenhoff B	Buchan M	Coppell	Greenhoff J 1	McCreery	Macari	Albiston	McIlroy replaced Houston
11 May	Stoke City	24,204	Victoria Ground	A	D	3–3	Stepney	Nicholl	Albiston	Jackson T	Greenhoff B	Buchan M	Coppell	McCreery 1	McGrath C	Macari	Hill 2	
14 May	Arsenal	53,232	Old Trafford	H	W	3–2	Stepney	Nicholl	Albiston	McIlroy	Greenhoff B	Buchan M	Coppell	Greenhoff J 1	Pearson SJ	Macari 1	Hill 1	McCreery replaced Pearson SJ
16 May	West Ham United	29,904	Upton Park	A	L	2–4	Roche	Nicholl	Albiston	McIlroy	Greenhoff B	Buchan M	Coppell	Greenhoff J	Pearson SJ 1	Macari	Hill 1	McCreery replaced Greenhoff J

FA Cup

Date	Opponents	Attendances	Venue	H/A	Result	Score	Players and Scores											Substitutions
8 Jan	Walsall	48,870	Old Trafford	H	W	1–0	Stepney	Nicholl	Houston	McIlroy	Greenhoff B	Buchan M	Coppell	Greenhoff J	Pearson SJ	Macari	Hill 1	Daly replaced Coppell
29 Jan	Queen's Park Rangers	57,422	Old Trafford	H	W	1–0	Stepney	Nicholl	Houston	McIlroy	Greenhoff B	Buchan M	Coppell	Greenhoff J	Pearson SJ	Macari 1	Hill	
26 Feb	Southampton	29,137	The Dell	A	D	2–2	Stepney	Nicholl	Houston	McIlroy	Greenhoff B	Buchan M	Coppell	Greenhoff J	Pearson SJ	Macari 1	Hill 1	McCreery replaced Greenhoff J
8 Mar	Southampton	58,103	Old Trafford	H	W	2–1	Stepney	Nicholl	Houston	McIlroy	Greenhoff B	Buchan M	Coppell	Greenhoff J 2	Pearson SJ	Macari	Hill	
19 Mar	Aston Villa	57,089	Old Trafford	H	W	2–1	Stepney	Nicholl	Houston 1	McIlroy	Greenhoff B	Buchan M	Coppell	Greenhoff J	Pearson SJ	Macari 1	Hill	McCreery replaced Greenhoff J
23 Apr	Leeds United	55,000	Hillsborough	A	W	2–1	Stepney	Nicholl	Houston	McIlroy	Greenhoff B	Buchan M	Coppell 1	Greenhoff J 1	Pearson SJ	Macari	Hill	
21 May	Liverpool	100,000	Wembley	A	W	2–1	Stepney	Nicholl	Albiston	McIlroy	Greenhoff B	Buchan M	Coppell	Greenhoff J 1	Pearson SJ 1	Macari	Hill	McCreery replaced Hill

FL Cup

Date	Opponents	Attendances	Venue	H/A	Result	Score	Players and Scores											Substitutions
1 Sep	Tranmere Rovers	37,586	Old Trafford	H	W	5–0	Stepney	Nicholl	Houston	Daly 2	Greenhoff B	Buchan M	Coppell	McIlroy	Pearson SJ 1	Macari 1	Hill 1	McCreery replaced McIlroy
22 Sep	Sunderland	46,170	Old Trafford	H	D	•2–2	Stepney	Nicholl	Houston	Daly	Greenhoff B	Buchan M	McCreery	McIlroy	Pearson SJ 1	Macari	Hill	
4 Oct	Sunderland	46,170	Roker Park	A	D	2–2	Stepney	Nicholl	Houston	Daly 1	Waldron	Buchan M	Coppell	McIlroy	McCreery	Greenhoff B 1	Hill	Albiston replaced Greenhoff B
6 Oct	Sunderland	47,689	Old Trafford	H	W	1–0	Stepney	Nicholl	Houston	Daly	Greenhoff B 1	Buchan M	Coppell	McIlroy	McCreery	Macari	Hill	Albiston replaced Hill
27 Oct	Newcastle United	52,002	Old Trafford	H	W	7–2	Stepney	Nicholl 1	Albiston	Daly	Greenhoff B	Houston 1	Coppell 1	McIlroy	Pearson SJ 1	Macari	Hill 3	McGrath C replaced Pearson SJ
1 Dec	Everton	57,738	Old Trafford	H	L	0–3	Stepney	Forsyth	Albiston	Daly	Paterson	Greenhoff B	Coppell	McIlroy	Pearson SJ	Jackson T	Hill	McCreery replaced Daly

UEFA Cup

Date	Opponents	Attendances	Venue	H/A	Result	Score	Players and Scores											Substitutions
15 Sep	Ajax	30,000	Olympisch Stadion	A	L	0–1	Stepney	Nicholl	Houston	Daly	Greenhoff B	Buchan M	Coppell	McIlroy	Pearson SJ	Macari	Hill	McCreery replaced Daly
29 Sep	Ajax	58,918	Old Trafford	H	W	2–0	Stepney	Nicholl	Houston	Daly	Greenhoff B	Buchan M	Coppell	McIlroy 1	McCreery	Macari 1	Hill	Albiston replaced Daly, Paterson replaced Hill
20 Oct	Juventus	59,000	Old Trafford	H	W	1–0	Stepney	Nicholl	Albiston	Daly	Greenhoff B	Houston	Coppell	McIlroy	Pearson SJ	Macari	Hill 1	McCreery replaced Daly
3 Nov	Juventus	66,632	Stadio Comunale	A	L	0–3	Stepney	Nicholl	Albiston	Daly	Greenhoff B	Houston	Coppell	McIlroy	Pearson SJ	Macari	Hill	McCreery replaced McIlroy, Paterson replaced Macari

Football League Division 1
P42 • W18 • D11 • L13 • F71 • A62 • PTS47
Position: 6

1977/78

Football League

Date	Opponents	Attendances	Venue	H/A	Result	Score	Players and Scores											Substitutions
20 Aug	Birmingham City	28,005	St Andrews	A	W	4–1	Stepney	Nicholl	Albiston	McIlroy	Greenhoff B	Buchan M	Coppell	McCreery	Pearson SJ	Macari 3	Hill 1	Grimes replaced Pearson SJ
24 Aug	Coventry City	55,726	Old Trafford	H	W	2–1	Stepney	Nicholl	Albiston	McIlroy	Greenhoff B	Buchan M	Coppell	McCreery 1	Pearson SJ	Macari	Hill 1	
27 Aug	Ipswich Town	57,904	Old Trafford	H	D	0–0	Stepney	Nicholl	Albiston	McIlroy	Greenhoff B	Buchan M	McGrath C	McCreery	Coppell	Macari	Hill	Grimes replaced McIlroy
3 Sep	Derby County	21,279	Baseball Ground	A	W	1–0	Stepney	Forsyth	Albiston	McIlroy	Nicholl	Buchan M	Coppell	McCreery	Pearson SJ	Macari 1	Hill	
10 Sep	Manchester City	50,856	Maine Road	A	L	1–3	Stepney	Forsyth	Albiston	McIlroy	Nicholl 1	Buchan M	Coppell	McCreery	Pearson SJ	Macari	Hill	McGrath C replaced Macari
17 Sep	Chelsea	54,951	Old Trafford	H	L	0–1	Stepney	Nicholl	Albiston	McIlroy	Greenhoff B	Buchan M	Coppell	McCreery	Pearson SJ	Macari	Hill	McGrath C replaced Buchan M
24 Sep	Leeds United	33,517	Elland Road	A	D	1–1	Stepney	Nicholl	Albiston	McIlroy	Greenhoff B	Houston	McGrath C	Coppell	Pearson SJ	Macari	Hill 1	
1 Oct	Liverpool	55,089	Old Trafford	H	W	2–0	Stepney	Nicholl	Albiston	McIlroy 1	Greenhoff B	Buchan M	McGrath C	Coppell	Greenhoff J	Macari 1	Hill	
8 Oct	Middlesbrough	26,822	Ayresome Park	A	L	1–2	Stepney	Nicholl	Albiston	McCreery	Greenhoff B	Buchan M	McGrath C	Greenhoff J	Coppell 1	Macari	Hill	
15 Oct	Newcastle United	55,056	Old Trafford	H	W	3–2	Stepney	Nicholl	Albiston	McIlroy	Houston	Buchan M	McGrath C	Greenhoff J 1	Coppell 1	Macari 1	Hill	
22 Oct	West Bromwich Alb.	27,526	The Hawthorns	A	L	0–4	Stepney	Forsyth	Rogers	McIlroy	Nicholl	Buchan M	Coppell	McCreery	Pearson SJ	Macari	Hill	McGrath C replaced McCreery
29 Oct	Aston Villa	39,144	Villa Park	A	L	1–2	Stepney	Nicholl 1	Albiston	McIlroy	Houston	Buchan M	McGrath C	Coppell	Pearson SJ	McCreery	Hill	Grimes replaced Hill
5 Nov	Arsenal	53,055	Old Trafford	H	L	1–2	Stepney	Nicholl	Albiston	McIlroy	Houston	Buchan M	McGrath C	Coppell	Pearson SJ	McCreery	Hill 1	Grimes replaced McGrath C
12 Nov	Nottingham Forest	30,183	City Ground	A	L	1–2	Roche	Nicholl	Houston	McIlroy	Greenhoff B	Buchan M	McGrath C	Coppell	Pearson SJ 1	McCreery	Hill	
19 Nov	Norwich City	48,729	Old Trafford	H	W	1–0	Roche	Nicholl	Houston	McIlroy	Greenhoff B	Buchan M	Coppell	Greenhoff J	Pearson SJ 1	Macari	Hill	McCreery replaced McIlroy
26 Nov	Queen's Park Rangers	25,367	Loftus Road	A	D	2–2	Roche	Nicholl	Houston	Grimes	Greenhoff B	Buchan M	Coppell	Greenhoff J	Pearson SJ	Macari	Hill 2	McGrath C replaced Macari
3 Dec	Wolverhampton Wan.	48,874	Old Trafford	H	W	3–1	Roche	Nicholl	Albiston	McIlroy 1	Greenhoff B	Houston	Coppell	Greenhoff J 1	Pearson SJ 1	Grimes	Hill	McGrath C replaced Grimes
10 Dec	West Ham United	20,242	Upton Park	A	L	1–2	Roche	Nicholl	Albiston	Coppell	Greenhoff B	Houston	McGrath C 1	Greenhoff J	Pearson SJ	Grimes	Hill	
17 Dec	Nottingham Forest	54,374	Old Trafford	H	L	0–4	Roche	Nicholl	Houston	McIlroy	Greenhoff B	Buchan M	Coppell	Greenhoff J	Pearson SJ	Macari	Hill	Grimes replaced Pearson SJ
26 Dec	Everton	48,335	Goodison Park	A	W	6–2	Roche	Nicholl	Houston	McIlroy 1	Greenhoff B	Buchan M	Coppell 1	Greenhoff J 1	Ritchie	Macari 2	Hill 1	Grimes replaced Greenhoff B
27 Dec	Leicester City	57,396	Old Trafford	H	W	3–1	Roche	Nicholl	Albiston	McIlroy	Houston	Buchan M	Coppell 1	Greenhoff J 1	Ritchie	Macari	Hill 1	
31 Dec	Coventry City	24,706	Highfield Road	A	L	0–3	Roche	Nicholl	Houston	McIlroy	Greenhoff B	Buchan M	Coppell	Greenhoff J	Ritchie	Macari	Hill	McGrath C replaced Houston
2 Jan	Birmingham City	53,501	Old Trafford	H	L	1–2	Roche	Nicholl	Albiston	McIlroy	Greenhoff B	Buchan M	Coppell	Greenhoff J 1	Ritchie	Macari	Hill	
14 Jan	Ipswich Town	23,321	Portman Road	A	W	2–1	Roche	Nicholl	Albiston	McIlroy 1	Houston	Buchan M	Coppell	Greenhoff J	Pearson SJ 1	Macari	Hill	
21 Jan	Derby County	57,115	Old Trafford	H	W	4–0	Roche	Nicholl	Albiston	McIlroy	Houston	Buchan M 1	Coppell	Greenhoff J	Pearson SJ 1	Macari	Hill 2	
8 Feb	Bristol City	43,457	Old Trafford	H	D	1–1	Roche	Nicholl	Albiston	McIlroy	Houston	Buchan M	Coppell	Jordan	Pearson SJ	Macari	Hill 1	Greenhoff J replaced Buchan M
11 Feb	Chelsea	32,849	Stamford Bridge	A	D	2–2	Roche	Nicholl	Albiston	McIlroy 1	Houston	Greenhoff B	Coppell	Jordan	Pearson SJ	Macari	Hill 1	
25 Feb	Liverpool	49,094	Anfield	A	L	1–3	Roche	Nicholl	Albiston	McIlroy 1	McQueen	Houston	Coppell	Jordan	Pearson SJ	Macari	Hill	
1 Mar	Leeds United	49,101	Old Trafford	H	L	0–1	Roche	Nicholl	Albiston	McIlroy	Greenhoff B	Houston	Coppell	Greenhoff J	Jordan	Macari	Hill	McGrath C replaced Hill
4 Mar	Middlesbrough	46,332	Old Trafford	H	D	0–0	Roche	Nicholl	Houston	McIlroy	McQueen	Greenhoff B	Coppell	Greenhoff J	Jordan	Macari	Hill	
11 Mar	Newcastle United	25,825	St James' Park	A	D	2–2	Roche	Nicholl	Houston	McIlroy	McQueen	Greenhoff B	Coppell	Greenhoff J	Jordan 1	Macari	Hill 1	
15 Mar	Manchester City	58,398	Old Trafford	H	D	2–2	Stepney	Nicholl	Houston	McIlroy	McQueen	Greenhoff B	Coppell	Greenhoff J	Jordan	Macari	Hill 2	Albiston replaced Jordan
18 Mar	West Bromwich Alb.	46,329	Old Trafford	H	D	1–1	Stepney	Nicholl	Houston	McIlroy	McQueen 1	Greenhoff B	Coppell	Greenhoff J	Pearson SJ	Macari	Hill	McGrath C replaced Hill
25 Mar	Leicester City	20,299	Filbert Street	A	W	3–2	Stepney	Nicholl	Houston	McIlroy	McQueen	Greenhoff B	Coppell	Greenhoff J 1	Pearson SJ 1	Macari	Hill 1	
27 Mar	Everton	55,277	Old Trafford	H	L	1–2	Stepney	Nicholl	Albiston	McIlroy	McQueen	Greenhoff B	Coppell	Greenhoff J	Pearson SJ	Macari	Hill 1	
29 Mar	Aston Villa	41,625	Old Trafford	H	D	1–1	Stepney	Greenhoff B	Houston	McIlroy 1	McQueen	Buchan M	Coppell	Greenhoff J	Pearson SJ	Macari	Jordan	McCreery replaced Greenhoff J
1 Apr	Arsenal	40,829	Highbury	A	L	1–3	Stepney	Greenhoff B	Houston	McIlroy	McQueen	Buchan M	Coppell	Jordan 1	Pearson SJ	Macari	Hill	McCreery replaced Hill
8 Apr	Queen's Park Rangers	42,677	Old Trafford	H	W	3–1	Stepney	Greenhoff B	Houston	McIlroy	McQueen	Buchan M	Coppell	Jordan	Pearson SJ 2	Grimes 1	McCreery	
15 Apr	Norwich City	19,778	Carrow Road	A	W	3–1	Stepney	Albiston	Houston	McIlroy 1	McQueen	Buchan M	Coppell 1	Jordan 1	Pearson SJ	Greenhoff B	McCreery	McGrath C replaced McCreery
22 Apr	West Ham United	54,089	Old Trafford	H	W	3–0	Stepney	Albiston	Houston	McIlroy 1	McQueen	Buchan M	Coppell	Jordan	Pearson SJ 1	Grimes 1	Greenhoff B	
25 Apr	Bristol City	26,035	Ashton Gate	A	W	1–0	Roche	Albiston	Houston	McIlroy	McQueen	Nicholl	Coppell	Jordan	Pearson SJ 1	Grimes	Greenhoff B	
29 Apr	Wolverhampton Wan.	24,774	Molineux	A	L	1–2	Stepney	Albiston	Houston	McIlroy	McQueen	Nicholl	Coppell	Jordan	Pearson SJ	Greenhoff B 1	Grimes	McCreery replaced Greenhoff B

FA Cup

Date	Opponents	Attendances	Venue	H/A	Result	Score	Players and Scores											Substitutions
7 Jan	Carlisle United	21,710	Brunton Park	A	D	1–1	Roche	Nicholl	Albiston	McIlroy	Greenhoff B	Buchan M	Coppell	Greenhoff J	Pearson SJ	Macari 1	Grimes	McCreery replaced Grimes
11 Jan	Carlisle United	54,156	Old Trafford	H	W	4–2	Roche	Nicholl	Albiston	McIlroy	Houston	Buchan M	Coppell	Greenhoff J	Pearson SJ 2	Macari 2	Hill	
28 Jan	West Bromwich Alb.	57,056	Old Trafford	H	D	1–1	Roche	Nicholl	Albiston	McIlroy	Houston	Buchan M	Coppell 1	Jordan	Pearson SJ	Macari	Hill	
1 Feb	West Bromwich Alb.	37,086	The Hawthorns	A	L	2–3	Roche	Nicholl	Albiston	McIlroy	Houston	Buchan M	Coppell	Jordan	Pearson SJ 1	Macari	Hill 1	Greenhoff J replaced Albiston

FL Cup

Date	Opponents	Attendances	Venue	H/A	Result	Score	Players and Scores											Substitutions
30 Aug	Arsenal	36,171	Highbury	A	L	2–3	Stepney	Nicholl	Albiston	Grimes	Greenhoff B	Buchan M	Coppell	McCreery 1	Pearson SJ 1	Macari	Hill	McGrath C replaced Greenhoff B

European Cup Winners' Cup

Date	Opponents	Attendances	Venue	H/A	Result	Score	Players and Scores											Substitutions
14 Sep	St Etienne	33,678	Geoffroy Guichard	A	D	1–1	Stepney	Nicholl	Albiston	McIlroy	Greenhoff B	Buchan M	McGrath C	McCreery	Pearson SJ	Coppell	Hill 1	Grimes replaced McIlroy, Houston replaced Greenhoff B
5 Oct	St Etienne	31,634	Plymouth	A	W	2–0	Stepney	Nicholl	Albiston	McIlroy	Greenhoff B	Buchan M	Coppell 1	Greenhoff J	Pearson SJ 1	Macari	Hill	McGrath C replaced Pearson SJ
19 Oct	Porto	70,000	Estadio das Antas	A	L	0–4	Stepney	Nicholl	Albiston	McIlroy	Houston	Buchan M	McGrath C	McCreery	Coppell	Macari	Hill	Forsyth replaced Houston, Grimes replaced McGrath C
2 Nov	Porto	51,831	Old Trafford	H	W	••5–2	Stepney	Nicholl 1	Albiston	McIlroy	Houston	Buchan M	McGrath C	Coppell 2	Pearson SJ	McCreery	Hill	

Football League Division 1
P42 • W16 • D10 • L16 • F67 • A63 • PTS42
Position: 10

1978/79

Football League

Date	Opponent	Attendances	Venue			Players and Scores											Substitutions
19 Aug	Birmingham City	56,139	Old Trafford	H W	1–0	Roche	Greenhoff B	Albiston	McIlroy	McQueen	Buchan M	Coppell	Greenhoff J	Jordan 1	Macari	McCreery	
23 Aug	Leeds United	36,845	Elland Road	A W	3–2	Roche	Greenhoff B	Albiston	McIlroy 1	McQueen 1	Buchan M	Coppell	Greenhoff J	Jordan	Macari 1	McCreery	
26 Aug	Ipswich Town	21,802	Portman Road	A L	0–3	Roche	Greenhoff B	Albiston	McIlroy	McQueen	Buchan M	Coppell	Greenhoff J	Jordan	Macari	McCreery	McGrath C replaced McCreery
2 Sep	Everton	53,982	Old Trafford	H D	1–1	Roche	Nicholl	Albiston	McIlroy	Greenhoff B	Buchan M 1	Coppell	Greenhoff J	Jordan	Macari	McCreery	Grimes replaced McCreery
9 Sep	Queen's Park Rangers	23,477	Loftus Road	A D	1–1	Roche	Greenhoff B	Albiston	McIlroy	McQueen	Buchan M	Coppell	Greenhoff J 1	Jordan	Macari	McCreery	
16 Sep	Nottingham Forest	53,039	Old Trafford	H D	1–1	Roche	Greenhoff B	Albiston	McIlroy	McQueen	Buchan M	Coppell	Greenhoff J 1	Jordan	Macari	McCreery	Grimes replaced McCreery
23 Sep	Arsenal	45,393	Highbury	A D	1–1	Roche	Albiston	Houston	Greenhoff B	McQueen	Buchan M	Coppell 1	Greenhoff J	Jordan	Macari	McIlroy	
30 Sep	Manchester City	55,301	Old Trafford	H W	1–0	Roche	Albiston	Houston	Greenhoff B	McQueen	Buchan M	Coppell	Greenhoff J	Jordan 1	Macari	McIlroy	
7 Oct	Middlesbrough	45,402	Old Trafford	H W	3–2	Roche	Albiston	Houston	McIlroy	McQueen	Buchan M	Coppell	Greenhoff J	Jordan 1	Macari 2	McCreery	Grimes replaced Greenhoff J
14 Oct	Aston Villa	36,204	Villa Park	A D	2–2	Roche	Albiston	Houston	McIlroy 1	McQueen	Buchan M	Coppell	Greenhoff J	Jordan	Macari 1	Grimes	
21 Oct	Bristol City	47,211	Old Trafford	H L	1–3	Roche	Albiston	Houston	McIlroy	McQueen	Buchan M	Coppell	Greenhoff J 1	Jordan	Macari	Grimes	Greenhoff B replaced McIlroy
28 Oct	Wolverhampton Wan.	23,141	Molineux	A W	4–2	Roche	Nicholl	Houston	Greenhoff B 1	McQueen	Buchan M	Coppell	Greenhoff J 2	Jordan 1	Macari	McIlroy	Grimes replaced McQueen
4 Nov	Southampton	46,259	Old Trafford	H D	1–1	Roche	Nicholl	Houston	McIlroy	Greenhoff B	Buchan M	Coppell	Greenhoff J 1	Jordan	Macari	Grimes	
11 Nov	Birmingham City	23,550	St Andrews	A L	1–5	Roche	Nicholl	Houston	McCreery	Greenhoff B	Buchan M	Coppell	Greenhoff J	Jordan 1	Macari	McIlroy	Albiston replaced Nicholl
18 Nov	Ipswich Town	42,109	Old Trafford	H W	2–0	Bailey	Albiston	Houston	Greenhoff B	McQueen	Buchan M	Coppell 1	Greenhoff J 1	Jordan	Sloan	McIlroy	McGrath C replaced Sloan
21 Nov	Everton	42,126	Goodison Park	A L	0–3	Bailey	Albiston	Houston	Greenhoff B	McQueen	Buchan M	Coppell	Greenhoff J	Jordan	Sloan	McIlroy	Macari replaced Sloan
25 Nov	Chelsea	28,162	Stamford Bridge	A W	1–0	Bailey	Greenhoff B	Houston	McIlroy	McQueen	Buchan M	Coppell	Greenhoff J 1	Jordan	Macari	Thomas M	
9 Dec	Derby County	23,180	Baseball Ground	A W	3–1	Bailey	Greenhoff B	Houston	McIlroy	McQueen	Buchan M	Coppell	Greenhoff J 1	Ritchie 2	Macari	Thomas M	Paterson replaced Houston
16 Dec	Tottenham Hotspur	52,026	Old Trafford	H W	2–0	Bailey	Greenhoff B	Houston	McIlroy 1	McQueen	Buchan M	Coppell	Greenhoff J	Ritchie 1	Macari	Thomas M	
22 Dec	Bolton Wanderers	32,390	Burnden Park	A L	0–3	Bailey	Greenhoff B	Connell	McIlroy	McQueen	Buchan M	Coppell	Greenhoff J	Ritchie	Macari	Thomas M	Nicholl replaced Greenhoff J
26 Dec	Liverpool	54,910	Old Trafford	H L	0–3	Bailey	Greenhoff B	Connell	McIlroy	McQueen	Buchan M	Coppell	Greenhoff J	Ritchie	Macari	Thomas M	
30 Dec	West Bromwich Alb.	45,091	Old Trafford	H L	3–5	Bailey	Greenhoff B 1	Houston	McIlroy 1	McQueen 1	Buchan M	Coppell	Greenhoff J	Ritchie	McCreery	Thomas M	Sloan replaced Greenhoff J
3 Feb	Arsenal	45,460	Old Trafford	H L	0–2	Bailey	Greenhoff B	Houston	Nicholl	McQueen	Buchan M	Coppell	Greenhoff J	Macari	McIlroy	Thomas M	Ritchie replaced Greenhoff J
10 Feb	Manchester City	46,151	Maine Road	A W	3–0	Bailey	Greenhoff B	Albiston	McIlroy	McQueen	Buchan M	Coppell 2	Greenhoff J	Ritchie 1	Macari	Thomas M	
24 Feb	Aston Villa	44,437	Old Trafford	H D	1–1	Bailey	Greenhoff B	Albiston	McIlroy	McQueen	Buchan M	Coppell	Greenhoff J 1	Ritchie	Macari	Thomas M	Nicholl replaced Macari
28 Feb	Queen's Park Rangers	36,085	Old Trafford	H W	2–0	Bailey	Greenhoff B	Albiston	McIlroy	McQueen	Buchan M	Coppell 1	Greenhoff J 1	Ritchie	Nicholl	Thomas M	
3 Mar	Bristol City	24,583	Ashton Gate	A W	2–1	Bailey	Nicholl	Albiston	McIlroy	McQueen 1	Buchan M	Coppell	Greenhoff J	Ritchie 1	Grimes	Thomas M	
20 Mar	Coventry City	25,382	Highfield Road	A L	3–4	Bailey	Nicholl	Albiston	McIlroy 1	McQueen	Buchan M	Coppell 2	Greenhoff J	Jordan	Greenhoff B	Thomas M	
24 Mar	Leeds United	51,191	Old Trafford	H W	4–1	Bailey	Nicholl	Albiston	McIlroy	McQueen	Buchan M	Coppell	Greenhoff J	Ritchie 3	Greenhoff B	Thomas M 1	Paterson replaced Greenhoff J
27 Mar	Middlesbrough	20,138	Ayresome Park	A D	2–2	Bailey	Nicholl	Albiston	McIlroy	McQueen 1	Buchan M	Coppell 1	Greenhoff J	Jordan	Greenhoff B	Thomas M	
7 Apr	Norwich City	19,382	Carrow Road	A D	2–2	Bailey	Albiston	Houston	McIlroy	McQueen 1	Buchan M	Coppell	Greenhoff J	Jordan	Macari 1	Thomas M	
11 Apr	Bolton Wanderers	49,617	Old Trafford	H L	1–2	Bailey	Nicholl	Albiston	McIlroy	McQueen	Buchan M 1	Coppell	Ritchie	Jordan	Macari	Thomas M	
14 Apr	Liverpool	46,608	Anfield	A L	0–2	Bailey	Nicholl	Albiston	McIlroy	Greenhoff B	Buchan M	Coppell	Ritchie	Jordan	Macari	Thomas M	Houston replaced Ritchie
16 Apr	Coventry City	46,035	Old Trafford	H D	0–0	Bailey	Nicholl	Albiston	McIlroy	McQueen	Buchan M	Coppell	Ritchie	Jordan	Greenhoff B	Thomas M	McCreery replaced Ritchie
18 Apr	Nottingham Forest	33,074	City Ground	A D	1–1	Bailey	Nicholl	Albiston	McIlroy	McQueen	Buchan M	Coppell	McCreery	Jordan 1	Greenhoff B	Thomas M	Grimes replaced Buchan M
21 Apr	Tottenham Hotspur	36,665	White Hart Lane	A D	1–1	Bailey	Nicholl	Albiston	McIlroy	McQueen 1	Greenhoff B	Coppell	McCreery	Jordan	Macari	Thomas M	Grimes replaced Thomas M
25 Apr	Norwich City	33,678	Old Trafford	H W	1–0	Bailey	Nicholl	Albiston	McIlroy	McQueen	Buchan M	Coppell	McCreery	Jordan	Macari 1	Thomas M	Grimes replaced Buchan M
28 Apr	Derby County	42,546	Old Trafford	H D	0–0	Bailey	McCreery	Albiston	McIlroy	Nicholl	Houston	Coppell	Ritchie	Jordan	Macari	Thomas M	Grimes replaced Ritchie
30 Apr	Southampton	21,616	The Dell	A D	1–1	Bailey	Albiston	Houston	Sloan	McQueen	Moran	Coppell	Paterson	Ritchie 1	Macari	Grimes	
5 May	West Bromwich Alb.	27,960	The Hawthorns	A L	0–1	Bailey	Albiston	Houston	McIlroy	McQueen	Greenhoff B	Coppell	Greenhoff J	Jordan	Macari	Thomas M	Grimes replaced Thomas M
7 May	Wolverhampton Wan.	39,402	Old Trafford	H W	3–2	Bailey	Nicholl	Albiston	Greenhoff B	Houston	Buchan M	Coppell 2	Ritchie 1	Jordan	Macari	Thomas M	Grimes replaced Greenhoff B
16 May	Chelsea	38,109	Old Trafford	H D	1–1	Bailey	Albiston	Houston	McIlroy	McQueen	Nicholl	Coppell 1	Greenhoff J	Jordan	McCreery	Thomas M	Grimes replaced McCreery

FA Cup

Date	Opponent	Attendances	Venue			Players and Scores											Substitutions
15 Jan	Chelsea	38,743	Old Trafford	H W	3–0	Bailey	Greenhoff B	Houston	McIlroy	McQueen	Buchan M	Coppell 1	Greenhoff J 1	Pearson SJ	Nicholl	Grimes 1	
31 Jan	Fulham	25,229	Craven Cottage	A D	1–1	Bailey	Greenhoff B	Houston	McIlroy	McQueen	Buchan M	Coppell	Greenhoff J 1	Pearson SJ	Macari	Thomas M	Nicholl replaced Pearson SJ
12 Feb	Fulham	41,200	Old Trafford	H W	1–0	Bailey	Greenhoff B	Albiston	McIlroy	McQueen	Buchan M	Coppell	Greenhoff J 1	Ritchie	Macari	Thomas M	
20 Feb	Colchester United	13,171	Layer Road	A W	1–0	Bailey	Greenhoff B	Albiston	McIlroy	McQueen	Buchan M	Coppell	Greenhoff J 1	Ritchie	Macari	Thomas M	
10 Mar	Tottenham Hotspur	51,800	White Hart Lane	A D	1–1	Bailey	Nicholl	Albiston	McIlroy	McQueen	Buchan M	Coppell	Greenhoff J	Ritchie	Macari	Thomas M 1	Nicholl replaced Greenhoff B
14 Mar	Tottenham Hotspur	55,584	Old Trafford	H W	2–0	Bailey	Nicholl	Albiston	McIlroy 1	McQueen	Buchan M	Coppell	Greenhoff J	Jordan 1	Grimes	Thomas M	Jordan replaced Ritchie
31 Mar	Liverpool	52,524	Maine Road	A D	2–2	Bailey	Nicholl	Albiston	McIlroy	McQueen	Buchan M	Coppell	Greenhoff J	Jordan 1	Greenhoff B 1	Thomas M	
4 Apr	Liverpool	53,069	Goodison Park	A W	1–0	Bailey	Nicholl	Albiston	McIlroy	McQueen	Buchan M	Coppell	Greenhoff J 1	Jordan	Macari	Thomas M	Ritchie replaced Macari
12 May	Arsenal	100,000	Wembley	A L	2–3	Bailey	Nicholl	Albiston	McIlroy 1	McQueen 1	Buchan M	Coppell	Greenhoff J	Jordan	Macari	Thomas M	

FL Cup

Date	Opponent	Attendances	Venue			Players and Scores											Substitutions
30 Aug	Stockport County	41,761	Old Trafford	H W	3–2	Roche	Greenhoff B	Albiston	McIlroy 1	McQueen	Buchan M	Coppell	Greenhoff J 1	Jordan 1	Macari	Grimes	
4 Oct	Watford	40,534	Old Trafford	H L	1–2	Roche	Albiston	Houston	Greenhoff B	McQueen	Buchan M	Coppell	Greenhoff J	Jordan 1	McIlroy	Grimes	McCreery replaced Greenhoff B

FOOTBALL LEAGUE DIVISION 1
P42 • W15 • D15 • L12 • F60 • A63 • PTS45
POSITION: 9

The 1980s

1979/80

Football League

Date	Opponent	Attendances	Venue			Players and Scores											Substitutions
18 Aug	Southampton	21,768	The Dell	A D	1–1	Bailey	Nicholl	Albiston	McIlroy	McQueen 1	Buchan M	Coppell	Wilkins	Jordan	Macari	Thomas M	
22 Aug	West Bromwich Alb.	53,377	Old Trafford	H W	2–0	Bailey	Nicholl	Albiston	McIlroy	McQueen 1	Buchan M	Coppell 1	Wilkins	Jordan	Macari	Thomas M	Ritchie replaced McIlroy
25 Aug	Arsenal	44,380	Highbury	A D	0–0	Bailey	Nicholl	Albiston	McIlroy	McQueen	Buchan M	Coppell	Wilkins	Jordan	Macari	Thomas M	Paterson replaced Coppell
1 Sep	Middlesbrough	51,015	Old Trafford	H W	2–1	Bailey	Nicholl	Albiston	McIlroy	McQueen	Buchan M	Coppell	Wilkins	Jordan	Macari 2	Thomas M	
8 Sep	Aston Villa	34,859	Villa Park	A W	3–0	Bailey	Nicholl	Albiston	McIlroy	McQueen	Buchan M	Coppell 1	Wilkins	Jordan	Macari	Thomas M 1	Grimes 1 replaced Jordan
15 Sep	Derby County	54,308	Old Trafford	H W	1–0	Bailey	Nicholl	Albiston	McIlroy	McQueen	Buchan M	Coppell	Wilkins	Ritchie	Macari	Grimes 1	
22 Sep	Wolverhampton Wan.	35,503	Molineux	A L	1–3	Bailey	Nicholl	Albiston	McIlroy	McQueen	Buchan M	Grimes	Wilkins	Coppell	Macari 1	Thomas M	
29 Sep	Stoke City	52,596	Old Trafford	H W	4–0	Bailey	Nicholl	Albiston	McIlroy 1	McQueen 2	Buchan M	Grimes	Wilkins 1	Coppell	Macari	Thomas M	Sloan replaced Macari
6 Oct	Brighton & Hove Alb.	52,641	Old Trafford	H W	2–0	Bailey	Nicholl	Albiston	McIlroy	McQueen	Buchan M	Grimes	Wilkins	Coppell 1	Macari 1	Thomas M	
10 Oct	West Bromwich Alb.	27,713	The Hawthorns	A L	0–2	Bailey	Nicholl	Albiston	McIlroy	McQueen	Buchan M	Grimes	Wilkins	Coppell	Macari	Thomas M	
13 Oct	Bristol City	28,305	Ashton Gate	A D	1–1	Bailey	Nicholl	Albiston	McIlroy	McQueen	Buchan M	Grimes	Wilkins	Coppell	Macari 1	Thomas M	
20 Oct	Ipswich Town	50,826	Old Trafford	H W	1–0	Bailey	Nicholl	Albiston	McIlroy	McQueen	Buchan M	Grimes 1	Wilkins	Coppell	Macari	Thomas M	
27 Oct	Everton	37,708	Goodison Park	A D	0–0	Bailey	Nicholl	Albiston	McIlroy	McQueen	Buchan M	Grimes	Wilkins	Coppell	Macari	Thomas M	Sloan replaced Albiston
3 Nov	Southampton	50,215	Old Trafford	H W	1–0	Bailey	Nicholl	Houston	McIlroy	Moran	Buchan M	Grimes	Wilkins	Coppell	Macari 1	Thomas M	
10 Nov	Manchester City	50,067	Maine Road	A L	0–2	Bailey	Nicholl	Houston	McIlroy	Moran	Buchan M	Grimes	Wilkins	Coppell	Macari	Thomas M	
17 Nov	Crystal Palace	52,800	Old Trafford	H D	1–1	Bailey	Nicholl	Houston	McIlroy	Moran	Buchan M	Coppell	Wilkins	Jordan 1	Macari	Thomas M	Grimes replaced Thomas M
24 Nov	Norwich City	46,540	Old Trafford	H W	5–0	Bailey	Nicholl	Grimes	McIlroy	Moran 1	Buchan M	Coppell 1	Wilkins	Jordan 2	Macari 1	Thomas M	
1 Dec	Tottenham Hotspur	51,389	White Hart Lane	A W	2–1	Bailey	Nicholl	Grimes	McIlroy	Moran	Buchan M	Coppell 1	Wilkins	Jordan	Macari 1	Thomas M	
8 Dec	Leeds United	58,348	Old Trafford	H D	1–1	Bailey	Nicholl	Grimes	McIlroy	Moran	Buchan M	Coppell	Wilkins	Jordan	Macari	Thomas M 1	
15 Dec	Coventry City	25,541	Highfield Road	A W	2–1	Bailey	Nicholl	Houston	McIlroy	McQueen 1	Buchan M	Coppell	Wilkins	Jordan	Macari 1	Thomas M	
22 Dec	Nottingham Forest	54,607	Old Trafford	H W	3–0	Bailey	Nicholl	Houston	McIlroy	McQueen 1	Buchan M	Coppell	Wilkins	Jordan 2	Macari	Thomas M	
26 Dec	Liverpool	51,073	Anfield	A L	0–2	Bailey	Nicholl	Houston	McIlroy	McQueen	Buchan M	Coppell	Wilkins	Jordan	Macari	Thomas M	Grimes replaced Thomas M
29 Dec	Arsenal	54,295	Old Trafford	H W	3–0	Bailey	Nicholl	Houston	McIlroy 1	McQueen 1	Buchan M	Coppell	Wilkins	Jordan 1	Macari	Thomas M	
12 Jan	Middlesbrough	30,587	Ayresome Park	A D	1–1	Bailey	Nicholl	Houston	McIlroy	McQueen	Buchan M	Coppell	Wilkins	Jordan	Macari	Thomas M 1	McGrath C replaced Thomas M
2 Feb	Derby County	27,783	Baseball Ground	A W	•3–1	Bailey	Nicholl	Houston	McIlroy 1	McQueen	Buchan M	Coppell	Jovanovic	Jordan	Macari	Thomas M 1	Grimes replaced Jovanovic
9 Feb	Wolverhampton Wan.	51,568	Old Trafford	H L	0–1	Bailey	Nicholl	Houston	McIlroy	McQueen	Buchan M	Coppell	Wilkins	Jordan	Macari	Thomas M	Grimes replaced Wilkins
16 Feb	Stoke City	28,389	Victoria Ground	A D	1–1	Bailey	Nicholl	Houston	McIlroy	McQueen	Buchan M	Coppell 1	Wilkins	Jordan	Macari	Grimes	Ritchie replaced Macari
23 Feb	Bristol City	43,329	Old Trafford	H W	•4–0	Bailey	Nicholl	Houston	McIlroy 1	McQueen	Buchan M	Coppell	Wilkins	Jordan 2	Macari	Grimes	Ritchie replaced McQueen
27 Feb	Bolton Wanderers	47,546	Old Trafford	H W	2–0	Bailey	Nicholl	Houston	McIlroy	McQueen 1	Buchan M	Coppell 1	Wilkins	Jordan	Macari	Grimes	Sloan replaced Wilkins
1 Mar	Ipswich Town	30,229	Portman Road	A L	0–6	Bailey	Nicholl	Houston	McIlroy	McQueen	Buchan M	Coppell	Sloan	Jordan	Macari	Grimes	Jovanovic replaced Nicholl
12 Mar	Everton	45,515	Old Trafford	H D	0–0	Bailey	Nicholl	Albiston	McIlroy	McQueen	Buchan M	Coppell	Wilkins	Jordan	Macari	Grimes	Greenhoff J replaced Macari
15 Mar	Brighton & Hove Alb.	29,621	Goldstone Ground	A D	0–0	Bailey	Nicholl	Albiston	McIlroy	McQueen	Buchan M	Coppell	Wilkins	Jordan	Macari	Grimes	
22 Mar	Manchester City	56,387	Old Trafford	H W	1–0	Bailey	Nicholl	Albiston	McIlroy	McQueen	Buchan M	Coppell	Wilkins	Jordan	Macari	Thomas M 1	Grimes replaced Thomas M
29 Mar	Crystal Palace	33,056	Selhurst Park	A W	2–0	Bailey	Nicholl	Albiston	McIlroy	McQueen	Buchan M	Coppell	Wilkins	Jordan 1	Macari	Thomas M 1	
2 Apr	Nottingham Forest	31,417	City Ground	A L	0–2	Bailey	Nicholl	Albiston	McIlroy	McQueen	Buchan M	Coppell	Wilkins	Jordan	Macari	Thomas M	
5 Apr	Liverpool	57,342	Old Trafford	H W	2–1	Bailey	Nicholl	Albiston	Greenhoff J 1	McQueen	Buchan M	Coppell	Wilkins	Jordan	Macari	Thomas M 1	
7 Apr	Bolton Wanderers	31,902	Burnden Park	A W	3–1	Bailey	Nicholl	Albiston	McIlroy	McQueen 1	Buchan M	Coppell 1	Wilkins	Jordan	Grimes	Thomas M 1	Ritchie replaced Wilkins
12 Apr	Tottenham Hotspur	53,151	Old Trafford	H W	4–1	Bailey	Nicholl	Albiston	McIlroy	McQueen	Buchan M	Coppell	Wilkins 1	Jordan	Ritchie 3	Thomas M	
19 Apr	Norwich City	23,274	Carrow Road	A W	2–0	Bailey	Nicholl	Albiston	McIlroy	Moran	Buchan M	Coppell	Wilkins	Jordan 2	Ritchie	Thomas M	
23 Apr	Aston Villa	45,201	Old Trafford	H W	2–1	Bailey	Nicholl	Albiston	McIlroy	Moran	Buchan M	Coppell	Greenhoff J	Jordan 2	Macari	Thomas M	
26 Apr	Coventry City	52,154	Old Trafford	H W	2–1	Bailey	Nicholl	Albiston	McIlroy 2	Moran	Buchan M	Coppell	Greenhoff J	Jordan	Macari	Thomas M	Sloan replaced Greenhoff J
3 May	Leeds United	39,625	Elland Road	A L	0–2	Bailey	Nicholl	Albiston	McIlroy	McQueen	Buchan M	Coppell	Greenhoff J	Jordan	Macari	Thomas M	Ritchie replaced Buchan M

FA Cup

Date	Opponent	Attendances	Venue			Players and Scores											Substitutions
5 Jan	Tottenham Hotspur	45,207	White Hart Lane	A D	1–1	Bailey	Nicholl	Houston	McIlroy 1	McQueen	Buchan M	Coppell	Wilkins	Jordan	Macari	Thomas M	
9 Jan	Tottenham Hotspur	53,762	Old Trafford	H L	0–1	Bailey	Nicholl	Houston	McIlroy	McQueen	Buchan M	Coppell	Wilkins	Jordan	Macari	Thomas M	

FL Cup

Date	Opponent	Attendances	Venue			Players and Scores											Substitutions
29 Aug	Tottenham Hotspur	29,163	White Hart Lane	A L	1–2	Bailey	Nicholl	Albiston	Paterson	McQueen	Buchan M	Ritchie	Wilkins	Jordan	Macari	Thomas M 1	
5 Sep	Tottenham Hotspur	48,292	Old Trafford	H W	•3–1	Bailey	Nicholl	Albiston	McIlroy	Houston	Buchan M	Coppell 1	Wilkins	Jordan	Macari	Thomas M 1	Ritchie replaced Houston
26 Sep	Norwich City	18,312	Carrow Road	A L	1–4	Bailey	Nicholl	Albiston	McIlroy 1	McQueen	Buchan M	Grimes	Wilkins	Coppell	Macari	Thomas M	Ritchie replaced McIlroy

FOOTBALL LEAGUE DIVISION 1
P42 • W24 • D10 • L8 • F65 • A35 • PTS58
POSITION: 2

Results

1980/81

Football League

		Attendances	Venue				Players and Scores											Substitutions
16 Aug	Middlesbrough	54,394	Old Trafford	H	W	3–0	Bailey	Nicholl	Albiston	McIlroy	Moran	Buchan M	Coppell	Greenhoff J	Jordan	Macari 1	Thomas M 1	Grimes 1 replaced Jordan
19 Aug	Wolverhampton Wan.	31,955	Molineux	A	L	0–1	Roche	Nicholl	Albiston	McIlroy	Moran	Buchan M	Grimes	Greenhoff J	Coppell	Macari	Thomas M	Ritchie replaced Grimes
23 Aug	Birmingham City	28,661	St Andrews	A	D	0–0	Roche	Nicholl	Albiston	McIlroy	Moran	Buchan M	McGrath C	Coppell	Ritchie	Macari	Thomas M	Duxbury replaced Moran
30 Aug	Sunderland	51,498	Old Trafford	H	D	1–1	Bailey	Nicholl	Albiston	McIlroy	Jovanovic 1	Buchan M	Coppell	Greenhoff J	Ritchie	Macari	Thomas M	
6 Sep	Tottenham Hotspur	40,995	White Hart Lane	A	D	0–0	Bailey	Nicholl	Albiston	McIlroy	Jovanovic	Buchan M	Coppell	Greenhoff J	Ritchie	Macari	Thomas M	Duxbury replaced Ritchie
13 Sep	Leicester City	43,229	Old Trafford	H	W	5–0	Bailey	Nicholl	Albiston	McIlroy	Jovanovic 2	Buchan M	Grimes 1	Greenhoff J	Coppell 1	Macari 1	Thomas M	McGarvey replaced Macari
20 Sep	Leeds United	32,539	Elland Road	A	D	0–0	Bailey	Nicholl	Albiston	McIlroy	Jovanovic	Buchan M	Grimes	Greenhoff J	Coppell	Macari	Thomas M	Duxbury replaced Macari
27 Sep	Manchester City	55,918	Old Trafford	H	D	2–2	Bailey	Nicholl	Albiston 1	McIlroy	McQueen	Buchan M	Grimes	Greenhoff J	Coppell 1	Duxbury	Thomas M	Sloan replaced Duxbury
4 Oct	Nottingham Forest	29,801	City Ground	A	W	2–1	Bailey	Nicholl	Albiston	McIlroy	Jovanovic	Moran	Duxbury	Coppell 1	Jordan	Macari 1	Thomas M	
8 Oct	Aston Villa	38,831	Old Trafford	H	D	3–3	Bailey	Nicholl	Albiston	McIlroy 2	Jovanovic	Moran	Duxbury	Coppell 1	Jordan	Macari	Thomas M	Greenhoff J replaced Macari
11 Oct	Arsenal	49,036	Old Trafford	H	D	0–0	Bailey	Nicholl	Albiston	McIlroy	Jovanovic	Moran	Grimes	Coppell	Jordan	Duxbury	Thomas M	
18 Oct	Ipswich Town	28,572	Portman Road	A	D	1–1	Bailey	Nicholl	Albiston	McIlroy 1	Jovanovic	Moran	Coppell	Duxbury	Jordan	Macari	Thomas M	
22 Oct	Stoke City	24,534	Victoria Ground	A	W	2–1	Bailey	Nicholl	Albiston	McIlroy	Jovanovic	Moran	Coppell	Birtles	Jordan 1	Macari 1	Thomas M	Duxbury replaced Jovanovic
25 Oct	Everton	54,260	Old Trafford	H	W	2–0	Bailey	Nicholl	Albiston	McIlroy	Moran	Duxbury	Coppell 1	Birtles	Jordan 1	Macari	Thomas M	
1 Nov	Crystal Palace	31,449	Selhurst Park	A	L	0–1	Bailey	Nicholl	Albiston	McIlroy	Jovanovic	Moran	Coppell	Birtles	Jordan	Macari	Thomas M	
8 Nov	Coventry City	42,794	Old Trafford	H	D	0–0	Bailey	Nicholl	Albiston	McIlroy	Jovanovic	Moran	Coppell	Birtles	Jordan	Macari	Thomas M	Sloan replaced Jovanovic
12 Nov	Wolverhampton Wan.	37,959	Old Trafford	H	D	0–0	Bailey	Nicholl	Albiston	McIlroy	Moran	Duxbury	Coppell	Birtles	Jordan	Macari	Thomas M	
15 Nov	Middlesbrough	20,606	Ayresome Park	A	D	1–1	Bailey	Nicholl	Albiston	McIlroy	Moran	Duxbury	Coppell	Birtles	Jordan 1	Macari	Thomas M	
22 Nov	Brighton & Hove Alb.	23,923	Goldstone Ground	A	W	4–1	Bailey	Nicholl	Albiston	McIlroy 1	Jovanovic	Moran	Coppell	Birtles	Jordan 2	Duxbury 1	Thomas M	Grimes replaced Birtles
29 Nov	Southampton	46,840	Old Trafford	H	D	1–1	Bailey	Jovanovic	Albiston	McIlroy	Moran	Duxbury	Coppell	Birtles	Jordan 1	Macari	Grimes	Whelan A replaced Moran
6 Dec	Norwich City	18,780	Carrow Road	A	D	•2–2	Bailey	Nicholl	Albiston	McIlroy	Jovanovic	Buchan M	Coppell 1	Greenhoff J	Jordan	Macari	Duxbury	
13 Dec	Stoke City	39,568	Old Trafford	H	D	2–2	Bailey	Nicholl	Albiston	McIlroy	Jovanovic	Moran	Coppell	Duxbury	Jordan 1	Macari 1	Thomas M	
20 Dec	Arsenal	33,730	Highbury	A	L	1–2	Bailey	Nicholl	Albiston	McIlroy	Jovanovic	Moran	Coppell	Duxbury	Jordan	Macari 1	Thomas M	
26 Dec	Liverpool	57,049	Old Trafford	H	D	0–0	Bailey	Nicholl	Albiston	McIlroy	Jovanovic	Moran	Coppell	Duxbury	Jordan	Macari	Thomas M	
27 Dec	West Bromwich Alb.	30,326	The Hawthorns	A	L	1–3	Bailey	Nicholl	Albiston	McIlroy	Jovanovic 1	Moran	Coppell	Duxbury	Jordan	Macari	Thomas M	
10 Jan	Brighton & Hove Alb.	42,208	Old Trafford	H	W	2–1	Bailey	Nicholl	Albiston	Wilkins	McQueen 1	Buchan M	Coppell	Birtles	Jordan	Macari 1	Thomas M	Duxbury replaced Wilkins
28 Jan	Sunderland	31,910	Roker Park	A	L	0–2	Bailey	Nicholl	Albiston	Duxbury	McQueen	Buchan M	Coppell	Birtles	Jordan	Macari	Thomas M	
31 Jan	Birmingham City	39,081	Old Trafford	H	W	2–0	Bailey	Nicholl	Albiston	Duxbury	McQueen	Buchan M	Coppell	Birtles	Jordan 1	Macari 1	Thomas M	McIlroy replaced Thomas M
7 Feb	Leicester City	26,085	Filbert Street	A	L	0–1	Bailey	Nicholl	Albiston	Duxbury	Jovanovic	Buchan M	Coppell	Birtles	Jordan	Macari	Thomas M	Wilkins replaced Jovanovic
17 Feb	Tottenham Hotspur	40,642	Old Trafford	H	D	0–0	Bailey	Nicholl	Albiston	Duxbury	Moran	Buchan M	Coppell	Wilkins	Birtles	Macari	McIlroy	
21 Feb	Manchester City	50,114	Maine Road	A	L	0–1	Bailey	Nicholl	Albiston	Duxbury	Moran	Buchan M	Coppell	Wilkins	Birtles	Macari	McIlroy	McGarvey replaced Duxbury
28 Feb	Leeds United	45,733	Old Trafford	H	L	0–1	Bailey	Nicholl	Albiston	Wilkins	Moran	Buchan M	Coppell	Birtles	Jordan	Macari	McIlroy	
7 Mar	Southampton	22,698	The Dell	A	L	0–1	Bailey	Nicholl	Albiston	Wilkins	Moran	Buchan M	Coppell	Birtles	Jordan	Macari	McIlroy	
14 Mar	Aston Villa	42,182	Villa Park	A	D	3–3	Bailey	Nicholl	Albiston	Wilkins	Moran	Buchan M	Coppell	Birtles	Jordan 2	Macari	McIlroy 1	
18 Mar	Nottingham Forest	38,205	Old Trafford	H	D	•1–1	Bailey	Nicholl	Albiston	Wilkins	Moran	Buchan M	Coppell	Birtles	Jordan	Macari	McIlroy	Duxbury replaced McIlroy
21 Mar	Ipswich Town	46,685	Old Trafford	H	W	2–1	Bailey	Nicholl 1	Albiston	Moran	McQueen	Buchan M	Coppell	Birtles	Jordan	Duxbury	Thomas M 1	
28 Mar	Everton	25,856	Goodison Park	A	W	1–0	Bailey	Nicholl	Albiston	Moran	McQueen	Buchan M	Coppell	Birtles	Jordan 1	Duxbury	Thomas M	Macari replaced Nicholl
4 Apr	Crystal Palace	37,954	Old Trafford	H	W	1–0	Bailey	Duxbury 1	Albiston	Moran	McQueen	Buchan M	Coppell	Birtles	Jordan	Macari	Thomas M	Wilkins replaced Thomas M
11 Apr	Coventry City	20,201	Highfield Road	A	W	2–0	Bailey	Duxbury	Albiston	Moran	McQueen	Buchan M	Coppell	Birtles	Jordan 2	Macari	Wilkins	
14 Apr	Liverpool	31,276	Anfield	A	W	1–0	Bailey	Duxbury	Albiston	Moran	McQueen 1	Buchan M	Coppell	Birtles	Jordan	Macari	Wilkins	
18 Apr	West Bromwich Alb.	44,442	Old Trafford	H	W	2–1	Bailey	Duxbury	Albiston	Moran	McQueen	Buchan M	Coppell	Birtles	Jordan 1	Macari 1	Wilkins	
25 Apr	Norwich City	40,165	Old Trafford	H	W	1–0	Bailey	Duxbury	Albiston	Moran	McQueen	Buchan M	Coppell	Birtles	Jordan 1	Macari	Wilkins	

FA Cup

3 Jan	Brighton & Hove Alb.	42,199	Old Trafford	H	D	2–2	Bailey	Nicholl	Albiston	McIlroy	Jovanovic	Moran	Coppell	Birtles	Jordan	Macari	Thomas M 1	Duxbury 1 replaced McIlroy
7 Jan	Brighton & Hove Alb.	26,915	Goldstone Ground	A	W	2–0	Bailey	Nicholl 1	Albiston	Wilkins	McQueen	Buchan M	Coppell	Birtles 1	Jordan	Macari	Thomas M	Duxbury replaced Wilkins
24 Jan	Nottingham Forest	34,110	City Ground	A	L	0–1	Bailey	Nicholl	Albiston	Wilkins	McQueen	Buchan M	Coppell	Birtles	Jordan	Macari	Thomas M	

FL Cup

27 Aug	Coventry City	31,656	Old Trafford	H	L	0–1	Bailey	Nicholl	Albiston	McIlroy	Jovanovic	Buchan M	Coppell	Greenhoff J	Ritchie	Macari	Thomas M	Sloan replaced Greenhoff J
2 Sep	Coventry City	18,946	Highfield Road	A	L	0–1	Bailey	Nicholl	Albiston	McIlroy	Jovanovic	Buchan M	Coppell	Greenhoff J	Ritchie	Macari	Thomas M	

UEFA Cup

17 Sep	Widzew Lodz	38,037	Old Trafford	H	D	1–1	Bailey	Nicholl	Albiston	McIlroy 1	Jovanovic	Buchan M	Grimes	Greenhoff J	Coppell	Macari	Thomas M	Duxbury replaced Nicholl
1 Oct	Widzew Lodz	40,000	Stadion TKS	A	D	0–0	Bailey	Nicholl	Albiston	McIlroy	Jovanovic	Buchan M	Grimes	Coppell	Jordan	Duxbury	Thomas M	Moran replaced Buchan M

Football League Division 1
P42 • W15 • D18 • L9 • F51 • A36 • PTS48
Position: 8

1981/82

Football League

		Attendances	Venue				Players and Scores											Substitutions
29 Aug	Coventry City	19,329	Highfield Road	A	L	1–2	Bailey	Gidman	Albiston	Wilkins	McQueen	Buchan M	Coppell	Birtles	Stapleton	Macari 1	McIlroy	
31 Aug	Nottingham Forest	51,496	Old Trafford	H	D	0–0	Bailey	Gidman	Albiston	Wilkins	McQueen	Buchan M	Coppell	Birtles	Stapleton	Macari	McIlroy	
5 Sep	Ipswich Town	45,555	Old Trafford	H	L	1–2	Bailey	Gidman	Albiston	Wilkins	McQueen	Buchan M	Coppell	Birtles	Stapleton 1	Macari	McIlroy	Duxbury replaced McIlroy
12 Sep	Aston Villa	37,661	Villa Park	A	D	1–1	Bailey	Gidman	Albiston	Wilkins	McQueen	Buchan M	Coppell	Birtles	Stapleton 1	Macari	McIlroy	
19 Sep	Swansea City	47,309	Old Trafford	H	W	1–0	Bailey	Gidman	Albiston	Wilkins	McQueen	Buchan M	Coppell	Birtles 1	Stapleton	Macari	McIlroy	Moses replaced McIlroy
22 Sep	Middlesbrough	19,895	Ayresome Park	A	W	2–0	Bailey	Gidman	Albiston	Wilkins	McQueen	Buchan M	Coppell	Birtles 1	Stapleton 1	Macari	Moses	Duxbury replaced Buchan M
26 Sep	Arsenal	39,795	Highbury	A	D	0–0	Bailey	Gidman	Albiston	Wilkins	McQueen	Buchan M	Coppell	Birtles	Stapleton	Macari	Moses	
30 Sep	Leeds United	47,019	Old Trafford	H	W	1–0	Bailey	Gidman	Albiston	Wilkins	McQueen	Buchan M	Coppell	Birtles	Stapleton 1	McIlroy	Moses	Duxbury replaced McQueen
3 Oct	Wolverhampton Wan.	46,837	Old Trafford	H	W	5–0	Bailey	Gidman	Albiston	Wilkins	Moran	Buchan M	Coppell	Birtles 1	Stapleton 1	McIlroy 3	Moses	
10 Oct	Manchester City	52,037	Maine Road	A	D	0–0	Bailey	Gidman	Albiston	Wilkins	Moran	Buchan M	Robson	Birtles	Stapleton	McIlroy	Moses	Coppell replaced Birtles
17 Oct	Birmingham City	48,800	Old Trafford	H	D	1–1	Bailey	Gidman	Albiston	Wilkins	Moran	Buchan M	Robson	Birtles	Stapleton	Moses	Coppell 1	
21 Oct	Middlesbrough	38,342	Old Trafford	H	W	1–0	Bailey	Gidman	Albiston	Wilkins	Duxbury	Buchan M	Robson	Birtles	Stapleton	Moses 1	Coppell	
24 Oct	Liverpool	41,438	Anfield	A	W	2–1	Bailey	Gidman	Albiston 1	Wilkins	Moran 1	Buchan M	Robson	Birtles	Stapleton	Moses	Coppell	
31 Oct	Notts County	45,928	Old Trafford	H	W	2–1	Bailey	Gidman	Albiston	Wilkins	Duxbury	Buchan M	Robson	Birtles 1	Stapleton	Moses 1	Coppell	Macari replaced Robson
7 Nov	Sunderland	27,070	Roker Park	A	W	5–1	Bailey	Gidman	Albiston	Wilkins	Moran 1	Buchan M	Robson 1	Birtles 1	Stapleton 2	Moses	Coppell	Duxbury replaced Gidman
21 Nov	Tottenham Hotspur	35,534	White Hart Lane	A	L	1–3	Roche	Duxbury	Albiston	Wilkins	Moran	Buchan M	Robson	Birtles 1	Stapleton	Moses	McIlroy	Nicholl replaced Buchan M
28 Nov	Brighton & Hove Alb.	41,911	Old Trafford	H	W	2–0	Roche	Gidman	Albiston	Wilkins	Moran	McQueen	Robson	Birtles 1	Stapleton 1	Moses	McIlroy	
5 Dec	Southampton	24,404	The Dell	A	L	2–3	Roche	Gidman	Albiston	Wilkins	Moran	McQueen	Robson 1	Birtles	Stapleton 1	Moses	McIlroy	
6 Jan	Everton	40,451	Old Trafford	H	D	1–1	Bailey	Gidman	Albiston	Wilkins	Moran	Buchan M	Robson	McGarvey	Stapleton 1	McIlroy	Coppell	
23 Jan	Stoke City	19,793	Victoria Ground	A	W	3–0	Bailey	Duxbury	Albiston	Wilkins	McQueen	Moran	Robson	Birtles 1	Stapleton 1	Macari	Coppell 1	
27 Jan	West Ham United	41,291	Old Trafford	H	W	1–0	Bailey	Duxbury	Albiston	Wilkins	Moran	McQueen	Robson	Birtles	Stapleton	Macari 1	Coppell	
30 Jan	Swansea City	24,115	Veitch Field	A	L	0–2	Bailey	Duxbury	Albiston	Wilkins	Moran	McQueen	Robson	Birtles	Stapleton	Macari	Coppell	Gidman replaced McQueen
6 Feb	Aston Villa	43,184	Old Trafford	H	W	4–1	Bailey	Gidman	Albiston	Wilkins	Moran 2	Buchan M	Robson 1	Birtles	Stapleton	Duxbury	Coppell 1	McGarvey replaced Birtles
13 Feb	Wolverhampton Wan.	22,481	Molineux	A	W	1–0	Bailey	Gidman	Albiston	Wilkins	Moran	Buchan M	Robson	Birtles 1	Stapleton	Duxbury	Coppell	
20 Feb	Arsenal	43,833	Old Trafford	H	D	0–0	Bailey	Gidman	Albiston	Wilkins	Moran	Buchan M	Robson	Birtles	Stapleton	Duxbury	Coppell	
27 Feb	Manchester City	57,830	Old Trafford	H	D	1–1	Bailey	Gidman	Albiston	Wilkins	Moran 1	Buchan M	Robson	Birtles	Stapleton	Duxbury	Coppell	
6 Mar	Birmingham City	19,637	St Andrews	A	W	1–0	Bailey	Gidman	Albiston	Wilkins	Moran	Buchan M	Robson	Birtles 1	Stapleton	Duxbury	Coppell	McGarvey replaced Moran
17 Mar	Coventry City	34,499	Old Trafford	H	L	0–1	Bailey	Gidman	Albiston	Wilkins	Moran	Buchan M	Robson	Birtles	Stapleton	Moses	Coppell	Duxbury replaced Robson
20 Mar	Notts County	17,048	County Ground	A	W	3–1	Bailey	Gidman	Albiston	Wilkins	Moran	Buchan M	Robson	Birtles	Stapleton 1	Moses	Coppell 2	McGarvey replaced Moran
27 Mar	Sunderland	40,776	Old Trafford	H	D	0–0	Bailey	Gidman	Albiston	Wilkins	McQueen	Buchan M	Robson	Birtles	Stapleton	Moses	Coppell	McGarvey replaced Birtles
3 Apr	Leeds United	30,953	Elland Road	A	D	0–0	Bailey	Duxbury	Albiston	Wilkins	Moran	Buchan M	Robson	McGarvey	Stapleton	Moses	Coppell	
7 Apr	Liverpool	48,371	Old Trafford	H	L	0–1	Bailey	Duxbury	Albiston	Wilkins	Moran	Buchan M	Robson	McGarvey	Stapleton	Moses	Coppell	Grimes replaced Buchan M
10 Apr	Everton	29,306	Goodison Park	A	D	3–3	Bailey	Gidman	Albiston	Wilkins	Moran	Duxbury	Robson	McGarvey	Stapleton	Moses	Coppell 2	Grimes 1 replaced Moses
12 Apr	West Bromwich Alb.	38,717	Old Trafford	H	W	1–0	Bailey	Gidman	Albiston	Wilkins	Moran 1	McQueen	Robson	McGarvey	Stapleton	Grimes	Coppell	
17 Apr	Tottenham Hotspur	50,724	Old Trafford	H	W	2–0	Bailey	Gidman	Albiston	Wilkins	Moran	McQueen	Robson	McGarvey 1	Stapleton	Grimes	Coppell 1	
20 Apr	Ipswich Town	25,744	Portman Road	A	L	1–2	Bailey	Gidman 1	Albiston	Wilkins	Moran	McQueen	Robson	McGarvey	Stapleton	Grimes	Duxbury	Birtles replaced McQueen
24 Apr	Brighton & Hove Alb.	20,750	Goldstone Ground	A	W	1–0	Bailey	Gidman	Albiston	Wilkins 1	Moran	McQueen	Robson	McGarvey	Stapleton	Grimes	Duxbury	Whiteside N replaced Duxbury
1 May	Southampton	40,038	Old Trafford	H	W	1–0	Bailey	Gidman	Albiston	Wilkins	Duxbury	McQueen	Robson	McGarvey 1	Stapleton	Grimes	Davies A	
5 May	Nottingham Forest	18,449	City Ground	A	W	1–0	Bailey	Gidman	Albiston	Wilkins	Moran	Duxbury	Robson	McGarvey	Stapleton 1	Grimes	Coppell	
8 May	West Ham United	26,337	Upton Park	A	D	1–1	Bailey	Gidman	Albiston	Wilkins	Moran 1	Duxbury	Moses	Birtles	Stapleton	Grimes	Coppell	McGarvey replaced Birtles
12 May	West Bromwich Alb.	19,707	The Hawthorns	A	W	3–0	Bailey	Gidman	Albiston	Wilkins	Moran	McQueen	Robson 1	Birtles 1	Stapleton	Grimes	Coppell 1	
15 May	Stoke City	43,072	Old Trafford	H	W	2–0	Bailey	Gidman	Albiston	Wilkins	Moran	McQueen	Robson 1	Birtles	Whiteside N 1	Grimes	Coppell	McGarvey replaced Birtles

FA Cup

2 Jan	Watford	26,104	Vicarage Road	A	L	0–1	Bailey	Gidman	Albiston	Wilkins	Moran	Buchan M	Robson	Birtles	Stapleton	Moses	McIlroy	Macari replaced Moses

FL Cup

7 Oct	Tottenham Hotspur	39,333	White Hart Lane	A	L	0–1	Bailey	Gidman	Albiston	Wilkins	Moran	Buchan M	Coppell	Birtles	Stapleton	McIlroy	Robson	Duxbury replaced Birtles
28 Oct	Tottenham Hotspur	55,890	Old Trafford	H	L	0–1	Bailey	Gidman	Albiston	Wilkins	Moran	Buchan M	Robson	Birtles	Stapleton	Moses	Coppell	

Football League Division 1
P42 • W22 • D12 • L8 • F59 • A29 • PTS78
Position: 3

1982/83

FOOTBALL LEAGUE

Date	Opponent	Attendances	Venue				Players and Scores											Substitutions
28 Aug	Birmingham City	48,673	Old Trafford	H	W	3–0	Bailey	Duxbury	Albiston	Wilkins	Moran 1	McQueen	Robson	Muhren	Stapleton 1	Whiteside N	Coppell 1	
1 Sep	Nottingham Forest	23,956	City Ground	A	W	3–0	Bailey	Duxbury	Albiston	Wilkins 1	Moran	McQueen	Robson 1	Muhren	Stapleton	Whiteside N 1	Coppell	
4 Sep	West Bromwich Alb.	24,928	The Hawthorns	A	L	1–3	Bailey	Duxbury	Albiston	Wilkins	Moran	McQueen	Robson 1	Muhren	Stapleton	Whiteside N	Coppell	
8 Sep	Everton	43,186	Old Trafford	H	W	2–1	Bailey	Duxbury	Albiston	Wilkins	Moran	McQueen	Robson 1	Muhren	Stapleton	Whiteside N 1	Coppell	
11 Sep	Ipswich Town	43,140	Old Trafford	H	W	3–1	Bailey	Duxbury	Albiston	Wilkins	Moran	McQueen	Robson	Muhren	Stapleton	Whiteside N 2	Coppell 1	
18 Sep	Southampton	21,700	The Dell	A	W	1–0	Bailey	Duxbury	Albiston	Wilkins	Buchan M	McQueen	Robson	Grimes	Stapleton	Whiteside N	Coppell	Macari 1 for Coppell
25 Sep	Arsenal	43,198	Old Trafford	H	D	0–0	Bailey	Duxbury	Albiston	Wilkins	Moran	McQueen	Robson	Grimes	Stapleton	Whiteside N	Macari	
2 Oct	Luton Town	17,009	Kenilworth Road	A	D	1–1	Bailey	Duxbury	Albiston	Wilkins	Moran	McQueen	Robson	Grimes 1	Stapleton	Whiteside N	Moses	
9 Oct	Stoke City	43,132	Old Trafford	H	W	1–0	Bailey	Duxbury	Albiston	Wilkins	Moran	McQueen	Robson 1	Grimes	Stapleton	Whiteside N	Moses	
16 Oct	Liverpool	40,853	Anfield	A	D	0–0	Bailey	Duxbury	Albiston	Wilkins	Moran	McQueen	Robson	Grimes	Stapleton	Whiteside N	Coppell	
23 Oct	Manchester City	57,334	Old Trafford	H	D	2–2	Bailey	Duxbury	Albiston	Wilkins	Moran	McQueen	Robson	Muhren	Stapleton 2	Whiteside N	Coppell	Macari for Muhren
30 Oct	West Ham United	31,684	Upton Park	A	L	1–3	Bailey	Duxbury	Albiston	Grimes	Moran 1	Buchan M	Robson	Muhren	Stapleton	Whiteside N	Coppell	
6 Nov	Brighton & Hove Alb.	18,379	Goldstone Ground	A	L	0–1	Bailey	Duxbury	Albiston	Moses	Moran	McQueen	Robson	Muhren	Stapleton	Whiteside N	Coppell	Macari for Moran
13 Nov	Tottenham Hotspur	47,869	Old Trafford	H	W	1–0	Bailey	Duxbury	Albiston	Moses	McGrath P	McQueen	Robson	Muhren 1	Stapleton	Whiteside N	Coppell	
20 Nov	Aston Villa	35,487	Villa Park	A	L	1–2	Bailey	Duxbury	Albiston	Moses	Moran	McQueen	Robson	Muhren	Stapleton 1	Whiteside N	Coppell	McGarvey for Whiteside N
27 Nov	Norwich City	34,579	Old Trafford	H	W	3–0	Bailey	Duxbury	Albiston	Moses	Moran	McQueen	Robson 2	Muhren 1	Stapleton	Whiteside N	Coppell	
4 Dec	Watford	25,669	Vicarage Road	A	W	1–0	Bailey	Duxbury	Albiston	Moses	Buchan M	McQueen	Robson	Muhren	Stapleton	Whiteside N 1	Coppell	
11 Dec	Notts County	33,618	Old Trafford	H	W	4–0	Bailey	Duxbury 1	Albiston	Moses	Moran	McQueen	Robson 1	Muhren	Stapleton 1	Whiteside N 1	Coppell	Grimes for Robson
18 Dec	Swansea City	15,748	Veitch Field	A	D	0–0	Bailey	Duxbury	Albiston	Moses	Moran	McQueen	Robson	Muhren	Stapleton	Whiteside N	Coppell	
27 Dec	Sunderland	47,783	Old Trafford	H	D	0–0	Bailey	Duxbury	Albiston	Moses	Moran	McQueen	Robson	Muhren	Stapleton	Whiteside N	Coppell	
28 Dec	Coventry City	18,945	Highfield Road	A	L	0–3	Bailey	Duxbury	Albiston	Moses	Moran	McQueen	Robson	Wilkins	Stapleton	McGarvey	Grimes	
1 Jan	Aston Villa	41,545	Old Trafford	H	W	3–1	Bailey	Duxbury	Albiston	Moses	Moran	McQueen	Robson	Muhren	Stapleton 2	Whiteside N	Coppell 1	
3 Jan	West Bromwich Alb.	39,123	Old Trafford	H	D	0–0	Bailey	Duxbury	Albiston	Moses	Moran	McQueen	Robson	Muhren	Stapleton	Whiteside N	Coppell	
15 Jan	Birmingham City	19,333	St Andrews	A	W	2–1	Bailey	Duxbury	Albiston	Moses	Moran	McQueen	Robson 1	Muhren	Stapleton	Whiteside N 1	Coppell	
22 Jan	Nottingham Forest	38,615	Old Trafford	H	W	2–0	Bailey	Duxbury	Albiston	Moses	Moran	McQueen	Robson	Muhren 1	Stapleton	Whiteside N	Coppell 1	
5 Feb	Ipswich Town	23,804	Portman Road	A	D	1–1	Bailey	Duxbury	Albiston	Moses	Moran	McQueen	Robson	Muhren	Stapleton 1	Whiteside N	Coppell	
26 Feb	Liverpool	57,397	Old Trafford	H	D	1–1	Bailey	Duxbury	Albiston	Moses	Moran	McQueen	Wilkins	Muhren 1	Stapleton	Whiteside N	Coppell	Macari for Moran
2 Mar	Stoke City	21,266	Victoria Ground	A	L	0–1	Bailey	Duxbury	Albiston	Moses	McGrath P	McQueen	Wilkins	Muhren	Stapleton	Whiteside N	Coppell	
5 Mar	Manchester City	45,400	Maine Road	A	W	2–1	Bailey	Duxbury	Albiston	Moses	McGrath P	McQueen	Wilkins	Muhren	Stapleton 2	Whiteside N	Coppell	
19 Mar	Brighton & Hove Alb.	36,264	Old Trafford	H	D	1–1	Bailey	Gidman	Albiston 1	Grimes	McGrath P	Duxbury	Wilkins	Muhren	Stapleton	Whiteside N	Coppell	Macari for Wilkins
22 Mar	West Ham United	30,227	Old Trafford	H	W	2–1	Bailey	Gidman	Albiston	Moses	McGrath P	Duxbury	Wilkins	Muhren	Stapleton 1	McGarvey 1	Coppell	Macari for Stapleton
2 Apr	Coventry City	36,814	Old Trafford	H	W	•3–0	Wealands	Duxbury	Albiston	Moses	McGrath P	McQueen	Wilkins	Muhren	Stapleton 1	Whiteside N	Coppell	Macari 1 for Whiteside N
4 Apr	Sunderland	31,486	Roker Park	A	D	0–0	Wealands	Duxbury	Albiston	Moses	McGrath P	McQueen	Wilkins	Muhren	Stapleton	Macari	Coppell	McGarvey for Macari
9 Apr	Southampton	37,120	Old Trafford	H	D	1–1	Bailey	Duxbury	Albiston	Moses	McGrath P	McQueen	Robson 1	Muhren	Stapleton	Whiteside N	Wilkins	
19 Apr	Everton	21,715	Goodison Park	A	L	0–2	Wealands	Duxbury	Albiston	Moses	McGrath P	McQueen	Robson	Wilkins	Stapleton	Whiteside N	Grimes	Cunningham L for Whiteside N
23 Apr	Watford	43,048	Old Trafford	H	W	2–0	Wealands	Duxbury	Albiston	Moses	McGrath P	McQueen	Robson	Wilkins	Stapleton	Whiteside N	Grimes 1	Cunningham L 1 for Albiston
30 Apr	Norwich City	22,233	Carrow Road	A	D	1–1	Bailey	Duxbury	Grimes	Moses	Moran	McQueen	Robson	Wilkins	Stapleton	Whiteside N 1	Cunningham L	
2 May	Arsenal	23,602	Highbury	A	L	0–3	Bailey	Duxbury	Grimes	Moses	Moran	McQueen	McGrath P	Wilkins	McGarvey	Whiteside N	Cunningham L	
7 May	Swansea City	35,724	Old Trafford	H	W	2–1	Bailey	Duxbury	Grimes	Wilkins	Moran	McQueen	Robson 1	Muhren	Stapleton 1	Whiteside N	Cunningham L	Davies A for Wilkins
9 May	Luton Town	34,213	Old Trafford	H	W	3–0	Bailey	Duxbury	Grimes	McGrath P 2	Moran	McQueen	Robson	Muhren	Stapleton 1	Whiteside N	Davies A	McGarvey for Whiteside N
11 May	Tottenham Hotspur	32,803	White Hart Lane	A	L	0–2	Bailey	Duxbury	Albiston	Moses	Moran	McGrath P	Robson	Muhren	Stapleton	Whiteside N	Grimes	McGarvey for Robson
14 May	Notts County	14,395	County Ground	A	L	2–3	Wealands	Gidman	Albiston	Moses	McGrath P 1	Duxbury	Wilkins	Muhren 1	Stapleton	Whiteside N	Davies A	

FA CUP

8 Jan	West Ham United	44,143	Old Trafford	H	W	2–0	Bailey	Duxbury	Albiston	Moses	Moran	McQueen	Robson	Muhren	Stapleton 1	Whiteside N	Coppell 1	
29 Jan	Luton Town	20,516	Kenilworth Road	A	W	2–0	Bailey	Duxbury	Albiston	Moses 1	Moran 1	McQueen	Robson	Muhren	Stapleton	Whiteside N	Coppell	
19 Feb	Derby County	33,022	Baseball Ground	A	W	1–0	Bailey	Duxbury	Albiston	Moses	Moran	McQueen	Robson	Muhren	Stapleton	Whiteside N 1	Coppell	
12 Mar	Everton	58,198	Old Trafford	H	W	1–0	Bailey	Duxbury	Albiston	Moses	Moran	McQueen	Wilkins	Muhren	Stapleton 1	Whiteside N	Coppell	Macari for Duxbury
16 Apr	Arsenal	46,535	Villa Park	A	W	2–1	Bailey	Duxbury	Albiston	Moses	Moran	McQueen	Robson 1	Wilkins	Stapleton	Whiteside N 1	Grimes	McGrath P for Moran
21 May	Brighton & Hove Alb.	100,000	Wembley	A	D	2–2	Bailey	Duxbury	Albiston	Wilkins 1	Moran	McQueen	Robson	Muhren	Stapleton 1	Whiteside N	Davies A	
26 May	Brighton & Hove Alb.	92,000	Wembley	A	W	4–0	Bailey	Duxbury	Albiston	Wilkins	Moran	McQueen	Robson 2	Muhren 1	Stapleton	Whiteside N 1	Davies A	

FL CUP

6 Oct	Bournemouth	22,091	Old Trafford	H	W	•2–0	Bailey	Duxbury	Albiston	Wilkins	Moran	McQueen	Robson	Grimes	Stapleton 1	Beardsley	Moses	Whiteside N for Beardsley
26 Oct	Bournemouth	13,226	Dean Court	A	D	2–2	Bailey	Duxbury	Albiston	Wilkins	Grimes	Buchan M	Robson	Muhren 1	Stapleton	Whiteside N	Coppell 1	Macari for Wilkins
10 Nov	Bradford City	15,568	Valley Parade	A	D	0–0	Bailey	Duxbury	Albiston	Moses	McGrath P	McQueen	Robson	Muhren	Stapleton	Whiteside N	Coppell	
24 Nov	Bradford City	24,507	Old Trafford	H	W	4–1	Bailey	Duxbury	Albiston 1	Moses 1	Moran 1	McQueen	Robson	Muhren	Stapleton	Macari	Coppell 1	Whiteside N for Coppell
1 Dec	Southampton	28,378	Old Trafford	H	W	2–0	Bailey	Duxbury	Albiston	Moses	Moran	McQueen 1	Robson	Muhren	Stapleton	Whiteside N 1	Coppell	
19 Jan	Nottingham Forest	44,413	Old Trafford	H	W	4–0	Bailey	Duxbury	Albiston	Moses	Moran	McQueen 2	Robson 1	Muhren	Stapleton	Whiteside N	Coppell 1	
15 Feb	Arsenal	43,136	Highbury	A	W	4–2	Bailey	Duxbury	Albiston	Moses	Moran	McQueen	Robson	Muhren	Stapleton 1	Whiteside N 1	Coppell 2	
23 Feb	Arsenal	56,635	Old Trafford	H	W	2–1	Bailey	Duxbury	Albiston	Moses	Moran 1	McQueen	Robson	Muhren	Stapleton	Whiteside N	Coppell 1	Wilkins for Robson
26 Mar	Liverpool	100,000	Wembley	A	L	1–2	Bailey	Duxbury	Albiston	Moses	Moran	McQueen	Wilkins	Muhren	Stapleton	Whiteside N 1	Coppell	Macari for Moran

UEFA CUP

15 Sep	Valencia	46,588	Old Trafford	H	D	0–0	Bailey	Duxbury	Albiston	Wilkins	Buchan M	McQueen	Robson	Grimes	Stapleton	Whiteside N	Coppell	
29 Sep	Valencia	35,000	Luis Casanova	A	L	1–2	Bailey	Duxbury	Albiston	Wilkins	Moran	Buchan M	Robson 1	Grimes	Stapleton	Whiteside N	Moses	Macari for Buchan M, Coppell for Moses

FOOTBALL LEAGUE DIVISION 1
P42 • W19 • D13 • L10 • F56 • A38 • PTS70
POSITION: 3

1983/84

FOOTBALL LEAGUE

Date	Opponent	Attendances	Venue				Players and Scores											Substitutions
27 Aug	Queen's Park Rangers	48,742	Old Trafford	H	W	3–1	Bailey	Duxbury	Albiston	Wilkins	Moran	McQueen	Robson	Muhren 2	Stapleton 1	Whiteside N	Graham A	Macari for Whiteside N
29 Aug	Nottingham Forest	43,005	Old Trafford	H	L	1–2	Bailey	Duxbury	Albiston	Wilkins	Moran 1	McQueen	Robson	Muhren	Stapleton	Whiteside N	Graham A	Macari for Duxbury
3 Sep	Stoke City	23,704	Victoria Ground	A	W	1–0	Bailey	Gidman	Albiston	Wilkins	Moran	McQueen	Robson	Muhren 1	Stapleton	Whiteside N	Graham A	
6 Sep	Arsenal	42,703	Highbury	A	W	3–2	Bailey	Gidman	Albiston	Wilkins	Moran 1	McQueen	Robson 1	Muhren	Stapleton 1	Whiteside N	Graham A	Moses for Graham A
10 Sep	Luton Town	41,013	Old Trafford	H	W	2–0	Bailey	Gidman	Albiston 1	Wilkins	Moran	McQueen	Robson	Muhren 1	Stapleton	Whiteside N	Graham A	Moses for Robson
17 Sep	Southampton	20,674	The Dell	A	L	0–3	Bailey	Duxbury	Albiston	Wilkins	Moran	McQueen	Moses	Muhren	Stapleton	Whiteside N	Graham A	
24 Sep	Liverpool	56,121	Old Trafford	H	W	1–0	Bailey	Duxbury	Albiston	Wilkins	Moran	McQueen	Robson	Muhren	Stapleton 1	Whiteside N	Graham A	
1 Oct	Norwich City	19,290	Carrow Road	A	D	3–3	Bailey	Duxbury	Albiston	Wilkins	Moran	McGrath P	Robson	Muhren	Stapleton 1	Whiteside N 2	Graham A	Moses for Muhren
15 Oct	West Bromwich Alb.	42,221	Old Trafford	H	W	3–0	Bailey	Duxbury	Albiston 1	Wilkins	Moran	McQueen	Robson	Muhren	Stapleton	Whiteside N 1	Graham A 1	
22 Oct	Sunderland	26,826	Roker Park	A	W	1–0	Bailey	Duxbury	Albiston	Wilkins 1	Moran	McQueen	Robson	Moses	Stapleton	Whiteside N	Graham A	Macari for Moran
29 Oct	Wolverhampton Wan.	41,880	Old Trafford	H	W	3–0	Bailey	Gidman	Albiston	Wilkins	Duxbury	McQueen	Robson 1	Muhren	Stapleton 2	Whiteside N	Graham A	Moses for Gidman
5 Nov	Aston Villa	45,077	Old Trafford	H	L	1–2	Bailey	Duxbury	Albiston	Wilkins	Moran	McQueen	Robson 1	Moses	Stapleton	Whiteside N	Graham A	Macari for Whiteside N
12 Nov	Leicester City	24,409	Filbert Street	A	D	1–1	Bailey	Duxbury	Albiston	Wilkins	Moran	McQueen	Robson 1	Moses	Stapleton	Whiteside N	Graham A	
19 Nov	Watford	43,111	Old Trafford	H	W	4–1	Bailey	Moses	Albiston	Wilkins	Duxbury	McQueen	Robson 1	Muhren	Stapleton 3	Crooks	Graham A	
27 Nov	West Ham United	23,355	Upton Park	A	D	1–1	Bailey	Moses	Albiston	Wilkins 1	Duxbury	McQueen	Robson	Muhren	Stapleton	Crooks	Graham A	Whiteside N for Muhren
3 Dec	Everton	43,664	Old Trafford	H	L	0–1	Bailey	Duxbury	Albiston	Wilkins	Moran	McQueen	Robson	Moses	Stapleton	Crooks	Whiteside N	
10 Dec	Ipswich Town	19,779	Portman Road	A	W	2–0	Bailey	Duxbury	Albiston	Wilkins	Moran	McQueen	Robson	Moses	Stapleton	Crooks 1	Graham A 1	
16 Dec	Tottenham Hotspur	33,616	Old Trafford	H	W	4–2	Bailey	Moses	Albiston	Wilkins	Moran 2	Duxbury	Robson	Muhren	Stapleton	Whiteside N	Graham A 2	Macari for Stapleton
26 Dec	Coventry City	21,553	Highfield Road	A	D	1–1	Wealands	Duxbury	Albiston	Wilkins	Moran	McQueen	Moses	Muhren 1	Stapleton	Crooks	Graham A	
27 Dec	Notts County	41,544	Old Trafford	H	D	3–3	Wealands	Duxbury	Albiston	Wilkins	Moran 1	McQueen 1	Moses	Muhren	Stapleton	Crooks 1	Graham A	Whiteside N for Crooks
31 Dec	Stoke City	40,164	Old Trafford	H	W	1–0	Bailey	Duxbury	Albiston	Wilkins	Moran	McQueen	Moses	Muhren	Stapleton	Whiteside N	Graham A 1	
2 Jan	Liverpool	44,622	Anfield	A	D	1–1	Bailey	Duxbury	Albiston	Wilkins	Moran	McQueen	Moses	Muhren	Stapleton	Whiteside N 1	Graham A	Crooks for Moran
13 Jan	Queen's Park Rangers	16,308	Loftus Road	A	D	1–1	Bailey	Duxbury	Moses	Wilkins	Moran	Hogg	Robson 1	Muhren	Stapleton	Whiteside N	Graham A	
21 Jan	Southampton	40,371	Old Trafford	H	W	3–2	Bailey	Duxbury	Moses	Wilkins	Moran	Hogg	Robson 1	Muhren 1	Stapleton 1	Whiteside N	Graham A	Hughes for Whiteside N
4 Feb	Norwich City	36,851	Old Trafford	H	D	0–0	Bailey	Moses	Albiston	Wilkins	Moran	Duxbury	Robson	Muhren	Stapleton	Whiteside N	Graham A	
7 Feb	Birmingham City	19,957	St Andrews	A	D	2–2	Bailey	Duxbury	Albiston	Wilkins	Moran	Hogg 1	Robson	Moses	Stapleton	Whiteside N 1	Graham A	
12 Feb	Luton Town	11,265	Kenilworth Road	A	W	5–0	Bailey	Duxbury	Albiston	Wilkins	Moran	Hogg	Robson 2	Muhren	Stapleton 1	Whiteside N 2	Moses	Graham A for Robson
18 Feb	Wolverhampton Wan.	20,676	Molineux	A	D	1–1	Bailey	Duxbury	Albiston	Wilkins	Moran	Hogg	Robson	Muhren	Stapleton	Whiteside N 1	Moses	Graham A for Wilkins
25 Feb	Sunderland	40,615	Old Trafford	H	W	2–1	Bailey	Duxbury	Albiston	Wilkins	Moran 2	Hogg	Robson	Muhren	Stapleton	Whiteside N	Moses	Graham A for Whiteside N
3 Mar	Aston Villa	32,874	Villa Park	A	W	3–0	Bailey	Duxbury	Albiston	Wilkins	McGrath P	Hogg	Robson 1	Muhren	Stapleton	Whiteside N 1	Moses 1	Graham A for Whiteside N
10 Mar	Leicester City	39,473	Old Trafford	H	W	2–0	Bailey	Duxbury	Albiston	Wilkins	Moran	Hogg	Robson	Muhren	Stapleton	Hughes 1	Moses 1	
17 Mar	Arsenal	48,942	Old Trafford	H	W	4–0	Bailey	Duxbury	Albiston	Wilkins	Moran	Hogg	Robson 1	Muhren 2	Stapleton 1	Whiteside N	Moses	Hughes for Whiteside N
31 Mar	West Bromwich Alb.	28,104	The Hawthorns	A	L	0–2	Bailey	Duxbury	Albiston	Wilkins	Moran	Hogg	Robson	Graham A	Stapleton	Whiteside N	Moses	
7 Apr	Birmingham City	39,896	Old Trafford	H	W	1–0	Bailey	Duxbury	Albiston	Wilkins	Moran	Hogg	Robson 1	Graham A	Stapleton	Whiteside N	Moses	Hughes for Whiteside N

continued on page 147

1983/84 continued

Football League continued

		Attendances	Venue			Players and Scores											Substitutions
14 Apr	Notts County	13,911	County Ground	H L	0–1	Bailey	Duxbury	Albiston	Wilkins	Moran	Hogg	McGrath P	Moses	Stapleton	Whiteside N	Davies A	Hughes for Davies A
17 Apr	Watford	20,764	Vicarage Road	A D	0–0	Bailey	Duxbury	Albiston	Wilkins	Moran	Hogg	McGrath P	Graham A	Stapleton	Whiteside N	Davies A	
21 Apr	Coventry City	38,524	Old Trafford	H W	4–1	Bailey	Duxbury	Albiston	Wilkins 1	Moran	Hogg	McGrath P 1	Moses	Stapleton	Hughes 2	Graham A	Whiteside N for Wilkins
28 Apr	West Ham United	44,124	Old Trafford	H D	0–0	Bailey	Duxbury	Albiston	Wilkins	Moran	Hogg	McGrath P	Moses	Stapleton	Hughes	Graham A	Whiteside N for McGrath P
5 May	Everton	28,802	Goodison Park	A D	1–1	Bailey	Duxbury	Albiston	Wilkins	Moran	Hogg	Robson	Moses	Stapleton 1	Hughes	Davies A	Whiteside N for Davies A
7 May	Ipswich Town	44,257	Old Trafford	H L	1–2	Bailey	Duxbury	Albiston	Wilkins	Moran	McGrath P	Robson	Moses	Stapleton	Hughes 1	Graham A	
12 May	Tottenham Hotspur	39,790	White Hart Lane	A D	1–1	Bailey	Duxbury	Albiston	Wilkins	Moran	McGrath P	Robson	Moses	Stapleton	Hughes	Graham A	Whiteside N 1 for Stapleton
16 May	Nottingham Forest	23,651	City Ground	A L	0–2	Bailey	Duxbury	Albiston	Wilkins	Moran	McGrath P	Robson	Blackmore C	Stapleton	Hughes	Graham A	Whiteside N for Graham A

FA Cup

7 Jan	Bournemouth	14,782	Dean Court	A L	0–2	Bailey	Moses	Albiston	Wilkins	Duxbury	Hogg	Robson	Muhren	Stapleton	Whiteside N	Graham A	Macari for Albiston

FL Cup

3 Oct	Port Vale	19,885	Vale Park	A W	1–0	Bailey	Duxbury	Albiston	Wilkins	Moran	McGrath P	Robson	Muhren	Stapleton 1	Whiteside N	Graham A	Moses for Duxbury
26 Oct	Port Vale	23,589	Old Trafford	H W	2–0	Bailey	Gidman	Albiston	Wilkins 1	Duxbury	McQueen	Robson	Moses	Stapleton	Whiteside N 1	Graham A	Hughes for Whiteside N
8 Nov	Colchester United	13,031	Layer Road	A W	2–0	Bailey	Duxbury	Albiston	Wilkins	Moran	McQueen 1	Robson	Moses 1	Stapleton	Whiteside N	Graham A	Macari for Whiteside N
30 Nov	Oxford United	13,739	Manor Ground	A D	1–1	Bailey	Duxbury	Albiston	Wilkins	Moran	McQueen	Robson	Moses	Stapleton	Whiteside N	Hughes 1	
7 Dec	Oxford United	27,459	Old Trafford	H D	1–1	Bailey	Duxbury	Albiston	Wilkins	Moran	McQueen	Robson	Moses	Stapleton 1	Whiteside N	Graham A	
19 Dec	Oxford United	13,912	Manor Ground	A L	1–2	Wealands	Moses	Albiston	Wilkins	Moran	Duxbury	Robson	Muhren	Stapleton	Whiteside N	Graham A 1	Macari for Robson

European Cup Winners' Cup

14 Sep	Dukla Prague	39,745	Old Trafford	H D	1–1	Bailey	Duxbury	Albiston	Wilkins 1	Moran	McQueen	Robson	Muhren	Stapleton	Macari	Graham A	Gidman for Robson, Moses for Muhren
27 Sep	Dukla Prague	28,850	Stadion Juliska	A D	2–2	Bailey	Duxbury	Albiston	Wilkins	Moran	McQueen	Robson 1	Muhren	Stapleton 1	Whiteside N	Graham A	
19 Oct	Spartak Varna	40,000	Stad Yuri Gagarin	A W	2–1	Bailey	Duxbury	Albiston	Wilkins	Moran	McQueen	Robson 1	Muhren	Stapleton	Whiteside N	Graham A 1	
2 Nov	Spartak Varna	39,079	Old Trafford	H W	2–0	Bailey	Duxbury	Albiston	Moses	Moran	McQueen	Robson	Macari	Stapleton 2	Whiteside N	Graham A	Dempsey for Moran, Hughes for Whiteside N
7 Mar	Barcelona	70,000	Estadio Camp Nou	A L	0–2	Bailey	Duxbury	Albiston	Wilkins	Moran	Hogg	Robson	Muhren	Stapleton	Hughes	Moses	Graham A for Hughes
21 Mar	Barcelona	58,547	Old Trafford	H W	3–0	Bailey	Duxbury	Albiston	Wilkins	Moran	Hogg	Robson 2	Muhren	Stapleton 1	Whiteside N	Moses	Hughes for Whiteside N
11 Apr	Juventus	58,171	Old Trafford	H D	1–1	Bailey	Duxbury	Albiston	McGrath P	Moran	Hogg	Graham A	Moses	Stapleton	Whiteside N	Gidman	Davies A 1 for Gidman
25 Apr	Juventus	64,655	Stadio Comunale	A L	1–2	Bailey	Duxbury	Albiston	Wilkins	Moran	Hogg	McGrath P	Moses	Stapleton	Hughes	Graham A	Whiteside N 1 for Stapleton

Football League Division 1
P42 • W20 • D14 • L8 • F71 • A41 • PTS74
Position: 4

1984/85

Football League

		Attendances	Venue			Players and Scores											Substitutions
25 Aug	Watford	53,668	Old Trafford	H D	1–1	Bailey	Duxbury	Albiston	Moses	Moran	Hogg	Robson	Strachan 1	Hughes	Brazil A	Olsen	Whiteside N for Brazil A
28 Aug	Southampton	22,183	The Dell	A D	0–0	Bailey	Duxbury	Albiston	Moses	Moran	Hogg	Robson	Strachan	Hughes	Brazil A	Olsen	
1 Sep	Ipswich Town	20,876	Portman Road	A D	1–1	Bailey	Duxbury	Albiston	Moses	Moran	Hogg	Robson	Strachan	Hughes 1	Brazil A	Olsen	Whiteside N for Brazil A
5 Sep	Chelsea	48,398	Old Trafford	H D	1–1	Bailey	Duxbury	Albiston	Moses	Moran	Hogg	Robson	Strachan	Hughes	Whiteside N	Olsen 1	
8 Sep	Newcastle United	54,915	Old Trafford	H W	5–0	Bailey	Duxbury	Albiston	Moses 1	Moran	Hogg	Robson	Strachan 2	Hughes 1	Whiteside N	Olsen 1	
15 Sep	Coventry City	18,312	Highfield Road	A W	3–0	Bailey	Duxbury	Albiston	Moses	Moran	Hogg	Robson 1	Strachan	Hughes	Whiteside N 2	Olsen	
22 Sep	Liverpool	56,638	Old Trafford	H D	1–1	Bailey	Duxbury	Albiston	Moses	Moran	Hogg	Robson	Strachan 1	Hughes	Whiteside N	Olsen	Muhren for Moran
29 Sep	West Bromwich Alb.	26,292	The Hawthorns	A W	2–1	Bailey	Duxbury	Albiston	Moses	Moran	Hogg	Robson 1	Strachan 1	Hughes	Brazil A	Olsen	
6 Oct	Aston Villa	37,131	Villa Park	A L	0–3	Bailey	Duxbury	Albiston	Moses	Moran	Hogg	Strachan	Muhren	Hughes	Brazil A	Olsen	
13 Oct	West Ham United	47,559	Old Trafford	H W	5–1	Bailey	Duxbury	Albiston	Moses 1	McQueen 1	Hogg	Robson	Strachan 1	Hughes 1	Brazil A 1	Olsen	
20 Oct	Tottenham Hotspur	54,516	Old Trafford	H W	1–0	Bailey	Gidman	Albiston	Moses	Moran	Hogg	Robson	Strachan	Hughes 1	Brazil A	Olsen	
27 Oct	Everton	40,742	Goodison Park	A L	0–5	Bailey	McQueen	Albiston	Moses	Moran	Hogg	Robson	Strachan	Hughes	Brazil A	Olsen	Stapleton for Moran
2 Nov	Arsenal	32,279	Old Trafford	H W	4–2	Bailey	Gidman	Albiston	Moses	Moran	Hogg	Robson 1	Strachan 2	Hughes 1	Stapleton	Olsen	
10 Nov	Leicester City	23,840	Filbert Street	A W	3–2	Bailey	Gidman	Albiston	Moses	Garton	Hogg	Robson	Strachan 1	Hughes 1	Brazil A 1	Olsen	Whiteside N for Olsen
17 Nov	Luton Town	41,630	Old Trafford	H W	2–0	Bailey	Gidman	Albiston	Moses	McQueen	Duxbury	Robson	Strachan	Hughes	Whiteside N 2	Olsen	Stapleton for Robson
24 Nov	Sunderland	25,405	Roker Park	A L	2–3	Bailey	Gidman	Duxbury	Moses	McQueen	Garton	Robson 1	Strachan	Hughes 1	Whiteside N	Olsen	Muhren for Olsen
1 Dec	Norwich City	36,635	Old Trafford	H W	2–0	Bailey	Gidman	Duxbury	Moses	McQueen	McGrath P	Robson 1	Strachan	Hughes 1	Whiteside N	Olsen	
8 Dec	Nottingham Forest	25,902	City Ground	A L	2–3	Bailey	Duxbury	Blackmore C	Moses	McQueen	McGrath P	Robson	Strachan 2	Stapleton	Brazil A	Muhren	
15 Dec	Queen's Park Rangers	36,134	Old Trafford	H W	3–0	Bailey	Gidman 1	Albiston	Moses	McQueen	Duxbury 1	Robson	Strachan	Stapleton	Brazil A 1	Olsen	
22 Dec	Ipswich Town	35,168	Old Trafford	H W	3–0	Bailey	Gidman 1	Albiston	Moses	McQueen	Duxbury	Robson 1	Strachan 1	Hughes	Stapleton	Olsen	
26 Dec	Stoke City	20,985	Victoria Ground	A L	1–2	Bailey	Gidman	Albiston	Moses	McQueen	Duxbury	Robson	Strachan	Hughes	Stapleton 1	Muhren	Brazil A for Strachan
29 Dec	Chelsea	42,197	Stamford Bridge	A W	3–1	Bailey	Duxbury	Albiston	Moses 1	McQueen	McGrath P	Robson	Strachan	Stapleton 1	Hughes 1	Muhren	
1 Jan	Sheffield Wednesday	47,625	Old Trafford	H L	1–2	Bailey	Duxbury	Albiston	Moses	McQueen	McGrath P	Robson	Strachan	Hughes 1	Brazil A	Muhren	
12 Jan	Coventry City	35,992	Old Trafford	H L	0–1	Pears	Duxbury	Albiston	Moses	McQueen	McGrath P	Robson	Strachan	Stapleton	Hughes	Muhren	Brazil A for Robson
2 Feb	West Bromwich Alb.	36,681	Old Trafford	H W	2–0	Pears	Gidman	Albiston	Moses	Moran	Hogg	McGrath P	Strachan 2	Hughes	Whiteside N	Olsen	
9 Feb	Newcastle United	32,555	St James' Park	A D	1–1	Pears	Gidman	Albiston	Moses	Moran 1	Hogg	McGrath P	Strachan	Whiteside N	Hughes	Olsen	Stapleton for Olsen
23 Feb	Arsenal	48,612	Highbury	A W	1–0	Bailey	Gidman	Albiston	Duxbury	Moran	Hogg	McGrath P	Strachan	Hughes	Stapleton	Olsen	Whiteside N 1 for Moran
2 Mar	Everton	51,150	Old Trafford	H D	1–1	Bailey	Gidman	Albiston	Duxbury	McGrath P	Hogg	Strachan	Brazil A	Hughes	Whiteside N	Olsen 1	
12 Mar	Tottenham Hotspur	42,908	White Hart Lane	A W	2–1	Bailey	Gidman	Albiston	Duxbury	McGrath P	Hogg	Strachan	Whiteside N 1	Hughes 1	Stapleton	Olsen	
15 Mar	West Ham United	16,674	Upton Park	A D	2–2	Bailey	Gidman	Albiston	Duxbury	McGrath P	Hogg	Strachan	Whiteside N	Hughes	Stapleton 1	Olsen	Robson 1 for Whiteside N
23 Mar	Aston Villa	40,941	Old Trafford	H W	4–0	Bailey	Gidman	Albiston	Whiteside N 1	McGrath P	Hogg	Robson	Strachan	Hughes 3	Stapleton	Olsen	
31 Mar	Liverpool	34,886	Anfield	A W	1–0	Bailey	Gidman	Albiston	Whiteside N	McGrath P	Hogg	Robson	Strachan	Hughes	Stapleton 1	Olsen	
3 Apr	Leicester City	35,590	Old Trafford	H W	2–1	Bailey	Gidman	Albiston	Whiteside N	McGrath P	Hogg	Robson 1	Strachan	Hughes	Stapleton 1	Olsen	
6 Apr	Stoke City	42,940	Old Trafford	H W	5–0	Bailey	Gidman	Albiston	Whiteside N 1	McGrath P	Hogg	Robson	Strachan	Hughes 2	Stapleton	Olsen 2	Duxbury for Robson
9 Apr	Sheffield Wednesday	39,380	Hillsborough	A L	0–1	Pears	Gidman	Albiston	Duxbury	McGrath P	Hogg	Robson	Strachan	Hughes	Stapleton	Olsen	Brazil A for Duxbury
21 Apr	Luton Town	10,320	Kenilworth Road	A L	1–2	Bailey	Gidman	Albiston	Whiteside N 1	McGrath P	Hogg	Robson	Muhren	Hughes	Stapleton	Olsen	
24 Apr	Southampton	31,291	Old Trafford	H D	0–0	Bailey	Gidman	Albiston	Whiteside N	McGrath P	Hogg	Robson	Strachan	Hughes	Stapleton	Olsen	Duxbury for Stapleton
27 Apr	Sunderland	38,979	Old Trafford	H D	2–2	Bailey	Gidman	Albiston	Whiteside N	McGrath P	Moran 1	Robson 1	Strachan	Hughes	Brazil A	Olsen	Duxbury for Gidman
4 May	Norwich City	15,502	Carrow Road	A W	1–0	Bailey	Gidman	Albiston	Whiteside N	McGrath P	Moran 1	Robson	Strachan	Hughes	Stapleton	Olsen	
6 May	Nottingham Forest	41,775	Old Trafford	H W	2–0	Bailey	Gidman 1	Albiston	Whiteside N	Moran	Hogg	McGrath P	Strachan	Stapleton 1	Brazil A	Olsen	Muhren for Moran
11 May	Queen's Park Rangers	20,483	Loftus Road	A W	3–1	Bailey	Gidman	Albiston	Whiteside N	McGrath P	Hogg	Duxbury	Strachan 1	Stapleton	Brazil A 2	Olsen	Muhren for Hogg
13 May	Watford	20,500	Vicarage Road	A L	1–5	Bailey	Gidman	Albiston	Whiteside N	McGrath P	Moran 1	Duxbury	Strachan	Hughes	Brazil A	Stapleton	Muhren for Whiteside N

FA Cup

5 Jan	Bournemouth	32,080	Old Trafford	H W	3–0	Bailey	Duxbury	Albiston	Moses	McQueen 1	McGrath P	Robson	Strachan 1	Stapleton 1	Hughes	Muhren	
26 Jan	Coventry City	38,039	Old Trafford	H W	2–1	Pears	Gidman	Albiston	Moses	Moran	Hogg	McGrath P 1	Strachan	Whiteside N	Hughes 1	Olsen	Brazil A for Hughes
15 Feb	Blackburn Rovers	22,692	Ewood Park	A W	2–0	Bailey	Gidman	Albiston	Moses	Moran	Hogg	McGrath P 1	Strachan 1	Hughes	Whiteside N	Olsen	
9 Mar	West Ham United	46,769	Old Trafford	H W	4–2	Bailey	Gidman	Albiston	Duxbury	McGrath P	Hogg	Strachan	Whiteside N 3	Hughes 1	Stapleton	Olsen	
13 Apr	Liverpool	51,690	Goodison Park	A D	2–2	Bailey	Gidman	Albiston	Whiteside N	McGrath P	Hogg	Robson 1	Strachan	Hughes	Stapleton 1	Olsen	
17 Apr	Liverpool	45,775	Maine Road	A W	2–1	Bailey	Gidman	Albiston	Whiteside N	McGrath P	Hogg	Robson 1	Strachan	Hughes 1	Stapleton	Olsen	
18 May	Everton	100,000	Wembley	A W	1–0	Bailey	Gidman	Albiston	Whiteside N 1	McGrath P	Moran	Robson	Strachan	Hughes	Stapleton	Olsen	Duxbury for Albiston

FL Cup

26 Sep	Burnley	28,383	Old Trafford	H W	4–0	Bailey	Duxbury	Albiston	Moses	Garton	Hogg	Robson 1	Muhren	Hughes 3	Whiteside N	Graham A	Brazil A for Whiteside N
9 Oct	Burnley	12,690	Turf Moor	A W	3–0	Bailey	Duxbury	Albiston	Moses	Moran	Hogg	Strachan	Blackmore C	Stapleton	Brazil A 2	Olsen 1	
30 Oct	Everton	50,918	Old Trafford	H L	1–2	Bailey	Gidman	Albiston	Moses	Moran	Hogg	Robson	Strachan	Hughes	Brazil A 1	Olsen	Stapleton for Olsen

UEFA Cup

19 Sep	Raba Vasas	33,119	Old Trafford	H W	3–0	Bailey	Duxbury	Albiston	Moses	Moran	Hogg	Robson 1	Muhren 1	Hughes 1	Whiteside N	Olsen	
3 Oct	Raba Vasas	26,000	Raba ETO Stadion	A D	2–2	Bailey	Duxbury	Albiston	Moses	Moran	Hogg	Robson	Muhren 1	Hughes	Brazil A 1	Olsen	Gidman for Robson
24 Oct	PSV Eindhoven	27,500	Philips Stadion	A D	0–0	Bailey	Gidman	Albiston	Moses	Moran	Hogg	Robson	Strachan	Hughes	Brazil A	Olsen	
7 Nov	PSV Eindhoven	39,281	Old Trafford	H W	1–0	Bailey	Gidman	Albiston	Moses	Moran	Hogg	Robson	Strachan 1	Hughes	Stapleton	Olsen	Garton for Moran, Whiteside N for Stapleton
28 Nov	Dundee United	48,278	Old Trafford	H D	2–2	Bailey	Gidman	Albiston	Moses	McQueen	Duxbury	Robson 1	Strachan 1	Hughes	Whiteside N	Olsen	Stapleton for Whiteside N
12 Dec	Dundee United	21,821	Tannadice Park	A W	•3–2	Bailey	Gidman	Albiston	Moses	McQueen	Duxbury	Robson	Strachan	Hughes 1	Stapleton	Muhren 1	
6 Mar	Videoton	35,432	Old Trafford	H W	1–0	Bailey	Gidman	Albiston	Duxbury	McGrath P	Hogg	Strachan	Whiteside N	Hughes	Stapleton 1	Olsen	
20 Mar	Videoton	25,000	Sosta Stadion	A L	0–1	Bailey	Gidman	Albiston	Duxbury	McGrath P	Hogg	Robson	Strachan	Hughes	Stapleton	Whiteside N	Olsen for Robson

Football League Division 1
P42 • W22 • D10 • L10 • F77 • A47 • PTS76
Position: 4

1985/86

Football League

		Attendances	Venue			Players and Scores											Substitutions
17 Aug	Aston Villa	49,743	Old Trafford	H W	4–0	Bailey	Gidman	Albiston	Whiteside N 1	McGrath P	Hogg	Robson	Moses	Hughes 2	Stapleton	Olsen 1	Duxbury for Hughes
20 Aug	Ipswich Town	18,777	Portman Road	A W	1–0	Bailey	Gidman	Albiston	Whiteside N	McGrath P	Hogg	Robson 1	Strachan	Hughes	Stapleton	Olsen	Duxbury for Gidman
24 Aug	Arsenal	37,145	Highbury	A W	2–1	Bailey	Duxbury	Albiston	Whiteside N	McGrath P 1	Hogg	Robson	Strachan	Hughes 1	Stapleton	Olsen	
26 Aug	West Ham United	50,773	Old Trafford	H W	2–0	Bailey	Duxbury	Albiston	Whiteside N	McGrath P	Hogg	Robson	Strachan 1	Hughes 1	Stapleton	Olsen	
31 Aug	Nottingham Forest	26,274	City Ground	A W	3–1	Bailey	Duxbury	Albiston	Whiteside N	McGrath P	Hogg	Robson	Strachan	Hughes 1	Stapleton 1	Barnes 1	Brazil A for Strachan
4 Sep	Newcastle United	51,102	Old Trafford	H W	3–0	Bailey	Duxbury	Albiston	Whiteside N	McGrath P	Hogg	Robson	Strachan	Hughes 1	Stapleton 2	Barnes	Brazil A for Stapleton
7 Sep	Oxford United	51,820	Old Trafford	H W	3–0	Bailey	Duxbury	Albiston	Whiteside N 1	McGrath P	Hogg	Robson 1	Strachan	Hughes	Stapleton	Barnes 1	Brazil A for Stapleton
14 Sep	Manchester City	48,773	Maine Road	A W	3–0	Bailey	Duxbury 1	Albiston 1	Whiteside N	McGrath P	Hogg	Robson 1	Strachan	Hughes	Stapleton	Barnes	Brazil A for Stapleton
21 Sep	West Bromwich Alb.	25,068	The Hawthorns	A W	5–1	Bailey	Duxbury	Albiston	Whiteside N	McGrath P	Hogg	Robson	Strachan 1	Stapleton 1	Brazil A 2	Blackmore C 1	Moran for Strachan
28 Sep	Southampton	52,449	Old Trafford	H W	1–0	Bailey	Duxbury	Albiston	Whiteside N	McGrath P	Moran	Robson	Moses	Hughes 1	Stapleton	Barnes	Brazil A for Whiteside N
5 Oct	Luton Town	17,454	Kenilworth Road	A D	1–1	Bailey	Duxbury	Albiston	Whiteside N	McGrath P	Moran	Robson	Moses	Hughes 1	Stapleton	Barnes	
12 Oct	Queen's Park Rangers	48,845	Old Trafford	H W	2–0	Bailey	Duxbury	Albiston	Whiteside N	McGrath P	Moran	Robson	Olsen 1	Hughes 1	Stapleton	Barnes	
19 Oct	Liverpool	54,492	Old Trafford	H D	1–1	Bailey	Duxbury	Albiston	Whiteside N	Moran	Hogg	McGrath P 1	Moses	Hughes	Stapleton	Olsen	Barnes for Moses
26 Oct	Chelsea	42,485	Stamford Bridge	A W	2–1	Bailey	Duxbury	Albiston	Whiteside N	Moran	Hogg	McGrath P	Olsen 1	Hughes 1	Stapleton	Barnes	
2 Nov	Coventry City	46,748	Old Trafford	H W	2–0	Bailey	Garton	Albiston	Whiteside N	Moran	Hogg	McGrath P	Olsen 2	Hughes	Stapleton	Barnes	
9 Nov	Sheffield Wednesday	48,105	Hillsborough	A L	0–1	Bailey	Gidman	Albiston	Whiteside N	McGrath P	Moran	Robson	Olsen	Hughes	Stapleton	Barnes	Strachan for Robson
16 Nov	Tottenham Hotspur	54,575	Old Trafford	H D	0–0	Bailey	Gidman	Albiston	Whiteside N	McGrath P	Moran	Strachan	Olsen	Hughes	Stapleton	Barnes	
23 Nov	Leicester City	22,008	Filbert Street	A L	0–3	Bailey	Gidman	Albiston	Whiteside N	Moran	Hogg	McGrath P	Strachan	Hughes	Stapleton	Olsen	Brazil A for Albiston
30 Nov	Watford	42,181	Old Trafford	H D	1–1	Bailey	Gidman	Gibson C	Whiteside N	Moran	Hogg	McGrath P	Strachan	Hughes	Stapleton	Olsen	Brazil A 1 for Moran
7 Dec	Ipswich Town	37,981	Old Trafford	H W	1–0	Bailey	Gidman	Gibson C	Whiteside N	McGrath P	Hogg	Dempsey	Strachan	Hughes	Stapleton 1	Olsen	Brazil A for Hughes
14 Dec	Aston Villa	27,626	Villa Park	A W	3–1	Turner C	Gidman	Gibson C	Whiteside N	McGrath P	Garton	Blackmore C 1	Strachan 1	Hughes 1	Stapleton	Olsen	Brazil A for Stapleton
21 Dec	Arsenal	44,386	Old Trafford	H L	0–1	Bailey	Gidman	Gibson C	Whiteside N	McGrath P	Garton	Blackmore C	Strachan	Hughes	Stapleton	Olsen	
26 Dec	Everton	42,551	Goodison Park	A L	1–3	Bailey	Gidman	Gibson C	Whiteside N	McGrath P	Hogg	Blackmore C	Strachan	Hughes	Stapleton 1	Olsen	Wood N for Olsen
1 Jan	Birmingham City	43,095	Old Trafford	H W	1–0	Turner C	Gidman	Albiston	Whiteside N	McGrath P	Garton	Blackmore C	Strachan	Hughes	Stapleton	Gibson C 1	Brazil A for McGrath P
11 Jan	Oxford United	13,280	Manor Ground	A W	3–1	Bailey	Gidman	Albiston	Whiteside N 1	Moran	Garton	Blackmore C	Strachan	Hughes 1	Stapleton	Gibson C 1	
18 Jan	Nottingham Forest	46,717	Old Trafford	H L	2–3	Bailey	Gidman	Albiston	Whiteside N	Moran	Garton	Olsen 2	Strachan	Hughes	Stapleton	Gibson C	
2 Feb	West Ham United	22,642	Upton Park	A L	1–2	Bailey	Gidman	Albiston	Whiteside N	McGrath P	Moran	Robson 1	Olsen	Hughes	Stapleton	Gibson C	Gibson T for Robson
9 Feb	Liverpool	35,064	Anfield	A D	1–1	Turner C	Gidman	Albiston	Whiteside N	McGrath P	Moran	Sivebaek	Gibson T	Hughes	Gibson C 1	Olsen	Stapleton for Olsen
22 Feb	West Bromwich Alb.	45,193	Old Trafford	H W	3–0	Turner C	Gidman	Albiston	Blackmore C	McGrath P	Moran	Strachan	Gibson C	Hughes	Stapleton	Olsen 3	Gibson T for Gidman
1 Mar	Southampton	19,012	The Dell	A L	0–1	Turner C	Duxbury	Albiston	Gibson C	McGrath P	Moran	Robson	Strachan	Hughes	Stapleton	Olsen	Gibson T for Olsen
15 Mar	Queen's Park Rangers	23,407	Loftus Road	A L	0–1	Turner C	Duxbury	Albiston	Blackmore C	McGrath P	Moran	Olsen	Strachan	Stapleton	Davenport	Gibson C	Gibson T for Blackmore C
19 Mar	Luton Town	33,668	Old Trafford	H W	2–0	Turner C	Duxbury	Albiston	Whiteside N	McGrath P 1	Moran	Gibson C	Strachan	Hughes 1	Davenport	Olsen	Stapleton for Moran
22 Mar	Manchester City	51,274	Old Trafford	H D	2–2	Turner C	Duxbury	Albiston	Whiteside N	McGrath P	Higgins M	Gibson C 1	Strachan 1	Hughes	Davenport	Barnes	Stapleton for Barnes
29 Mar	Birmingham City	22,551	St Andrews	A D	1–1	Turner C	Gidman	Albiston	Whiteside N	McGrath P	Higgins M	Robson 1	Strachan	Hughes	Davenport	Gibson C	Stapleton for Gibson C
31 Mar	Everton	51,189	Old Trafford	H D	0–0	Turner C	Gidman	Albiston	Whiteside N	McGrath P	Higgins M	Robson	Strachan	Hughes	Davenport	Gibson C	Stapleton for Davenport
5 Apr	Coventry City	17,160	Highfield Road	A W	3–1	Turner C	Gidman	Albiston	Whiteside N	McGrath P	Higgins M	Robson 1	Strachan 1	Hughes	Davenport	Gibson C 1	Stapleton for Gibson C
9 Apr	Chelsea	45,355	Old Trafford	H L	1–2	Turner C	Gidman	Albiston	Duxbury	McGrath P	Higgins M	Robson	Strachan	Hughes	Davenport	Olsen 1	Stapleton for Strachan
13 Apr	Sheffield Wednesday	32,331	Old Trafford	H L	0–2	Turner C	Gidman	Albiston	Duxbury	McGrath P	Higgins M	Robson	Sivebaek	Hughes	Davenport	Olsen	Gibson T for Davenport
16 Apr	Newcastle United	31,840	St James' Park	A W	4–2	Turner C	Gidman	Albiston	Whiteside N 1	McGrath P	Garton	Robson 1	Gibson T	Hughes 2	Stapleton	Blackmore C	Sivebaek for Gibson T
19 Apr	Tottenham Hotspur	32,357	White Hart Lane	A D	0–0	Turner C	Gidman	Albiston	Whiteside N	McGrath P	Garton	Duxbury	Davenport	Hughes	Stapleton	Blackmore C	Olsen for Davenport
26 Apr	Leicester City	38,840	Old Trafford	H W	4–0	Turner C	Gidman	Albiston	Whiteside N	McGrath P	Garton	Duxbury	Davenport 1	Hughes 1	Stapleton 1	Blackmore C 1	Olsen for Whiteside N
3 May	Watford	18,414	Vicarage Road	A D	1–1	Turner C	Garton	Albiston	Whiteside N	McGrath P	Hogg	Duxbury	Davenport	Hughes 1	Stapleton	Blackmore C	Olsen for Davenport

FA Cup

9 Jan	Rochdale	40,223	Old Trafford	H W	2–0	Turner C	Duxbury	Albiston	Whiteside N	Higgins M	Garton	Blackmore C	Strachan	Hughes 1	Stapleton 1	Gibson C	Olsen for Hughes
25 Jan	Sunderland	35,484	Roker Park	A D	0–0	Bailey	Gidman	Albiston	Whiteside N	McGrath P	Moran	Robson	Strachan	Stapleton	Blackmore C	Olsen	
29 Jan	Sunderland	43,402	Old Trafford	H W	3–0	Bailey	Gidman	Albiston	Whiteside N 1	McGrath P	Moran	Robson	Strachan	Stapleton	Olsen 2	Gibson C	Blackmore C for Strachan
5 Mar	West Ham United	26,441	Upton Park	A D	1–1	Turner C	Duxbury	Albiston	Whiteside N	McGrath P	Moran	Robson	Strachan	Hughes	Stapleton 1	Gibson C	Olsen for Robson
9 Mar	West Ham United	30,441	Old Trafford	H L	0–2	Turner C	Duxbury	Albiston	Whiteside N	McGrath P	Higgins M	Olsen	Strachan	Hughes	Stapleton	Gibson C	Blackmore C for Higgins M

FL Cup

24 Sep	Crystal Palace	21,507	Selhurst Park	A W	1–0	Bailey	Duxbury	Albiston	Whiteside N	McGrath P	Moran	Robson	Blackmore C	Stapleton	Brazil A	Barnes 1	
9 Oct	Crystal Palace	26,118	Old Trafford	H W	1–0	Bailey	Duxbury	Albiston	Whiteside N 1	McGrath P	Moran	Robson	Olsen	Hughes	Stapleton	Barnes	Brazil A for Hughes
29 Oct	West Ham United	32,056	Old Trafford	H W	1–0	Bailey	Duxbury	Albiston	Whiteside N 1	Moran	Hogg	McGrath P	Olsen	Hughes	Stapleton	Barnes	Brazil A for Duxbury
26 Nov	Liverpool	41,291	Anfield	A L	1–2	Bailey	Gidman	Blackmore C	Whiteside N	Moran	Hogg	McGrath P 1	Strachan	Stapleton	Brazil A	Olsen	

Football League Division 1
P42 • W22 • D10 • L10 • F70 • A36 • PTS76
Position: 4

1986/87

Football League

		Attendances	Venue			Players and Scores											Substitutions
23 Aug	Arsenal	41,382	Highbury	A L	0–1	Turner C	Duxbury	Albiston	Whiteside N	McGrath P	Moran	Strachan	Blackmore C	Stapleton	Davenport	Gibson C	Olsen for Gibson C
25 Aug	West Ham United	43,306	Old Trafford	H L	2–3	Turner C	Duxbury	Albiston	Whiteside N	McGrath P	Moran	Strachan	Blackmore C	Stapleton 1	Davenport 1	Gibson C	Olsen for Gibson C
30 Aug	Charlton Athletic	37,544	Old Trafford	H L	0–1	Turner C	Duxbury	Albiston	Whiteside N	McGrath P	Moran	Strachan	Blackmore C	Stapleton	Davenport	Olsen	Gibson T for Whiteside N
6 Sep	Leicester City	16,785	Filbert Street	A D	1–1	Turner C	Sivebaek	Albiston	Whiteside N 1	McGrath P	Hogg	Strachan	Duxbury	Stapleton	Gibson T	Olsen	Davenport for Gibson T
13 Sep	Southampton	40,135	Old Trafford	H W	5–1	Turner C	Sivebaek	Albiston	Whiteside N 1	McGrath P	Moran	Robson	Strachan	Stapleton 2	Davenport 1	Olsen 1	Gibson T for Strachan
16 Sep	Watford	21,650	Vicarage Road	A L	0–1	Turner C	Sivebaek	Albiston	Moses	McGrath P	Moran	Robson	Blackmore C	Stapleton	Davenport	Olsen	
21 Sep	Everton	25,843	Goodison Park	A L	1–3	Turner C	Sivebaek	Albiston	Whiteside N	McGrath P	Moran	Robson 1	Strachan	Stapleton	Davenport	Moses	Olsen for Whiteside N
28 Sep	Chelsea	33,340	Old Trafford	H L	0–1	Turner C	Sivebaek	Albiston	Whiteside N	McGrath P	Moran	Robson	Strachan	Stapleton	Davenport	Moses	Olsen for Moses
4 Oct	Nottingham Forest	34,828	City Ground	A D	1–1	Turner C	Sivebaek	Albiston	Whiteside N	McGrath P	Moran	Robson 1	Strachan	Stapleton	Davenport	Olsen	
11 Oct	Sheffield Wednesday	45,890	Old Trafford	H W	3–1	Turner C	Sivebaek	Albiston	Whiteside N 1	McGrath P	Hogg	Robson	Strachan	Stapleton	Davenport 2	Barnes	
18 Oct	Luton Town	39,927	Old Trafford	H W	1–0	Turner C	Sivebaek	Albiston	Whiteside N	McGrath P	Hogg	Robson	Strachan	Stapleton 1	Davenport	Barnes	Gibson T for Strachan
26 Oct	Manchester City	32,440	Maine Road	A D	1–1	Turner C	Sivebaek	Albiston	Whiteside N	McGrath P	Hogg	Robson	Moses	Stapleton 1	Davenport	Barnes	
1 Nov	Coventry City	36,946	Old Trafford	H D	1–1	Turner C	Sivebaek	Albiston	Whiteside N	McGrath P	Hogg	Robson	Strachan	Stapleton	Davenport 1	Olsen	Moses for Robson
8 Nov	Oxford United	13,545	Manor Ground	A L	0–2	Turner C	Duxbury	Albiston	Moran	McGrath P	Hogg	Blackmore C	Moses	Stapleton	Davenport	Barnes	Olsen for McGrath P
15 Nov	Norwich City	22,634	Carrow Road	A D	0–0	Turner C	Sivebaek	Duxbury	Moses	McGrath P	Hogg	Olsen	Blackmore C	Stapleton	Davenport	Barnes	Moran for Sivebaek
22 Nov	Queen's Park Rangers	42,235	Old Trafford	H W	1–0	Turner C	Sivebaek 1	Duxbury	Moses	McGrath P	Hogg	Olsen	Blackmore C	Stapleton	Davenport	Barnes	Strachan for Barnes
29 Nov	Wimbledon	12,112	Plough Lane	A L	0–1	Turner C	Sivebaek	Duxbury	Moses	McGrath P	Moran	Olsen	Blackmore C	Stapleton	Davenport	Barnes	Robson for Barnes
7 Dec	Tottenham Hotspur	35,957	Old Trafford	H D	3–3	Turner C	Sivebaek	Duxbury	Moses	McGrath P	Moran	Robson	Strachan	Whiteside N 1	Davenport 2	Olsen	Stapleton for McGrath P
13 Dec	Aston Villa	29,205	Villa Park	A D	3–3	Walsh	Sivebaek	Duxbury	Moses	Moran	Hogg	Robson	Strachan	Whiteside N 1	Davenport 2	Olsen	Stapleton for Davenport
20 Dec	Leicester City	34,180	Old Trafford	H W	2–0	Walsh	Sivebaek	Gibson C 1	O'Brien L	Moran	Hogg	Robson	Strachan	Whiteside N	Davenport	Olsen	Stapleton 1 for O'Brien L
26 Dec	Liverpool	40,663	Anfield	A W	1–0	Walsh	Sivebaek	Gibson C	Whiteside N 1	Moran	Duxbury	Robson	Strachan	Stapleton	Davenport	Olsen	
27 Dec	Norwich City	44,610	Old Trafford	H L	0–1	Walsh	Sivebaek	Gibson C	Whiteside N	Garton	Duxbury	Robson	Strachan	Stapleton	Davenport	Olsen	O'Brien L for Robson
1 Jan	Newcastle United	43,334	Old Trafford	H W	•4–1	Turner C	Sivebaek	Gibson C	O'Brien L	Garton	Moran	Duxbury	Strachan	Whiteside N 1	Davenport	Olsen 1	Stapleton 1 for Whiteside N
3 Jan	Southampton	20,409	The Dell	A D	1–1	Turner C	Duxbury	Gibson C	O'Brien L	Garton	Moran	Gill	Strachan	Stapleton	Gibson T	Olsen 1	Davenport for Gill
24 Jan	Arsenal	51,367	Old Trafford	H W	2–0	Turner C	Sivebaek	Duxbury	Whiteside N	Garton	Moran	Blackmore C	Strachan 1	Stapleton	Gibson T 1	Olsen	McGrath P for Duxbury
7 Feb	Charlton Athletic	15,482	The Valley	A D	0–0	Turner C	Sivebaek	Gibson C	Duxbury	Garton	Moran	Robson	Strachan	Stapleton	Gibson T	Olsen	Davenport for Gibson T
14 Feb	Watford	35,763	Old Trafford	H W	3–1	Turner C	Garton	Gibson C	Duxbury	McGrath P 1	Moran	Robson	Strachan 1	Davenport 1	Gibson T	Olsen	Stapleton for Garton
21 Feb	Chelsea	26,516	Stamford Bridge	A D	1–1	Bailey	Duxbury	Gibson C	Whiteside N	McGrath P	Moran	Robson	Strachan	Davenport 1	Gibson T	Olsen	Stapleton for Olsen
28 Feb	Everton	47,421	Old Trafford	H D	0–0	Bailey	Duxbury	Gibson C	Whiteside N	McGrath P	Moran	Robson	Hogg	Davenport	Gibson T	Strachan	O'Brien L for Davenport
7 Mar	Manchester City	43,619	Old Trafford	H W	•2–0	Bailey	Sivebaek	Gibson C	Duxbury	McGrath P	Moran	Robson 1	Strachan	Whiteside N	Gibson T	O'Brien L	Davenport for Strachan
14 Mar	Luton Town	12,509	Kenilworth Road	A L	1–2	Bailey	Sivebaek	Gibson C	Duxbury	McGrath P	Moran	Robson 1	Strachan	Whiteside N	Gibson T	O'Brien L	Davenport for Gibson C
21 Mar	Sheffield Wednesday	29,888	Hillsborough	A L	0–1	Bailey	Garton	Duxbury	O'Brien L	McGrath P	Moran	Robson	Strachan	Whiteside N	Davenport	Gibson C	Gibson T for Garton
28 Mar	Nottingham Forest	39,182	Old Trafford	H W	2–0	Walsh	Sivebaek	Gibson C	O'Brien L	McGrath P 1	Duxbury	Robson 1	Moses	Stapleton	Whiteside N	Wood N	Albiston for Wood N
4 Apr	Oxford United	32,443	Old Trafford	H W	3–2	Walsh	Sivebaek	Gibson C	O'Brien L	McGrath P	Duxbury	Robson 1	Moses	Stapleton	Wood N	Davenport 2	Albiston for Wood N
14 Apr	West Ham United	23,486	Upton Park	A D	0–0	Walsh	Duxbury	Gibson C	Moses	McGrath P	Moran	Robson	Strachan	Stapleton	Gibson T	Davenport	Albiston for Robson
18 Apr	Newcastle United	32,706	St James' Park	A L	1–2	Walsh	Duxbury	Gibson C	Moses	McGrath P	Moran	O'Brien L	Strachan 1	Gibson T	Whiteside N	Davenport	Stapleton for Gibson T
20 Apr	Liverpool	54,103	Old Trafford	H W	1–0	Walsh	Sivebaek	Albiston	Moses	McGrath P	Moran	Duxbury	Strachan	Davenport 1	Whiteside N	Gibson C	Stapleton for Albiston
25 Apr	Queen's Park Rangers	17,414	Loftus Road	A D	1–1	Walsh	Duxbury	Albiston	Moses	McGrath P	Moran	Robson	Strachan 1	Whiteside N	Davenport	Gibson C	Sivebaek for Moses
2 May	Wimbledon	31,686	Old Trafford	H L	0–1	Walsh	Duxbury	Albiston	Moses	McGrath P	Moran	Robson	Strachan	Davenport	Olsen	Gibson C	Stapleton for Moses
4 May	Tottenham Hotspur	36,692	White Hart Lane	A L	0–4	Walsh	Sivebaek	Gibson C	Duxbury	McGrath P	Moran	Robson	Strachan	Gibson T	Whiteside N	Olsen	Blackmore C for Sivebaek
6 May	Coventry City	23,407	Highfield Road	A D	1–1	Walsh	Garton	Albiston	Duxbury	McGrath P	Moran	Robson	Strachan	Whiteside N 1	Davenport	Gibson C	Blackmore C for Strachan
9 May	Aston Villa	35,179	Old Trafford	H W	3–1	Walsh	Garton	Albiston	Duxbury 1	McGrath P	Moran	Robson 1	Blackmore C 1	Whiteside N	Davenport	Gibson C	Olsen for Whiteside N

FA Cup

10 Jan	Manchester City	54,294	Old Trafford	H W	1–0	Turner C	Sivebaek	Gibson C	Whiteside N 1	Garton	Moran	Duxbury	Strachan	Stapleton	Davenport	Olsen	Gibson T for Davenport
31 Jan	Coventry City	49,082	Old Trafford	H L	0–1	Turner C	Sivebaek	Duxbury	Whiteside N	Garton	Moran	Blackmore C	Strachan	Stapleton	Gibson T	Olsen	McGrath P for Blackmore C, Davenport for Stapleton

FL Cup

24 Sep	Port Vale	18,906	Old Trafford	H W	2–0	Turner C	Duxbury	Albiston	Whiteside N 1	McGrath P	Moran	Robson	Strachan	Stapleton 1	Davenport	Moses	
7 Oct	Port Vale	10,486	Vale Park	A W	5–2	Turner C	Sivebaek	Albiston	Moses 2	McGrath P	Moran	Robson	Strachan	Stapleton 1	Davenport 1	Barnes 1	Whiteside N for Moran, Gibson T for Stapleton
29 Oct	Southampton	23,639	Old Trafford	H D	0–0	Turner C	Duxbury	Albiston	Whiteside N	McGrath P	Hogg	Robson	Moses	Stapleton	Davenport	Barnes	Olsen for Moses, Gibson T for Davenport
4 Nov	Southampton	17,915	The Dell	A L	1–4	Turner C	Duxbury	Albiston	Whiteside N	McGrath P	Hogg	Moses	Olsen	Stapleton	Davenport 1	Gibson C	Wood N for Whiteside N, Moran for Gibson C

Football League Division 1
P42 • W14 • D14 • L14 • F52 • A45 • PTS56
Position: 11

1987/88

Football League

		Attendances	Venue			Players and Scores											Substitutions
15 Aug	Southampton	21,214	The Dell	A D	2–2	Walsh	Anderson V	Duxbury	Moses	McGrath P	Moran	Robson	Strachan	McClair	Whiteside N 2	Olsen	Albiston replaced Moses, Davenport replaced Olsen
19 Aug	Arsenal	42,890	Old Trafford	H D	0–0	Walsh	Anderson V	Duxbury	Moses	McGrath P	Moran	Robson	Strachan	McClair	Whiteside N	Olsen	
22 Aug	Watford	38,582	Old Trafford	H W	2–0	Walsh	Anderson V	Duxbury	Moses	McGrath P 1	Moran	Robson	Strachan	McClair 1	Whiteside N	Olsen	Davenport replaced Strachan, Albiston replaced Olsen
29 Aug	Charlton Athletic	14,046	Selhurst Park	A W	3–1	Walsh	Anderson V	Duxbury	Moses	McGrath P 1	Moran	Robson 1	Strachan	McClair 1	Whiteside N	Olsen	Gibson C replaced Strachan, Davenport replaced Olsen
31 Aug	Chelsea	46,478	Old Trafford	H W	3–1	Walsh	Anderson V	Albiston	Moses	McGrath P	Moran	Duxbury	Strachan 1	McClair 1	Whiteside N 1	Olsen	Gibson C replaced Albiston
5 Sep	Coventry City	27,125	Highfield Road	A D	0–0	Walsh	Anderson V	Albiston	Moses	McGrath P	Moran	Duxbury	Strachan	McClair	Whiteside N	Olsen	Gibson C replaced Albiston, Davenport replaced Olsen
12 Sep	Newcastle United	45,137	Old Trafford	H D	2–2	Walsh	Anderson V	Duxbury	Moses	McGrath P	Moran	Robson	Strachan	McClair 1	Whiteside N	Olsen 1	Davenport replaced Olsen
19 Sep	Everton	38,439	Goodison Park	A L	1–2	Walsh	Anderson V	Duxbury	Moses	McGrath P	Hogg	Robson	Strachan	McClair	Whiteside N 1	Olsen	Garton replaced Hogg, Davenport replaced Strachan
26 Sep	Tottenham Hotspur	47,601	Old Trafford	H W	1–0	Walsh	Anderson V	Gibson C	Garton	McGrath P	Duxbury	Robson	Strachan	McClair 1	Whiteside N	Olsen	Blackmore C replaced Anderson V, Davenport replaced Strachan
3 Oct	Luton Town	9,137	Kenilworth Road	A D	1–1	Walsh	Blackmore C	Gibson C	Garton	McGrath P	Duxbury	Robson	Strachan	McClair 1	Whiteside N	Olsen	O'Brien L replaced Blackmore C
10 Oct	Sheffield Wednesday	32,779	Hillsborough	A W	4–2	Walsh	Garton	Gibson C	Duxbury	McGrath P	Moran	Robson 1	Strachan	McClair 2	Whiteside N	Olsen	Blackmore C 1 replaced Moran, Davenport replaced Strachan
17 Oct	Norwich City	39,345	Old Trafford	H W	2–1	Walsh	Garton	Gibson C	Duxbury	McGrath P	Blackmore C	Robson 1	Davenport 1	McClair	Whiteside N	Olsen	Moran replaced Garton, O'Brien L replaced Blackmore C
25 Oct	West Ham United	19,863	Upton Park	A D	1–1	Walsh	Anderson V	Gibson C 1	Duxbury	McGrath P	Moran	Robson	Strachan	McClair	Davenport	Olsen	Blackmore C replaced Strachan
31 Oct	Nottingham Forest	44,669	Old Trafford	H D	2–2	Walsh	Anderson V	Gibson C	Duxbury	Garton	Moran	Robson 1	Davenport	McClair	Whiteside N 1	Olsen	Strachan replaced Whiteside N
15 Nov	Liverpool	47,106	Old Trafford	H D	1–1	Walsh	Anderson V	Gibson C	Duxbury	Blackmore C	Moran	Robson	Strachan	McClair	Whiteside N 1	Olsen	Davenport replaced Moran
21 Nov	Wimbledon	11,532	Plough Lane	A L	1–2	Walsh	Anderson V	Duxbury	Moses	Blackmore C 1	Moran	Robson	Graham D	McClair	Whiteside N	Olsen	Albiston replaced Duxbury, O'Brien L replaced Graham D
5 Dec	Queen's Park Rangers	20,632	Loftus Road	A W	2–0	Turner C	Duxbury	Albiston	Moses	Moran	O'Brien L	Robson 1	Strachan	McClair	Davenport 1	Olsen	
12 Dec	Oxford United	34,709	Old Trafford	H W	3–1	Turner C	Duxbury	Gibson C	Moses	Moran	Davenport	Robson	Strachan 2	McClair	Whiteside N	Olsen 1	Albiston replaced Robson
19 Dec	Portsmouth	22,207	Fratton Park	A W	2–1	Turner C	Duxbury	Gibson C	Bruce	Moran	Moses	Robson 1	Strachan	McClair 1	Whiteside N	Olsen	Davenport replaced Olsen
26 Dec	Newcastle United	26,461	St James' Park	A L	0–1	Turner C	Duxbury	Gibson C	Bruce	Moran	Moses	Robson	Strachan	McClair	Whiteside N	Davenport	Anderson V replaced Gibson C, Olsen replaced Moses
28 Dec	Everton	47,024	Old Trafford	H W	2–1	Turner C	Anderson V	Gibson C	Bruce	Moran	Duxbury	Robson	Strachan	McClair 2	Whiteside N	Olsen	Moses replaced Strachan, Davenport replaced Whiteside N
1 Jan	Charlton Athletic	37,257	Old Trafford	H D	0–0	Turner C	Anderson V	Gibson C	Bruce	Duxbury	Moses	Robson	Strachan	McClair	Davenport	Olsen	O'Brien L replaced Moses, Blackmore C replaced Olsen
2 Jan	Watford	18,038	Vicarage Road	A W	1–0	Turner C	Anderson V	Albiston	Bruce	Moran	Duxbury	Robson	Strachan	McClair 1	Whiteside N	Gibson C	Davenport replaced Albiston, O'Brien L replaced Moran
16 Jan	Southampton	35,716	Old Trafford	H L	0–2	Turner C	Anderson V	Gibson C	Bruce	Moran	Moses	Robson	Duxbury	McClair	Davenport	Olsen	Strachan replaced Gibson C, O'Brien L replaced Moran
24 Jan	Arsenal	29,392	Highbury	A W	2–1	Turner C	Anderson V	Duxbury	Bruce	Blackmore C	Hogg	Robson	Strachan 1	McClair 1	Whiteside N	Olsen	O'Brien L replaced Blackmore C
6 Feb	Coventry City	37,144	Old Trafford	H W	1–0	Turner C	Anderson V	Duxbury	Bruce	O'Brien L 1	Hogg	Robson	Strachan	McClair	Whiteside N	Olsen	Albiston replaced O'Brien L
10 Feb	Derby County	20,016	Baseball Ground	A W	2–1	Turner C	Anderson V	Duxbury	Bruce	O'Brien L	Hogg	Robson	Strachan 1	McClair	Whiteside N 1	Olsen	Albiston replaced Duxbury, Davenport replaced Olsen
13 Feb	Chelsea	25,014	Stamford Bridge	A W	2–1	Turner C	Anderson V	Albiston	Bruce 1	O'Brien L 1	Hogg	Robson	Davenport	McClair	Whiteside N	Gibson C	Blackmore C replaced Gibson C
23 Feb	Tottenham Hotspur	25,731	White Hart Lane	A D	1–1	Turner C	Anderson V	Duxbury	Bruce	O'Brien L	Hogg	Davenport	Blackmore C	McClair 1	Whiteside N	Gibson C	Strachan replaced Hogg, Olsen replaced Anderson V
5 Mar	Norwich City	19,129	Carrow Road	A L	0–1	Turner C	Blackmore C	Duxbury	Bruce	O'Brien L	Moran	Robson	Strachan	McClair	Davenport	Gibson C	Olsen replaced Duxbury
12 Mar	Sheffield Wednesday	33,318	Old Trafford	H W	4–1	Turner C	Blackmore C 1	Gibson C	Bruce	Duxbury	Hogg	Robson	Strachan	McClair 2	Davenport 1	Olsen	O'Brien L replaced Olsen
19 Mar	Nottingham Forest	27,598	City Ground	A D	0–0	Turner C	Anderson V	Blackmore C	Bruce	Duxbury	Hogg	Whiteside N	Olsen	McClair	Davenport	Gibson C	O'Brien L replaced Gibson C, McGrath P replaced Hogg
26 Mar	West Ham United	37,269	Old Trafford	H W	3–1	Turner C	Anderson V 1	Blackmore C	Bruce	McGrath P	Duxbury	Robson 1	Strachan 1	McClair	Davenport	Gibson C	Olsen replaced Strachan
2 Apr	Derby County	40,146	Old Trafford	H W	4–1	Turner C	Anderson V	Blackmore C	Hogg	McGrath P	Duxbury	Robson	Strachan	McClair 3	Davenport	Gibson C 1	Olsen replaced Davenport, O'Brien L replaced McGrath P
4 Apr	Liverpool	43,497	Anfield	A D	3–3	Turner C	Anderson V	Blackmore C	Bruce	McGrath P	Duxbury	Robson 2	Strachan 1	McClair	Davenport	Gibson C	Olsen replaced Duxbury, Whiteside N replaced Blackmore C
12 Apr	Luton Town	28,830	Old Trafford	H W	3–0	Turner C	Anderson V	Blackmore C	Bruce	McGrath P	Duxbury	Robson 1	Strachan	McClair 1	Davenport 1	Gibson C	Olsen replaced Gibson C
30 Apr	Queen's Park Rangers	35,773	Old Trafford	H W	•2–1	Turner C	Anderson V	Blackmore C	Bruce 1	McGrath P	Duxbury	Robson	Strachan	McClair	Davenport	Olsen	O'Brien L replaced Blackmore C
2 May	Oxford United	8,966	Manor Ground	A W	2–0	Turner C	Anderson V 1	Gibson C	Bruce	McGrath P	Duxbury	Robson	Strachan 1	McClair	Davenport	Olsen	Blackmore C replaced Anderson V
7 May	Portsmouth	35,105	Old Trafford	H W	4–1	Turner C	Anderson V	Gibson C	Bruce	McGrath P	Duxbury	Robson 1	Strachan	McClair 2	Davenport 1	Olsen	Hogg replaced McGrath P, Blackmore C replaced Anderson V
9 May	Wimbledon	28,040	Old Trafford	H W	2–1	Turner C	Duxbury	Blackmore C	Bruce	McGrath P	Moses	Robson	Strachan	McClair 2	Davenport	Gibson C	Martin L replaced Moses

FA Cup

10 Jan	Ipswich Town	23,012	Portman Road	A W	•2–1	Turner C	Anderson V 1	Duxbury	Bruce	Moran	Moses	Robson	Strachan	McClair	Whiteside N	Gibson C	Olsen replaced Moses, Davenport replaced Gibson C
30 Jan	Chelsea	50,716	Old Trafford	H W	2–0	Turner C	Anderson V	Duxbury	Bruce	Blackmore C	Hogg	Robson	Strachan	McClair 1	Whiteside N 1	Olsen	O'Brien L replaced Blackmore C
20 Feb	Arsenal	54,161	Highbury	A L	1–2	Turner C	Anderson V	Gibson C	Bruce	Duxbury	Hogg	Davenport	Strachan	McClair 1	Whiteside N	Olsen	O'Brien L replaced Hogg, Blackmore C replaced Olsen

FL Cup

23 Sep	Hull City	25,041	Old Trafford	H W	5–0	Walsh	Anderson V	Gibson C	Moses	McGrath P 1	Duxbury	Robson	Strachan 1	McClair 1	Whiteside N 1	Davenport 1	Garton replaced Moses
7 Oct	Hull City	13,586	Boothferry Park	A W	1–0	Turner C	Blackmore C	Gibson C	Garton	McGrath P	Duxbury	Robson	Strachan	McClair 1	Whiteside N	Olsen	O'Brien L replaced Gibson C, Graham D replaced Duxbury
28 Oct	Crystal Palace	27,283	Old Trafford	H W	2–1	Turner C	Anderson V	Gibson C	Duxbury	Garton	Moran	Robson	Strachan	McClair 2	Whiteside N	Davenport	Blackmore C replaced Robson, Olsen replaced Davenport
18 Nov	Bury	33,519	Old Trafford	H W	2–1	Walsh	Anderson V	Gibson C	Duxbury	Blackmore C	Davenport	Robson	Strachan	McClair 1	Whiteside N 1	Olsen	O'Brien L replaced Gibson C, Moses replaced Davenport
20 Jan	Oxford United	12,658	Manor Ground	A L	0–2	Turner C	Anderson V	Gibson C	Blackmore C	Moran	Duxbury	Robson	Strachan	McClair	Whiteside N	Olsen	Hogg replaced Moran, Davenport replaced Strachan

Football League Division 1
P40 • W23 • D12 • L5 • F71 • A38 • PTS81
Position: 2

1988/89

Football League

		Attendances	Venue			Players and Scores											Substitutions
27 Aug	Queen's Park Rangers	46,377	Old Trafford	H D	0–0	Leighton	Blackmore C	Martin L	Bruce	McGrath P	McClair	Robson	Strachan	Davenport	Hughes	Olsen	O'Brien L replaced Davenport
3 Sep	Liverpool	42,026	Anfield	A L	0–1	Leighton	Anderson V	Blackmore C	Bruce	McGrath P	Duxbury	Robson	Strachan	McClair	Hughes	Olsen	Garton replaced McGrath P, Davenport replaced Strachan
10 Sep	Middlesbrough	40,422	Old Trafford	H W	1–0	Leighton	Garton	Blackmore C	Bruce	McGrath P	Duxbury	Robson 1	Strachan	McClair	Hughes	Olsen	
17 Sep	Luton Town	11,010	Kenilworth Road	A W	2–0	Leighton	Garton	Blackmore C	Bruce	McGrath P	Duxbury	Robson 1	Davenport 1	McClair	Hughes	Olsen	
24 Sep	West Ham United	39,941	Old Trafford	H W	2–0	Leighton	Blackmore C	Sharpe L	Bruce	Garton	Duxbury	Robson	Strachan	McClair	Hughes 1	Davenport 1	Olsen replaced Sharpe L, Beardsmore replaced Garton
1 Oct	Tottenham Hotspur	29,318	White Hart Lane	A D	2–2	Leighton	Garton	Sharpe L	Bruce	McGrath P	Duxbury	Robson	Strachan	McClair 1	Hughes 1	Davenport	Olsen replaced Davenport, Anderson V replaced Garton
22 Oct	Wimbledon	12,143	Plough Lane	A D	1–1	Leighton	Blackmore C	Sharpe L	Bruce	Garton	Duxbury	Robson	Strachan	McClair	Hughes 1	Davenport	Beardsmore replaced Strachan, Robins replaced Davenport
26 Oct	Norwich City	36,998	Old Trafford	H L	1–2	Leighton	Blackmore C	Sharpe L	Bruce	Garton	Duxbury	Robson	Strachan	McClair	Hughes 1	Davenport	Olsen replaced Davenport
30 Oct	Everton	27,005	Goodison Park	A D	1–1	Leighton	Garton	Blackmore C	Bruce	Duxbury	Donaghy M	Robson	Strachan	McClair	Hughes 1	Olsen	Gibson C replaced Strachan, O'Brien L replaced Donaghy M
5 Nov	Aston Villa	44,804	Old Trafford	H D	1–1	Leighton	Blackmore C	Gibson C	Bruce 1	O'Brien L	Donaghy M	Robson	Strachan	McClair	Hughes	Olsen	Duxbury replaced Gibson C
12 Nov	Derby County	24,080	Baseball Ground	A D	2–2	Leighton	Garton	Blackmore C	Bruce	Duxbury	Donaghy M	Robson	Strachan	McClair 1	Hughes 1	Sharpe L	Olsen replaced Duxbury
19 Nov	Southampton	37,277	Old Trafford	H D	2–2	Leighton	Garton	Blackmore C	Bruce	Milne	Donaghy M	Robson 1	Strachan	McClair	Hughes 1	Sharpe L	Gill replaced Sharpe L
23 Nov	Sheffield Wednesday	30,867	Old Trafford	H D	1–1	Leighton	Garton	Blackmore C	Bruce	Milne	Donaghy M	Robson	Strachan	McClair	Hughes 1	Sharpe L	Gill replaced Strachan, Wilson D replaced Blackmore C
27 Nov	Newcastle United	20,350	St James' Park	A D	0–0	Leighton	Garton	Blackmore C	Bruce	Gill	Donaghy M	Robson	Milne	McClair	Hughes	Sharpe L	Martin L replaced Milne, Robins replaced Sharpe L
3 Dec	Charlton Athletic	31,173	Old Trafford	H W	3–0	Leighton	Garton	Martin L	Bruce	Blackmore C	Donaghy M	Robson	Strachan	McClair 1	Hughes 1	Milne 1	
10 Dec	Coventry City	19,936	Highfield Road	A L	0–1	Leighton	Garton	Martin L	Bruce	Blackmore C	Donaghy M	Robson	Strachan	McClair	Hughes	Sharpe L	Gill replaced Garton, Milne replaced Garton
17 Dec	Arsenal	37,422	Highbury	A L	1–2	Leighton	Martin L	Sharpe L	Bruce	Blackmore C	Donaghy M	Robson	Strachan	McClair	Hughes 1	Milne	Gill replaced Blackmore C, Beardsmore replaced Martin L
26 Dec	Nottingham Forest	39,582	Old Trafford	H W	2–0	Leighton	Martin L	Sharpe L	Bruce	Beardsmore	Donaghy M	Robson	Strachan	McClair	Hughes 1	Milne 1	
1 Jan	Liverpool	44,745	Old Trafford	H W	3–1	Leighton	Martin L	Sharpe L	Bruce	Beardsmore 1	Donaghy M	Robson	Strachan	McClair 1	Hughes 1	Milne	McGrath P replaced Martin L, Robins replaced Strachan
2 Jan	Middlesbrough	24,411	Ayresome Park	A L	0–1	Leighton	Gill	Sharpe L	Bruce	McGrath P	Donaghy M	Robson	Beardsmore	McClair	Hughes	Milne	Wilson D replaced Beardsmore, Robins replaced Gill
14 Jan	Millwall	40,931	Old Trafford	H W	3–0	Leighton	Martin L	Sharpe L	Bruce	Beardsmore	Donaghy M	Gill 1	Blackmore C 1	McClair	Hughes 1	Milne	Wilson D replaced Beardsmore, Maiorana replaced Milne
21 Jan	West Ham United	29,822	Upton Park	A W	3–1	Leighton	Gill	Martin L 1	Bruce	Blackmore C	Donaghy M	Robson	Strachan 1	McClair 1	Hughes	Milne	Sharpe L replaced Strachan
5 Feb	Tottenham Hotspur	41,423	Old Trafford	H W	1–0	Leighton	Martin L	Sharpe L	Bruce	Blackmore C	Donaghy M	Robson	Strachan	McClair 1	Hughes	Milne	McGrath P replaced Sharpe L, Beardsmore replaced Strachan
11 Feb	Sheffield Wednesday	34,820	Hillsborough	A W	2–0	Leighton	McGrath P	Martin L	Bruce	Blackmore C	Donaghy M	Robson	Strachan	McClair 2	Hughes	Milne	Beardsmore replaced Hughes
25 Feb	Norwich City	23,155	Carrow Road	A L	1–2	Leighton	Blackmore C	Sharpe L	Bruce	McGrath P 1	Donaghy M	Robson	Strachan	McClair	Hughes	Milne	Martin L replaced Milne, Beardsmore replaced Blackmore C
12 Mar	Aston Villa	28,332	Villa Park	A D	0–0	Leighton	Beardsmore	Martin L	Bruce	McGrath P	Donaghy M	Robson	Strachan	McClair	Hughes	Sharpe L	Blackmore C replaced Beardsmore, Milne replaced Martin L
25 Mar	Luton Town	36,335	Old Trafford	H W	2–0	Leighton	Martin L	Blackmore C 1	Bruce	McGrath P	Donaghy M	Robson	Beardsmore	McClair	Hughes	Milne 1	Maiorana replaced Beardsmore
27 Mar	Nottingham Forest	30,092	City Ground	A L	0–2	Leighton	Anderson V	Blackmore C	Bruce	McGrath P	Donaghy M	Robson	Beardsmore	McClair	Hughes	Milne	Martin L replaced McGrath P, Gill replaced Milne
2 Apr	Arsenal	37,977	Old Trafford	H D	•1–1	Leighton	Anderson V	Donaghy M	Bruce	McGrath P	Whiteside N	Robson	Beardsmore	McClair	Hughes	Maiorana	Martin L replaced Maiorana, Blackmore C replaced Beardsmore
8 Apr	Millwall	17,523	The Den	A D	0–0	Leighton	Anderson V	Donaghy M	Bruce	McGrath P	Whiteside N	Robson	Beardsmore	McClair	Hughes	Martin L	Maiorana replaced McGrath P
15 Apr	Derby County	34,145	Old Trafford	H L	0–2	Leighton	Anderson V	Martin L	Bruce	McGrath P	Donaghy M	Robins	Beardsmore	McClair	Hughes	Maiorana	Duxbury replaced Beardsmore, Wilson D replaced Anderson V
22 Apr	Charlton Athletic	12,055	Selhurst Park	A L	0–1	Leighton	Duxbury	Donaghy M	Bruce	McGrath P	Whiteside N	Robson	Beardsmore	McClair	Hughes	Milne	Robins replaced Milne
29 Apr	Coventry City	29,799	Old Trafford	H L	0–1	Leighton	Duxbury	Donaghy M	Bruce	McGrath P	Whiteside N	Robson	Beardsmore	McClair	Hughes	Martin L	Robins replaced Martin L
2 May	Wimbledon	23,368	Old Trafford	H W	1–0	Leighton	Duxbury	Donaghy M	Bruce	McGrath P	Whiteside N	Robson	Beardsmore	McClair 1	Hughes	Martin L	Maiorana replaced Whiteside N
6 May	Southampton	17,021	The Dell	A L	1–2	Leighton	Duxbury	Donaghy M	Bruce	McGrath P	Whiteside N	Robson	Beardsmore 1	McClair	Hughes	Martin L	Sharpe L replaced Martin L, Milne replaced Robson
8 May	Queen's Park Rangers	10,017	Loftus Road	A L	2–3	Leighton	Duxbury	Sharpe L	Bruce 1	Blackmore C 1	Donaghy M	Milne	Beardsmore	McClair	Hughes	Martin L	Robins replaced Sharpe L
10 May	Everton	26,722	Old Trafford	H L	1–2	Leighton	Duxbury	Sharpe L	Bruce	Blackmore C	Donaghy M	Milne	Beardsmore	McClair	Hughes 1	Martin L	Robins replaced Blackmore C, Brazil D replaced Duxbury
13 May	Newcastle United	30,379	Old Trafford	H W	2–0	Leighton	Duxbury	Martin L	Bruce	Blackmore C	Donaghy M	Robson 1	Beardsmore	McClair 1	Hughes	Milne	Robins replaced Milne, Sharpe L replaced Blackmore C

FA Cup

7 Jan	Queen's Park Rangers	36,222	Old Trafford	H D	0–0	Leighton	Gill	Martin L	Bruce	Beardsmore	Donaghy M	Robson	Robins	McClair	Hughes	Milne	Wilson D replaced Robson
11 Jan	Queen's Park Rangers	22,236	Loftus Road	A D	2–2	Leighton	Martin L	Sharpe L	Bruce	Beardsmore	Donaghy M	Gill 1	Blackmore C	McClair	Hughes	Milne	Graham D 1 replaced Sharpe L, Wilson D replaced Blackmore C
23 Jan	Queen's Park Rangers	46,257	Old Trafford	H W	3–0	Leighton	Martin L	Sharpe L	Bruce	Blackmore C	Donaghy M	Robson 1	Strachan	McClair 2	Hughes	Milne	Beardsmore replaced Blackmore C, McGrath P replaced Milne
28 Jan	Oxford United	47,754	Old Trafford	H W	•4–0	Leighton	Blackmore C	Sharpe L	Bruce 1	McGrath P	Donaghy M	Robson 1	Strachan	McClair	Hughes 1	Milne	Beardsmore replaced Sharpe L, Gill replaced McGrath P
18 Feb	Bournemouth	12,500	Dean Court	A D	1–1	Leighton	Blackmore C	Martin L	Bruce	McGrath P	Donaghy M	Robson	Strachan	McClair	Hughes 1	Milne	Sharpe L replaced Martin L
22 Feb	Bournemouth	52,422	Old Trafford	H W	1–0	Leighton	Blackmore C	Sharpe L	Bruce	McGrath P	Donaghy M	Robson	Strachan	McClair 1	Hughes	Milne	Gill replaced Milne
18 Mar	Nottingham Forest	55,052	Old Trafford	H L	0–1	Leighton	Beardsmore	Sharpe L	Bruce	McGrath P	Donaghy M	Robson	Strachan	McClair	Hughes	Milne	Martin L replaced Sharpe L, Blackmore C replaced Milne

FL Cup

28 Sep	Rotherham United	12,592	Millmoor Ground	A W	1–0	Leighton	Blackmore C	Sharpe L	Bruce	McGrath P	Duxbury	Robson	Strachan	McClair	Hughes	Davenport 1	Beardsmore replaced Sharpe L, Olsen replaced Strachan
12 Oct	Rotherham United	20,597	Old Trafford	H W	5–0	Leighton	Beardsmore	Blackmore C	Bruce 1	Garton	Duxbury	Robson 1	Strachan	McClair 3	Hughes	Sharpe L	Robins replaced Duxbury, Davenport replaced Robson
2 Nov	Wimbledon	10,864	Plough Lane	A L	1–2	Leighton	Blackmore C	Gibson C	Bruce	Garton	Duxbury	Robson 1	O'Brien L	McClair	Hughes	Olsen	Strachan replaced Duxbury, Anderson V replaced Olsen

Football League Division 1
P38 • W13 • D12 • L13 • F45 • A35 • PTS51
Position: 11

The 1990s

1989/90

Football League		Attendances	Venue				Players and Scores											Substitutions
19 Aug	Arsenal	47,245	Old Trafford	H	W	4–1	Leighton	Duxbury	Blackmore C	Bruce 1	Phelan	Donaghy M	Robson	Webb 1	McClair 1	Hughes 1	Sharpe L	Martin L replaced Sharpe L
22 Aug	Crystal Palace	22,423	Selhurst Park	A	D	1–1	Leighton	Duxbury	Blackmore C	Bruce	Phelan	Donaghy M	Robson 1	Webb	McClair	Hughes	Sharpe L	
26 Aug	Derby County	22,175	Baseball Ground	A	L	0–2	Leighton	Duxbury	Martin L	Bruce	Phelan	Blackmore C	Robson	Webb	McClair	Hughes	Sharpe L	Graham D replaced Martin L
30 Aug	Norwich City	39,610	Old Trafford	H	L	0–2	Leighton	Duxbury	Blackmore C	Bruce	Phelan	Pallister	Robson	Webb	McClair	Hughes	Sharpe L	Martin L replaced Robson, Robins replaced Blackmore C
9 Sep	Everton	37,916	Goodison Park	A	L	2–3	Leighton	Duxbury	Martin L	Bruce	Phelan	Pallister	Donaghy M	Blackmore C	McClair 1	Hughes	Sharpe L	Anderson V replaced Duxbury, Beardsmore 1 replaced Martin L
16 Sep	Millwall	42,746	Old Trafford	H	W	5–1	Leighton	Anderson V	Donaghy M	Bruce	Phelan	Pallister	Robson 1	Ince	McClair	Hughes 3	Sharpe L 1	Duxbury replaced Ince, Beardsmore replaced Bruce
23 Sep	Manchester City	43,246	Maine Road	A	L	1–5	Leighton	Anderson V	Donaghy M	Duxbury	Phelan	Pallister	Beardsmore	Ince	McClair	Hughes 1	Wallace	Sharpe L replaced Beardsmore
14 Oct	Sheffield Wednesday	41,492	Old Trafford	H	D	0–0	Leighton	Duxbury	Donaghy M	Bruce	Phelan	Pallister	Robson	Ince	McClair	Hughes	Wallace	Martin L replaced Duxbury, Sharpe L replaced Wallace
21 Oct	Coventry City	19,605	Highfield Road	A	W	4–1	Leighton	Donaghy M	Martin L	Bruce 1	Phelan 1	Pallister	Robson	Ince	McClair	Hughes 2	Sharpe L	Duxbury replaced Ince, Maiorana replaced Sharpe L
28 Oct	Southampton	37,122	Old Trafford	H	W	2–1	Leighton	Donaghy M	Martin L	Bruce	Phelan	Pallister	Robson	Ince	McClair 2	Hughes	Sharpe L	Blackmore C replaced Ince
4 Nov	Charlton Athletic	16,065	Selhurst Park	A	L	0–2	Leighton	Donaghy M	Martin L	Bruce	Phelan	Pallister	Robson	Ince	McClair	Hughes	Sharpe L	Blackmore C replaced Sharpe L, Wallace replaced Donaghy M
12 Nov	Nottingham Forest	34,182	Old Trafford	H	W	1–0	Leighton	Blackmore C	Martin L	Bruce	Phelan	Pallister 1	Robson	Ince	McClair	Hughes	Wallace	Sharpe L replaced Wallace
18 Nov	Luton Town	11,141	Kenilworth Road	A	W	3–1	Leighton	Blackmore C 1	Martin L	Bruce	Phelan	Pallister	Robson	Ince	McClair	Hughes 1	Wallace 1	
25 Nov	Chelsea	47,106	Old Trafford	H	D	0–0	Leighton	Blackmore C	Martin L	Bruce	Phelan	Pallister	Robson	Ince	McClair	Hughes	Wallace	Duxbury replaced Martin L, Beardsmore replaced Wallace
3 Dec	Arsenal	34,484	Highbury	A	L	0–1	Leighton	Blackmore C	Martin L	Bruce	Phelan	Pallister	Robson	Ince	McClair	Hughes	Wallace	Beardsmore replaced Blackmore C
9 Dec	Crystal Palace	33,514	Old Trafford	H	L	1–2	Leighton	Beardsmore 1	Martin L	Bruce	Phelan	Pallister	Robson	Ince	McClair	Sharpe L	Wallace	Hughes replaced Sharpe L, Blackmore C replaced Phelan
16 Dec	Tottenham Hotspur	36,230	Old Trafford	H	L	0–1	Leighton	Beardsmore	Sharpe L	Bruce	Phelan	Pallister	Robson	Ince	McClair	Hughes	Wallace	Anderson V replaced Bruce, Blackmore C replaced Beardsmore
23 Dec	Liverpool	37,426	Anfield	A	D	0–0	Leighton	Blackmore C	Martin L	Bruce	Phelan	Pallister	Robson	Ince	McClair	Hughes	Wallace	Sharpe L replaced Wallace
26 Dec	Aston Villa	41,247	Villa Park	A	L	0–3	Leighton	Anderson V	Martin L	Bruce	Phelan	Pallister	Blackmore C	Ince	McClair	Hughes	Sharpe L	Duxbury replaced Martin L, Robins replaced Blackmore C
30 Dec	Wimbledon	9,622	Plough Lane	A	D	2–2	Leighton	Anderson V	Martin L	Bruce	Phelan	Pallister	Blackmore C	Ince	McClair	Hughes 1	Robins 1	Sharpe L replaced Ince
1 Jan	Queen's Park Rangers	34,824	Old Trafford	H	D	0–0	Leighton	Anderson V	Martin L	Bruce	Phelan	Pallister	Sharpe L	Blackmore C	McClair	Hughes	Robins	Duxbury replaced Sharpe L, Beardsmore replaced Blackmore C
13 Jan	Derby County	38,985	Old Trafford	H	L	1–2	Leighton	Anderson V	Martin L	Bruce	Phelan	Pallister 1	Beardsmore	Blackmore C	McClair	Hughes	Robins	Duxbury replaced Blackmore C, Milne replaced Beardsmore
21 Jan	Norwich City	17,370	Carrow Road	A	L	0–2	Leighton	Anderson V	Martin L	Bruce	Phelan	Pallister	Robins	Ince	McClair	Hughes	Wallace	Beardsmore replaced Ince, Blackmore C replaced Phelan
3 Feb	Manchester City	40,274	Old Trafford	H	D	1–1	Leighton	Anderson V	Martin L	Donaghy M	Phelan	Pallister	Blackmore C 1	Duxbury	McClair	Hughes	Wallace	Beardsmore replaced Donaghy M, Robins replaced Wallace
10 Feb	Millwall	15,491	The Den	A	W	2–1	Leighton	Anderson V	Martin L	Beardsmore	Phelan	Pallister	Blackmore C	Duxbury	McClair	Hughes 1	Wallace 1	Brazil D replaced Anderson V, Robins replaced Blackmore C
24 Feb	Chelsea	29,979	Stamford Bridge	A	L	0–1	Leighton	Anderson V	Martin L	Bruce	Phelan	Pallister	Duxbury	Ince	McClair	Hughes	Wallace	Beardsmore replaced Duxbury, Donaghy M replaced Anderson V
3 Mar	Luton Town	35,327	Old Trafford	H	W	4–1	Leighton	Anderson V	Martin L	Bruce	Phelan	Pallister	Robins 1	Ince	McClair 1	Hughes 1	Wallace 1	Beardsmore replaced Wallace
14 Mar	Everton	37,398	Old Trafford	H	D	0–0	Leighton	Duxbury	Martin L	Bruce	Phelan	Pallister	Robins	Ince	McClair	Hughes	Wallace	Beardsmore replaced Hughes, Blackmore C replaced Robins
18 Mar	Liverpool	46,629	Old Trafford	H	L	•1–2	Leighton	Anderson V	Martin L	Bruce	Phelan	Pallister	Blackmore C	Ince	McClair	Hughes	Wallace	Duxbury replaced Anderson V, Beardsmore replaced Wallace
21 Mar	Sheffield Wednesday	33,260	Hillsbrough	A	L	0–1	Leighton	Donaghy M	Martin L	Bruce	Phelan	Pallister	Beardsmore	Gibson C	McClair	Hughes	Blackmore C	Ince replaced Blackmore C, Wallace replaced Beardsmore
24 Mar	Southampton	20,510	The Dell	A	W	2–0	Leighton	Donaghy M	Martin L	Bruce	Phelan	Pallister	Gibson C 1	Ince	McClair 1	Hughes	Wallace	Webb replaced Gibson C, Robins 1 replaced Hughes
31 Mar	Coventry City	39,172	Old Trafford	H	W	3–0	Leighton	Donaghy M	Gibson C	Bruce	Phelan	Pallister	Webb	Ince	McClair	Hughes 2	Wallace	Martin L replaced Donaghy M, Robins 1 replaced Wallace
14 Apr	Queen's Park Rangers	18,997	Loftus Road	A	W	2–1	Sealey	Ince	Martin L	Bruce	Phelan	Pallister	Robson	Webb 1	McClair	Hughes	Wallace	Gibson C replaced Bruce, Robins 1 replaced Hughes
17 Apr	Aston Villa	44,080	Old Trafford	H	W	2–0	Sealey	Anderson V	Gibson C	Robins 2	Phelan	Pallister	Robson	Webb	McClair	Hughes	Wallace	Beardsmore replaced Anderson V, Blackmore C replaced Gibson C
21 Apr	Tottenham Hotspur	33,317	White Hart Lane	A	L	1–2	Leighton	Robins	Martin L	Bruce 1	Phelan	Pallister	Robson	Webb	McClair	Hughes	Wallace	Beardsmore replaced Wallace, Blackmore C replaced Webb
30 Apr	Wimbledon	29,281	Old Trafford	H	D	0–0	Bosnich	Anderson V	Martin L	Bruce	Phelan	Pallister	Beardsmore	Ince	Robins	Hughes	Gibson C	Wallace replaced Robins, Blackmore C replaced Gibson C
2 May	Nottingham Forest	21,186	City Ground	A	L	0–4	Leighton	Duxbury	Blackmore C	Bruce	Phelan	Pallister	Beardsmore	Webb	McClair	Robins	Wallace	
5 May	Charlton Athletic	35,389	Old Trafford	H	W	1–0	Leighton	Ince	Martin L	Bruce	Phelan	Pallister 1	Robson	Webb	McClair	Hughes	Wallace	

FA Cup																		
7 Jan	Nottingham Forest	23,072	City Ground	A	W	1–0	Leighton	Anderson V	Martin L	Bruce	Phelan	Pallister	Beardsmore	Blackmore C	McClair	Hughes	Robins 1	Duxbury replaced Blackmore C
28 Jan	Hereford United	13,777	Edgar Street	A	W	1–0	Leighton	Anderson V	Martin L	Donaghy M	Duxbury	Pallister	Blackmore C 1	Ince	McClair	Hughes	Wallace	Beardsmore replaced Ince
18 Feb	Newcastle United	31,748	St James' Park	A	W	3–2	Leighton	Anderson V	Martin L	Bruce	Phelan	Pallister	Robins 1	Duxbury	McClair 1	Hughes	Wallace 1	Beardsmore replaced Robins 1, Ince replaced Duxbury
11 Mar	Sheffield United	34,344	Bramall Lane	A	W	1–0	Leighton	Anderson V	Martin L	Bruce	Phelan	Pallister	Robins	Ince	McClair 1	Hughes	Wallace	Duxbury replaced Anderson V
8 Apr	Oldham Athletic	44,026	Maine Road	A	D	3–3	Leighton	Martin L	Gibson C	Bruce	Phelan	Pallister	Robson 1	Ince	McClair	Hughes	Webb 1	Robins replaced Martin L, Wallace 1 replaced Robson
11 Apr	Oldham Athletic	35,005	Maine Road	A	W	2–1	Leighton	Ince	Martin L	Bruce	Phelan	Pallister	Robson	Webb	McClair 1	Hughes	Wallace	Robins 1 replaced Martin L
12 May	Crystal Palace	80,000	Wembley	A	D	3–3	Leighton	Ince	Martin L	Bruce	Phelan	Pallister	Robson 1	Webb	McClair	Hughes 2	Wallace	Blackmore C replaced Martin L, Robins replaced Pallister
17 May	Crystal Palace	80,000	Wembley	A	W	1–0	Sealey	Ince	Martin L 1	Bruce	Phelan	Pallister	Robson	Webb	McClair	Hughes	Wallace	

FL Cup																		
20 Sep	Portsmouth	18,072	Fratton Park	A	W	3–2	Leighton	Anderson V	Donaghy M	Beardsmore	Phelan	Pallister	Robson	Ince 2	McClair	Hughes	Wallace 1	Duxbury replaced Robson, Sharpe L replaced McClair
3 Oct	Portsmouth	26,698	Old Trafford	H	D	0–0	Leighton	Duxbury	Donaghy M	Bruce	Phelan	Pallister	Robson	Ince	McClair	Hughes	Wallace	
25 Oct	Tottenham Hotspur	45,759	Old Trafford	H	L	0–3	Leighton	Donaghy M	Martin L	Bruce	Phelan	Pallister	Robson	Ince	McClair	Hughes	Sharpe L	Maiorana replaced Martin L

Football League Division 1
P38 • W13 • D9 • L16 • F46 • A47 • PTS48
Position: 13

1990/91

Football League		Attendances	Venue				Players and Scores											Substitutions
25 Aug	Coventry City	46,715	Old Trafford	H	W	2–0	Sealey	Irwin	Donaghy M	Bruce 1	Phelan	Pallister	Webb 1	Ince	McClair	Hughes	Blackmore C	
28 Aug	Leeds United	29,172	Elland Road	A	D	0–0	Sealey	Irwin	Donaghy M	Bruce	Phelan	Pallister	Webb	Ince	McClair	Hughes	Blackmore C	Beardsmore replaced Ince
1 Sep	Sunderland	26,105	Roker Park	A	L	1–2	Sealey	Irwin	Donaghy M	Bruce	Phelan	Pallister	Webb	Ince	McClair 1	Hughes	Blackmore C	Beardsmore replaced Hughes, Robins replaced Donaghy M
4 Sep	Luton Town	12,576	Kenilworth Road	A	W	1–0	Sealey	Irwin	Blackmore C	Bruce	Phelan	Pallister	Webb	Ince	McClair	Robins 1	Beardsmore	Hughes replaced Robins, Donaghy M replaced Beardsmore
8 Sep	Queen's Park Rangers	43,427	Old Trafford	H	W	3–1	Sealey	Irwin	Blackmore C	Bruce	Phelan	Pallister	Webb	Ince	McClair 1	Robins 2	Beardsmore	
16 Sep	Liverpool	35,726	Anfield	A	L	0–4	Sealey	Irwin	Blackmore C	Bruce	Phelan	Pallister	Webb	Ince	McClair	Hughes	Robins	Beardsmore replaced Ince, Donaghy M replaced Pallister
22 Sep	Southampton	41,228	Old Trafford	H	W	3–2	Sealey	Irwin	Donaghy M	Anderson V	Phelan	Pallister	Webb	Robins	McClair 1	Hughes 1	Blackmore C 1	Beardsmore replaced Robins, Sharpe L replaced Irwin
29 Sep	Nottingham Forest	46,766	Old Trafford	H	L	0–1	Sealey	Irwin	Blackmore C	Donaghy M	Phelan	Pallister	Webb	Ince	McClair	Robins	Beardsmore	Hughes replaced Robins, Martin L replaced Beardsmore
20 Oct	Arsenal	47,232	Old Trafford	H	L	0–1	Sealey	Irwin	Blackmore C	Bruce	Phelan	Pallister	Webb	Ince	McClair	Hughes	Sharpe L	Robins replaced Sharpe L, Martin L replaced Irwin
27 Oct	Manchester City	36,427	Maine Road	A	D	3–3	Sealey	Irwin	Martin L	Bruce	Blackmore C	Pallister	Webb	Ince	McClair 2	Hughes 1	Sharpe L	Wallace replaced Sharpe L
3 Nov	Crystal Palace	45,724	Old Trafford	H	W	2–0	Sealey	Irwin	Blackmore C	Bruce	Phelan	Pallister	Webb 1	Ince	McClair	Wallace 1	Sharpe L	Martin L replaced Wallace
10 Nov	Derby County	21,115	Baseball Ground	A	D	0–0	Sealey	Irwin	Blackmore C	Bruce	Phelan	Pallister	Webb	Ince	McClair	Hughes	Sharpe L	Wallace replaced Sharpe L, Donaghy M replaced Irwin
17 Nov	Sheffield United	45,903	Old Trafford	H	W	2–0	Sealey	Irwin	Blackmore C	Bruce 1	Phelan	Pallister	Webb	Ince	McClair	Hughes 1	Sharpe L	Wallace replaced Irwin
25 Nov	Chelsea	37,836	Old Trafford	H	L	2–3	Sealey	Irwin	Blackmore C	Bruce	Phelan	Pallister	Webb	Ince	McClair	Hughes 1	Wallace 1	Martin L replaced Blackmore C, Sharpe L replaced Phelan
1 Dec	Everton	32,400	Goodison Park	A	W	1–0	Sealey	Irwin	Blackmore C	Donaghy M	Phelan	Pallister	Sharpe L 1	Ince	McClair	Hughes	Wallace	Martin L replaced Sharpe L, Webb replaced Ince
8 Dec	Leeds United	40,927	Old Trafford	H	D	1–1	Sealey	Irwin	Blackmore C	Donaghy M	Phelan	Pallister	Sharpe L	Webb 1	McClair	Hughes	Wallace	Robson replaced Irwin, Donaghy M replaced Phelan
15 Dec	Coventry City	17,106	Highfield Road	A	D	2–2	Sealey	Blackmore C	Sharpe L	Bruce	Phelan	Pallister	Webb	Ince	McClair	Hughes 1	Wallace 1	Robson replaced Sharpe L, Irwin replaced Ince
22 Dec	Wimbledon	9,744	Plough Lane	A	W	3–1	Sealey	Blackmore C	Donaghy M	Bruce 2	Phelan	Pallister	Robson	Ince	McClair	Hughes 1	Webb	Wallace replaced Blackmore C
26 Dec	Norwich City	39,801	Old Trafford	H	W	3–0	Sealey	Irwin	Blackmore C	Bruce	Webb	Pallister	Robson	Ince	McClair 2	Hughes 1	Sharpe L	Phelan replaced Robson, Donaghy M replaced Sharpe L
29 Dec	Aston Villa	47,485	Old Trafford	H	D	1–1	Sealey	Irwin	Blackmore C	Bruce 1	Webb	Pallister	Robson	Ince	McClair	Hughes	Sharpe L	Phelan replaced Robson
1 Jan	Tottenham Hotspur	29,399	White Hart Lane	A	W	2–1	Sealey	Irwin	Blackmore C	Bruce 1	Phelan	Pallister	Webb	Ince	McClair 1	Hughes	Sharpe L	Robins replaced Phelan, Martin L replaced Irwin
12 Jan	Sunderland	45,934	Old Trafford	H	W	3–0	Sealey	Irwin	Blackmore C	Bruce	Webb	Pallister	Robson	Ince	McClair 1	Hughes 2	Sharpe L	Phelan replaced Webb, Robins replaced Ince
19 Jan	Queen's Park Rangers	18,544	Loftus Road	A	D	1–1	Sealey	Irwin	Martin L	Bruce	Phelan 1	Donaghy M	Beardsmore	Webb	McClair	Hughes	Blackmore C	Robins replaced Beardsmore, Sharpe L replaced Martin L
3 Feb	Liverpool	43,690	Old Trafford	H	D	1–1	Sealey	Irwin	Blackmore C	Bruce 1	Phelan	Pallister	Robson	Webb	McClair	Hughes	Sharpe L	Wallace replaced Webb, Martin L replaced Phelan
26 Feb	Sheffield United	27,570	Bramall Lane	A	L	1–2	Walsh	Irwin	Martin L	Webb	Donaghy M	Pallister	Robson	Ince	McClair	Blackmore C 1	Wallace	Robins replaced Robson, Ferguson D replaced Webb
2 Mar	Everton	45,656	Old Trafford	H	L	0–2	Sealey	Irwin	Martin L	Ferguson D	Donaghy M	Pallister	Sharpe L	Ince	McClair	Blackmore C	Wallace	Beardsmore replaced Martin L, Giggs replaced Irwin
9 Mar	Chelsea	22,818	Stamford Bridge	A	L	2–3	Sealey	Blackmore C	Martin L	Donaghy M	Phelan	Pallister	Robson	Ince	McClair 1	Hughes 1	Sharpe L	Wallace replaced Blackmore C
13 Mar	Southampton	15,701	The Dell	A	D	1–1	Sealey	Whitworth	Martin L	Donaghy M	Phelan	Pallister	Beardsmore	Ince 1	McClair	Wallace	Sharpe L	Robins replaced Beardsmore, Ferguson D replaced Whitworth
16 Mar	Nottingham Forest	23,859	City Ground	A	D	1–1	Sealey	Irwin	Martin L	Bruce	Phelan	Pallister	Robson	Ince	Blackmore C 1	Hughes	Wallace	Donaghy M replaced Martin L
23 Mar	Luton Town	41,752	Old Trafford	H	W	4–1	Sealey	Irwin	Blackmore C	Bruce 2	Phelan	Pallister	Robson	Wallace	McClair 1	Hughes	Sharpe L	Robins 1 replaced Wallace
30 Mar	Norwich City	18,282	Carrow Road	A	W	3–0	Sealey	Irwin	Blackmore C	Bruce 2	Phelan	Pallister	Robson	Ince 1	Webb	Hughes	Sharpe L	McClair replaced Irwin, Robins replaced Sharpe L
2 Apr	Wimbledon	36,660	Old Trafford	H	W	2–1	Walsh	Irwin	Donaghy M	Bruce 1	Phelan	Pallister	Webb	Ince	McClair 1	Blackmore C	Sharpe L	Robins replaced Sharpe L, Wratten replaced Bruce
6 Apr	Aston Villa	33,307	Villa Park	A	D	1–1	Sealey	Irwin	Donaghy M	Bruce	Phelan	Pallister	Robson	Webb	McClair	Hughes	Sharpe L 1	Robins replaced Phelan
16 Apr	Derby County	32,776	Old Trafford	H	W	3–1	Bosnich	Irwin	Donaghy M	Bruce	Webb	Pallister	Robson 1	Ince	Blackmore C 1	Hughes	Wallace	McClair 1 replaced Webb
4 May	Manchester City	45,286	Old Trafford	H	W	1–0	Walsh	Irwin	Blackmore C	Bruce	Phelan	Pallister	Robson	Webb	McClair	Hughes	Giggs 1	Donaghy M replaced Giggs
6 May	Arsenal	40,229	Highbury	A	L	1–3	Walsh	Phelan	Blackmore C	Bruce 1	Webb	Donaghy M	Robson	Ince	McClair	Hughes	Robins	Beardsmore replaced Robson, Ferguson D replaced Hughes
11 May	Crystal Palace	25,301	Selhurst Park	A	L	0–3	Walsh	Irwin	Donaghy M	Bruce	Webb	Pallister	Kanchelskis	Ince	Robins	Ferguson D	Wallace	Beardsmore replaced Pallister, Wratten replaced Robins

7 Jan	Queen's Park Rangers	35,065	Old Trafford	H	W	2–1	Sealey	Irwin	Blackmore C	Bruce	Webb	Pallister	Robson	Ince	McClair 1	Hughes 1	Sharpe L	
26 Jan	Bolton Wanderers	43,293	Old Trafford	H	W	1–0	Sealey	Irwin	Blackmore C	Bruce	Phelan	Pallister	Robson	Webb	McClair	Hughes 1	Sharpe L	Robins replaced Phelan
18 Feb	Norwich City	23,058	Carrow Road	A	L	1–2	Sealey	Irwin	Martin L	Bruce	Blackmore C	Pallister	Robson	Ince	McClair 1	Hughes	Sharpe L	Wallace replaced Martin L

FL Cup																		
26 Sep	Halifax Town	7,500	Shay Ground	A	W	3–1	Leighton	Irwin	Blackmore C 1	Donaghy M	Phelan	Pallister	Webb 1	Ince	McClair 1	Hughes	Beardsmore	Martin L replaced Ince, Robins replaced Hughes
10 Oct	Halifax Town	22,295	Old Trafford	H	W	2–1	Sealey	Anderson V 1	Blackmore C	Bruce 1	Phelan	Pallister	Webb	Irwin	McClair	Hughes	Martin L	Wallace replaced Blackmore C, Robins replaced Irwin
31 Oct	Liverpool	42,033	Old Trafford	H	W	3–1	Sealey	Irwin	Blackmore C	Bruce 1	Phelan	Pallister	Webb	Ince	McClair	Hughes 1	Sharpe L 1	Donaghy M replaced Phelan, Wallace replaced Hughes
28 Nov	Arsenal	40,884	Highbury	A	W	6–2	Sealey	Irwin	Blackmore C 1	Bruce	Phelan	Pallister	Sharpe L 3	Ince	McClair	Hughes 1	Wallace 1	Donaghy M replaced Bruce
16 Jan	Southampton	21,011	The Dell	A	D	1–1	Sealey	Donaghy M	Blackmore C	Bruce	Phelan	Pallister	Robson	Webb	McClair	Hughes 1	Sharpe L	Irwin replaced Webb
23 Jan	Southampton	41,093	Old Trafford	H	W	3–2	Sealey	Irwin	Blackmore C	Bruce	Phelan	Pallister	Robson	Webb	McClair	Hughes 3	Sharpe L	Donaghy M replaced Irwin, Robins replaced Sharpe L
10 Feb	Leeds United	34,050	Old Trafford	H	W	2–1	Sealey	Irwin	Martin L	Bruce	Blackmore C	Pallister	Robson	Ince	McClair 1	Hughes	Sharpe L 1	Donaghy M replaced Irwin, Wallace replaced Martin L
24 Feb	Leeds United	32,014	Elland Road	A	W	1–0	Sealey	Donaghy M	Blackmore C	Webb	Phelan	Pallister	Robson	Ince	McClair	Hughes	Sharpe L 1	Martin L replaced Webb
21 Apr	Sheffield Wednesday	80,000	Wembley	A	L	0–1	Sealey	Irwin	Blackmore C	Bruce	Webb	Pallister	Robson	Ince	McClair	Hughes	Sharpe L	Phelan replaced Webb

European Cup Winners' Cup																		
19 Sep	Pecsi Munkas	26,411	Old Trafford	H	W	2–0	Sealey	Irwin	Blackmore C 1	Bruce	Phelan	Pallister	Webb 1	Ince	McClair	Robins	Beardsmore	Hughes replaced Robins, Sharpe L replaced Ince
3 Oct	Pecsi Munkas	15,000	PMSC Stadion	A	W	1–0	Sealey	Anderson V	Donaghy M	Bruce	Phelan	Pallister	Webb	Blackmore C	McClair 1	Hughes	Martin L	Sharpe L replaced Martin L
23 Oct	Wrexham	29,405	Old Trafford	H	W	3–0	Sealey	Blackmore C	Martin L	Bruce 1	Sharpe L	Pallister 1	Webb	Ince	McClair 1	Hughes	Wallace	Beardsmore replaced Ince, Robins replaced Wallace
7 Nov	Wrexham	13,327	The Racecourse	A	W	2–0	Sealey	Irwin	Blackmore C	Bruce 1	Phelan	Pallister	Webb	Ince	McClair	Robins 1	Wallace	Donaghy M replaced Ince, Martin L replaced McClair
6 Mar	Montpellier	41,942	Old Trafford	H	D	1–1	Sealey	Blackmore C	Martin L	Donaghy M	Phelan	Pallister	Robson	Ince	McClair 1	Hughes	Sharpe L	Wallace replaced Martin L
19 Mar	Montpellier	20,500	Stade de la Masson	A	W	2–0	Sealey	Irwin	Blackmore C 1	Bruce 1	Phelan	Pallister	Robson	Ince	McClair	Hughes	Sharpe L	Martin L replaced Ince
10 Apr	Legia Warsaw	17,500	Wojska Polskiego	A	W	3–1	Sealey	Irwin	Blackmore C	Bruce 1	Phelan	Pallister	Webb	Ince	McClair 1	Hughes 1	Sharpe L	Donaghy M replaced Phelan
24 Apr	Legia Warsaw	44,269	Old Trafford	H	D	1–1	Walsh	Irwin	Blackmore C	Bruce	Phelan	Pallister	Robson	Webb	McClair	Hughes	Sharpe L 1	Donaghy M replaced Blackmore C
15 May	Barcelona	45,000	Feyenoord Stadion	A	W	2–1	Sealey	Irwin	Blackmore C	Bruce	Phelan	Pallister	Robson	Ince	McClair	Hughes 2	Sharpe L	

Football League Division 1
P38 • W16 • D12 • L10 • F58 • A45 • PTS59

1991/92

Football League

Date	Opponent	Attendances	Venue			Players and Scores											Substitutions
17 Aug	Notts County	46,278	Old Trafford	H	W	2–0	Schmeichel	Irwin	Blackmore C	Bruce	Ferguson D	Parker P	Robson 1	Ince	McClair	Hughes 1	Kanchelskis	Pallister replaced Ince, Giggs replaced Ferguson D
21 Aug	Aston Villa	39,995	Villa Park	A	W	1–0	Schmeichel	Irwin	Blackmore C	Bruce 1	Donaghy M	Parker P	Robson	Ince	McClair	Hughes	Kanchelskis	
24 Aug	Everton	36,085	Goodison Park	A	D	0–0	Schmeichel	Irwin	Blackmore C	Bruce	Donaghy M	Parker P	Robson	Ince	McClair	Hughes	Giggs	Webb replaced Irwin, Pallister replaced Blackmore C
28 Aug	Oldham Athletic	42,078	Old Trafford	H	W	1–0	Schmeichel	Parker P	Irwin	Bruce	Webb	Pallister	Robson	Ince	McClair 1	Hughes	Giggs	Blackmore C replaced Ince, Ferguson D replaced Webb
31 Aug	Leeds United	43,778	Old Trafford	H	D	1–1	Schmeichel	Parker P	Irwin	Bruce	Webb	Pallister	Robson 1	Ince	McClair	Hughes	Blackmore C	Giggs replaced Ince, Phelan replaced Bruce
3 Sep	Wimbledon	13,824	Selhurst Park	A	W	2–1	Schmeichel	Parker P	Donaghy M	Bruce	Phelan	Pallister 1	Robson	Webb	McClair	Hughes	Blackmore C 1	Irwin replaced Phelan
7 Sep	Norwich City	44,946	Old Trafford	H	W	3–0	Schmeichel	Parker P	Irwin 1	Bruce	Webb	Pallister	Robson	Kanchelskis	McClair 1	Hughes	Giggs 1	Blackmore C replaced Kanchelskis, Phelan replaced Webb
14 Sep	Southampton	19,264	The Dell	A	W	1–0	Schmeichel	Phelan	Irwin	Bruce	Webb	Pallister	Robson	Kanchelskis	McClair	Hughes 1	Giggs	Ince replaced Kanchelskis
21 Sep	Luton Town	46,491	Old Trafford	H	W	5–0	Schmeichel	Phelan	Irwin	Bruce 1	Webb	Pallister	Robson	Ince 1	Blackmore C	Hughes 1	Giggs	McClair 2 replaced Blackmore C
28 Sep	Tottenham Hotspur	35,087	White Hart Lane	A	W	2–1	Schmeichel	Phelan	Irwin	Bruce	Kanchelskis	Pallister	Robson 1	Ince	McClair	Hughes 1	Giggs	Blackmore C replaced Kanchelskis
6 Oct	Liverpool	44,997	Old Trafford	H	D	0–0	Schmeichel	Phelan	Irwin	Bruce	Blackmore C	Pallister	Robson	Ince	McClair	Hughes	Giggs	Kanchelskis replaced Phelan, Donaghy M replaced Ince
19 Oct	Arsenal	46,594	Old Trafford	H	D	1–1	Schmeichel	Blackmore C	Irwin	Bruce 1	Webb	Pallister	Robson	Ince	McClair	Hughes	Giggs	Kanchelskis replaced Webb
26 Oct	Sheffield Wednesday	38,260	Hillsborough	A	L	2–3	Schmeichel	Parker P	Irwin	Bruce	Webb	Pallister	Robson	Kanchelskis	McClair 2	Blackmore C	Giggs	Martin L replaced Bruce
2 Nov	Sheffield United	42,942	Old Trafford	H	W	•2–0	Schmeichel	Parker P	Blackmore C	Bruce	Webb	Donaghy M	Kanchelskis 1	Ince	McClair	Robins	Giggs	Robson replaced Kanchelskis, Pallister replaced Giggs
16 Nov	Manchester City	38,180	Maine Road	A	D	0–0	Schmeichel	Parker P	Irwin	Bruce	Webb	Pallister	Robson	Blackmore C	McClair	Hughes	Giggs	Ince replaced Webb
23 Nov	West Ham United	47,185	Old Trafford	H	W	2–1	Schmeichel	Parker P	Irwin	Bruce	Webb	Pallister	Robson 1	Kanchelskis	McClair	Hughes	Giggs 1	Blackmore C replaced Parker P
30 Nov	Crystal Palace	29,017	Selhurst Park	A	W	3–1	Schmeichel	Parker P	Irwin	Bruce	Webb 1	Pallister	Robson	Kanchelskis 1	McClair 1	Hughes	Giggs	Blackmore C replaced Irwin
7 Dec	Coventry City	42,549	Old Trafford	H	W	4–0	Schmeichel	Parker P	Irwin	Bruce 1	Webb 1	Pallister	Kanchelskis	Ince	McClair 1	Hughes 1	Giggs	Blackmore C replaced Parker P
15 Dec	Chelsea	23,120	Stamford Bridge	A	W	3–1	Schmeichel	Parker P	Irwin 1	Bruce 1	Webb	Pallister	Kanchelskis	Ince	McClair 1	Hughes	Giggs	Blackmore C replaced Giggs
26 Dec	Oldham Athletic	18,947	Boundary Park	A	W	6–3	Schmeichel	Parker P	Irwin 2	Bruce	Webb	Pallister	Robson	Ince	McClair 2	Hughes	Kanchelskis 1	Blackmore C replaced Robson, Giggs 1 replaced Irwin
29 Dec	Leeds United	32,638	Elland Road	A	D	1–1	Schmeichel	Parker P	Blackmore C	Bruce	Webb 1	Pallister	Kanchelskis	Ince	McClair	Hughes	Giggs	Sharpe L replaced Blackmore C, Donaghy M replaced Kanchelskis
1 Jan	Queen's Park Rangers	38,554	Old Trafford	H	L	1–4	Schmeichel	Parker P	Blackmore C	Bruce	Webb	Pallister	Phelan	Ince	McClair 1	Hughes	Sharpe L	Giggs replaced Phelan
11 Jan	Everton	46,619	Old Trafford	H	W	1–0	Schmeichel	Parker P	Blackmore C	Bruce	Webb	Pallister	Kanchelskis 1	Ince	McClair	Hughes	Giggs	Donaghy M replaced Blackmore C
18 Jan	Notts County	21,055	County Ground	A	D	1–1	Schmeichel	Parker P	Irwin	Bruce	Webb	Pallister	Kanchelskis	Ince	McClair	Hughes	Giggs	Blackmore C 1 replaced Bruce, Robins replaced Giggs
22 Jan	Aston Villa	45,022	Old Trafford	H	W	1–0	Schmeichel	Donaghy M	Irwin	Bruce	Webb	Pallister	Robson	Ince	McClair	Hughes 1	Kanchelskis	
1 Feb	Arsenal	41,703	Highbury	A	D	1–1	Schmeichel	Donaghy M	Irwin	Parker P	Webb	Pallister	Robson	Ince	McClair 1	Hughes	Kanchelskis	Giggs replaced Ince
8 Feb	Sheffield Wednesday	47,074	Old Trafford	H	D	1–1	Schmeichel	Giggs	Irwin	Donaghy M	Webb	Pallister	Robson	Ince	McClair 1	Hughes	Kanchelskis	Sharpe L replaced Giggs, Phelan replaced Webb
22 Feb	Crystal Palace	46,347	Old Trafford	H	W	2–0	Schmeichel	Donaghy M	Irwin	Giggs	Webb	Pallister	Robson	Ince	McClair	Hughes 2	Kanchelskis	Sharpe L replaced Kanchelskis, Parker P replaced Webb
26 Feb	Chelsea	44,872	Old Trafford	H	D	1–1	Walsh	Donaghy M	Irwin	Giggs	Webb	Pallister	Robson	Ince	McClair	Hughes 1	Kanchelskis	Blackmore C replaced Robson, Parker P replaced Kanchelskis
29 Feb	Coventry City	23,967	Highfield Road	A	D	0–0	Walsh	Parker P	Irwin	Donaghy M	Webb	Pallister	Kanchelskis	Ince	McClair	Hughes	Giggs	Blackmore C replaced Kanchelskis
14 Mar	Sheffield United	30,183	Bramall Lane	A	W	2–1	Schmeichel	Parker P	Irwin	Bruce	Phelan	Pallister	Robson	Ince	McClair 1	Sharpe L	Kanchelskis	Blackmore C 1 replaced Bruce
18 Mar	Nottingham Forest	28,062	City Ground	A	L	0–1	Schmeichel	Blackmore C	Irwin	Bruce	Webb	Pallister	Phelan	Ince	McClair	Hughes	Sharpe L	Kanchelskis replaced Hughes, Giggs replaced Webb
21 Mar	Wimbledon	45,428	Old Trafford	H	D	0–0	Schmeichel	Blackmore C	Irwin	Bruce	Webb	Pallister	Kanchelskis	Ince	McClair	Hughes	Giggs	Sharpe L replaced Webb
28 Mar	Queen's Park Rangers	22,603	Loftus Road	A	D	0–0	Schmeichel	Donaghy M	Irwin	Bruce	Phelan	Pallister	Robson	Kanchelskis	McClair	Hughes	Giggs	Sharpe L replaced Kanchelskis
31 Mar	Norwich City	17,489	Carrow Road	A	W	3–1	Schmeichel	Donaghy M	Irwin	Bruce	Giggs	Pallister	Robson	Ince 2	McClair 1	Hughes	Sharpe L	Blackmore C replaced Robson
7 Apr	Manchester City	46,781	Old Trafford	H	D	1–1	Schmeichel	Donaghy M	Irwin	Bruce	Blackmore C	Pallister	Giggs 1	Ince	McClair	Hughes	Sharpe L	Kanchelskis replaced Blackmore C
16 Apr	Southampton	43,972	Old Trafford	H	W	1–0	Schmeichel	Parker P	Irwin	Bruce	Phelan	Pallister	Kanchelskis 1	Ince	McClair	Hughes	Giggs	Webb replaced Ince
18 Apr	Luton Town	13,410	Kenilworth Road	A	D	1–1	Schmeichel	Parker P	Irwin	Bruce	Phelan	Pallister	Giggs	Webb	McClair	Hughes	Sharpe L 1	Kanchelskis replaced Hughes, Blackmore C replaced Parker P
20 Apr	Nottingham Forest	47,576	Old Trafford	H	L	1–2	Schmeichel	Blackmore C	Irwin	Bruce	Phelan	Pallister	Kanchelskis	Webb	McClair 1	Giggs	Sharpe L	Hughes replaced Webb, Donaghy M replaced Sharpe L
22 Apr	West Ham United	24,197	Upton Park	A	L	0–1	Schmeichel	Irwin	Donaghy M	Bruce	Phelan	Pallister	Giggs	Blackmore C	McClair	Hughes	Sharpe L	Kanchelskis replaced Blackmore C, Ferguson D replaced Donaghy M
26 Apr	Liverpool	38,669	Anfield	A	L	0–2	Schmeichel	Irwin	Donaghy M	Bruce	Kanchelskis	Pallister	Robson	Ince	McClair	Hughes	Giggs	Phelan replaced Pallister
2 May	Tottenham Hotspur	44,595	Old Trafford	H	W	3–1	Schmeichel	Ferguson D	Irwin	Bruce	Phelan	Donaghy M	Kanchelskis	Ince	McClair 1	Hughes 2	Giggs	Sharpe L replaced Ince

FA Cup

Date	Opponent	Attendances	Venue														Substitutions
15 Jan	Leeds United	31,819	Elland Road	A	W	1–0	Schmeichel	Parker P	Irwin	Bruce	Webb	Pallister	Kanchelskis	Ince	McClair	Hughes 1	Giggs	
27 Jan	Southampton	19,506	The Dell	A	D	0–0	Schmeichel	Parker P	Irwin	Donaghy M	Webb	Pallister	Robson	Ince	McClair	Hughes	Blackmore C	Giggs replaced Blackmore C
5 Feb	Southampton	33,414	Old Trafford	H	D	2–2	Schmeichel	Parker P	Irwin	Donaghy M	Webb	Pallister	Robson	Ince	McClair 1	Giggs	Kanchelskis 1	Sharpe L replaced Donaghy M, Hughes replaced Kanchelskis

FL Cup

Date	Opponent	Attendances	Venue														Substitutions
25 Sep	Cambridge United	30,934	Old Trafford	H	W	3–0	Walsh	Phelan	Irwin	Bruce 1	Webb	Pallister	Robson	Ince	McClair 1	Hughes	Blackmore C	Giggs 1 replaced Webb
9 Oct	Cambridge United	9,248	Abbey Stadium	A	D	1–1	Wilkinson I	Donaghy M	Irwin	Bruce	Blackmore C	Pallister	Robson	Ince	McClair 1	Hughes	Martin L	Robins replaced Pallister, Giggs replaced Martin L
30 Oct	Portsmouth	29,543	Old Trafford	H	W	3–1	Schmeichel	Parker P	Irwin	Bruce	Webb	Pallister	Donaghy M	Kanchelskis	McClair	Blackmore C	Giggs	Robson 1 replaced Pallister, Robins 2 replaced Irwin
4 Dec	Oldham Athletic	38,550	Old Trafford	H	W	2–0	Schmeichel	Parker P	Irwin	Bruce	Webb	Pallister	Robson	Kanchelskis 1	McClair 1	Hughes	Giggs	Ince replaced Robson, Blackmore C replaced Giggs
8 Jan	Leeds United	28,886	Elland Road	A	W	3–1	Schmeichel	Parker P	Blackmore C 1	Bruce	Webb	Pallister	Kanchelskis 1	Ince	McClair	Hughes	Giggs 1	Sharpe L replaced Kanchelskis, Donaghy M replaced Giggs
4 Mar	Middlesbrough	25,572	Ayresome Park	A	D	0–0	Schmeichel	Parker P	Irwin	Donaghy M	Webb	Pallister	Robson	Ince	McClair	Hughes	Giggs	Phelan replaced Donaghy M, Sharpe L replaced Ince
11 Mar	Middlesbrough	45,875	Old Trafford	H	W	2–1	Schmeichel	Parker P	Irwin	Bruce	Webb	Pallister	Robson	Ince	McClair	Sharpe L 1	Giggs 1	Robins replaced Sharpe L
12 Apr	Nottingham Forest	76,810	Wembley	A	W	1–0	Schmeichel	Parker P	Irwin	Bruce	Phelan	Pallister	Kanchelskis	Ince	McClair 1	Hughes	Giggs	Sharpe L replaced Kanchelskis

European Cup Winners' Cup

Date	Opponent	Attendances	Venue														Substitutions
18 Sep	Athinaikos	9,500	Apostolos Nikolaid	A	D	0–0	Schmeichel	Phelan	Irwin	Bruce	Webb	Pallister	Robins	Ince	McClair	Hughes	Beardsmore	Wallace replaced Beardsmore
2 Oct	Athinaikos	35,023	Old Trafford	H	W	2–0	Schmeichel	Phelan	Martin L	Bruce	Kanchelskis	Pallister	Robson	Ince	McClair 1	Hughes 1	Wallace	Beardsmore replaced Martin L, Robins replaced Wallace
23 Oct	Atletico Madrid	52,000	Vicente Calderon	A	L	0–3	Schmeichel	Parker P	Irwin	Bruce	Webb	Pallister	Robson	Ince	McClair	Hughes	Phelan	Martin L replaced Ince, Beardsmore replaced Phelan
6 Nov	Atletico Madrid	39,654	Old Trafford	H	D	1–1	Walsh	Parker P	Blackmore C	Bruce	Webb	Phelan	Robson	Robins	McClair	Hughes 1	Giggs	Martin L replaced Phelan, Pallister replaced Robins

Football League Division 1
P42 • W21 • D15 • L6 • F63 • A33 • PTS78
Position: 2

1992/93

Premier League

Date	Opponent	Attendances	Venue			Players and Scores											Substitutions
15 Aug	Sheffield United	28,070	Bramall Lane	A	L	1–2	Schmeichel	Irwin	Blackmore C	Bruce	Ferguson D	Pallister	Kanchelskis	Ince	McClair	Hughes 1	Giggs	Phelan replaced Ince, Dublin replaced Kanchelskis
19 Aug	Everton	31,901	Old Trafford	H	L	0–3	Schmeichel	Irwin	Blackmore C	Bruce	Ferguson D	Pallister	Kanchelskis	Ince	McClair	Hughes	Giggs	Phelan replaced Ince, Dublin replaced Giggs
22 Aug	Ipswich Town	31,704	Old Trafford	H	D	1–1	Schmeichel	Irwin 1	Blackmore C	Bruce	Ferguson D	Pallister	Kanchelskis	Phelan	McClair	Hughes	Giggs	Dublin replaced Blackmore C, Webb replaced Kanchelskis
24 Aug	Southampton	15,623	The Dell	A	W	1–0	Schmeichel	Phelan	Irwin	Bruce	Ferguson D	Pallister	Dublin 1	Ince	McClair	Hughes	Giggs	
29 Aug	Nottingham Forest	19,694	City Ground	A	W	2–0	Schmeichel	Phelan	Irwin	Bruce	Ferguson D	Pallister	Dublin	Ince	McClair	Hughes 1	Giggs 1	Kanchelskis replaced Hughes, Blackmore C replaced Phelan
2 Sep	Crystal Palace	29,736	Old Trafford	H	W	1–0	Schmeichel	Blackmore C	Irwin	Bruce	Ferguson D	Pallister	Dublin	Ince	McClair	Hughes 1	Giggs	Kanchelskis replaced Dublin
6 Sep	Leeds United	31,296	Old Trafford	H	W	2–0	Schmeichel	Blackmore C	Irwin	Bruce 1	Ferguson D	Pallister	Kanchelskis 1	Ince	McClair	Hughes	Giggs	
12 Sep	Everton	30,002	Goodison Park	A	W	2–0	Schmeichel	Irwin	Blackmore C	Bruce 1	Ferguson D	Pallister	Kanchelskis	Ince	McClair 1	Hughes	Giggs	
19 Sep	Tottenham Hotspur	33,296	White Hart Lane	A	D	1–1	Schmeichel	Irwin	Blackmore C	Bruce	Ferguson D	Pallister	Kanchelskis	Ince	McClair	Hughes	Giggs 1	Wallace replaced Kanchelskis
26 Sep	Queen's Park Rangers	33,287	Old Trafford	H	D	0–0	Schmeichel	Irwin	Blackmore C	Bruce	Ferguson D	Pallister	Kanchelskis	Ince	McClair	Hughes	Giggs	Wallace replaced Kanchelskis
3 Oct	Middlesbrough	24,172	Ayresome Park	A	D	1–1	Schmeichel	Irwin	Phelan	Bruce 1	Ferguson D	Pallister	Blackmore C	Ince	McClair	Hughes	Giggs	Kanchelskis replaced Phelan, Robson replaced Hughes
18 Oct	Liverpool	33,243	Old Trafford	H	D	2–2	Schmeichel	Parker P	Irwin	Bruce	Ferguson D	Pallister	Kanchelskis	Ince	McClair	Hughes 2	Giggs	Blackmore C replaced Kanchelskis
24 Oct	Blackburn Rovers	20,305	Ewood Park	A	D	0–0	Schmeichel	Parker P	Irwin	Bruce	Ferguson D	Pallister	Blackmore C	Ince	McClair	Hughes	Giggs	Kanchelskis replaced Ferguson D
31 Oct	Wimbledon	32,622	Old Trafford	H	L	0–1	Schmeichel	Parker P	Blackmore C	Bruce	Ferguson D	Pallister	Kanchelskis	Ince	McClair	Hughes	Giggs	Robson replaced Kanchelskis
7 Nov	Aston Villa	39,063	Villa Park	A	L	0–1	Schmeichel	Parker P	Blackmore C	Bruce	Ferguson D	Pallister	Robson	Ince	Sharpe L	Hughes	Giggs	McClair replaced Ferguson D
21 Nov	Oldham Athletic	33,497	Old Trafford	H	W	•3–0	Schmeichel	Parker P	Irwin	Bruce	Sharpe L	Pallister	Robson	Ince	McClair 1	Hughes 1	Giggs	Phelan replaced Irwin, Butt replaced Ince
28 Nov	Arsenal	29,739	Highbury	A	W	1–0	Schmeichel	Parker P	Irwin	Bruce	Sharpe L	Pallister	Robson	Ince	McClair	Hughes 1	Giggs	
6 Dec	Manchester City	35,408	Old Trafford	H	W	2–1	Schmeichel	Parker P	Irwin	Bruce	Sharpe L	Pallister	Robson	Ince 1	McClair	Hughes 1	Giggs	Cantona replaced Giggs
12 Dec	Norwich City	34,500	Old Trafford	H	W	1–0	Schmeichel	Parker P	Irwin	Bruce	Sharpe L	Pallister	Cantona	Ince	McClair	Hughes 1	Giggs	
19 Dec	Chelsea	34,464	Stamford Bridge	A	D	1–1	Schmeichel	Parker P	Irwin	Bruce	Phelan	Pallister	Cantona 1	Ince	McClair	Hughes	Sharpe L	Kanchelskis replaced Phelan
26 Dec	Sheffield Wednesday	37,708	Hillsborough	A	D	3–3	Schmeichel	Parker P	Irwin	Bruce	Sharpe L	Pallister	Cantona 1	Ince	McClair 2	Hughes	Giggs	Kanchelskis replaced Giggs
28 Dec	Coventry City	36,025	Old Trafford	H	W	5–0	Schmeichel	Parker P	Irwin 1	Bruce	Sharpe L 1	Pallister	Cantona 1	Ince	McClair	Hughes 1	Giggs 1	Kanchelskis replaced Giggs, Phelan replaced Bruce
9 Jan	Tottenham Hotspur	35,648	Old Trafford	H	W	4–1	Schmeichel	Parker P 1	Irwin 1	Bruce	Sharpe L	Pallister	Cantona 1	Ince	McClair 1	Hughes	Giggs	Kanchelskis replaced Giggs, Phelan replaced Ince
18 Jan	Queen's Park Rangers	21,117	Loftus Road	A	W	3–1	Schmeichel	Parker P	Irwin	Bruce	Sharpe L	Pallister	Kanchelskis 1	Ince 1	McClair	Hughes	Giggs 1	Phelan replaced Hughes
27 Jan	Nottingham Forest	36,085	Old Trafford	H	W	2–0	Schmeichel	Parker P	Irwin	Bruce	Sharpe L	Pallister	Cantona	Ince 1	McClair	Hughes 1	Giggs	
30 Jan	Ipswich Town	22,068	Portman Road	A	L	1–2	Schmeichel	Parker P	Irwin	Bruce	Sharpe L	Pallister	Cantona	Ince	McClair 1	Hughes	Giggs	Kanchelskis replaced Sharpe L
6 Feb	Sheffield United	36,156	Old Trafford	H	W	2–1	Schmeichel	Parker P	Irwin	Bruce	Sharpe L	Pallister	Cantona 1	Ince	McClair 1	Hughes	Giggs	Kanchelskis replaced Giggs
8 Feb	Leeds United	34,166	Elland Road	A	D	0–0	Schmeichel	Parker P	Irwin	Bruce	Sharpe L	Pallister	Cantona	Ince	McClair	Hughes	Giggs	Kanchelskis replaced Giggs
20 Feb	Southampton	36,257	Old Trafford	H	W	2–1	Schmeichel	Parker P	Irwin	Bruce	Sharpe L	Pallister	Cantona	Ince	McClair	Hughes	Giggs 2	
27 Feb	Middlesbrough	36,251	Old Trafford	H	W	3–0	Schmeichel	Parker P	Irwin 1	Bruce	Sharpe L	Pallister	Cantona 1	Ince	McClair	Hughes	Giggs 1	
6 Mar	Liverpool	44,374	Anfield	A	W	2–1	Schmeichel	Parker P	Irwin	Bruce	Sharpe L	Pallister	Kanchelskis	Ince	McClair 1	Hughes 1	Giggs	
9 Mar	Oldham Athletic	17,106	Boundary Park	A	L	0–1	Schmeichel	Parker P	Irwin	Bruce	Sharpe L	Pallister	Kanchelskis	Ince	McClair	Hughes	Giggs	Dublin replaced Kanchelskis
14 Mar	Aston Villa	36,163	Old Trafford	H	D	1–1	Schmeichel	Parker P	Irwin	Bruce	Sharpe L	Pallister	Cantona	Ince	McClair	Hughes 1	Giggs	
20 Mar	Manchester City	37,136	Maine Road	A	D	1–1	Schmeichel	Parker P	Irwin	Bruce	Sharpe L	Pallister	Cantona 1	Ince	McClair	Hughes	Giggs	
24 Mar	Arsenal	37,301	Old Trafford	H	D	0–0	Schmeichel	Parker P	Irwin	Bruce	Sharpe L	Pallister	Cantona	Ince	McClair	Hughes	Giggs	Robson replaced Hughes
5 Apr	Norwich City	20,582	Carrow Road	A	W	3–1	Schmeichel	Parker P	Irwin	Bruce	Sharpe L	Pallister	Cantona 1	Ince	McClair	Kanchelskis 1	Giggs 1	Robson replaced Kanchelskis
10 Apr	Sheffield Wednesday	40,102	Old Trafford	H	W	2–1	Schmeichel	Parker P	Irwin	Bruce 2	Sharpe L	Pallister	Cantona	Ince	McClair	Hughes	Giggs	Robson replaced Parker P
12 Apr	Coventry City	24,429	Highfield Road	A	W	1–0	Schmeichel	Parker P	Irwin 1	Bruce	Sharpe L	Pallister	Cantona	Ince	McClair	Hughes	Giggs	Robson replaced Cantona
17 Apr	Chelsea	40,139	Old Trafford	H	W	•3–0	Schmeichel	Parker P	Irwin	Bruce	Sharpe L	Pallister	Cantona 1	Ince	McClair	Hughes 1	Giggs	Robson replaced McClair, Kanchelskis replaced Giggs
21 Apr	Crystal Palace	30,115	Selhurst Park	A	W	2–0	Schmeichel	Parker P	Irwin	Bruce	Kanchelskis	Pallister	Cantona	Ince 1	McClair	Hughes 1	Giggs	Robson replaced Kanchelskis
3 May	Blackburn Rovers	40,447	Old Trafford	H	W	3–1	Schmeichel	Parker P	Irwin	Bruce	Sharpe L	Pallister 1	Cantona	Ince 1	McClair	Hughes	Giggs 1	Robson replaced Sharpe L, Kanchelskis replaced McClair
9 May	Wimbledon	30,115	Selhurst Park	A	W	2–1	Schmeichel	Parker P	Irwin	Bruce	Sharpe L	Pallister	Robson 1	Ince 1	McClair	Hughes	Cantona	Giggs replaced Irwin

FA Cup

Date	Opponent	Attendances	Venue														Substitutions
5 Jan	Bury	30,668	Old Trafford	H	W	2–0	Schmeichel	Parker P	Irwin	Bruce	Sharpe L	Pallister	Cantona	Gillespie K 1	McClair	Hughes	Phelan 1	Blackmore C replaced Irwin, Robson replaced McClair
23 Jan	Brighton & Hove Alb.	33,610	Old Trafford	H	W	1–0	Schmeichel	Parker P	Irwin	Bruce	Sharpe L	Pallister	Wallace	Ince	McClair	Phelan	Giggs 1	Gillespie K replaced Ince
14 Feb	Sheffield United	27,150	Bramall Lane	A	L	1–2	Schmeichel	Parker P	Irwin	Bruce	Sharpe L	Pallister	Kanchelskis	Ince	McClair	Hughes	Giggs 1	

FL Cup

Date	Opponent	Attendances	Venue														Substitutions
23 Sep	Brighton & Hove Alb.	16,649	Goldstone Ground	A	D	1–1	Walsh	Irwin	Martin L	Bruce	Webb	Pallister	Kanchelskis	Ince	McClair	Hughes	Wallace 1	Beckham replaced Kanchelskis
7 Oct	Brighton & Hove Alb.	25,405	Old Trafford	H	W	1–0	Schmeichel	Parker P	Irwin	Bruce	Kanchelskis	Pallister	Robson	Ince	McClair	Hughes 1	Giggs	
28 Oct	Aston Villa	35,964	Villa Park	A	L	0–1	Schmeichel	Parker P	Irwin	Bruce	Ferguson D	Pallister	Blackmore C	Ince	McClair	Hughes	Giggs	Kanchelskis replaced Irwin

UEFA Cup

Date	Opponent	Attendances	Venue														Substitutions
16 Sep	Torpedo Moscow	19,998	Old Trafford	H	D	0–0	Walsh	Irwin	Martin L	Bruce	Blackmore C	Pallister	Kanchelskis	Webb	McClair	Hughes	Wallace	Neville G replaced Martin L
29 Sep	Torpedo Moscow	11,357	Torpedo Stadion	A	D	0–0	Schmeichel	Irwin	Phelan	Bruce	Webb	Pallister	Wallace	Ince	McClair	Hughes	Giggs	Parker P replaced Phelan, Robson replaced Wallace

Premier League
P42 • W24 • D12 • L6 • F67 • A31 • PTS84

1993/94

Premiership

Date	Opponent	Attendances	Venue		Score	Players and Scores											Substitutions
15 Aug	Norwich City	19,705	Carrow Road	A W	2–0	Schmeichel	Parker P	Irwin	Bruce	Kanchelskis	Pallister	Robson 1	Ince	Keane	Hughes	Giggs 1	
18 Aug	Sheffield United	41,949	Old Trafford	H W	3–0	Schmeichel	Parker P	Irwin	Bruce	Kanchelskis	Pallister	Robson	Ince	Keane 2	Hughes 1	Giggs	McClair replaced Robson
21 Aug	Newcastle United	41,829	Old Trafford	H D	1–1	Schmeichel	Parker P	Irwin	Bruce	Kanchelskis	Pallister	Robson	Ince	Keane	Hughes	Giggs 1	McClair replaced Kanchelskis, Sharpe L replaced Parker P
23 Aug	Aston Villa	39,624	Villa Park	A W	2–1	Schmeichel	Parker P	Irwin	Bruce	Kanchelskis	Pallister	Giggs	Ince	Keane	Hughes	Sharpe L 2	
28 Aug	Southampton	16,189	The Dell	A W	3–1	Schmeichel	Parker P	Irwin 1	Bruce	Sharpe L 1	Pallister	Cantona 1	Ince	Keane	Hughes	Giggs	McClair replaced Giggs, Kanchelskis replaced Keane
1 Sep	West Ham United	44,613	Old Trafford	H W	3–0	Schmeichel	Parker P	Irwin	Bruce 1	Sharpe L 1	Pallister	Cantona 1	Ince	Keane	Kanchelskis	Giggs	McClair replaced Ince, Robson replaced Kanchelskis
11 Sep	Chelsea	37,064	Stamford Bridge	A L	0–1	Schmeichel	Parker P	Irwin	Bruce	Sharpe L	Pallister	Cantona	Ince	Keane	Robson	Giggs	McClair replaced Robson
19 Sep	Arsenal	44,009	Old Trafford	H W	1–0	Schmeichel	Parker P	Irwin	Bruce	Sharpe L	Pallister	Cantona 1	Ince	Keane	Hughes	Giggs	McClair replaced Hughes
25 Sep	Swindon Town	44,583	Old Trafford	H W	4–2	Schmeichel	Parker P	Irwin	Bruce	Sharpe L	Pallister	Cantona 1	Ince	Keane	Hughes 2	Kanchelskis 1	McClair replaced Sharpe L, Giggs replaced Kanchelskis
2 Oct	Sheffield Wednesday	34,548	Hillsborough	A W	3–2	Schmeichel	Parker P	Irwin	Bruce	Sharpe L	Pallister	Cantona	Ince	Keane	Hughes 2	Giggs 1	Kanchelskis replaced Giggs
16 Oct	Tottenham Hotspur	44,655	Old Trafford	H W	2–1	Schmeichel	Parker P	Irwin	Bruce	Sharpe L 1	Pallister	Robson	Cantona	Keane 1	Hughes	Giggs	McClair replaced Robson, Butt replaced Giggs
23 Oct	Everton	35,455	Goodison Park	A W	1–0	Schmeichel	Martin L	Irwin	Bruce	Sharpe L 1	Pallister	Cantona	Ince	McClair	Hughes	Keane	
30 Oct	Queen's Park Rangers	44,663	Old Trafford	H W	2–1	Schmeichel	Parker P	Irwin	Bruce	Sharpe L	Phelan	Cantona 1	Ince	Keane	Hughes 1	Giggs	
7 Nov	Manchester City	35,155	Maine Road	A W	3–2	Schmeichel	Parker P	Irwin	Bruce	Sharpe L	Pallister	Cantona 2	Ince	Keane 1	Hughes	Kanchelskis	Giggs replaced Kanchelskis
20 Nov	Wimbledon	44,748	Old Trafford	H W	3–1	Schmeichel	Parker P	Irwin	Bruce	Sharpe L	Pallister 1	Cantona	Ince	Robson	Hughes 1	Kanchelskis 1	Phelan replaced Robson
24 Nov	Ipswich Town	43,300	Old Trafford	H D	0–0	Schmeichel	Parker P	Irwin	Bruce	Sharpe L	Pallister	Cantona	Ince	Robson	Hughes	Kanchelskis	Giggs replaced Kanchelskis, Ferguson D replaced Robson
27 Nov	Coventry City	17,009	Highfield Road	A W	1–0	Schmeichel	Parker P	Irwin	Bruce	Sharpe L	Pallister	Cantona 1	Ince	Ferguson D	Hughes	Giggs	
4 Dec	Norwich City	44,694	Old Trafford	H D	2–2	Schmeichel	Parker P	Irwin	Bruce	Kanchelskis	Pallister	Cantona	Ince	McClair 1	Hughes	Giggs 1	Sharpe L replaced Hughes
7 Dec	Sheffield United	26,744	Bramall Lane	A W	3–0	Schmeichel	Parker P	Irwin	Bruce	Sharpe L 1	Pallister	Cantona 1	Ince	McClair	Hughes 1	Giggs	Keane replaced McClair
11 Dec	Newcastle United	36,332	St James' Park	A D	1–1	Schmeichel	Parker P	Irwin	Bruce	Sharpe L	Pallister	Cantona	Ince 1	McClair	Hughes	Giggs	Keane replaced McClair, Kanchelskis replaced Hughes
19 Dec	Aston Villa	44,499	Old Trafford	H W	3–1	Schmeichel	Parker P	Irwin	Bruce	Sharpe L	Pallister	Cantona 2	Ince 1	Keane	Hughes	Kanchelskis	Giggs replaced Sharpe L
26 Dec	Blackburn Rovers	44,511	Old Trafford	H D	1–1	Schmeichel	Parker P	Irwin	Bruce	Sharpe L	Pallister	Cantona	Ince 1	Keane	Hughes	Giggs	McClair replaced Parker P, Ferguson D replaced Hughes
29 Dec	Oldham Athletic	16,708	Boundary Park	A W	5–2	Schmeichel	Parker P	Irwin	Bruce 1	Sharpe L	Pallister	Cantona 1	Ince	Keane	Kanchelskis 1	Giggs 2	McClair replaced Cantona, Robson replaced Ince
1 Jan	Leeds United	44,724	Old Trafford	H D	0–0	Schmeichel	Parker P	Irwin	Bruce	Kanchelskis	Pallister	Cantona	Robson	McClair	Keane	Giggs	
4 Jan	Liverpool	42,795	Anfield	A D	3–3	Schmeichel	Parker P	Irwin 1	Bruce 1	Kanchelskis	Pallister	Cantona	Ince	McClair	Keane	Giggs 1	
15 Jan	Tottenham Hotspur	31,343	White Hart Lane	A W	•1–0	Schmeichel	Parker P	Irwin	Bruce	Kanchelskis	Pallister	Cantona	Ince	Keane	Hughes	Giggs	McClair replaced Hughes
22 Jan	Everton	44,750	Old Trafford	H W	1–0	Schmeichel	Parker P	Irwin	Bruce	Kanchelskis	Pallister	Cantona	Ince	Keane	Hughes	Giggs 1	
5 Feb	Queen's Park Rangers	21,267	Loftus Road	A W	3–2	Schmeichel	Parker P	Irwin	Bruce	Kanchelskis 1	Pallister	Cantona 1	Ince	Keane	Hughes	Giggs 1	
26 Feb	West Ham United	28,832	Upton Park	A D	2–2	Schmeichel	Parker P	Irwin	Bruce	Kanchelskis	Pallister	Cantona	Ince 1	McClair	Hughes 1	Keane	Dublin replaced Kanchelskis, Thornley replaced Irwin
5 Mar	Chelsea	44,745	Old Trafford	H L	0–1	Schmeichel	Parker P	Irwin	Bruce	Kanchelskis	Pallister	Keane	Ince	McClair	Hughes	Giggs	Dublin replaced Parker P, Robson replaced McClair
16 Mar	Sheffield Wednesday	43,669	Old Trafford	H W	5–0	Schmeichel	Parker P	Irwin	Bruce	Kanchelskis	Pallister	Cantona 2	Ince 1	Keane	Hughes 1	Giggs 1	McClair replaced Giggs 1, Robson replaced Kanchelskis
19 Mar	Swindon Town	18,102	County Ground	A D	2–2	Schmeichel	Parker P	Irwin	Bruce	Keane 1	Pallister	Cantona	Ince 1	McClair	Hughes	Giggs	
22 Mar	Arsenal	36,203	Highbury	A D	2–2	Schmeichel	Parker P	Irwin	Bruce	Sharpe L 2	Pallister	Cantona	Ince	Keane	Hughes	Giggs	McClair replaced Sharpe L
30 Mar	Liverpool	44,751	Old Trafford	H W	1–0	Schmeichel	Parker P	Irwin	Bruce	Sharpe L	Pallister	Cantona	Ince 1	Keane	Hughes	Kanchelskis	Giggs replaced Sharpe L, Robson replaced Cantona
2 Apr	Blackburn Rovers	20,866	Ewood Park	A L	0–2	Schmeichel	Parker P	Irwin	Bruce	Sharpe L	Pallister	Kanchelskis	Ince	Keane	Hughes	Giggs	McClair replaced Parker P
4 Apr	Oldham Athletic	44,686	Old Trafford	H W	3–2	Schmeichel	Irwin	Sharpe L	Bruce	Keane	Pallister	Kanchelskis	Ince 1	McClair	Hughes	Giggs 1	Dublin 1 replaced McClair
16 Apr	Wimbledon	28,553	Selhurst Park	A L	0–1	Schmeichel	Parker P	Irwin	Bruce	Kanchelskis	Pallister	Robson	Ince	McClair	Hughes	Giggs	Sharpe L replaced Robson, Dublin replaced Parker P
23 Apr	Manchester City	44,333	Old Trafford	H W	2–0	Schmeichel	Parker P	Irwin	Bruce	Kanchelskis	Pallister	Cantona 2	Ince	Keane	Hughes	Sharpe L	Giggs replaced Sharpe L
27 Apr	Leeds United	41,127	Elland Road	A W	2–0	Schmeichel	Parker P	Irwin	Bruce	Kanchelskis 1	Pallister	Cantona	Ince	Keane	Hughes	Giggs 1	
1 May	Ipswich Town	22,468	Portman Road	A W	2–1	Schmeichel	Parker P	Irwin	Bruce	Kanchelskis	Pallister	Cantona 1	Ince	Keane	Hughes	Giggs 1	Sharpe L replaced Giggs, Walsh replaced Schmeichel
4 May	Southampton	44,705	Old Trafford	H W	2–0	Walsh	Irwin	Sharpe L	Parker P	Kanchelskis 1	Pallister	Cantona	Ince	Keane	Hughes 1	Giggs	
8 May	Coventry City	44,717	Old Trafford	H D	0–0	Walsh	Neville G	Irwin	Bruce	Sharpe L	Pallister	Cantona	Robson	McClair	Dublin	McKee	Parker P replaced Bruce, Keane replaced McKee

9 Jan	Sheffield United	22,019	Bramall Lane	A W	1–0	Schmeichel	Parker P	Irwin	Bruce	Kanchelskis	Pallister	Cantona	Ince	Keane	Hughes 1	Giggs	
30 Jan	Norwich City	21,060	Carrow Road	A W	2–0	Schmeichel	Parker P	Irwin	Bruce	Kanchelskis	Pallister	Cantona 1	Ince	Keane 1	Hughes	Giggs	McClair replaced Hughes
20 Feb	Wimbledon	27,511	Selhurst Park	A W	3–0	Schmeichel	Parker P	Irwin 1	Bruce	Kanchelskis	Pallister	Cantona 1	Ince 1	Keane	Hughes	Giggs	McClair replaced Cantona, Dublin replaced Hughes
12 Mar	Charlton Athletic	44,347	Old Trafford	H W	3–1	Schmeichel	Parker P	Irwin	Bruce	Kanchelskis 2	Pallister	Cantona	Ince	Keane	Hughes 1	Giggs	Sealey replaced Parker P
10 Apr	Oldham Athletic	56,399	Wembley	A D	1–1	Schmeichel	Parker P	Irwin	Bruce	Sharpe L	Pallister	McClair	Ince	Dublin	Hughes 1	Giggs	Butt replaced Parker P, Robson replaced Dublin
13 Apr	Oldham Athletic	32,211	Maine Road	A W	4–1	Schmeichel	Parker P	Irwin 1	Bruce	Kanchelskis 1	Pallister	Robson 1	Ince	Keane	Hughes	Giggs 1	McClair replaced Keane, Sharpe L replaced Hughes
14 May	Chelsea	79,634	Wembley	A W	4–0	Schmeichel	Parker P	Irwin	Bruce	Kanchelskis	Pallister	Cantona 2	Ince	Keane	Hughes 1	Giggs	Sharpe L replaced Irwin, McClair 1 replaced Cantona

FL Cup

22 Sep	Stoke City	23,327	Victoria Ground	A L	1–2	Schmeichel	Martin L	Irwin	Phelan	Kanchelskis	Pallister	Robson	Ferguson D	McClair	Hughes	Dublin 1	Bruce replaced Phelan, Sharpe L replaced Robson
6 Oct	Stoke City	41,387	Old Trafford	H W	2–0	Schmeichel	Irwin	Martin L	Bruce	Sharpe L 1	Pallister	Robson	Kanchelskis	McClair 1	Hughes	Keane	Giggs replaced Martin L
27 Oct	Leicester City	41,344	Old Trafford	H W	5–1	Schmeichel	Phelan	Martin L	Bruce 2	Sharpe L 1	Pallister	Robson	Kanchelskis	McClair 1	Hughes 1	Keane	Giggs replaced Sharpe L, Irwin replaced Pallister
30 Nov	Everton	34,052	Goodison Park	A W	2–0	Schmeichel	Parker P	Irwin	Bruce	Kanchelskis	Pallister	Cantona	Ince	Robson	Hughes 1	Giggs 1	Ferguson D replaced Robson
12 Jan	Portsmouth	43,794	Old Trafford	H D	2–2	Schmeichel	Parker P	Irwin	Bruce	Kanchelskis	Pallister	Cantona 1	Robson	McClair	Hughes	Giggs 1	Dublin replaced McClair, Keane replaced Hughes
26 Jan	Portsmouth	24,950	Fratton Park	A W	1–0	Schmeichel	Parker P	Irwin	Bruce	Kanchelskis	Pallister	Cantona	Ince	McClair 1	Keane	Giggs	
13 Feb	Sheffield Wednesday	43,294	Old Trafford	H W	1–0	Schmeichel	Parker P	Irwin	Bruce	Kanchelskis	Pallister	Cantona	Ince	Keane	Hughes	Giggs 1	
2 Mar	Sheffield Wednesday	34,878	Hillsborough	A W	4–1	Schmeichel	Parker P	Irwin	Bruce	Kanchelskis 1	Pallister	Keane	Ince	McClair 1	Hughes 2	Giggs	
27 Mar	Aston Villa	77,231	Wembley	A L	1–3	Sealey	Parker P	Irwin	Bruce	Kanchelskis	Pallister	Cantona	Ince	Keane	Hughes 1	Giggs	McClair replaced Bruce, Sharpe L replaced Giggs

European Cup

15 Sep	Kispest Honved	9,000	Jozsef Bozsik	A W	3–2	Schmeichel	Parker P	Irwin	Bruce	Sharpe L	Pallister	Robson	Ince	Cantona 1	Keane 2	Giggs	Phelan replaced Giggs
29 Sep	Kispest Honved	35,781	Old Trafford	H W	2–1	Schmeichel	Parker P	Irwin	Bruce 2	Sharpe L	Pallister	Robson	Ince	Cantona	Hughes	Giggs	Martin L replaced Irwin, Phelan replaced Ince
20 Oct	Galatasaray	39,396	Old Trafford	H D	•3–3	Schmeichel	Martin L	Sharpe L	Bruce	Keane	Pallister	Robson 1	Ince	Cantona 1	Hughes	Giggs	Phelan replaced Robson
3 Nov	Galatasaray	40,000	Ali Sam Yen	A D	0–0	Schmeichel	Phelan	Irwin	Bruce	Parker P	Sharpe L	Robson	Ince	Cantona	Keane	Giggs	Neville G replaced Phelan, Dublin replaced Keane

Premiership
P42 • W27 • D11 • L4 • F80 • A38 • PTS92
Position: 1

1994/95

Premiership

Date	Opponent	Attendances	Venue		Score	Players and Scores											Substitutions
20 Aug	Queen's Park Rangers	43,214	Old Trafford	H W	2–0	Schmeichel	May	Irwin	Bruce	Sharpe L	Pallister	Kanchelskis	Ince	McClair 1	Hughes 1	Giggs	Parker P replaced May, Keane replaced Sharpe L
22 Aug	Nottingham Forest	22,072	City Ground	A D	1–1	Schmeichel	May	Irwin	Bruce	Sharpe L	Pallister	Kanchelskis 1	Ince	McClair	Hughes	Giggs	Keane replaced Giggs
27 Aug	Tottenham Hotspur	24,502	White Hart Lane	A W	1–0	Schmeichel	May	Irwin	Bruce 1	Sharpe L	Pallister	Kanchelskis	Ince	McClair	Hughes	Giggs	
31 Aug	Wimbledon	43,440	Old Trafford	H W	3–0	Schmeichel	May	Irwin	Bruce	Sharpe L	Pallister	Cantona 1	Kanchelskis	McClair 1	Hughes	Giggs 1	
11 Sep	Leeds United	39,120	Elland Road	A L	1–2	Schmeichel	May	Irwin	Bruce	Kanchelskis	Pallister	Cantona 1	Ince	McClair	Hughes	Giggs	Sharpe L replaced Giggs, Butt replaced McClair
17 Sep	Liverpool	43,740	Old Trafford	H W	2–0	Schmeichel	May	Irwin	Bruce	Sharpe L	Pallister	Kanchelskis 1	Ince	Cantona	Hughes	Giggs	McClair 1 replaced Hughes
24 Sep	Ipswich Town	22,553	Portman Road	A L	2–3	Walsh	Irwin	Sharpe L	Bruce	Keane	Pallister	Kanchelskis	Ince	McClair	Cantona 1	Giggs	Scholes 1 replaced Sharpe L, Butt replaced McClair
1 Oct	Everton	43,803	Old Trafford	H W	2–0	Schmeichel	May	Irwin	Bruce	Sharpe L 1	Pallister	Cantona	Ince	Keane	Hughes	Kanchelskis 1	McClair replaced Hughes
8 Oct	Sheffield Wednesday	32,616	Hillsborough	A L	0–1	Schmeichel	Parker P	Irwin	Bruce	Sharpe L	Pallister	Keane	Ince	McClair	Hughes	Gillespie K	May replaced Parker P, Scholes replaced Gillespie K
15 Oct	West Ham United	43,795	Old Trafford	H W	1–0	Schmeichel	May	Irwin	Bruce	Sharpe L	Pallister	Kanchelskis	Ince	Cantona 1	Hughes	Giggs	Butt replaced May
23 Oct	Blackburn Rovers	30,260	Ewood Park	A W	4–2	Schmeichel	Keane	Irwin	Bruce	Sharpe L	Pallister	Kanchelskis 2	Ince	Cantona 1	Hughes 1	Butt	McClair replaced Butt
29 Oct	Newcastle United	43,795	Old Trafford	H W	2–0	Schmeichel	Keane	Irwin	Bruce	Kanchelskis	Pallister 1	Cantona	Ince	McClair	Hughes	Giggs	Gillespie K 1 replaced Giggs
6 Nov	Aston Villa	32,136	Villa Park	A W	2–1	Walsh	Keane	Irwin	Bruce	Kanchelskis 1	Pallister	Scholes	Ince 1	Cantona	Butt	Giggs	McClair replaced Butt, Gillespie K replaced Scholes
10 Nov	Manchester City	43,738	Old Trafford	H W	5–0	Schmeichel	Keane	Irwin	Bruce	Kanchelskis 3	Pallister	Cantona 1	Ince	McClair	Hughes 1	Giggs	Scholes replaced Giggs
19 Nov	Crystal Palace	43,788	Old Trafford	H W	3–0	Schmeichel	Neville G	Irwin 1	May	Kanchelskis 1	Pallister	Cantona 1	Ince	McClair	Hughes	Davies S	Gillespie K replaced Kanchelskis, Scholes replaced Davies S, Pilkington replaced Schmeichel
26 Nov	Arsenal	38,301	Highbury	A D	0–0	Walsh	Neville G	Irwin	May	Kanchelskis	Pallister	Cantona	Ince	McClair	Hughes	Gillespie K	Butt replaced Kanchelskis, Davies S replaced Gillespie K
3 Dec	Norwich City	43,789	Old Trafford	H W	1–0	Walsh	Neville G	Irwin	May	Kanchelskis	Pallister	Cantona 1	Ince	McClair	Hughes	Davies S	Gillespie K replaced Davies S, Butt replaced Cantona
10 Dec	Queen's Park Rangers	18,948	Loftus Road	A W	3–2	Walsh	Neville G	Irwin	Bruce	Keane 1	Pallister	Kanchelskis	Ince	McClair	Scholes 2	Davies S	Gillespie K replaced Neville G, Butt replaced Davies S
17 Dec	Nottingham Forest	43,744	Old Trafford	H L	1–2	Walsh	Keane	Irwin	Bruce	Kanchelskis	Pallister	Cantona 1	Ince	McClair	Hughes	Giggs	Butt replaced Giggs, Neville G replaced Kanchelskis
26 Dec	Chelsea	31,139	Stamford Bridge	A W	3–2	Walsh	Keane	Irwin	Bruce	Butt	Pallister	Cantona 1	Ince	McClair 1	Hughes 1	Giggs	Kanchelskis replaced Butt, Neville G replaced Ince
28 Dec	Leicester City	43,789	Old Trafford	H D	1–1	Walsh	Neville G	Irwin	Bruce	Kanchelskis 1	Pallister	Cantona	Keane	McClair	Hughes	Giggs	Scholes replaced Hughes
31 Dec	Southampton	15,204	The Dell	A D	2–2	Walsh	May	Neville G	Bruce	Keane	Pallister 1	Cantona	Butt 1	McClair	Hughes	Giggs	Gillespie K replaced McClair
3 Jan	Coventry City	43,120	Old Trafford	H W	2–0	Walsh	Neville G	Irwin	Bruce	Gillespie K	Pallister	Cantona 1	Keane	Scholes 1	Butt	Giggs	McClair replaced Keane
15 Jan	Newcastle United	34,471	St James' Park	A D	1–1	Schmeichel	Keane	Irwin	Bruce	Sharpe L	Pallister	Cantona	Butt	McClair	Hughes 1	Giggs	May replaced Butt, Scholes replaced Hughes
22 Jan	Blackburn Rovers	43,742	Old Trafford	H W	1–0	Schmeichel	Keane	Irwin	Bruce	Sharpe L	Pallister	Cantona 1	Ince	McClair	Cole	Giggs	Kanchelskis replaced Sharpe L
25 Jan	Crystal Palace	18,224	Selhurst Park	A D	1–1	Schmeichel	Keane	Irwin	May 1	Sharpe L	Pallister	Cantona	Ince	McClair	Cole	Giggs	Kanchelskis replaced Sharpe L
4 Feb	Aston Villa	43,795	Old Trafford	H W	1–0	Schmeichel	Neville G	Irwin	Bruce	Sharpe L	Pallister	Scholes	Ince	McClair	Cole 1	Giggs	May replaced Neville G, Kanchelskis replaced Giggs
11 Feb	Manchester City	26,368	Maine Road	A W	3–0	Schmeichel	Neville P	Irwin	Bruce	Sharpe L	Pallister	Kanchelskis 1	Ince 1	McClair	Cole 1	Giggs	May replaced Kanchelskis, Scholes replaced Neville P
22 Feb	Norwich City	21,824	Carrow Road	A W	2–0	Schmeichel	Keane	Sharpe L	Bruce	Kanchelskis 1	Pallister	Cole	Ince 1	McClair	Hughes	Giggs	
25 Feb	Everton	40,011	Goodison Park	A L	0–1	Schmeichel	Irwin	Sharpe L	Bruce	Keane	Pallister	Cole	Ince	McClair	Hughes	Giggs	Kanchelskis replaced McClair
4 Mar	Ipswich Town	43,804	Old Trafford	H W	9–0	Schmeichel	Keane 1	Irwin	Bruce	Kanchelskis	Pallister	Cole 5	Ince 1	McClair	Hughes 2	Giggs	Sharpe L replaced Kanchelskis, Butt replaced Bruce
7 Mar	Wimbledon	18,224	Selhurst Park	A W	1–0	Schmeichel	Neville G	Irwin	Bruce 1	Sharpe L	Pallister	Cole	Ince	McClair	Hughes	Giggs	
15 Mar	Tottenham Hotspur	43,802	Old Trafford	H D	0–0	Schmeichel	Irwin	Sharpe L	Bruce	Kanchelskis	Pallister	Cole	Ince	McClair	Hughes	Giggs	Butt replaced McClair
19 Mar	Liverpool	38,906	Anfield	A L	0–2	Schmeichel	Irwin	Sharpe L	Bruce	Keane	Pallister	Kanchelskis	Ince	McClair	Hughes	Giggs	Cole replaced Sharpe L, Butt replaced Keane
22 Mar	Arsenal	43,623	Old Trafford	H W	3–0	Schmeichel	Keane	Irwin	Bruce	Sharpe L 1	Pallister	Kanchelskis 1	Ince	Cole	Hughes 1	Giggs	
2 Apr	Leeds United	43,712	Old Trafford	H D	0–0	Schmeichel	Neville G	Irwin	Beckham	Keane	Pallister	Cole	Ince	McClair	Hughes	Giggs	
15 Apr	Leicester City	21,281	Filbert Street	A W	4–0	Schmeichel	Neville G	Irwin	Bruce	Sharpe L 1	Pallister	Cole 2	Ince 1	McClair	Hughes	Butt	Scholes replaced Hughes, Beckham replaced Sharpe L
17 Apr	Chelsea	43,728	Old Trafford	H D	0–0	Schmeichel	Neville G	Irwin	Bruce	Beckham	Pallister	Cole	Ince	McClair	Hughes	Butt	Scholes replaced Butt, Davies S replaced Beckham
1 May	Coventry City	21,858	Highfield Road	A W	3–2	Schmeichel	Neville G	Irwin	May	Sharpe L	Pallister	Butt	Cole 2	McClair	Hughes	Scholes 1	Beckham replaced Scholes
7 May	Sheffield Wednesday	43,868	Old Trafford	H W	1–0	Schmeichel	Neville G	Irwin	May 1	Sharpe L	Pallister	Cole	Ince	McClair	Hughes	Scholes	Butt replaced Scholes, Neville P replaced May
10 May	Southampton	43,479	Old Trafford	H W	2–1	Schmeichel	Neville G	Irwin 1	Bruce	Sharpe L	Pallister	Cole 1	Ince	McClair	Hughes	Butt	Scholes replaced Hughes
14 May	West Ham United	24,783	Upton Park	A D	1–1	Schmeichel	Neville G	Irwin	Bruce	Sharpe L	Pallister	Cole	Ince	McClair 1	Keane	Butt	Hughes replaced Butt, Scholes replaced Keane

RESULTS

1994/95 continued

FA Cup

Date	Opponent	Attendances	Venue			Players and Scores											Substitutions
9 Jan	Sheffield United	22,322	Bramall Lane	A W	2–0	Schmeichel	O'Kane	Irwin	Bruce	Keane	Pallister	Cantona 1	Butt	McClair	Hughes 1	Giggs	Sharpe L replaced O'Kane, Scholes replaced McClair
28 Jan	Wrexham	43,222	Old Trafford	H W	•5–2	Schmeichel	Neville P	Irwin 2	May	Sharpe L	Pallister	Keane	Ince	McClair 1	Scholes	Giggs 1	Kanchelskis replaced Keane, Beckham replaced McClair
19 Feb	Leeds United	42,744	Old Trafford	H W	3–1	Schmeichel	Keane	Irwin	Bruce 1	Sharpe L	Pallister	Kanchelskis	Ince	McClair 1	Hughes 1	Giggs	
12 Mar	Queen's Park Rangers	42,830	Old Trafford	H W	2–0	Schmeichel	Neville G	Irwin 1	Bruce	Sharpe L 1	Pallister	Kanchelskis	Ince	McClair	Hughes	Giggs	Keane replaced Giggs
9 Apr	Crystal Palace	38,256	Villa Park	A D	2–2	Schmeichel	Neville G	Irwin 1	Keane	Sharpe L	Pallister 1	Beckham	Ince	McClair	Hughes	Giggs	Butt replaced Beckham
12 Apr	Crystal Palace	17,987	Villa Park	A W	2–0	Schmeichel	Neville G	Irwin	Bruce 1	Sharpe L	Pallister 1	Butt	Ince	Keane	Hughes	Giggs	McClair replaced Giggs
20 May	Everton	79,592	Wembley	A L	0–1	Schmeichel	Neville G	Irwin	Bruce	Sharpe L	Pallister	Keane	Ince	McClair	Hughes	Butt	Giggs replaced Bruce, Scholes replaced Sharpe L

FL Cup

Date	Opponent	Attendances	Venue			Players and Scores											Substitutions
21 Sep	Port Vale	18,605	Vale Park	A W	2–1	Walsh	Neville G	Irwin	Butt	May	Keane	Gillespie K	Beckham	McClair	Scholes 2	Davies S	Sharpe L replaced Butt, O'Kane replaced Neville G
5 Oct	Port Vale	31,615	Old Trafford	H W	2–0	Walsh	Casper	O'Kane	Butt	May 1	Pallister	Gillespie K	Beckham	McClair 1	Scholes	Davies S	Tomlinson replaced Gillespie K, Neville G replaced Davies S
26 Oct	Newcastle United	34,178	St James' Park	A L	0–2	Walsh	Neville G	Irwin	Bruce	Gillespie K	Pallister	Beckham	Scholes	McClair	Butt	Davies S	Sharpe L replaced Irwin, Tomlinson replaced Irwin

European Cup

Date	Opponent	Attendances	Venue			Players and Scores											Substitutions
14 Sep	IFK Gothenburg	33,625	Old Trafford	H W	4–2	Schmeichel	May	Irwin	Bruce	Sharpe L 1	Pallister	Kanchelskis 1	Ince	Butt	Hughes	Giggs 2	
28 Sep	Galatasaray	35,000	Ali Sami Yen Stadi	A D	0–0	Schmeichel	May	Sharpe L	Bruce	Kanchelskis	Pallister	Butt	Ince	Keane	Hughes	Giggs	Parker P replaced Giggs
19 Oct	Barcelona	40,064	Old Trafford	H D	2–2	Schmeichel	May	Irwin	Parker P	Sharpe L 1	Pallister	Kanchelskis	Ince	Keane	Hughes 1	Butt	Bruce replaced Parker P, Scholes replaced Butt
2 Nov	Barcelona	114,432	Estadio Camp Nou	A L	0–4	Walsh	Parker P	Irwin	Bruce	Kanchelskis	Pallister	Butt	Ince	Keane	Hughes	Giggs	Scholes replaced Giggs
23 Nov	IFK Gothenburg	36,350	Nya Ulevi Stadio	A L	1–3	Walsh	May	Irwin	Bruce	Kanchelskis	Pallister	Cantona	Ince	McClair	Hughes 1	Davies S	Neville G replaced May, Butt replaced Davies S
7 Dec	Galatasaray	39,220	Old Trafford	H W	•4–0	Walsh	Neville G	Irwin	Bruce	Keane 1	Pallister	Cantona	Beckham 1	McClair	Butt	Davies S 1	

Premiership
P42 • W26 • D10 • L6 • F77 • A28 • PTS88
Position: 2

1995/96

Premiership

Date	Opponent	Attendances	Venue			Players and Scores											Substitutions
19 Aug	Aston Villa	34,655	Villa Park	A L	1–3	Schmeichel	Neville P	Irwin	Parker P	Neville G	Pallister	Butt	Keane	McClair	Scholes	Sharpe L	Beckham 1 replaced Neville P, O'Kane replaced Pallister
23 Aug	West Ham United	31,966	Old Trafford	H W	2–1	Schmeichel	Neville G	Irwin	Bruce	Sharpe L	Pallister	Butt	Keane 1	McClair	Scholes 1	Beckham	Cole replaced Scholes, Thornley replaced McClair
26 Aug	Wimbledon	32,226	Old Trafford	H W	3–1	Schmeichel	Neville G	Irwin	Bruce	Sharpe L	Pallister	Butt	Keane 2	Cole 1	Scholes	Beckham	Giggs replaced Cole, Davies S replaced Scholes
28 Aug	Blackburn Rovers	29,843	Ewood Park	A W	2–1	Schmeichel	Neville G	Irwin	Bruce	Sharpe L 1	Pallister	Butt	Keane	Cole	Scholes	Beckham 1	Giggs replaced Scholes, Davies S replaced Beckham
9 Sep	Everton	39,496	Goodison Park	A W	3–2	Schmeichel	Neville G	Irwin	Bruce	Sharpe L 2	Pallister	Butt	Keane	Cole	Scholes	Beckham	Giggs 1 replaced Scholes, Davies S replaced Cole
16 Sep	Bolton Wanderers	32,812	Old Trafford	H W	3–0	Schmeichel	Parker P	Neville P	Bruce	Sharpe L	Pallister	Butt	Cooke	Scholes 2	Beckham	Giggs 1	Davies S replaced Cooke
23 Sep	Sheffield Wednesday	34,101	Hillsborough	A D	0–0	Schmeichel	Parker P	Irwin	Bruce	McClair	Pallister	Butt	Davies S	Scholes	Beckham	Giggs	Cooke replaced Davies S
1 Oct	Liverpool	34,934	Old Trafford	H D	2–2	Schmeichel	Neville G	Neville P	Bruce	Sharpe L	Pallister	Cantona 1	Keane	Cole	Butt 1	Giggs	Scholes replaced Neville P, Beckham replaced Butt
14 Oct	Manchester City	35,707	Old Trafford	H W	1–0	Schmeichel	Neville G	Neville P	Bruce	Keane	Pallister	Butt	Beckham	Cole	Scholes 1	Giggs	McClair replaced Keane, Sharpe L replaced Scholes
21 Oct	Chelsea	30,192	Stamford Bridge	A W	4–1	Schmeichel	Neville G	Irwin	Bruce	Keane	Pallister	Cantona	Butt	Cole	Scholes 2	Giggs 1	McClair 1 replaced Scholes
28 Oct	Middlesbrough	36,580	Old Trafford	H W	2–0	Schmeichel	Neville G	Irwin	Bruce	Keane	Pallister 1	Cantona	Butt	Cole 1	Scholes	Giggs	McClair replaced Scholes
4 Nov	Arsenal	38,317	Highbury	A L	0–1	Schmeichel	Neville G	Irwin	Bruce	Keane	Pallister	Cantona	Butt	Cole	Scholes	Giggs	Sharpe L replaced Butt, McClair replaced Irwin, Beckham replaced Scholes
18 Nov	Southampton	39,301	Old Trafford	H W	4–1	Schmeichel	Neville G	Irwin	Bruce	Beckham	Pallister	Cantona	Butt	Cole 1	Scholes 1	Giggs 2	Neville P replaced Irwin, McClair replaced Scholes, Sharpe L replaced Giggs
22 Nov	Coventry City	23,344	Highfield Road	A W	4–0	Schmeichel	Neville G	Irwin 1	Bruce	Beckham 1	Pallister	Cantona	McClair 2	Cole	Butt	Giggs	Neville P replaced Neville G, Sharpe L replaced Butt, May replaced Irwin
27 Nov	Nottingham Forest	29,263	City Ground	A D	1–1	Schmeichel	Neville G	Irwin	Bruce	Butt	Pallister	Cantona 1	McClair	Cole	Beckham	Giggs	Scholes replaced McClair, Sharpe L replaced Beckham
2 Dec	Chelsea	42,019	Old Trafford	H D	1–1	Pilkington	Neville G	Irwin	Bruce	Sharpe L	May	Cantona	McClair	Cole	Scholes	Beckham 1	Cooke replaced Cole
9 Dec	Sheffield Wednesday	41,849	Old Trafford	H D	2–2	Pilkington	Neville G	Neville P	Bruce	Sharpe L	May	Cantona 2	McClair	Cole	Scholes	Beckham	Davies S replaced Scholes, Cooke replaced Sharpe L
17 Dec	Liverpool	40,546	Anfield	A L	0–2	Schmeichel	Neville G	Irwin	Bruce	Sharpe L	May	Cantona	McClair	Cole	Beckham	Giggs	Scholes replaced Cole
24 Dec	Leeds United	39,801	Elland Road	A L	1–3	Schmeichel	Neville G	Irwin	Bruce	Keane	Parker P	Cantona	McClair	Cole 1	Butt	Beckham	Scholes replaced Beckham, Neville P replaced Bruce, May replaced Parker P
27 Dec	Newcastle United	42,024	Old Trafford	H W	2–0	Schmeichel	Neville P	Irwin	May	Beckham	Neville G	Cantona	Keane 1	Cole 1	Butt	Giggs	McClair replaced May
30 Dec	Queen's Park Rangers	41,890	Old Trafford	H W	2–1	Schmeichel	Irwin	Neville P	Prunier	Keane	Neville G	Cantona	Beckham	Cole 1	Butt	Giggs 1	Parker P replaced Neville P, McClair replaced Cole, Sharpe L replaced Beckham
1 Jan	Tottenham Hotspur	32,852	White Hart Lane	A L	1–4	Schmeichel	Parker P	Neville P	Neville G	Keane	Prunier	Cantona	Beckham	Cole 1	Butt	Giggs	McClair replaced Keane, Sharpe L replaced Neville P, Pilkington replaced Schmeichel
13 Jan	Aston Villa	42,667	Old Trafford	H D	0–0	Schmeichel	Irwin	Neville P	Bruce	Sharpe L	Neville G	Cantona	Keane	Cole	Butt	Giggs	Scholes replaced Sharpe L
22 Jan	West Ham United	24,197	Upton Park	A W	1–0	Schmeichel	Neville G	Irwin	Bruce	Sharpe L	Neville P	Cantona 1	Keane	Cole	Butt	Giggs	Beckham replaced Cole
3 Feb	Wimbledon	25,423	Selhurst Park	A W	•4–2	Schmeichel	Irwin	Neville P	Bruce	Sharpe L	Neville G	Cantona 2	Keane	Cole 1	Butt	Giggs	Beckham replaced Bruce
10 Feb	Blackburn Rovers	42,681	Old Trafford	H W	1–0	Schmeichel	Irwin	Neville P	May	Sharpe L 1	Pallister	Cantona	Keane	Cole	Beckham	Giggs	
21 Feb	Everton	42,459	Old Trafford	H W	2–0	Schmeichel	Irwin	Neville P	Bruce	Sharpe L	Pallister	Cantona	Keane 1	Cole	Butt	Giggs 1	Beckham replaced Sharpe L
25 Feb	Bolton Wanderers	21,381	Burnden Park	A W	6–0	Schmeichel	Irwin	Neville P	Bruce 1	Beckham 1	Pallister	Cantona	Keane	Cole 1	Butt 1	Giggs	McClair replaced Giggs, Scholes 2 replaced Cantona
4 Mar	Newcastle United	36,584	St James' Park	A W	1–0	Schmeichel	Irwin	Neville P	Bruce	Sharpe L	Neville G	Cantona 1	Keane	Cole	Butt	Giggs	
16 Mar	Queen's Park Rangers	18,817	Loftus Road	A D	1–1	Schmeichel	Neville G	Irwin	Bruce	Keane	May	Cantona 1	McClair	Cole	Beckham	Giggs	Butt replaced May, Scholes replaced McClair, Sharpe L replaced Beckham
20 Mar	Arsenal	50,028	Old Trafford	H W	1–0	Schmeichel	Neville G	Neville P	Bruce	Sharpe L	May	Cantona 1	Keane	Cole	Butt	Giggs	Scholes replaced Cole
24 Mar	Tottenham Hotspur	50,508	Old Trafford	H W	1–0	Schmeichel	Neville G	Neville P	Bruce	Sharpe L	May	Cantona 1	Keane	Cole	Butt	Giggs	McClair replaced Cole, Beckham replaced Neville P
6 Apr	Manchester City	29,688	Maine Road	A W	3–2	Schmeichel	Irwin	Neville P	Bruce	Keane	Neville G	Cantona 1	Beckham	Cole 1	Butt	Giggs 1	Sharpe L replaced Cole, May replaced Bruce
8 Apr	Coventry City	50,332	Old Trafford	H W	1–0	Schmeichel	Irwin	Sharpe L	Beckham	Neville G	May	Cantona 1	McClair	Cole	Butt	Giggs	
13 Apr	Southampton	15,262	The Dell	A L	1–3	Schmeichel	Irwin	Sharpe L	Bruce	Neville G	Beckham	Cantona	Keane	Cole	Butt	Giggs 1	Scholes replaced Butt, May replaced Sharpe L
17 Apr	Leeds United	48,382	Old Trafford	H W	1–0	Schmeichel	Irwin	Neville P	Bruce	Keane 1	Pallister	Cantona	McClair	Cole	Beckham	Giggs	Scholes replaced McClair, Sharpe L replaced Cole, May replaced Bruce
28 Apr	Nottingham Forest	53,926	Old Trafford	H W	5–0	Schmeichel	Irwin	Neville P	May	Sharpe L	Pallister	Cantona 1	Keane	Scholes 1	Beckham 2	Giggs 1	Neville G replaced Neville P
5 May	Middlesbrough	29,922	Riverside Stadium	A W	3–0	Schmeichel	Irwin	Neville P	May 1	Keane	Pallister	Cantona	Beckham	Scholes	Butt	Giggs 1	Cole 1 replaced Scholes

FA Cup

Date	Opponent	Attendances	Venue			Players and Scores											Substitutions
6 Jan	Sunderland	41,563	Old Trafford	H D	2–2	Pilkington	Neville G	Irwin	Bruce	Keane	Pallister	Cantona 1	Butt 1	Cole	Beckham	Giggs	Neville P replaced Neville G, Sharpe L replaced Beckham
16 Jan	Sunderland	21,378	Roker Park	A W	2–1	Schmeichel	Parker P	Irwin	Bruce	Neville P	Neville G	Cantona	Keane	Cole 1	Butt	Giggs	Sharpe L replaced Parker P, Scholes 1 replaced Butt
27 Jan	Reading	14,780	Elm Park	A W	3–0	Schmeichel	Neville G	Irwin	Bruce	Sharpe L	Neville P	Cantona 1	Keane	Cole	Butt	Giggs 1	Parker P 1 replaced Neville P
18 Feb	Manchester City	42,692	Old Trafford	H W	2–1	Schmeichel	Irwin	Neville P	Bruce	Sharpe L 1	Pallister	Cantona 1	Keane	Cole	Butt	Giggs	
11 Mar	Southampton	45,446	Old Trafford	H W	2–0	Schmeichel	Neville P	Irwin	Bruce	Sharpe L 1	Neville G	Cantona 1	Keane	Cole	Butt	Giggs	
31 Mar	Chelsea	38,421	Villa Park	A W	2–1	Schmeichel	Neville P	Sharpe L	Keane	Neville G	May	Cantona	Beckham 1	Cole 1	Butt	Giggs	
11 May	Liverpool	79,007	Wembley	A W	1–0	Schmeichel	Irwin	Neville P	May	Keane	Pallister	Cantona 1	Beckham	Cole	Butt	Giggs	Neville G replaced Beckham, Scholes replaced Cole

FL Cup

Date	Opponent	Attendances	Venue			Players and Scores											Substitutions
20 Sep	York City	29,049	Old Trafford	H L	0–3	Pilkington	Parker P	Irwin	McGibbon	Sharpe L	Pallister	Neville P	Beckham	McClair	Davies S	Giggs	Cooke replaced Neville P, Bruce replaced Davies S
3 Oct	York City	9,386	Bootham Crescent	A W	3–1	Schmeichel	Neville G	Sharpe L	Bruce	Cooke 1	Pallister	Cantona	Beckham	Cole	Scholes 2	Giggs	Neville P replaced Sharpe L, Keane replaced Cooke

UEFA Cup

Date	Opponent	Attendances	Venue			Players and Scores											Substitutions
12 Sep	Rotor Volgograd	40,000	Central Stadion	A D	0–0	Schmeichel	Neville G	Irwin	Bruce	Sharpe L	Pallister	Butt	Keane	Scholes	Beckham	Giggs	Davies S replaced Keane, Parker P replaced Scholes
26 Sep	Rotor Volgograd	29,724	Old Trafford	H D	2–2	Schmeichel 1	Neville P	O'Kane	Bruce	Sharpe L	Pallister	Butt	Keane	Cole	Beckham	Giggs	Scholes 1 replaced O'Kane, Cooke replaced Beckham

Premiership
P38 • W25 • D7 • L6 • F73 • A35 • PTS82
Position: 1

1996/97

Premiership

Date	Opponent	Attendances	Venue			Players and Scores											Substitutions
17 Aug	Wimbledon	25,786	Selhurst Park	A W	3–0	Schmeichel	Irwin 1	Neville P	May	Keane	Pallister	Cantona 1	Butt	Scholes	Beckham 1	Cruyff	Johnsen replaced Butt, McClair replaced Cantona
21 Aug	Everton	54,943	Old Trafford	H D	•2–2	Schmeichel	Irwin	Neville P	May	Poborsky	Pallister	Cantona	Butt	Cruyff 1	Beckham	Giggs	McClair replaced Poborsky
25 Aug	Blackburn Rovers	54,178	Old Trafford	H D	2–2	Schmeichel	Irwin	Neville P	May	Johnsen	Pallister	Cantona	McClair	Cruyff 1	Beckham	Giggs	Neville G replaced Neville P, Solskjaer 1 replaced May
4 Sep	Derby County	18,025	Baseball Ground	A D	1–1	Schmeichel	Neville G	Irwin	May	Johnsen	Pallister	Cantona	Butt	Cruyff	Beckham 1	Giggs	Scholes replaced Cruyff, Solskjaer replaced May
7 Sep	Leeds United	39,694	Elland Road	A W	•4–0	Schmeichel	Neville G	Irwin	May	Poborsky 1	Johnsen	Cantona 1	Butt 1	Cruyff	Beckham	Giggs	McClair replaced Beckham, Solskjaer replaced Poborsky, Cole replaced Cruyff
14 Sep	Nottingham Forest	54,984	Old Trafford	H W	4–1	Schmeichel	Neville G	Irwin	Johnsen	Poborsky	Pallister	Cantona 2	Butt	Solskjaer 1	Beckham	Giggs 1	McClair replaced Butt, Cole replaced Solskjaer
21 Sep	Aston Villa	39,339	Villa Park	A D	0–0	Gouw, van der	Neville G	Irwin	Johnsen	Keane	Pallister	Cantona	Solskjaer	Cruyff	Beckham	Giggs	Poborsky replaced Cruyff, Cole replaced Solskjaer
29 Sep	Tottenham Hotspur	54,943	Old Trafford	H W	2–0	Schmeichel	Neville G	Irwin	May	Poborsky	Pallister	Cantona	Butt	Solskjaer 2	Beckham	Giggs	Scholes replaced Poborsky, Cruyff replaced Giggs
12 Oct	Liverpool	55,128	Old Trafford	H W	1–0	Schmeichel	Neville G	Irwin	May	Poborsky	Johnsen	Cantona	Butt	Solskjaer	Beckham 1	Cruyff	Scholes replaced Poborsky, Giggs replaced Solskjaer
20 Oct	Newcastle United	36,579	St James' Park	A L	0–5	Schmeichel	Neville G	Irwin	May	Johnsen	Pallister	Cantona	Butt	Solskjaer	Beckham	Poborsky	Scholes replaced Johnsen, Cruyff replaced Solskjaer, McClair replaced Poborsky
26 Oct	Southampton	15,256	The Dell	A L	3–6	Schmeichel	Neville G	Neville P	May 1	Keane	Pallister	Cantona	Butt	Scholes 1	Beckham 1	Cruyff	Irwin replaced Pallister, Solskjaer replaced Cruyff, McClair replaced Butt
2 Nov	Chelsea	55,198	Old Trafford	H L	1–2	Schmeichel	Irwin	Neville P	May 1	Keane	Johnsen	Cantona	Butt	Scholes	Beckham	Solskjaer	Poborsky replaced Scholes
16 Nov	Arsenal	55,210	Old Trafford	H W	•1–0	Schmeichel	Neville G	Neville P	May	Poborsky	Johnsen	Cantona	Butt	Solskjaer	Beckham	Giggs	
23 Nov	Middlesbrough	30,063	Riverside Stadium	A D	2–2	Schmeichel	Clegg	O'Kane	May 1	Keane 1	Johnsen	Cantona	Butt	Scholes	Beckham	Thornley	Cruyff replaced Thornley, McClair replaced O'Kane
30 Nov	Leicester City	55,196	Old Trafford	H W	3–1	Schmeichel	Neville G	Irwin	May	Keane	Pallister	Cantona	Butt 2	Cruyff	Beckham	Giggs	Solskjaer 1 replaced Cruyff, Poborsky replaced Giggs
8 Dec	West Ham United	25,045	Upton Park	A D	2–2	Schmeichel	Johnsen	Irwin	May	McClair	Pallister	Cantona	Poborsky	Solskjaer 1	Beckham 1	Giggs	Neville P replaced Poborsky
18 Dec	Sheffield Wednesday	37,671	Hillsborough	A D	1–1	Schmeichel	Neville G	Irwin	May	Johnsen	Pallister	Cantona	Butt	Scholes 1	Solskjaer	Giggs	Neville P replaced Johnsen, Beckham replaced Neville G
21 Dec	Sunderland	55,081	Old Trafford	H W	5–0	Schmeichel	Neville G	Neville P	May	Irwin	Pallister	Cantona 2	Butt 1	Solskjaer 2	Scholes	Giggs	Poborsky replaced Solskjaer, McClair replaced Pallister, Thornley replaced Neville P
26 Dec	Nottingham Forest	29,032	City Ground	A W	4–0	Schmeichel	Neville G	Irwin	May	Scholes	Johnsen	Cantona	Butt 1	Solskjaer 1	Beckham 1	Giggs	Poborsky replaced Giggs, McClair replaced Butt, Cole 1 replaced Solskjaer
28 Dec	Leeds United	55,256	Old Trafford	H W	1–0	Schmeichel	Neville G	Irwin	May	Keane	Johnsen	Cantona 1	Scholes	Solskjaer	Beckham	Giggs	Butt replaced Scholes, Cole replaced Solskjaer
1 Jan	Aston Villa	55,133	Old Trafford	H D	0–0	Schmeichel	Neville G	Irwin	May	Keane	Johnsen	Cantona	Butt	Solskjaer	Beckham	Giggs	Scholes replaced Butt, Cole replaced Solskjaer
12 Jan	Tottenham Hotspur	33,026	White Hart Lane	A W	2–1	Schmeichel	Neville G	Johnsen	May	Keane	Pallister	Cantona	Scholes	Solskjaer 1	Beckham 1	Giggs	Poborsky replaced Scholes, Cole replaced Solskjaer, Casper replaced Johnsen
18 Jan	Coventry City	23,080	Highfield Road	A W	2–0	Schmeichel	Neville G	Irwin	Johnsen	Keane	Pallister	Cantona	Scholes	Solskjaer 1	Poborsky	Giggs 1	Casper replaced Johnsen
29 Jan	Wimbledon	55,314	Old Trafford	H W	2–1	Schmeichel	Clegg	Irwin	Neville G	Keane	Pallister	Cantona	Scholes	Solskjaer	Beckham	Giggs 1	Cole 1 replaced Scholes
1 Feb	Southampton	55,269	Old Trafford	H W	2–1	Schmeichel	Clegg	Irwin	Neville G	Keane	Pallister 1	Cantona 1	Poborsky	Solskjaer	Beckham	Giggs	Johnsen replaced Clegg, Cole replaced Poborsky
19 Feb	Arsenal	38,172	Highbury	A W	2–1	Schmeichel	Neville G	Irwin	Johnsen	Keane	Pallister	Solskjaer 1	Poborsky	Cole 1	Beckham	Giggs	Butt replaced Poborsky, McClair replaced Butt
22 Feb	Chelsea	28,324	Stamford Bridge	A D	1–1	Schmeichel	Neville G	Irwin	Johnsen	Keane	Pallister	Solskjaer	McClair	Cole	Beckham 1	Giggs	May replaced Johnsen, Cruyff replaced Giggs

Continued on page 154

1996/97 continued

Premiership continued

Date	Opponent	Attendances	Venue			Players and Scores											Substitutions
15 Mar	Sheffield Wednesday	55,267	Old Trafford	H W	2–0	Schmeichel	Neville G	Irwin	May	Butt	Pallister	Cantona	Solskjaer	Cole 1	Beckham	Giggs	Scholes for Solskjaer, Poborsky 1 for Cole
22 Mar	Everton	40,079	Goodison Park	A W	2–0	Schmeichel	Irwin	Neville P	May	Keane	Pallister	Cantona 1	Butt	Solskjaer 1	Beckham	Giggs	Johnsen for Pallister, McClair for Beckham
5 Apr	Derby County	55,243	Old Trafford	H L	2–3	Schmeichel	Neville G	Neville P	Johnsen	Keane	Pallister	Cantona 1	Butt	Cole	Beckham	Giggs	Irwin for Neville G, Scholes for Pallister, Solskjaer 1 for Butt
12 Apr	Blackburn Rovers	30,476	Ewood Park	A W	3–2	Gouw, van der	Neville G	Neville P	Johnsen	Keane	Pallister	Cantona 1	Butt	Cole 1	Scholes 1	Solskjaer	Beckham for Scholes
19 Apr	Liverpool	40,892	Anfield	A W	3–1	Schmeichel	Neville G	Neville P	Johnsen	Keane	Pallister 2	Cantona	Butt	Cole 1	Beckham	Scholes	McClair for Scholes
3 May	Leicester City	21,068	Filbert Street	A D	2–2	Schmeichel	Neville G	Neville P	May	Keane	Pallister	Cantona	Butt	Cole	Solskjaer 2	Scholes	Beckham for Butt, Johnsen for Solskjaer
5 May	Middlesbrough	54,589	Old Trafford	H D	3–3	Schmeichel	Neville G 1	Irwin	May	Johnsen	Pallister	Cantona	Keane 1	Cole	Beckham	Solskjaer 1	Scholes for Johnsen
8 May	Newcastle United	55,236	Old Trafford	H D	0–0	Schmeichel	Neville G	Neville P	May	Keane	Johnsen	Cantona	Poborsky	Cole	Beckham	Scholes	Solskjaer for Cole, McClair for Keane
11 May	West Ham United	55,249	Old Trafford	H W	2–0	Schmeichel	Irwin	Neville P	May	Poborsky	Johnsen	Cantona	Butt	Solskjaer 1	Beckham	Scholes	Cruyff 1 for Scholes, McClair for Poborsky, Clegg for Irwin

FA Cup

5 Jan	Tottenham Hotspur	52,495	Old Trafford	H W	2–0	Schmeichel	Neville G	Irwin	May	Keane	Johnsen	Cantona	Scholes 1	Cole	Beckham 1	Giggs	McClair for Irwin, Solskjaer for Cole
25 Jan	Wimbledon	53,342	Old Trafford	H D	1–1	Schmeichel	Clegg	Irwin	Casper	Keane	Neville G	Cantona	McClair	Scholes 1	Poborsky	Giggs	Solskjaer for McClair, Cole for Poborsky
4 Feb	Wimbledon	25,601	Selhurst Park	A L	0–1	Schmeichel	Neville G	Irwin	Johnsen	Keane	Pallister	Cantona	Poborsky	Cole	Beckham	Giggs	McClair for Irwin, Solskjaer for Poborsky

FL Cup

23 Oct	Swindon Town	49,305	Old Trafford	H W	2–1	Gouw, van der	Neville G	Neville P	May	Keane	Casper	Thornley	Appleton	McClair	Scholes 1	Poborsky 1	Davies S for Appleton
27 Nov	Leicester City	20,428	Filbert Street	A L	0–2	Gouw, van der	O'Kane	Clegg	May	Keane	Casper	Cruyff	McClair	Scholes	Poborsky	Thornley	Appleton for O'Kane, Cooke for Poborsky, Davies S for Thornley

European Cup

11 Sep	Juventus	50,000	Delle Alpi	A L	0–1	Schmeichel	Neville G	Irwin	Johnsen	Poborsky	Pallister	Cantona	Butt	Cruyff	Beckham	Giggs	Solskjaer for Poborsky, Cole for Cruyff, McClair for Giggs
25 Sep	Rapid Vienna	51,831	Old Trafford	H W	2–0	Schmeichel	Neville G	Irwin	Johnsen	Keane	Pallister	Cantona	Poborsky	Solskjaer 1	Beckham 1	Giggs	May for Johnsen, Butt for Poborsky, Cole for Solskjaer
16 Oct	Fenerbahce	26,200	Fenerbahce	A W	2–0	Schmeichel	Neville G	Irwin	May	Johnsen	Pallister	Cantona 1	Butt	Solskjaer	Beckham 1	Cruyff	Poborsky for Cruyff
30 Oct	Fenerbahce	53,297	Old Trafford	H L	0–1	Schmeichel	Neville G	Irwin	May	Keane	Johnsen	Cantona	Butt	Poborsky	Beckham	Cruyff	Neville P for Neville G, Scholes for Poborsky, Solskjaer for Cruyff
20 Nov	Juventus	53,529	Old Trafford	H L	0–1	Schmeichel	Neville G	Neville P	May	Keane	Johnsen	Cantona	Butt	Solskjaer	Beckham	Giggs	McClair for Neville P, Cruyff for Solskjaer
4 Dec	Rapid Vienna	45,000	Hanappi Stadion	A W	2–0	Schmeichel	Neville G	Irwin	May	Keane	Pallister	Cantona 1	Butt	Solskjaer	Beckham	Giggs 1	Casper for Neville G, McClair for Keane, Poborsky for Butt
5 Mar	Porto	53,415	Old Trafford	H W	4–0	Schmeichel	Neville G	Irwin	May1	Johnsen	Pallister	Cantona 1	Solskjaer	Cole 1	Beckham	Giggs 1	
19 Mar	Porto	40,000	das Antas	A D	0–0	Schmeichel	Neville G	Irwin	May	Keane	Pallister	Cantona	Butt	Solskjaer	Beckham	Johnsen	Neville P for Irwin, Scholes for Solskjaer, Poborsky for Beckham
9 Apr	Borussia Dortmund	48,500	Westfalenstadion	A L	0–1	Gouw, van der	Neville G	Irwin	Johnsen	Keane	Pallister	Cantona	Butt	Solskjaer	Beckham	Giggs	Cole for Solskjaer, Scholes for Giggs
23 Apr	Borussia Dortmund	53,606	Old Trafford	H L	0–1	Schmeichel	Neville G	Neville P	May	Johnsen	Pallister	Cantona	Butt	Cole	Beckham	Solskjaer	Scholes for May, Giggs for Solskjaer

Premiership
P38 • W21 • D12 • L5 • F76 • A44 • PTS75
Position: 1

1997/98

Premiership

Date	Opponent	Attendances	Venue			Players and Scores											Substitutions
10 Aug	Tottenham Hotspur	26,359	White Hart Lane	A W	•2–0	Schmeichel	Irwin	Neville P	Johnsen	Butt 1	Pallister	Keane	Scholes	Cruyff	Sheringham	Giggs	Beckham for Scholes
13 Aug	Southampton	55,008	Old Trafford	H W	1–0	Schmeichel	Irwin	Neville P	Johnsen	Butt	Pallister	Keane	Scholes	Cruyff	Sheringham	Giggs	Beckham 1 for Scholes, Berg for Johnsen
23 Aug	Leicester City	21,221	Filbert Street	A D	0–0	Schmeichel	Neville G	Irwin	Berg	Butt	Pallister	Keane	Beckham	Cruyff	Sheringham	Giggs	Scholes for Cruyff
27 Aug	Everton	40,079	Goodison Park	A W	2–0	Schmeichel	Neville G	Irwin	Berg	Butt	Pallister	Keane	Beckham 1	Scholes	Sheringham 1	Giggs	Cole for Sheringham
30 Aug	Coventry City	55,074	Old Trafford	H W	3–0	Schmeichel	Neville G	Neville P	Berg	Butt	Pallister	Keane 1	Beckham	Cole 1	Sheringham	Giggs	Poborsky 1 for Cole, Irwin for P Neville
13 Sep	West Ham United	55,068	Old Trafford	H W	2–1	Schmeichel	Neville G	Pallister	Berg	Butt	Beckham	Keane 1	Neville P	Cole	Scholes 1	Giggs	Poborsky for Giggs, McClair for Cole
20 Sep	Bolton Wanderers	25,000	Reebok Stadium	A D	0–0	Schmeichel	Neville G	Irwin	Berg	Butt	Pallister	Keane	Beckham	Cole	Scholes	Poborsky	Neville P for Poborsky, Solskjaer for Scholes
24 Sep	Chelsea	55,163	Old Trafford	H D	2–2	Schmeichel	Neville G	Irwin	Berg	Butt	Pallister	Keane	Beckham	Cole	Scholes 1	Poborsky	Giggs for Neville G, Solskjaer 1 for Poborsky, Sheringham for Scholes
27 Sep	Leeds United	39,952	Elland Road	A L	0–1	Schmeichel	Neville G	Irwin	Berg	Beckham	Pallister	Keane	Scholes	Poborsky	Sheringham	Solskjaer	Neville P for Neville G, Johnsen for Scholes, Thornley for Poborsky
4 Oct	Crystal Palace	55,143	Old Trafford	H W	•2–0	Schmeichel	Neville G	Johnsen	Berg	Butt	Pallister	Beckham	Neville P	Scholes	Sheringham 1	Giggs	Irwin for Neville P, Poborsky for Johnsen
18 Oct	Derby County	30,014	Pride Park	A D	2–2	Schmeichel	Neville G	Irwin	Berg	Butt	Pallister	Beckham	Scholes	Solskjaer	Sheringham 1	Giggs	Neville P for Irwin, Johnsen for Butt, Cole 1 for Scholes
25 Oct	Barnsley	55,142	Old Trafford	H W	7–0	Schmeichel	Neville G	Neville P	Curtis	Butt	Pallister	Beckham	Scholes 1	Cole 3	Solskjaer	Giggs 2	Wallwork for Pallister, Poborsky 1 for Beckham, Cruyff for Scholes
1 Nov	Sheffield Wednesday	55,259	Old Trafford	H W	6–1	Schmeichel	Neville G	Neville P	Berg	Butt	Pallister	Beckham	Scholes	Cole 2	Sheringham 2	Solskjaer 2	McClair for Butt, Poborsky for Scholes, Curtis for Berg
9 Nov	Arsenal	38,203	Highbury	A L	2–3	Schmeichel	Neville G	Neville P	Berg	Butt	Pallister	Beckham	Scholes	Cole	Sheringham 2	Giggs	Johnsen for Pallister, Solskjaer for Giggs
22 Nov	Wimbledon	26,309	Selhurst Park	A W	5–2	Schmeichel	Neville G	Johnsen	Berg	Butt 1	Pallister	Neville P	Scholes 1	Cole 1	Sheringham	Giggs	Beckham 2 for Neville G
30 Nov	Blackburn Rovers	55,175	Old Trafford	H W	••4–0	Schmeichel	Neville G	Neville P	Berg	Butt	Pallister	Beckham	Solskjaer 2	Cole	Sheringham	Giggs	Poborsky for Pallister, Johnsen for Butt, McClair for Sheringham
6 Dec	Liverpool	41,027	Anfield	A W	3–1	Schmeichel	Neville G	Johnsen	Berg	Butt	Pallister	Beckham 1	Neville P	Cole 2	Sheringham	Giggs	
15 Dec	Aston Villa	55,151	Old Trafford	H W	1–0	Schmeichel	Neville G	Johnsen	Neville P	Butt	Pallister	Beckham	Solskjaer	Cole	Sheringham	Giggs 1	McClair for Solskjaer
21 Dec	Newcastle United	36,767	St James' Park	A W	1–0	Schmeichel	Neville G	Johnsen	Neville P	Butt	Pallister	Beckham	Scholes	Cole 1	Sheringham	Giggs	McClair for Sheringham, Solskjaer for Scholes
26 Dec	Everton	55,167	Old Trafford	H W	2–0	Pilkington	Neville G	Johnsen	Berg 1	Butt	Pallister	Beckham	Neville P	Cole 1	Scholes	Solskjaer	McClair for Pallister, Poborsky for Beckham, Curtis for Neville P
28 Dec	Coventry City	23,054	Highfield Road	A L	2–3	Pilkington	Neville G	Johnsen	Berg	Beckham	Pallister	Scholes	Solskjaer 1	Cole	Sheringham 1	Giggs	Curtis for Johnsen, Butt for Solskjaer
10 Jan	Tottenham Hotspur	55,281	Old Trafford	H W	2–0	Schmeichel	Neville G	Irwin	Johnsen	Beckham	Pallister	Scholes	Solskjaer	Cole	Sheringham	Giggs 2	
19 Jan	Southampton	15,241	The Dell	A L	0–1	Schmeichel	Neville G	Irwin	Johnsen	Butt	Pallister	Beckham	Solskjaer	Cole	Scholes	Giggs	Nevland for Neville G, McClair for Butt
31 Jan	Leicester City	55,156	Old Trafford	H L	0–1	Schmeichel	Neville G	Irwin	Johnsen	Butt	Pallister	Beckham	Solskjaer	Cole	Scholes	Giggs	Sheringham for Berg for Johnsen, Neville P for Scholes
7 Feb	Bolton Wanderers	55,156	Old Trafford	H D	1–1	Schmeichel	Neville G	Irwin	P Neville	Beckham	Pallister	Scholes	Solskjaer	Cole 1	Sheringham	Giggs	Berg for Sheringham
18 Feb	Aston Villa	39,372	Villa Park	A W	2–0	Schmeichel	Neville G	Irwin	Berg	Butt	Pallister	Beckham 1	McClair	Cole	Sheringham	Giggs 1	Neville P for McClair
21 Feb	Derby County	55,170	Old Trafford	H W	2–0	Schmeichel	Neville G	Irwin 1	Berg	Butt	Pallister	Beckham	Neville P	Cole	Sheringham	Giggs 1	Clegg for Irwin, Cruyff for Cole, McClair for Giggs
28 Feb	Chelsea	34,511	Stamford Bridge	A W	1–0	Schmeichel	Neville G	Irwin	Johnsen	Butt	Pallister	Beckham	Neville P 1	Cole	Sheringham	Scholes	Berg for Pallister
7 Mar	Sheffield Wednesday	39,427	Hillsborough	A L	0–2	Gouw, van der	Neville G	May	Berg	Butt	Johnsen	Beckham	Neville P	Cole	Sheringham	Solskjaer	Scholes for Johnsen, McClair for Cole, Curtis for Neville P
11 Mar	West Ham United	25,892	Upton Park	A D	1–1	Schmeichel	Neville G	Irwin	Berg	Butt	May	Beckham	McClair	Cole	Sheringham	Scholes 1	Curtis for Butt, Solskjaer for Cole, Thornley for McClair
14 Mar	Arsenal	55,174	Old Trafford	H L	0–1	Schmeichel	Neville G	Irwin	Berg	Curtis	Johnsen	Beckham	Neville P	Cole	Sheringham	Scholes	May for Johnsen, Solskjaer for Neville P, Thornley for Curtis
28 Mar	Wimbledon	55,306	Old Trafford	H W	2–0	Gouw, van der	Neville G	Irwin	Berg	May	Johnsen 1	Beckham	Neville P	Cole	Scholes 1	Solskjaer	Thornley for Solskjaer, McClair for Cole
6 Apr	Blackburn Rovers	30,547	Ewood Park	A W	3–1	Schmeichel	Neville G	Irwin	Johnsen	P Neville	Pallister	Beckham 1	Scholes 1	Cole 1	Solskjaer	Giggs	Butt for Solskjaer
10 Apr	Liverpool	55,171	Old Trafford	H D	1–1	Schmeichel	Neville G	Irwin	Johnsen 1	Butt	Pallister	Beckham	Neville P	Cole	Scholes	Giggs	May for Johnsen, Thornley for Giggs, Sheringham for Neville P
18 Apr	Newcastle United	55,194	Old Trafford	H D	1–1	Schmeichel	Neville G	Irwin	May	Butt	Pallister	Beckham 1	Neville P	Cole	Sheringham	Giggs	Gouw, van der for Schmeichel, Solskjaer for Neville G, Scholes for Butt
27 Apr	Crystal Palace	26,180	Selhurst Park	A W	3–0	Schmeichel	Irwin	May	Neville P	Butt 1	Pallister	Beckham	Scholes 1	Cole 1	Sheringham	Giggs	Clegg for Irwin
4 May	Leeds United	55,167	Old Trafford	H W	3–0	Gouw, van der	Neville G	Irwin 1	May	Butt	Pallister	Beckham 1	Scholes	Cole	Sheringham	Giggs 1	Neville P for Irwin, Brown for May, McClair for Sheringham
10 May	Barnsley	18,694	Oakwell	A W	2–0	Gouw, van der	May	Curtis	Berg	Butt	Clegg	Brown	Mulryne	Cole 1	Sheringham 1	Giggs	Higginbotham for Clegg

FA Cup

4 Jan	Chelsea	34,792	Stamford Bridge	A W	5–3	Schmeichel	Neville G	Irwin	Johnsen	Butt	Pallister	Beckham 2	Scholes	Cole 2	Sheringham 1	Giggs	Solskjaer for Scholes
24 Jan	Walsall	54,669	Old Trafford	H W	5–1	Schmeichel	Neville G	Irwin	Berg	Johnsen 1	Thornley	Beckham	McClair	Cole 2	Scholes	Solskjaer 2	Clegg for Irwin, Mulryne for Scholes, Nevland for Thornley
15 Feb	Barnsley	54,700	Old Trafford	H D	1–1	Schmeichel	Clegg	Irwin	Berg	Johnsen	Pallister	Nevland	Neville P	McClair	Sheringham 1	Giggs	Beckham for Johnsen, Neville G for McClair, Cruyff for Nevland
25 Feb	Barnsley	18,655	Oakwell	A L	2–3	Schmeichel	Neville G	May	Neville P	Clegg	Pallister	Beckham	Nevland	Cole 1	McClair	Thornley	Sheringham 1 for Nevland, Irwin for McClair, Twiss for Clegg

FL Cup

14 Oct	Ipswich Town	22,173	Portman Road	A L	0–2	Gouw, van der	Curtis	Neviile P	May	Johnsen	Mulryne	Thornley	McClair	Cole	Cruyff	Poborsky	Scholes for Thornley, Nevland for Mulryne, Irwin for Johnsen

European Cup

17 Sep	Kosice	10,000	Kosice	A W	3–0	Schmeichel	Neville G	Irwin 1	Berg 1	Butt	Pallister	Keane	Beckham	Cole 1	Scholes	Poborsky	McClair for Beckham
1 Oct	Juventus	53,428	Old Trafford	H W	3–2	Schmeichel	Neville G	Irwin	Berg	Butt	Pallister	Johnsen	Beckham	Solskjaer	Sheringham 1	Giggs 1	Scholes 1 for Butt, Neville P for Solskjaer
22 Oct	Feyenoord	53,188	Old Trafford	H W	2–1	Schmeichel	Neville G	Irwin 1	Neville P	Butt	Pallister	Beckham	Scholes 1	Cole	Sheringham	Giggs	Solskjaer for Cole
5 Nov	Feyenoord	51,000	Feyenoord	A W	3–1	Schmeichel	Neville G	Irwin	Berg	Butt	Pallister	Beckham	Scholes	Cole 3	Sheringham	Giggs	Poborsky for Scholes, Solskjaer for Cole, Neville P for Irwin
27 Nov	Kosice	53,535	Old Trafford	H W	•3–0	Schmeichel	Neville G	Johnsen	Neville P	Butt	Pallister	Beckham	Scholes	Cole 1	Sheringham 1	Giggs	Solskjaer for Butt, Poborsky for Giggs, Berg for Neville P
10 Dec	Juventus	47,786	Delle Alpi	A L	0–1	Schmeichel	Neville G	Neville P	Berg	Johnsen	Pallister	Beckham	Poborsky	Solskjaer	Sheringham	Giggs	Cole for Solskjaer, McClair for Poborsky
4 Mar	Monaco	15,000	Monaco	A D	0–0	Schmeichel	Neville G	Irwin	Berg	Johnsen	Butt	Beckham	Neville P	Cole	Sheringham	Scholes	McClair for Irwin
18 Mar	Monaco	53,683	Old Trafford	H D	1–1	Gouw, van der	Neville G	Irwin	Neville P	Johnsen	Butt	Beckham	Scholes	Cole	Sheringham	Solskjaer 1	Berg for Neville G, Clegg for Scholes

Premiership
P38 • W23 • D8 • L7 • F73 • A26 • PTS77
Position: 2

1998/99

Premiership

Date	Opponent	Attendances	Venue			Players and Scores											Substitutions
15 Aug	Leicester City	55,052	Old Trafford	H D	2–2	Schmeichel	Neville G	Irwin	Johnsen	Stam	Keane	Beckham 1	Butt	Scholes	Cole	Giggs	Berg for Stam, Sheringham 1 replace Neville G
22 Aug	West Ham United	26,039	Upton Park	A D	0–0	Schmeichel	Neville G	Irwin	Johnsen	Berg	Keane	Beckham	Butt	Cole	Yorke	Giggs	Neville P for Neville G, Sheringham for Cole
9 Sep	Charlton Athletic	55,147	Old Trafford	H W	4–1	Schmeichel	Irwin	Johnsen	Stam	Neville P	Keane	Beckham	Scholes	Blomqvist	Solskjaer 2	Yorke 2	Berg for Irwin, Sheringham for Yorke, Cole for Solskjaer
12 Sep	Coventry City	55,193	Old Trafford	H W	2–0	Schmeichel	Neville G	Johnsen 1	Stam	Neville P	Keane	Beckham	Scholes	Solskjaer	Yorke 1	Giggs	Butt for Beckham, Blomqvist for Giggs, Berg for Johnsen
20 Sep	Arsenal	38,142	Highbury	A L	0–3	Schmeichel	Neville G	Irwin	Stam	Berg	Beckham	Butt	Keane	Blomqvist	Yorke	Giggs	
24 Sep	Liverpool	55,181	Old Trafford	H W	2–0	Schmeichel	Neville G	Irwin 1	Stam	Neville P	Keane	Beckham	Scholes 1	Solskjaer	Yorke	Giggs	Cole for Solskjaer, Butt for Scholes
3 Oct	Southampton	15,251	The Dell	A W	3–0	van der Gouw	Neville G	Irwin	Stam	Neville P	Beckham	Butt	Keane	Blomqvist	Cole 1	Yorke 1	Cruyff 1 for Yorke, Sheringham for Blomqvist, Brown for Irwin
17 Oct	Wimbledon	55,265	Old Trafford	H W	5–1	van der Gouw	Neville G	Brown	Stam	Neville P	Keane	Beckham 1	Blomqvist	Cole 2	Yorke 1	Giggs 1	Cruyff for Beckham, Scholes for Giggs, Curtis for Neville P
24 Oct	Derby County	30,867	Pride Park	A D	1–1	Schmeichel	Neville G	Brown	Stam	Neville P	Beckham	Butt	Keane	Cole	Yorke	Giggs	Scholes for Neville G, Cruyff 1 for Giggs, Blomqvist for Butt
31 Oct	Everton	40,079	Goodison Park	AW*	4–1	Schmeichel	Neville G	Brown	Stam	Neville P	Keane	Beckham	Scholes	Blomqvist 1	Cole 1	Yorke 1	Irwin for Neville P
8 Nov	Newcastle United	55,174	Old Trafford	H D	0–0	Schmeichel	Neville G	Brown	Irwin	Stam	Keane	Beckham	Scholes	Blomqvist	Cole	Yorke	Johnsen for Brown, Butt for Johnsen, Solskjaer for Blomqvist
14 Nov	Blackburn Rovers	55,198	Old Trafford	H W	3–2	Schmeichel	Neville G	Stam	Curtis	Neville P	Beckham	Butt	Scholes 2	Blomqvist	Cole	Yorke 1	Cruyff for Scholes, Solskjaer for Blomqvist, Keane for Cruyff
21 Nov	Sheffield Wed	39,475	Hillsborough	A L	1–3	Schmeichel	Neville G	Irwin	Stam	Neville P	Keane	Beckham	Scholes	Blomqvist	Cole 1	Yorke	Brown for Irwin, Butt for Blomqvist, Solskjaer for Keane
29 Nov	Leeds United	55,172	Old Trafford	H W	3–2	Schmeichel	Neville G	Brown	Stam	Neville P	Butt 1	Keane 1	Scholes	Cole	Solskjaer 1	Yorke	Giggs for Cole, Sheringham for Scholes, Berg for Stam
5 Dec	Aston Villa	39,241	Villa Park	A D	1–1	Schmeichel	Neville G	Brown	Irwin	Stam	Keane	Beckham	Scholes 1	Blomqvist	Cole	Yorke	Giggs for Blomqvist, Butt for Cole
12 Dec	Tottenham Hotspur	36,079	White Hart Lane	A D	2–2	Schmeichel	Neville G	Johnsen	Stam	Neville P	Keane	Beckham	Butt	Sheringham	Solskjaer 2	Giggs	Berg for Solskjaer, Cole for Sheringham, Blomqvist for Giggs
16 Dec	Chelsea	55,159	Old Trafford	H D	1–1	Schmeichel	Neville G	Brown	Irwin	Stam	Butt	Keane	Scholes	Blomqvist	Cole 1	Yorke	Beckham for Yorke, Giggs for Blomqvist, Sheringham for Scholes
19 Dec	Middlesbrough	55,152	Old Trafford	H L	2–3	Schmeichel	Neville G	Irwin	Johnsen	Neville P	Beckham	Butt 1	Keane	Cole	Sheringham	Giggs	Scholes 1 for Beckham, Solskjaer for Neville P
26 Dec	Nottingham Forest	55,216	Old Trafford	H W	3–0	Schmeichel	Irwin	Johnsen 2	Berg	Neville P	Keane	Beckham	Butt	Scholes	Sheringham	Giggs 1	Solskjaer for Scholes, Greening for Keane, Blomqvist for Giggs
29 Dec	Chelsea	34,741	Stamford Bridge	A D	0–0	Schmeichel	Neville G	Irwin	Johnsen	Stam	Beckham	Butt	Keane	Scholes	Cole	Giggs	Sheringham for Scholes
10 Jan	West Ham United	55,180	Old Trafford	H W	4–1	van der Gouw	Brown	Irwin	Stam	Berg	Keane	Butt	Blomqvist	Cole 2	Yorke 1	Giggs	Johnsen for Brown, Solskjaer 1 for Butt, Cruyff for Keane
16 Jan	Leicester City	22,091	Filbert Street	A W	6–2	Schmeichel	Brown	Irwin	Stam 1	Berg	Keane	Beckham	Blomqvist	Cole 2	Yorke 3	Giggs	Neville P for Brown
31 Jan	Charlton Athletic	20,043	The Valley	A W	1–0	Schmeichel	Neville G	Irwin	Stam	Berg	Beckham	Butt	Keane	Cole	Yorke 1	Giggs	Solskjaer for Beckham, Scholes for Butt
3 Feb	Derby County	55,174	Old Trafford	H W	1–0	Schmeichel	Neville G	Irwin	Stam	Johnsen	Keane	Butt	Scholes	Solskjaer	Yorke 1	Giggs	Blomqvist for Giggs

1998/99 continued

Premiership continued

Date	Opponent	Attendances	Venue			Score	Players and Scores											Substitutions
6 Feb	Nottingham Forest	30,025	City Ground	A	W	8–1	Schmeichel	Neville G	Johnsen	Stam	Neville P	Keane	Beckham	Scholes	Blomqvist	Cole 2	Yorke 2	Solskjaer 4 for Keane, Curtis for Yorke, Butt for Blomqvist
17 Feb	Arsenal	55,171	Old Trafford	H	D	1–1	Schmeichel	Neville G	Johnsen	Stam	Neville P	Keane	Beckham	Butt	Blomqvist	Cole 1	Yorke	Scholes for Blomqvist, Giggs for Butt
20 Feb	Coventry City	22,596	Highfield Road	A	W	1–0	Schmeichel	Neville G	Irwin	Stam	Johnsen	Keane	Beckham	Scholes	Cole	Yorke	Giggs 1	Berg for Stam, Solskjaer for Cole, Neville P for Yorke
27 Feb	Southampton	55,316	Old Trafford	H	W	2–1	Schmeichel	Neville G	Johnsen	Berg	Neville P	Beckham	Butt	Scholes	Solskjaer	Yorke 1	Giggs	Keane 1 for Butt, Cole for Solskjaer, Irwin for Neville P
13 Mar	Newcastle United	36,776	St James' Park	A	W	2–1	Schmeichel	Neville G	Irwin	Stam	Berg	Keane	Beckham	Scholes	Cole 2	Yorke	Giggs	van der Gouw for Schmeichel, Johnsen for Giggs, Neville P for Scholes
21 Mar	Everton	55,182	Old Trafford	H	W	3–1	Schmeichel	Neville G 1	Johnsen	Stam	Berg	Neville P	Beckham 1	Butt	Cole	Solskjaer 1	Yorke	Greening for Beckham, Sheringham for Cole, Curtis for Solskjaer
3 Apr	Wimbledon	26,121	Selhurst Park	A	D	1–1	Schmeichel	Neville G	Irwin	Johnsen	Berg	Beckham 1	Keane	Scholes	Blomqvist	Cole	Yorke	Solskjaer for Blomqvist
17 Apr	Sheffield Wed	55,270	Old Trafford	H	W	3–0	van der Gouw	Neville G	Brown	Stam	Neville P	Keane	Butt	Scholes 1	Blomqvist	Sheringham 1	Solskjaer 1	May for Stam, Greening for Keane, Irwin for Blomqvist
25 Apr	Leeds United	40,255	Elland Road	A	D	1–1	Schmeichel	Neville G	Brown	Irwin	May	Keane	Beckham	Butt	Blomqvist	Cole 1	Yorke	Neville P for Irwin, Sheringham for Blomqvist, Scholes for Beckham
1 May	Aston Villa	55,189	Old Trafford	H	W*	2–1	Schmeichel	Neville G	Irwin	May	Johnsen	Beckham 1	Butt	Scholes	Blomqvist	Sheringham	Yorke	Neville P for Blomqvist, Brown for May
5 May	Liverpool	44,702	Anfield	A	D	2–2	Schmeichel	Neville G	Irwin 1	Stam	Johnsen	Keane	Beckham	Scholes	Blomqvist	Cole	Yorke 1	Butt for Cole, Neville P for Blomqvist
9 May	Middlesbrough	34,665	Riverside Stadium	A	W	1–0	Schmeichel	Neville G	Irwin	May	Stam	Beckham	Keane	Scholes	Blomqvist	Sheringham	Yorke 1	Butt for Keane, Cole for Blomqvist, Neville P for Scholes
12 May	Blackburn Rovers	30,436	Ewood Park	A	D	0–0	Schmeichel	Neville G	Irwin	Stam	Johnsen	Neville P	Beckham	Butt	Cole	Yorke	Giggs	May for Stam, Sheringham for Cole, Scholes for Neville P
16 May	Tottenham Hotspur	55,189	Old Trafford	H	W	2–1	Schmeichel	Neville G	Irwin	May	Johnsen	Keane	Beckham 1	Scholes	Sheringham	Yorke	Giggs	Cole 1 for Sheringham, Butt for Scholes, Neville P for Giggs

FA Cup

Date	Opponent	Attendances	Venue			Score	Players and Scores											Substitutions
3 Jan	Middlesbrough	52,232	Old Trafford	H	W	3–1	Schmeichel	Brown	Irwin 1	Stam	Berg	Keane	Butt	Blomqvist	Cole 1	Yorke	Giggs 1	Solskjaer for Blomqvist, Neville P for Brown, Sheringham for Cole
24 Jan	Liverpool	54,591	Old Trafford	H	W	2–1	Schmeichel	Neville G	Irwin	Stam	Berg	Keane	Beckham	Butt	Cole	Yorke 1	Giggs	Scholes for Butt, Solskjaer 1 for Irwin, Johnsen for Berg
14 Feb	Fulham	54,798	Old Trafford	H	W	1–0	Schmeichel	Neville G	Irwin	Stam	Berg	Neville P	Beckham	Butt	Cole 1	Yorke	Solskjaer	Greening for Irwin, Blomqvist for Solskjaer, Johnsen for Cole
7 Mar	Chelsea	54,587	Old Trafford	H	D	0–0	Schmeichel	Neville G	Brown	Irwin	Berg	Neville P	Keane	Beckham	Blomqvist	Scholes	Solskjaer	Yorke for Neville P, Cole for Blomqvist, Sheringham for Solskjaer
10 Mar	Chelsea	33,075	Stamford Bridge	A	W	2–0	Schmeichel	Neville G	Irwin	Stam	Berg	Keane	Beckham	Scholes	Cole	Yorke 2	Giggs	Neville P for Cole, Blomqvist for Giggs, Solskjaer for Yorke
11 Apr	Arsenal	39,217	Villa Park	A	D	0–0	Schmeichel	Neville G	Johnsen	Irwin	Stam	Keane	Beckham	Butt	Cole	Yorke	Giggs	Neville P for Irwin, Solskjaer for Giggs, Scholes for Cole
14 Apr	Arsenal	30,223	Villa Park	A	W	2–1	Schmeichel	Neville G	Johnsen	Stam	Neville P	Keane	Beckham 1	Butt	Sheringham	Solskjaer	Blomqvist	Giggs 1 for Blomqvist, Scholes for Sheringham, Yorke for Solskjaer
22 May	Newcastle United	79,101	Wembley	A	W	2–0	Schmeichel	Neville G	Johnsen	May	Neville P	Keane	Beckham	Scholes 1	Cole	Solskjaer	Giggs	Sheringham 1 for Keane, Yorke for Cole, Stam for Scholes

FL Cup

Date	Opponent	Attendances	Venue			Score	Players and Scores											Substitutions
28 Oct	Bury	52,495	Old Trafford	H	W	2–0	van der Gouw	May	Neville P	Curtis	Clegg	Cruyff	Berg	Mulryne	Wilson	Greening	Solskjaer 1	Nevland 1 for Mulryne, Brown for Clegg, Scholes for Wilson
11 Nov	Nottingham Forest	37,337	Old Trafford	H	W	2–1	van der Gouw	Clegg	Curtis	May	Berg	Wilson	Greening	Butt	Cruyff	Mulryne	Solskjaer 2	Wallwork for May
2 Dec	Tottenham Hotspur	35,702	White Hart Lane	A	L	1–3	van der Gouw	Clegg	Johnsen	Neville P	Curtis	Berg	Butt	Solskjaer	Greening	Sheringham 1	Giggs	Notman for Butt, Beckham for Curtis, Blomqvist for Greening

European Cup

Date	Opponent	Attendances	Venue			Score	Players and Scores											Substitutions
12 Aug	LKS Lodz	50,906	Old Trafford	H	W	2–0	Schmeichel	Neville G	Irwin	Johnsen	Stam	Keane	Beckham	Butt	Cole 1	Scholes	Giggs 1	Solskjaer for Scholes
26 Aug	LKS Lodz	8,000	Lodz	A	D	0–0	Schmeichel	Irwin	Neville P	Johnsen	Stam	Keane	Beckham	Butt	Sheringham	Scholes	Giggs	Solskjaer for Giggs
16 Sep	Barcelona	53,601	Old Trafford	H	D	3–3	Schmeichel	Neville G	Irwin	Stam	Berg	Keane	Beckham 1	Solskjaer	Scholes 1	Yorke	Giggs 1	Butt for Solskjaer, Neville P for Irwin, Blomqvist for Giggs
30 Sep	Bayern Munich	53,000	Olympic Stadium	A	D	2–2	Schmeichel	Neville G	Irwin	Stam	Neville P	Keane	Beckham	Scholes 1	Sheringham	Yorke 1	Blomqvist	Cruyff for Blomqvist
21 Oct	Brondby	40,530	Brondby	A	W	6–2	Schmeichel	Neville G	Brown	Stam	Neville P	Keane 1	Blomqvist	Scholes	Cole 1	Yorke 1	Giggs 2	Solskjaer 1 for Cole, Cruyff for Giggs, Wilson for Yorke
4 Nov	Brondby	53,250	Old Trafford	H	W	5–0	Schmeichel	Neville G	Irwin	Stam	Neville P 1	Keane	Beckham 1	Scholes 1	Cole 1	Yorke 1	Blomqvist	Brown for Neville P, Cruyff for Blomqvist, Solskjaer for Cole
25 Nov	Barcelona	67,648	Nou Camp	A	D	3–3	Schmeichel	Neville G	Irwin	Stam	Brown	Keane	Beckham	Scholes	Cole 1	Yorke 2	Blomqvist	Butt for Beckham
9 Dec	Bayern Munich	54,434	Old Trafford	H	D	1–1	Schmeichel	Neville G	Irwin	Stam	Brown	Keane 1	Beckham	Scholes	Cole	Yorke	Giggs	Johnsen for Irwin, Butt for Yorke
3 Mar	Internazionale	54,430	Old Trafford	H	W	2–0	Schmeichel	Neville G	Irwin	Johnsen	Stam	Keane	Beckham	Scholes	Cole	Yorke 2	Giggs	Butt for Scholes, Berg for Johnsen
17 Mar	Internazionale	79,528	Milan	A	D	1–1	Schmeichel	Neville G	Irwin	Johnsen	Stam	Berg	Keane	Beckham	Cole	Yorke	Giggs	Scholes 1 for Johnsen, Neville P for Giggs
7 Apr	Juventus	54,487	Old Trafford	H	D	1–1	Schmeichel	Neville G	Irwin	Stam	Berg	Keane	Beckham	Scholes	Cole	Yorke	Giggs 1	Johnsen for Berg, Sheringham for Yorke
21 Apr	Juventus	64,500	Delle Alpi	A	W	3–2	Schmeichel	Neville G	Irwin	Johnsen	Stam	Keane 1	Beckham	Butt	Cole 1	Yorke 1	Blomqvist	Scholes for Blomqvist
26 May	Bayern Munich	90,000	Nou Camp	A	W	2–1	Schmeichel	Neville G	Irwin	Johnsen	Stam	Beckham	Butt	Blomqvist	Cole	Yorke	Giggs	Sheringham 1 for Blomqvist, Solskjaer 1 for Cole

Premiership
P38 • W22 • D13 • L3 • F80 • A37 • PTS79
Position: 1

1999/2000

Premiership

Date	Opponent	Attendances	Venue			Score	Players and Scores											Substitutions
8 Aug	Everton	39,141	Goodison Park	A	D	1–1	Bosnich	Neville P	Irwin	Berg	Keane	Stam	Beckham	Scholes	Cole	Yorke 1	Solskjaer	Butt for. York
11 Aug	Sheffield Wednesday	54,941	Old Trafford	H	W	4–0	Bosnich	Neville P	Irwin	Berg	Keane	Stam	Beckham	Scholes 1	Cole 1	Yorke 1	Giggs	Sheringham for. Yorke, Butt for. Beckham, Solskjaer 1 for. Giggs
14 Aug	Leeds United	55,187	Old Trafford	H	W	2–0	Bosnich	Neville P	Irwin	Berg	Keane	Stam	Beckham	Scholes	Cole	Yorke 2	Giggs	van der Gouw for. Bosnich, Butt for. Scholes, Sheringham for. Yorke
22 Aug	Arsenal	38,147	Highbury	A	W	2–1	van der Gouw	Neville P	Irwin	Berg	Keane 2	Stam	Beckham	Scholes	Cole	Yorke	Giggs	Butt for. Scholes, Sheringham for. Cole, Culkin for. van der Gouw
25 Aug	Coventry City	22,024	Highfield Road	A	W	2–1	van der Gouw	Neville P	Irwin	Berg	Keane	Stam	Beckham	Butt	Yorke 1	Sheringham	Giggs	Scholes 1 for. Butt, Solskjaer for. Sheringham, Curtis for. Neville P
30 Aug	Newcastle United	55,190	Old Trafford	H	W	5–1	van der Gouw	Neville G	Neville P	Berg	Scholes	Stam	Beckham	Butt	Cole 4	Yorke	Giggs 1	Fortune for. Scholes, Sheringham for. Beckham, Clegg for. Neville G
11 Sep	Liverpool	44,929	Anfield	A	W	**3–2	Taibi	Neville P	Silvestre	Berg	Scholes	Stam	Beckham	Butt	Cole 1	Yorke	Giggs	Wallwork for. Butt, Clegg for. Neville P
18 Sep	Wimbledon	55,189	Old Trafford	H	D	1–1	Taibi	Irwin	Silvestre	Berg	Neville P	Stam	Scholes	Solskjaer	Yorke	Sheringham	Giggs	Cruyff 1 for. Giggs, Cole for. Solskjaer
25 Sep	Southampton	55,249	Old Trafford	H	D	3–3	Taibi	Irwin	Silvestre	Berg	Scholes	Stam	Beckham	Butt	Yorke 2	Sheringham 1	Solskjaer	
3 Oct	Chelsea	34,909	Stamford Bridge	A	L	0–5	Taibi	Irwin	Silvestre	Berg	Neville P	Stam	Beckham	Butt	Cole	Yorke	Scholes	Solskjaer for. Cole, Sheringham for. Scholes, Wilson for. Beckham
16 Oct	Watford	55,188	Old Trafford	H	W	4–1	Bosnich	Neville P	Irwin 1	Silvestre	Scholes	Stam	Beckham	Butt	Cole 2	Yorke 1	Giggs	Keane for. Stam, Solskjaer for. Cole, Greening for. Giggs
23 Oct	Tottenham Hotspur	36,072	White Hart Lane	A	L	1–3	Bosnich	Irwin	Neville P	Silvestre	Keane	Stam	Beckham	Scholes	Cole	Yorke	Giggs 1	Solskjaer for. Beckham, Greening for. Irwin
30 Oct	Aston Villa	55,211	Old Trafford	H	W	3–0	Bosnich	Neville P	Irwin	Silvestre	Keane 1	Stam	Beckham	Scholes 1	Cole 1	Yorke	Giggs	Solskjaer for. Yorke, Cruyff for. Giggs, Wilson for. Cole
6 Nov	Leicester City	55,191	Old Trafford	H	W	2–0	Bosnich	Neville P	Higginbotham	Silvestre	Keane	Stam	Scholes	Solskjaer	Cole 2	Yorke	Giggs	May for. Higginbotham, Berg for. Neville P
20 Nov	Derby County	33,370	Pride Park	A	W	2–1	van der Gouw	Neville G	Neville P	Silvestre	Keane	Stam	Beckham	Butt 1	Cole 1	Yorke	Giggs	Berg for. Silvestre, Solskjaer for. Beckham
4 Dec	Everton	55,193	Old Trafford	H	W	5–1	Bosnich	Neville G	Irwin 1	Silvestre	Keane	Stam	Scholes	Butt	Solskjaer 4	Sheringham	Giggs	van der Gouw for. Bosnich, Neville P for. Silvestre, Cole for. Giggs
18 Dec	West Ham United	26,037	Upton Park	A	W	4–2	van der Gouw	Neville G	Irwin	Silvestre	Keane	Stam	Beckham	Scholes	Yorke 2	Sheringham	Giggs 2	Neville P for. Irwin, Butt for. Beckham
26 Dec	Bradford City	55,188	Old Trafford	H	W	4–0	Bosnich	Neville G	Neville P	Silvestre	Keane 1	Stam	Scholes	Butt	Solskjaer	Sheringham	Fortune 1	Wallwork for. Stam, Yorke 1 for. Scholes, Cole 1 for. Sheringham
28 Dec	Sunderland	42,026	Stadium of Light	A	D	2–2	Bosnich	Neville G	Irwin	Silvestre	Keane 1	Stam	Beckham	Butt 1	Cole	Yorke	Giggs	Sheringham for. Irwin, Solskjaer for. Beckham, Neville P for. Cole
24 Jan	Arsenal	58,293	Old Trafford	H	D	1–1	Bosnich	Neville G	Irwin	Silvestre	Keane	Stam	Beckham	Butt	Cole	Yorke	Giggs	Neville P for. Irwin, Sheringham 1 for. Cole
29 Jan	Middlesbrough	61,267	Old Trafford	H	W	1–0	Bosnich	Neville G	Irwin	Silvestre	Keane	Stam	Beckham 1	Butt	Yorke	Sheringham	Giggs	Scholes for. Neville G, Solskjaer for. Irwin, Cole for. Sheringham
2 Feb	Sheffield Wednesday	39,640	Hillsborough	A	W	1–0	Bosnich	Neville G	Irwin	Silvestre	Keane	Stam	Beckham	Butt	Yorke	Sheringham 1	Giggs	Scholes for. Butt
5 Feb	Coventry City	61,380	Old Trafford	H	W	3–2	Bosnich	Neville G	Neville P	Silvestre	Keane	Stam	Beckham	Solskjaer	Cole 2	Sheringham	Scholes 1	Butt for. Solskjaer, Cruyff for. Sheringham
12 Feb	Newcastle United	36,470	St James' Park	A	L	0–3	Bosnich	Neville G	Irwin	Silvestre	Keane	Stam	Beckham	Scholes	Cole	Sheringham	Giggs	Butt for. Irwin, Solskjaer for. Sheringham
20 Feb	Leeds United	40,160	Elland Road	A	W	1–0	Bosnich	Neville G	Irwin	Silvestre	Keane	Stam	Scholes	Butt	Cole 1	Yorke	Giggs	Sheringham for. Yorke
26 Feb	Wimbledon	26,129	Selhurst Park	A	D	2–2	Bosnich	Neville G	Neville P	Silvestre	Butt	Stam	Beckham	Cruyff 1	Cole 1	Sheringham	Giggs	Berg for. Neville P, Solskjaer for. Cruyff
4 Mar	Liverpool	61,592	Old Trafford	H	D	1–1	van der Gouw	Neville G	Irwin	Silvestre	Keane	Stam	Beckham	Butt	Solskjaer 1	Yorke	Giggs	Cole for. Solskjaer, Sheringham for. Yorke
11 Mar	Derby County	61,619	Old Trafford	H	W	3–1	Bosnich	Neville G	Neville P	Silvestre	Keane	Berg	Beckham	Fortune	Solskjaer	Yorke 3	Scholes	Butt for. Fortune, Wallwork for. Keane
18 Mar	Leicester City	22,170	Filbert Street	A	W	2–0	Bosnich	Neville G	Irwin	Berg	Keane	Stam	Beckham 1	Scholes	Cole	Yorke 1	Giggs	Sheringham for. Cole, Butt for. Giggs
25 Mar	Bradford City	18,276	Valley Parade	A	W	4–0	Bosnich	Neville G	Neville P	Silvestre	Keane	Berg	Beckham 1	Scholes 1	Cole 1	Yorke 2	Giggs	Wallwork for. Keane, Solskjaer for. Giggs
1 Apr	West Ham United	61,611	Old Trafford	H	W	7–1	Bosnich	Neville G	Irwin 1	Silvestre	Keane	Stam	Beckham 1	Scholes 3	Cole 1	Yorke	Fortune	Butt for. Keane, Sheringham for. Cole, Solskjaer 1 for. Scholes
10 Apr	Middlesbrough	34,775	Riverside Stadium	A	W	4–3	Bosnich	Neville G	Irwin	Berg	Keane	Stam	Beckham	Scholes 1	Cole 1	Yorke	Giggs 1	Silvestre for. Irwin, Butt for. Keane, Fortune 1 for. Giggs
15 Apr	Sunderland	61,612	Old Trafford	H	W	4–0	Bosnich	Neville G	Neville P	Silvestre	Keane	Stam	Scholes	Butt 1	Solskjaer 2	Sheringham	Fortune	van der Gouw for. Bosnich, Berg 1 for. Stam, Beckham for. Scholes
22 Apr	Southampton	15,245	The Dell	A	W	*3–1	van der Gouw	Neville G	Neville P	Silvestre	Keane	Stam	Beckham 1	Butt	Cole	Solskjaer 1	Giggs	Johnsen for. Giggs, Sheringham for. Solskjaer, Yorke for. Cole
24 Apr	Chelsea	61,593	Old Trafford	H	W	3–2	van der Gouw	Neville G	Neville P	Silvestre	Keane	Johnsen	Beckham	Butt	Solskjaer 1	Yorke 2	Giggs	Berg for. Neville G, Scholes for. Keane, Cruyff for. Solskjaer
29 Apr	Watford	20,250	Vicarage Road	A	W	3–2	van der Gouw	Neville P	Silvestre	Berg	Wilson	Johnsen	Greening	Butt	Solskjaer	Sheringham	Giggs 1	Yorke 1 for. Wilson, Higginbotham for. Johnsen, Cruyff 1 for. Greening
6 May	Tottenham Hotspur	61,629	Old Trafford	H	W	3–1	van der Gouw	Neville P	Irwin	Silvestre	Scholes	Stam	Beckham 1	Butt	Solskjaer 1	Sheringham 1	Giggs	Berg for. Stam, Greening for. Butt, Cruyff for. Solskjaer
14 May	Aston Villa	39,217	Villa Park	A	W	1–0	van der Gouw	Irwin	Higginbotham	Berg	Neville P	Silvestre	Scholes	Solskjaer	Yorke	Sheringham 1	Giggs	Cruyff for. Solskjaer, Wallwork for. Higginbotham

FA Cup

United withdrew, see p.36

FL Cup

Date	Opponent	Attendances	Venue			Score	Players and Scores											Substitutions
13 Oct	Aston Villa	33,815	Villa Park	A	L	0–3	Bosnich	Clegg	Curtis	Higginbotham	Wallwork	O'Shea	Twiss	Cruyff	Solskjaer	Greening	Chadwick	Healy for. Higginbotham, Wellens for. Twiss

Club World Championship

Date	Opponent	Attendances	Venue			Score	Players and Scores											Substitutions
6 Jan	Nexaca	26,000	Rio	A	D	1–1	Bosnich	Neville G	Irwin	Silvestre	Keane	Stam	Beckham	Butt	Cole	Yorke 1	Giggs	Solskjaer for. Irwin, Neville P for. Butt, Sheringham for. Cole
8 Jan	Vasco da Gama	5,000	Rio	A	L	1–3	Bosnich	Neville G	Irwin	Silvestre	Keane	Stam	Neville P	Butt 1	Solskjaer	Yorke	Giggs	Sheringham for. Solskjaer, Cruyff for. Stam, Fortune for. Giggs
11 Jan	South Melbourne	25,000	Rio	A	W	2–0	van der Gouw	Neville P	Higginbotham	Berg	Wallwork	Wilson	Greening	Cruyff	Cole	Solskjaer	Fortune 2	Beckham for. Wilson, Rachubka for. van der Gouw

European Cup

Date	Opponent	Attendances	Venue			Score	Players and Scores											Substitutions
14 Sep	Croatia Zagreb	53,250	Old Trafford	H	D	0–0	van der Gouw	Clegg	Neville P	Berg	Wilson	Stam	Beckham	Scholes	Cole	Yorke	Giggs	Fortune for. Clegg, Sheringham for. Wilson
22 Sep	Sturm Graz	16,480	Graz	A	W	3–0	van der Gouw	Neville P	Irwin	Berg	Keane 1	Stam	Beckham	Scholes	Cole 1	Yorke 1	Cruyff	Wilson for. Stam, Solsjkaer for. Cole, Sheringham for. Cruyff
29 Sep	Marseille	53,993	Old Trafford	H	W	2–1	van der Gouw	Neville P	Irwin	Berg	Stam	Scholes 1	Beckham	Butt	Cole 1	Yorke	Solskjaer	Sheringham for. Berg, Fortune for. Solsjkaer, Clegg for. Cole
19 Oct	Marseille	57,745	Marseille	A	L	0–1	Bosnich	Neville P	Irwin	Berg	Keane	Stam	Beckham	Scholes	Cole	Yorke	Giggs	Solskjaer for. Berg
27 Oct	Croatia Zagreb	38,000	Zagreb	A	W	2–1	Bosnich	Neville P	Irwin	Berg	Keane 1	Stam	Beckham 1	Scholes	Cole	Yorke	Giggs	Solskjaer for. Yorke, Greening for. Scholes, Cruyff for. Cole
2 Nov	Sturm Graz	53,745	Old Trafford	H	W	2–1	Bosnich	Neville G	Irwin	Berg	Keane 1	May	Greening	Wilson	Cole	Solskjaer 1	Giggs	Neville P for. Wilson, Cruyff for. Greening, Higginbotham for. Irwin
23 Nov	Fiorentina	40,000	Fiorentina	A	L	0–2	Bosnich	Neville G	Irwin	Berg	Keane	Stam	Beckham	Scholes	Cole	Yorke	Giggs	Neville P for. Berg, Fortune for. Cole, Solskjaer for. Yorke
8 Dec	Valencia	54,606	Old Trafford	H	W	3–0	van der Gouw	Neville G	Irwin	Neville P	Keane 1	Stam	Beckham	Scholes 1	Cole	Solskjaer 1	Giggs	Butt for. Scholes, Yorke for. Cole
1 Mar	Bordeaux	59,786	Old Trafford	H	W	2–0	van der Gouw	Neville G	Irwin	Silvestre	Keane	Stam	Beckham	Butt	Cole	Sheringham 1	Giggs 1	Neville P for. Cole, Fortune for. Keane, Solskjaer for. Giggs
7 Mar	Bordeaux	33,100	Bordeaux	A	W	2–1	van der Gouw	Neville G	Irwin	Silvestre	Keane 1	Stam	Beckham	Butt	Cole	Sheringham	Giggs	Yorke for. Sheringham, Solskjaer 1 for. Irwin, Berg for. Cole
15 Mar	Fiorentina	59,926	Old Trafford	H	W	3–1	Bosnich	Neville G	Irwin	Berg	Keane 1	Stam	Beckham	Scholes	Cole 1	Yorke 1	Giggs	
21 Mar	Valencia	48,432	Valencia	A	D	0–0	Bosnich	Neville G	Irwin	Berg	Keane	Stam	Scholes	Butt	Solskjaer	Sheringham	Fortune	Cruyff for. Solskjaer
4 Apr	Real Madrid	64,119	Madrid	A	D	0–0	Bosnich	Neville G	Irwin	Berg	Keane	Stam	Beckham	Scholes	Cole	Yorke	Giggs	Sheringham for. Yorke, Butt for. Scholes, Silvestre for. Irwin
19 Apr	Real Madrid	59,178	Old Trafford	H	L	2–3	van der Gouw	Neville G	Irwin	Berg	Keane	Stam	Beckham 1	Scholes 1	Cole	Yorke	Giggs	Silvestre for. Irwin, Sheringham for. Berg, Solskjaer for. Cole

Premiership
P38 •W28 •D7 •L3 •F97 •A45 •PTS91
Position: 1

2000/01

PREMIERSHIP

Date	Opponent	Attendances	Venue				Players and Scores											Substitutions
20 Aug	Newcastle United	67,477	Old Trafford	H	W	2-0	Barthez	Neville G	Neville P	Stam	Johnsen 1	Beckham	Keane	Scholes	Cole 1	Sheringham	Giggs	Wallwork for. Johnsen, Yorke for. Sheringham, Solskjaer for. Cole
22 Aug	Ipswich Town	22,007	Portman Road	A	D	1-1	Barthez	Neville G	Neville P	Stam	Wallwork	Beckham 1	Keane	Scholes	Solskjaer	Yorke	Giggs	Cole for. Solskjaer, Silvestre for. Neville P, Sheringham for. Yorke
26 Aug	West Ham United	25,998	Upton Park	A	D	2-2	Barthez	Neville G	Neville P	Stam	Silvestre	Beckham 1	Keane	Scholes	Cole 1	Sheringham	Giggs	Berg for. Stam
5 Sep	Bradford City	66,447	Old Trafford	H	W	6-0	Barthez	Neville G	Johnsen	Wallwork	Silvestre	Beckham 1	Butt	Greening	Fortune 2	Cole 1	Sheringham 2	Solskjaer for. Cole, Neville P for. Johnsen, Scholes for. Butt
9 Sep	Sunderland	67,503	Old Trafford	H	W	3-0	Barthez	Neville G	Johnsen	Stam	Silvestre	Beckham	Butt	Scholes 2	Cole	Sheringham 1	Giggs	Irwin for. Stam, Solskjaer for. Cole
16 Sep	Everton	38,541	Goodison Park	A	W	3-1	Barthez	Neville G	Irwin	Brown	Silvestre	Beckham	Butt 1	Scholes	Solskjaer 1	Sheringham	Giggs 1	Yorke for. Giggs, Neville P for. Scholes, van der Gouw for. Barthez
23 Sep	Chelsea	67,568	Old Trafford	H	D	3-3	van der Gouw	Neville G	Irwin	Johnsen	Silvestre	Beckham 1	Keane	Scholes 1	Cole	Sheringham 1	Giggs	Butt for. Sheringham, Brown for. Irwin, Solskjaer for. Cole
1 Oct	Arsenal	38,146	Highbury	A	L	0-1	Barthez	Neville G	Irwin	Johnsen	Silvestre	Beckham	Keane	Scholes	Cole	Sheringham	Giggs	Yorke for. Sheringham, Solskjaer for. Giggs
14 Oct	Leicester City	22,132	Filbert Street	A	W	3-0	Barthez	Brown	Irwin	Johnsen	Silvestre	Fortune	Keane	Butt	Solskjaer 1	Sheringham 2	Yorke	Giggs for. Sheringham
21 Oct	Leeds United	67,525	Old Trafford	H	W	*3-0	Barthez	Neville G	Neville P	Johnsen	Silvestre	Fortune	Keane	Scholes	Butt	Yorke 1	Solskjaer	Beckham 1 for. Keane, Brown for. Johnsen
28 Oct	Southampton	67,581	Old Trafford	H	W	5-0	Barthez	Neville G	Irwin	Brown	Neville P	Beckham	Butt	Scholes	Cole 2	Sheringham 3	Giggs	Wallwork for. Neville G, Yorke for. Cole, Solskjaer for. Sheringham
4 Nov	Coventry City	21,079	Highfield Road	A	W	2-1	Barthez	Neville G	Irwin	Brown	Neville P	Beckham 1	Keane	Scholes	Cole 1	Sheringham	Giggs	Solskjaer for. Scholes, Yorke for. Sheringham
11 Nov	Middlesbrough	67,576	Old Trafford	H	W	2-1	Barthez	Neville G	Neville P	Brown	Silvestre	Beckham	Keane	Scholes	Butt 1	Yorke	Solskjaer	Sheringham 1 for. Solskjaer, Wallwork for. Brown, Chadwick for. Yorke
18 Nov	Manchester City	34,429	Maine Road	A	W	1-0	Barthez	Neville G	Irwin	Brown	Neville P	Beckham 1	Keane	Scholes	Butt	Sheringham	Yorke	Giggs for. Sheringham
25 Nov	Derby County	32,910	Pride Park	A	W	3-0	Barthez	Neville G	Irwin	Brown	Silvestre	Butt 1	Keane	Scholes	Chadwick	Sheringham 1	Yorke 1	Solskjaer for. Chadwick, Fortune for. Scholes, van der Gouw for. Barthez
2 Dec	Tottenham Hotspur	67,583	Old Trafford	H	W	2-0	Barthez	Neville G	Neville P	Brown	Silvestre	Beckham	Keane	Scholes 1	Butt	Sheringham	Yorke	Giggs for. Yorke, Solskjaer 1 for. Butt
9 Dec	Charlton Athletic	20,043	The Valley	A	D	3-3	van der Gouw	Neville G	Neville P	Brown	Silvestre	Beckham	Keane 1	Chadwick	Butt	Solskjaer 1	Giggs 1	Scholes for. Chadwick, Greening for. Keane, Sheringham for. Beckham
17 Dec	Liverpool	67,533	Old Trafford	H	L	0-1	Barthez	Neville G	Irwin	Brown	Silvestre	Beckham	Keane	Scholes	Butt	Solskjaer	Giggs	Greening for. Butt, Chadwick for. Irwin
23 Dec	Ipswich Town	67,597	Old Trafford	H	W	2-0	Barthez	Neville G	Neville P	Brown	Silvestre	Beckham	Keane	Scholes	Giggs	Solskjaer 2	Fortune	Healy for. Giggs, Wallwork for. Beckham, Greening for. Keane
26 Dec	Aston Villa	40,889	Villa Park	A	W	1-0	Barthez	Neville G	Irwin	Brown	Silvestre	Beckham	Keane	Scholes	Butt	Solskjaer 1	Giggs	Neville P for. Silvestre, Wallwork for. Irwin
30 Dec	Newcastle United	52,134	St James' Park	A	D	1-1	Barthez	Neville G	Neville P	Brown	Silvestre	Beckham 1	Keane	Butt	Solskjaer	Yorke	Giggs	Wallwork for. Silvestre, Scholes for. Solskjaer, Chadwick for. Butt
1 Jan	West Ham United	67,603	Old Trafford	H	W	*3-1	Barthez	Neville P	Neville G	Brown	Silvestre	Beckham	Keane	Scholes	Solskjaer 1	Yorke 1	Giggs	Greening for. Giggs, Wallwork for. Keane, Butt for. Scholes
13 Jan	Bradford City	20,551	Valley Parade	A	W	3-0	Barthez	Neville G	Irwin	Stam	Silvestre	Beckham	Keane	Neville P	Solskjaer	Sheringham 1	Giggs 1	Brown for. Neville P, Chadwick 1 for. Stam, Cole for. Solskjaer
20 Jan	Aston Villa	67,533	Old Trafford	H	W	2-0	Barthez	Neville G 1	Irwin	Stam	Neville P	Greening	Keane	Butt	Solskjaer	Sheringham 1	Giggs	Chadwick for. Greening, Cole for. Solskjaer
31 Jan	Sunderland	48,260	Stadium of Light	A	W	1-0	Barthez	Neville G	Brown	Stam	Silvestre	Beckham	Keane	Scholes	Cole 1	Sheringham	Giggs	Solskjaer for. Sheringham, Butt for. Scholes, Neville P for. Silvestre
3 Feb	Everton	67,528	Old Trafford	H	W	*1-0	Barthez	Neville P	Brown	Stam	Silvestre	Beckham	Irwin	Scholes	Chadwick	Cole	Yorke	Giggs for. Scholes, Wallwork for. Beckham, Sheringham for. Chadwick
10 Feb	Chelsea	34,960	Stamford Bridge	A	D	1-1	van der Gouw	Neville G	Brown	Stam	Silvestre	Beckham	Keane	Scholes	Cole 1	Solskjaer	Giggs	
25 Feb	Arsenal	67,535	Old Trafford	H	W	6-1	Barthez	Neville G	Brown	Stam	Silvestre	Beckham	Keane 1	Butt	Scholes	Yorke 3	Solskjaer 1	Chadwick for. Keane, Sheringham 1 for. Yorke
3 Mar	Leeds United	40,055	Elland Road	A	D	1-1	Barthez	Neville G	Brown	Stam	Neville P	Beckham	Scholes	Butt	Irwin	Sheringham	Solskjaer	Chadwick 1 for. Butt, Yorke for. Sheringham
17 Mar	Leicester City	67,516	Old Trafford	H	W	2-0	Rachubka	Neville G	Irwin	Stam	Neville P	Greening	Keane	Scholes	Butt	Sheringham	Solskjaer	Yorke 1 for. Greening, Chadwick for. Butt, Silvestre 1 for. Neville P
31 Mar	Liverpool	44,806	Anfield	A	L	0-2	Barthez	Neville G	Irwin	Brown	Neville P	Beckham	Keane	Butt	Yorke	Sheringham	Giggs	Chadwick for. Sheringham. Silvestre for. Irwin, Scholes for. Butt
10 Apr	Charlton Athletic	67,505	Old Trafford	H	W	2-1	Barthez	Neville G	Irwin	Brown	Silvestre	Scholes	Keane	Butt	Cole 1	Yorke	Giggs	Solskjaer 1 for. Yorke, Sheringham for. Butt, Neville P for. Irwin
14 Apr	Coventry City	67,637	Old Trafford	H	W	4-2	Goram	Neville G	Brown	Stam	Silvestre	Scholes 1	Keane	Butt	Giggs 1	Cole	Yorke 2	van der Gouw for. Goram, Beckham for. Butt, Solskjaer for. Cole
21 Apr	Manchester City	67,535	Old Trafford	H	D	1-1	Barthez	Neville G	Brown	Stam	Neville P	Beckham	Keane	Scholes	Chadwick	Sheringham 1	Solskjaer	Giggs for. Chadwick, Silvestre for. Brown, Butt for. Scholes
28 Apr	Middlesbrough	34,417	Riverside Stadium	A	W	2-0	van der Gouw	Neville P 1	Brown	Stam	Johnsen	Beckham 1	Stewart	Butt	Fortune	Sheringham	Solskjaer	Giggs for. Fortune, Cole for. Solskjaer, Chadwick for. Stewart
5 May	Derby County	67,526	Old Trafford	H	L	0-1	Barthez	Irwin	Wallwork	Johnsen	Neville P	Beckham	Stewart	Butt	Chadwick	Cole	Sheringham	Giggs for. Stewart, Silvestre for. Neville P, van der Gouw for. Barthez
13 May	Southampton	15,246	The Dell	A	L	1-2	Goram	Irwin	Brown	Johnsen	Neville P	Chadwick	Stewart	Wallwork	Fortune	Yorke	Giggs 1	van der Gouw for. Goram, May for. Wallwork
19 May	Tottenham Hotspur	36,072	White Hart Lane	A	L	1-3	van der Gouw	Irwin	May	Johnsen	Silvestre	Neville P	Butt	Scholes 1	Cole	Sheringham	Giggs	Djordjc for. Irwin

FA CUP

7 Jan	Fulham	19,178	Craven Cottage	A	W	2-1	van der Gouw	Neville G	Brown	Neville P	Silvestre	Beckham	Keane	Butt	Solskjaer 1	Yorke	Giggs	Wallwork for. Butt, Sheringham 1 for. Yorke, Chadwick for. Beckham
28 Jan	West Ham United	67,029	Old Trafford	H	L	0-1	Barthez	Neville G	Irwin	Stam	Silvestre	Beckham	Keane	Butt	Cole	Sheringham	Giggs	Yorke for. Butt, Solskjaer for. Irwin

FL CUP

31 Oct	Watford	18,871	Vicarage Road	A	W	3-0	van der Gouw	Clegg	Neville P	Brown	O'Shea	Wallwork	Fortune	Greening	Chadwick	Yorke 1	Solskjaer 2	Stewart for. Wallwork, Rachubka for. Fortune
28 Nov	Sunderland	47,543	Stadium of Light	A	L	1-2	van der Gouw	Clegg	Neville P	Johnsen	O'Shea	Wallwork	Fortune	Greening	Chadwick	Yorke 1	Solskjaer	Stewart for. Johnsen, Healy for. Chadwick, Webber for. Wallwork

EUROPEAN CUP

13 Sep	RSC Anderlecht	62,749	Old Trafford	H	W	5-1	Barthez	Neville G	Irwin 1	Johnsen	Silvestre	Beckham	Keane	Scholes	Cole 3	Sheringham 1	Giggs	Solskjaer for. Giggs, Neville P for. Irwin, Yorke for. Cole
19 Sep	Dinamo Kiev	60,000	Kiev	A	D	0-0	van der Gouw	Neville G	Irwin	Johnsen	Silvestre	Beckham	Keane	Butt	Cole	Yorke	Giggs	Sheringham for. Yorke, Solskjaer for. Cole
26 Sep	PSV Eindhoven	33,500	Eindhoven	A	L	1-3	van der Gouw	Neville G	Neville P	Brown	Silvestre	Butt	Keane	Scholes 1	Greening	Yorke	Solskjaer	Giggs for. Greening, Beckham for. Scholes, Wallwork for. Silvestre
18 Oct	PSV Eindhoven	66,316	Old Trafford	H	W	3-1	Barthez	Neville G	Irwin	Johnsen	Silvestre	Beckham	Keane	Scholes 1	Cole	Sheringham 1	Giggs	Yorke 1 for. Sheringham, Brown for. Irwin, Butt for. Beckham
24 Oct	RSC Anderlecht	28,000	Anderlecht	A	L	1-2	Barthez	Neville G	Irwin 1	Johnsen	Silvestre	Beckham	Butt	Scholes	Cole	Yorke	Giggs	Brown for. Silvestre, Solskjaer for. Irwin
8 Nov	Dinamo Kiev	66,776	Old Trafford	H	W	1-0	Barthez	Neville G	Irwin	Brown	Neville P	Beckham	Keane	Butt	Cole	Sheringham 1	Giggs	Fortune for. Giggs, Yorke for. Sheringham, Silvestre for. Fortune
21 Nov	Panathinaikos	65,024	Old Trafford	H	W	3-1	Barthez	Neville G	Brown	Neville P	Silvestre	Beckham	Keane	Butt	Scholes 2	Sheringham 1	Yorke	
6 Dec	Sturm Graz	16,500	Graz	A	W	2-0	Barthez	Neville G	Irwin	Brown	Silvestre	Beckham	Keane	Butt	Scholes 1	Sheringham	Yorke	Giggs 1 for. Butt, Solskjaer for. Yorke, Neville P for. Irwin
14 Feb	Valencia	51,000	Valencia	A	D	0-0	Barthez	Neville G	Brown	Stam	Silvestre	Beckham	Keane	Scholes	Cole	Sheringham	Giggs	Butt for. Beckham, Solskjaer for. Cole
20 Feb	Valencia	66,715	Old Trafford	H	D	1-1	Barthez	Neville G	Brown	Stam	Silvestre	Beckham	Keane	Scholes	Cole 1	Sheringham	Giggs	Butt for. Giggs, Solskjaer for. Sheringham
7 Mar	Panathinaikos	27,231	Spiros Louis Stadium	A	D	1-1	Barthez	Neville G	Brown	Stam	Silvestre	Beckham	Keane	Scholes 1	Cole	Neville P	Yorke	Chadwick for. Silvestre, Solskjaer for. Cole, Sheringham for. Neville P
13 Mar	Sturm Graz	66,404	Old Trafford	H	W	3-0	Barthez	Neville G	Irwin	Stam	Silvestre	Chadwick	Keane 1	Butt 1	Scholes	Sheringham 1	Solskjaer	Greening for. Scholes
3 Apr	Bayern Munich	66,584	Old Trafford	H	L	0-1	Barthez	Neville G	Brown	Stam	Silvestre	Beckham	Keane	Scholes	Solskjaer	Cole	Giggs	Yorke for. Beckham
18 Apr	Bayern Munich	60,000	Olympic Stadium	A	L	1-2	Barthez	Neville G	Brown	Stam	Silvestre	Scholes	Keane	Butt	Yorke	Cole	Giggs 1	Sheringham for. Yorke, Solskjaer for. Butt, Chadwick for. Brown

PREMIERSHIP
P38 • W24 • D8 • L6 • F79 • A31 • PTS80
POSITION: 1

Index

Acknowledgements

PICTURE SOURCES:
l=left; r=right; c=centre; b=bottom; a=above; br=bottom right; bl=bottom left; cr=centre right; cl=centre left; tr=top right; tl=top left; tcr=top centre right.

Action Images: TT p.1lc, rc; p.2bl; p.3; p.7b; rc, 2, 20bl, 21c, 22br, 30tl, 30tr, 31tr, 35b, 36tr, 37bl, 39b 39t, 54bc, 56lc, 57br, 59br, 60c, 62, 67tl, 67lc, 72bl, 73cr, 76, 81tr, 83tr, 87bc, 89tl, 91b, 92tl, 92, 93tl, 94c, 95tr, 96c, 96tl, 98tl, 100tc, 101bl, 101lc, 103cr, 104cl, 104br, 105cl, 106t, 109tl, 110tl, 111bl, 111tr, 113b, 114tr, 117cl, 117br, 122tl.

Allsport/Hulton Deutsch: TT p.2bl; p.5b; p.5t; p.6b; p.8br: 10br, 11c, 18tr, 20br, 21tl, 23c, 25t, 26br, 28bl, 29tl, 29bl, 29br, 31c, 33bc, 36c, 42tl, 44cr, 45c, 53c, 55tr, 56br, 63br, 64bl, 70tr, 74c, 74tl, 75bl, 75cr, 76c, 86c, 88lc, 108cr, 110c, 114c, 114lc, 26/99d, 26tl/99tl, 33ctr

Colorsport: TT p.5b; 9br, 10tl, 10c, 12r1, 12r3, 12r4, 13bl, 15bl, 16bl, 17br, 17b, 17/54bc, 17/106tr, 18bl, 18lc, 19bc, 19c, 20tr, 21c, 27bl, 27c, 27t, 28tl, 30tl, 30tr, 34tl, 34c, 36b, 37cr, 38bl, 38c, 38br, 39tl, 42tl, 48tr, 48cr, 50br, 52tr, 54tl, 54lc, 56tl, 61bl, 62tr, 64tl, 64cr, 65c, 65br, 66lc, 67c, 69tr, 70tl, 70c, 71cr, 73tl, 76tr, 77lc, 78tr, 78tl, 80tl, 80lc, 80cr, 81tl, 85c, 86c, 88cr, 89cl, 89c, 90bl, 90c, 93c, 93br, 94bl, 96tr, 97b, 98tr, 99br, 101br, 102, 103c, 104tl, 111tl, 112cr, 115br, 116bl, 117tl, 117tr, 118tl, 118tr, 119cr, 120tl, 120bl, 120c, 121c

Empics: TT p.4t; p6.t; p.7t; p.8t: 22cr, 22tl, 22bc, 35tl, 38bl, 42c, 43c, 52c, 60tl, 65tl, 69tl, 72cr, 73br, 85br, 96b, 115tr, 122cr

Express Newspapers: 58tl, 84

Hulton Getty: 102cr

John Peters: TT p.1c; p.2tr; 22b, 29, 31bl, 31cr, 41tl, 44c, 44br, 45tr, 48bl, 48bc, 48br, 49c, 49bc, 49cr, 50c, 50c, 50c, 50cr, 51tl, 51cb, 51lc, 51cr, 51br, 58b, 58br, 60b, 60bc, 61tc, 61tr, 61cr, 61bl, 63tc, 63tlc, 69lc, 79tl, 79cl, 88tl, 94cr, 94tl, 95tl, 95bl, 100c, 100cl, 101tr, 104t, 104b, 105tr, 105c, 105cl, 107b, 113tl, 114tr, 116tl, 116tr, 117 cl, 121cl, 121cr, 121br,

Mirror Syndication International: 6c, 19tr, 26bl, 41tr

MUFC: 3c, 8c, 8tl, 9bl, 9tr, 12tl, 12r2, 12r5, 14bl, 15tr, 15c, 16b, 16b2, 17, 46cr, 54c, 54c, 55tr, 57tr, 57c, 57bl, 57c, 62c, 62, 66bc, 68tl, 68, 69c, 79c, 79cr, 82bl, 82c, 83c, 83bl, 83tl, 86tl, 87cr, 89t, 91c, 103b, 100c, 100c, 103bl, 106bl, 106r, 107bl, 109c, 112tl, 113tr, 113cl, 116br, 121t, 121tr, 123b

MUFC: 44lc, 57tc, 66cl, 66bc, 81bl, 113cr, 123c

News Team International: 11t, 13t, 24bl, 25br, 41c, 41br, 44tr, 54tr, 56tr, 56bl, 119lc, 110tr

Oldham Evening Chronicle: 77tr

PA News: 75c

Popperfoto: TT (REUTERS)p.8bl: 7, 14tr, 16tr, 17c, 24tr, 32c, 33lc, 34tr, 34br, 36tl, 37t, 40tr, 42bl, 48c, 49tr, 50tl, 50bl, 50bl, 54bl, 55lc, 71tl, 75tl, 76bl, 84tl, 84, 85tl, 92bl, 98c, 102cr, 108lc/tl, 122tr, 52br

The Illustrated London News: 11c

Tom Tyrrell: 11br, 51lc

Umbro: 49br

Untraceable: 8tl, 13r, 40bl, 54tc, 55br

Zone: 17tr, 45br, 46br, 46c, 47bl, 47br, 50bc, 56c, 58bc, 58br, 59lc, 59tr, 59bl, 51tr, 52tr

COVER IMAGES SUPPLIED BY:
**Action Images: Colorsport:
Allsport/Hulton Deutsch:** Empics
Sporting Pictures: Zone/John Peters

Please note that every effort has been made to check the accuracy of the information contained in this book, and to trace and credit the copyright holders correctly. Andre Deutsch and Picthall and Gunzi apologize for any unintentional errors or omissions, and would be happy to include revisions to content and/or acknowledgements in subsequent editions of this book.

BIBLIOGRAPHY:
Always in the Running, Jim White, Mainstream Publishing, Edinburgh 1996

Fergie's Ultimate United (video), Alex Ferguson, VCI, 1997

Football Wizard: The Billy Meredith Story, John Harding, Robson Books, London 1998

Glory, Glory Man United magazine

Golden Heroes: 50 Seasons of Footballer of the Year, Denis Signy and Norman Giller, Chameleon, 1997

Grimsby Town: A Complete Record, Les Triggs, David Hepton and Sid Woodhead, Breedon Books, Derby 1992

Hamlyn Illustrated History of Manchester United 1878-1996, Tom Tyrrell and David Meek, Hamlyn, London 1996

Insider Guide, Sam Pilger and Justyn Barnes, André Deutsch, London 1997

Just Champion, Alex Ferguson, Sport for Choice (Zone Ltd), London 1993

Manchester United - A Complete Record 1878-1986, Ian Morrison and Alan Shury, Breedon Books, Derby 1990

Manchester United Family Tree, Pete Frame, André Deutsch, London 1996

Manchester United Greats, David Meek, Sportspring Publishing, Edinburgh 1989

Manchester United magazine Published under contract by Zone

Manchester United Official Yearbook 1998, Cliff Butler, Manchester United Football Club plc, Manchester 1998

Manchester United Player by Player, Ivan Ponting, Hamlyn, London 1997

Manchester United: The Official Review '95/96, Zone Ltd, London 1996

Manchester United: The Official Review '96/97, Zone Ltd, London 1997

Manchester United - The Quest for Glory, Tommy Docherty, Sidgwick and Jackson (Macmillan), London 1991

Matt Busby's Manchester United Scrapbook, Matt Busby, Souvenir Press Ltd, London 1980

Old Trafford Encyclopedia Stephen F. Kelly, Mainstream Publishing, Edinburgh 1993

Rothmans Football Yearbook 1997-98, Jack Rollin (Ed.), Headline Book Publishing, London 1997

Sir Matt Busby: A Tribute, Rick Glanvill, MUFC/Virgin Publishing, London 1994

Soccer Who's Who, Maurice Golesworthy, Robert Hale Ltd, London 1964

Sporting Profiles, Michael Parkinson, Pavilion, London 1995

Umbro Book of Quotations, Ebury Press (Random House), London 1996

United Alphabet: A Complete Who's Who of Manchester United F.C., Garth Dykes, ACL & Polar Publishing, Leicester 1994

Results were taken from the *Soccer Data* database © Alan Shury and Tony Brown 2001

Quotations were mostly taken from sources listed in the bibliography, and from newspapers, including the *Daily Mirror,* the *News Chronicle,* the *Sunday Telegraph,* the *Independent,* the *Manchester Evening News,* the *Athletic News* and the *Times.* Quotations were also taken from *Manchester United* magazine. In some cases we were unable to trace quoted material to any published source, and have had to rely on the memory of individuals.

OTHER SOURCES:
www.manutd.com
www.soccerbase.com
www.soccerdata.com
www.matchfacts.com

Picthall & Gunzi Ltd would particularly like to thank the following individuals and organizations for their invaluable help with the production of this publication:

Justyn Barnes, Jane Bawden, Adam Bostock, Lynn Bresler, Tony Brown, Cliff Butler, David Clowes, Cognitive Applications, Tony Cutting, Garth Dykes, the Football Associations of England, Northern Ireland, the Republic of Ireland, Scotland and Wales, Annie Frankland, James Freedman, Elaine Hide, Kim Hide, Ciaran Hughes, Margaret Hynes, Sam Izzard, Manchester City Council, Manchester United FC, Manchester United Museum, David Meek, Andy Mitten, Faith Mowbray, Deborah Murrell, James Parker, Sam Pilger, Louise Pritchard, Floyd Sayers, Jill Somerscales, Tony Somerscales, Betty Stewart, Frank Taylor, Tom Tyrrell, Wilstead Lower School, Mark Wylie, Zone, Dominic Zwemmer.

Garth Dykes' *The United Alphabet: A Complete Who's Who of Manchester United F.C.* has been an invaluable source of information for this publication.

Data-base consultant
Simon Lewis

Computer support
Belinda Ellington

Index
Lynn Bresler

Picture Research
Maria Gibbs
Matt Turner
Dominic Zwemmer

USEFUL ADDRESSES:
Manchester United Museum
Old Trafford
Manchester
M16 0RA

United Review
Manchester United F.C.
Old Trafford
Manchester
M16 0RA

The Definitive Newton Heath, published by Soccer Data, lists all known line-ups and goal scorers for the club up to its transformation into Manchester United, in 1902. The book contains a full list of player details, including their other clubs where known, and is available from Tony Brown, 4 Adrian Close, Beeston, Nottingham NG9 6FL

Tony Brown is a football statistician who specialises in computer databases of the game, including the complete match-by-match record of Manchester United on CD-Rom.

The Players' A-Z section of this book does not claim to be a definitive record of Manchester United players' careers, since compiling such information is sometimes hampered by a lack of official records, especially for the early years, and conflicting sources of published information. Researching facts about Manchester United players' careers is a continuing process. Cliff Butler, the club statistician, would be pleased to receive details of any inaccuracies, omissions or further information by post, at Manchester United Football Club plc, Old Trafford, Manchester M16 0RA.

> *As great a coach as he was a player, with an uncannily brilliant eye for young local players' possibilities*
>
> **The *Manchester Guardian* on Matt Busby, after Roger Byrne's debut**